The Definitive Guide to Samba 3

RODERICK W. SMITH

The Definitive Guide to Samba 3
Copyright © 2004 by Roderick W. Smith

ISBN (pbk): 1-59059-277-8

Printed and bound in the United States of America 10987654321

Trademarked names may appear in this book. Rather than use a trademark symbol with every occurrence of a trademarked name, we use the names only in an editorial fashion and to the benefit of the trademark owner, with no intention of infringement of the trademark.

Technical Reviewers: Christopher Hertel, Will Iverson

Editorial Board: Steve Anglin, Dan Appleman, Gary Cornell, James Cox, Tony Davis, John Franklin, Chris Mills, Steve Rycroft, Dominic Shakeshaft, Julian Skinner, Jim Sumser, Karen Watterson, Gavin Wray, John Zukowski

Lead Editors: Martin Streicher, James Cox

Developmental Editor: Robert J. Denn

Project Manager: Kylie Johnston

Copy Manager: Nicole LeClerc

Copy Editor: Kim Wimpsett

Production Manager: Kari Brooks

Production Editor: Kelly Winquist

Compositor: Susan Glinert

Proofreader: Christy Wagner

Indexer: Valerie Haynes Perry

Artist: Kinetic Publishing Services, LLC

Cover Designer: Kurt Krames

Manufacturing Manager: Tom Debolski

Distributed to the book trade in the United States by Springer-Verlag New York, Inc., 175 Fifth Avenue, New York, NY 10010 and outside the United States by Springer-Verlag GmbH & Co. KG, Tiergartenstr. 17, 69112 Heidelberg, Germany.

In the United States: phone 1-800-SPRINGER, e-mail orders@springer-ny.com, or visit http://www.springer-ny.com. Outside the United States: fax +49 6221 345229, e-mail orders@springer.de, or visit http://www.springer.de.

For information on translations, please contact Apress directly at 2560 Ninth Street, Suite 219, Berkeley, CA 94710. Phone 510-549-5930, fax 510-549-5939, e-mail info@apress.com, or visit http://www.apress.com.

*For Amy, with a belated congratulations
for finishing her doctorate.*

Contents at a Glance

Contents

Part Three Advanced Samba Operations 217

About the Author

Roderick W. Smith is a consultant and the author or coauthor of a dozen books on Linux, Unix, and networking. His previous titles include *Linux Samba Server Administration* (Sybex, 2000), *Advanced Linux Networking* (Addison-Wesley, 2002), and *Linux Power Tools* (Sybex, 2003). He also writes the "Guru Guidance" column for *Linux Magazine*.

Acknowledgments

ALTHOUGH ONE PERSON'S name may be prominent on the cover, books are collaborative efforts. Without the help of many other people, a book such as the one you're holding would not exist, or would be a much lesser work. I would like to thank Editors Martin Streicher and James Cox, who got the ball rolling on this book and helped shepherd it through to the end. Developmental Editor Robert J. Denn helped with broad comments about the shape of the text and oversaw the chapter-by-chapter development. Technical Reviewers Christopher R. Hertel and Will Iverson corrected technical errors (although any that remain are my own). Copy Editor Kim Wimpsett helped keep my prose readable. Production Editor Kelly Winquist coordinated the production team. Project Manager Kylie Johnston was the "glue" holding everything together. Neil Salkind and others at Studio B helped get the book off to a good start. Finally, all the members of the Samba Team deserve thanks—without their efforts, books about Samba would be limited to dance manuals!

Introduction

MOST OFFICES RELY on file-sharing protocols, and arguably the most popular of these is the Server Message Block (SMB), a.k.a. the Common Internet File System (CIFS), which is the native file-sharing protocol of Microsoft Windows. What if you want to use Unix, though? Are you left out of the SMB/CIFS party? Not at all! An open-source package called Samba enables Unix systems to communicate via SMB/CIFS. This package has many advantages over the standard Windows file-sharing tools, particularly on the server side. Samba provides many more fine-tuning options than does Windows' native file-sharing server software. Samba on Unix is, by many measures, faster and more reliable than Windows and its native SMB/CIFS support. Samba enables you to use a single system as both an SMB/CIFS server and a server for Unix-centric features, such as remote text-mode logins. Running Samba, particularly on an open-source OS such as FreeBSD or Linux, is likely to be less expensive than running Windows. If these features appeal to you, Samba is worth investigating.

In addition to its core server features, Samba provides client capabilities. You can use tools such as smbclient to access SMB/CIFS shares, and on many platforms, additional tools (such as smbmount and mount_smbfs) enable you to mount SMB/CIFS shares on a Unix directory tree. Thus, Samba is often worth using even if you don't need its server features. An isolated Unix system can participate as a client on a Windows-dominated network with the help of Samba. Indeed, you can even use Samba between two Unix systems, although in many cases other protocols are better suited to this task.

With the release of Samba 3.0.0 in September 2003, the server has achieved a new level of maturity. This new version includes better Active Directory (AD) integration, new security systems, better Unicode support, better Windows NT/200x/XP printing support, tools to help migrate a domain from Windows NT control, a new net utility, and many behind-the-scenes changes. (Appendix A, which lists Samba's configuration parameters, provides icons identifying the new parameters.) These improved features can make Samba appealing to those who might have dismissed it before. Some of these features provide opportunities (and perhaps a few challenges) to experienced Samba administrators, too. All of these features are covered in this book, along with the traditional Samba features from 2.2.x and earlier lines of the server.

Who Should Buy This Book

This book is intended for experienced Unix system administrators who want to run a Samba server for the benefit of Windows, OS/2, Mac OS, Unix, or other clients. Although Samba server duties dominate the book, some chapters also cover Samba's client tools, as well as non-Samba SMB/CIFS client tools. The emphasis, though, is on running a Samba server on a Unix-like OS. In writing the book, I used Linux, FreeBSD, and Mac OS X systems as models, although the underlying OS could be AIX, HPUX, IRIX, Solaris, or any of several others, as well—most Samba features don't vary much from one OS to another. Samba can also run on a variety of non-Unix platforms, such as AmigaOS, BeOS, OS/2, VMS, or others. Samba's capabilities are usually somewhat limited on these platforms, though, and this book doesn't cover their idiosyncrasies in great detail.

My assumption is that you're at least moderately familiar with Unix in general and with your specific Unix-like OS in particular. You should understand how to perform tasks such as configuring your computer with an IP address, installing software, adding and deleting user accounts, and starting servers. Some of these topics are described briefly in this book, particularly as they directly influence Samba, but overall these are basic Unix system administration tasks that I assume you know how to perform. If your experience is in the Windows, Mac OS Classic, or other non-Unix world and you want to learn Unix while implementing Samba on your Unix OS, you can do so, but you'll need to supplement this book with documentation on your OS of choice. Example books include John P. Lathrop's *Linux in Small Business: A Practical User's Guide* (Apress, 2002), my *FreeBSD: The Complete Reference* (Osborne/McGraw-Hill, 2003), or David Pogue's *Mac OS X: The Missing Manual, Panther Edition* (O'Reilly, 2003). If you're learning Unix from scratch, you shouldn't try to use Samba for any mission-critical tasks at first; the learning curve of Unix and Samba combined is great enough that you're likely to run into problems. If you have several weeks or months to learn, though, or if you want to use Samba initially for a low-priority system, you may be able to dive into the Samba world with little or no Unix experience.

How This Book Is Organized

This book is organized in a way that should facilitate your implementation of a basic Samba server. Depending upon your background and needs, you can get Samba up and running, performing useful work, after reading just a few chapters. Overall, the book has eighteen chapters organized into four parts. A fifth part contains two appendixes. The parts are as follows:

> **Understanding SMB/CIFS:** This part contains two chapters and introduces SMB/CIFS and Samba. The first chapter describes the SMB/CIFS protocol in broad strokes. Unix administrators who are unfamiliar with SMB/CIFS should read this chapter first because the SMB/CIFS protocols have several unique and, from a Unix perspective, peculiar characteristics. The second chapter describes how Samba integrates SMB/CIFS with the underlying Unix OS. Again, Unix administrators who are unfamiliar with SMB/CIFS should be sure to read this chapter, but you can skip it if you're already familiar with SMB/CIFS or are in a hurry to get started.

> **Basic Samba Operations:** The second part contains five chapters that cover basic Samba configuration—obtaining and running the software, setting global Samba options, configuring file shares, configuring printer shares, and managing accounts. You'll be able to set up a basic file server after reading just the first three chapters of this section; however, the information in the first part will help you understand what you're doing, and subsequent chapters may be necessary for configuring Samba in many specific roles.

Advanced Samba Operations: The third part consists of five chapters that describe how to configure Samba to perform many more advanced or esoteric tasks. These are configuring a master browser, configuring a NetBIOS name server, configuring a domain controller, securing Samba, and configuring Samba to work with non-Samba servers and protocols.

Samba Tips and Tricks: The six chapters that make up the fourth part describe assorted tools and techniques that will help you get the most out of Samba. Topics covered are using GUI configuration tools, writing Samba scripts, migrating a Windows domain to Samba control, performing network backups with Samba, troubleshooting Samba, and using SMB/CIFS clients.

Appendixes: This book comes with two appendixes. The first is a complete listing of Samba configuration options. The second is a description of the new net utility.

If you're new to Samba and SMB/CIFS, I recommend you start reading with Chapter 1 and continue through until at least Chapter 4. You can then read Chapters 5, 6, and any additional chapters you need to read in order to do whatever you want to do with Samba. If you already understand SMB/CIFS, you can probably skip Chapter 1 and perhaps Chapter 2. If you're an old hand with Samba and need to get caught up on Samba 3.0 features, concentrate on Chapter 7, Chapter 10, Chapter 15, and Appendix B; these chapters contain the most information on changed Samba 3.0 features. Some additional information on Samba changes is scattered throughout the book, though.

Conventions Used in This Book

Books about computers and computer programs frequently make heavy use of certain special types of computer-related words, such as variables, computer names, filenames, and usernames. This book also uses special elements to help draw your attention to important information or to break off information that's incidental to the main thread of a section. Understanding these conventions will help you get the most from this book.

Text and Font Conventions

To help distinguish unusual non-English words from the rest of the text, this book uses special formatting conventions, including the following:

Normal text: Most of the book's text appears in a normal proportionally spaced font, such as this one.

Code font: Words that refer to special on-computer constructs are designated by use of a monospaced font, such as this one. This font is used for variable names, filenames (including program executable names), usernames, computer names (NetBIOS names and DNS hostnames), URLs, the contents of configuration files, and interactions between the computer and a user (as, for instance, when changing a password with smbpasswd). Code font may appear within a paragraph or on separate lines, where it's typically used in code listings or to illustrate multiline program output or multiple commands.

Italics: Italics can be used for emphasis or to signify a new word that's used for the first time in a chapter. It can also be used, particularly in conjunction with code font, to denote a variable—information that's likely to be different on different systems or when different conditions are met. For instance, a username in a program's output might be italicized.

Bold: Bold can be used in some style elements, such as bulleted list heads. Used in conjunction with code font, it denotes something that you or a user type into a computer. This convention helps you see what you're supposed to type and what the computer displays in lengthy interaction examples.

In the case of text-mode computer/user interactions, the computer typically displays a prompt for the user, and the user enters a command at the prompt. In this book, the prompt is most often your Unix shell prompt, such as a bash or tcsh prompt. This book uses a single dollar sign ($) as the prompt for an ordinary user login and a hash mark (#) as the prompt for a superuser (root) login. In practice, your prompt is likely to include other information, such as your username and current directory, and it may not even include a dollar sign or hash mark. User-mode commands can usually be typed as root, but superuser commands won't work correctly when typed as an ordinary user. When interacting with a program other than the shell, the appropriate prompt is shown. For instance, an interaction might look like this:

```
$ su
Password:
# smbclient //TAP/SHARED -U GROGERS
added interface ip=192.168.1.3 bcast=192.168.1.255 nmask=255.255.255.0
Got a positive name query response from 192.168.1.1 ( 192.168.1.1 172.24.21.1 )
Password:
Domain=[STUDIO] OS=[Unix] Server=[Samba 3.0.0]
smb: \> exit
```

This example starts with a user-mode dollar sign prompt, but the su command prompts for a password (which doesn't echo and therefore isn't shown), whereupon the user acquires superuser privileges and a hash mark prompt. Using this account, the example uses smbclient to connect to a remote share (as described in Chapter 18), and after some information is displayed, the smbclient prompt, smb: \>, appears and a command is typed at this prompt. Note that this particular example accomplishes nothing; it's presented here merely to illustrate the formatting conventions.

When using GUI programs (running in X under Unix, or under Windows or some other OS's GUI environment), menu selections are separated by an arrow character (➤). For instance, the text might refer to picking the File ➤ Save ➤ To Network menu item. This means to locate the File menu item on the menu bar, move to (and possibly click, depending on the GUI) the Save option on that menu, then to move to and click the To Network item on the Save submenu.

IP Addresses and Names

Many IP addresses are assigned to real computers. Even if an address is unused today, it may be assigned to somebody tomorrow. Thus, to avoid confusion, this book uses three special address ranges that are reserved for private network use when IP addresses are needed in examples. These address ranges are 192.168.0.0–192.168.255.255, 172.16.0.0–172.31.255.255, and 10.0.0.0–10.255.255.255. Anybody is free to use these addresses on private networks that don't connect to the Internet or that connect to the Internet only via a proxy server or Network Address Translation (NAT) router. A computer that's directly connected to the Internet isn't likely to use an address in these ranges, and unless otherwise stated, the procedures and examples described in this book work equally well for private and public networks.

Like IP addresses, DNS domain names that are unused today may be registered for use tomorrow. For this reason, three domain names (example.com, example.net, and example.org) are reserved for use in documentation. I use these domain names in this book, but they're a bit boring, and sometimes an example calls for two clearly unrelated domains. Therefore, I also sometimes use clearly fictitious names in the .edu top-level domain, which isn't likely to expand to include my examples—namely, luna.edu and pangaea.edu. Given that lunar colonies don't yet exist and Pangaea was a supercontinent that existed more than 200 million years before universities were invented, these names seem safe for the moment.

This book uses various dances and types of dance for most example machine names. When they appear in uppercase (for example, TAP or CHARLESTON), the names refer to NetBIOS names. When they're in lowercase (tap or charleston), the names refer to DNS hostnames. In most cases the two are equivalent. NetBIOS domain names aren't registered with any central authority, so I use whatever is convenient when I need to refer to them.

Special Text Elements

Some text elements are offset to provide emphasis or to isolate a comment that's peripheral from the main flow of the text. These text elements take special formatting:

NOTE A note provides expanded information that's usually a bit of a tangent from the main thrust of the surrounding text. For instance, a note might provide pointers to outdated methods of achieving a goal in older versions of Samba.

TIP A tip provides a pointer that's likely to save you time or effort. For instance, a tip might give advice on how to configure Samba to optimize its performance for particular clients.

CAUTION A caution advises you of potential problems that could waste your time, damage your data, or even lead to legal trouble. For instance, a caution might warn against configuring Samba in a way that's likely to result in security breaches.

Sidebar

A sidebar is like a note, but it's longer. Notes are typically only a paragraph long, but sidebars are longer and provide more information.

Contacting Me

I welcome any comments you have about this book. You may contact me at
rodsmith@rodsbooks.com or view my page about this book at
http://www.rodsbooks.com/samba3/.

Part One

Understanding SMB/CIFS

CHAPTER 1

Understanding SMB/CIFS

THIS BOOK DESCRIBES Samba, a file- and printer-sharing tool for Unix and Unix-like operating systems (OSs). (In practice, Samba is also available on some OSs that are rather remote from the Unix mold, such as VMS and OS/2.) Samba is an independent implementation of the Server Message Block (SMB) protocol, which is also known as the Common Internet File System (CIFS). SMB/CIFS is common on Windows-dominated networks, but you can use it even between Unix and Unix-like systems. If you're a Unix administrator who's familiar with Unix but not skilled with Windows, chances are certain SMB/CIFS features will seem strange. Even if you're a Windows administrator, you may not fully understand all of the important SMB/CIFS features. This chapter addresses these issues by describing SMB/CIFS—why it exists, how it compares to other file- and printer-sharing protocols, what the important SMB/CIFS features are, and what components exist on an SMB/CIFS network. The next chapter expands on these issues and ties them explicitly to Samba, describing the core components of Samba. Together, these first two chapters provide the necessary background information for understanding Samba.

The File-Sharing Problem

File sharing is a common feature of many local area networks (LANs). To understand SMB/CIFS, and hence to understand Samba, it's necessary to understand the motivations behind file sharing and the features file-sharing software must implement. These motivations and features influence the design of file-sharing protocols (such as SMB/CIFS) and of the software that implements these protocols (such as Samba).

Why Share Files and Printers?

To start, definitions are in order. *File sharing* enables files stored on one computer to be accessed from a second computer as if the files were stored locally on the second computer. File sharing enables users to work on other users' documents, either stored on other users' computers or stored on a common server system. (Upcoming sections in this chapter elaborate on these options.) *Printer sharing* enables many users to access common printers. Using printer sharing, a department or small workgroup can purchase just one or two printers and share that equipment among dozens of employees. Printer sharing lets printerless workstations print and enables users to print on specialized communal printers, such as fast black-and-white laser printers or high-quality color laser printers.

Ultimately, the reason to implement file- and printer-sharing tools is to enhance efficiency. For instance, if a work environment requires employees working on widely separated computers to frequently collaborate on documents, file sharing can facilitate cooperation and collaboration by enabling users to access the same files. Similarly, if users normally roam from one computer to another, file sharing can enable users to access their files from any computer on the network. Printer sharing can improve efficiency and productivity by giving users easy access to the best printer for the job.

You can also measure efficiency in terms of cost. If a workgroup needs access to a large collection of files, storing those files on a single server may be more cost-effective than upgrading all the users' hard disks to store multiple copies of the files. Given a workgroup of, say, 24, it's clearly much less expensive to buy and run a single printer than two dozen, even if the single printer must be of a higher quality to meet the demands of many users. You can also use Samba as a backup tool, obviating the need to buy expensive tape or other backup hardware for every computer.

You can use file- and printer-sharing tools, and particularly Samba, in fairly unusual ways to implement solutions to other problems, too. For instance, you can use Samba to seamlessly turn a low-cost non-PostScript inkjet printer into a PostScript printer. You can turn a Samba server into a tool for automatically creating CD-R discs from collections of files prepared on other computers. Samba can even automatically update a Domain Name System (DNS) server's records to keep DNS lookups correct on a network that uses the Dynamic Host Configuration Protocol (DHCP) for Internet Protocol (IP) address assignment. Such unusual uses of Samba are described in various chapters, but particularly in Chapter 12 and in Chapter 14.

Of course, file and printer sharing aren't without their risks. One risk is the single point of failure. If you store many critical files on a single server, your data are at greater risk of loss in the event of a system crash or hardware failure than if redundant copies are stored on dozens of computers. Similarly, the breakdown of a single printer can be more disruptive than the failure of one printer among two dozen. Another risk is security. Samba is a network server, and like all network servers, it poses some risk of a security breach. (Throughout this book, I point out potential security pitfalls, and Chapter 11 covers this important topic in greater detail.)

On the whole, sharing files and printers often makes sense for networks of more than a handful of computers. The benefits of centralizing data storage, providing users with easy access to other users' files, sharing printers, and implementing unusual tricks through file- and printer-sharing tools far outweigh the risks of a single point of failure and of the potential for security breaches. Of course, this analysis assumes you take adequate precautions. If you store all your files on a single computer with an old hard disk and never back it up, or if you don't implement appropriate security on your network, you're asking for trouble!

Requirements for File Sharing

Because they must present files to clients as if they were local files, file-sharing servers pose certain unique challenges. Some of these challenges are particularly tricky for Samba because different OSs provide different filesystem features, requiring Samba to emulate features that may not be present on the underlying filesystem. Some noteworthy requirements of file sharing protocols include the following:

Exchange of file metadata: Many programs rely upon file *metadata*—that is, data associated with the file, such as the filename, file creation date and time, ownership, permissions, and so on. Thus, file-sharing protocols must transfer the metadata in addition to ordinary file data. In the case of Samba, the metadata supported by SMB/CIFS doesn't perfectly match the metadata provided by the filesystems used by Unix-like OSs, so Samba must make substitutions, which sometimes aren't optimal. Several Samba options enable you to adjust how it handles metadata.

Share identification: Clients need to be able to tell the server which shared directories they need to access. Although share data aren't technically metadata, such as a filename is, they're similar to a filename in that they help users locate the file. Samba provides the ability to define many different file shares, all of which can reside on a single server computer.

Random access: Some network protocols don't support random access to files stored on the server, but most local filesystems do support random access. To work as a networked filesystem, SMB/CIFS must support this feature. Fortunately, its implementation is largely hidden in the guts of Samba; you don't need to configure options to enable it or to tweak it.

File locking: Some programs require exclusive access to files. Many OSs provide a *locking* mechanism, in which one program can claim temporary exclusive access to a file. File-sharing protocols must support these mechanisms. As with metadata, these mechanisms don't always match between Unix systems and Samba clients, so Samba must bridge the gap.

Security: Different file server protocols take different approaches to security. SMB/CIFS uses usernames and passwords, and it supports an optional centralized security system in the form of *domains*. Samba supports these features and also provides access restrictions based on IP address and interactions of Samba usernames with Unix file permissions.

One of the advantages of running Samba atop a Unix-like OS is that Samba provides fine-grained control over many of these file-sharing requirements. For instance, you can adjust parameters that influence how Samba treats usernames and passwords. Such options aren't readily altered when using a Windows system and its built-in SMB/CIFS server.

Requirements for Printer Sharing

SMB/CIFS treats printer sharing much like file sharing, and in fact the Samba configurations for the two types of shares are virtually identical. Many of the same features and requirements of file sharing therefore also apply to printer shares. In most cases, though, the needs for sharing printers are simpler. For instance, printer sharing involves the transfer of print jobs from the client to the server; clients don't need to read print jobs from the server. This fact simplifies printer share configuration for features such as metadata, random access, and file locking. Nonetheless, printer shares have some unique requirements:

Identification as a printer share: SMB/CIFS provides mechanisms that enable a server to specify which shares are ordinary file shares and which are printer shares.

Printer driver delivery: In the simplest case, from the point of view of the server, users or client administrators are responsible for locating and installing drivers. SMB/CIFS, though, provides tools to help automate delivery of drivers for particular printer shares, and Samba supports these features. Chapter 6 describes these tools in more detail.

Of course, in practice printer shares are used quite differently than are file shares, at least from the user's perspective. From the point of view of configuring a Samba server, though, the two are remarkably similar.

One feature of most Unix systems is that they rely upon PostScript printers. Unix systems that don't have PostScript printers typically use Ghostscript (http://www.cs.wisc.edu/~ghost/) to convert PostScript into a format that the printer can understand. This characteristic means that Samba can share a non-PostScript printer either "raw" (using the printer's native drivers on clients) or via Ghostscript (using PostScript drivers on clients). Chapter 6 describes these options in greater detail.

Common File-Sharing Software

To understand Samba, its features, and whether to use it, you should understand, at least in broad strokes, some of the alternatives to Samba. The first part of this task is to understand the difference between file-sharing and file-serving software. After describing this difference, I cover several other popular file- and printer-sharing protocols: Network File System (NFS), Line Printer Daemon (LPD), Internet Printing Protocol (IPP), AppleTalk, NetWare, and SMB/CIFS.

TIP   You can run multiple file servers on a single computer. For instance, you can run both Samba and Netatalk to give users of both Windows and Mac OS computers access to the same files using the clients' native protocols. You can even re-export a share—mount a share using one protocol and then use another server program to share the mounted directory tree with systems that don't understand the first protocol. (A similar process is possible with printer shares, too.) Chapter 12 describes this process for some protocol combinations involving SMB/CIFS.

File Sharing vs. File Serving

All network protocols involve the transfer of data, and many involve the transfer of files. One of the most popular and oldest of these protocols is the File Transfer

Protocol (FTP), which is often used for making files available to anonymous clients on the Internet at large and also for distributing files within organizations. The Hypertext Transfer Protocol (HTTP), upon which the World Wide Web is based, is another popular file-transfer protocol, although it's most often used to transfer files in one direction only (from the server to the client). The Secure Shell (SSH) protocol provides secure file-transfer capabilities through utilities such as scp.

These protocols are examples of *file-serving* protocols, or protocols that transfer or copy a file from one system to another. Typically, a user can't use a file-serving protocol to load, say, a word processing file from an FTP server directly into a word processor. The reason is that these protocols provide limited support for some of the important file-sharing protocol features described earlier in "Requirements for File Sharing." To work on the file, the user must launch a file-transfer client, transfer the file, edit it, and then transfer it back to the server.

File-sharing protocols, by contrast, are designed to treat files on remote systems as if they were stored on the local system. This support means that client software can be better integrated into the client OS as a whole, enabling the file server's shares to be treated like filesystems on a logical level. Users can then load data files directly into application programs, rather than using specialized file-transfer programs to retrieve files from servers and send the results back to the server. This characteristic gives file-sharing protocols a great advantage for many uses in office environments: file operations are streamlined, improving productivity.

Of course, as with many things in life, reality isn't all that simple. In practice, the line between file-serving protocols and file-sharing protocols can be quite blurry. For instance, Samba provides an SMB/CIFS client program known as smbclient, which works like common text-mode FTP clients. You can use smbclient to access SMB/CIFS servers from client OSs for which better-integrated SMB/CIFS client support is non-existent, but there's little advantage to using smbclient over an FTP client for ordinary file transfers. (You can use smbclient as part of a script to back up a system or print files, though, which isn't as easy with FTP clients.) On the other side, a few projects exist to add support for file-serving protocols to OS kernels, effectively turning these protocols into file-sharing protocols. For instance, the Linux Userland File System (LUFS; http://lufs.sourceforge.net/lufs/) adds support to the Linux kernel for FTP and SSH, enabling you to treat servers running these protocols as if they were file-sharing servers. Of course, the lack of critical file-sharing protocol features means that you may run into glitches with some programs or performance may suffer.

NFS

In the Unix world, one of the most popular file-sharing protocols is NFS. Several versions of this protocol exist, and the version number often appears after the *NFS* abbreviation, as in *NFSv3* or *NFSv4*. In early 2004, NFSv2 is common, but NFSv3 is gaining popularity. NFSv4 is still relatively new but is used by some sites.

Unlike most file-sharing protocols, basic NFS relies on the User Datagram Protocol (UDP) for data transport rather than the more complex Transmission Control Protocol (TCP). NFSv3 adds support for TCP, but UDP is still common even with NFSv3 and later. UDP has lower overhead than TCP, so in theory it can produce faster data transfers. On the other hand, UDP also lacks error-correcting mechanisms built into TCP, so

UDP can cause delays and other problems if network connections between the server and client are flaky. For this reason, UDP is best used on small local networks.

Sun Microsystems developed NFS explicitly for use with Unix systems. Thus, NFS fully supports common Unix filesystem metadata, such as ownership (including both user and group ownership), Unix-style permissions, symbolic links, and so on. This feature makes NFS an excellent file-sharing protocol for use between Unix and Unix-like OSs, particularly when support for file ownership, permissions, and other features is important. One potential complication regarding these features is that NFS's ownership mapping is based on user IDs (UIDs). Instead of passing a username with the file, NFS passes a UID number. (The equivalent is true of groups and group IDs, as well.) Thus, if users have accounts on both the client and the server, and if users' UID numbers differ between these two systems, users may not see the correct ownership and per-mission information between computers. A similar problem can occur if users try to access their files from multiple clients. For instance, the user andrew may see his files on the server as being owned by claire, and claire may see her files as owned by dale. Various solutions to this problem exist, such as keeping UID and group ID (GID) numbers manually synchronized across computers, using tools such as the Network Information System (NIS) to automatically synchronize UIDs and GIDs, and using special client- or server-side tools to modify the interpretation of UID and GID numbers. Not all of these solutions work on all platforms, though. In practice, keeping UID and GID numbers synchronized is usually the best approach. If you want to link up systems that had not previously been tied together using NFS or other tools that rely on this mapping, the hassle involved may be great enough that using another protocol, such as SMB/CIFS, may make sense even for Unix-to-Unix communications.

Another important feature of NFS is its method of authentication. Unlike many network protocols, which rely upon usernames and passwords for authentication, NFS uses only client IP addresses for this purpose. The server computer is configured to trust particular clients by IP address (or occasionally by hostname, NIS netgroup name, or a similar method that ultimately reduces to IP addresses). Some servers support adding caveats, such as "squashing" access from particular users to give them restricted access or trusting access only if it originates from a port numbered below 1024. The assumption is that the client computer is properly secured, so the server gives the client the responsibility of controlling access to files using the client's normal authentication tools. This approach is reasonable in low-security environments or on networks to which access is highly restricted. Unfortunately, one problem with this approach is that a miscreant who breaks into one computer on a network or who manages to gain physical access to the network can easily spoof or hijack an IP address, gaining full access to all exported files on the server. This feature makes NFS unsuitable for use on the Internet as a whole and even on large networks or those to which access is easily obtained. If you run an NFS server, it's vital that you restrict access to the server, both physically and in terms of logical and (if possible) physical network topology, to prevent abuse of that server.

Most modern Unix-like OSs ship with NFS implementations for both client and server functions, but these tools have varying pedigrees. Some work well, but others are less reliable. Interoperation is usually possible and not too difficult, but you may need to debug problems that are specific to certain combinations. Configuration details also differ from one client or server to another. NFS implementations for most non-Unix OSs also exist, although some are extra-cost add-ons. In practice, it's often easier and less expensive to get a Unix-like OS to "talk" the protocol that's native to another system than vice versa, although there are exceptions to this rule. (For instance, there's no reliable AppleTalk client for most Unix-like OSs.)

In practice, NFS is usually fairly reliable, but details differ from one OS to another. Because of its reliance on UDP, NFS clients can "hang" if a server goes down. The client keeps retrying the transfer until the server responds. When this happens, applications may become unresponsive until the server comes back online. Some NFS clients offer options to alter this behavior at the expense of reliability—saving or retrieving files may fail, much as if a disk had gone bad.

Overall, NFS is a good choice for use on Unix-dominated networks or when you need Unix-style ownership, permissions, or other metadata. On the other hand, NFS's security model is deficient by modern standards, and its mapping of users is inflexible. These can be serious drawbacks, even in a Unix-only environment. When clients are non-Unix systems, other servers for Unix provide better mapping of features to the clients' expectations.

LPD and IPP

NFS provides no tools for sharing printers; it's a file-only protocol. Of course, Unix systems have a need for sharing printers, so other protocols exist for that purpose. Traditionally, the LPD program, and a protocol of the same name, has handled this task. (Several other printing programs, such as LPRng, also support the LPD protocol.) Like NFS, LPD relies upon IP-based authentication, which is convenient but not as secure as may be desired on some networks. Unix systems have traditionally used LPD or similar programs for both local and network printing, so configuring local and remote printers is similar. Typically, a file called /etc/printcap handles both tasks. A local print server can accept remote jobs, provided authentication is permitted in the /etc/hosts.lpd file. (The authentication method is likely to be different for programs other than the original LPD.)

In recent years, a new printing protocol, IPP, has been gaining popularity. This protocol is most commonly implemented in a printing package known as the Common Unix Printing System (CUPS; http://www.cups.org). Like NFS and LPD, IPP provides passwordless access to printers, but it also supports using passwords, as well as administering the server remotely, detecting network printers semiautomatically, passing printer information between clients and servers, and communicating printer information to applications. For these reasons, IPP is harder to configure on the server than most LPD-based packages, but configuring many CUPS clients can actually be easier than configuring many LPD clients.

If you're configuring a network filled with Unix systems, sticking with LPD, LPRng, or CUPS for printing is generally the simplest course of action. If you want to use passwords, though, using CUPS or SMB/CIFS may be preferable. You must also know at least a little about your server's local LPD or CUPS daemon when you configure a Samba print server because Samba passes its print job to the printer using this system. Chapter 6 describes these issues in more detail.

AppleTalk

In the mid-1980s, Apple developed its own networking tools for its Macintosh line of computers. Initially, the name *AppleTalk* applied to both the hardware and the software, and even today some references use the name in both ways. Officially, though, the name *LocalTalk* now applies to the original hardware (which is now quite rare), and *AppleTalk* applies to the protocol suite. Modern Macintoshes use Ethernet rather than LocalTalk, and the combination of AppleTalk over Ethernet is sometimes referred to as *EtherTalk*. Yet another name associated with this package is *AppleShare*, which refers to the file-sharing portions of the AppleTalk suite.

Originally, AppleTalk was both a protocol stack roughly equivalent to TCP/IP and a set of protocols for sharing files and printers, roughly equivalent to NFS or SMB/CIFS. Today, AppleTalk has added support for operation over TCP/IP, so it's possible to operate an AppleTalk network over the Internet or without passing low-level AppleTalk packets over the network. Macintoshes still rely on the AppleTalk protocol stack for a few operations, though, such as name resolution.

In the Unix world, support for AppleTalk is provided by a few packages, the most popular of which are Netatalk (`http://netatalk.sourceforge.net`) and the Columbia AppleTalk Package (CAP; `http://www.cs.mu.oz.au/appletalk/cap.html`). Both of these packages provide servers to enable Apple Macintosh users to access files stored on the Unix server and to print to printers connected to the Unix server (either directly or via another network protocol). Both packages also provide tools that enable a Unix system to print to an AppleTalk printer, but neither provides any means for a Unix system to function as a client to another AppleTalk file server. Mac OS X, which is built around a Unix-like core, supports AppleTalk in both client and server mode using its own AppleTalk implementation.

AppleTalk uses usernames and passwords to enable authentication for file access, but printer access doesn't require this security level. In practice, you can use firewall software to provide IP-based restrictions as well, but the servers themselves don't usually implement these restrictions. The AppleTalk protocols support encrypting usernames and passwords, but this feature is optional, and many Unix Netatalk and CAP binaries omit this support.

Mac OS Classic (that is, versions prior to Mac OS X) doesn't support Unix-style file ownership or permission information, so neither does AppleTalk. Mac OS Classic does rely heavily on certain filesystem features that aren't available in most Unix-like OSs, though. Specifically, Mac OS splits files into two *forks*: a *data fork*, which contains ordinary file data such as a word processor's text; and a *resource fork*, which contains specialized resources that the OS or a program may use, such as font data, program executable code, or icons. (In some sense, the resource fork is a repository for extended and arbitrary file metadata.) Unix AppleTalk servers typically store the data fork as an ordinary file in the expected location and then store the resource fork as a hidden file or a file in a hidden subdirectory. This solution works but is awkward in some ways. For instance, if a shared directory is accessed both via AppleTalk and in some other way (say, via NFS or SMB/CIFS), it's possible for a user to create a file via AppleTalk and then to delete only the data fork via the other method. The result can be an accumulation of old and undeleted resource fork data.

In addition to resource forks, Mac OS uses some file metadata that Unix systems don't use, or use in different ways. Most AppleTalk implementations are limited to 31-character filenames, for instance, and Mac OS has traditionally treated these filenames in a case-insensitive manner. Recent versions of Mac OS, even before the release of Mac OS X, can handle case-sensitive filenames, though. Recent versions of AppleTalk also support up to 255-character filenames, but this support is currently quite rare outside of Mac OS X.

If your network supports systems running Mac OS Classic, you can run Netatalk, CAP, Mac OS X's AppleTalk server, or some other server to support these systems. Doing so won't interfere with the use of NFS, SMB/CIFS, or other protocols, but you and your users may encounter some oddities, such as files with names longer than 31 characters that don't appear to AppleTalk users and the accumulation of "orphaned" resource forks. You may also want to use AppleTalk merely to use an old networked printer that works with AppleTalk but not other protocols. If your Macintoshes are running Mac OS X, though, other protocols may work better than AppleTalk, and if you don't have many Macintosh clients, chances are there's no need to run this protocol.

NOTE   A client package for Mac OS Classic, known as DAVE (http://www.thursby.com/products/dave.html), enables Mac OS Classic systems to use SMB/CIFS shares. If your network is dominated by Windows systems but has a few Macs running older versions of Mac OS, you can use DAVE to enable all the systems to use the same file- and printer-sharing protocols. Mac OS X includes native SMB/CIFS client support, but DAVE for Mac OS X extends this support. Chapter 18 describes both DAVE and Mac OS X's native SMB/CIFS support in greater detail.

NetWare

Novell (http://www.novell.com) developed its NetWare product in the mid-1980s. Like AppleTalk, NetWare uses its own protocol stack. This stack consists of the Internet Packet Exchange (IPX) and the Sequenced Packet Exchange (SPX), which are roughly equivalent to the IP and TCP portions, respectively, of TCP/IP. Atop these protocols rests the NetWare Core Protocol (NCP), which is the file-sharing protocol.

NetWare was developed primarily for DOS networks and has since been adapted for use with Windows, Mac OS, and other OSs. As such, it implements support for DOS-style metadata but lacks support for Unix-style ownership and permissions.

You can find NetWare support for Unix-like OSs in the form of two packages. The first, Mars_nwe, is based at http://systemhaus.gkdmedien.de/mars_nwe/. (This page is in German, but the download links are obvious. English documentation is available at http://en.tldp.org/HOWTO/IPX-HOWTO-10.html.) Mars_nwe provides NetWare server support for various Unix-like OSs. The second NetWare package for Unix-like systems is ncpfs (ftp://platan.vc.cvut.cz/pub/linux/ncpfs/), which is a NetWare client for Linux. In addition, Novell offers and has offered some limited NetWare support for some Unix-like systems, sometimes through third parties. For instance, Novell once licensed Caldera to provide a NetWare product for Linux, but that product is no longer available.

On the whole, NetWare is most comparable to SMB/CIFS in scope and target market. As a product designed with DOS and its descendents in mind, NetWare works well with a set of OSs much like those that work well with SMB/CIFS. From a Unix perspective, though, NetWare isn't as desirable simply because the common Unix-based NetWare software isn't as sophisticated as Samba.

SMB/CIFS

SMB/CIFS evolved through several stages at various companies, with the most important of these being IBM and Microsoft. Today SMB/CIFS is most strongly associated with Microsoft, which uses the protocol for its Windows family of OSs. As originally developed in the 1980s, SMB/CIFS was built atop the Network Basic Input/Output System (NetBIOS), which is an application programming interface (API) for network file access, and the NetBIOS Extended User Interface (NetBEUI), which functioned as a protocol stack similar to TCP/IP. Modern networks often use SMB/CIFS atop TCP/IP rather than NetBEUI. Two configurations are common for this: NetBIOS over TCP/IP (NBT), which attempts to preserve many NetBIOS features such as NetBIOS-style computer names, and a "raw" mode that discards many of the NetBIOS conventions. The latter was introduced with Windows 2000, and recent versions of Samba also support it. Earlier systems use NBT or non-TCP/IP systems exclusively.

Like AppleTalk and NetWare, SMB/CIFS provides both file- and printer-sharing tools. Most SMB/CIFS servers rely upon usernames and passwords for authentication for both file and printer sharing. You can configure these servers to perform authentication themselves or to rely upon a centralized authentication database located on a computer known as a *domain controller*, described in more detail in the upcoming section "Domain Controllers." Although most configuration details are unaffected by the use of a domain controller, the decision of whether to use one has profound security implications for your network.

Modern versions of SMB/CIFS were developed for use with DOS, Windows, and OS/2. As such, the protocol supports the types of file metadata required by these OSs. These features include both short and long filenames, a read-only flag, and a few special DOS-style flags. SMB/CIFS also supports file ownership information and access control lists (ACLs), which can be used to limit who may access a file. ACLs serve a function similar to Unix-style permissions, but mapping between the two is a nontrivial undertaking. Older clients, such as DOS and Windows 9x/Me systems, didn't use the SMB/CIFS ACL features, so Samba has historically been able to get by with fairly crude ACL support. Windows NT/200x/XP, though, uses ACLs, and because Windows XP is now the Microsoft desktop OS of choice, Samba ACL support is more important than it once was. Samba versions 2.2 and 3.0 have improved ACL support, but this support is partially dependent upon the local filesystem on which files are stored. If you're just now setting up a computer to function as a Samba server, be sure you use a filesystem that supports ACLs natively or for which an appropriate add-on is available. Examples include ext2fs or ext3fs in Linux, XFS in Linux or IRIX, and FFS in FreeBSD 5.0 or later. Chapter 5 provides more information about ACL mapping options.

NOTE   To fully support ACLs, you need only use an ACL-supported filesystem for the Samba file share directories. The Samba executables and configuration files themselves, as well as the bulk of the OS, need not reside on ACL-enabled filesystems.

Some SMB/CIFS extensions enable it to support most Unix-style metadata, including hard and symbolic links, ownership, and Unix-style permissions. Samba 3.0 supports these extensions, but as of early 2004, few clients do. (The 2.6.*x* Linux kernel's new CIFS driver is an important exception to this rule.)

Like many protocols, SMB/CIFS has evolved over time. SMB/CIFS clients and servers must negotiate the appropriate level of support to interoperate. Which level is used is partly responsible for determining which features work when a client and server communicate with one another. Table 1-1 summarizes the most important levels of the SMB/CIFS protocol.

Table 1-1. Levels of the SMB/CIFS Protocol

Name	Description
CORE	Original SMB/CIFS protocol. Usernames and long filenames aren't supported.
COREPLUS	Similar to CORE, but some operations are handled more efficiently.
LANMAN1	Adds support for some new features, such as usernames and long filenames. This was first used by OS/2.
LANMAN2.1	Enhanced variant of LANMAN1.
NT1	Variant of LANMAN dialect used by Windows NT. (The *NT1* name is as used by certain Samba options. Its more technically correct name is *NT LM 0.12*.)

NOTE   Because early SMB/CIFS protocols, such as CORE and COREPLUS, lack support for usernames, using Samba with very old clients that support only these protocols requires changing your Samba configuration to not require usernames. Samba can work with such clients once so configured, though.

Ordinarily, SMB/CIFS is best used on networks on which many clients are DOS, Windows, or OS/2 systems. In some cases, though, you can use SMB/CIFS with other clients, including Unix-like systems, Mac OS, and so on. Unix-like clients will suffer from a lack of Unix-specific metadata unless both the client and server support the Unix extensions, but sometimes this problem is minor. For instance, if the purpose is sharing user data files such as word processing files and spreadsheets, these filesystem features may not be important. (Sharing a directory used for software development can be a problem, though, because the execute bit won't map correctly.) Although Unix lacks some filesystem metadata and other features normally required by SMB/CIFS clients, Samba includes extensive tools to implement these features in ways that should be transparent to clients. In the process, Samba provides configuration options that enable you to manipulate these features in unusual ways. This flexibility can be a big bonus of Samba compared to a Windows file server.

Features of SMB/CIFS

The function of SMB/CIFS sounds simple: It enables sharing files and printers across a network. As with many computer issues, though, considerable complexity lurks just beneath the surface. In the case of SMB/CIFS, much of this complexity derives from the need to support legacy modes of operation, such as short filenames for DOS programs as well as long filenames for more modern OSs and programs. Additional complexity results from the need to operate in a networked environment generally. As such, you must deal with issues such as naming computers.

This section describes many of the implementation details of SMB/CIFS that create the complexity inherent in the protocol. These issues begin with the underlying network tools, NetBEUI and NetBIOS. Understanding how SMB/CIFS clients and servers locate one another is also critically important because this feature isn't the same as ordinary TCP/IP addressing. SMB/CIFS provides several different user authentication tools, and knowing how these tools work can also be important. Finally, SMB/CIFS supports its own set of file metadata, and understanding this issue is important, particularly when it comes to Samba, because Samba must bridge the gap between SMB/CIFS metadata and the metadata provided by the underlying Unix-like OS.

The Role of NetBEUI

For this book's purposes, NetBEUI is of interest mainly for historical reasons because Samba can't normally be used in conjunction with NetBEUI. NetBEUI is important, though, because it's used by some Windows-only LANs, and in the 1980s and early 1990s, NetBEUI was the dominant means of implementing NetBIOS and SMB/CIFS.

 NOTE   At least one set of tools to implement NetBEUI with Samba does exist. Originally developed by Procom Technology (http://www.procom.com), the code includes patches to both Samba and the Linux kernel. This code appears to have languished, though, and has not become mainstream or officially updated since Samba 2.0.*x* and the 2.0.*x* Linux kernels. One site that includes unofficial updates for Samba 2.2.*x* and the 2.4.*x* Linux kernels is http://zhubr.tamb.ru/samba/. Because these patches are far from common, I don't describe them further in this book.

What is NetBEUI, though? One way of thinking about it is to refer to the traditional Open System Interconnection (OSI) model of networking, as depicted in Figure 1-1. In this model, each computer implements a series of software components, known as *layers*, that handle specific functions needed for transferring data between computers. (The Physical layer consists of actual network hardware, though.) NetBEUI is a Transport-layer component. In many modern networking protocols, TCP/IP—and in particular TCP and UDP—monopolizes this layer, so using NetBEUI means that TCP/IP is *not* in use, at least not by the software that uses NetBEUI.

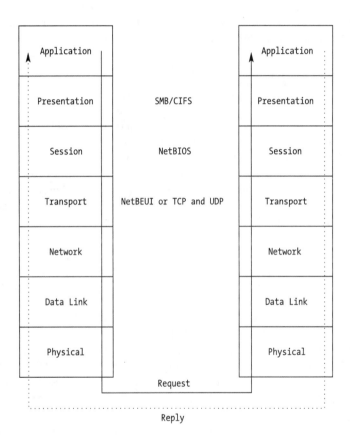

Figure 1-1. The OSI model is a way of describing the operation of TCP/IP or other network stacks.

As a Transport-layer component, NetBEUI is responsible for ensuring that data are delivered intact between computers. NetBEUI is concerned with sending and receiving individual packets but not with higher-level "conversations" between the two systems. That task is handled by NetBIOS and SMB/CIFS at the Session and Presentation layers, respectively.

In a network that uses NetBEUI, that protocol effectively replaces TCP/IP, at least as a means for handling NetBIOS and SMB/CIFS. NetBEUI isn't nearly as complex or capable as TCP/IP, though. Most notably, NetBEUI lacks any means of routing packets between subnets. For this reason, NetBEUI is inadequate for use on large networks or those that are broken up geographically. In both cases, routers are likely to lie between individual systems on the network, making TCP/IP the protocol stack of choice. On the other hand, this limitation can be an advantage. If a computer's SMB/CIFS server uses only NetBEUI and not TCP/IP, the server software becomes very difficult to compromise from anything but the local network. For this reason, some network administrators like to use NetBEUI for SMB/CIFS file and printer sharing as a security measure. You can gain similar advantages, though, by blocking the TCP/IP ports associated with SMB/CIFS services at the network's router. Samba also provides controls based on IP addresses, which can help improve security. Chapter 11 describes Samba security measures in greater detail.

The Role of NetBIOS

As depicted in Figure 1-1, NetBIOS resides above NetBEUI or TCP in the OSI protocol stack model. Historically, NetBIOS was developed before NetBEUI; the latter was a formalized description of network packet structures, which was helpful in expanding NetBIOS services across multiple types of network hardware. The name *NetBIOS* bears a resemblance to the acronym for the Basic Input/Output System (BIOS), the low-level boot and system control software for x86 computers. This isn't a coincidence; NetBIOS was conceived as a network-enabled equivalent to the BIOS, providing an interface to networking operations for applications.

Today, SMB/CIFS is the only major protocol that relies upon NetBIOS. Other common protocols, such as HTTP, the Simple Mail Transfer Protocol (SMTP), and SSH, all use TCP/IP without the intervention of NetBIOS, although, of course, the OSI Session layer is still used by these protocols. Although it was originally developed in conjunction with what is now NetBEUI, today NetBIOS can use any of several Transport-layer and lower protocols for data transport. NetBIOS can use NetBEUI, TCP/IP, SPX/IPX, and other protocols. The most common underlying protocol stack is TCP/IP, with NetBEUI placing second. As noted earlier, Samba is designed to work only with TCP/IP.

Samba is generally referred to as an implementation of SMB/CIFS, which Figure 1-1 shows as residing on a separate OSI layer than NetBIOS. You might therefore think that Samba relies upon another software component to implement NetBIOS functions. This isn't true, though; in reality, Samba handles the NetBIOS functions as well as the SMB/CIFS functions. In truth, NetBIOS is less of a protocol stack layer than it is a set of OS calls for applications. For this reason, there's little need to formally implement NetBIOS for Unix-like systems. Instead, Samba uses its own internal calls and OS interfaces to handle what NetBIOS does for DOS and Windows.

When NetBIOS uses TCP/IP, the resulting protocol is sometimes called NetBIOS over TCP/IP (NetBT or NBT for short). Thus, Samba is effectively an implementation of NBT as well as an SMB/CIFS implementation. IBM often refers to NBT as TCPBEUI, although, despite what the name seems to imply, NetBEUI isn't involved. Technically, NBT is responsible for handling three specific tasks:

The name service: To communicate with one another, computers must be able to call each other by name. This task is described in more detail in the next section, "Machine Addressing."

The datagram service: NetBIOS provides the means to send data in a connectionless manner. When used in conjunction with TCP/IP, this method of data transmission maps logically onto UDP, so UDP packets are used for this purpose.

The session service: In addition to connectionless data transfers, NetBIOS provides session-based data-transfer pipes. In a TCP/IP context, this task is best handled by TCP, so NBT uses TCP for most file-sharing tasks.

NBT is assigned a total of six ports: three TCP ports and three UDP ports, numbered 137 through 139, although in practice only three of these six total ports are commonly used. UDP port 137 handles name resolution (in theory, TCP port 137 may also be used for this purpose, but in practice it seldom is), UDP port 138 handles the datagram service, and TCP port 139 handles the session service. In practice, UDP port 137 and TCP port 139 are the most important ports for SMB/CIFS, but browse lists (in Network Neighborhood or My Network Places on a Windows client) are propagated via the datagram service on UDP port 138.

Technically, NetBIOS isn't really required for SMB/CIFS operation, and some implementations, including Samba, support using SMB/CIFS directly over TCP/IP. In this mode of operation, SMB/CIFS uses TCP port 445 rather than TCP port 139. This operation is rare, though. By default, even when making a Unix-to-Unix connection (using smbclient or some other Unix SMB/CIFS client program and a Samba server), the standard behavior is to use TCP port 139 and NBT.

Machine Addressing

One of the most peculiar aspects of SMB/CIFS, particularly for those who are already familiar with TCP/IP networking, is name resolution. Because NetBIOS and SMB/CIFS were originally developed without reference to TCP/IP, these protocols provide their own means of name resolution. As described in Chapter 4 and Chapter 9, Samba can use standard DNS name resolution mechanisms instead of or in addition to traditional NetBIOS names, at least in some contexts. To operate on a Windows network properly, though, Samba must also implement the traditional NBT methods of name resolution. Several methods of name resolution exist, some of which parallel the methods provided by DNS. You should also understand the limited hierarchical organization that's provided by NetBIOS in the form of workgroups and domains.

Machine Names

Most computer networking technologies use numbers to identify computers. Examples include the 6-byte media access control (MAC) address that's built into Ethernet cards and the 4-byte IPv4 address used by TCP/IP. NetBIOS uses computer names more directly, and a computer's NetBIOS name need not bear much resemblance to the same computer's DNS hostname.

NetBIOS names can be up to 15 characters in length. They can contain uppercase and lowercase letters (although the protocols are case-insensitive), numbers, and the following symbols:

! @ # $ % ^ & ( ) - ' { } . ~

Avoiding symbols, and especially dots (.), is generally wise because they can be confusing and can cause problems if you want to use the same name for a NetBIOS name as for a DNS hostname. As a general rule, making these two names match is a good idea. For instance, if a computer's DNS hostname is waltz.pangaea.edu, you might make its NetBIOS name WALTZ. In principle, you could make the NetBIOS name GURGLE, F#27IOU, or any other legal NetBIOS name that's not already in use on the network, but the mismatch is likely to cause confusion.

NOTE   This book displays most DNS hostnames entirely in lowercase and NetBIOS names entirely in uppercase. This practice should help make it clear which type of name is in use. Exceptions include Web site uniform resource locators (URLs) that use mixed case in their official links or examples in which demonstrating case effects (or the lack of effects) is important.

NetBIOS includes its own name-handling routines, so it's not directly compatible with DNS hostnames. NetBIOS also knows nothing about the IP addresses used with TCP/IP. Of course, when NetBIOS is used over TCP/IP, it must link those names to IP addresses. You can accomplish this task in one or more of several ways:

Broadcast resolution: A client that wants to locate a given server can broadcast a plea to locate the target system. Assuming a system by the specified name exists on the local network, it responds to the query, in the process revealing its IP address. This approach is known as *B mode* name resolution.

Using NBNS: The NetBIOS Name Server (NBNS), also known as the Windows Internet Name Service (WINS), is a service that's roughly equivalent to DNS. If you configure a computer to handle NBNS duties, and if you then tell other SMB/CIFS clients and servers to use the NBNS computer, those clients will register with the NBNS system and then ask it for the IP addresses of computers they want to contact. This approach is known as *P mode* (for *point-to-point*) name resolution.

Using lmhosts: The computer can use the lmhosts file, which is typically located in /etc/samba or a similar directory for Samba systems, in the C:\WINDOWS directory or its equivalent on Windows 9*x*/Me systems, or in the C:\WINNT\SYSTEM32\DRIVERS\ETC directory or its equivalent on Windows NT/200*x*/XP systems. This file works much like the /etc/hosts file for TCP/IP name resolution; it contains lines that begin with IP addresses and end with NetBIOS names.

Using DNS: You can configure computers to use DNS (although it's not part of NBT) instead of or in addition to traditional NBT name resolution methods. Ordinarily, the computer making the name lookup adds its own domain name to the specified NetBIOS name and then requests a name lookup. For instance, if a lookup for WALTZ is done on tango.pangaea.edu, the system tries to find waltz.pangaea.edu in the DNS records. Samba can use this approach, as can the Windows NT/200*x*/XP family. This approach isn't an option for DOS and Windows 9*x*/Me, though.

Typically, Windows 9*x*/Me systems use a combination of one or more of the first three methods. The first two methods can be combined in either order. A *hybrid (H) node* is a computer that's configured to try an NBNS system and, if that fails, to try a broadcast. A *mixed (M) node* tries a broadcast first and then looks for an NBNS system. The default configuration for Windows 9*x*/Me systems is to use B mode, but Windows 200*x*/XP systems use DNS by default. Chapter 9 describes how to configure Samba to function as an NBNS system, as well as how to configure Windows clients to use this server.

One important difference between NetBIOS names and DNS hostnames is that computers register their own NetBIOS names, whereas DNS hostnames are assigned centrally in a DNS server. When a computer that uses NetBIOS boots, it broadcasts the name it has been given in its configuration files or sends that name to the NBNS system. If no other computer is using that name, the computer keeps it. (Of course, this approach can cause conflicts if some computers on the network use a lmhosts file that lists names that another computer tries to claim.)

Although you can think of each computer as having a single NetBIOS name, each computer typically registers several distinct network resources, which may correspond to specific types of services the system offers. Each resource uses the master name plus a 1-byte code that identifies the resource type. You can scan an individual computer to learn what resources it makes available by using Samba's nmblookup utility from a Unix system:

```
$ nmblookup -SR NESSUS
querying NESSUS on 192.168.1.255
192.168.1.3 NESSUS<00>
Looking up status of 192.168.1.3
        NESSUS          <00> -          B <ACTIVE>
        NESSUS          <03> -          B <ACTIVE>
        NESSUS          <20> -          B <ACTIVE>
        RINGWORLD       <00> - <GROUP> B <ACTIVE>
        RINGWORLD       <1e> - <GROUP> B <ACTIVE>
```

This output identifies three resources offered by NESSUS, numbered (in hexadecimal) 0x00, 0x03, and 0x20. Two additional resources using the name RINGWORLD also appear; these are related to the workgroup or domain, as described in the next section, "Workgroups and Domains." Table 1-2 summarizes some of the important NetBIOS machine resources by number.

Table 1-2. Common NetBIOS Machine Resource IDs

Number	Name	Function
00	Standard Workstation Service	Computer's NetBIOS name.
03	Messenger (WinPopUp) Service	Text messaging service; sends messages that appear in a window on the recipient's screen.
06	RAS Server Service	Enables remote access to a Windows server via a modem. Samba doesn't support this service.
1B	Domain Master Browser Service	The domain master browser collects data on computers available on the network for the benefit of network browsers. Chapter 8 describes this service in more detail.
1D	Master Browser Service	Similar to the Domain Master Browser Service but functions on a single network segment. Chapter 8 describes this service.
1F	NetDDE Service	Network Dynamic Data Exchange. Enables sharing data across applications run on multiple computers. Samba doesn't support this service.
20	File or Print Service	Sharing of files or printers. Chapters 5 and 6 describe this service.
21	RAS Client Service	A remote access client that connects to the RAS Server (resource code 06).
BE	Network Monitor Agent	A method of monitoring the performance of a network. Samba doesn't support this service.
BF	Network Monitor Utility	Similar to the Network Monitor Agent (resource code BE). Samba doesn't support this service.

Workgroups and Domains

Internet hostnames are multitiered in nature. At the top of the hierarchy are top-level domains (TLDs), such as edu, com, and tw. A limited number of TLDs exist, and changes to the collection of TLDs tend to be rare. Below TLDs are domain names. Depending upon the TLD, the domain name may be owned by an individual or an organization or be controlled by the authority responsible for the TLD. In any event, the domain name is written before the TLD, with a dot (.) separating the two, as in pangaea.edu or example.com. The domain name may be optionally split into subdomains, as in physics.pangaea.edu, and these may be split into sub-subdomains and so on to an arbitrary depth. In the case of domains that are controlled by the TLD authority, at least one split is more or less mandatory. For instance, the uk TLD is split into domains for commercial, educational, and other purposes, so an organization may register threeroomco.co.uk but not threeroomco.uk or co.uk. However the domains are organized, the most fine-grained option, which appears on the extreme left part of the domain name, is the machine name, such as waltz in waltz.physics.pangaea.edu.

This review of Internet domain names is important because SMB/CIFS also supports domains, but these domains are entirely unrelated to Internet domains. Actually, SMB/CIFS supports two very similar ways of organizing computers: workgroups and domains. (They're actually the same thing, but domains support a few features that aren't present on workgroups.)

Unlike Internet domains, SMB/CIFS workgroups and domains support only two tiers of organization: the machine name and the workgroup or domain name. (Even these two tiers are more apparent than real; the structure is built at the user interface level, not built into the underlying data structures.) For instance, you might call your SMB/CIFS workgroup or domain PHYSICS and name the computers in that workgroup or domain WALTZ, FOXTROT, and so on. No further layers of organization are possible, though; there's no equivalent to the Internet's TLDs, and you can't break the PHYSICS workgroup or domain into subdomains as you can an Internet domain. Furthermore, SMB/CIFS workgroups and domains are fairly local constructs. Ordinarily, workgroups are confined to a single physical network segment, but Samba provides mechanisms that can extend a workgroup to a limited degree. SMB/CIFS domains can span multiple physical network segments, but to do so, you must configure a computer as a *domain controller* and tell all the computers in the domain to refer to that system; Chapter 10 covers this topic. The topics of master browser configuration and NBNS configuration, described in Chapters 8 and 9, are related to this issue, as well.

In practice, workgroups and domains can be a useful way to organize computers in a network of a few dozen computers. From their network browsers, users will most easily see the computers in their own workgroup or domain. Users can still access computers in other workgroups or domains, but doing so requires extra browsing steps. Isolating computers in this fashion can be a good way to reduce clutter, much like storing files in separate directories.

 NOTE In addition to reusing the word *domain*, SMB/CIFS reuses the word *browser*. This word often refers to Web browsers, but in an SMB/CIFS context, it refers to a tool provided in Windows as *Network Neighborhood* or *My Network Places*. This tool enables browsing of file and printer shares for easy access. Each new release of Windows has further blurred the lines between SMB/CIFS browsing and Web browsing, so the distinction isn't always clear to end users. The servers used to handle these two types of browsing are different, though.

In addition to their handling of separate physical subnetworks, workgroups and domains differ in terms of authentication. Workgroups rely on individual servers to authenticate user access, whereas domains use a centralized domain controller to authenticate user access to all of a domain's resources. This configuration can greatly simplify network administration if your network supports many servers, but it can be more tedious to set up initially. Chapter 10 describes this process in more detail.

Referring to the `nmblookup` command presented earlier in "Machine Names," you see that this command returned the workgroup or domain name (RINGWORLD) in addition to the target computer's NetBIOS name. As with the NetBIOS name, computers can offer services for the workgroup or domain as a whole. Table 1-3 summarizes some of these.

Table 1-3. Common NetBIOS Group Resource IDs

Number	Name	Function
00	Standard Workstation Group	Workgroup or domain to which the computer belongs.
1C	Logon Server	Identifies a server that provides authentication services for a domain.
1E	Normal Group Name	Workgroup or domain name used by the computer during master browser elections, as described in Chapter 8.
20	Group Name	If present, this value normally duplicates the Standard Workstation Group (00) number.

User Authentication

Security is an important part of any network protocol. SMB/CIFS provides security through username/password authentication, but several twists on this basic method exist:

Workgroup vs. domain authentication: As described in the previous section, "Workgroups and Domains," workgroups leave the task of authentication to individual servers, whereas domains centralize this job in the domain controller.

Need for usernames: Windows 9*x*/Me SMB/CIFS servers don't use local usernames at all, although they can use usernames in conjunction with network resources. Thus, these servers don't require the use of a username. Instead, they assign unique passwords to each share. Indeed, the early CORE and COREPLUS versions of SMB/CIFS don't support usernames at all. Windows NT/200*x*/XP, by contrast, use usernames and passwords much like Unix systems do, so they require both features for SMB/CIFS shares. Samba can emulate either system.

Encryption: Ideally, network protocols that use passwords encrypt them to prevent miscreants with network sniffers from stealing the passwords. SMB/CIFS supports password encryption, but its use isn't required by the protocol. In practice, encryption is required for Windows 95 Original Equipment Manufacturer (OEM) Service Release 2 (OSR2), Windows NT 4.0 Service Pack 3 (SP3), and later releases, but you can change this requirement. Samba supports both encrypted and unencrypted passwords; however, SMB/CIFS encryption is incompatible with that used by most Unix password databases, so when using encrypted passwords, you must maintain separate Unix and Samba password databases. This topic is covered in greater detail in Chapter 4 and in Chapter 7.

Most Unix-like systems use case-sensitive passwords—an a is different from an A, for example. SMB/CIFS passwords, though, may be either case-sensitive or case-insensitive, depending upon the authentication protocol used—an a may be treated identically to an A. This difference is unimportant when using encrypted SMB/CIFS passwords because Samba provides a password database of its own that stores appropriate hashes for the SMB/CIFS authentication methods. When using unencrypted passwords, though, you can configure Samba to try several variants on a provided password in an effort to match the case-insensitive SMB/CIFS password to the case-sensitive Unix password.

In addition to authenticating users with a username and password, other methods of authentication are possible. One of these methods is to use IP addresses, much as NFS does. You can implement such controls by using firewall tools or by using special Samba options. If you like, you can even disable the normal password requirements and use IP-based authentication alone, but such configurations are generally quite risky. You may want to accept such risks on a system that provides publicly available shares, though.

Although SMB/CIFS provides for the encryption of passwords, it doesn't provide any means to encrypt nonpassword data. This deficiency makes SMB/CIFS alone an unsuitable protocol for transferring highly sensitive data across any but the most secure local networks. Of course, you can set up a virtual private network (VPN) if you need to share files across the Internet. Another option is to use a Secure Sockets Layer (SSL) addition to Samba versions prior to 3.0 (this option has been removed with this version of the server) or to tunnel the protocol through SSH. Chapter 11 describes these options. Another option related to authentication, security, and encryption is Kerberos (http://web.mit.edu/kerberos/www/). Samba supports Kerberos, but only if you compile the program with appropriate support. Most precompiled Samba binaries lack this support.

File Metadata

As a protocol for sharing files and printers for DOS, Windows, and OS/2 systems, SMB/CIFS provides support for file metadata associated with these OSs. Some of the specific features provided by SMB/CIFS include the following:

Filename length: SMB/CIFS supports two types of filenames: short filenames, which are eight characters in length followed by an optional three-character extension (therefore sometimes called *8.3 filenames*), and long filenames, which can be up to 127 characters in length. Most Unix-like systems support filenames of at least 127 characters, and often twice that, but details vary from one OS and filesystem to another. Samba's challenge comes in creating 8.3 filenames when the file's real filename is longer than this. Samba must do this on the fly and consistently so a client can use the same filename for the same file time after time.

Legal filename characters: DOS is fairly restrictive in what characters are legal in its filenames, so when dealing with DOS clients, filenames must sometimes be altered. This task is akin to creating 8.3 filenames from long filenames.

Filename case-sensitivity: DOS uses uppercase-only filenames. Windows uses mixed-case filenames but handles them in a case-insensitive manner. Unix-like OSs, by contrast, use case-sensitive filenames. Mapping these two systems can be tricky, particularly if a directory contains files that differ only in case. Samba does a good job of handling this task, though. Its work is helped if a directory is used primarily or exclusively through Samba, meaning that files that differ in case only are unlikely to be created.

File date and time stamps: All modern OSs include date and time stamps on their files. Many applications ignore this data, but it can sometimes be useful to users in searching for the correct file. A few programs, such as some software development tools, also rely on time stamps. Unix systems store the date and time in Coordinated Universal Time (UCT) format, which is similar to the better-known Greenwich mean time (GMT): the time in Greenwich, England. SMB/CIFS, by contrast, uses local time. Fortunately, this conversion is fairly straightforward, but you may run into problems if your time zone is set incorrectly. You may also want to use a tool to coordinate the clocks on all your computers. SMB/CIFS provides a time-setting protocol, and you can use another tool, known as the Network Time Protocol (NTP), to set a Samba server's clock to an external source. Chapter 12 covers this topic.

File ownership: Early versions of the SMB protocol included no concept of file ownership. With the development of Windows NT, though, file ownership information was added to SMB/CIFS. This information isn't identical to Unix ownership, but a mapping can be set up. Since Samba 2.2, the software has done more to handle this mapping appropriately.

ACLs: The earlier section "SMB/CIFS" introduced the concept of ACLs, which are supported by recent versions of the SMB/CIFS protocol. Samba 2.2 and later supports ACLs on Unix systems that provide this support. Earlier versions of Samba could only map SMB/CIFS ACLs to Unix-style permission modes.

Read-only bits: In the DOS heritage, files can be written to by default, and a special metadata flag, the *read-only bit*, identifies files that shouldn't be modified. This concept is the inverse of the Unix-style write permission bit, and Samba performs this mapping. Some additional complications arise because Unix provides three write permission bits and because DOS and Unix treat the ability to delete write-protected files differently. Samba provides various options that enable you to customize how these differences are handled.

Hidden bits: DOS and its descendents enable you to mark a file as *hidden* using a special metadata bit. When this bit is present, most programs won't display the file as present. This concept is similar to Unix *dot files*, whose filenames begin with a dot (.). Samba can enable the hidden bit on dot files and store the hidden bit using the world execute bit, which has no direct counterpart in SMB/CIFS. Ordinarily, Samba hides dot files, but applications can't set the hidden bit on arbitrary files. You can change this behavior if you like, though.

System bits: The *system bit* is a piece of metadata that identifies a file as being of special importance to the OS. Such files are unlikely to be stored on an SMB/CIFS server, but the protocol supports this bit nonetheless. Samba can map it to the group execute bit, which has no direct equivalent in SMB/CIFS. As with the hidden bit mapping, you can enable or disable this mapping. The default settings disable storage of this bit.

Archive bits: When you back up a DOS or Windows system, the backup software can clear the *archive bit*. This bit is set when you create or restore data and cleared when a backup is made of the file. SMB/CIFS supports this bit, and Samba can map it to the owner execute bit, which has no equivalent in SMB/CIFS. The default Samba settings mean that files created by clients will have the owner's execute bit set on all files, which can be confusing if the directory is used both from Samba and directly on the Linux server or via NFS. As with the hidden and system bits, you can change Samba's handling of this bit if you like.

File streams: *File streams* are similar to the forks used by Mac OS, but streams are more flexible. A given file can support an arbitrary number of named streams, each of which can hold particular types of data. Samba doesn't support file streams as of version 3.0, because this feature is seldom used in the Windows world, and programs that do use it almost invariably don't require it. Support for this feature may be added in the future but will probably require an underlying filesystem that also supports it, such as the Journaled File System (JFS) under AIX or Linux or the Extents Filesystem (XFS) under IRIX or Linux.

Samba provides many options related to the handling of file metadata. The default settings work well for most installations, but you may want to fine-tune these options by enabling or disabling support for specific metadata bits, by changing filename case options, and so on. Chapter 5 covers most of these options.

When used with OSs that are outside of the DOS/Windows family, you may encounter unusual file metadata needs. For instance, Unix-like clients work best with case-sensitive filenames. Some file metadata options can be changed to help out with such clients. Other clients provide other unusual needs. For instance, Mac OS Classic systems may need to store resource fork data. In this specific case, the special need is handled by the Mac OS Classic SMB/CIFS client, which creates special directories in which the resource forks are stored. This solution is similar to the approach used by CAP or Netatalk, but it's done by the client rather than the server. Chapter 18 describes some of the needs of specific SMB/CIFS client OSs.

Handling Subnets and Routing

Linking SMB/CIFS to TCP/IP involves connecting components that weren't originally designed to be compatible. Some of the problems and solutions of this integration have already been described, such as the different methods used to name computers and the assignment of TCP/IP port numbers to NetBIOS services. One topic that requires more elaboration is how to handle subnets and routing. The original NetBEUI protocols weren't designed to handle more than a few dozen computers on a single physical network, but TCP/IP is perfectly capable of working across large internets. Adapting SMB/CIFS to work on internets requires making some changes and extensions to its basic features.

NOTE Capitalization is important for the word *internet*. Used with a lowercase *i*, the word refers to any collection of physical networks, typically linked by routers. An internet might link together networks in different wings of a building or across buildings, even when these networks aren't tied to any other network. When capitalized, the word *Internet* refers to the globe-spanning network of networks that's become so important to daily life in the past decade. The Internet is the single largest internet ever created. From an SMB/CIFS point of view, the Internet is just another internet, albeit a huge one.

As used in this section, the assumption is that a subnet is more or less synonymous with a LAN. A LAN is a portion of a network where the computers are connected more or less directly to one another. Most important, no routers lie between two computers on a LAN. Some network types, such as the common twisted-pair Ethernet, typically place hubs or switches between computers, but these devices are very low level, don't interfere with the passage of broadcast packets, and require no special configuration to handle TCP/IP, NetBEUI, or other protocol stacks' data. A *subnet* is a set of computers that lie in the same TCP/IP address space, as defined by their IP addresses and *subnet masks* (also known as *netmasks*). In most cases, the two terms describe the same set of computers, but it's possible to create a network that's a single LAN but that contains multiple subnets or otherwise doesn't map the two constructs in a one-to-one manner. As a general rule, such networks can be tricky to configure properly, so most network administrators avoid them.

The original NetBEUI and NetBIOS implementations worked well across a single subnet but provided no means for routing packets between subnets. TCP/IP's routing capabilities add a complication to NBT because some of the assumptions of NetBIOS don't map well to a routable environment. The most important of these assumptions is the original handling of name resolution. As described earlier in "Machine Names," NBT uses broadcasts for resolving names. As implemented in TCP/IP, such broadcasts seldom pass beyond a subnet's router to other subnets. For this reason, computers on one subnet may not be able to reach computers on another subnet by name. For instance, consider the small internet depicted in Figure 1-2. If MAMBO wants to contact TANGO, there's no problem because these two systems are on the same subnet. If MAMBO tries to contact FOXTROT, though, the broadcast to locate the name fails because it's not passed by the router between the two subnets.

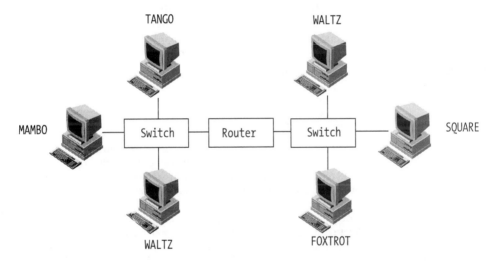

Figure 1-2. An SMB/CIFS network can span multiple subnets with the help of special configurations.

The problem with SMB/CIFS and internets isn't in the core protocols, though, at least not when TCP/IP is the protocol stack in use. MAMBO can certainly direct packets at the SMB/CIFS ports on FOXTROT, and FOXTROT can reply in kind. The main problem is one of machine addressing. Several solutions exist to this problem:

Using IP addresses directly: If the client uses IP addresses directly rather than using a NetBIOS name, there's no problem.

Name servers: If you configure a system to handle NBNS duties, and if all the computers use the NBNS system, the problem vanishes. The NBNS computer knows about all six computers on the network depicted in Figure 1-2 and can return an appropriate IP address.

Special router configurations: If the router is configured to pass broadcasts, or at least NBT name broadcasts, between networks, the problem goes away. Most routers aren't so configured by default, but you can reconfigure any but the simplest routers to do the job.

Using DNS or lmhosts: These two methods of NetBIOS name resolution aren't affected by intervening routers. Samba and Windows NT/200*x*/XP systems can all use DNS, and most SMB/CIFS clients can use lmhosts, so these options are good ones in many environments.

Proxying: A computer on each network can be configured as a proxy. When a NetBIOS name proxy receives a name broadcast and doesn't notice a reply, the proxy can forward the request on to an NBNS system located on the other subnet or can send a directed broadcast to the other network. If the proxy receives a reply, it can pass the information on to the original requesting system. You can configure Samba to function in this way.

Certain complications can arise from some of these options. For instance, consider Figure 1-2 again. Both subnets include a computer called WALTZ. This configuration is perfectly legal when using broadcasts for name resolution because neither WALTZ computer is visible from the other's subnet. Assuming that all the systems use the same workgroup or domain name, though, this name conflict will cause confusion at best when the subnets are linked together via most of the preceding methods. (Direct use of IP addresses is an exception.)

NOTE The fact that SMB/CIFS systems require special configuration to work across subnets can increase administrative demands, but it also helps avoid global confusion. Because of the limited range of NetBIOS name broadcasts and other SMB/CIFS broadcasts, no coordination of NetBIOS names or of workgroup or domain names is needed between organizations on the Internet. For instance, both pangaea.edu and example.com could have workgroups called PHYSICS and even use duplicate NetBIOS names without fear of interference. (This assumes, of course, that the two organizations operate physically separate networks.) This contrasts with DNS hostnames, which must be registered with the appropriate authorities before they're used on the Internet.

Other parts of the SMB/CIFS system can also be adversely affected by splitting a network into subnets. Most notably, network browsing relies on one computer, the master browser, having data on all the network's computers. Much of this information is gleaned from broadcasts, and clients locate the local master browser by sending a broadcast to find it. In practice, browsing across subnets is possible, but it requires special configuration. Typically, one computer on each subnet is assigned to be the subnet's local master browser, and those local master browsers are then linked together. Configuring the router to pass broadcasts or using a proxy can also solve the problem.

Traditionally, Windows networks have solved all of these problems by using a domain rather than a workgroup. Domains include explicit mechanisms to handle name resolution and browsing across subnets. As a general rule, this is the best approach to the problem, but Samba is more flexible. Samba can implement a domain, but it can also provide proxying solutions that enable a workgroup to function across subnets. This approach can be handy if you have an existing workgroup configuration that works well but you need to extend it to a new subnet. Chapters 8, 9, and 10 describe these issues in more detail.

The Components of an SMB/CIFS Network

Although SMB/CIFS is, in principle, just like any other network protocol, in practice an SMB/CIFS network includes several components not used by most other protocols. These components include SMB/CIFS servers, SMB/CIFS clients, NBNS systems, master browsers, and domain controllers.

SMB/CIFS Servers

Most computers that run Samba function as SMB/CIFS servers. As defined here, an SMB/CIFS server is a computer that makes file or printer shares available to other computers. As such, an SMB/CIFS server is closely equivalent in function to an NFS server, an AppleTalk server, or any other type of file or print server. On a TCP/IP network, the SMB/CIFS server listens on TCP port 139 for connection requests and responds to those requests as its configuration mandates. In principle, an SMB/CIFS server need only listen on this one port. In practice, UDP port 137 and possibly UDP port 138 are also important. As described earlier in "The Role of NetBIOS," UDP port 137 handles name resolution tasks. If the network uses broadcast name resolution, the server must listen to port 137 to hear these broadcasts. If it doesn't, clients may not be able to contact the server by name.

A single SMB/CIFS server can provide several file and printer shares. For instance, you might provide one file share that holds common program files, a second file share that delivers templates and other documents that all users at a site must access, and a printer share for printing to a workgroup printer. File servers can also hold users' data files, which is convenient for backup purposes, reduces the need for large hard drives on client computers, and enables users to more readily move from one computer to another on a network. Each share is named and can be accessed by name from a client's SMB/CIFS browser, as shown in Figure 1-3, which presents seven file shares and five printer shares on a single server.

Figure 1-3. A single SMB/CIFS server can provide many file and printer shares.

All recent versions of Windows include SMB/CIFS server software, typically installed as "file and printer sharing for Microsoft networks" or something similar. Although configuring a Windows system to share files isn't the primary focus of this book, the topic is touched upon in Chapter 16 because some backup methods require the systems to be backed up to function as file-sharing servers.

An SMB/CIFS server can be anything from a fast and powerful dedicated server computer with huge hard disks to a lowly desktop system running an old OS. Of course, you wouldn't use these two systems similarly. The dedicated server would be just that, whereas the underpowered desktop system might be used as a fallback server or in a peer-to-peer networking environment, as described in the upcoming sidebar, "Client/Server vs. Peer-to-Peer Networks."

Samba uses a daemon called smbd to provide the file- and printer-sharing service. This daemon listens on TCP port 139 (and 445 for non-NBT operation) and provides support for the file-exchange protocols and various support functions. A separate daemon, nmbd, handles the name resolution and browse support functions.

SMB/CIFS Clients

SMB/CIFS client computers function in a way analogous to other network clients. These systems initiate data-transfer requests involving SMB/CIFS servers, usually as a result of the activities of users who sit at the client computers. SMB/CIFS clients are often user desktop systems. Typically, users run common office programs on the clients, sometimes from program files stored on SMB/CIFS servers. Data files may also be stored either locally or on SMB/CIFS servers.

In the case of printer operations, the client converts a document into a format that's suitable for printing using whatever printing language the printer supports and then sends the document as a file to the SMB/CIFS print server.

To initiate a connection, an SMB/CIFS client normally performs name resolution using broadcasts, an NBNS system, or some other method, as described earlier in "Machine Names." Frequently, SMB/CIFS clients are also configured as SMB/CIFS servers, although this configuration isn't always necessary and can be a security risk.

SMB/CIFS clients are frequently Windows computers, but SMB/CIFS clients for many other OSs are also available. Examples include Unix-like or some other OSs running Samba clients, OS/2, BeOS, Mac OS Classic running DAVE, and Mac OS X's native SMB/CIFS client. This list isn't exhaustive, though. Chapter 18 describes SMB/CIFS clients for several OSs.

An SMB/CIFS browser, such as the one depicted in Figure 1-3, is an important part of the SMB/CIFS client package on many OSs. The browser enables users to scan a network for nearby SMB/CIFS servers and to access the shares on the server. In most client OSs, file shares can be accessed directly, as if they were on the local computer. Printer shares must normally be accessed by installing a printer driver, giving the resulting printer object a name, and linking it to the share name.

In most cases, including Windows, the SMB/CIFS client is tightly integrated into the OS. This integration enables the client OS to present the files stored on the file server as if they were local files. A few SMB/CIFS clients, such as the smbclient program that ships with Samba, provide a more aloof interaction model. In this case, the client is a separate program, requiring special operations within that program to move files back and forth.

Client/Server vs. Peer-to-Peer Networks

Most network operations involve clients and servers. Frequently, a single server computer functions primarily as a server for many client computers. For instance, a typical Web server delivers Web pages to dozens, hundreds, thousands, or more clients each day. In this *client/server* model of networking, a central resource (the server) is frequently much more powerful than the clients it serves. An SMB/CIFS server probably needs lots of disk space, a fast disk subsystem, and good network connections. Particularly if it handles lots of clients, it may also need a lot of RAM and a fast CPU; however, file sharing is inherently more disk-intensive than RAM- or CPU-intensive, so a system with a modest amount of RAM and CPU speed may suffice on many networks. SMB/CIFS clients, as desktop workstations, typically need good display subsystems and may have site-specific requirements, such as a fast CPU if the computers are to be used for CPU-intensive work. In an SMB/CIFS client/server network, one or more servers hold many critical user files, interface to printers, and so on.

Another model of overall network operations is the *peer-to-peer* network. In this arrangement, most computers function as both clients and servers. Instead of storing user files on a single server, users store their files locally but make them available to other users on other computers on an ad-hoc basis. Printers can be shared in a similar way. Essentially, a peer-to-peer network distributes the work of the server in a client/server network across most or all of the clients. Note that a peer-to-peer model still uses client programs and server programs, but a given computer is likely to run both types of programs.

Peer-to-peer networking is common in small offices. Particularly when using Windows and its standard SMB/CIFS support, configuring a peer-to-peer network is fairly straightforward. As the number of computers on the network rises, though, the peer-to-peer configuration can become an administrative nightmare. For instance, if a user leaves the organization, you may need to delete that user's password on dozens of individual computers, particularly if you use a workgroup rather than a domain. The security risks of running servers on every user's desktop computer can be quite substantial as well. For these reasons, a client/server network configuration is generally preferred for all but the smallest networks.

Samba can integrate well with both client/server and peer-to-peer networks, but Samba's greatest strength is in its server side, so it often forms the core of a client/server network. You configure the Samba server and the Samba client in the same way for either network type; the difference is in one of the overall mix of clients and servers on the network, not in the configuration of any one computer.

Master Browsers

SMB/CIFS networks normally sport at least one master browser. As noted earlier in "Workgroups and Domains," the master browser is responsible for keeping track of the computers available on the network—or more precisely, the computers that have announced themselves to the master browser as offering services. The master browser computer may or may not also keep track of the computers' IP addresses (it does so only if it also functions as an NBNS or other name-resolution server). Rather, the function of the master browser is to maintain a list of available computers that are ultimately displayed in clients' SMB/CIFS browsers. Users can then click a computer to see what resources it makes available.

SMB/CIFS provides mechanisms to automatically determine which computer will function as the master browser. This process is known as a *browser election*, and it follows specific rules related to the OS each computer runs, what other functions on the SMB/CIFS network the system performs, and so on. Chapter 8 describes this process. If a master browser is shut down or becomes inaccessible, the remaining computers will notice this fact and hold a new election. Thus, there's no need to explicitly name a master browser, although you can "rig" the election when using Samba, as described in Chapter 8.

Master browser elections take place on a single subnet and determine which computer functions as the *local master browser*. Another type of master browser coordinates browse lists across subnets in a domain configuration and is known as the *domain master browser*. Chapter 8 also describes this type of master browser, including how to configure Samba to fill this role.

NBNS Servers

NBNS systems are optional components of an SMB/CIFS network. As described earlier in "Machine Names," NBT provides several methods of name resolution, and some SMB/CIFS implementations expand upon this list. NBNS systems are just one of these methods, albeit a convenient method.

If your network sports an NBNS system, clients register their names with the server when they boot, so the NBNS computer doesn't need much in the way of explicit configuration. This feature contrasts with a DNS server, which must be updated whenever you add a new computer to a network or change a computer's IP address. For this reason, NBNS configuration is fairly transparent—at least, in theory. In practice, several complications can make your life more difficult. For instance, you may want to tie together NBNS and DNS, enabling your NBNS computer to add or change entries on your DNS server's database. (The DNS server may or may not run on the same computer that hosts the NBNS software.) Another important issue is telling your SMB/CIFS clients about the NBNS system. In practice, this task is handled in much the same way as configuring a TCP/IP client computer to use a DNS server: by entering an IP address in a configuration screen or file. Windows clients can also accept this information as part of their DHCP configurations, but only if the DHCP server is told the NBNS computer's IP address.

Chapter 9 covers NBNS configuration in more detail, including information on linking NBNS and DNS. Unlike master browsers, NBNS systems require explicit configuration as such; there's no equivalent to the master browser election to automatically elevate a computer to NBNS status. If you specify multiple NBNS systems, you must ensure that they can communicate to exchange their lists of machines on the local network.

Domain Controllers

If you want centralized login or traditional Windows-style operation across subnets, you must normally configure a domain. Doing so requires setting aside a computer as a domain controller. Ordinarily, the domain controller also functions as a domain master browser and as an NBNS system. (The domain controller and domain master browser functions *must* be handled by the same system; NBNS functions can be, but usually aren't, handled by another system.) The domain controller must host usernames and passwords for all users of the domain; it's responsible for accepting user login requests and providing authorizations based on usernames and passwords.

In the simplest case, a domain contains a single domain controller, which must be explicitly configured as such. This system is sometimes called the *primary domain controller* (PDC). As a precaution against its failure and to help distribute the load, many networks also sport a *backup domain controller* (BDC), which synchronizes its data with that of the PDC. If the PDC becomes inaccessible, computers on the network automatically switch to the BDC. Samba has long been able to function as a PDC, although Samba hasn't supported all PDC functions. Samba's ability to function as a BDC is more constrained. Although Samba interfaces with normal SMB/CIFS clients and servers as a PDC, its internal handling of this task is different enough from that of Windows that Samba can't exchange the data files to enable it to function as a BDC. Methods do exist to let Samba function as a BDC to a Samba PDC, though.

Complicating domain configuration is the fact that different versions of Windows make different requirements of the domain controller. For this reason, the procedures for configuring and using a domain controller for different versions of Windows are different. The distinctions between Windows 9*x*/Me and Windows NT/200*x*/XP are particularly great.

Summary

SMB/CIFS has a history spanning roughly 20 years. In that time, the protocol has evolved considerably, including substantial changes to enable it to operate over network stacks for which it wasn't designed, additions to support new types of file metadata, and improved authentication methods. This history is partially hidden from network administrators and is almost completely hidden from users, but the history sometimes obtrudes itself in the form of configuration options to enable or disable particular features. Understanding some of the goals of the file-sharing system, its contrasts to other file-sharing systems, and general features and components of the system can be important in configuring Samba.

#### CHAPTER 2

Samba and SMB/CIFS

CHAPTER 1 INTRODUCED the SMB/CIFS protocol in general terms, with only occasional references to Samba specifically. This chapter looks more closely at Samba as an example of an SMB/CIFS implementation. This chapter starts with an overview of Samba's history because this information can help in understanding why Samba works as it does. The next topic is a close look at the differences between Unix and Windows in file metadata requirements because so many Samba options relate to these differences. Password authentication also presents challenges for bridging the gap between Unix and SMB/CIFS, so that topic is up next. As a Unix server, Samba runs as daemons, so an examination of the Samba daemons and their functions is a critical topic. Following in the Unix tradition, Samba uses text-mode configuration files, and knowing where to look for these files and understanding their basic formats is critical for configuring and using Samba. This chapter concludes with a look at running Samba on a few non-Unix systems.

The Birth of Samba

Chances are you already have a good idea of how and why you want to deploy Samba. If you're typical, you want to use a reliable Unix box, possibly running an inexpensive open-source OS, such as FreeBSD or Linux, to function as a file or print server for a network of Windows boxes. Chances are you have experience with, or at least have heard about, the reliability of Unix and Unix-like OSs, and you want to harness this reliability for your file server. OS cost and your own experience with the server OS may also fit into this equation, as might Samba's extreme configurability.

 NOTE You can use various non-Windows clients with Samba, but Windows clients are the most common type. What's more, the history of both SMB/CIFS and Samba is tied to Windows and closely related OSs, such as DOS and OS/2.

These reasons are all perfectly valid today, but Samba's history predates the explosion in popularity of Linux and other open-source OSs. In fact, Samba is part of the reason for Linux's popularity; Linux infiltrated many organizations as a platform for running Samba.

Understanding Samba's history isn't strictly necessary for running the server, but the story is interesting to those who enjoy such tales, and knowing how Samba came to be can help you understand its current development environment and feature set.

The Need for Samba

Like many open-source software projects, Samba began life as a way to solve one person's problems. The person in this case was a student named Andrew Tridgell at the Australian National University in Canberra, and the problem was getting three computers—a PC running DOS, a Sun workstation, and a DECstation 3100 running Digital Unix—to communicate using one protocol. At that time (1991), the Sun and the DECstation could share files via NFS, and a program known as Pathworks enabled the DECstation to share files with the DOS box. (Tridgell didn't know it at the time, but Pathworks was an early SMB implementation for VMS systems.) Three-way file sharing wasn't easy with this setup, but that's what Tridgell wanted to do. Being a good hacker, he decided to take matters into his own hands and reverse engineer the protocol used by DOS and Pathworks.

NOTE   The term *hacker* has come to mean a computer miscreant—somebody who breaks into others' computers, often maliciously and almost always illegally. This meaning, though, is a fairly recent phenomenon and is promulgated by the popular media. The word has an older and more honorable meaning, referring to individuals who are skilled with computers, particularly with computer programming, and who enjoy using those skills for productive and legal purposes. Many open-source programmers consider themselves hackers in this positive sense, and this is how I use the term in this book, albeit infrequently because of the possibility of confusion. I use the term *cracker* when referring to computer miscreants.

Tridgell used packet sniffers to spy on the packets sent between his DOS system and his DECstation, and over the course of a few days, he pieced together how the protocol worked and wrote software for the Sun workstation to implement the protocol. Soon, he was able to do what he wanted to do. Like many hackers, Tridgell decided to share his code, so he posted it to the Internet and then largely forgot about it.

Early Samba Development

Although Tridgell had set aside his initial SMB server software, others were downloading it and trying it. Some of these users asked questions, such as whether the software could be made to work with the fledgling Linux OS, which also began life in 1991. Tridgell became intrigued by Linux and quickly ported his software. He renewed his coding project under various names, such as NetBIOS for Unix and SMB Server, but he nixed the latter name because it had already been trademarked for another product. Thus, Tridgell searched for a name that included the letters *S*, *M*, and *B* in that order, and *Samba* sprung up. This event brings us to 1994 and version 1.6 of the software.

As with many open-source projects, Samba's popularity grew initially among developers. Individuals contacted Tridgell to ask questions, contribute code, and so on. Eventually, they joined mailing lists and read Usenet newsgroups dedicated to Samba. The Samba documentation claims that the individual developers are now "too numerous to mention."

Much of the early work on Samba was devoted to implementing core features. As outlined in Chapter 1, the long history of SMB/CIFS guarantees compatibility problems. For instance, Samba must negotiate the protocol level with each of its partners and then implement the appropriate protocol variant. In some cases, Samba must work around—or reproduce—bugs in specific SMB/CIFS implementations. Even handling the DOS and Windows families alone is a challenge, given the number of releases of these OSs that are available. The challenges facing the Samba Team, as the Samba developers came to be collectively called, were substantial.

By 1999 and the 1.9.*x* Samba series, the server was quite reliable at handling basic file-serving tasks in a wide variety of environments. It's impossible to say just when Samba began to be noticed in the broader community, in part because awareness of the server grew slowly. Samba's growth and popularity also tracked that of Linux. Many Samba developers used (and continue to use) Linux as their primary development platform, and the two made a natural pair as low-cost software to replace or supplement much pricier Microsoft Windows installations in many institutions' server rooms. Of course, Samba continued to be available on other Unix-like OSs, and projects sprang up over the years to make the software available on non-Unix OSs. Official Samba binaries are available for 16 platforms. Five of these are different Linux distributions, and most of the rest are commercial Unix platforms, such as AIX, IRIX, and Solaris. Samba is available precompiled for some non-Unix platforms, such as VMS. The software can compile on or has been ported to still more platforms, such as BeOS, OS/2, and Plan 9.

NOTE Samba is available for Mac OS X and in fact ships with the OS. Despite its unique graphical user interface (GUI) and configuration tools, Mac OS X is built atop a Unix-like core, so in most respects running Samba on Mac OS X is like running Samba on any other Unix-like OS. Samba isn't available for pre-X versions of Mac OS, although a commercial package called DAVE (http://www.thursby.com) is available for these older versions of Mac OS.

Samba's Widespread Deployment

In 1999, Samba 2.0 was released. This version added many important features, of course, but the shift to a new major version number was psychologically important as well. Linux was drawing increasing attention in the computer media and eventually in the mainstream media. Samba both rode this wave and fueled it.

Open-source advocate and historian Eric S. Raymond has called Samba Linux's "stealth weapon." Corporate IT staff, pressed to accomplish as much as possible with as little money as possible, often turned to Samba running on Linux, FreeBSD, or other open-source OSs as a cost-saver—sometimes without corporate approval. Samba could hold its own against Windows NT (and, later, Windows 200*x*) servers, and end users sitting at workstations wouldn't even know their files were stored on Samba servers. As a bonus, the Unix-like OS running Samba generally took less effort to administer, on a per-user basis, than did Windows NT servers, so administrators had more time to devote to other tasks.

The open secret of Samba deployment soon became anything but secret, and the Samba Team set its sights on greater integration with Windows networks. Samba 2.0 had provided some limited support for Windows domains, and that support was expanded with Samba 2.2 and again with Samba 3.0. As Microsoft is wont to do, each time it has released a new OS, it has broken compatibility with Samba servers. This tendency has kept the Samba developers busy, but the inconveniences are usually minor and short-lived.

Samba 3.0 is the latest new version of the software. This version includes many improvements:

Active Directory support: Active Directory is Microsoft's latest authentication and network services management system and is tied to Kerberos. A Samba 3.0 server can join an Active Directory domain to authenticate users against the Active Directory server.

Unicode support: Unicode is an increasingly important method of encoding text, including filenames. Unicode supports most of the world's printed languages, including Asian languages, unlike the older American Standard Code for Information Interchange (ASCII), which was designed with English in mind, and supports most other western European languages reasonably well, albeit not always perfectly.

Authentication changes: The new authentication system is largely an internal rewrite, but some alterations to configuration options have been made to support these changes.

New filename mangling system: Filename *mangling* is the procedure by which Samba translates filenames when the host OS and the client have different requirements. Samba 2.2.*x* and earlier used one mangling system, but version 3.0 has made substantial changes to this system.

New net command: The Samba developers have written a new utility, called net, which is similar to the command of the same name in Windows. The ultimate goal is to replace several other Samba commands, such as smbpasswd, but this task isn't yet complete.

NT-style status32 codes: These codes help improve error handling. Their use is transparent to Samba administration.

Improved Windows 200*x*/XP printer support: Samba has long provided better support for certain ancillary printing features for Windows 9*x*/Me than for the Windows NT/200*x*/XP family. Version 3.0 narrows this gap.

Domain migration: Samba now includes tools that enable migrating an existing Windows NT domain to Samba control.

Domain trust relationships: Samba 3.0 provides improved mechanisms for establishing trust relationships with Windows NT 4.0 domain controllers. This advance helps better integrate Samba into a Windows-controlled domain.

Of course, Samba development isn't finished. Microsoft continues to modify and expand SMB/CIFS, and Samba must continue to change to keep up. The Samba Team is also working to close the gap on features such as better domain integration. Although Samba can function as a domain controller or as a client on a Samba- or Windows-controlled domain, this integration is still imperfect. Andrew Tridgell has suggested that post-3.0 versions of Samba are likely to include substantial code rewrites to improve Samba's implementation of some of these features.

Overall, Samba has become an important horse in the Unix server stable. Samba 3.0 provides several improvements, particularly to domain and Active Directory integration. Future versions will continue these improvements, enabling Samba to keep up in the busy world of file sharing.

Unix and Windows File Metadata Differences

Samba as an SMB/CIFS implementation faces many challenges because of the platform on which the server runs. The problem isn't that Unix is deficient when compared to Windows; it's just that Unix is *different*. Many of these differences relate to file *metadata*— data that describe a file, but that aren't the file's contents. Examples of file metadata include filenames, ownership, permissions, and file streams. The following sections outline these differences. Configuration options that tell Samba how to handle these features are covered in upcoming chapters, particularly in Chapter 5.

Filename Case

In the Americas and western Europe, most filenames are encoded in ASCII, which is a fairly straightforward encoding system. Every character is tied to a specific 8-bit number, with different numbers assigned to uppercase and lowercase letters. In the Unix world, most ASCII characters are legal in filenames, although there are some exceptions, such as the slash (/), which functions as a directory name separator. Furthermore, Unix-like systems treat filenames in a *case-sensitive* manner. For instance, if a file called upper.txt exists on the disk, an attempt to load the file by specifying its name as UPPER.TXT, Upper.txt, or any other variation that differs only in case will fail. Another aspect of case-sensitivity is that a single directory can hold two or more files with names that differ only in case. Although this practice is somewhat uncommon, it's not unprecedented.

Windows, by contrast, uses *case-retentive* filenames. Windows retains the case you specify for files, so if you tell the OS to create a file called UpPeR.tXt, it will do so, preserving the case of all the letters in the filename. In a case-retentive system, though, case doesn't matter in subsequent accesses. For instance, if you subsequently specify the filename as Upper.txt, UPPER.TXT, or any other case-only variant, Windows will happily load the same file. One consequence of this fact is that a single directory can't hold two files whose names differ only in case. If you try to create a new file with a name that differs only in case from one that already exists, Windows overwrites the existing file rather than creating a new one.

NOTE   In practice, Windows programs often play fast and loose with filename case. Programs may convert filenames to all uppercase, all lowercase, or lowercase with an initial capital. These changes may occur when you create the file or when filenames are displayed. Such changes may interact with filename length; short filenames may be more likely to be modified than long filenames. Such changes are the result of tampering by Windows programs; the underlying Windows filesystems, which Samba must emulate at some level, are case-retentive as just described.

Further complicating matters is the fact that DOS uses a wholly *case-insensitive* file-naming system. Lowercase letters simply aren't legal in DOS filenames. If you type a filename with lowercase letters, the program converts those letters to uppercase. (Some programs convert all filenames to lowercase for display purposes, though.) In such an environment, it's meaningless to have two filenames that differ only in case in a single directory.

To support case-retentive and case-insensitive OSs using a case-sensitive filesystem, Samba must do extra work. When asked to open or otherwise modify a file, the server must check for the file using the specified case and all possible variants. If only one variant is found, Samba can use the file. If two or more files match the specification (say, because they were created directly on the server computer or via a case-sensitive protocol such as NFS), Samba must decide which file to access. From the user's point of view, this decision can be arbitrary and, therefore, potentially wrong. When a client creates a file, Samba must decide what to do about the file's case—preserve it or convert it to all uppercase or all lowercase. (The latter is an option because all lowercase is more common on most Unix systems and so will look better if the file is subsequently accessed from the server's shell or from another Unix system via a file server.)

One further complication is the fact that Samba can share directories that correspond to non-Unix filesystems. For instance, you might mount and share a floppy disk that was originally created in Windows. This disk's file-naming conventions match those of SMB/CIFS but must be interpreted through the Unix host OS. Fortunately, this process is unlikely to cause additional filename complications; because both SMB/CIFS and the Windows floppy disk are treated in a case-retentive way, everything works smoothly.

As described in Chapter 5, Samba provides options that affect its treatment of filename case. Some of these options determine how Samba passes filenames between itself and its clients, and others relate to how the server records filenames on the local disk.

Unicode Filenames

ASCII is a 7-bit encoding system, meaning that it supports a total of 128 possible symbols. (In practice, though, ASCII is encoded in 8-bit bytes, for a total of 256 possible symbols.) Although that's plenty for uppercase and lowercase Roman letters, numbers, and common punctuation, it's wholly inadequate when one adds variants such as characters with umlauts, scientific symbols, non-Roman alphabets such as Cyrillic and Arabic, Kanji, and so on. In the past, alternative 8-byte encodings have been used for some of these symbol sets, but this practice has led to an unmanageable mish-mash of encoding systems. The solution is *Unicode*, a single encoding system that aims to be adequate for encoding all alphabets and other symbol systems. Unicode comes in several variants, but the form used by Windows and Samba is a 16-bit encoding, meaning that it supports 65,536 characters—enough to completely encode quite a few alphabets, semi-ideographic languages, and special symbols.

Unicode is great in theory, but implementing Unicode support requires changing a lot of software, including filesystems and file-sharing software such as Samba. Prior to Samba 3.0, the software supported non-ASCII characters by using a *character set*. Each character set corresponds to a particular encoding system, many of which are variants on ASCII. Samba couldn't negotiate this detail automatically, though, so you had to ensure that the server and all of its clients were set to use the same character set. If mismatches occurred, you'd find files with odd names on some clients but not on others. With Samba 3.0, the software has acquired the ability to use Unicode. Of course, the client must understand Unicode as well for this support to do any good. With Unicode, changes in filenames across systems should go away, and a single server should be able to store files with filenames in multiple alphabets, such as Roman, Cyrillic, and Arabic filenames all in a single directory.

Samba's ability to speak to the client in Unicode is only part of the battle. To store Unicode filenames, either the filesystem must support them or Samba must re-encode the filename using two or more characters for every character in the filename. The latter approach might not look very good if the file is subsequently accessed using a non-SMB/CIFS method, but it should be fine if the directories in question are accessed only from Samba.

NOTE   Samba's Unicode support (or lack thereof, if you disable it) affects Samba's filename handling; it *doesn't* affect how data are stored inside data files. That detail is independent of Samba or of the filesystem.

Filename Length Limits

SMB was originally designed for use by DOS, which uses filenames that are extremely limited by modern standards. As noted earlier, DOS filenames are entirely uppercase. (In practice, most DOS programs can handle lowercase filenames, but DOS doesn't normally present such filenames to its programs.) A further limit is that DOS filenames can be no longer than eight characters with an optional three-character extension (the so-called *8.3* filename length limit). In expanding this limit for Windows 95, Microsoft developed an unusual extension to DOS's primary filesystem, the File Allocation Table (FAT): Multiple filename entries are combined into one. The first entry contains an 8.3 filename and could be used by DOS. Subsequent entries are tied to the first and contain a long filename. This FAT extension is known as the Virtual File Allocation Table (VFAT) filesystem. Explicit support for both short and long filenames is also present in the New Technology File System (NTFS) used by Windows NT/200*x*/XP, as well as in the SMB/CIFS protocols.

Unix, by contrast, has long had a heritage of supporting long filenames. The details vary from one Unix variant and filesystem to another, but most filesystems used on Unix-like systems today support filenames of at least 127 characters and usually 255 or 256 characters. No common Unix-like OS today provides explicit support for both long filenames and 8.3 variant filenames on the same files. Even when mounting VFAT partitions, these OSs provide direct access only to long filenames. Of course, when the OS stores files on a VFAT partition, it must create a short filename to go along with the long one, but this detail is hidden from user programs—including Samba.

As a result of the filename length demands of SMB/CIFS, Samba provides mechanisms to simulate the long- and short-filename features of VFAT and NTFS. This process is known as filename *mangling*, and it involves creating a shortened version of a filename on the fly using a *hashing algorithm*, which converts data from one form to another in a way that's not reversible. Filename mangling can also be used when characters in a filename aren't supported by the client. One potential problem with hashes is that they can create *collisions*—given two long filenames, Samba might generate identical mangled versions of these filenames. When this happens, one file will be inaccessible to the client. Fortunately, mangling collisions are uncommon.

You can see the effect of filename mangling from a DOS prompt on a Windows computer. Assign a drive letter to a Samba share, as described in Chapter 18, and then change to a directory that contains long filenames. Type **DIR** to see a directory listing. The result might resemble the following, although of course the specific filenames and associated data you see will differ:

```
E:\jp1\keymap-master> DIR

 Volume in drive E is RODSMITH
 Directory of E:\jp1\keymap-master

.               <DIR>        06-12-03  1:33p .
..              <DIR>        06-12-03  1:53a ..
KEZB1H~Q TXT       30,222    06-07-03  7:37p keymap-master-readme.txt
K9OIBN~R XLS    2,326,528    06-11-03 11:56p keymap-master-v7.37.xls
keymap   txt          374    06-12-03  1:33p keymap.txt
KOTYXB~R TXT       16,332    06-07-03  7:37p keymap-master-protocols.txt
         4 file(s)    2,373,456 bytes
         2 dir(s)     7,501.00 MB free
```

The complete long filename appears in the rightmost column of this output while the mangled 8.3 filename appears in the leftmost column. This output demonstrates a few characteristics of Samba's filename mangling:

Few collisions, even for similar names: The four files in this directory all begin with the same string, keymap, and three share the same extension, txt. Despite these similarities, Samba has generated mangled names that are unique, albeit uninspiring.

Mangling can seriously distort filenames: In this example, none of the mangled names bears much resemblance to the original filename. All of the mangled filename bases end in a tilde (~) and a single letter. (Windows uses a tilde and a number or letter to distinguish short filenames on FAT partitions.) In Samba versions prior to version 3.0, more of the base was likely to survive; for instance, one of these mangled names might have been KEYMA~2X.TXT.

Mangling converts lowercase to uppercase: The mangled portions of the filename are entirely uppercase for the benefit of the client OS.

Mangling isn't used on 8.3 filenames: Filenames that already conform to the 8.3 length limits aren't normally mangled. (Some Samba options permit mangling of names that don't conform to the target OS's case requirements, though.)

When a client asks for access to a file using a mangled name that Samba recognizes, such as KEZB1H~Q.TXT from the preceding directory listing, Samba substitutes the correct matching long filename (keymap-master-readme.txt) for local calls on the Unix system. Essentially, Samba translates between short and long filenames.

Overall, filename mangling is a very powerful tool for use on Windows networks, particularly when old and new clients or programs are in simultaneous use on the network. (If, say, only DOS clients are present, they won't create long filenames, so most mangling features will become unimportant.)

File Ownership

Older SMB/CIFS clients, such as DOS and Windows 9x/Me systems, have no concept of file ownership. When used with such clients, Samba can do whatever it likes regarding file ownership, and in fact Samba offers several options that manipulate file ownership or Samba's access to files owned by particular users. By default, Samba applies the username the user gave to obtain access to a share to determine whether to grant access to a file. For instance, if a user sent the fastaire username, files that the user creates will be owned by fastaire, and the user will be able to access all files that fastaire could read locally, if the user logged onto the server via an SSH or Telnet session. If this user tries to access a file owned by grogers, and if that file has 0600 (-rw------) permissions, then fastaire will be unable to access the file. (The next section, "File Permissions and ACLs," briefly summarizes the meaning of Unix file permission strings.)

This default behavior is convenient for system administrators who are familiar with Unix-style ownership and permissions. You can use normal local file ownership and permissions rules, including setting options on entire directories, changing ownership of shared files that should be read-only, and so on, much as you would if users were to use the computer as an ordinary workstation or multiuser system via Telnet, SSH, or the like.

Samba is much more flexible than this description suggests, though. The server includes options that enable you to force the username that Samba uses to access files. For instance, you could design a share that always creates new files using the grogers username, even if fastaire (or any other user) accesses the share. Such a share also gives access to existing files as if grogers was using the share, even when it's another user doing the work. Such a system can be handy for a directory to which all users should have easy write access. Another use for this feature is when users belong to a variety of groups with different local access to directories but which they should all be able to access via Samba.

Newer SMB/CIFS clients, such as Windows NT/200x/XP, support user accounts locally and can, therefore, communicate this information with Samba. Samba doesn't tightly integrate its own local account access rules with the client's account system, though; instead, it relies on the ownership rules established for less-sophisticated clients. For instance, Samba doesn't care if a client's configuration normally enables grogers to read fastaire's files; if that access isn't permitted on the Samba server, the client can't override it, except by mounting a share under both usernames. When Samba provides full ACL support, as described in the next section, "File Permissions and ACLs," users of Windows NT/200x/XP systems can read the owner of a file as they can read the owner of a file on a local NTFS partition. Samba doesn't permit users to acquire ownership of a file on a Samba server, though. This restriction is largely because of the fact that changing the ownership of a file can be done only by root under Unix, not by ordinary users.

File Permissions and ACLs

Unix-like OSs use a permissions system that grants read, write, and execute permissions to each of three tiers of users: a file's owner, a group of users, and all users (a.k.a. *world* access). The meanings of read and write access are fairly obvious. Execute permission is applied to executable files, such as binary program files and scripts. These permissions can be written as a set of letters representing read (r), write (w), and execute (x) permissions or a dash (-) to indicate that a permission is missing. These codes are grouped together for the owner, group, and world. For instance, rwxr-x--- indicates that the owner may read, write, or execute the file; members of the file's group may read or execute the file but not write to it; and all other users have no access to the file.

The permissions can also be represented numerically as a set of three octal (base-8) numbers, each of which is three bits in size. The most significant bit (octal 4) refers to read access, the next bit (octal 2) refers to write access, and the least significant bit (octal 1) refers to execute access. These numbers can be added together for each of the three scopes (owner, group, and world) and strung together as a three-digit octal number. Thus, rwxr-x--- can also be expressed as 750.

In addition to these major permission modes, Unix supports several specific file types. The most common of these apply to ordinary files, and this file type is often indicated by a leading dash on symbolic permission specifications or as a leading 0 in the octal mode, as in -rwxr-x--- or 0750. Other file types include directories, character and block device files, symbolic links, and a few more exotic file types. Most of these file types can be indicated by special leading symbols in the symbolic mode expression.

Set user ID (SUID) and *set group ID* (SGID) files are variants on ordinary executables in which the program is run with the permissions of the file owner rather than of the user who runs the program. These can be indicated by an s rather than an x in the owner and group symbolic mode or by an octal 4 or 2 being added before the three-digit octal permission string, as in 4750 for an SUID file or 6750 for a file that's both SUID and SGID.

Directories are unusual because they treat the execute bit in a peculiar way. Specifically, the execute bit grants the ability to search a directory for information using tools such as find. Indeed, even some ls options require the execute bit. Most directories that should be readable have both read and execute bits set. Unix treats directories as files, so making changes to a directory (such as adding or deleting files) requires write access to the directory, but not to the file being deleted, if that's the operation in question.

Directories can also have their *sticky bits* set, which adds an octal 1 to the start of the numeric code, as in 1750. Sticky bits are also indicated by a t in place of the world x permission bit. When the sticky bit is present, only the file's owner may delete a file, although the owner must still have write permission to the directory. This bit is normally present on world-writeable temporary directories such as /tmp and /var/tmp.

Some of these Unix concepts carry over to the world of DOS, Windows, and SMB/CIFS. One of the closest of these parallels is the write permission bit. SMB/CIFS supports this concept although its meaning is inverted: A file carries a *read-only bit* if it shouldn't be modified. DOS and Windows systems normally expect a file's read-only bit to control whether it can be deleted, though, and this isn't true of Unix-like systems. Samba, therefore, provides options to emulate the behavior that clients are likely to expect. SMB/CIFS also supports directories, so Unix directories can be handled by Samba in a way that's logically very natural.

Other Unix-style permissions are largely lost on SMB/CIFS. Symbolic links aren't supported as such, although Samba can provide access to the linked-to files as if they were regular files. Device files and other exotic file types have no direct counterparts in SMB/CIFS. Execute permission is meaningless to most SMB/CIFS clients, as is the distinction between owner, group, and world permissions. In practice, Samba employs the user's local access rights, as described earlier, to determine whether it should give access to a file.

Instead of Unix-style permissions, Windows NT/200x/XP systems support *access control lists* (ACLs), which provide a fine-grained method of granting access to a file. Suppose that fastaire has created a file but that grogers should be able to read it. With a system that uses ACLs, fastaire can add an ACL specifying that grogers should be able to read the file. The equivalent action on a Unix system would be to add grogers to a particular group, give group ownership of the file to that group, and ensure that the group permissions for the file include read access. The file's owner probably doesn't have the administrative rights to create groups or add users to groups, so ACLs give users more control over who may access their files.

Traditionally, Samba has bridged the gap between ACLs and Unix-style permissions by using ACLs as an access method for manipulating a file's standard Unix permissions. (Logically speaking, you can think of Unix-style permissions as providing a subset of broader ACL functionality.) This approach gives users some control over Unix-style permissions on their files, but it's an imperfect solution. Samba 2.2 supports ACLs more directly, provided the underlying filesystem does so as well. When this option is properly configured, users can give other users access to their files much as they could when using a Windows NT–series SMB/CIFS server.

File Streams

NTFS, the preferred filesystem for Windows NT/200*x*/XP, supports file streams—effectively, multiple files stored under a single name. Each stream is named (essentially, a subname of the filename) and can be used to store application-specific data. In principle, applications can use file streams to quickly and easily access bundles of related data. For instance, an audio file format might include audio data in the primary stream and information about the audio file, such as the name of the performers in a music track, in another stream. Using file streams would enable a program to easily change the supporting text information without touching the main audio file data. If the data were in a single conventional file, doing so might require computation- or time-intensive copying operations.

Streams are a good idea in theory, but they haven't been widely used. Programs that do use streams typically use them only as an option. In the Windows world, filesystems such as FAT, which don't support streams, are still common, so most programs can't require the use of streams.

Most Unix filesystems haven't traditionally supported streams. For this reason, Samba doesn't support streams, despite the fact that SMB/CIFS does. Lack of streams support hasn't been a major problem for Samba because so few programs truly require it. This situation could change in the future, though, and the Samba Team is studying streams and considering how to implement them. Chances are any future streams implementation will require the use of a filesystem that also supports streams.

Unix and Windows Password Authentication

Because SMB/CIFS normally uses passwords to authorize access to a server, Samba must implement SMB/CIFS password hashing. On the surface, this appears to be no problem; after all, Unix systems have also long used passwords for authentication. Unfortunately, tapping into the Unix password database isn't always possible. To understand why, some background in standard Unix passwords is necessary, along with information on encrypted and unencrypted (a.k.a. *cleartext*) passwords in Samba. As with many such differences, Samba provides multiple methods of bridging the gap between the two worlds.

Unix Password Databases and Hashes

Traditionally, Unix systems store both usernames and passwords in a file called /etc/passwd. This file is a plain-text file that contains critical information about user accounts, including passwords. Each line corresponds to one account and resembles the following:

```
grogers:$1$cOyMg83f$RxJIf7fatdrDAFW3.d9VS1:503:506::/home/grogers:/bin/bash
```

Each field is separated from its neighbors by a single colon (:). For the purposes of this discussion, the most important fields are the first two, which contain the username (grogers) and an encrypted (technically, a hashed) version of the password (the long string beginning 1 in this example). In theory, any of several hashes can be used for Unix passwords. In practice, two systems have been commonly employed:

DES: The Data Encryption Standard (DES) is a popular password hash on many Unix-like systems. It supports passwords of up to eight characters in length.

MD5: The Message Digest 5 (MD5) algorithm generates longer hashes than does DES and supports passwords of up to 128 characters in length.

DES used to be the most common password hash on Unix-like systems, but MD5 has been growing in popularity in recent years. In both cases, passwords are case-sensitive. Both systems also commonly *salt* their passwords, which involves adding some extra data to the password before encrypting it. Using a salt makes a *dictionary attack*—in which an attacker tries every word in a dictionary as a potential password, comparing the results to the encrypted password file—more difficult to implement. (Salting doesn't prevent a dictionary attack from succeeding, though; it just adds to the time required to test all the possible variants.)

Because a one-way hash is used, passwords can't be easily recovered from a passwd file. (Dictionary attacks may succeed with poorly chosen passwords, though.) This point is critically important for understanding why Samba handles encrypted passwords the way it does, so keep it in mind.

The /etc/passwd file is potentially vulnerable to attack because it must be readable to many users. The original thought was that this wasn't a problem because passwords were stored in a hashed form; however, the proliferation of password-cracking tools that use dictionary attacks has made a traditional /etc/passwd file quite dangerous. Any user on a Unix system can copy /etc/passwd and run a dictionary attack on it, thus uncovering other users' passwords.

For this reason, most systems today employ *shadow passwords*. Details vary from one OS to another, but the basic idea is that the password is removed from /etc/passwd and stored in another file, such as /etc/shadow. This file is readable only by root, so to run a password-cracking program on the file, a miscreant must first obtain at least limited root privileges or otherwise overcome system security. In a shadow password system, the password field in /etc/passwd is replaced by a special code character—typically an asterisk (*) or an x. An asterisk may also denote an account that should not accept logins, as might be the case for special system accounts.

One method of implementing shadow passwords and other password authentication systems is to use the Pluggable Authentication Module (PAM). Traditionally, any server or login program that requires access to passwords reads this information directly from /etc/passwd. This practice made any changes to the password system, such as a shift from DES to MD5, very difficult to implement because potentially dozens of programs had to be changed. PAM adds an intermediate layer so that individual servers don't need to know the details of how authentication occurs. Instead, the servers call PAM, and PAM does the work of checking /etc/passwd, the shadow password file, or any other authentication mechanism. Using PAM makes it easier to implement new authentication methods without requiring changes to any server source code, assuming that all the servers that need authentication services use PAM. Samba uses PAM when it's configured to accept cleartext passwords, but encrypted passwords require an authentication mechanism that's independent of PAM.

Other Unix authentication systems are still more complex. For instance, many networks use the Network Information Service (NIS) or similar tools for storing account information for many systems on a single computer. Mac OS X uses an authentication system that can integrate several different databases. It's unusual in that it can integrate Unix and Samba encrypted passwords better than can most Unix systems, at least short of explicitly configuring sophisticated integration systems.

SMB/CIFS Cleartext and Encrypted Passwords

In the early days, SMB/CIFS used unencrypted (cleartext) passwords. Passwords were exchanged between clients and servers without any form of encryption. This approach was simple, but it was also dangerous, particularly on networks whose physical security couldn't be guaranteed. On the other hand, cleartext passwords enable Samba to authenticate would-be users against the normal Unix password system (typically via PAM). When Samba receives a username and password, the server hashes the password and checks it against the password database. If the hashed values match, the user is granted access.

In practice, though, this process can be more complex than just described. One issue is case-sensitivity. Recall that Unix passwords are case-sensitive. Some SMB/CIFS passwords, though, aren't case-sensitive. Specifically, older clients (through Windows Me) use a case-insensitive password hash, and clients might alter the case of the cleartext passwords they send to the server. Therefore, to test passwords, Samba must sometimes try several variants in case. For instance, suppose the user's Unix password is YI3wtT^d. Some SMB/CIFS clients might convert this value to YI3WTT^D, the hash of which wouldn't match anything in the Unix password database. For this reason, Samba provides options that support converting the case of up to a specified number of letters and checking these variants. This process can slow down authentication, but it's sometimes the only way to enable users to authenticate themselves.

Since Windows 95 OEM Service Release 2 (OSR2) and Windows NT Service Pack 3 (SP3), Windows has used encrypted passwords by default in its SMB/CIFS transactions, with no provision to automatically fall back on cleartext passwords. The Windows 9x/Me encrypted passwords use a DES hash, but the way the hash is used is incompatible with the hash used by some Unix systems. For instance, passwords are treated in a case-insensitive way, and no salt is applied. Windows NT/200x/XP uses another hash, Message Digest 4 (MD4), which is also incompatible with Unix's DES or MD5 hashes, although these NT hashes are case-sensitive. For these reasons, SMB/CIFS encrypted passwords and Unix's stored encrypted passwords are incompatible. When Samba communicates with clients using an encrypted password system, the server can't verify the password against its stored password database.

NOTE Encrypting passwords does nothing to encrypt other data you might transfer, such as your files. If you're concerned about snooping for nonpassword data, you should consider encrypting your entire SMB/CIFS connection using a tool such as an SSH tunnel. Chapter 11 covers this topic in more detail.

Methods of Bridging the Gap

One method of solving the problem of SMB/CIFS encrypted passwords is to disable them on the clients. Chapter 7 describes how to do this. Of course, this solution isn't without its downsides. One of these problems is that you give up the benefits of encrypted passwords; anybody who manages to intercept a logon request can obtain a password. Another problem is that all recent versions of Windows use encrypted passwords by default, so using cleartext passwords on a large network requires changing the password default on many clients—a potentially time-consuming and tedious proposition. On the whole, this approach is best used on small, private networks.

Another tool for bridging the gap lies in Samba's support for SMB/CIFS encrypted passwords. This support requires that you maintain a separate Samba password database (smbpasswd, typically stored in /etc/samba). This database contains Samba password hashes for all the accounts that should have access to the Samba server. These passwords might or might not be identical to the computer's ordinary logon passwords. This approach nets you the security benefits of encrypted passwords, and it can improve your system's authentication flexibility. For instance, you can give some users access to the Samba system by giving them Samba passwords but prevent others who have regular Unix accounts from using Samba by excluding them from the Samba password database. On the other hand, using Samba encrypted passwords increases administrative complexity because two password databases must be maintained. As described in Chapter 7, some Samba password tools help reduce this burden by enabling you to maintain both Samba passwords and the system passwords using the same programs.

A variant on using encrypted passwords is to have the Samba server defer to a domain controller for password authentication. In this case, no Samba password database needs to be maintained locally, but you must maintain such a database on the domain controller system. Samba actually provides two ways to accomplish this goal. One method involves fully joining the domain, and the other method involves merely forwarding authentication requests to the domain controller.

A twist on SMB/CIFS vs. Unix-style passwords that deserves mention is methods that enable closer integration of the Unix and SMB/CIFS sides of the authentication equation. Some variations on this approach include the following:

Domain authentication: Various tools, such as the old pam_smb (`http://pamsmb.sourceforge.net`) and the newer Winbind (part of Samba), turn a Unix system into a node in a Windows domain. These systems are PAM modules that perform authentication against a Windows domain. To simplify account maintenance, you can run a Windows NT/200x or a Samba domain controller that houses all information on user accounts. If you then equip your Unix systems with pam_smb or Winbind and configure Samba servers to authenticate against the domain controller, you need only maintain that one account database.

Kerberos and Active Directory authentication: Kerberos (`http://web.mit.edu/kerberos/www/`) is a network security and authentication tool that features a centralized login database. It's possible to configure Samba with Kerberos support, and Kerberos is closely related to Active Directory as used by Windows. Using these tools enables you to implement a centralized account database similar in broad strokes to a domain's centralized account database.

As a general rule, using standard Samba encrypted passwords in conjunction with the other account information stored in the ordinary Unix password database is the best approach on small and many midsize networks. As a network grows in size and acquires many users and individual server computers, though, the benefits of a centralized system also grow. Chances are such a system will have an SMB/CIFS domain, so domain authentication can be a good match. Kerberos and Active Directory can take more effort to configure but may be appropriate when a higher level of integration or security are in order.

Samba Daemons

Most servers on Unix-like OSs are implemented as *daemons*—programs that run in the background, with little or no direct access from the console aside from appearing in ps listings or the like. This arrangement is true of Samba; however, unlike many servers, Samba actually consists of several different daemons. Understanding a bit about what each of these daemons does will help you plan your server's operation and diagnose problems.

 NOTE   This section describes the Samba daemons in general terms. Chapter 3 describes how to start the Samba daemons running.

---

smbd

Most of the core Samba functionality resides in the smbd daemon. This server binds to TCP port 139 and handles the actual file- and printer-sharing tasks. In principle, a Samba server computer could run nothing but smbd and be useful. Clients could connect to the server directly by using an IP address, DNS hostname, or other mechanism to identify the server computer and specify a share name directly. Such use is possible, and sometimes practical, for some clients, including the Samba smbclient program. For instance, the following command will connect to a server that runs only smbd, enabling the transfer of files using commands similar to those in text-mode FTP programs:

```
$ smbclient //waltz.pangaea.edu/fastaire
```

Note that this command specified a DNS hostname (waltz.pangaea.edu) rather than a NetBIOS name (such as WALTZ). In practice, the two might be impossible to tell apart if the domain portion of the DNS hostname were omitted (as in waltz). If the Samba server isn't running nmbd (as described shortly) and if the client only uses NetBIOS broadcasts or an NBNS system, a NetBIOS name won't work.

In addition to handling file and printer shares, smbd also provides the authentication support required by these services, as well as time services. Although it's not a huge part of the SMB/CIFS protocol, one feature it supports is the ability to synchronize clocks between systems, and this duty is handled by smbd. Chapter 12 describes this function of Samba in more detail.

Essentially, running smbd alone is much like running an ordinary FTP or NFS server; the computer responds to SMB/CIFS logon requests and enables the transfer of files and print jobs.

nmbd

As described in Chapter 1, SMB/CIFS provides more than just file-exchange services. In particular, SMB/CIFS provides a series of tools that help users locate servers and shares on their local networks. Some of the vital support functions provided by nmbd include the following:

Response to name broadcasts: When an SMB/CIFS system operates as a broadcast (B) node, as described in Chapter 1, it sends name queries to all computers on the local network. One of nmbd's jobs is to respond to these queries when they match the computer's NetBIOS name. This name defaults to being the first component of the computer's TCP/IP hostname, but you can override this setting in the Samba configuration file.

Registering a NetBIOS name: A Samba system's nmbd daemon registers the computer's NetBIOS name with other systems. In the case of a B node, nmbd broadcasts its configured NetBIOS name when it starts, and if no other system claims the name, nmbd responds to broadcast queries for that name, as just described. When the computer is configured as a P node, it registers the name with the NBNS system, which then handles name resolution. H- and M-node operations employ both mechanisms, with differing priorities, as described in Chapter 1.

NBNS system: If you configure a Samba server as an NBNS system, it's nmbd that handles this duty. When so configured, nmbd keeps track of the computers that have registered with it and responds to name query requests directed at it by other computers. This function requires that nmbd run continuously; it won't make a good NBNS system if it's run from a super server. Chapter 9 describes NBNS configuration in more detail.

NBNS proxy: Samba provides several options that enable it to function as a proxy for computers on the local or distant subnets. These configurations can simplify the addition of a few distant computers to a network that otherwise consists solely of machines on a single subnet or can help work around other name resolution problems. Chapter 9 describes these configurations in more detail.

Master browser: Chapter 1 described the role of a master browser in an SMB/CIFS network. Samba can function as a master browser, and it's nmbd that's responsible for this operation. This duty also entails several subduties, such as participating in browser elections. As with NBNS functions, master browser functions require nmbd to maintain a list of computers, so this function works poorly if nmbd is run via a super server.

Most of these functions work via UDP port 137, although master browser duties are mostly handled via UDP port 138. Because these services are also ones that should be accessible to anybody on a network, nmbd also functions without authentication. This fact means that a security flaw in nmbd is potentially more serious than a flaw in smbd, which might be exploitable only to authorized users. On the other hand, nmbd doesn't give users direct and arbitrary access to files on the computer. Nonetheless, using firewall rules to restrict access to TCP and UDP ports 137 and 138 from any but authorized systems is a wise precaution.

Samba TNG

This book emphasizes the official Samba project, and particularly the 3.0 version of this server suite, headquartered at http://www.samba.org. Occasionally, though, major software projects *fork*, meaning that two independent teams take what was once one code base and develop it in different directions. This has happened with Samba; the forked project is known as Samba the Next Generation (Samba TNG) and is based at http://www.samba-tng.org.

Samba TNG is much like Samba 2.2 or 3.0 in most respects, but it differs in some of the details of the protocols it supports. The emphasis of Samba TNG development is on domain control features. Compared to Samba 2.2, Samba TNG is arguably a better domain controller. Samba 3.0, though, improves the mainstream Samba project's support for domain features. Nonetheless, if domain control is important to you, you may want to check both projects' Web pages to determine which one provides the best match of features to your needs.

One other notable difference between the mainstream Samba and Samba TNG is in the number of daemons each project uses. Samba uses two major daemons plus the optional SWAT. Samba TNG, by contrast, uses about ten daemons. The smbd and nmbd daemons are both present, but they rely upon numerous smaller daemons to implement specific functionality. Consult the Samba TNG documentation for details.

SWAT

To be called a Samba server computer, a system needs to run smbd, and nmbd is a practical necessity in most networks. A third server, the Samba Web Administration Tool (SWAT), isn't necessary for a system to be a Samba server, but it can be a useful addition. As its name implies, SWAT provides administrative access to the server. Most important, it enables you to edit the Samba configuration file, smb.conf, using a Web browser, either from the Samba server itself or from another computer. (Figure 2-1 shows SWAT in action.) SWAT also provides tools that enable ordinary users to view information on the status of the Samba server and to change their passwords.

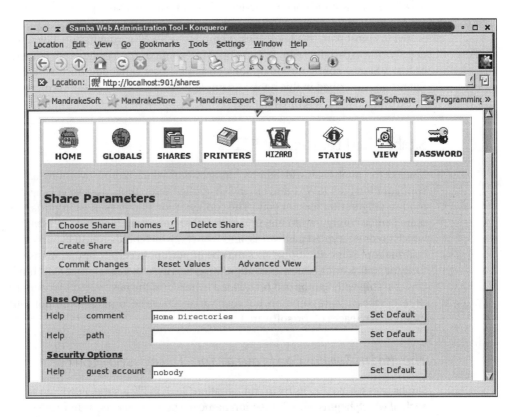

Figure 2-1. SWAT enables you to configure a Samba server using a Web browser.

CAUTION SWAT can be a handy administrative tool, but it's also a potentially very serious security risk. To use SWAT for Samba administration, you must normally send your root password unencrypted over the network—a potentially very risky proposition. For this reason, if you want to use SWAT for Samba administration, I strongly recommend you use it only from the Samba server itself or from computers on the same physical network. In the latter case, use it only if you're quite certain that your local network is physically secure. Be sure to use super server options, TCP Wrappers, or firewall rules to block access to the SWAT server from any but authorized computers.

SWAT is often started separately from the main smbd and nmbd daemons. In fact, many OSs package SWAT separately from the bulk of Samba so that you can leave SWAT completely uninstalled even if you install the main Samba server. SWAT can be a useful tool for those who are new to Samba configuration because it helps those unfamiliar with the server learn about its options, and it can prevent some types of configuration blunders, such as typos in configuration options. On the other hand, SWAT can tie the hands of an experienced administrator, making it difficult or impossible to achieve advanced effects.

For the most part, this book doesn't emphasize SWAT configuration. If you want to use SWAT, you certainly can. In fact, the SWAT configuration options are named after ordinary Samba configuration options, so a SWAT user can follow the text-based configurations described in this book and implement them using SWAT. If you want to give SWAT a try, it's described in Chapter 13.

Samba Configuration Files

Much of this book deals with Samba configuration, which is done by editing text-mode configuration files. (SWAT and other GUI configuration tools work by editing the text-mode configuration files for you.) The configuration file that's most important is the main Samba configuration file, smb.conf. Other important files include smbpasswd, which holds encrypted passwords, and lmhosts, which holds NetBIOS name lookup information. Some additional files may be important in certain situations as well.

By default, Samba places its configuration files in /usr/local/samba/lib, but many OSs that ship with Samba use /etc/samba instead. (In the past, variant locations such as /etc/samba.d were common, but such variants have become less common with the 2.2 and 3.0 releases of the software.)

The Main Samba Configuration File, smb.conf

Samba uses smb.conf as its main configuration file. This file is subdivided into sections, each of which begins with the section name in square brackets, as in [global] or [lexmark]. Three section types exist:

The global section: This section is identified as [global] and contains settings that affect the operation of the Samba server as a whole, such as access restrictions based on IP address and the server's NetBIOS name. The global section also contains default settings—options that normally appear inside sections devoted to shares, but that can be changed for all shares by being placed in the global section. The global section is the first section of the smb.conf file.

File share sections: Sections after the global section define shares. By default, these sections describe file shares and tell the server about directories that Samba is to make available to clients. Options include the directory to be shared, comments that can be associated with it, user-by-user access restrictions, how to handle file metadata differences such as filename case, and so on.

Printer share sections: Printer shares are much like file shares, but they include one or more of a handful of special options that tell Samba to treat the share as a file share.

In the case of file and printer share sections, the name within brackets is the share name. Except for a couple of special shares, unless you override the name with special options, the share appears in clients' browsers by the name within brackets. For instance, the [lexmark] printer share appears in browse lists as LEXMARK.

NOTE   Client software may alter the case of share names. As with NetBIOS names, I present share names in uppercase in this book, except for their bracketed names within the smb.conf file, which I present in lowercase.

Aside from the share names or [global] section name, options in the smb.conf file take the following form:

parameter = Value

The *parameter* is the name of the option that's to be set, such as netbios name or directory. The *Value* is the value that's to be assigned to the option. Typically, Samba parameter lines are indented relative to the section name. This practice isn't required, but it makes it easier to spot where new sections begin. Depending upon the option, the *Value* can take any of several different forms:

Strings: Some parameters take arbitrary alphanumeric strings as values, such as a NetBIOS name or a directory specification. Strings can include letters, numbers, and sometimes other symbols. If a string includes spaces, you don't need to do anything special such as enclosing the string in quotes, but if you do include quotes around a string, the quotes will be omitted. If a line ends in a backslash (\), Samba treats the next line as a continuation of the first, which can be convenient when you must specify a particularly long string.

Numbers: Some values are numbers, such as a time or a maximum or minimum number of bytes to be applied in some way.

Booleans: A *Boolean* value is a way to specify one of two states. Samba understands the strings Yes, True, and 1 as synonyms for one state and No, False, and 0 as synonyms for the opposite state. A handful of parameters accept Boolean values plus something else, such as Auto to set an option automatically.

Variables: Samba supports several variables, which are summarized in Table 2-1. When a variable is used, the parameter is set to the value it references. You can also use variables as part of a larger string.

Lists: Some parameters can accept several values of other types, such as several numbers or strings, separated by spaces or commas. For instance, when restricting access by IP address using the hosts allow parameter, you separate IP addresses or hostnames by commas, as in

hosts allow = 192.168.7.9, 192.168.7.10.

Table 2-1. Samba Variables

Variable	Meaning
%a	Operating system running on client. Possible values are OS2 (OS/2), Samba, UNKNOWN, WfWg (Windows for Workgroups or DOS), Win2K (Windows 2000), Win95 (Windows 9x/Me), or WinNT (Windows NT).
%c	The number of pages in a print job (if known).
%d	Process ID of the daemon.
%D	Workgroup or domain name of the client.
%f	The sender of a WinPopUp message.
%g	Primary group of %u.
%G	Primary group of %U.
%h	DNS name of the server.
%H	Home directory of %u.
%I	IP address of the client.
%J	The name of a print job.
%L	NetBIOS name of the server.
%m	NetBIOS name of the client.
%M	DNS name of the client.
%N	NIS home directory server.
%p	If the share is automounted, path to its root directory.

Table 2-1. Samba Variables (Continued)

Variable	Meaning
%P	Path to the share's root directory.
%R	SMB protocol level, as described in Chapter 1. Legal values are CORE, COREPLUS, LANMAN1, LANMAN2, and NT1.
%s	The name of a file; used in printer shares to identify the filename of a file to be printed and with WinPopUp messages to identify a file containing the text to be displayed to the user.
%S	Name of the share.
%t	The destination of a WinPopUp message.
%T	Current date and time.
%u	Effective Unix username.
%U	Requested username.
%v	Samba version number.
%z	The size of a print job, in bytes.
%$(*envvar*)	The value of the Unix environment variable *envvar*.

For the most part, the smb.conf file is case-insensitive; read only = yes is equivalent to READ ONLY = Yes or any other variant. For consistency, I present parameter names in lowercase and, unless some other case would make the string easier to parse, I specify values with an initial capital, as in read only = Yes. A few values are exceptions to the case-insensitivity rule; for instance, if a parameter takes a local Unix directory or filename as a value, that directory or filename is case-sensitive.

In addition to section names and parameter/value lines, smb.conf supports comments. These are indicated by a hash mark (#) or semicolon (;). Most administrators place comments on separate lines, but you can place a comment after other information on the same line as a Samba parameter; Samba ignores the comment character and everything appearing after it on a line.

TIP If you want to remove a parameter but think you might want to add it back later, comment it out by placing a comment character at the start of the line. If you comment out an entire share definition, you must comment out *every* line in the share definition, not just the line containing the share name. Instead of commenting out a share, you can set the available = No parameter within the share, which has the effect of removing it from the server's list of active shares.

As an example, consider Listing 2-1. This listing shows a simple but complete smb.conf file. This file sets the computer's NetBIOS name to RUMBA and the workgroup or domain name to RINGWORLD, while telling Samba to use encrypted passwords. It defines a single share, [homes], with options that set a comment visible to clients in their network browsers, make the share writeable, and prevent the share from showing up as HOMES in network browsers. (The [homes] share is special; it corresponds to each user's home directory. Chapter 5 describes this and other file shares in more detail.) In practice, most smb.conf files are much longer than the one presented in Listing 2-1.

Listing 2-1. A Sample smb.conf *File*

```
[global]
    workgroup = RINGWORLD
    netbios name = RUMBA
    encrypt passwords = Yes
[homes]
    comment = Home Directories
    writeable = Yes
    browseable = No
```

Many Samba binary packages ship with default smb.conf files that define [homes] shares, printer shares corresponding to the computer's standard printers, and possibly additional shares. These default files often include extensive comments to help you make changes without knowing a great deal about Samba, but other default files are much more sparsely commented. In any event, chances are the default file won't work quite correctly for you. Two settings are particularly likely to need adjustment for your network:

Workgroup name: If the workgroup parameter is set incorrectly, clients on the network may not be able to find your computer, or at best, they'll have to browse to the unfamiliar workgroup name to find it. If your network uses a domain rather than a workgroup, set its name using this parameter.

Password encryption: Prior to version 3.0, Samba defaulted to using cleartext passwords, and most default smb.conf files didn't change this setting. Because modern versions of Windows require encrypted passwords, this mismatch has caused many failures to connect. Samba 3.0 changes the default to use encrypted passwords, but even with that setting (or if it's changed on a Samba 2.2 or earlier system), you must create an smbpasswd file. This file is described in the next section, and the process of manipulating it is covered in more detail in Chapter 7.

In addition to these two very common sources of problems, many other parameters may need adjustments for particular network types. For instance, if your network uses a domain, you must configure Samba to be a member of that domain, or at least to authenticate users against the domain controller, if you want to use the domain controller for authentication. File metadata settings may need to be adjusted if you're using unusual clients, although the default settings usually work at least to some extent. Chances are you'll want to create additional shares beyond the default ones. The rest of this book is devoted to making these and other important changes to your Samba configuration.

Once you've created an smb.conf file, you may want to test its validity using the testparm program:

```
# testparm /etc/samba/smb.conf
```

This command returns information on potential problems with the file. For instance, it might warn you if you mistype the comment parameter as coment. The program will also point out blatant violations of smb.conf syntax requirements, such as specifying Maybe for a Boolean parameter. Of course, testparm can't test that the file will create the results you expect; a configuration file may be perfectly valid and yet define a server that won't do what you want it to do. For instance, testparm can't check for typos in your workgroup or NetBIOS name specification.

The Samba Password File, smbpasswd

If you use encrypted passwords, Samba stores its SMB/CIFS passwords in its own password file, smbpasswd. This file is similar in broad strokes to the standard Unix passwd file (described earlier in "Unix Password Databases and Hashes"), but the details differ. As with passwd, smbpasswd stores data one line per account, using colon-delimited fields. The fields are as follows:

username:UID:LANMAN hash:NT hash:flags:change time

Each field has a particular meaning:

username: This field contains the Unix username. Unless you take steps to map the SMB/CIFS username to another Unix username, this is the username that the user must use to access the server.

UID: The *user ID* (UID) is a number associated with the account. The server computer uses this number internally rather than the username, although most programs use the username as input and output. The UID should match the UID for the user in the /etc/passwd file.

LANMAN hash: This field looks like alphanumeric gibberish. It contains the LANMAN hash of the password, as used by Windows 9x/Me clients. If the string begins with the characters NO PASSWORD, no password is present on the account. A hash consisting entirely of X characters indicates a disabled account.

NT hash: This field also looks like gibberish to the naked eye. It contains the MD4-hashed password, as used by Windows NT/200x/XP. NT hashes are case-sensitive, unlike LANMAN hashes. This hash is harder to break than the LANMAN hash, but it's still very sensitive.

flags: This field contains flags that describe the nature of the account. It's surrounded by square bracket characters ([ ]) and contains eleven characters between the brackets. Currently, four flags exist: U indicates an ordinary user account, N means that the account has no password, D means that the account is disabled for Samba access, and W means that the account is a *workstation trust* account, which is used by computers (not users) in NT domains. This list of flags may be expanded in the future.

change time: The final field starts with the string LCT- and holds the time of the last change to the account, expressed as seconds since 1970.

 CAUTION   Both the LANMAN hash and the NT hash are extremely sensitive values. Given the way SMB/CIFS exchanges encrypted passwords over the network, anybody who obtains the smbpasswd file can impersonate any user specified in the file. For this reason, you must take extra care to protect this file from prying eyes. It should *never* be readable by anybody but root. Some installations place it in a directory that's readable only by root as an added precaution.

As a general rule, there's no need to directly edit the smbpasswd file. Instead, tools such as the smbpasswd program and, in Samba 3.0, the net program enable you to edit the smbpasswd file indirectly. You can use these programs to add users, change passwords, and so on. Chapter 7 describes these operations in more detail.

Ordinarily, all Samba users must have normal Unix accounts. That is, every username and UID specified in smbpasswd must also have an entry in /etc/passwd. The reverse isn't true, though, and in fact many ordinary Unix accounts should *not* exist in smbpasswd. Unix systems typically host several specialized accounts used exclusively for automated or semi-automated system maintenance or by daemons. For instance, you might find accounts called daemon, bin, mail, and nobody in your /etc/passwd file. These accounts should almost certainly *not* have counterparts in smbpasswd. The same is true of the root account, which is simply too powerful to be given access via Samba.

 TIP   If you really need to have root access to files via Samba, you may be able to accomplish the goal by creating a special share with access limited to just one user via the valid users parameter and by using the force user parameter to give the user of this share root privileges. You may want to create a special ordinary user account for using this share alone. This approach at least restricts access to other shares so that a miscreant who obtains the root or special user's password can't do damage to other shares.

The Hostname Lookup File, lmhosts

The lmhosts file works much like the standard Unix /etc/hosts file except that lmhosts maps NetBIOS names, rather than TCP/IP hostnames, to IP addresses. The format of lines in this file is quite simple:

```
IP-address   NetBIOS-name
```

The two fields are separated by any amount of whitespace (spaces or tabs). Lines that begin with a hash mark (#) are comments, which are ignored. As an example, Listing 2-2 presents a sample lmhosts file.

Listing 2-2. Sample lmhosts *File*

```
# NetBIOS name mappings for my network
192.168.7.9    WALTZ
192.168.7.10   RUMBA
192.168.7.20   BALLET#20
```

The first two entries, for WALTZ and RUMBA, are straightforward; they map these computers to the 192.168.7.9 and 192.168.7.10 IP addresses, respectively. The final entry, for BALLET, adds an extra component. In the context of a NetBIOS name in this file, a hash mark is *not* a comment; instead, it tells the system to map that name only if the computer is looking for a system with the specified name using the resource of the specified number, expressed in hexadecimal. For instance, BALLET#20 matches only the Server Service (resource type 0x20; both file and printer shares use this resource type) on the computer called BALLET. (Chapter 1 describes NetBIOS resource types. Refer in particular to Table 1-2.) Chances are you'll have no need to use this syntax because it effectively reduces the amount of access the local computer has to the named remote system; for instance, it might prevent the local computer from accessing another system's WinPopUp or master browser services.

As with /etc/hosts, lmhosts is of limited utility on most networks. Samba supports NetBIOS name resolution systems that are simpler to configure than lmhosts, such as broadcast name resolution, NBNS, and even DNS. The best use of lmhosts is on computers that are separated from the rest of a NetBIOS network by routers and when DNS doesn't do the job. In such a case, setting up lmhosts to point to systems on the main network can obviate the need to set up an NBNS computer or use other workarounds. As the number of computers using lmhosts rises, though, or as changes to the network become more frequent, the effort involved in maintaining lmhosts becomes problematic.

Additional Configuration Files

Although smb.conf, smbpasswd, and lmhosts are the most important Samba configuration files, there are others, and some of these files can be important in some circumstances. Some of these files include the following:

smbusers: This file contains mappings from SMB/CIFS usernames to Unix usernames. (In practice, this filename is just a convention; you point to the file using the `username map` parameter.) By default, Samba doesn't perform such mapping, but you can enable it if you want to tie together an existing Unix system to an existing NetBIOS network that uses different usernames for the same users.

Included files: The `include` parameter enables you to reference supplemental configuration files from the main `smb.conf` file. You might use this option in conjunction with a variable, such as those described in Table 2-1, to have Samba work differently for different clients. For instance, you might use different included files for DOS, Windows, and Unix clients that set different filename mangling and case-handling options.

Running Samba on Non-Unix Systems

Samba was designed as an SMB/CIFS server for Unix and Unix-like systems. Many of its options and assumptions are built around the need to implement SMB/CIFS features on Unix-like hosts. Nonetheless, Samba's robustness and power have drawn the attention of many developers outside of the Unix world. These individuals have managed to port the Samba server to assorted non-Unix platforms. Some notable ports include the following:

Mac OS X: This OS is built atop a Unix core, unlike its earlier Mac OS Classic predecessors. Thus, in some sense Mac OS X doesn't quality as a non-Unix host. Nonetheless, Mac OS, even Mac OS X, tends to be perceived as distinct from Unix. In fact, Mac OS X ships with Samba, although it's not enabled by default. Subsequent chapters of this book describe some of the quirks of running Samba atop Mac OS X.

VMS: Digital Equipment Corporation's (DEC's) Virtual Machine/Storage (VMS) OS was a popular OS on DEC's minicomputers and Alpha workstations. DEC no longer exists as a separate company, but VMS remains a viable OS, although it's not an extraordinarily popular one. Some of VMS's features parallel those of Unix, so some of Samba's features map well onto VMS's capabilities. As I write, the current version of Samba for VMS is 2.0.3, which is substantially out of date. You can learn more at http://www.ifn.ing.tu-bs.de/ifn/sonst/samba-vms.html.

OS/2: IBM's OS/2 was a moderately popular workstation and server OS for *x*86 computers in the 1990s, and it remains in use at many sites. OS/2 includes native SMB/CIFS support, but Samba has also been ported to the OS and is available from http://hobbes.nmsu.edu/pub/os2/apps/internet/util/. Why run Samba on an OS that includes its own SMB/CIFS support? The main reason is to gain access to some of Samba's unique features, such as IP-based access restrictions. As with VMS, though, the OS/2 version of Samba is old (2.0.7 as I write), and some Samba features don't work because of OS feature mismatches.

BeOS: Be, Inc., developed an entirely new OS in the 1990s. BeOS ran on
dedicated Be hardware, Apple PowerMacs, and *x*86 systems. This OS wasn't
closely related to or a clone of any existing OS, although it borrowed ideas
from many different OSs. Unfortunately, Be didn't fare well and was bought
by Palm. BeOS may be getting a new lease on life under a pseudonym, Zeta,
from YellowTAB (http://www.yellowtab.com). BeOS has shipped with Samba
in the past, although these Samba versions are particularly elderly—they
date back to the 1.9.*x* series.

AmigaOS: The Amiga was a 680*x*0-based computer and matching OS introduced in 1985 to compete with the early Macintosh systems. The AmigaOS
was ahead of its time for a desktop system; for instance, it supported full pre-
emptive multitasking. Over the years, more powerful Amiga systems have
been introduced, up to the present with systems such as the PowerPC-based
AmigaOne (http://www.eyetech.co.uk/amigaone/). Ports of Samba to AmigaOS
are available; check http://www.amigasamba.org for details. The latest
version as I write is 2.2.5, although that version is considered experimental.
The latest stable version is 2.0.7.

Samba has also been ported to many additional OSs. Go to the Samba Web page
(http://www.samba.org), click a local mirror, and click the *download* link. The Ports
area lists several OSs to which Samba has been ported, but that list is incomplete. Try
typing the name of your OS and **Samba** into a Web search engine if you want to learn
about running Samba on a particularly exotic OS.

With the exception of Mac OS X, many OSs lack certain key Unix features, and the
corresponding Samba functionality is, therefore, missing. For instance, most of these
OSs lack support for user accounts and Unix-style permissions. Thus, authentication
mechanisms may be crude. For instance, the OS/2 version of Samba requires you to
set a single username in the OS/2 CONFIG.SYS file. Samba will then accept accesses
using that username and no others. Features such as the mapping of hidden and
archive bits onto Unix execute bits aren't supported. VMS supports more Unix-like
features, including user accounts, but some features may be missing nonetheless. For
instance, the VMS version of Samba doesn't support encrypted passwords. Even
when features are present, you may need to cope with peculiar implementations. For
instance, you might need to hunt to find the smb.conf file or use OS-specific configuration tools such as OS/2's CONFIG.SYS file. You should definitely read any OS-specific
documentation you can find with the port of Samba to your OS.

Overall, Samba is best run on a Unix-like OS, and in fact Samba should compile
and run on just about any such OS. The rest of this book assumes you're running Samba
on such an OS, but much of this information applies to many ports of Samba on other
platforms. You may need to make adjustments for your specific situation, though.

You may also want to keep in mind that Samba isn't the only non-Microsoft implementation of SMB/CIFS. Indeed, as described earlier in "The Need for Samba," the
server began life through Andrew Tridgell's use of SMB/CIFS software for DOS and a
DECstation. These programs were from different vendors and had different names.
Today, tools such as Thursby's DAVE for Mac OS Classic (http://www.thursby.com)
and Objective Development's Sharity for various Unix systems (http://www.obdev.at/
products/sharity/) provide alternatives to Samba. Some of these products, such as

DAVE, run on platforms on which Samba doesn't run. Chapter 18 describes interfacing some of these programs' clients with a Samba server.

Summary

Considered as a tool for integrating Unix-like systems with Windows systems, Samba functions as a sort of translator. This translator, like a translator of human languages, must bridge the gap between different assumptions made by the two parties. In the case of Samba, these differences include numerous file metadata differences and password authentication differences. To run on Unix-like systems, Samba is implemented as a pair of daemons, smbd and nmbd, with SWAT serving as an optional Web-based configuration tool. You can also edit configuration files directly, but of course doing so means that you must understand something about the format of these files. Finally, although Samba is primarily a Unix program, ports to other platforms exist and enable Samba to serve as a translator for them, as well—albeit a translator with a strong figurative accent, making some features impossible to use.

Part Two

Basic Samba Operations

CHAPTER 3

Obtaining, Installing, and Running Samba

BEFORE YOU CAN configure and use Samba, you must obtain it, install it on your system, and at least know how to get it running. These tasks are similar to the equivalent procedures for many other servers, so if you're familiar with your OS, chances are you won't run into any major problems with Samba.

Of course, Samba does have its own peculiarities and specific features that can benefit from some explanation. This is particularly true of compilation options, requirements for methods of starting Samba, and Samba runtime options. This chapter describes these issues. If you follow along at your own computer, you should have a Samba server that's running, even if it's not responding correctly on your network, by the time you finish the chapter.

NOTE   As described in Chapter 2, you must change some Samba configuration options for the server to work correctly on any particular network. Chapter 4 describes the options you're most likely to need to adjust to get Windows systems to recognize the Samba server.

Sources for Samba

To install Samba, you must first know where to find it. The two most common places to get Samba are from official Samba sites on the Internet and from media or other sites associated with the OS you're running.

Official Samba Sites

The primary Samba Web site is at http://www.samba.org. If you enter that URL into a Web browser, though, you'll see a page that consists of little more than links to other sites, listed by geography. Most of these links fall into two categories: Web sites and download sites. The former are sites that contain documentation, announcements, additional links, and so on. Download sites are direct links to Web or FTP sites that hold Samba itself. Therefore, if you want to obtain Samba, you should click a link in the download area. Select a site that's near to you geographically. This action will be likely to result in the quickest download time because downloading a large package such as Samba from across the globe is usually slow. When you click a link to a Samba download site, you'll see a list of files and directories. You can also use an FTP client to get to these files by entering the same hostname you see as part of the URL. For instance, if the URL has led you to us2.samba.org, using an FTP client to connect to that site should also work. In most cases, the Samba files are in the /pub/samba subdirectory.

Whether you access the files via a Web browser or FTP client, the latest version of Samba is generally available as samba-latest.tar.gz or samba-latest.tar.bz2. These files are links to the latest stable version of Samba, which is also accessible via a filename with the version number embedded in the filename, as in samba-3.0.1.tar.bz2 for Samba 3.0.1. These files contain the entire source code for the Samba distribution, including the primary Samba servers, Samba client software, the Samba Web Administration Tool (SWAT), assorted documentation, and so on.

NOTE   Files whose names end in .gz are compressed with gzip, and filename extensions of .bz2 indicate files compressed with bzip2. The bzip2 program generates smaller files, but not all computers have bzip2 or its dedicated uncompresser, bunzip2, installed. (The official home of bzip2 is http://sources.redhat.com/bzip2/.) File packages created with tar and compressed with either program are often called *tarballs*.

If you want an older version of Samba for some reason, it's accessible from the old-versions subdirectory. Some of these versions date back to 1999. Development versions are likely to be available in the alpha, beta, and rc subdirectories. *Alpha* software is likely to be unstable but may be the only way to get certain advanced features. After the alpha software has been tested for a while, it's considered more stable, and its status is elevated to that of *beta* software. Even beta software is likely to contain bugs, though, so you should only use beta software if you must have a feature it contains. *Release candidate* (RC) versions of Samba are close to being final but may still contain more bugs than final versions. Check the dates on the files to determine whether the alpha, beta, RC, or final release software is the most recent.

You may also want to look for announcements from the *development* link on the main Samba page for your region. This page should provide information about the features that are under development, what the latest development (alpha, beta, or RC) software is, and so on.

TIP   To keep up to date with Samba developments, consider subscribing to a mailing list. The samba-announce list hosts announcements about new releases and other important information. Check the Samba Web page's *mailing lists* link for details about how to subscribe.

The Samba packages I've just described (for old, current, and development versions) are distributed as source code. To use this software, you must compile it on your system, as described in the upcoming section "Installing from Source Code." Installing from source code has its advantages, such as optimizing the software for your system, enabling you to set compile-time options to suit your preferences, and perhaps running a more recent version than you could otherwise run.

Installing precompiled binaries is generally simpler and less time-consuming than compiling the software from source code. In many cases, the advantages of compiling Samba yourself are slim. For these reasons, the Samba download sites also offer precompiled binaries. These are in subdirectories of the `bin-pkgs` directory. (`Binary_Packages` is a link to this directory.) As I write, this directory holds 16 subdirectories. Five of these subdirectories are for popular Linux distributions, and many of the rest are for popular Unix and Unix-like OSs, such as AIX, IRIX, and Solaris. A few subdirectories are devoted to non-Unix systems, such as VMS. Precisely what you'll find in these subdirectories varies substantially. Some include further subdirectories for different CPU architectures, such as the `Intel` and `Sparc` subdirectories under the `solaris` directory. Some include subdirectories for different OS versions. Some provide source and binary subdirectories. The source code may include OS-specific patches or be distributed in forms that benefit the OS, such as source RPM Package Manager (RPM) files for Red Hat Linux. Some OSs' subdirectories provide binaries packaged as tarballs. Others use OS-specific formats, such as Debian packages for Debian GNU/Linux or RPMs for most other Linux distributions.

Another way to get to Samba download sites is to go to the main Samba Web site for your area and click the *download* link. The Web page that pops up describes how to obtain Samba. This page also includes a Ports section with links to a few non-Unix ports of Samba.

However you obtain Samba, you may want to check the authenticity of what you've just downloaded (this is a good idea for all code you download). To check validity of the code, follow these steps:

1. In addition to the Samba tarball, download the `samba-pubkey.asc` file and the `samba-version.tar.asc` file, where `version` is the Samba version number.

2. Type the command `gunzip samba-version.tar.gz` or `bunzip2 samba-version.tar.bz2`, as appropriate. This command undoes the compression because the verification signature is made with the uncompressed files.

3. Type the command `gpg --verify --keyserver wwwkeys.pgp.net samba-version.tar.asc`. If all goes well, the result should be several lines of output that begin something like this, albeit with different details:

```
Signature made Sat 07 Jun 2003 02:23:27 PM EDT using DSA key ID 2F87AF6F
gpg: Good signature from "Samba Distribution Verification Key➥
<samba-bugs@samba.org>"
```

The output is likely to continue for a few more lines, ultimately concluding that the key isn't certified with a trusted signature. Unless you're very paranoid, you shouldn't be concerned with this message. The GNU Privacy Guard (GPG) system provides several layers of identity checks. The first message about a good signature indicates that the signatures in the tarball and in the files downloaded in step 1 match those found on the wwwkeys.pgp.net public key site. The remaining warnings indicate that gpg can't verify that the public key site is who it should be. Unless a miscreant has managed to compromise both the Samba Web site and the public key site, there should be no problem.

Using CVS

This chapter emphasizes obtaining Samba through a tarball or other prepackaged form. Another approach is possible, though: the Concurrent Versioning System (CVS). CVS is a tool that enables developers to coordinate their development efforts. A CVS server contains an entire source code tree and enables developers to "check out" specific files to work on them and then "check in" those same files and their changes. The idea is to prevent the chaos that might result from multiple developers trying to make changes to the same files. Non-developers can also use CVS to obtain the very latest version of Samba—more recent even than whatever alpha or beta software is present on the Samba Web or FTP site.

Because CVS is of interest primarily to developers or those who need the absolute latest features, I don't describe it in great detail in this book. Consult http://us3.samba.org/samba/cvs.html (or the equivalent file on another Samba Web site) for information about using CVS to obtain Samba. If you use CVS, the remaining configuration and compilation procedures described in this chapter still apply; only your method of downloading Samba is different.

Samba Distributed with OSs

A second method of obtaining Samba is using the version that came with your OS. Most Unix-like OSs today ship with Samba, but the Samba version sometimes lags the latest available from the Samba Web site by a few months. Using an OS-provided Samba package offers several advantages over using the original package. These advantages boil down to convenience—the OS-provided Samba package is likely to be easier to install and run because it will use the OS's native package management tools, and it may ship with SysV or other startup scripts necessary to start Samba. In some cases, an OS distributor may patch Samba to fix bugs or work around compatibility problems. Such patches are particularly likely if the OS in question is on the fringes of the Unix world or outside it entirely. Apple ships a version of Samba with Mac OS X, for instance, that's been tweaked to work in the Mac OS X environment. In such situations, you're well advised to not try recompiling Samba yourself unless you have a compelling reason, such as a need for a new feature. Some of the benefits of Samba distributed with an OS accrue to binary packages obtained from the Samba Web site, though. For instance, Red Hat Linux RPMs from the Samba Web site include SysV startup scripts that can help you start Samba automatically whenever the system boots.

OS Samba packages are sometimes split into multiple files. For instance, the OS may include separate files for the base Samba tools (sometimes called samba or samba-server), another file for Samba clients (typically samba-clients), another package for documentation (samba-docs), and perhaps more packages for specialized or related tools, such as SWAT. You should check your installation media or OS's distribution FTP site for all files containing the string samba. (The SWAT package may be called swat and not contain the string samba.)

OS-provided packages almost invariably come in precompiled binary form, although many OSs also provide source code. Some OS-specific distribution methods, such as FreeBSD's ports system, rely upon source code as the primary distribution form. The upcoming section "Installing from a Binary Package" describes how to install a Samba binary package in several popular formats. If your OS uses some other format, you should consult your OS-specific documentation.

In addition to official OS-sponsored sites, you may be able to find Samba on FTP or Web sites that are unofficial repositories for your OS of choice. For instance, many OS/2 files, including Samba, are available from ftp://hobbes.nmsu.edu. (Samba for OS/2 is in the /pub/os2/apps/internet/util directory.) This site isn't run by IBM, OS/2's publisher, but it's a common repository for OS/2 files. If you can't find a precompiled version of Samba on the Samba Web or FTP site, and if it doesn't come with your OS and isn't available on your OS's official sites, you may want to look for it on popular archive sites for your OS. Looking for Samba in this way is particularly important for exotic OSs because the plain Samba source code may not compile cleanly on your target platform.

Installing Samba

Depending upon how you do it, installing Samba involves unpacking an archive file, configuring a compilation routine, performing a compilation, and moving binary program files to appropriate locations. Some installation methods, particularly for binary distributions, can greatly simplify the process by using OS-specific installation tools. The ultimate goal in all cases is the same, though: You must place critical Samba files, such as the smbd binary and the smb.conf configuration file, in appropriate locations in your OS's directory tree. Once this is done, it becomes possible to run the binaries, as described in the upcoming section "Running Samba."

Installing from Source Code

The earlier section "Official Samba Sites" described how to obtain Samba source code. Once you've done so, you can unpack the code and compile it. This process involves several steps and is likely to take several minutes to complete even on a new computer. The result is a binary that's optimized to run on your particular CPU and with the Samba compile-time options that are important to you.

NOTE This section describes compiling source code obtained from an official Samba source. Some OSs provide customized binary compilation procedures. For instance, Linux distributions that use RPMs support compiling *source RPMs*, which contain source code and any changes the distribution maintainer provides. FreeBSD uses a *ports* system, which enables you to easily download original program source code and changes to that code and to automatically compile and install the source code. Consult the OS-specific documentation to learn about such options.

CAUTION As noted earlier, it's often better to install Samba using binary packages, as described in the upcoming section "Installing from a Binary Package." This is particularly true when an OS's publisher tightly integrates Samba into its system and maintains it with security updates, as, for instance, Apple does with the Samba it ships with Mac OS X. Compiling your own version of Samba in such an environment can cause problems integrating Samba into OS-specific control mechanisms or can omit OS-specific bug fixes that are distributed by the OS's publisher but that have yet to find their way into the main Samba package.

Preparing for the Build

Compiling Samba (or any source code package) requires that your system have certain software components installed. Most important, you need a *compiler*—a program that converts source code into machine code. Most compilers ship with a collection of related programs, such as assemblers and linkers.

Samba is written primarily in C, so it needs a C compiler. Samba is most commonly compiled using the popular open-source GNU Compiler Collection (GCC). GCC ships with most open-source OSs, such as Linux and FreeBSD. It's also available for most commercial OSs, although commercial Unix-like OSs almost always ship with their own compilers as well. If you're not sure if your system has a C compiler installed, you can try following the directions in the next two sections. If they fail and you believe the cause might be a lack of a compiler, check the main GCC Web page, http://gcc.gnu.org, as well as the GCC binaries Web page, http://gcc.gnu.org/install/binaries.html. Samba may compile with non-GCC compilers, but the safest bet is to use GCC.

In addition to GCC, Samba relies upon a series of *libraries*, which are collections of code that provide support functions used by other programs. Libraries aren't technically programs themselves; rather, they provide features that many other programs might want to use. Precisely what libraries you need depends in part on the configuration options you choose, as described in the next section, "Configuring the Compilation."

In theory, this process should detect the presence or absence of necessary libraries and warn you if your libraries are out of date or nonexistent. Unfortunately, this process sometimes doesn't go right, so you may encounter problems only when you try to compile Samba.

Many OSs provide collections of packages related to software development. You may want to go through your OS's software installation tools and pick software development options. On the other hand, doing this may cause a large number of packages to be installed that won't be used. The result is a lot of wasted disk space, and it may be a modest security risk. An intruder might be able to abuse your own development tools to compile cracking programs on your system. An alternative is to try compiling Samba and then respond to any error messages you see.

NOTE   To *use* Samba, you need the binary forms of libraries. To *compile* Samba, you need these binary forms, but you also need programming interfaces, known as *development libraries* or *header files*. If you encounter error messages about the lack of libraries, it could be that the development libraries are missing, not the binary libraries.

Configuring the Compilation

The first step in compiling source code is to extract the files from the tarball. You can do this in any convenient directory, such as your home directory or /usr/src. If you uncompressed your tarball to check its GPG signature, as described earlier in "Official Samba Sites," the tarball is now uncompressed, and you should be able to extract it using a command like this:

```
$ tar -xvf samba-version.tar
```

NOTE   You can, and for safety reasons probably should, extract the Samba source code and compile it as an ordinary user. You will need root privileges to install the compiled binaries in their ultimate locations.

If you didn't uncompress the tarball to check its signature, you can perform both steps with a single command:

```
$ tar -xvzf samba-version.tar.gz
```

If you downloaded a tarball compressed with bzip2, substitute j for z in the string -xvzf, and of course make the appropriate substitution in the Samba tarball's filename. In any event, the result should be a directory called samba-*version*, where *version* is the Samba version number. Change into this directory, and read the README and WHATSNEW.txt files for any important information that might be new. The source subdirectory contains the main Samba source code. Change into this directory to perform the remaining configuration, compilation, and installation tasks.

The source subdirectory holds a file called configure. This file is a script that scans your system to determine what software is installed on it, what type of OS and CPU you have, and so on. The result is a customized file (called Makefile) that controls the compilation process.

To help you customize the Samba binary you build for your system, the configure script supports several options. Most of these options take the form --with-*package* or --without-*package*, where *package* is a Samba subcomponent that should or should not be included. A few take other forms, such as --enable-*feature* or --disable-*feature*. Some take options after an equals sign, such as --with-*path=pathname*, to set the directory in which a file is stored. Specified in their default states, some of the more important of these options are as follows:

--enable-shared: By default, Samba builds itself using shared (a.k.a. dynamic) libraries, which minimizes the server's memory load. You can change this behavior by using the --enable-static option, or you can add an equals sign and a package name to build specific libraries dynamically or statically.

--disable-debug: Samba's build scripts normally disable the compiler's debugging features. Enabling these features is most likely to be useful if you're compiling Samba on a platform that uses an unusual compiler or with a new version of GCC or if you're compiling an alpha or beta release of Samba.

--disable-developer: This option controls whether developer warnings and debugging information should be displayed.

--enable-cups: The Common Unix Printing System (CUPS) is a relatively new printing subsystem for Unix-like systems. The configure script normally autodetects the presence of CUPS and enables support if CUPS is installed on your system. You can force the issue by using the appropriate option, though. Samba can print using CUPS even if you specify --disable-cups, but Samba will take better advantage of CUPS if you enable this option.

--without-smbwrapper: smbwrapper is a tool that enables Samba to simulate a mounted filesystem, giving a computer running Samba the ability to access remote SMB/CIFS servers as file-sharing servers. Some OSs, such as Linux, FreeBSD, and Mac OS X, provide their own tools to implement these features, so smbwrapper is seldom used with them. This feature may be useful on some other platforms, though.

--without-smbmount: smbmount is Linux's native method of mounting remote SMB/CIFS shares. This support also requires similar options to be enabled in the Linux kernel.

--with-ads: This option enables support for Active Directory, which is an increasingly important authentication and network information system on Windows networks. Active Directory is related to Kerberos.

--with-krb5=*directory*: This option tells Samba where to look to find the Kerberos support directory tree. The default value is /usr.

--without-pam: As described in Chapter 2, the Pluggable Authentication Module (PAM) is a mechanism for providing user authentication for servers and other login tools. If your OS uses PAM, you should activate this support in Samba, particularly if you plan to use unencrypted passwords.

--without-pam_smbpass: If you enable this option, the build process will build PAM modules that authenticate users against the Samba encrypted password file.

--with-ldap: The Lightweight Directory Access Protocol (LDAP) provides an alternative method of storing encrypted passwords. This option is most important if your network uses Samba primary and backup domain controllers or if you use LDAP for Unix authentication and want to better integrate Unix and Samba password databases.

--without-syslog: Ordinarily, Samba creates its own log files, but if you change this option, you can tell Samba to log data via the syslogd server.

--without-quotas: Some computers implement *quotas*, in which the amount of disk space any given user can consume is limited. To work well on such systems, you should enable quota support in Samba.

--with-libsmbclient: The smbclient program can be built using shared libraries or statically. The default depends on the setting for shared libraries generally (--enable-shared or --disable-shared).

--without-acl-support: To better interact with Windows NT/200*x*/XP clients, you should enable support for access control lists (ACLs).

--with-winbind: Winbind is a tool that enables a Unix system to authenticate local users against a Windows domain. By default, this option is included if the underlying OS supports it.

--without-fhs: The Filesystem Hierarchy Standard (FHS) is a standardized layout of directories and their contents. If you enable FHS support, Samba adjusts some of its default directory locations.

--prefix=*directory*: This option sets the directory that's used as a base for many other directory locations. The default value is /usr/local/samba.

--exec-prefix=*directory*: This option sets the location of architecture-dependent subdirectories, such as those used to store compiled Samba binaries. The default is the value set with --prefix.

--with-privatedir=*directory*: This option sets the default location of the smbpasswd and other sensitive Samba files. The default is /usr/local/samba/lib/private.

--with-lockdir=*directory*: Samba stores files that relate to *locking* files in the directory specified with this option. The default value is /usr/local/samba/var/locks. File locking is a tool to prevent two programs from trampling over each other when they both try to modify a single file.

--with-piddir=*directory*: Samba stores its process ID (PID) number in a file stored in the directory you specify with this option. The default value is /usr/local/samba/var/locks.

This list of options isn't complete. Most of the rest are geared toward Samba developers or relate to relatively obscure options that you're unlikely to need to change. Nonetheless, you may want to peruse the configure script to learn about some of these options. A list of options appears near the start of the file, along with brief descriptions of their effects. You can also type **configure --help** to produce a list of options, although it's not quite complete.

As an example of configure in action, consider compiling Samba on a Linux system. Linux-related options you're likely to want to change from their defaults include support for smbmount and PAM. You might also want to enable other options, such as support for syslog and ACLs. Thus, you can type the following command to configure Samba for this system:

```
$ ./configure --with-smbmount --with-pam --with-syslog --with-acl-support
```

After you type this command, the system should respond with a series of lines indicating the features that configure is checking or setting. These messages will scroll past fairly rapidly and be difficult to follow. The process is likely to take anywhere from a minute or so to several minutes. If all goes well, the system will conclude with no error messages and a statement that several files have been created, including one called Makefile and the include/config.h file. You're now ready to compile Samba. If you later decide you need a feature you omitted from the configuration step, you must go back and rerun the configuration.

Sometimes, the configuration process fails. This may occur if you're missing basic configuration tools that are used by configure or because the script has found you're missing tools that are required to compile Samba. If this happens, read any error messages you see and do a Web search on the appropriate keywords.

Compiling Samba

Most of the work of compiling Samba is actually in the configuration step. Once you've created a Makefile using configure, you need only type a single command to build all of Samba:

```
$ make
```

After you type this command, you'll see a series of summary commands scroll past. Most of these simply read compiling *filename*, where *filename* is the file that's being compiled. Samba is a large program (actually, a series of programs), so this compilation process is likely to take several minutes and possibly more than an hour on older or heavily loaded systems. Some configuration options can affect the compile time, as well; for instance, adding support for smbmount and ACLs involves compiling some additional files, which adds a small amount of time to the process.

Unfortunately, compilation doesn't always go smoothly, particularly with alpha or beta versions of Samba. Sometimes, the problem is a missing library. When this happens, you're likely to encounter an error such as the following near the end of the compilation messages:

```
lib/pam_errors.c:24: security/pam_appl.h: No such file or directory
make: *** [lib/pam_errors.o] Error 1
```

This error indicates that a file, security/pam_appl.h, is missing. With any luck, the filenames involved will give you a clue about the cause. In this case, the fact that both the missing filename and the file that called it (pam_errors.c) have names beginning with pam suggests the file is related to PAM. Perhaps the system needs some PAM library files. This particular error message appeared on a Debian GNU/Linux system, so I searched the Debian file list at http://www.debian.org/distrib/packages for packages related to PAM and discovered a likely candidate: libpam0g-dev. After installing this package, the compilation proceeded further.

Unfortunately, even when you've installed all the necessary packages, compilation doesn't always succeed. For instance, the installation of libpam0g-dev did indeed clear the error message I reported, but when I tried again, the system responded (after several minutes churning away) with a long series of error messages beginning with this:

```
Compiling nsswitch/pam_winbind.c with -fPIC
nsswitch/pam_winbind.c:60: parse error before `*'
nsswitch/pam_winbind.c: In function `converse':
nsswitch/pam_winbind.c:67: `pamh' undeclared (first use in this function)
```

This example indicates a more serious flaw—a *parse error* usually means there's a bug in the code or at least that the code is seriously mismatched with the compiler's capabilities. This particular example comes from a beta version of Samba, so chances are it's related to the unstable nature of the version I was trying to compile. In this case, I was able to work around the problem by rerunning the configure script and telling it not to use PAM at all. Once that change was made, Samba compiled smoothly. When this happens, the compilation process peters out with a few uninspiring messages about compiling, linking, and building various components.

When Samba finishes compiling, the programs are available in binary form. These binaries, though, include debugging symbols that greatly expand the size of the binaries. If you're running an alpha or beta version of Samba, or if you're running into problems you think may be related to bugs, you may want to leave these debugging symbols intact. Otherwise, you may want to remove them from the binary files using the strip command:

```
$ strip bin/*
```

As an example of the impact of this command, consider smbd on a couple of test systems. On one *x*86 system, smbd went from 39MB to 2MB. On a PowerPC system, the effect was less dramatic but still large, reducing the size of the executable from 6MB to 2MB. After you've stripped the files, you can begin installing them—or you can do so without stripping the files if you prefer. Unfortunately, a successful compilation is no guarantee that everything will work perfectly, although chances are good that they will, particularly if you're using a final release version of Samba on a common platform.

Installing the Binaries

To install the Samba program files, you'll likely need root privileges. Thus, you should use su, use sudo, log out and log in again as root, or do whatever else you must to become the superuser. Then, change to the Samba source code directory (if you're not already there), and type the following command:

```
# make install
```

This command tells the system to compile the program, if necessary (it shouldn't be because the program has just been compiled), and to copy programs, configuration files, documentation files, and so on to various locations specified by defaults or by configure options such as --exec-prefix and --prefix. If all goes well, the make utility will report on its progress in copying individual files to their final destinations.

At this point, Samba is installed, but depending upon your system's defaults and the options you passed to configure, the programs may be installed in an odd location. By default, Samba's binary files reside in /usr/local/samba/sbin and /usr/local/samba/bin. (Servers reside in the former location, whereas clients, support programs, and administrative tools reside in the latter location.) Chances are these directories aren't on your system's path, so you may need to add them to the path or create symbolic links from these files to directories that are on your path. Similarly, the Samba scripts place the man pages in subdirectories of /usr/local/samba/man, so you may want to edit /etc/man.config and add a MANPATH entry pointing to /usr/local/samba/man.

Once the binaries are installed and paths set appropriately, you can try running Samba, as described in the upcoming section "Running Samba." The sections between this point and that section all relate to installing binary packages. If you've successfully compiled and installed Samba from source code, installing from a binary package is unnecessary, so you can skip those sections. (If the binary you compiled doesn't work as you expect, though, you may want to delete it and try a prepackaged binary program.)

Installing from a Binary Package

Installing a binary package is usually easier than installing a source package. All the tedious precompilation configuration has already been done, presumably in a way that's optimized for your platform. The package maintainer has also worked out any obnoxious configuration kinks. On the downside, if you need to enable some unusual Samba feature, you may have no choice but to compile the package yourself.

In any event, the following sections describe three popular methods of binary package distribution: Binary tarballs, RPMs, and Debian packages. Binary tarballs come in several varieties; there are "generic" tarballs, which work the same on many platforms, as well as tarballs that contain special information or are formatted in a way that's helpful for OS-specific package installation routines.

NOTE   Some OSs install Samba by default. For instance, Mac OS X installs a binary version of Samba as part of the system installation, so you shouldn't need to do the job manually.

Installing a Tarball

Tarballs are the most universal form of package distribution. As described earlier in "Official Samba Sites," Samba's source code is distributed in tarball form. The tools used to extract data from a binary tarball are the same as those used to handle a tarball that contains source code: tar and a compression program such as gzip or bzip2 (or their decompression counterparts, gunzip or bunzip2). Some commercial Unix systems don't ship with either of these programs; instead, they use a program called compress. Tarballs created with compress have .tar.Z filename extensions. How you install a tarball depends on the OS you're using.

Installing a Basic Tarball

In the conceptually simplest case, a tarball must be unpacked from the root (/) directory. To do so, you download a file, change to the root directory, and unpack the file:

```
# tar -xvzf /path/to/samba-version.tar.gz
```

You may need to change the filename and path, and if the tarball is compressed with bzip2, change z to j in the -xvzf options. The result of this command is that the tarball will be extracted into the current directory. If it stores its files in directories based off the root directory, the files will end up in reasonable locations. At this point, Samba is installed.

CAUTION   Before extracting any tarball, and particularly when doing the job from the root directory or as the root user, you should check the contents of the tarball. Replace x in the -xvzf option in the tar command with l (that's a lowercase L) to view the contents of the tarball without extracting them. If the contents include directories that match those that appear in your root directory, it's designed to be unpacked from there. If you're not positive the tarball is intended for your OS, unpack it in another directory so you can study the files. You can subsequently unpack the tarball from the root directory if the package is okay.

One problem with basic tarball installation is that you can't be sure whether the files you unpack will overwrite existing files. If you're installing Samba for the first time, this probably won't be an issue, but it might be—some unrelated program might happen to use a filename that Samba uses. If this happens, or if you happen to download a bogus Samba package created by somebody who wants to wreak havoc, you might overwrite another valid program. This is one of the reasons so many systems have shifted away from using raw binary tarballs as a binary software distribution format.

Installing a FreeBSD Package

FreeBSD ships with packages stored as tarballs. (FreeBSD 4.*x* and earlier use filename extensions of .tgz for gzip-compressed tarballs, and FreeBSD 5.0 and later use filename extensions of .tbz for bzip2-compressed tarballs.) To install one of these packages directly, including the Samba package, you use the pkg_add or sysinstall utility.

To use pkg_add, pass it the name of the package. For instance, to install samba-*version*.tbz, you would type this:

```
# pkg_add samba-version.tbz
```

This program completes its work silently; if it doesn't present any error messages, Samba was installed correctly.

Although pkg_add is fairly straightforward, it does require you to obtain a copy of an appropriate FreeBSD tarball. To help in this task and further automate the procedure, you can use another tool, sysinstall. Type **sysinstall** at a root command prompt, and you'll see a text-mode menu system. Select Configure ➤ Packages. You can then pick a source to search, such as your installation CD-ROM or a FreeBSD FTP site. Depending upon your selection, you may need to select additional options, such as the name of the FTP site. Once that's done, select the Net package area and locate the Samba package, as shown in Figure 3-1. This figure shows a late Samba 3.0 alpha package selected; above it is Samba 2.2.7a, the latest stable version when the screen shot was taken. To select a package, press the space bar; an X will toggle on and off with each press. When you've finished selecting packages, press the Tab key to highlight OK and press the Enter key. On the next screen, highlight Install and press the Enter key. The sysinstall tool then asks you to confirm that you want to install the package or packages you selected, and installation proceeds. Once this is done, you can exit from the sysinstall utility.

Once you've installed a tarball through pkg_add or sysinstall, FreeBSD keeps track of the files the tarball contains. Later, you can use pkg_delete or sysinstall to delete a package, and the package management tools will warn you about any conflicting files. Other FreeBSD package management tools, such as the ports tools, also interface with pkg_add and its related database. One limitation to this system is that it doesn't work with any random tarball you might stumble across. FreeBSD package tarballs include special files that help the package system do what it needs to do.

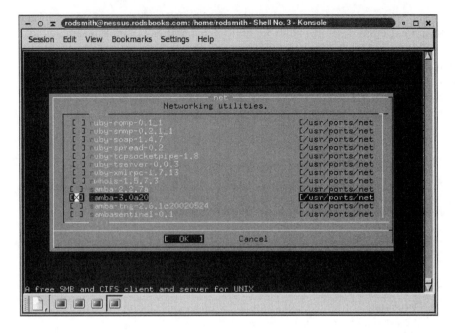

Figure 3-1. FreeBSD's sysinstall *provides a text-mode menu system with which you can install Samba.*

Installing an RPM

Many Linux distributions use RPM to handle packages. Binary RPMs are basically compressed cpio archives with some extra bits added. These extra features help the OS keep a database of installed packages and files similar to the one FreeBSD maintains with the help of its package tools.

If you want to install a Samba binary, either from your Linux distribution or from the Samba Web or FTP site, you can do so with the rpm command. This command takes several options, but for installing a package, the most common set of options is -Uvh followed by the package name:

```
# rpm -Uvh samba-version-minorversion.arch.rpm
```

In this example, *version* is the Samba version number, such as 2.2.7a or 3.0.1. The *minorversion* is an additional revision component that describes changes made by the package maintainer as opposed to the Samba Team. Distribution maintainers may use these numbers to track revisions such as changes to their custom SysV startup scripts. Finally, *arch* is an architecture code, such as i586 for Pentium-class *x*86 CPUs or ppc for PowerPC. Many distributions provide only i386 optimizations for their packages. This practice creates packages that work on all 32-bit *x*86 CPUs, but their performance may suffer slightly compared to i586 or better optimizations when run on Pentium or faster CPUs.

Most RPM-based Linux distributions also provide GUI tools that can aid in package installation. Details differ from one distribution to another, but most resemble the Red Hat Package Management tool shown in Figure 3-2. In this case, Samba is merely identified as the Windows File Server. (Clicking the Details button shows you the names of the individual packages to be installed, though.) After you select Samba, click Update. The system checks its RPM database and prompts you to insert a disc, whereupon it installs Samba.

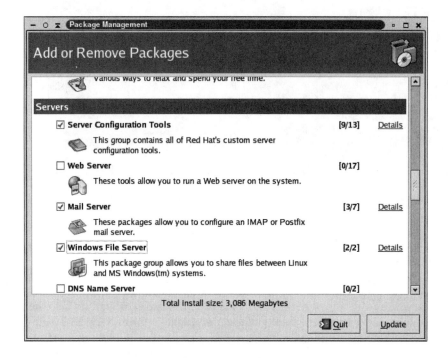

Figure 3-2. Red Hat's Package Management tool provides a GUI interface for selecting packages that ship with Red Hat Linux.

Most RPM-based distributions split Samba into several binary packages, such as a split of the server from the client or the binaries from the documentation. There may also be a separate package for SWAT. The details differ substantially from one distribution to another, though. This type of split enables you to install only those components you need on your system, which can save space and possibly even improve security.

Installing a Debian Package

Debian GNU/Linux and its derivatives include package management tools that are roughly equivalent to the RPM tools created by Red Hat or FreeBSD's package management tools. Debian packages, though, use yet another file format. Debian ships with an unusually large collection of software, including Samba. Debian is also one of the distributions whose packages can be obtained from the Samba Web and FTP sites.

The core tool for package installation under Debian is dpkg. This program functions much like rpm or pkg_add and its related tools. To install a package you've downloaded, use the -i option to dpkg:

```
# dpkg -i samba_version-minorversion.deb
```

As in RPMs, *version* and *minorversion* refer to the Samba version number and any minor changes created by the Debian package maintainer. Some Debian packages also include an architecture code similar to the RPM architecture code.

As with RPM-based distributions, Debian splits its Samba files into multiple packages. In particular, the OS ships with samba-common, samba, samba-doc, and swat packages. Chances are you need to install at least samba-common and samba.

Rather than hunt for a package, you may be able to use the apt-get tool, which searches a database built from your installation media and, optionally, one or more FTP or Web sites. To install Samba using apt-get, you would type this:

```
# apt-get install samba
```

This command should locate and install the samba package as well as any packages upon which it depends, such as samba-common. This command will only work if the Advanced Package Tools (APT) utilities are properly configured, though. A basic configuration involves editing the /etc/apt/sources.list file to refer to the installation CD-ROMs or some appropriate FTP sites. For more information, consult the APT HOWTO document at http://www.debian.org/doc/manuals/apt-howto/.

Debian also supports both text-based and GUI configuration tools that provide a point-and-click (or keyboard-and-click) interface to package selection. The standard text-based tool is dselect. If you installed Debian yourself, this tool should be familiar because Debian uses it during installation. A GUI equivalent, shown in Figure 3-3, is the Storm Package Manager, which originated with the now-defunct Storm distribution. This tool has been picked up by Debian itself and remains useful today.

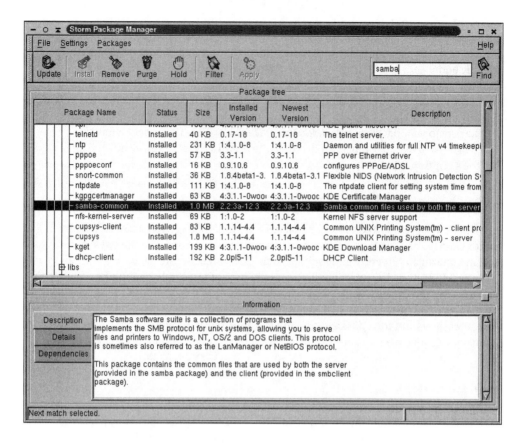

Figure 3-3. The Storm Package Manager provides a GUI interface for package selection in Debian and related Linux distributions.

Running Samba

Whether you install Samba by compiling it from source code or by installing it from a binary package, your next job is to start it running. Typically, this means running the smbd and nmbd daemons, so this is the task to which the rest of this chapter is devoted. Additional tools, such as the SWAT server and various SMB/CIFS clients, must be run in different ways. These topics are covered in subsequent chapters, such as Chapter 13 and Chapter 18.

You can run Samba in any of several ways. The following sections describe running Samba manually, as when testing it; running it via SysV or local startup scripts; running it from a super server; and using Samba's runtime options, which you can adjust to tweak Samba's behavior without modifying its configuration file.

NOTE When you install Samba as part of a base OS or using a package provided by the OS, chances are good that it will already be configured to run automatically. Most Unix-like systems, including most Linux distributions and FreeBSD, use SysV or local startup scripts for this job. Mac OS X uses a super server configuration, which you can enable or disable using the Sharing panel in System Preferences, as described further in Chapter 13.

Running Samba Manually

When you first install Samba, chances are you want to get it running without rebooting the computer. The simplest way to do this is to run it by typing the daemon names, each of which should be followed by -D to tell it to run in daemon mode:

```
# nmbd -D
# smbd -D
```

NOTE Depending upon how Samba was installed, you may need to add the complete path to the program files, as in /usr/local/samba/ sbin/nmbd instead of simply nmbd.

After you type these commands, use ps to verify that the servers are running:

```
# ps ax | grep mbd
18066 ?        S      0:00 /usr/local/samba/sbin/nmbd -D
18068 ?        S      0:00 /usr/local/samba/sbin/smbd -D
```

If you see no output, or only the grep command itself, chances are Samba can't find its configuration file, smb.conf. Check the locations where it should reside. If you installed from source code and didn't change any defaults, check /usr/local/samba/lib. If you installed a precompiled binary package, check /etc/samba, /usr/local/etc/samba, or whatever location would be appropriate for your OS. You can also use the find command to try to locate the file:

```
# find / -name "smb.conf"
```

If the file isn't present where it should be, create it. Use Listing 2-1 from Chapter 2 as a starting point. If you can't determine where Samba is looking for its configuration file, you may need to tell it to look wherever you've put the file by using the -s parameter, as described in the upcoming section "Samba Runtime Options."

At this point, chances are your Samba installation won't be very useful. You may not be able to browse to the Samba server from clients, and even if you can, the server might not properly authenticate users or present useful shares. Making the server do these things is the point of the next several chapters of this book. If both nmbd and smbd show up in a ps listing, it's working well.

To stop the servers, you can use the kill command, along with the PIDs listed in the first column of the ps output shown earlier:

```
# kill 18066
# kill 18068
```

Some Unix-like OSs provide a command called killall that enables you to kill processes by name rather than by PID. For instance, to kill nmbd and smbd, you would type this:

```
# killall nmbd
# killall smbd
```

CAUTION   On some Unix-like OSs, such as Solaris, killall doesn't kill processes by name; instead, and more in fitting with the command's name, killall kills *all* active processes. Therefore, you should *never* issue a killall command unless you're *absolutely positive* that the command does what you think it does. If there's any doubt in your mind, type **man killall** or check other documentation for your OS to learn what the command does.

If your computer uses SysV startup scripts, you can use those scripts manually rather than start and stop the servers by typing their names. For instance, the following commands start and stop, respectively, the Samba servers on a Red Hat Linux system:

```
# /etc/rc.d/init.d/smb start
# /etc/rc.d/init.d/smb stop
```

SysV Startup Scripts

AT&T's System V version of Unix has been a model for many subsequent versions and variants of Unix. One of System V's features that's now used pervasively is its startup script system, which has come to be known as *SysV startup scripts*. Systems that use SysV startup scripts use a series of scripts, one per server or subsystem, typically in /etc/rc.d, /etc/init.d, or a subdirectory of one of these directories, to start and stop many OS subsystems.

When a SysV startup script is passed a start parameter, the script starts the associated service; when it's passed a stop parameter, the script stops the service. The scripts may also respond to other parameters, such as restart to restart the service or status to report on the service's status. OSs that use SysV startup scripts include most

Linux distributions and Solaris. As noted shortly, FreeBSD borrows some SysV features, but it doesn't use runlevels.

Computers that use SysV startup scripts also usually implement several *runlevels*, which are numbered system states that correspond to different conditions or sets of servers. Typically, runlevel 0 halts the system, runlevel 1 is a special single-user mode, and runlevel 6 reboots the system. Runlevels 2 through 5 correspond to normal operating modes, with details differing from one OS to another. In practice, runlevels are created by using special directories (subdirectories of the SysV startup script directory or subdirectories placed directly in /etc) in which symbolic links to SysV startup scripts reside. When a service should be started, the link's name begins with S; when it should be killed, the link's name begins with K. When entering a runlevel, the OS executes the SysV startup scripts pointed to by the links in the associated directory, passing start or stop parameters depending upon the first letter of the link's name.

Samba binary packages created for OSs that use SysV startup scripts typically ship with appropriate scripts. This is one of the benefits of using such precompiled packages on these OSs. If you've compiled Samba yourself, you must use the SysV startup scripts from a precompiled Samba package, create a script yourself, or use another method of starting Samba, such as a local startup script.

Listing 3-1 shows a simple SysV startup script for launching Samba (both nmbd and smbd). This script is only a basic starting point; it may work acceptably for you, but it's decidedly bare-bones. It provides no feedback about the success of starting or stopping the servers, for instance. It relies upon the presence of the servers' correct PIDs being stored in the specified PID files. If your OS uses sophisticated SysV startup scripts, you may want to try modifying one of them to do the job rather than using Listing 3-1 as a guide.

Listing 3-1. Sample SysV Startup Script for Launching Samba

```
#!/bin/sh
case "$1" in
    start)
        /usr/local/samba/sbin/nmbd -D
        /usr/local/samba/sbin/smbd -D
        ;;
    stop)
        kill `cat /usr/local/samba/var/locks/nmbd.pid`
        kill `cat /usr/local/samba/var/locks/smbd.pid`
        ;;
    restart)
        $0 stop
        $0 start
        ;;
esac
```

FreeBSD is unusual in that it uses SysV-style scripts, but it doesn't employ them in runlevels. The standard FreeBSD Samba startup script is called /usr/local/etc/rc.d/samba.sh. FreeBSD's Samba package ships with this script but calls it samba.sh.sample rather than samba.sh. To start Samba automatically when the system boots, you must rename the script to samba.sh.

Local Startup Scripts

Instead of or in addition to SysV startup scripts, some Unix systems provide one or more monolithic startup scripts. These scripts can launch many servers, but they aren't used to stop servers, as SysV startup scripts can do. These scripts frequently contain the word local in their names, and so I refer to them as *local startup scripts*. Examples include /etc/rc.d/rc.local in Red Hat and related Linux distributions, /etc/init.d/boot.local in SUSE Linux, and /etc/rc.local in FreeBSD. (FreeBSD's developers discourage using this script, though.) Local startup scripts tend to be easy ways to start Samba running because you need only add a couple of lines to these scripts, such as these:

```
/usr/local/samba/sbin/nmbd -D
/usr/local/samba/sbin/smbd -D
```

When the local startup script executes as part of the normal boot process, Samba starts. The problem with this approach is that it provides no easy way to shut down or restart Samba. If you need to make changes to your Samba configuration, you must manually kill the servers and then restart them, as described earlier in "Running Samba Manually." Nonetheless, if you're having problems creating a SysV startup script, you might want to at least try a local startup script.

Running Samba from a Super Server

A *super server* is a single server that runs and listens to the ports used by a potentially very large number of target servers. When the super server detects a connection request for a particular server, the super server launches the target server, which wasn't running until that moment. Two common super servers are inetd and xinetd.

The advantage of using a super server is that an infrequently used server need not consume memory space on the server computer until a client tries to access the server. The super server itself consumes relatively little memory and can stand in for quite a few memory-hungry servers. Super servers also offer security benefits; inetd is frequently paired with the TCP Wrappers tool for controlling access by IP address, and xinetd includes functionality similar to that of TCP Wrappers.

Super servers aren't without their drawbacks, though, and some of these are important for Samba. First, clients connecting to super servers notice a delay between the connection attempt and the initial reply. This delay results from the need to launch the target server. For a small server, such as a typical Telnet server, this delay is tiny; but for a server such as Samba, it can be much more substantial. A second problem is that super servers make it difficult or impossible for servers that must maintain information across connections to do so. This drawback is particularly important for nmbd, which handles NetBIOS Name Server (NBNS), browser, and similar functions for Samba. Some servers just plain don't work under super servers. For instance, although smbd can work under a super server, nmbd is very tricky to get working, particularly with xinetd. Finally, super servers are best employed for servers that are used infrequently. When a server is used heavily, the memory benefits of using a super server fade to nothing. The security screening benefits might still remain, but firewall rules can be used to similar effect. Samba also offers similar rules, so the benefits of a super server's security screening are limited at best.

As a general rule, Samba isn't well suited to use from a super server. I only recommend such use for smbd alone, leaving nmbd running via a SysV or local startup script. The primary reasons to run smbd from a super server are if the computer has few SMB/CIFS clients, if they connect infrequently, and if memory is tight on this computer. For instance, the server might function primarily as an NFS server, with perhaps one SMB/CIFS client connecting every few days. In such a situation, you might try using a super server configuration.

A few OSs, such as Debian GNU/Linux, give you the option of running Samba from a super server upon installation. Mac OS X 10.3 is one of the rare OSs that runs Samba from a super server by default (it uses xinetd), although the usual method of controlling Samba's running from Mac OS X is to use its GUI controls. (Chapter 13 covers these tools in more detail.) Although I recommend avoiding use of super servers for running Samba generally, Mac OS X seems to run well with this configuration, and trying to bypass this configuration is likely to lead to trouble, or at least confusion, when using the GUI controls.

If you're using inetd, you must edit the /etc/inetd.conf file. This file contains a series of lines, one per server, that describe the servers inetd is to launch. To handle *both* smbd and nmbd, this file should contain lines like the following:

```
netbios-ssn stream tcp  nowait  root  /usr/local/samba/sbin/smbd   smbd
netbios-ns  dgram  udp  wait    root  /usr/local/samba/sbin/nmbd   nmbd
```

Your /etc/services file should also contain the following entries:

```
netbios-ns    137/tcp                  # NETBIOS Name Service
netbios-ns    137/udp
netbios-dgm   138/tcp                  # NETBIOS Datagram Service
netbios-dgm   138/udp
netbios-ssn   139/tcp                  # NETBIOS session service
netbios-ssn   139/udp
```

In fact, the 137/udp and 139/tcp entries are the most important, and they're the only ones required for the inetd.conf entries specified earlier. In practice, running nmbd from inetd is a tricky proposition at best; you might find that your Samba server won't show up in browse lists. A configuration such as this one should work for smbd, though, and this might be adequate if you can run nmbd directly or if you only want to access the Samba server using more direct means, such as the smbclient program from a Unix-like system.

If you use xinetd, you must create equivalent /etc/xinetd.conf entries to the /etc/inetd.conf lines shown earlier. The xinetd.conf file presents much of the same information as does inetd.conf, but it uses a multiline format. In fact, some OSs that ship with xinetd by default, such as the Mandrake and Red Hat Linux distributions and Mac OS X, split individual server definitions into separate files, which are stored in the /etc/xinetd.d directory.

For instance, this directory might have separate nmbd and smbd files corresponding to the like-named Samba daemons; or the directory might have a single samba file that holds entries for both servers. Listing 3-2 shows such a listing. (It can be split in two to create a pair of files with the same effect.) Enter Listing 3-2 into a file called samba (or anything else you like) in /etc/xinetd.d, and xinetd will, once restarted, take over handling the Samba ports. As with the inetd configuration, you must also create the /etc/services entries described earlier, if they don't already exist.

Listing 3-2. Sample xinetd *Entries for Launching Samba*

```
service netbios-ssn
{
    socket_type     = stream
    protocol        = tcp
    wait            = no
    user            = root
    server          = /usr/local/samba/sbin/smbd
}

service netbios-ns
{
    socket_type     = dgram
    protocol        = udp
    wait            = yes
    user            = root
    server          = /usr/local/samba/sbin/nmbd
}
```

Whether you use inetd or xinetd, in order for your changes to take effect, you must perform the following steps:

1. Shut down any running smbd and nmbd processes, as described earlier in "Running Samba Manually."

2. Find the PID of the inetd or xinetd process. On most systems, typing **ps ax | grep inetd** should do the job.

3. Pass a HUP signal to the inetd or xinetd process, as in **kill -HUP 8239** if step 2 revealed that the relevant PID was 8239.

Instead of steps 2 and 3, if your system launches the super server via a SysV script, you may be able to use it to restart the super server. For instance, on a Red Hat Linux system, you could type **/etc/rc.d/init.d/xinetd restart** to do the job.

Once you make these changes, the smbd server will probably respond normally. You can test this behavior by using smbclient from the same or a different Unix-like system:

```
$ smbclient //localhost/sharename
added interface ip=192.168.1.3 bcast=192.168.1.255 nmask=255.255.255.0
Password:
Domain=[RINGWORLD] OS=[Unix] Server=[Samba 3.0.1]
```

NOTE Of course, you'll only be able to access the server if other aspects of its configuration are working. As noted earlier, this may not be the case until you've set options described in the next several chapters, particularly in Chapters 4 and 5.

Chances are good that your network browsing will become unreliable if you use a super server for nmbd. If this happens, you should switch back to stand-alone operation via a SysV or local startup script, at least for nmbd. You can judge for yourself whether the delays in starting smbd are a problem.

Samba Runtime Options

Samba, like many Unix programs, accepts options on its command line to alter the way it operates. Most of Samba's options are best set in its main configuration file, smb.conf; however, you may want to override some options on a case-by-case basis. For this purpose, command-line options are invaluable. Table 3-1 presents the most important Samba command-line options.

Table 3-1. Summary of Samba Command-Line Arguments

Argument	Used by Daemon(s)	Meaning
-D	smbd, nmbd	Run the server as a daemon; it runs in the background and doesn't output data to the terminal from which it was launched.
-F	smbd, nmbd	Run the server in the foreground (that is, not as a daemon). This mode is useful for debugging and for running from certain diagnostic programs.
-S	smbd, nmbd	Send log data to standard output (the terminal, if launched from one) rather than to a log file.
-i	smbd, nmbd	Run the server interactively. This is similar to specifying both the -S and -F options.
-h	smbd, nmbd	Print a summary of command-line options. (This option is broken in at least early versions of Samba 3.0.*x*.)
-V	smbd, nmbd	Print the daemon's version number.
-d *debug-level*	smbd, nmbd	Sets the amount of data to be logged. If *debug-level* is 0, only critical errors are logged. A *debug-level* of 10 creates *huge* amounts of data. In practice, levels between 0 and 3 are best for production systems.

Table 3-1. Summary of Samba Command-Line Arguments (Continued)

Argument	Used by Daemon(s)	Meaning
-H *lmhosts-file*	nmbd	Sets the location and name of the lmhosts file, as described in Chapter 2. The nmbd server uses this file to resolve queries made by local clients, not to respond to queries made by remote systems.
-l *logfile*	smbd, nmbd	For nmbd, sets the filename for log files. (The extension .client will be added to the specified filename.) For smbd, sets the directory in which the log.smb file will be stored.
-s *config-file*	smbd, nmbd	Specifies the location and name of the configuration file (typically smb.conf).
-n *netbios-name*	nmbd	Sets the base NetBIOS name used by the computer.
-p *port-num*	smbd, nmbd	Sets the port to which the server listens.
-O *socket-option*	smbd	Sets socket options that may be used to optimize Samba performance.

You can specify any of these options you want if you want to override the default options set in smb.conf. You can even use the -s option to point Samba to an alternate smb.conf file or to tell the server where to look for the file in the first place if you don't care for the default location set when the server was compiled. You can use these options when launching the server manually or include them in SysV or local startup scripts or super server configurations.

Summary

Samba is widely available for many platforms. Many Unix-like OSs ship with Samba, and for many others, precompiled binaries are available on the Samba Web page or FTP site or on third-party sites. Thus, obtaining Samba is seldom a problem, although you may need to hunt to find precompiled binaries for particularly exotic OSs.

Once you've obtained Samba, installing it can be as easy as clicking a few buttons in a GUI or issuing one or two commands at a text-mode shell. If you want or need to compile Samba yourself, though, the process becomes more complex. You must uncompress the source code, configure it, compile it, and install it. These steps can go fairly smoothly, but if you run into problems, you'll have to study the error messages and look for a solution.

Once the software is installed, you must be able to run it. You can do this in any of several ways, ranging from manually starting the servers to creating startup scripts or super server configurations to have the servers start automatically whenever you boot the computer.

#### CHAPTER 4

Global Samba Configuration

MANY SAMBA CONFIGURATION options apply to the server as a whole or set defaults that are picked up by all file and printer shares that don't override these defaults. This chapter describes the most basic and important of these parameters; several subsequent chapters describe global parameters that have more specialized purposes.

This chapter begins with a look at the structure of the smb.conf file, emphasizing the difference between global and share parameters. Next up is information on identifying your server—giving it a name, setting its workgroup or domain, telling Samba what OS to emulate, and so on. Samba offers several password options, and these are quite important; they determine whether and how clients can authenticate to the server. Finally, this chapter examines Samba's logging options—features that determine where Samba stores information about its operation and what information it records.

Samba Configuration File Format

Chapter 2, and particularly the section "The Main Samba Configuration File, smb.conf" of that chapter, introduced the basic structure of the smb.conf file. If you compiled Samba from source code using standard configuration options, this file will reside in /usr/local/samba/lib, although you won't find a default file in that location. Precompiled Samba packages for many OSs place the file in /etc, /etc/samba, /usr/local/etc, or a similar location. If your precompiled Samba package places its configuration file in a particular location, you should probably leave it there.

TIP If you can't determine where your Samba binaries expect to find smb.conf, you can specify a location and filename using the -s parameter, as in smbd -s /etc/samba/smb.conf to have the smbd server read /etc/samba/smb.conf as its configuration file. This parameter works with smbd, nmbd, net, and smbclient. The smbpasswd utility uses the -c parameter to achieve this same effect. As a general rule, though, it's best to put the configuration file in the default location for your OS; GUI configuration tools and the like may expect to find the file in a particular place and won't work correctly if it's moved.

If your Samba package or OS ships with a default `smb.conf` file, you may want to use it as a starting point for modification. These sample files often contain optimizations for your particular system. For instance, they may include printer options to help Samba use the printing system installed on your computer. These sample files may also be heavily commented, which can help you decide which options should be changed. If you can't find a sample file, you can use Listing 4-1 as a starting point. This bare-bones listing doesn't include many of the options described in this chapter, much less other chapters, but it may be a useful starting point.

Listing 4-1. A Sample `smb.conf` *File*

```
[global]
   workgroup = RINGWORLD
   netbios name = RUMBA
   encrypt passwords = Yes
[homes]
   comment = Home Directories
   writeable = Yes
   browseable = No
[printers]
   comment = All Printers
   writeable = Yes
   browseable = No
   printable = Yes
```

NOTE The default `smb.conf` files that ship with most binary Samba packages are likely to include options not shown in Listing 4-1 and some that aren't covered in this chapter. If you're curious about specific options, consult Appendix A or look up the parameter in the index.

Listing 4-1 is broken into three sections: `[global]`, `[homes]`, and `[printers]`. The first of these sections, `[global]`, defines global parameters, such as those described in this chapter. The next two sections define a file share and a printer share, respectively, as described in Chapter 5 and Chapter 6. These particular shares (`[homes]` and `[printers]`) are special; they define file shares that correspond to specific users' home directories and printer shares for all the printers defined on the server, respectively.

Some parameters have synonyms or antonyms, and you may encounter these rather than the parameter names shown in Listing 4-1 or elsewhere in this book. For instance, the `writeable` parameter has synonyms of `write ok` and `writable`; these parameters have the same effect as `writeable`. An antonym is `read only`; setting `read only = No` has the same effect as setting `writeable = Yes`. Appendix A notes the synonyms and antonyms for particular parameters.

Broadly speaking, parameters have one of two *scopes*: *global* or *share*. Parameters with global scope can be used *only* in the [global] section. These parameters set features that affect the server as a whole, such as the server's NetBIOS name and whether the server should function as a domain controller. Global parameters simply don't make sense when applied to individual shares. Many, but not all, of the parameters described in this chapter are global parameters.

> **NOTE** Global parameters may also influence the behavior of Samba clients, such as smbclient. Not all global parameters make sense in the context of clients, though.

Share parameters, by contrast, often appear in file or printer share definitions. These parameters set values that need not apply to all the shares on a server. For instance, a share parameter might make one share read-only, but another share might pass a different option to the same parameter to make it read/write. Share parameters, though, aren't confined to use in file and printer share definitions. When these parameters appear in the [global] section, their effects apply to all of a Samba server's shares unless they're overridden by the same parameter (or a synonym or antonym for that parameter) in a specific file or printer share definition. For instance, if a server holds ten file shares, all but one of which should have read/write access, then you could place a writeable = Yes parameter in the [global] section, omit this parameter from most of the file shares, and place a writeable = No parameter in the one share that should not be writeable by ordinary users.

Most parameters, both global and share, have default values compiled into the Samba binary. If you omit the parameter, the default value applies. You can change some of these compiled-in defaults by altering compile-time options, as described in Chapter 3. You can't change other defaults in this way, although of course you could modify the source code if you wanted to do so. On rare occasion, the Samba Team alters the default value with a new release of the software. For instance, the default password encryption value changed between the 2.2.*x* and 3.0.*x* series, as described in the upcoming section "Setting Password Options."

Identifying Your Server

Some of the most basic Samba configuration options relate to machine identification. As described in Chapter 1, SMB/CIFS and NetBIOS rely on methods of system identification that are distinct from those used by most TCP/IP applications. For this reason, you must tell your Samba server software how to identify itself to other SMB/CIFS clients and servers. One such identification involves the workgroup or domain association. Another is the computer's NetBIOS name. Identifying the server software type can also be important in some situations, as can a few miscellaneous settings.

NOTE Server identification options, and particularly the NetBIOS name, are most important for clients that use NetBIOS name resolution methods. As described in Chapter 9, some clients can use Domain Name System (DNS) name resolution or some other method to locate servers, and some do so by default. Most clients, including all versions of Windows, OS/2, Samba, and Mac OS, can use NetBIOS names.

Setting the Workgroup or Domain Name

Chapter 1 introduces the concept of NetBIOS workgroups and domains, and you should review that chapter if you need detailed information on this topic. In brief, workgroups and domains are similar methods of breaking logically related collections of computers into smaller coherent wholes. For instance, suppose your network spans five floors in an office building, with each floor holding 20 computers. Users who need to browse this network might have a hard time finding their target computers from a list of 100 systems. To make the job easier, you could break up the network into five workgroups or domains, each corresponding to the systems on a single floor of the building. If users are more likely to need to access resources stored on computers on their own floors, this arrangement will improve the overall accessibility of the network because searching through 20 computers is a lot easier than scanning 100 of them. If a user needs to access a system on another floor, this can still be done but may take more mouse clicks to find the target system in a network browser.

Of course, for this arrangement to work, each computer must know to which workgroup or domain it belongs. In the case of Samba, this task is accomplished with the workgroup parameter, which is used in Listing 4-1 to assign the computer to the RINGWORLD workgroup or domain. Despite the name, the workgroup parameter works equally well for workgroups and domains. A domain is essentially a workgroup with a few extra features, so the same Samba parameter sets both the workgroup and the domain name.

Even if your network has just a single workgroup or domain, it must be named. The default name if none is specified is most likely WORKGROUP, unless your Samba version has been modified to change this default. Most sample smb.conf files include the workgroup parameter, so you should locate that line and adjust it to match the name used on your network. If you're unsure of what your local workgroup or domain name is, you must consult the settings on a computer that already runs on this workgroup or domain. If the network supports another Samba server, you can check the workgroup parameter in its smb.conf file. In the case of an all-Windows network, you must examine the network settings from a working Windows system. For instance, in Windows XP, you should open the Control Panel, double-click the System icon, and click the Computer Name tab, as shown in Figure 4-1. This tab provides information about the computer's name settings, including its workgroup or domain name (on the Workgroup line—RINGWORLD in Figure 4-1).

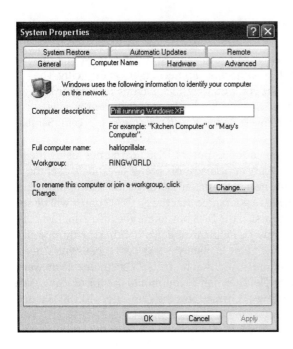

Figure 4-1. You can learn what workgroup name to use in Samba by examining the settings of existing computers on your network.

If you haven't already set up your network, you must decide upon a workgroup or domain name. Workgroup or domain names follow the same naming rules as do NetBIOS names, as described in Chapter 1. Specifically, they are case-insensitive, may be up to 15 characters in length, and may contain letters, numbers, and various punctuation symbols. As a general rule, it's best to keep the workgroup names fairly short and to use only letters and numbers. Punctuation can be confusing in some contexts, and overly long names may not fit in short display fields.

Remember that the computer's NetBIOS workgroup or domain name is logically distinct from the machine's DNS domain name on the Internet. In practice, these two names may be identical, and in some cases making them match with domain or sub-domain names makes a great deal of sense. For instance, a college might split its DNS domain into subdomains named after departments, such as psych.pangaea.edu, chemistry.pangaea.edu, and so on. Using equivalent NetBIOS workgroup or domain names (PSYCH, CHEMISTRY, and so on) can avoid confusion. Some organizations may be large but not use DNS subdomains, though, in which case the NetBIOS workgroup or domain names may not have equivalents in the DNS structure. If your network is entirely private and has no DNS domain name on the Internet, of course, you'll need to create a workgroup or domain name. You can use anything you like within the constraints of length and permitted characters; you won't conflict with another network, even if that network happens to use the same workgroup or domain name as you use.

Setting the NetBIOS Name

Unlike the workgroup or domain name, which you almost certainly must set explicitly in `smb.conf`, the computer's NetBIOS name may not need to be set explicitly. The reason for this is that Samba uses the computer's DNS hostname (minus the DNS domain name) as the default NetBIOS name. For instance, if your computer is `rumba.example.com`, and if you don't override the NetBIOS name in `smb.conf`, Samba uses `RUMBA` as its NetBIOS name.

Depending upon how you set up your computers' DNS hostnames, using the default setting may be adequate. Many administrators prefer to explicitly set the computer's NetBIOS name, though, even if the default setting should be appropriate. Setting this option explicitly provides a guarantee that the NetBIOS name will be set properly even if the method used to assign the DNS hostname goes awry (for instance, if a changed DHCP server setting causes a failure to assign a DNS hostname automatically). On the other hand, setting the name explicitly in `smb.conf` means you'll need to explicitly change the NetBIOS name in addition to the DNS hostname if you want both to change. To explicitly set the NetBIOS name, you should use the `netbios name` parameter, as demonstrated in Listing 4-1, which sets the computer's NetBIOS name to `RUMBA`.

NOTE   Technically, a NetBIOS name consists of a base name, which is set using the `netbios name` parameter, and a one-byte code that identifies the type of service the computer offers. A computer can register several NetBIOS names using a single base name. The workgroup name is also the basis of NetBIOS names registered in this way. This all happens transparently, though—Samba automatically creates the full NetBIOS name based on the base name and the appropriate code for whatever service it's registering. Administrators frequently refer to the NetBIOS base name as *the NetBIOS name*.

Samba is unusually flexible when it comes to its NetBIOS names. If you like, you can configure Samba to respond to multiple NetBIOS names. To do so, you can set one using `netbios name` or rely on the automatic use of the DNS hostname. You can then use the `netbios aliases` parameter to have the system advertise additional names for browsing and name resolution purposes. For instance, if you want a computer to respond to the names `RUMBA`, `TANGO`, and `CHICKENDANCE`, you might include the following lines in `smb.conf`:

```
netbios name = RUMBA
netbios aliases = TANGO, CHICKENDANCE
```

The effect of these lines is that the three names you specify will appear in clients' network browsers. For instance, Figure 4-2 shows a Windows XP browser opened on a network that includes a computer configured to use these three names. (In Windows XP's network browser, the NetBIOS name appears in parentheses.) Note that each of these aliases is also identified as *DNS name is nessus* using a comment, as described shortly in "Setting Additional Identifications." Each of these names, when clicked, will show the same set of shares unless you perform some extra configuration, described shortly.

Figure 4-2. A single Samba server can appear under multiple NetBIOS names if you use the netbios aliases *parameter.*

Why would you want to create multiple entries for a single Samba server? One answer is that you may want to consolidate multiple servers in one. For instance, suppose you've got three old servers and want to replace them with just one more modern server. You can have Samba handle all the original servers' shares and take over all three servers' original names. Doing so will simplify life for your users because they won't need to change any shortcuts, print queues, or whatnot they may already have on their systems. To your users, their preferred servers will simply seem to have sprouted additional shares. Of course, this approach may not work if the original servers had duplicate share names, but in many cases Samba's ability to respond to multiple NetBIOS names can greatly simplify network reconfiguration. Even if the servers have duplicate share names, you may be able to work around the problem by customizing the configuration on a per-alias basis using the include parameter.

If you want to create shares that appear only to users who call the server by a particular name, you can use the include parameter with the %L variable (see Table 2-1 in Chapter 2) to create shares that are unique to particular hostnames. For instance, suppose you want to create shares that are visible only to users of CHICKENDANCE. You might include the following line in smb.conf:

```
include = %L.conf
```

You would then create a file called chickendance.conf in the same directory as smb.conf and place any share definitions unique to CHICKENDANCE in this file. (Note that Samba converts the NetBIOS name to lowercase when you use the %L variable.)

You can create additional files named after other NetBIOS names, such as `tango.conf` and `rumba.conf`, to provide shares that should appear only on these computers. Using this technique, you can make the computer look very much like multiple systems. The main reason for doing this is to prevent your users from becoming confused by the appearance of shares they don't expect to see if you consolidate multiple servers' shares into one. You can also define shares that have the same name under each alias but that refer to different directories, thus overcoming one of the potential problems of consolidating multiple servers into one.

Even aside from the use of an alias-sensitive `include` parameter, Samba doesn't respond *quite* identically to all its aliases. Specifically, Samba doesn't advertise the alias names as a master browser or a logon server if the computer is configured to fill these roles; Samba restricts these functions to the name set via `netbios name`. In most cases, you don't need to be concerned with this fact, but if you use `include` to set up alias-sensitive options, you should be sure to put options relating to these features in the main `smb.conf` file or in the file called for the primary NetBIOS name.

Setting the OS Level

Chapter 1 mentions *browser elections*, which are described more fully in Chapter 8. In brief, most SMB/CIFS clients provide a method of locating available resources via a network browser (which isn't necessarily related to a Web browser). The network browser obtains a list of servers from a system known as the *master browser*, whose function it is to collect such information from other computers. SMB/CIFS provides a means to automatically designate one computer as the master browser—a browser election.

In a browser election, each computer advertises certain characteristics, such as whether it's currently serving some other important duty in the SMB/CIFS network. One of these characteristics is the computer's *OS level*—basically a code number for the OS version the computer runs. In fact, the OS level is a critically important factor in determining which computer is likely to win a browser election.

The default OS level for Samba is 20, but you can override this value with the `os level` parameter. Chapter 8 covers the meanings of various OS levels in more detail, but for now you should know that a Samba server with an OS level of 20 will win a master browser election against most Windows systems, including all versions of Windows 9*x*/Me, Windows NT Workstation, and Windows 2000/XP Professional. The Server versions of Windows NT/200*x* will beat out a Samba server with default settings, though.

The upshot of all this is that you may want to adjust the `os level` parameter if you want Samba to win—or not to win—a browser election. As a general rule, if your network's browsing works to your satisfaction prior to adding a Samba server, and if the Samba server you're configuring isn't replacing a system that functions as the master browser, you may want to consider setting `os level = 0` to assure that Samba won't win a browser election, potentially disrupting a working browsing setup. (Setting `local master = No` is another way to accomplish this goal; consult Chapter 8 for details.) On the other hand, if your Samba server is taking over domain controller duties, or if it's replacing the only Windows NT/200*x* servers on your network, you may want to leave the `os level` parameter unchanged (that is, not include it in smb.conf at all). If you want the Samba server to win even against Windows NT/200*x* Server systems, you should boost the os level setting to 33 or above. (Windows systems use power-of-2 OS levels, so some administrators like to use os level = 64.) To force Samba to call for an election when it starts, you must also set preferred master = Yes.

CAUTION Various misconfigurations can cause recurring browse problems. For instance, a computer can lock itself into a loop in which it repeatedly calls for—and then loses—master browser elections. The result is that browse lists on clients appear and disappear frequently. To be sure this doesn't happen because of your addition of a Samba server, set preferred master = No or be sure that this parameter *isn't* present in smb.conf (the default value is No).

The idea behind OS levels is that more reliable computers, and those that are likely to be running continuously for long periods of time, are best suited to function as master browsers, and thus should be most likely to win browser elections. A dedicated Samba or Windows NT/200*x* server computer is likely to be up for days or even months before being rebooted and is, therefore, likely to be able to maintain browse information over time without gaps. If the master browser is shut down or reboots frequently, clients are likely to have problems because the master browser will become inaccessible. This can result in incomplete browse lists or delays in which browse lists are completely unavailable.

Two additional parameters that are similar in some respects to os level are announce as and announce version. These parameters collectively tell Samba what OS to claim to be. The announce as parameter accepts values of NT, NT Server (which is synonymous with NT), NT Workstation, Win95, and WfW (Windows for Workgroups). The default value of NT works well in most cases and makes the Samba server appear to be a Windows NT system.

The announce version parameter takes a number as a value. The default value for Samba 2.2.*x* and 3.0.*x* is 4.9. Samba 2.0.*x* and earlier used a default version of 4.2. In most cases, you shouldn't change either the announce as parameter or the announce version parameter. In fact, changing these values has the potential to cause problems. For instance, Samba's handling of browser elections is modeled after that of Windows NT, so setting announce as to other values can cause problems if Samba also tries to participate in browser elections. Setting announce version = 5.0 can cause problems because other systems will then try to treat Samba as a Windows 2000 server, which Samba won't handle well.

Setting Additional Identifications

You may want to set a few additional options that can help your clients identify the server. These options include the following:

lm announce: This parameter determines whether Samba periodically generates a LAN Manager (LM) browsing announcement, which is required by OS/2 clients. You can set a value of Yes, No, or Auto. The final option is the default and works well on most networks—Samba listens for LM announcements and generates them if and only if Samba detects them. Using Yes or No overrides this behavior with an absolute setting.

lm interval: LM announcements occur at the interval specified by this parameter, whose value defaults to 60, for 60 seconds. Shorter intervals increase network bandwidth consumed by these broadcasts but make the Samba server appear more quickly on OS/2 clients' network browsers.

netbios scope: NetBIOS supports a seldom-used feature known as *scope*. If your network uses NetBIOS scopes, you can completely isolate two groups of computers by giving them different scope IDs. If you do this, you must tell Samba what scope to use by specifying it with this option, which takes a string as a value.

protocol: As described in Chapter 1, SMB/CIFS comes in several different versions. You can set the maximum protocol level for Samba to use with this parameter, which takes values of CORE, COREPLUS, CORE+ (which is identical to COREPLUS), LANMAN1, LANMAN2, and NT1. (The last of these is the default.) Chances are you won't need to change this value, but it's conceivable that an obscure older SMB/CIFS implementation might work better with a lower protocol setting. A synonym of this parameter is max protocol.

remote announce: Ordinarily, Samba, like most SMB/CIFS implementations, announces its presence when it starts, but only to the systems on the local subnet. You can provide network addresses to this parameter to change this behavior and have Samba announce itself to master browsers on the remote networks you specify. This trick can be handy if you want to add a single Samba server to one or more networks separated from the server by a router. In some cases, doing this may be enough to obviate the need to create a domain configuration instead of using a simpler workgroup setup. Chapter 8 describes this parameter's use in more detail.

server string: This option sets a free-form string that appears in many network browsers along with the server's name. For instance, Figure 4-2 shows the result of using server string = DNS name is %h on the computer with the DNS hostname of nessus. This example uses the %h variable to insert the DNS hostname into the server string. Note that the share-level comment parameter performs a similar job, but it sets a comment that's associated with a specific share; the global server string sets a comment for the server as a whole.

CAUTION Many sample smb.conf files ship with server string set to Samba server %v or something similar. Using the %v variable, which produces the Samba version number, in a server string parameter is unwise because it advertises the exact server version number to everybody—potentially even miscreants who might want to break into the computer and who might know of a security flaw in the version of Samba you're running. For this reason, I strongly recommend you set server string to something that doesn't provide any information about the server software you're running. Potential miscreants might still be able to learn what you're running through other means, but doing so will take more knowledge and effort if you don't advertise the information.

Of these options, server string is the one you're most likely to want to set. Depending upon the client OS and its settings, the server string value may be more or less prominent than shown in Figure 4-2. The remaining options are mostly of limited interest—they're best for use on a network with OS/2 clients or one that uses NetBIOS scopes, for instance.

Setting Password Options

Passwords may be the single greatest source of problems for new Samba administrators. As described in Chapter 2's "Unix and Windows Password Authentication" section, the encryption technique used by SMB/CIFS isn't compatible with the most common Unix password systems. For this reason, using encrypted passwords requires using a separate Samba password database. Alternatively, you can add Samba to an existing Windows domain, handing this task off to another computer. Either approach requires explicit configuration of your Samba server. Although this chapter introduces some of these options and provides enough detail to get some systems up and running, this topic is complex enough that it comes up again in several subsequent chapters—most notably, Chapter 7 and Chapter 10.

To Encrypt or Not to Encrypt

You must first decide whether to use encrypted passwords. As described in Chapter 2, encrypted passwords can provide an added measure of security; when your SMB/CIFS clients and servers use encrypted passwords, miscreants who manage to use network sniffers are less likely to be able to decipher your SMB/CIFS passwords. (The older LM hash, used by Windows 9x/Me, is easy to break by today's standards and so provides little protection, though.) Without these passwords, such individuals can't easily gain full entry to shares to which they shouldn't have access. On the downside, using encrypted passwords requires maintaining a separate password database for Samba alone or configuring your entire network to use a domain (or at least setting up one system that will handle all Samba authentication requests).

As a practical matter, encrypted passwords are generally preferable to unencrypted passwords. In addition to the security benefits, most modern Windows systems ship by default to use encrypted passwords and don't fall back on unencrypted passwords. Specifically, this has been the default starting with Windows 95 Original Equipment Manufacturer (OEM) Service Release 2 (OSR2) and Windows NT 4.0 Service Pack 3 (SP3). All versions of Windows 98, Me, XP, 2000, and 2003 use encrypted passwords by default. As a result, if you want to use unencrypted passwords with Windows clients, you must either use a very old version of Windows or alter the Windows configuration to use unencrypted passwords, as described in Chapter 7.

Setting the Authentication Method

Samba 3.0.*x* uses encrypted passwords by default, whereas Samba 2.2.*x* and earlier used unencrypted passwords by default. Given this option's importance, you may want to set it explicitly, even if your setting merely reiterates the default. You can do this with the global encrypt passwords parameter, which accepts a Boolean value as an option. If you set this parameter to Yes, you must also create a Samba password database, as described in the next section, "Using Encrypted Passwords."

Another Samba option that's critical to authentication is the security parameter, which determines what method Samba uses to authenticate users. Samba supports four possible values for this parameter:

Share: This method emulates the behavior of a Windows 9*x*/Me server. Clients need not send a username to connect to the server; instead, passwords are associated with specific shares. Internally, though, Samba must use usernames, so Samba tries several different usernames, as described shortly. This method tends to be confusing to use on a Samba server, but it's sometimes useful.

User: This method is the default, and it causes Samba to authenticate users against their local Unix accounts. Depending upon the setting of the encrypt passwords parameter, Samba may use the normal Unix password database or the Samba encrypted password database. Clients must send both a username and a password to log onto a server that uses user-level security.

Server: From the client's point of view, server-level authentication is identical to user-level authentication. The difference is that Samba passes the username and password to another SMB/CIFS server (typically a Windows NT/200*x* or Samba domain controller) for authentication. You give Samba the NetBIOS name or IP address of the remote authentication server using the password server parameter, as in password server = CHARLESTON. If this server fails to respond, Samba falls back to user-level authentication.

Domain: This authentication method is indistinguishable from user-level authentication to clients. Like server-level authentication, domain-level authentication requires that you give Samba the NetBIOS name or IP address of a domain controller with the password server parameter. The difference is that in this method, the Samba server must fully join the domain, a task that's described in Chapter 10. This method also requires that encrypt passwords be set to Yes.

The simplest Samba configuration employs user-level security. This method maps well onto the underlying Unix username/password security system, and you can implement it without setting up additional computers to handle authentication. Share-level security can be convenient with older clients (such as some DOS clients) that can't send usernames or when you don't want to have to maintain user accounts for all users on your network. For instance, suppose your Samba server shares a couple of printers and a repository of common files to which all your users should have access (say, templates and utility programs used by everybody on the network). In such a situation, you might configure Samba with share-level security so that you can simply assign passwords to each shared resource and not maintain accounts for each user. Server-level security is helpful if you have an existing Windows NT/200*x* or Samba server with a complete set of authenticated users and you don't want to have to reproduce these passwords. Domain-level security is much like server-level security, but it requires tighter integration into a domain. User-, server-, and domain-level security all require that users have ordinary Unix accounts on the Samba server system. Share-level security is less demanding in this respect, but ultimately, Samba must still use an account for every access, so you may need to create special accounts for Samba's use.

TIP   You can use the `include` parameter along with any of several variables, such as %a, %D, %I, %m, or %M, to set the security level differently for different clients. For instance, you might set share-level security for older clients or for those running on certain workgroups or domains while using user-level security for other clients.

Share-level security is confusing in part because Samba uses several different techniques to determine which local account to use for each access attempt. These methods are as follows:

1. **Guest account**: If a share sets the `guest only = Yes` parameter, then Samba tries to use the guest account (set with the `guest account` parameter). In this case, no other username is tried.

2. **Client-provided username**: Some clients pass a username even when share-level security is in place. In such cases, Samba tries using the provided username.

3. **Prior login**: If the client computer has already opened another share, Samba tries the username associated with that previously opened share.

4. **Share name**: The name of the share being accessed is tried as a username.

5. **Client name**: Samba tries the client's NetBIOS name as a username.

6. **User list**: You can provide a list of users with the `username` parameter, and Samba will try them in sequence.

Samba tries each of these methods in turn. For instance, suppose that the guest only parameter is not set to Yes, the client doesn't provide a username, and the client hasn't previously accessed a share. If the access attempt is to the PRINTER share and from the RUMBA computer, Samba will try the username printer and, if that fails, the username rumba. If you provide a list of users for a share with the username parameter, and if earlier methods failed to authenticate the access attempt, Samba tries each of the usernames listed as a last resort.

You can use this chain of access attempts to your advantage. For instance, you may want to create accounts named after each of the resources you want to share and then tell your users what the passwords are for each of these shares. Alternatively, if your clients simply don't support usernames, you can create accounts named after each of the clients' NetBIOS names and use the NetBIOS name as a stand-in for true usernames. This approach may be quite handy on a network with older DOS clients, particularly if each individual uses just one computer to access the Samba server.

Using Encrypted Passwords

Aside from setting the encrypt passwords option, using encrypted passwords requires creating a separate Samba password database. This database is normally stored in a file called smbpasswd, which typically resides in the same directory that holds smb.conf, in a subdirectory of that directory, or in a directory called private that's near to the directory holding smb.conf. You can change the file that Samba uses for this purpose by providing a filename to the smb passwd file parameter.

NOTE   You can configure Samba to store its encrypted passwords on a Lightweight Directory Access Protocol (LDAP) server. This is most often done in conjunction with primary and backup domain controllers, so Chapter 10 covers this topic. Storing passwords in an smbpasswd file is the simplest way to handle encrypted passwords in Samba.

NOTE   Recent versions of Mac OS X are unusual in that they provide an integrated username and password database for both local logins and Samba access, even when using encrypted passwords. This system is called *Open Directory*, and its use is specified using the auth methods and passdb backend global parameters. Unless you want to tie a Mac OS X Samba server into a domain or have some other compelling reason to unlink the Mac OS X and Samba passwords, you should leave these parameters alone on a Mac OS X system.

The simplest way to create a Samba password file is to use the smbpasswd utility with its -a option, which tells the program to create a new entry for the user. For instance, you can type the following command to create an entry for mikhail:

```
# smbpasswd -a mikhail
New SMB password:
Retype new SMB password:
Password changed for user mikhail.
```

The first time you run this command, you may receive an error message to the effect that the utility was unable to open the password file. Don't be concerned by this error; smbpasswd squawks loudly, but it silently creates the file, so all is well. If you see an error to the effect that the program was unable to add the account without a Unix identity, then the problem is more serious. Samba won't let you create a password database entry for an account that doesn't exist on the Samba server. Thus, if you're just setting up a Samba server computer, you should first create regular Unix accounts for your users with whatever tool your variety of Unix provides. These could be GUI system administration tools, text-mode tools such as useradd, or even manual editing of /etc/passwd or related files. Samba doesn't require that the Unix accounts be useable in any practical way; for instance, they might have expired or invalid passwords. The accounts must exist, though.

Chapter 7 describes Samba account maintenance in greater detail. If you need to perform more sophisticated account maintenance, consult that chapter.

Setting the Password and Username Levels

If you use unencrypted passwords, Samba must deal with the fact that Unix passwords are case-sensitive but SMB/CIFS passwords aren't. Sometimes this is unimportant; some clients deliver passwords without changing their case. Others, though, convert passwords to all uppercase. (Windows for Workgroups does this when using the LANMAN1 protocol but not when using COREPLUS, for instance. Windows 9*x* also tends to convert passwords to uppercase.)

To help work around this problem, Samba includes a mechanism to try case variants on the cleartext password sent by the client. For instance, if the client sends the password RHYTHM, Samba can try case variants, such as rhythm, Rhythm, rHythm, and so on. You can provide some control over this process with the password level parameter, which accepts as its value the maximum number of uppercase letters in the password. For instance, if password level = 1, Samba tries rhythm and all variants that use a single uppercase letter but not variants that include additional uppercase letters (except for the original password as delivered by the client). If password level = 2, Samba tries the original, rhythm, Rhythm, RHythm, RhYthm, and so on. The default password level value is 0, which causes Samba to use the original password as delivered to it and its all-lowercase variant.

Of course, attempting to authenticate a user with several login passwords, even if they differ only in case, has certain drawbacks. For one thing, this process takes time. The time required increases as the password length increases and as the `password level` value increases. If Samba needs to try multiple accounts (as is likely with share-level security), this problem is exacerbated. In practice, this effect is likely to be small on modern hardware and for typical passwords, but it's possible some of your users will notice login delays if this option is required. Another problem with this approach is that it decreases security. Unix passwords are case-sensitive because making them so improves security, at least if users take advantage of case-sensitive passwords. If Samba tries dozens of password variants, crackers are more likely to be able to successfully guess a user's password, particularly if that password is a poor one, such as the example I've just used—RHYTHM is a very poor password because it's a dictionary word.

NOTE   The `password level` option is meaningful only when using unencrypted passwords. If you use encrypted passwords, this option has no effect because Samba uses its own password database, which better matches the form of the passwords sent by clients.

An option that's similar to `password level` is `username level`. This option works just like `password level`, except that it applies to usernames rather than unencrypted passwords. Ordinarily, the default value of 0 is suitable because most Unix systems employ all-lowercase usernames. If your usernames are mixed case, though, you may need to set a higher `username level`. This action is most likely to be required if your network contains DOS clients because these clients are most likely to modify username case before sending usernames to the server. As with `password level`, setting a high `username level` and using mixed-case usernames may increase the time required to process a login request. Depending upon whether you try to keep usernames secret, you can reduce security by using this parameter for much the same reasons that `password level` affects security.

Logging Options

Like most servers, Samba supports saving information on its routine activity—and any errors it encounters—to a *log file*. In fact, Samba supports *several* log files, as well as additional logging options. Knowing how to adjust these options can be crucial when you need to solve a problem. If Samba's doing something you don't expect, there's a chance that a log file will provide a clue to help you resolve the problem. Samba's logging options include the following:

debug pid: Samba doesn't normally include its process ID (PID) number in log files, but this information is sometimes helpful when multiple Samba processes are busily logging data. To include this information, set debug pid = Yes. This option also requires that debug timestamp be set to Yes (as it is by default).

debug timestamp: Samba ordinarily includes time stamps on all the messages it sends to log files. If you set debug timestamp = No, Samba disables time stamps, which can improve legibility of log files at the expense of providing less information.

debug uid: Samba performs various operations using different user IDs (UIDs). Knowing what UID Samba is using for a logged operation is sometimes helpful, and setting debug uid = Yes provides this information. This option defaults to No, and when set to Yes, it requires that debug timestamp also be Yes.

log file: This option tells Samba what files to use for logging. The default is a compile-time option, but most packages use /var/log/samba or a similar location for log files. This parameter takes a *filename* as an option, though, and many sample smb.conf files use the %m parameter to include the client's NetBIOS name in the log filenames. This practice creates a separate log file for the activities of each client.

log level: Samba can log anywhere from no information to so much information that it will seriously degrade Samba's performance. The default, which is equivalent to log level = 1, logs a modest amount of data. Setting log level = 0 logs nothing, and setting this parameter to higher values logs more data, up to the maximum of 10. (You can specify higher values, and Samba's developers sometimes ask for the output when log level = 100, simply to guarantee getting everything.) In practice, settings between 1 and 3 work best for most production servers; higher values are intended for Samba developers as they track down bugs in the Samba code itself. A synonym for this parameter is debug level. In Samba 3.0 and later, you can provide a list of subsystems and log levels. For instance, log level = 3 winbind:5 auth:1 sets the log level to 3 for most systems but to 5 for winbind and 1 for auth.

max log size: This option sets the maximum size of Samba's log files in kilobytes. When a file exceeds this size, Samba renames it with an extension of .old and starts a new log file. The default value is 5000 (approximately 5MB). If you prefer to use some other method of controlling log file size, such as a systemwide log rotation utility, you can set max log size = 0 to disable this mechanism.

status: Samba provides a utility, smbstatus, that displays information on Samba's currently active connections. To operate, though, Samba must be able to create a special status file. To do this, the status parameter must be set to Yes, which is its default state. You should never need to change this option, unless you want to shut off all access to Samba's status information. This parameter is no longer valid in Samba 3.0.

syslog only: This parameter takes a Boolean value and defaults to No. If set to Yes, Samba doesn't create its own log files, as set with the log file parameter; instead, Samba uses the Unix system logger, syslogd, for all logging.

syslog: This parameter takes an integer as a value. Samba logs messages lower than this value via the syslogd utility in addition to or (if syslog only = True) instead of using Samba's own logging features. The default value is 1. To use this parameter, you must compile Samba with the --with-syslog option to configure, and you must configure your system logging tool to accept Samba's messages. On many systems, a line such as the following in /etc/syslog.conf should do the trick:

```
daemon.*    /var/log/messages
```

As a general rule, Samba's default logging options work reasonably well. You might want to use the log file, log level, and max log size parameters, though, to tweak these details. For a typical installation, the default log level of 1 works well, but increasing this parameter to 2 or 3 may be helpful if you're running into problems. If you're short on disk space or need particularly long-lived logs, you may need to adjust the max log size parameter. Remember that Samba may create multiple log files, depending upon what, if any, variables you use in log file. On a large network, this fact can result in many megabytes of disk space being tied up in Samba log files.

Summary

Before you can configure specific file or printer shares, you must set at least basic global Samba options. These options identify the server to other computers and determine how the server handles passwords. Chances are you'll have to do something with both these classes of options before Samba will work even minimally on your network. You may also want to adjust a few logging options. These changes may not be strictly necessary, but they can make Samba fit in better with your network as a whole or make it easier to use Samba, either as an end user or as a system administrator.

Where you go from here depends on your specific needs. If your network's configuration is relatively simple, you may want to proceed directly to configuring file and printer shares, as described in the next two chapters. You can then add more users to your Samba accounts, as described in Chapter 7. Other networks, though, are more complex and may require additional changes to your global configuration or the addition of custom shares. Integrating Samba into an existing domain, for instance, requires additional work. These topics are covered in Part III of this book.

CHAPTER 5
Configuring File Shares

THE PROTOTYPICAL USE for a Samba system is as a *file server*—a computer on which files are stored for the benefit of other computers. For this reason, a great many Samba options apply to file shares, which are the topic of this chapter. Before proceeding with this chapter, though, you should read Chapter 4. Some global options must be set to fit your network before you can use any file share. Chapter 4 also describes a few share-level parameters that are commonly used in the [global] section but that are also often used in file shares.

This chapter begins with a look at naming options—for the share itself and for files served by the share. Many Samba options influence filenames to work around differences between SMB/CIFS and how Unix handles these features. Next up is a look at special permission bits, such as the SMB/CIFS read-only bit and the hidden bit. Samba also provides a mechanism for preventing two or more programs from causing problems for each other when trying to access a single file simultaneously, but this mechanism requires integration with the underlying Unix file handling mechanisms, so Samba provides options to help implement that fit. Although security is an important enough topic to merit its own chapter (Chapter 11), some security options apply most directly to individual file shares, so this chapter covers them. This chapter also looks at the practice of setting certain share-level defaults in the [global] section, which can simplify your overall Samba configuration. Finally, this chapter presents several example shares that demonstrate the options described here, including a special type of share, known as a *home share*, that's commonly used to store individual users' files.

Setting Names and Directories

The core of a Samba share is the share's name. You specify the share name implicitly; Samba uses the section name within brackets as the share name. Just as important as the share name is the specification of the Unix directory you want to share. This detail you must ordinarily set explicitly although you *can* omit it (Samba uses the /tmp directory as the default directory location).

Setting the Share Name

In principle, an smb.conf share definition can consist of nothing more than the share name in brackets:

```
[sample]
```

This line defines a Samba share called SAMPLE, which takes on the default share-level values specified in the [global] section and, for those parameters not specified in the [global] section, the defaults set in the Samba binaries. (Descriptions in this book, including the summaries in Appendix A, specify the defaults for parameters.) If you don't override them in your [global] section, the defaults for a share include that it be a file share (as opposed to a printer share), that it point to files in /tmp, and that it be read-only. These options aren't terribly useful in most cases, so you'll almost always see Samba parameters on the lines following a share definition. These lines are conventionally indented for readability, but this formatting isn't required. All lines until the next share definition or the end of the file are part of the share definition.

NOTE   An include parameter can theoretically include share definitions, but this use is confusing amid share definitions and so should be avoided. If you want to place share definitions within an included file (say, to have Samba deliver different shares for different clients, as described in Chapter 4), the least confusing placement of the include parameter is at the end of the [global] section.

Share names can be quite long, but older clients are unlikely to be able to access shares with names longer than 12 characters. (Because of a bug in Samba through at least version 3.0.1, up to 13 characters may appear in a file browser for shares with longer names, but such shares are inaccessible.) Share names can contain letters, numbers, and assorted punctuation characters. You can use lowercase, uppercase, or a mixture of both types of letters, but case is irrelevant to SMB/CIFS share names, and most clients regularize the names in one way or another, usually converting to all uppercase, all lowercase, or lowercase with an initial capital letter. A few share names have special meaning and so shouldn't be used unless you want to invoke the special meanings. These are the most important of these special cases:

[homes]: This share maps to each user's home directory and is described in greater detail in the upcoming section "Creating a Home Share."

[printers]: This name is reserved for the automatic creation of printer shares corresponding to all the printers defined on the system's underlying printing system. Chapter 6 describes this share in greater detail.

Variables: You can use certain variables (summarized in Chapter 2's Table 2-1) in share names. Variables are identified by a leading percent symbol (%), so this symbol carries special meaning in share definitions.

Trailing dollar signs ($): Share names that end in dollar signs frequently have special meanings. For instance, they may be associated with domain logons or automatic distribution of printer driver files. Microsoft's OSs hide such shares in file browsers but may use them for behind-the-scenes operations.

As a general rule, share names that consist entirely of letters, or perhaps letters and numbers, are the least likely to cause problems. Some symbols are likely to cause problems with at least some clients. For instance, although you can specify a share name with a slash (/), in practice it won't work; clients are likely to report that the share can't be found or otherwise fails to connect.

In addition to the share's name, you can set a comment that's associated with a share by using the comment parameter. This share-level parameter takes a string (with or without surrounding quote marks) as an option. The default value is a null string. The comment you specify might or might not appear in association with the share name, depending upon your client and the options you're using to browse shares. Windows clients display the comment only if you select View ➤ Details from the network browser's window, which produces a display similar to that shown in Figure 5-1.

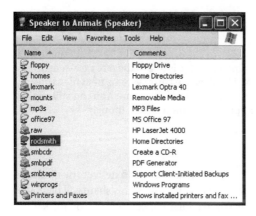

Figure 5-1. Share comments often elaborate on a share's name to clarify its purpose.

Another share naming option is volume. Under Windows and most other SMB/CIFS clients, disk devices can have names. These names are normally not very noticeable to users and are unimportant to fundamental Samba operation. On the other hand, they are used as volume identifiers in some OSs (such as Mac OS), they appear in the My Computer window when you assign a drive letter to a volume, and they appear when you perform a directory listing from a DOS prompt window:

```
C:\>DIR E:

Volume in drive E is WINDOWS
Directory of E:\

.               <DIR>        06-17-03  9:03p .
..              <DIR>        06-17-03  9:03p ..
MYPICT~1        <DIR>        06-17-03  9:35p My Pictures
MYMUSI~1        <DIR>        06-17-03  9:35p My Music
        0 file(s)              0 bytes
        4 dir(s)     512,327,680 bytes free
```

In this example, the volume label is WINDOWS, as reported on the first line of output. By default, Samba uses the share name as the volume label, and this practice normally works acceptably. Sometimes, though, you might need to override this default. For instance, some software installers that run from a CD-ROM look for a specific volume label, so if you want to share such an installer via Samba, you may need to change the volume label appropriately.

Setting the Share's Path

If you don't change it, the default directory that Samba shares is /tmp. Of course, chances are you don't want to use this directory, so most shares include a directory parameter, which sets the path to any directory you like on your computer:

```
directory = /usr/share/icons
```

> **NOTE** The directory parameter's value is one of the rare case-sensitive values in Samba's smb.conf file. Because Unix systems treat filenames in a case-sensitive way, the same is true of this value. You can still use any case for the directory parameter name itself, though.

This line, when included in a share definition, tells Samba to deliver the contents of /usr/share/icons as the root of the file share. How the files in this share will be made available depends upon the client software. For instance, consider the file on the WALTZ server /usr/share/icons/gv.png, delivered via a share called IMAGES, using the directory parameter presented earlier. This file might be accessible in any of these ways:

- Directly as gv.png from a user-mode access client such as Samba's own smbclient. Of course, you must tell the client to connect to WALTZ's IMAGES share first.

- As \\WALTZ\IMAGES\gv.png from a Windows file browser window. Variants on this method may be possible, such as specifying a DNS hostname rather than the WALTZ NetBIOS name.

- As *X*:\gv.png, where *X* is a drive letter, after associating the \\WALTZ\IMAGES share with *X*: in Windows.

- As */mount/point/*gv.png from a Unix client that supports mounting SMB/CIFS shares, after mounting the share at */mount/point*.

Minor variants on these methods are available in some OSs. For instance, Mac OS Classic clients mount shares using the share name rather than a drive letter and use colons (:) as directory delimiters. Chapter 18 describes methods of accessing Samba shares in more detail. The main point to note now is that you can't control precisely where on the client computer the shared files will appear. The purpose of the directory parameter is to determine what files you want to share from the server.

NOTE Different clients use different characters to separate directory elements. In particular, DOS, Windows, and OS/2 use a backslash (\); Unix (including Mac OS X) uses a forward slash (/); and Mac OS Classic uses a colon (:). These characters may be used as part of the specification of the share name or in separating directory names within a Samba share. GUIs sometimes hide the use of these directory-separation characters.

Each share is tied to a single directory; you shouldn't include multiple `directory` parameters in a single share or attempt to list multiple directories on a single `directory` line. If you want to share multiple directories, such as `/usr/share/icons` and `/usr/share/sounds`, you can do so in any of several ways:

Create multiple shares: You can create one share for each directory you want to make available. In many respects this approach is the cleanest, but if you want to share many unrelated directories, it can be a tedious approach because clients may have to mount or otherwise locate multiple shares.

Share a parent directory: You can share a parent directory of the directories you want to make available. For instance, rather than sharing `/usr/share/icons` and `/usr/share/sounds`, you could share `/usr/share`. This approach is simple, but it has the drawback that it may share more than you'd like.

Create links: You can create links between directories, either directly or by using a special share directory for the purpose. For instance, you might create a new directory for sharing (say, `/usr/share/samba`), share it, and create links in that directory to the directories you want to share. This approach is flexible and convenient, but if you want to disable links for security purposes, as described in the upcoming section "Controlling Links," it may not work.

NOTE A synonym for the `directory` parameter is `path`. Both keywords work equally well and are fully interchangeable.

Setting Filename Options

Because of the differences between Unix and SMB/CIFS filename assumptions described in Chapter 2, Samba must sometimes translate filenames in various ways. There is, however, no single best way to do this; the optimum approach can vary depending upon the client, the share, the user, and so on. For this reason, Samba provides a large number of filename-handling options. You may want to set them differently for one share than for another; or you may prefer setting the options in the [global] section so that they apply to all shares, as described in the upcoming section "Setting Share Defaults Globally." The following pages describe options relating to filename case, filename length, and mapping non-ASCII characters in filenames. I also describe how Samba's filename handling interacts with the local Unix filesystem because some filesystems have peculiarities you should consider when using Samba.

Samba Case Options

Samba provides several options related to filename case in order to better integrate Samba and its primarily Unix hosts with the mainly Windows clients that use it. As described in Chapter 2, Unix typically treats filenames in a case-sensitive manner, whereas most SMB/CIFS clients treat filenames as case-retentive—that is, filename case is preserved but ignored in matching filenames the user enters. These are some of the filename case options you might want to set:

> **case sensitive**: This option defaults to No, meaning that Samba ignores case when matching filenames. This behavior is appropriate for DOS, Windows, OS/2, and Mac OS Classic clients. If your server has primarily Unix clients, you might want to change this option's default to Yes. A synonym for this option is casesignnames.
>
> **default case**: This option sets the case in which files are stored when the preserve case option is set to No. Valid values are Lower and Upper.
>
> **mangle case**: If set to No (the default), Samba doesn't alter filenames if they differ from the default case. If set to Yes, Samba applies filename mangling rules, as described in Chapter 2 and the upcoming section, "Samba Filename Length Options," when filenames don't match the default case.
>
> **preserve case**: When this option is set to Yes (the default), Samba preserves the case of filenames specified by clients. If you set this value to No, Samba converts filename case as specified by default case.
>
> **short preserve case**: This option works just like preserve case, but it applies specifically to short (8.3) filenames. The default value is Yes.

For the most part, the default case options work reasonably well. The trickiest part of case handling for Samba is implementing case-sensitivity, and the default value of the case sensitive option (No) works well for this option. You might want to change this default to Yes if your clients are primarily Unix systems, though. The remaining options are mostly useful for cosmetic purposes—ensuring that files created by DOS clients appear in a consistent form, for instance, via the default case and preserve case parameters. The mangle case option is most likely to be needed for rare DOS client programs that choke on filenames that differ from the all-uppercase convention of that OS.

Samba Filename Length Options

Because Unix hosts typically support very long filenames (frequently up to 256 characters) but Samba clients sometimes don't support such long filenames, Samba provides options to create shortened filenames to stand in for long ones—a practice known as *name mangling*. This procedure is a requirement for DOS clients, which accept only eight-character filenames with three-character extensions (so-called *8.3 filenames* or *short filenames*). Windows clients sometimes use the 8.3 filenames *in addition to* the full long filename. This practice is helpful when a Windows client runs older DOS or Windows 3.1 software. Such software can't handle long filenames, despite the fact that the underlying OS can. Some clients have intermediate needs. Mac OS Classic, for instance, supports filenames of up to 31 characters. Recent versions of Thursby Software's (http://www.thursby.com) DAVE client for Mac OS Classic can perform its own name mangling from the SMB/CIFS long filenames to create 31-character filenames, so Samba doesn't need to do so. This means that name mangling for Mac OS Classic clients isn't controlled by Samba. The previous section, "Samba Case Options," described the mangle case option because this option relates to filename case. This option also relates to filename mangling, though. Samba generates a mangled filename much as Windows does when it uses a VFAT filesystem. On VFAT, as handled by Windows, the base name is shortened to six characters, a tilde (~) is added, and a number is appended to this. If the filename extension doesn't exceed three characters, it's left alone. For instance, longfilename.txt might become LONGFI~1.TXT. Samba is similar in broad strokes, but depending upon the options chosen, as few as one character may be preserved from the original base name, there may be changes before the tilde, the tilde may be replaced by another character, and non-numeric codes may follow the tilde. For instance, longfilename.txt may become LNHQX6~C.TXT. In either case, DOS clients can use the short filename while more capable clients can use the long filename. Some additional mangling options include the following:

> **mangled names:** If set to Yes (the default), this option causes Samba to generate short (8.3) filenames for clients that request them, even for files whose names are longer than this. (In the case of Windows clients, if you set this option to Yes, it has access to both short and long filenames.)

> **mangling method:** This parameter takes one of two values, hash or hash2. When using hash2 and the default mangle prefix value, the hashed filename is likely to bear little resemblance to the long filename, such as LNHQX6~C.TXT for longfilename.txt. The hash algorithm is likely to generate a short filename with a closer resemblance to the original filename, such as LONGF~A7.TXT; but the hash algorithm is more likely to produce *collisions*—two shortened filenames that happen to be identical but based on different original filenames. Samba 3.0 uses the hash2 algorithm by default, but earlier Samba versions used hash by default.

mangle prefix: This parameter sets the number of characters from the original filename to use in the mangled filename. The default value is 1, which produces filenames that bear little resemblance to the original. This option is valid only when using hash2 as the mangling method. Valid values range from 1 to 6.

mangled map: This option creates a customized mangling for particular filename patterns, as described shortly. Unlike other mangling options, this one applies to all filenames, not just those that would otherwise require a shortened 8.3 filename.

mangling char: Filename mangling normally uses a tilde (~) as part of the shortened filename, but you can change this character with the mangling char parameter, as in mangling char = ^ to use a carat (^). This option works only with the hash algorithm, not hash2.

strip dot: This Boolean parameter was valid through Samba 2.2.*x* but has been dropped with Samba 3.0. In Samba 2.2.*x* and earlier, it controlled whether a trailing dot (.) in a filename was stripped from the filename for interactions with clients.

mangled stack: This global parameter used to control how many mangled names Samba caches in memory. The more mangled names are cached, the less likely it is that filenames will be mangled differently on two accesses or create collisions. This parameter hasn't been valid since 1998, though; recent versions of Samba use new ways of mangling filenames that make it unnecessary. (References to it remain in the smb.conf man page through at least Samba 3.0.1, though.)

Ordinarily, filename mangling proceeds automatically whenever a filename exceeds the 8.3 filename limit. Note that this does *not* mean that the long filename becomes inaccessible, only that the short filename becomes available *in addition to* the long filename, for the benefit of clients such as DOS that require 8.3 filenames. The mangled map parameter modifies the way Samba maps filenames that meet a specified criterion. One common use of this parameter is to map filename extensions that are longer than the three characters permitted by DOS onto three-character extensions, without modifying the 8-character base. For instance, on Unix systems, the .html extension is often used on Hypertext Markup Language (HTML) files, but on DOS, the .htm extension is commonly used for such files. You can tell Samba to shorten the filename in this way by providing paired original and destination filename specifications within parentheses as the value of the mangled map parameter:

```
mangled map = (*.html *.htm) (*.jpeg *.jpg) (*;1 *)
```

This example converts .html extensions to .htm, turns .jpeg extensions into .jpg, and strips a trailing ;1 from files (these characters appear on CD-ROMs on some OSs). Such conversions can greatly simplify cross-OS operations by creating saner mangled filenames when specific shortenings make more sense than the odd ones that Samba might otherwise generate.

Handling Multiple Alphabets

On a fundamental level, all computers work exclusively with numbers. A few years ago, most computers in the Western world used the American Standard Code for Information Interchange (ASCII) as a method of encoding letters as numbers. Unfortunately, ASCII is limited. It's a 7-bit code that's usually stored in 8-bit bytes, meaning that it supports a maximum of 256 symbols (128 for ASCII proper and 128 for any extensions the OS may provide). This is an acceptable limit for encoding the Roman alphabet (both uppercase and lowercase), numbers, common punctuation, and some special-purpose computer codes. A single 8-bit code is inadequate for supporting all the world's alphabets, though. An interim solution has been to use separate *code pages*— essentially, ASCII and similar codes for different alphabets—for each language. Today, though, a 16-bit encoding system, known as *Unicode*, is gaining in popularity. Chapter 2 introduced Unicode in principle, but now it's time to look at how Samba uses Unicode.

SMB/CIFS supports Unicode, but not all SMB/CIFS clients and servers do. In practice, you need only provide Unicode support for Windows NT, 200*x*, and XP clients; DOS and Windows 9*x*/Me clients still use the old code page system. (Samba and related clients, including Mac OS X, can use either Unicode or the old code page system, depending upon what version of Samba is used and what its options are.) Telling Samba what system to use will keep your filenames looking reasonable when accessed from the server and may help prevent problems between clients as well, particularly if your site uses a mixture of different clients.

 NOTE Samba's alphabet encoding options relate to filenames and to the characters that the Samba Web Administration Tool (SWAT) displays. These options don't affect the data stored in files.

Implementing Code Pages

Through the 2.2.*x* series, Samba supported a set of global options to translate between SMB/CIFS code pages and the underlying host's filenames:

character set: To translate these filenames to appropriate filenames on the underlying Unix host, Samba needs to know what the host uses. This parameter specified the host's character set, as specified in Table 5-1.

client code page: This parameter told the server what code page to use when encoding filenames. Unfortunately, SMB/CIFS provides no mechanism for negotiating a code page between client and server, so you must ensure that clients and servers use the same code page. Table 5-2 summarizes the values you can assign to the client code page parameter, along with their meanings. The default value of 850 works acceptably on most installations in North America and Western Europe.

valid chars: This parameter told Samba to accept unusual additional characters, which you specified as the value of this parameter, in addition to the characters Samba normally accepts. Ordinarily, this parameter wasn't required, but if you had problems storing files whose names contain unusual characters, you might want to try it.

Table 5-1. Samba Character Sets

Character Set Value	Meaning
ISO8859-1	Latin 1
ISO8859-2	Latin 2
ISO8859-5	Latin/Cyrillic
ISO8859-7	Latin/Greek
KOI8-R	Russian (Cyrillic)

Table 5-2. Samba Code Pages

Code Page Value	Meaning
437	Latin U.S.
737	Greek
850	Latin 1
852	Latin 2
861	Icelandic
866	Cyrillic
932	Japanese SJIS
936	Simplified Chinese
949	Korean Hangul
950	Traditional Chinese

All three of these parameters have been superseded by other options as of Samba 3.0. These options continue to use the character sets specified in Table 5-1, though.

Implementing Unicode

As of version 3.0, Samba supports Unicode. There are actually several aspects to Unicode support, and this fact is reflected in the multiple parameters that affect its implementation:

display charset: This global option tells Samba and support programs such as SWAT what character set to use. It's usually set to the same value as unix charset. The default value is ASCII.

dos charset: This global option is roughly equivalent to Samba 2.2.*x*'s client code page option; it tells Samba what character set to use for clients, such as DOS and Windows 9*x*/Me, that don't understand Unicode. This option accepts the values listed in Table 5-2, with the string CP prepended to the start of the value. The default value depends on your installed code pages but is usually CP850 with a fallback to ASCII.

unicode: This global Boolean option tells Samba whether to accept Unicode filenames from clients that can generate them. The default value is Yes.

unix charset: This global option specifies the character set that Samba's host uses for filenames. The default value is UTF8 (which stands for *Unicode Transformation Format-8*, a method of encoding Unicode in an 8-bit format that can be viewed as if it were ASCII).

The display charset and unix charset options accept as values the character sets specified in Table 5-1 and some additional values, such as ASCII and UTF8. For most installations, the default settings work well, particularly with Windows NT/200*x*/XP clients. If you have DOS or Windows 9*x*/Me clients and need support for non-Roman alphabets, you may need to adjust the dos charset parameter.

NOTE Unfortunately, Samba's support for Japanese character sets is still quite limited as of version 3.0.1. If you need to support Japanese filenames, consult http://www.monyo.com/technical/samba/docs/.

Interactions with Local Filesystems

Most Samba file-naming options are built around the assumption of typical Unix-style file-naming conventions—long filenames (often up to 256 characters), case-sensitive filename handling, ASCII filenames, and so on. If your local filesystems conform to these assumptions, as do most Samba server filesystems, Samba should work as designed in terms of creating appropriate local filenames. These assumptions aren't always met, though. Many Unix-like OSs can mount filesystems from a wide variety of sources. These filesystems might not implement all of the features that Samba expects of local filesystems, so some features may not work as you'd like. This can sometimes cause confusion for users. Some specific concerns include the following:

FAT with short filenames: If you share a FAT filesystem (say, from a removable disk), and if you mount that filesystem in such a way that the host OS sees only the 8.3 filenames, the same restriction will be present on clients. If you try to copy a file with a longer name to the shared volume, the original filename will be truncated. Furthermore, FAT is case-insensitive, so all filenames will be converted to all lowercase or all uppercase, depending upon the host OS and mount options. Even if you use a case-sensitive client, you won't be able to store files whose names differ only in case.

FAT with long filenames: If you share a FAT filesystem that's mounted using VFAT long filename support, you won't run into filename length issues as when you share the same disk mounted using only 8.3 filenames. Filename case will be preserved on these shares, but you won't be able to create two files with names that differ only in case, even from a case-sensitive client.

HFS and HFS+: These filesystems are the native ones for Mac OS Classic, and many Mac OS X installations use them as well. Although HFS+ is very Unix-like in its filename requirements, HFS is more restricted; it supports filenames with a maximum length of 31 characters, and it treats them in a case-insensitive manner. Thus, if you share such a volume, you won't be able to create filenames longer than this limit, and you won't be able to create files whose names differ only in case, even from a case-sensitive client.

ISO-9660: This filesystem is the standard for CD-ROMs. It comes in three different *levels*. Level 1's limits are similar to those of FAT with short filenames. Level 2 supports single-case filenames up to 31 characters. Level 3 is similar to Level 2; its additional features are designed to aid in CD-R creation and don't impact Samba. In all three cases, the Unix host may present the single case as uppercase or lowercase, depending upon the OS and mount options. Some OSs also add a semicolon (;) and number (typically 1) to ISO-9660 filenames as a file version number. These characters can cause unnecessary name mangling unless you use the `mangled map` parameter to strip this file version information, as described earlier in "Samba Filename Length Options."

Rock Ridge: This standard exists to provide Unix-like filenames and metadata on CD-ROMs. Shared Rock Ridge CD-ROMs should behave exactly like read-only Unix filesystems.

Joliet: This filesystem frequently appears alongside ISO-9660 on CD-ROMs; it's Microsoft's method of providing long filenames and other extensions to ISO-9660. It should work much like a VFAT partition shared in a read-only fashion.

For the most part, these unusual filesystems don't pose great challenges to sharing via Samba, particularly if they're shared in a read-only fashion. The limits of FAT with 8.3 filenames and, to a lesser extent, HFS and VFAT, relate to the creation of new files. If users are aware of the limits, they shouldn't have problems as a result. Most modern Unix-like OSs support VFAT, and this filesystem was designed with backward compatibility in mind. Thus, even if you share a disk that must subsequently be read by an 8.3-only OS such as DOS, you can mount and share it as VFAT. The DOS client will see oddly truncated filenames, but this is no worse than would be the case if the files had been copied to the disk using a Windows computer.

Handling Special Permission Bits

As described in Chapter 2, SMB/CIFS and Unix both provide assorted file permission bits, but each system supports different types of metadata. The default Samba settings work well for many shares, but you may find it necessary to adjust the settings for some shares. Samba provides tools that can help you achieve these goals.

Unix and Windows Read-Only Files

The concepts of read/write and read-only access are shared between Unix and Windows although they're implemented somewhat differently. As a security measure, Samba makes read-only access the default; if an administrator forgets to set this option, users can't abuse write access to delete other users' files or alter the system configuration. For some servers, though, making read/write access the default may be sensible. For instance, printer shares are useless unless they're read/write, so Samba overrides read-only settings for printer shares. Other options also relate to read-only vs. read/write access:

delete readonly: As described in Chapter 2, Unix looks to the permissions on a file's directory to determine who may delete files. If a user has write access to the directory in question, that user may delete files in the directory, even if the user doesn't have write access to the file. Samba implements this behavior when the delete readonly option is set to Yes. The default setting is No, which emulates normal DOS behavior: A file may be deleted only if the user has write access to the file. This default setting is less likely to cause confusion for typical DOS users, but it imposes more overhead on Samba. (Under most versions of Windows, the GUI file manager automatically removes the read-only option when you delete a file, so this option has no obvious effect when using the file manager. It still has an effect when deleting files from a DOS prompt and some other programs, though.)

dos filemode: This option's purpose is similar to that of delete readonly, in that it alters who may change files' permissions to better conform to the expectations of a Windows user. Ordinarily, Unix permits only a file's owner to change the file's permissions, but from a Windows user's perspective, this may be confusing because, with certain underlying Unix permissions and ownership, the read-only bit might be immutable despite the user having write access to the file. Setting dos filemode = Yes changes this behavior so that any user who can write to a file can also change its permissions. The default value is No.

read only: This option's default value is Yes, which makes it impossible for users to create or modify files in the share. A read only value of No permits the share's users to write to the share. Many Samba parameters have synonyms. This one has several antonyms: write ok, writable, and writeable. You can change the read-only status of shares by setting write ok = Yes, for instance, instead of read only = No.

wide links: This option doesn't control read-only or read/write access in quite the sense that the preceding options do. Rather, this parameter controls how Samba treats symbolic links. If wide links = Yes (the default), a symbolic link that points to a file or directory outside of the share's normal directory tree is followed. If wide links = No, Samba denies access to such links. For instance, consider a share that provides access to /home/fastaire and a link in that directory that points to /etc/fstab. If wide links = Yes, Samba enables access to this file; if the option is No, access is denied. Setting wide links = No tends to slow access to files because Samba must do more checks. Setting this option can improve security by reducing the risk that a user could create a link pointing to files to which the user shouldn't have access. Ordinarily, this security risk is low (after all, if the user can create the link via a login session or the like, the user can probably access the linked-to file from that session). If you use other Samba options to change file-access permissions, though, the combination can be dangerous.

As a general rule, the default options work well. You're most likely to want to change the read only option (or one of its antonyms), but the default setting of read only = Yes is best from a security perspective. Changing the other options may be desirable to improve performance, to improve integration with Windows clients, or to improve security.

One critical consideration is that the Unix permissions, the Samba permissions options, and the user's account all interact in determining whether a user has read-only or read/write access to a share's files. Specifically, Samba uses the Unix permissions for the account with which the user accesses the share to determine whether to give a user access to the files. For instance, consider a file owned by fastaire and the tap group with Unix permissions of 0664 (-rw-rw-r--). If fastaire or any member of that group logs onto the share, the user will have read/write access to the file. Users who are not fastaire or members of the tap group, though, will be able to read but not write the file.

NOTE   Samba provides options, such as force user, that can change the rules about who has what types of access to a file. The upcoming section "Adjusting Access Rights" describes these parameters.

The Archive and System Bits

DOS and Windows computers use special permission bits to mark files that haven't been backed up, that are hidden from most directory listings, and that carry special meaning to the OS. These permission bits are known as the *archive*, *hidden*, and *system* bits, respectively. The hidden bit is complex enough that it's covered in its own section, "Hiding Files," but you can control the archive and system bits with these options:

map archive: When set to Yes (the default), this parameter causes the DOS archive bit, as described in Chapter 1, to be stored on the underlying Unix filesystem using the file's owner execute bit.

map system: When set to Yes (the default is No), this parameter causes the DOS system bit, as described in Chapter 1, to be stored on the underlying Unix filesystem using the file's group execute bit. If you enable this option, you must also change the create mask option to add the group execute bit to files. Samba will enable that bit only if the client sets the system bit, though.

Both of these options interact with the create mask setting, which is described in the upcoming section "Setting Default Unix Permissions." These mapping options work in both directions. If a file's Unix owner or group execute permissions are set because the file should be executable in Unix, the file will be mapped as having been archived or being a system file, if the map archive or map system bits are set. Unless you run backup software on the DOS or Windows client, the archive bit is unlikely to be important. Many programs hide system files, though, much as they hide hidden files. Thus, setting the system bit unnecessarily can have negative consequences. Because system files are unlikely to be stored on SMB/CIFS file servers, the default setting of map system = No is generally appropriate. If you install software on your server that requires some of its files to have their system bits set, though, you may need to adjust this option.

Hiding Files

SMB/CIFS and many SMB/CIFS clients provide a *hidden bit*. When this bit is set on a file, most programs don't display the file in file selector dialog boxes, file browsers, and the like. Unix doesn't provide an equivalent bit. To support this feature, Samba enables you to map the hidden bit to an execute permission bit that's otherwise unused by traditional SMB/CIFS clients. Instead of providing a hidden bit, most Unix systems use *dot files*—files whose names begin with a dot (.). Samba, therefore, provides an option to set the hidden bit on these dot files. Finally, Samba provides an extra-strong hiding option: the ability to *veto* files, making them completely inaccessible to clients. Each of these file-hiding options has its place on a Samba server.

NOTE   Some SMB/CIFS clients, including Samba's smbclient and most Unix-like systems that can mount SMB/CIFS shares, ignore the hidden bit. These settings are, therefore, irrelevant to such clients.

Mapping to Unix Permissions

If your users expect to be able to hide files using standard DOS or Windows tools, or if the applications you run expect to be able to do so, chances are you want to tell

Samba to support the hidden bit as directly as possible. You do this by setting the share-level map hidden parameter to Yes, which tells Samba to use the Unix world execute bit as a stand-in for the hidden bit. Files that aren't set to be world executable are visible to users, whereas those that are set to be world executable are hidden. (Of course, the client must be configured to actually hide the files from the user; Samba still includes these files in its directory listings.)

The map hidden = Yes option only works, though, if you also set the create mask option to enable use of the world execute bit. (The upcoming section "Setting Default Unix Permissions" describes this parameter.)

NOTE Supporting the SMB/CIFS hidden bit can create some permissions that are very peculiar from a traditional Unix file permissions perspective. Typically, world execute permissions exist only when world read permissions also exist. Likewise, Unix files with world execute permissions also typically give group and owner execute permissions. These features might not be desirable in the context of a Samba share with hidden files. A file with 0601 permissions, for instance, provides read and write access to the owner and no access to others but hides the file even from its owner. A program might use a hidden file for configuration data, and you might choose to block access to all users, but the file's owner on the Samba server as a security measure, thus creating such a configuration.

Supporting the hidden bit in this way works in both directions. For instance, suppose you share users' home directories, and suppose that users can log onto the Samba server and use it for software development. The programs that users develop may have world execute permissions. If you set map hidden = Yes, one consequence of this action is that the users' program files will appear to be hidden from Windows clients. This consequence may not be a major problem, particularly for binary executables; but if users need to copy the files using the Windows client, or if the programs are scripts that should be usable from Windows, hiding them may be unacceptable.

Hiding Unix Dot Files

Instead of using a hidden bit, Unix systems traditionally hide files whose names begin with a dot (.). If a directory is to be used solely as a Samba share, chances are you needn't be too concerned with this fact; however, if a directory is likely to be accessed from both Unix and Windows, you may want to consider what to do with dot files. This question is particularly relevant when sharing users' home directories, as described in the upcoming section "Creating a Home Share." When used from Unix, home directories almost invariably collect a large number of dot files because Unix user programs store program-specific settings in such files. (Some programs use subdirectories that are hidden using the same dot-name convention as dot files.)

By default, Samba sets the hidden bit on all dot files. Thus, most Samba clients won't display dot files. As a general rule, this approach works well; Unix dot files typically contain information that's not needed by SMB/CIFS clients. What's more, if this weren't done, users who are unfamiliar with the minutiae of Unix and Windows file-hiding techniques might mistakenly delete their Unix dot files when accessing a share from Windows and then become confused by the loss of default settings in their Unix programs.

On rare occasion, though, you may want to disable the hiding of dot files. For instance, if a Windows program creates files whose names begin with dots, but if those files shouldn't be hidden, the default Samba behavior could cause problems. Likewise, if your users understand the nature of Unix dot files and want to easily edit them from Windows clients, you may want to display them. (On the other hand, such users probably know enough to enable the display of hidden files using Windows' own settings.) To disable the hiding of dot files, set hide dot files = No for the share or shares in question. This setting overrides the Samba default.

Hiding Arbitrary Files

Sometimes you may want to hide arbitrary files from your clients. You might want to hide files that are likely to confuse users but that are necessary on the share, for instance. Several methods exist to hide arbitrary files:

Using the mapped hidden bit: If you set map hidden = Yes and an appropriate create mask, as described earlier in "Mapping to Unix Permissions," you can set the hidden bit using a DOS or Windows client or set the world execute bit from the Unix server. The effect will be a hidden file.

Turning the file into a dot file: You can rename the file as a dot file; for instance, change README.TXT into .README.TXT. Using the default Samba options, this will hide the file from SMB/CIFS clients that honor the hidden bit. Unfortunately, this approach will also cause problems if a program expects to access the file (even if it's hidden) using a particular name; Samba does *not* strip the leading dot from hidden dot files' names.

Hiding special files: By default, Samba doesn't hide "special" files—those that have unusual file type codes set, such as device files or sockets. To hide such files from clients, set hide special files = Yes. This parameter is new with Samba 3.0.

Hiding unreadable files: Under Unix, a file may exist and appear in a directory entry but be unreadable because the user lacks read access to the file. This behavior may seem strange to Windows users (particularly those familiar with Windows 9x/Me), so you can tell Samba to hide these files by setting hide unreadable = Yes. (The default value is No, which causes unreadable files to appear in directory listings.)

Hiding unwriteable files: You can hide files to which the user can't write by setting hide unwriteable = Yes. (The default value is No, which causes unwriteable files to appear in directory listings.) This parameter doesn't affect the appearance of directories to which the user lacks write access, though, just files. This parameter is new with Samba 3.0.

Using hide files: The hide files parameter can specify particular files you want to hide using the SMB/CIFS hidden bit, as described shortly.

To use the hide files parameter, you pass it a list of filenames, each of which is terminated by a slash (/). Each entry may contain spaces, as well as * and ? wildcards. The filenames are case-sensitive. For instance, consider the following parameter:

```
hide files = *.ufo/roswell.txt/black helicopters.???/
```

This entry hides all files with .ufo extensions, the file roswell.txt, and all files named black helicopters with a three-character extension. As with other hidden files, users can still access these files (assuming Unix permissions or other factors don't prevent such access). One problem with this approach is that it slows down Samba's directory accesses; Samba must search through directory entries and match them against the hidden files list, which takes time, even if no files actually match the restrictions. For this reason, if you want to hide arbitrary files, it's generally better to use the mapped hidden bit, unless you have some compelling reason not to do so, such as avoiding the confusion to users on the host Unix system of having nonprogram files with the execute bit set or if files that should *not* be hidden should be world executable on the underlying Unix system.

Vetoing Files

Sometimes hiding files isn't enough. A directory might contain files that Windows clients shouldn't be able to access under any circumstances. Ordinarily, the best way to deal with this situation is to avoid sharing the directory in question but to share instead another directory that contains duplicates of or links to the desirable files. Sometimes this approach isn't practical, though. For instance, if a directory is shared both via Samba and via Netatalk, the Netatalk server will generate a directory called .AppleDouble in which Macintosh resource forks are stored. If a Windows user accidentally alters files in this directory, the results can be very negative for the Macintosh users. Thus, you may want to *veto* the .AppleDouble directory—that is, make it completely inaccessible to Samba clients.

The veto files parameter works just like the hide files parameter; it takes a list of files, separated by slashes (/), that Samba should make unavailable to clients. Like hide files, veto files accepts wildcards and spaces within its filenames. Clients will not see the files under any circumstances, though, even if users set their computers to display hidden files. The veto files parameter is also effective with clients that don't support the hidden bit at all, such as smbclient.

As with hide files, one drawback to veto files is that it slows Samba down. Another potential problem is that it can interfere with deleting subdirectories. If a subdirectory contains a vetoed file, and if a Samba client attempts to delete that directory, Samba will be unable to comply because the vetoed file will exist, but the client won't be able to delete it. The solution is to set delete veto files = Yes. This parameter tells Samba to recursively delete all files in a directory that the client deletes, even if some of those files have been vetoed. The result might or might not be desirable, depending upon your purpose in vetoing the files. Of course, this parameter is unimportant on a read-only share.

Setting Security Options

You should always keep security in mind when configuring Samba (or any other server, for that matter). Sloppy security options can provide malicious individuals with unauthorized access to your server, resulting in sensitive data being stolen, loss of data, or other problems. Samba offers quite a few security options, and Chapter 11 describes many of these options. Some security options are quite fundamental to initial share configuration, though, so I describe them here. Prime among these options are parameters that set read-only or read/write access to a share. Another set of options relates to the security settings Samba employs when giving users access to shares. Windows NT, 200*x*, and XP systems offer *access control lists* (ACLs), and in order to implement ACLs, Samba needs to jump through some unusual hoops. Finally, Unix-style links pose unique security concerns that interact with share definitions.

Setting Read-Only or Read/Write Access

The most basic setting relating to read-only vs. read/write access is the read only parameter and its antonyms, write ok, writable, and writeable. The default is read only = Yes (or, equivalently, write ok = No). If a server functions primarily as a means for enabling users to store their own files, you might set the default for the entire server to read only = No in the [global] section; however, this practice is potentially risky. If you make such a change and then forget to set read only = Yes in a specific file share that should provide mere read-only access, users could damage files stored on the server. For this reason, it's probably best to not use read only or any of its antonyms in the [global] section and to explicitly set read only = No or one of its antonyms in every share to which read/write access should be granted. Following this practice will minimize the chance of an accidental misconfiguration causing problems.

TIP The read only = No parameter doesn't make an otherwise read-only filesystem or file read/write. For instance, if you mount a filesystem read-only using the host OS's mount command, setting read only = No won't make it possible for users to write to the filesystem. Depending upon your partition layout, you can use this fact as an added layer of protection by mounting data that should never be changed using your OS's read-only mount options.

Samba enables fine-tuning write access to shares through the use of a pair of extra options:

read list: This parameter accepts a list of usernames as its value. These users are granted read-only access to a share to which other users have read/write access.

write list: This parameter is the logical opposite of read list; it specifies users who should have write access to a share that's read-only to other users.

Typically, read list is used to restrict access to a small number of special access accounts, such as guest accounts. Such accounts are limited in number compared to ordinary user accounts, and most users should have fuller access to the share. The write list parameter, by contrast, might be used to grant a small number of users administrative access to a share. These users might be authorized to install software, templates, or other common files on a share from which most users need to only read data.

Adjusting Access Rights

Unix's permissions system depends upon the use of usernames and group names— or more precisely, user IDs (UIDs) and group IDs (GIDs), which are numerical equivalents of usernames and group names. Ordinarily, a process, such as a user program or a server, runs with a specific UID and GID. This identification, in conjunction with the ownership and permissions on files, determines whether and how that process may access the files. Similarly, the OS marks files that the process creates using the UID and GID of the process.

Normally, Samba operates within this conventional Unix security model, using the UID and GID of the user who logged on. For instance, if a user logs on as fastaire, that user can read files that fastaire could read and can write files that fastaire could write when logged onto the console or via some other logon tool, such as a Telnet or Secure Shell (SSH) logon.

One potential complication to this model is the authentication method you set with the security parameter. As described in Chapter 4, this parameter lets you use an authentication model that requires no username; however, Samba still needs a username for file accesses, so it picks one using the methods described in Chapter 4. You can apply a similar change to the username and group name used for accessing files for any share, no matter what security model you use, by applying special parameters:

> force user: This parameter takes a username as a value. Once the user has authenticated, all file accesses are performed using the specified username rather than the username used to connect to the server. (This effect doesn't modify the restrictions of write list or read list, though; if force user is used in conjunction with either of these parameters, the write list and read list parameters work from the user's real logon account, not the account set by force user.) Since Samba 2.0.5, the group used for accesses is also changed to the primary group of the forced user, as specified in /etc/passwd or some other user database.

> force group: This parameter takes a group name as a value. Once the user has authenticated, all file accesses are performed using the specified group name rather than the primary group of the user who logged on. If you also specify a force user parameter, the group specified by force group takes precedence over the group associated with the forced username. In Samba 2.0.5 and later, if you precede a group name with a plus sign (+), as in +tap, the group is forced only if the user is a member of the specified group (tap in this example). A synonym for this parameter is group.

valid users: Sometimes you may want to make a share available to just some users. This parameter enables you to do this; you pass it the usernames of users who should be able to access the share. Other users, although they can see the share in browse lists, can't access the share.

invalid users: This parameter is the opposite of valid users. Pass the names of users who should *not* have access to a share to this parameter, and they'll be unable to log onto the share.

As an example of these parameters, consider a share that includes the following lines:

```
force user = guest
force group = nobody
invalid users = flaky, shifty
```

A user connecting to this share must normally provide a username and password (although this might not be the case, depending upon other parameters' values). Suppose the user logs on as fastaire, who is a member of the tap group and no others. This user provides fastaire's password and is authenticated. If this user then creates files, they're owned by the guest user and the nobody group. (The guest account isn't present by default on many Unix installations, but you might create it to support guest access to Samba or other servers. The nobody group is common on Unix systems and is often used for low-access groups of users.) If an existing file in the share is owned by fastaire and has 0600 (-rw------) permissions, the user will be unable to read or write the file because Samba will use the guest and nobody user and group to control access to the file. This occurs despite the fact that the same user could access this file when logging on via SSH or Telnet. The users flaky and shifty are denied access to the share; they can't log on at all.

You can use the force user and force group parameters to fine-tune a system's security. You might use these options for "downgrade" access via Samba to reduce the risk that users could damage common file areas. You might also use these options to provide access to common areas using uniform ownership and permissions, which can reduce the risk that files that should be accessible to all will be inaccessible to some because of peculiar ownership and permissions. Keep in mind that these options are fairly weak as general system security measures; a user who logs on via Telnet, SSH, the console, or some other means isn't restricted in any way by the Samba options. These parameters are most useful as a means of fine-tuning Samba's file handling features. To fully restrict access to files, you should rely on standard Unix security practices and ensure that the Samba options don't provide a way around these features.

 CAUTION The force user and force group parameters are potentially quite risky. Be particularly wary about using force user = root, which gives users of the share superuser power within the share without entering the root password.

Setting Default Unix Permissions

Unix systems use permissions, as described in Chapter 2, as a method of controlling access to files. Because DOS, Windows, OS/2, Mac OS Classic, and many other clients don't use permissions, smb.conf parameters exist to set the permissions on files created via Samba. You can adjust these parameters on a share-by-share basis, but these options often appear in the [global] section, as described in the upcoming section "Setting Share Defaults Globally." Some other parameters, such as the permission bit mapping options described in the earlier section "The Archive and System Bits" interact with these options. Parameters that affect the permissions of new files include the following:

> **create mask**: This option sets the maximum permissions for a file, expressed as an octal value. For instance, if you set create mask = 0644, permissions on files created with this mask will never exceed 0644 (-rw-r--r--)—nobody will have execute permission, and only the file's owner will have write permission. The client may reduce permissions further (typically by eliminating any write permissions granted by the mask). The default value for this parameter is 0744. A synonym for this option is create mode.

> **directory mask**: This option works much like create mask, but it applies to permissions on directories. Because Unix relies upon the presence of execute bits for certain types of directory accesses, it's common for the directory mask to include the execute bit whenever the read bit is also active. The default value for this parameter is 0755. A synonym for this parameter is directory mode.

> **force create mode**: This parameter sets Unix permission bits (specified in octal) that Samba forces on. It does this *after* the create mask parameter is applied. The default value is 0000, so Samba doesn't force any bits on. If you wanted to force files created in a share to be readable to all users on the system, you might set force create mode = 0004.

> **force directory mode**: This parameter works just like force create mode, except that it applies to directories rather than ordinary files. Because directories are normally executable whenever they're readable, common values for the octal digits of this parameter are 0 (nothing forced on), 5 (forced readable), and 7 (forced readable and writeable).

> **inherit permissions**: This Boolean parameter, when set to Yes (the default is No), overrides the create mask and directory mask options. When this happens, new files and directories acquire permissions based on those of the parent directory. New directories' permissions exactly mirror those of the parent. New files' read and write bits are taken from those of the parent directory, but the execute bits are set by the value of the map archive, map hidden, and map system parameters.

unix extensions: This Boolean parameter doesn't affect permissions *per se*, but it does change the types of metadata that Samba delivers. Specifically, if unix extensions = Yes, Samba delivers symbolic links, file ownership, and some other Unix metadata in a way that similarly enabled clients can better handle. (Such clients are currently rare, but the new CIFS filesystem support in the 2.6.*x* Linux kernel supports it.) This option isn't of use to Windows clients, and its default value is No.

Setting the create mask option can be very important if you want to use the map system or map hidden parameters. Specifically, you must adjust create mask to support the relevant execute permission bits, or you won't be able to do so using the mapping options. You might also want to adjust create mask if the execute bit that appears on most files because of the map archive setting is a problem. The presence of the user execute bit on all files, including files that almost certainly are *not* executable in Unix, can be confusing if the share is accessed in any other way, such as directly on the server or via a Network File System (NFS) server from another Unix system. For this reason, when Samba is used as one of several ways of accessing files, it's common to set create mask = 0644. Alternatively, you can set map archive = No to achieve the same effect. You might also want to reduce the permissions if you want to use Unix-style permissions and ownership on the local computer as a method of controlling file access. For instance, using create mask = 0600 will ensure that only the file's owner will be able to read or write it. (You can use other parameters, most notably force user, to work around such restrictions, though.)

 CAUTION If you set create mask to eliminate the execute permission bit, the map archive option will become useless. Thus, if any software you run relies on the archive bit, you *shouldn't* remove the user execute bit via create mask.

Because readable directories' execute bits are normally set, the default directory mask most likely doesn't need to be changed to remove a potentially confusing execute bit. You might want to change the default value in order to better fit in with your Unix permission scheme, though.

On some systems, setting inherit permissions = Yes is desirable. This option enables users to control the permissions on their files by creating directories that have varying permissions. Of course, this presupposes that the users have access to their home directories in some other way, such as through a text-mode login or NFS. Alternatively, you could create ready-made subdirectories for users yourself, each with a different set of Unix permissions that would be mirrored in files created in the directory.

Implementing ACLs

Windows NT/200x/XP systems use ACLs instead of Unix-style permissions. Samba's ACL support has become more complete over time, but the most sophisticated Samba ACL features in Samba 3.0 and later require underlying OS support. This support remains unavailable on many platforms, so you may have to make do with a comparatively simple mapping of Unix-style permissions onto Windows ACLs.

NOTE   Samba's ACL features are inaccessible from older DOS and Windows 9x/Me clients, as well as from the Home edition of Windows XP. If you use such clients exclusively, you can safely ignore Samba's ACL features.

NOTE   To use Samba's ACL support, you must compile the server using the `--with-acl-support` option, which is described in Chapter 3. Not all binary versions of Samba ship with this option enabled.

Mapping ACLs on ACL-Ignorant Systems

Traditional Unix filesystems don't support ACLs, and if you use such a filesystem, you have little choice but to use no Samba ACL features or Samba features designed to map Unix-style permissions onto SMB/CIFS ACLs. In early 2004, examples of filesystems without ACL support include Linux's ReiserFS, the original Linux ext2fs and ext3fs (but extensions add ACL support to these filesystems), the original Unix FFS (extensions for some OSs add ACL support to FFS, though), and FAT. Note that filesystem developments may add ACL support to filesystems that had previously not supported this feature, so it's possible ACL support will be more common in the future.

If you're using a filesystem that doesn't support ACLs, or if you don't want to use the ACL support, you can create a mapping of Unix-style ownership and permissions onto SMB/CIFS ACLs using the following parameters:

`nt acl support`: When set to Yes (the default), this option enables Samba's mapping of Unix permissions to SMB/CIFS ACLs.

`security mask`: This parameter tells Samba what bits of the Unix permissions on ordinary files a client may modify. The default value is the same as the `create mask` parameter. Setting this value to 0777 gives clients the ability to modify any bit in the Unix security mode.

`directory security mask`: This parameter works like `security mask` but applies to directories rather than ordinary files. The default value mirrors the `directory mask` parameter.

force security mode: This parameter is akin to the force create mode parameter and uses its value as a default. It tells Samba which permission bits on ordinary files to force on when a client tries to change ACLs.

force directory security mode: This parameter works like force security mode but applies to directories. It takes its default from the force directory mode parameter.

Keep in mind that these options can give clients access to the Unix execute bits, but these bits may be mapped to the SMB/CIFS archive, system, and hidden bits, depending upon the settings of the map archive, map system, and map hidden parameters.

To access the Unix permissions from Windows NT/200x/XP, right-click the file and select Properties from the resulting context menu. The result is a Properties dialog box; the Security tab of this dialog box provides access to the permissions, as shown in Figure 5-2. You can control the permissions, within restrictions imposed by Samba and the limits of the underlying Unix permissions scheme, by clicking one of the three permission sets in the Name area and then clicking the appropriate box in the Allow column of the Permissions area.

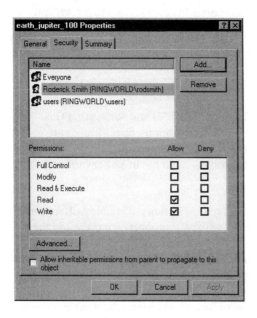

Figure 5-2. Windows provides point-and-click access to its ACL tools.

NOTE The details of ACL control vary from one version of Windows to another. Figure 5-2 shows a Windows 2000 system. Windows NT 4.0 used a more complex system involving multiple dialog boxes, but it was still accessed by selecting the Properties for a file. The Home edition of Windows XP doesn't provide a Security tab, so you can't employ ACLs with this version of Windows.

Using Samba in this way provides very restricted access to the Windows ACL features. For instance, if you click the Add button and try to give particular users access to the file, the action will fail. Depending upon precisely what you attempt to do, it may at first appear to work, but Windows will then display a dialog box telling you it was unable to update the ACLs when you try to complete the operation. Other operations will simply fail outright. Only the Read, Write, and Read & Execute items in Figure 5-2 have meaning when the underlying filesystem doesn't support ACLs; the Full Control and Modify items aren't implemented.

Using Native Unix ACLs

Some Unix filesystems support ACLs, either directly or through optional add-on packages. Filesystems that provide such support include:

XFS: This filesystem, available for Silicon Graphics' (SGI's) IRIX and for Linux, supports ACLs natively; no special options are required.

ext2fs and ext3fs: These closely related filesystems have long been the standard for Linux. They don't support ACLs through the 2.4.*x* kernel series, but you can find patches to add this support at `http://acl.bestbits.at`, and ACL support is a compile-time option with the 2.6.*x* kernels.

JFS: This filesystem, available for IBM's AIX and Linux, doesn't support ACLs natively; however, Linux patches to enable this support are available at `http://oss.software.ibm.com/developerworks/patch/?group_id=35` and have been added as a compile-time option to 2.6.*x* kernels.

UFS: This filesystem, which is the default in FreeBSD and some other OSs, can be made to support ACLs via compile-time options. Specifically, you must enable the `options UFS_ACL` setting in the kernel configuration file. This option is available in FreeBSD 5.0 and later, but not in earlier versions of FreeBSD.

Some of these filesystems require special mount options to enable ACL support. For instance, with ext2fs and ext3fs patched with ACL support, you must add the `acl` option. Once you've mounted the filesystem, Windows should provide additional ACL options from the Properties dialog box (Figure 5-2). This dialog box won't actually look different, but more of its buttons will work as users familiar with Microsoft's New Technology File System (NTFS) expect. In particular, you should be able to add ACLs by clicking the Add button. Samba won't allow you to add users who don't exist on the server, though. Users who can be added appear at the bottom of the list.

NOTE   Samba's ACL support works best in user- and domain-level security modes. Setting `security = server` is likely to cause problems because the chain between the client and the authentication database, including the list of authorized users who can be added as ACLs, is too convoluted. Attempting to use `security = share` is likely to result in confusion because usernames may not match expectations.

One additional ACL option that's most useful on systems that support ACLs is inherit acls. When set to Yes, Samba copies a directory's ACLs when creating subdirectories within it. The default value of No sets directory permissions according to the directory mask, force directory mode, and inherit permissions options instead.

Using ACLs from Unix

If you want to access ACLs from the Unix host, you can do so. The usual tools for this job are getfacl and setfacl. They may or may not be installed by default; they're often part of a separate package in support of filesystem ACLs. Check the site from which you obtained such support if it didn't come with your OS. To check on the ACLs present on a file, use getfacl:

```
$ getfacl zathras.wav
# file: zathras.wav
# owner: grogers
# group: users
user::rw-
user:fastaire:rw-
group::r--
mask::rw-
other::r--
```

The first three lines of output, each of which begins with a hash mark (#), specify the filename, owner, and group of the file. You can obtain the same information from a long directory listing (as in ls -l zathras.wav). The traditional Unix permission bits for the owner, group, and world also appear in subsequent lines of output. This example shows an ACL that's been added giving fastaire read/write access to the file.

To change ACLs, you can use the setfacl command. The -m option enables you to change an ACL, the -x option removes an ACL, and --set replaces an ACL. For instance, suppose you wanted to add an ACL for a new user. You might type the following command:

```
$ setfacl -m cachafaz:rw zathras.wav
```

This command gives the user cachafaz read/write access to the zathras.wav file. Of course, both setfacl and getfacl provide more options than I've described here. You should consult their man pages for more information on their operation.

Controlling Links

Native Unix filesystems invariably support *links*—special files that point to other files. These files can be created using the ln command in Unix. Two types of links are common:

Symbolic links: Also known as *soft links*, these links are really ordinary files with a special metadata bit set that identify them as links. The link file contains the name of another file, and when an ordinary program tries to access the file, the linked-to file is accessed instead. Symbolic links can point to ordinary files, directories, device files, and other special file types. The pointed-to file can reside on the same or a different filesystem—even on a filesystem of a different type. For instance, a symbolic link on an XFS partition can point to a file on a FAT partition.

Hard links: Hard links exist when two or more directory entries point to a single *inode* (a filesystem data structure that contains vital information on a file, such as its size, time stamps, and location on the disk). No one link name has any special claim to being the "real" or "primary" name for the file, except insofar as one was created first. Many systems limit the types of files that can be hard links; most notably, directories often can't be referenced via hard links. Hard links also can't point across filesystems, so both directory entries must reside on the same partition. Because only one lookup is involved, accessing hard links is faster than accessing symbolic links, although this difference is trivial in most cases.

Windows doesn't support the Unix concept of links, although Windows does support a similar concept, known as a *shortcut*. Windows shortcuts are most similar to Unix symbolic links; they're special files that contain the path to another file. Unfortunately, Samba can't dynamically map either symbolic or hard links to shortcuts, so Samba must handle links in other ways. Likewise, Samba needs to support Windows shortcuts. Fortunately, handling shortcuts is easy because the filesystem needn't be actively involved in this task. Rather, Windows gives shortcuts .LNK filename extensions and handles them distinctly without special filesystem support. Therefore, users can create Windows shortcuts on Samba shares without enabling any special Samba features.

NOTE   Other OSs support features similar to Unix's symbolic links and Windows' shortcuts. OS/2 uses *shadows*, and Mac OS Classic uses *aliases*, for instance. In most cases, these almost-link features aren't supported in Samba for these clients although these clients can follow symbolic links on the server following the same rules as Windows clients. Mac OS X, being based on Unix, supports symbolic links but can't create them on the Samba server. Hard links created in a Samba share through some non-Samba means work fine from Samba clients. To the client, each link appears to be an independent but identical file. (It's possible for one hard link to be in a shared directory while another hard link is in an unshared directory, in which case the Windows user won't even realize the link exists.) If a user changes one of the files, though, the other will change as well. For this reason, hard links can be confusing to Windows users, at least when users have write access to the files.

Samba's support for symbolic links is more complex and is handled through two parameters:

`follow symlinks`: This Boolean parameter defaults to Yes, and with this setting, Samba treats symbolic links like regular files—when a client accesses a link, the client "sees" the linked-to file. Windows clients will be unable to distinguish between original files and symbolic links. Setting this parameter to No tells Samba not to look up the target file when a client tries to access a symbolic link. The link still appears in directory listings, but it won't be accessible.

`wide links`: This Boolean parameter also defaults to Yes and is similar to `follow symlinks` in its actions; however, `wide links` affects only links that point outside of the share's directory tree. For instance, consider a share that's based on /usr/share/images. If `wide links` = No, a link from /usr/share/images/shoe.jpg to /usr/share/images/slipper.jpg will work; but a link to /usr/local/images/shoe.jpg won't work.

The default values of Yes for both `follow symlinks` and `wide links` result in maximum speed. Setting either value to No increases the time Samba takes to deliver files' contents because it must first check to see that the file isn't a prohibited link. On the other hand, taking this speed hit may be an acceptable consequence in some cases. Setting `wide links` to No can be desirable from a security point of view because it can reduce the risk that a user might create a link to an inappropriate file. Setting `follow symlinks` = No can reduce the confusion that might result if users tried editing or deleting files that are really symbolic links.

CAUTION   Some editors don't actually edit the original file; when you save a file, these editors rename the original and save a new file. When using such an editor on a symbolic link, the symbolic link will be renamed and a new file will be created, but the original file won't be affected. This result can be highly confusing to users, particularly if they don't fully understand the nature of links. Much the same result will occur with hard links in this situation, so they aren't better in this respect.

Overall, if a directory is to be used primarily or exclusively from Windows clients via Samba, you aren't likely to need to support links. The Windows users might create shortcuts, but no special configuration is required for these. You can disable links via `follow symlinks` or `wide links` if you like; you must judge for yourself whether the improved security is worth the speed hit.

In theory, using the global `unix extensions` = Yes parameter, described in the earlier section "Setting Default Unix Permissions," enables Unix clients to use both hard and symbolic links directly on a Samba server, much as could be done using NFS. In practice, though, this option requires support on the client as well as on the Samba server, and this support is still rare in early 2004. The most common tool that provides this support is the new CIFS driver in the Linux 2.6.*x* kernel. (The Linux SMB filesystem support doesn't work with unix extensions.) Even when Unix extensions support is present, it may not work quite as you'd expect. For instance, as of Samba 3.0.1 and the 2.6.1 Linux kernel, creating symbolic links between directories fails, although creating symbolic links within a directory or hard links between directories works. Existing hard and symbolic links both work as you'd expect, at least within a share. (Symbolic links pointing to files outside of a share will access like-named files on the client, if they exist. This behavior is similar to the default handling of symbolic links on many NFS configurations.) If you want the Unix extensions support for Unix clients, you should test its functionality before deploying it.

Locking Files

File servers such as Samba frequently field requests from multiple clients attempting to access the same files. Such accesses pose few or no problems when the clients merely want to read the files, but when the clients want to write the files, problems can ensue. Specifically, if two clients try to write data to one file simultaneously, or even in succession, the result can be file corruption or one user's changes overwriting the other user's changes.

To avoid this problem, most file-sharing servers and multitasking OSs employ a feature known as *file locking*. Before a program tries to write to a file, or even open it for read/write access, the program requests a *lock* on the file. This lock prevents other processes or clients from opening the file, at least for write access. As always, Samba's challenge is to integrate the SMB/CIFS file-locking mechanism with the underlying Unix file-locking systems. You can control this task through several smb.conf parameters:

share modes: This parameter enables support for several file-open options that implement locking features for Windows clients. These modes aren't directly supported by Unix, but Samba finds ways to simulate the effect using shared memory or lock files. The default value is Yes, and you should never change this option to No because some Windows applications will misbehave if you disable this option.

locking: This option enables basic file-locking behavior. The default value is Yes, and normally there's no need to change this parameter. Setting this option to No causes Samba to report that it has locked files even when it hasn't. This behavior is likely to cause program misbehavior, except possibly on read-only media such as CD-ROMs, so setting locking = No is inadvisable.

strict locking: This option controls whether Samba checks for the presence of file locks if a client doesn't request such a check. Most programs request these checks when necessary, so setting strict locking = No works well. A few programs fail to check for locks, though, which can cause problems with this option. Setting strict locking = Yes causes Samba to check for file locks on every file access, which improves reliability with some client programs but also degrades Samba's performance. In Samba 2.2.*x* and earlier, the default value was No, but Samba 3.0 changes this default to Yes.

`posix locking`: Ordinarily, Samba maintains a list of locks granted to its clients and coordinates this list with locks granted by the OS to local processes. Setting `posix locking = No` disconnects Samba's locks from those maintained by the OS. This is a potentially risky action, so leaving this parameter at its default value of Yes is advisable.

`blocking locks`: Many client programs, when they fail to obtain a lock, will begin *polling*—repeatedly requesting the lock until it's granted. Polling can be time-consuming, so this option enables an alternative that many clients support: The server will notify the client when it becomes possible to grant the requested lock. The default value of Yes works well in most cases; chances are you won't have to disable this feature.

`lock spin count`: This parameter controls how many times Samba attempts to acquire a lock on a byte range within a file. The default value of 2 works well, but some applications may work better with other values.

`lock spin time`: This parameter is the time in microseconds between attempts to gain a lock, when `lock spin count` is set greater than 1. The default value of 10 works well in most cases.

`oplocks`: An *opportunistic lock*, or *oplock* for short, enables clients to cache file accesses, which can improve network performance. This option, which defaults to Yes, enables Samba to support oplocks. In most cases, you should leave this option at its default value, but oplocks can cause problems on unreliable networks.

`kernel oplocks`: This option enables server-side programs to break a Samba oplock. The result is improved data consistency when files are accessed both via Samba and via local processes or an NFS server. Unfortunately, not all Unix-like systems support this feature; as of Samba 3.0.1, only the Linux 2.4.*x* and later kernels and IRIX are known to support it. The default value of this parameter is Yes, but on servers that don't support it, the feature is quietly disabled. You shouldn't need to disable this feature, although doing so can improve performance in some cases when `level2 oplocks = Yes`, as described next.

`level2 oplocks`: This feature enables Samba to downgrade an oplock from read/write to read-only status when a second client accesses a file, rather than revoking an oplock entirely. The result is improved performance in many environments. Thus, the default value of this parameter is Yes; however, this option is overridden and set to No if `kernel oplocks = Yes` and if the kernel supports oplocks. Setting `kernel oplocks = No` may, therefore, improve performance slightly when `level2 oplocks = Yes` but at the cost of greater potential for data corruption should both Samba and native Unix applications try to access a file simultaneously.

`oplock contention limit`: This parameter tells Samba to deny oplocks when the number of clients requesting access to a file exceeds the specified limit. This is an advanced tuning parameter, and the Samba documentation strongly advises against its use unless you have an intimate understanding of Samba's oplock mechanisms. The default value is 2.

fake oplocks: Early versions of Samba didn't support oplocks; instead, you could tell Samba to report that oplock requests succeeded even when they didn't by setting this parameter to Yes. This option has remained in Samba because it can improve performance; however, its use can also cause data corruption if multiple clients attempt to simultaneously open a single file for read/write access. For this reason, you should be *very* cautious about using this option. You might use it on read-only media, such as CD-ROMs, or if you're positive a share will be accessed only from a single client. The default (and safe) value is No.

veto oplock files: This parameter accepts a slash-delimited list of files and wildcards, similar to those used by veto files and hide files, for which Samba will never grant an oplock. You might use this parameter to list files that are likely to be very heavily used and for which oplocks are, therefore, likely to degrade performance.

As a general rule, the default options work well. You can set any of these options in the [global] section or on a per-share basis, so you can fine-tune your locking options for specific shares. Because of the change in the default between Samba 2.2.*x* and 3.0, I recommend setting strict locking explicitly to avoid the possibility of confusion when you review a Samba configuration. If files served by Samba are never accessed from the server itself or via another server (such as NFS), you may want to set kernel oplocks = No to let the level2 oplocks = Yes parameter function, improving perfor- mance. The added safety of kernel oplocks = Yes, when supported, is generally worth the slight degradation in speed of the necessary disabling of Level 2 oplocks, though. Using fake oplocks = Yes can improve speed on read-only media, but its use elsewhere is risky at best.

Miscellaneous Share Options

A few share-level parameters defy categorization but deserve some coverage:

available: Ordinarily and by default, this parameter is set to Yes, which makes a share accessible. If you want to quickly make a share disappear, you can set available = No, which has an effect similar to deleting an entire share definition from smb.conf. You might use this feature to temporarily disable a share if you discover a problem with it that will take some time to correct. Another possible use of this parameter is to define a share that you use very rarely and that you'd normally prefer not be available at all. Set available = No, and when you need to access the share, redefine it to Yes and restart Samba, pass smbd a SIGHUP signal, or wait for it to notice the changed file (it checks the file every minute for changes).

browseable: This parameter determines whether a share appears in browse lists on clients. The default value of Yes causes a share to appear and is usually appropriate. You can hide a share by setting this parameter to No; however, be aware that this setting doesn't make a share unavailable, only hidden from casual browsing. A user who knows the share's name can still connect to it even if it's not browseable. A synonym for this parameter is browsable.

copy: You can use this parameter to simplify the creation of a new share. Give it the name of an existing share, and the share you're defining takes on all the options of the specified share. You can then modify just the parameters you want to change for the new share.

csc policy: This option name stands for *client side caching policy*, and it defines how clients may cache files on the server. Valid values are manual (the default), documents, programs, and disable.

dont descend: This parameter specifies a comma-delimited list of directories that Samba should show as empty. This option can be useful both as a security measure and as a way of preventing access to recursive directories or those that could never be of interest to clients, such as /proc. This option tends to be fussy about the format of its values; for instance, you may need to specify ./proc rather than /proc. You should, therefore, test your entries once you create them to be sure they work as you expect.

dos filetime resolution: This Boolean parameter determines whether Samba reports file time stamps using a one-second or a two-second granularity. The default value of No causes one-second resolution, which is fine for most cases. Some programs, though, rely on the two-second resolution of the FAT filesystem. For instance, the default setting can cause Microsoft's Visual C++ to believe that files have been modified when in fact they haven't been changed. In this case, setting this option to Yes can correct the problem.

dos filetimes: Under Unix, only the owner of a file or root may alter the file's time stamp. Under DOS and Windows, though, any user who can write to a file can change its time stamp. If your clients use programs that rely on this feature, you may want to set dos filetimes = Yes, which overrides the default Samba behavior of honoring Unix standards on this matter.

fake directory create times: This parameter defaults to No, which causes Samba to report the earliest available time stamp for a directory as the directory's creation time. This behavior can cause problems for some programs, though, such as Visual C++, which mistakenly believes that directories have been modified when they haven't been. Setting this parameter to Yes causes Samba to report every directory's creation time as January 1, 1980, as a workaround for this problem.

fstype: SMB/CIFS enables clients to query the server about the filesystem used on a share. By default, Samba returns NTFS as this value, which works well in most cases. You can change this value to something else, though, such as FAT or Samba. If you believe an application is being unusually fussy about the filesystems used on the server, you can experiment with this parameter.

max connections: You can limit the number of connections that can be made to a specific share with this parameter. The default value of 0 stands for no limit. You might set this value to 1 if the share's contents are very sensitive and shouldn't be changed by more than a single user at a time or to some higher but finite value, such as 10, to limit the possibility of performance problems resulting from too many connections, particularly to an under-powered server. Windows 9*x*/Me clients usually don't disconnect promptly when told to do so, though, so this parameter can limit access more severely than you might initially expect.

lock directory: This global parameter sets a directory in which Samba stores information relevant to implementing the max connections access controls. A synonym for this parameter is lock dir.

max disk size: Although this parameter is global in scope and, therefore, appears only in the [global] section of smb.conf, it affects the apparent size of individual shares. Some clients have problems with shares that are larger than a particular size (typically 1GB), so this parameter lets you set a maximum reported disk size that the clients can handle. The default value of 0 imposes no limit, and higher values set a size in megabytes. Thus, a 1GB apparent size cap could be imposed by setting max disk size = 1024.

strict allocate: When set to No (the default), this parameter causes Samba to allocate space only for the parts of a file written by a client, even if the client has told Samba that the file will ultimately be larger. This behavior is faster than actually allocating the requested disk space, but Windows servers allocate disk space immediately and so return out-of-space errors earlier than Samba does by default. Setting this parameter to Yes causes Samba to emulate the standard Windows behavior, which impairs performance slightly but may improve compatibility with some clients. This change is particularly important if your system implements per-user disk space quotas.

strict sync: This parameter's default value of No causes Samba to ignore clients' disk-sync requests. This setting improves performance but increases the risk of data loss should Samba's host OS crash. If this small risk is unacceptable, you can set strict sync = Yes, which reduces the chance of data loss in a server crash at the cost of reduced disk performance.

sync always: When this parameter is set to No (the default), Samba honors applications' instructions on whether to report that a write operation has completed until the data has been sent to the disk (as opposed to cached in a write buffer). Setting this parameter to Yes causes Samba to always wait for the OS to finish writing data to disk before reporting an operation is complete. (This behavior also requires strict sync = Yes.) The result is reduced performance but a reduced chance of data loss should the server crash.

 NOTE   Much of the rest of this book describes more complex topics, many of which involve specific share-level parameters. These parameters are described in the relevant chapters of this book.

As with most Samba options, the default values of these miscellaneous parameters are acceptable in most cases. Some of these options may improve (or degrade) Samba's performance, though. Others may improve (or degrade) Samba's compatibility with specific clients or programs running on clients. Use the preceding descriptions as a guide, and experiment if you're unsure of the utility of a particular option. In many cases, the only way to know whether an option will be beneficial is to try it on your own system.

Setting Share Defaults Globally

Share parameters are frequently found in share definitions, but they can also appear in the [global] section of smb.conf. When used in this way, parameters set defaults that apply to all shares unless they're explicitly overridden in specific shares. You can place such parameters in [global] to avoid having to place them in every share definition you create, thus reducing the odds of causing problems by missing one.

Samba's default filename-handling options are optimal for Windows and OS/2 clients. They also work for DOS, Unix, and other platform clients, but tweaking these options sometimes improves performance on these platforms. Specifically, setting case sensitive = Yes for Unix clients can improve compatibility with them, albeit with a danger: If a Unix client creates files whose names differ only in case, other clients may not be able to access both files. Changing the case preservation options can help you keep consistent filename case if your network serves primarily DOS clients. Most clients aren't sensitive to filename case, but if you suspect problems because of case, you can set default case = Upper and mangle case = Yes to force the client to receive nothing but uppercase filenames. This combination is likely to make some filenames look like gibberish, though.

TIP   You can use the include parameter along with a variable such as %a within the [global] section to create custom configurations for particular OSs. For instance, you might include different case-sensitivity or case mangling options for DOS, Windows, and Unix clients. (Samba doesn't recognize all OSs, though. Table 18-1 in Chapter 18 summarizes the values of this variable.)

Some defaults make sense to change for all shares because you have no need to fine-tune them on a share-by-share basis. For instance, you might want to change the global file-locking options, as described earlier in "Locking Files." You can certainly do so, but there is a danger: If you set a share-level option globally, you may forget this fact and mistakenly believe that a specific share is using the normal default value when you examine the configuration file or create a new share later. Such an error is sometimes potentially risky. For instance, if you set read only = No in [global] and then forget that you've changed the default, you might mistakenly create a new share that you intend to be read-only but forget to set read only = Yes in the share. For this reason, I recommend you consider what might happen if you forget you've made a change before implementing it globally. If serious performance or security problems could result, make the change in each individual share rather than globally, even if doing so means redoing the same configuration change in many individual shares.

Common File Share Examples

The preceding presentation may be overwhelming; quite a few parameters were presented, so seeing how they're used in context may be helpful. The rest of this chapter is, therefore, devoted to this task; I don't show the context for every parameter, but I do present a sampling of useful share types. The first of these is a very common share type that's also treated in a special way by Samba: a home share, in which users store their personal files. Next up is a share for holding Windows executables, templates, or other files that most users shouldn't need to write. Finally, I present options for creating shares in which users may exchange files.

Creating a Home Share

Most file shares follow the rules laid out in this chapter. One share, though, is special: the home share. This share is denoted by a share name of [homes] in smb.conf, and it's unique in several ways. You'll see the unusual features of home shares both in the way they're defined in smb.conf and in the way they're accessed from clients.

Special Rules for a Home Share

A home share looks much like any other share in smb.conf except that it must appear under the share heading of [homes]. These shares provide users with access to the Unix home directories. Listing 5-1 shows a typical [homes] share.

Listing 5-1. A Typical [homes] *Share*

```
[homes]
    comment = Home Directories
    browseable = No
    read only = No
    wide links = No
```

Listing 5-1 illustrates several important points about home shares:

No directory specification: Samba uses the user's home directory, as specified in /etc/passwd, as the path for a [homes] share. For this reason, you won't find a directory specification (or its synonym, path) in a typical [homes] share. (This parameter may still be used, but there's seldom any need to do so.)

Share browseability: Most home shares bear the browseable = No parameter. This parameter works somewhat differently on home shares than on most shares. In the case of home shares, browseable = No tells Samba not to make a share called HOMES visible in browse listings. Part of the home share definition that's handled automatically, however, is to make the share visible in browsers under the user's name. For instance, fastaire will see a share called FASTAIRE on the server, and grogers will see a share called GROGERS. Neither user will see the other's home share. Either user can type the other's username as a share name to access the other's share, though, within limits imposed by Unix and Samba ownership and permissions rules.

Read/write access: Although a home share *could* be made available in read-only form, it's more common to see these shares in read/write form. Thus, a read only = No parameter or one of its antonyms is likely to be present in these shares.

Home shares are typically used to provide individual users on a network with file storage space for their own documents. Users can then access their home directories from any computer on the network, which helps to untie users from specific workstations. For instance, a university's computing center might use home shares to enable students to access their own files from any workstation in a public computing area. You might also use Samba and home directories to provide more disk space for all users by upgrading a single computer's (that is, the server's) hard disk or to make it easier to back up users' data files by storing them on a single computer.

Home shares are so important that many sample Samba configuration files include a [homes] section. These sections provide a lot of functionality for a fairly simple configuration. Of course, they're not without their pitfalls. If users can log onto the server through some means other than Samba, users' home directories are likely to contain files that are irrelevant to Samba clients. For instance, many local Unix programs create dot files to hold configuration options. Thus, you may want to ensure that hide dot files = Yes in home shares. (This setting is the default, but if you've overridden the default in the [global] section, changing it back in the [homes] section is probably advisable.)

Home shares are also important in the maintenance of *roaming profiles*, which are a feature available on domains. Roaming profiles enable users to store personal configuration information, such as preferred desktop backgrounds, icons, and so on, on the Samba server rather than on the local computer. Roaming profiles, therefore, extend the customizability of shared workstations; users can see the settings they like no matter what workstation they use. Chapter 14 describes roaming profiles in more detail.

Accessing a Home Share

Precisely how you access a home share depends on your client. Chapter 18 describes various SMB/CIFS clients. As a general rule, when you browse to the server, you'll see a share named after your username. For instance, Figure 5-3 shows a share called RODSMITH, which, when opened, shows the contents of the home directory assigned to the user rodsmith on the server.

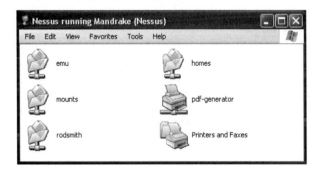

Figure 5-3. Most SMB/CIFS browsers display home shares under the user's name.

Displaying a home directory named after the user depends on the server knowing the username, though. A few clients, such as the BeOS SMB/CIFS client, don't ask for the username until you attempt to connect to a share. Such systems might not display a user's home directory at all unless you set browseable = Yes in the [homes] section of smb.conf. If this option is set, a share called HOMES will appear. Figure 5-3 also shows this share. Opening this share produces precisely the same effect as opening the share named after the user, except that the path to files (displayed in file open dialog boxes and the like) includes the string HOMES rather than the username. If all your clients are Windows clients, you shouldn't need to set browseable = Yes, and leaving this parameter set to No will reduce the number of shares that appear in share lists, which can simplify users' tasks of finding their own files.

Whatever the setting of the browseable parameter, users can manually enter either the username or the string HOMES as a share name in many SMB/CIFS clients. For instance, you might access rodsmith's home share on the NESSUS server using Samba's own smbclient from the rodsmith account by typing either of the following two commands:

```
$ smbclient //NESSUS/RODSMITH
$ smbclient //NESSUS/HOMES
```

Many GUI SMB/CIFS browsers also provide some way to enter a path to a share by typing it. For instance, in Windows XP, be sure the View ➤ Address Bar menu option is selected in a file browser window. You can then type the NetBIOS name and share name into the address field, such as \\NESSUS\HOMES, to access the share. (This format is referred to as the *Universal Naming Convention*, or UNC.)

You can use a similar technique to access other users' home shares. For instance, grogers might type \\TAP\FASTAIRE into a Windows XP file browser address field to access fastaire's home directory on TAP. Samba's home directory implementation doesn't allow grogers to see fastaire's home directory in a share browser window such as the one shown in Figure 5-3, though—or at least, other users' shares are ordinarily hidden from view in this way. Also, Unix and Samba access control mechanisms are always in play. If fastaire's files all have 0600 (-rw-------) permissions, grogers won't be able to read the files. Indeed, if fastaire's home directory doesn't grant grogers the ability to read it, grogers will receive a "permission denied" error when attempting to even view the fastaire home directory.

CAUTION If a user accesses a home share using a particular client and then walks away from the client, chances are the client will continue to provide access to the user's home share. In most versions of Windows, you can select Start ➤ Log Off, which will shut down the client's access to the Samba server, enabling a new user to authenticate and log on. In an environment that uses public workstations, be sure to educate your users about the risks of leaving a computer unattended without logging off. You may also want to add appropriate client-specific software to automatically log off after a period of inactivity.

A Windows Executable or Templates Share

On many networks, a Samba server delivers program files, templates, or other read-only files to users. Typically, most users don't need to be able to write to such a share, but a few may need write access so that they may update the share's contents—to upgrade software to the latest version, to add or update templates, and so on. Listing 5-2 shows such a share.

Listing 5-2. A Common Read-Only Share Definition

```
[programs]
    comment = Windows Program Files
    volume = WINPROGS
    browseable = Yes
    directory = /home/samba/winprg
    read only = Yes
    write list = grogers, fastaire
    force user = grogers
    invalid users = macky
```

A share such as the one shown in Listing 5-2 should work well for DOS, Windows, or OS/2 program storage (as the comment and share name in Listing 5-2 suggest), for template storage, or for various other purposes. These are some features worth noting in Listing 5-2:

Share identification: The share has a fairly descriptive name and a more descriptive comment parameter to help users locate it. The volume parameter probably isn't necessary unless a program on the share is particularly picky about its volume name. The browseable = Yes line restates the default for that parameter, so it's also probably not necessary. Restating it does no harm, though.

Directory location: This example locates the share in /home/samba/winprogs. This directory must exist, of course. In practice, you could locate it anywhere that's convenient, such as a subdirectory of /var or a nonstandard shares directory off the root directory (/samba/shares/programs, say). Note that the directory name needn't be the same as either the share name or the volume name. In practice, though, using the same name for all three may reduce the chance of causing confusion.

Share maintenance: The read only = Yes parameter restates the default, but doing so is wise in this case. The write list parameter gives two users the right to create and modify files in the directory. The force user parameter causes both users' files to be owned by just one user (grogers), though, which enables both users to modify each other's files. Other users do *not* acquire write privileges, despite the presence of the force user parameter. This type of arrangement is useful for shares that are maintained by multiple users. Alternatively, you could set create mask = 0660 (or higher) and directory mask = 0770 (or higher), omit the force user parameter, and ensure that both share administrators are in the same group. This approach would enable you to use Unix file permissions to restrict access to the share. Because of the force user parameter, everybody who may access the share may read the files it contains—at least, assuming no non-Samba changes to files' permissions.

Share access control: The invalid users parameter blocks the user macky from accessing the share. Normally, a common Windows program share wouldn't include such a parameter. You might use it to keep users from accessing files they'd find useless, though; for instance, perhaps macky is the office's one Mac OS user, who, therefore, can't run the Windows programs on the share. Granting macky access to the share probably won't do any harm; the files will just be useless. Keeping macky out might prevent confusion, though.

Before you can use this share, you must be sure to create the directory. Furthermore, if fastaire and grogers are to be able to add programs to it, the directory must be writeable by grogers (the user specified by force users). It could be owned by this user, or it could be owned by another user but with appropriate group or world write permissions. Note that fastaire does *not* need Unix-side permission to write to the share's directory. After the share administrators add a few programs to the share, a directory listing from Unix might look something like this:

```
$ ls -l /home/samba/winprg/
total 144
drwxr-xr-x    7 grogers  users         4096 May 10 12:59 Games
drwxr-xr-x    2 grogers  users         4096 May 10 15:05 Installers
drwxr-xr-x    3 grogers  users         4096 May 10 14:54 Lib
-rwxr--r--    1 grogers  users          151 May 10 14:54 Liprefs.js
drwxr-xr-x   17 grogers  users         4096 May 10 13:14 Program Files
drwxr-xr-x    2 grogers  users         4096 May 10 13:29 Utilities
```

Because no create mask or directory mask parameters were present, the files and directories take on default permissions: 0744 (rwxr--r--) for files and 0755 (rwxr-xr-x) for directories. All files in all subdirectories will have identical permissions. All files and directories are owned by grogers, even if fastaire created them. These details are all hidden from the share's users, though, including fastaire and grogers. (Users may be able to use ACL dialog boxes on Windows NT/200x/XP clients to glean some of this information, though.)

A File-Exchange Share

Suppose you want to create a configuration in which users' home shares are very private—only the owner of a home share may read it. You could create a configuration such as this by setting 0700 (rwx------) permissions on users' home directories and perhaps setting create mask = 0600 and directory mask = 0700 in the [homes] share definition. Such a setup provides good local security, but it complicates file exchange. If users need to collaborate and swap files, you'll need another share in which they can drop these files. Such a share might resemble Listing 5-3.

Listing 5-3. A File-Exchange Example Share

```
[transfers]
    comment = Transfer Files Here
    browseable = Yes
    directory = /home/samba/transfers
    read only = No
    invalid users = print
    nt acl support = Yes
    inherit permissions = Yes
```

Notable features of Listing 5-3 include the following:

Identification: As with Listing 5-2, the share is browseable although the `browseable` parameter merely reiterates the default. In this example, the share name and the directory name are related, although this need not be the case. The `comment` parameter also describes the share's purpose.

Access control: The purpose of the share requires that it be writeable, so the share definition specifies `read only = No`. The share is off-limits to the `print` user. The idea is that this is an account that was created for printer shares on the same server. This account doesn't correspond to a real user and so has no business accessing the share. Restricting this user's access could limit damage should a cracker break in using the `print` account.

File permissions: This share uses the `inherit permissions = Yes` parameter to set file permissions based on those of the parent directory. You can use this option to create initial access control features, as described shortly. The `nt acl support = Yes` parameter gives users of Windows NT/200x/XP clients some control over permissions, particularly if the `/home/samba/transfers` directory resides on an ACL-enabled filesystem.

To use Listing 5-3, you must first create the `/home/samba/transfers` directory. Precisely how you do this has substantial consequences for the security of the share. For instance:

- You can give the directory 0777 (`rwxrwxrwx`) permissions. If you do this, all users will be able to access the share without restrictions. Given the `inherit permissions = Yes` parameter, all users will be able to read and write others' files unless they use NT ACLs to restrict access or log onto the server using a shell account and change files' permissions.

- You can give the directory restrictive permissions, such as 0755, and create subdirectories with varying ownership and permissions. For instance, you could create a subdirectory for each user, giving it 0755 or 0750 permissions. Users could then place files in these directories for others to read but not write. Instead of or in addition to such a scheme, you could create subdirectories with varying group ownership and 0770, 0775, or 0777 permissions. Users could place files in these directories for others to read and modify.

Summary

File shares represent the core Samba functionality. Many Samba parameters exist to help define and fine-tune the operation of file shares in order to interface between an underlying Unix host and the expectations of an SMB/CIFS client. Options you're likely to set in a typical file share include those related to file naming, permissions, security, and file locking. A few miscellaneous options are also potentially important. File shares can point to any directory you like on the Samba server, but one particular type of file share deserves special attention because it points to a different directory for each user: the [homes] share. This share is typically used to provide a network of users with personal data storage space, independent of the workstation from which the user accesses it.

#### CHAPTER 6

Configuring Printer Shares

MOST SAMBA SYSTEMS function primarily or exclusively as file servers, storing files on the server for the benefit of clients. Samba can fulfill other functions, though. Some of Samba's additional services, such as delivering an accurate time, are described in subsequent chapters of this book. Others, such as handling NetBIOS name resolution, are also described later and are necessary only in support of other Samba functions. The purpose that's most closely tied to file sharing, though, is printer sharing. Printer shares enable clients to print to printers connected to the Samba server or even print indirectly to other printers that the Samba server can access. Internally, Samba treats printer shares much like file shares but with some important differences—most important, files delivered to Samba for local storage are passed to the server's print queue for printing.

This chapter describes how to set up printer shares. If you haven't already read them, you should first read Chapter 4 and Chapter 5 because those chapters describe necessary preliminary configuration and information on Samba shares generally. This chapter follows the trail with a look at global printer options, which are set in the [global] section of smb.conf. Next up is a look at what it takes to create a bare-bones printer share, as well as how to create a share that automatically handles all of a server's printers. Because many Unix systems work best with PostScript printers, this chapter describes how Samba treats PostScript and non-PostScript printers. Next up is a look at the print command parameter, which enables you to modify how Samba processes print jobs. Finally, most clients require printer drivers in order to print, and this chapter describes Samba's tools to help deliver these drivers to some popular printing clients.

TIP An old unused computer (even a 486 system) can make a good dedicated print server. Run a free Unix-like OS on it, such as FreeBSD or Linux, install Samba, and connect printers to the server. (You may need to add extra parallel-port cards or a Universal Serial Bus, or USB, card.) Your new dedicated Samba print server can then make printers available to all the computers on your network. This task need not be very resource-intensive, so it can be a good way to get some use out of old computers that would otherwise gather dust. Converting PostScript to printer-specific codes can chew some CPU time, though, as described in the upcoming section "PostScript and Non-PostScript Printers."

Setting Global Printer Options

The first step in configuring printer sharing (aside from the basic Samba configuration steps described in Chapter 4) is to set global printing options. Most important, Samba must know which of several common Unix printing systems you're using so Samba can submit print jobs using the correct utilities and options for that system. You must also tell Samba where to look to learn about the printers that are actually defined on your system.

Setting Your Printing System

Over the years, several different printing systems have been developed for Unix. Each of these systems implements a local print *queue*—a holding area for files that are to be processed. Typically, a printing daemon runs in the background and accepts files that should be printed, either from local programs or from programs run on remote systems. The daemon places the incoming print jobs in the queue, processes them, and sends each to the printer in turn. Various commands exist to list print jobs in the queue, re-order them, delete specific jobs, and so on. Examples of printing systems in common use are as follows:

BSD LPD: The printing system developed for the Berkeley Software Distribution (BSD) is often called the *line printer daemon* (LPD) and is an old but popular printing system. Many other printing systems emulate the BSD LPD commands.

CUPS: The Common Unix Printing System (CUPS; http://www.cups.org) was designed to address the shortcomings of the BSD LPD system and others of that age. It's much more complex than BSD LPD, it's becoming common on Linux distributions, and it's used on Mac OS X 10.2 and later.

LPRng: This printing system, based at http://www.lprng.com, is designed as a next-generation replacement of BSD LPD. Many of its configuration tools and methods are similar to those of BSD LPD. LPRng is common on some Linux distributions, but CUPS is quickly gaining ground in the Linux world.

SysV: This printing system originated with AT&T's SysV Unix and is popular with certain commercial Unix versions derived from SysV.

Other printing systems exist, but these four are the most common, and most others are modeled after one of these four. In order to print, Samba must know what printing system is in use on the server—or, at least, what programs and options to use to submit print jobs and perform other print job management tasks. Several Samba parameters enable you to set the overall system as well as the specific commands used for particular tasks:

printing: This global parameter sets the printing system used by the host OS. Essentially, this option modifies the defaults for the more specific printing parameters, such as print command. As of Samba 3.0.0, nine values are supported: BSD, AIX, LPRng, PLP, SysV, HPUX, QNX, SoftQ, and CUPS. In most respects, including the critical print command value, BSD, AIX, QNX, LPRng, and PLP are equivalent; SysV and HPUX are equivalent; SoftQ is unique but similar to SysV; and CUPS is unique but may be similar to SysV, depending upon Samba compile-time options. The default printing system is a compile-time option. If you're using a Samba binary that shipped with your OS, chances are the default value is fine, so you shouldn't need to use this parameter. If you compiled Samba yourself, though, or if you're using a binary created for a different OS or distribution, you may need to set this parameter.

NOTE The --enable-cups compile-time option (described in Chapter 3) tells Samba to use CUPS-specific tools to submit print jobs when printing = CUPS. If Samba is compiled without this support, Samba uses CUPS's SysV emulation mode for submitting print jobs.

print command: This share parameter sets the command that Samba uses to submit a job to the local print queue. Table 6-1 shows the default values of print command based on the setting of the printing parameter. How Samba treats printing when you use CUPS depends on the setting of the CUPS support compile-time option (--disable-cups or --enable-cups), as described in Chapter 2. You can change the print command parameter to achieve special results, as described in the upcoming section "Using the print command Parameter."

Table 6-1. Default print command *Values*

printing **Value**	print command **Value**
BSD, AIX, QNX, LPRng, or PLP	lpr -r -P%p %s
SysV or HPUX	lp -c -d%p %s; rm %s
SoftQ	lp -d%p -s %s; rm %s
CUPS without special CUPS support	lp -d'%p' %s; rm %s
CUPS with special CUPS support	Uses CUPS API

lpq command: Most Unix printing systems provide a command called lpq, which displays a list of queued print jobs. Ideally, Samba should be able to feed similar information back to clients that request it. You can specify a command Samba can use for this purpose with this share parameter.

lpq cache time: Samba caches information received from a call to lpq (or another program specified with lpq command) for a period of time (in seconds) specified with this global parameter. The default value is 10.

lprm command: Most Unix printing systems provide a command called lprm, which removes a job from the print queue. Samba can enable clients to remove jobs they've submitted, but only if Samba knows what command to issue.

lppause command: Windows enables users to pause a print job. Unix printing systems may not provide an exact equivalent to this feature, but you can usually achieve a similar effect by setting the printing priority for a job very low. The lppause command share parameter lets you set a command that will do this.

lpresume command: This share parameter specifies a command that Samba issues to undo the effect of lppause command when a client tells Samba to resume printing of the paused file.

queuepause command: Windows clients can pause all printing in a specified queue, and this share parameter points to a local command to achieve this effect. Not all printing systems define it.

queueresume command: This share parameter specifies a command that Samba issues to undo the effect of queuepause command when a client tells Samba to resume printing from the paused queue.

min print space: You can specify a minimum amount of disk space, in kilobytes, that must be present before Samba will accept a print job. The default value of 0 means that Samba won't check available disk space before accepting a print job. You can set this value to some higher value to minimize the risk of Samba running out of disk space while processing a print job. The exact amount required depends on the type of printer and varies from one print job to another, though, so it's impossible to give a good rule of thumb for this share parameter's optimum setting.

Although most of these parameters are share-level, they're often set in the [global] section so that they apply to all the print queues you define. You can override any of these settings except for printing and lpq cache time in specific shares, though, to customize the operation of particular printer shares.

The printing command parameters' default values are all determined by the print command parameter's setting. If you've set this parameter correctly, chances are you won't need to adjust the more specific commands. You might make an exception to this rule if you want to achieve a special effect (such as sending an e-mail to an administrator if a job is removed from a queue) or to provide the complete path to a command to ensure it executes even if Samba's default path doesn't include the directory in which the executable file resides.

NOTE Samba inherits whatever path is used by whatever shell, script, or program launches it. This path usually includes the path to relevant printing and other system tools, but this isn't guaranteed. If printing features aren't working, you might consider adjusting these parameters so they include the complete path to the relevant utilities. Note that the path Samba inherits when you launch the program from a shell may not be the same as the path Samba inherits when it's launched from a SysV or other startup script.

Many of these commands pass variables as options, such as the queue name (%p), the job number (%j), the job name (%J), the filename (%s), the number of printed pages (%c), and the size of the print job in bytes (%z). Samba keeps track of any necessary translations between names and numbers as used locally and as used by the Samba clients; when specifying commands, simply place the appropriate variable in whatever command you need to specify.

As a general rule, setting the printing system is fairly straightforward. You may not need to include any parameters at all. If you can't seem to get Samba to print, though, and if you're sure local printing works, you may want to try specifying your local printing system. For example:

```
printing = LPRng
```

If this doesn't work, you may want to try specifying a complete printing command, including the complete path to your printing binary:

```
print command = /usr/bin/lpr -r -P%p %s
```

CAUTION Some printing commands delete the input file (%s) automatically when printing is finished; that's the function of the -r parameter to lpr, for instance. Other printing commands don't delete the input file, though. To prevent Samba's printer share directories from overflowing, you must ensure that you delete these files yourself if your printing command doesn't do the job. You can separate commands with semicolons (;) and remove a file with rm after the semicolon, if necessary, as in lpr -P%p %s; rm %s, to achieve this end.

If manually specifying a print command works, you should check the operation of functions such as pausing and deleting print jobs from your clients. If they don't work, specifying them manually may be necessary if you want these features to work.

If using print command doesn't get printing working, you may want to try using custom commands or scripts as the print command to help debug the printing system. For instance, print command = cp %s /tmp/testprint.prn should copy the print job to

/tmp/testprint.prn. If the print job appears at that location, you at least know that Samba is receiving it, and you should re-examine the functionality of your local printing system. If the file doesn't appear, check Samba's log files and perform other network diagnostics to look for communication problems between the client and the server.

Loading Printers

The BSD LPD, LPRng, and similar printing systems use a file called /etc/printcap to store information on local printers, such as queue names and locations. Many local programs rely upon this file to provide a list of printers to the user, and Samba is such a program, particularly when you create a [printers] share (described in the upcoming section "Defining a Share for All Printers").

Some printing systems, though, don't use printcap or use it in an odd way. You may also have cause to create a bogus printcap file that omits printers you don't want Samba to use. In all of these cases, the global printcap name parameter is useful; it lets you tell Samba where to find this critical configuration file. Three classes of values for this parameter are common:

The actual printcap name: You can point to an actual printcap file, with complete path, as in printcap name = /etc/printcap. If this file is in some unusual location or is known by an odd name, this use enables you to point to the correct file. Likewise, you can point to an edited file if your real one causes problems or if you want to create one that omits certain printers.

The special value for CUPS: If your system uses CUPS for printing, specifying printcap name = cups causes Samba to read the "dummy" printcap file created by CUPS (usually /etc/printcap).

The special value for SysV: SysV printing systems support a tool called lpstat that enables programs to learn what printers are available. Samba will use this tool if you specify printcap name = lpstat, so setting this value may be necessary on systems using SysV printing systems.

The AIX printing system uses a file called /etc/qconfig instead of /etc/printcap. If the printcap name parameter points to a file called qconfig, Samba interprets it as a qconfig file rather than a printcap file; otherwise, Samba tries to read the file in printcap format.

Another global printing parameter is load printers. This Boolean parameter tells Samba whether to load all printers from printcap (or its equivalent) for browsing. This parameter isn't sufficient to do anything by itself, though; it must be combined with a [printers] share, as described in the upcoming section "Defining a Share for All Printers."

Testing Local Printing

Before you can hope to use Samba as a print server, you must usually configure the server to print locally. Precisely how you do this depends on the printing system you're using—BSD LPD, LPRng, CUPS, SysV, and other printing systems each have their own features. Furthermore, individual OSs often have text-based or GUI tools to facilitate printer configuration. For instance, many Linux systems ship with a printer configuration utility called `printtool`; you can configure Mac OS X systems via the Print Center tool (available in the Utilities folder); CUPS includes a Web-based configuration tool that can be accessed by typing `http://localhost:631` into a Web browser on the server; and various tools, such as Webmin (`http://www.webmin.net`) and Apsfilter (`http://www.apsfilter.org`), facilitate configuring BSD LPD and similar queues.

In most cases, the best way to set up a Samba print server is to first configure the printer for local printing to be sure that it works and only then to proceed with creating Samba printer shares. This approach makes it easier to troubleshoot problems because you'll be able to isolate local printing problems to non-Samba systems, as well as SMB/CIFS problems to Samba and its interactions with the client and with the local printing system.

Unfortunately, this approach doesn't always work. Unix systems work best with PostScript printers or with printers that are supported by Ghostscript (`http://www.cs.wisc.edu/~ghost/`), which turns PostScript into forms that can be understood by many printers. You can share non-PostScript printers either via Ghostscript or directly, as described in the upcoming section "PostScript and Non-PostScript Printers." You can even share some printers that Ghostscript doesn't support using native drivers on your clients. Unfortunately, in this case you won't be able to test local printing. If possible, test local printing using a PostScript printer using the physical port to which you intend to connect the ultimate destination printer, even if you only connect the PostScript printer temporarily. When you switch to the non-PostScript printer and change the clients' drivers, you'll eliminate some possible sources of problems, simplifying debugging. In all cases, you can use lights and other displays on the printers as a diagnostic tool. If a light blinks soon after you submit a print job, you can at least be confident that the printer has received the print job, even if it has become corrupted and can't print properly. If no lights blink when they should, chances are Samba or your local print queue is somehow losing the print job. Many printers can print status pages when you select appropriate options from their panels, and these may also offer clues for debugging printing problems. Consult your printer's documentation for details on how to interpret lights, create status page printouts, and so on.

Defining a Printer Share

Once you've set the global options necessary to support your local printing system, you can move on to defining a printer share. These share definitions are very similar to file shares, as described in Chapter 5, but they use a handful of additional parameters and are treated in unique ways by Samba and its clients.

A Basic Printer Share Definition

In many respects, printer shares are simpler than file shares, but many Samba options can be used on both types of shares. Some differences are important and may influence how you create printer shares:

Access: Printer shares *must* be accessible for read/write access. You might think this means you must specify read only = No or one of its antonyms, but this isn't so. Instead, Samba provides a special access option for printer shares: printable (or its synonym, print ok). When set to Yes (the default value is No), Samba accepts print access to the share. Files submitted for printing are printed via the print command. In essence, the printable parameter alone defines a share as a printer share. Everything else is elaboration.

Printer name: If you don't provide any special parameters for specifying the printer, Samba tries to print to a queue with the same name as the share name. For instance, if you create a share called [laser], Samba tries to print files to a local queue called laser. You can override this setting by using the printer name parameter (or its synonym, printer), as in printer name = hp5000 to print jobs to the local queue called hp5000.

Spool directory: Like all Samba shares, a printer share is associated with a directory on the Linux system. The default directory is /tmp, but you can specify another directory with the directory or path parameters, as described in Chapter 5. In the case of printer shares, this directory is known as the *Samba spool directory.* Unix printing systems also have spool directories, but the Samba spool directory is distinct from these local print queue spool directories. You can safely use a single Samba spool directory for all of a server's printer queues, or you can use separate directories if you prefer. When it's submitted for printing, a file is first stored in the Samba spool directory, then passed via the printing system to its spool directory, and then sent to the printer.

Local permissions: Typically, the Samba spool directory must be writeable to all users, or at least to everybody who's authorized to use the share. Another good practice is to set the *sticky bit* on the Samba spool directory (by typing chmod o+t */path/to/dir*, where */path/to/dir* is the Samba spool directory name). Setting the sticky bit ensures that only root and the file's owner may delete or rename a file in the directory. This feature is a useful security tool on directories in which many users store files, such as a Samba spool directory and the /tmp directory.

Print file permissions: Printed files sometimes contain sensitive data. To protect such data from being read by unauthorized individuals, you might want to set create mask = 0600 in a Samba printer share definition. This parameter, described in Chapter 5, prevents anybody but root and the file's owner from reading the file. Of course, in printing, physical security around the printer may be necessary when printing sensitive data, or else electronic security on the server will be for naught.

In practice, a typical Samba printer share looks like this:

```
[laser]
    comment = Laser printer in Room 343
    path = /var/spool/samba
    browseable = Yes
    writeable = No
    printable = Yes
    create mask = 0600
```

This share stores files in /var/spool/samba as Samba spools them to the local print queue called laser. Of course, the spool directory must exist and should have appropriate permissions. Typing the following commands will do well:

```
# mkdir /var/spool/samba
# chmod 0777 /var/spool/samba
# chmod o+t /var/spool/samba
```

Defining a Share for All Printers

Frequently, a Samba server handles several printers, and each share definition would look much like every other. As an aid to Samba configuration, the server provides a unique share name that automatically creates Samba print queues for every printer defined on the local server. Using this share name works much like defining an ordinary print queue, but with a few special differences. Knowing about these—and about when to use and when not to use this feature—can help simplify your Samba printer configuration.

Creating a [printers] Share

The special name for handling all your local printers is called, appropriately enough, [printers]. In many respects, this share is analogous to the [homes] share that creates shares for every user's home directory. Unlike the [homes] definition, though, the [printers] share creates an entry that every user can see for every printer on the server. For instance, if your /etc/printcap file (or its equivalent) defines print queues known as laser, inkjet, and dotmatrix, clients will see printer shares of these names if you include a [printers] share.

Actually defining the [printers] share is much like creating any other printer share. Specific factors you should consider include the following:

Loading the printers: Before you create a [printers] share, you should add the line load printers = Yes to your [global] section. This parameter is required to teach Samba the names of your local print queues.

Browseability: Like the [homes] share, the [printers] share typically includes a browseable = No parameter to prevent a share called PRINTERS from appearing in clients' browse lists.

Share names: The /etc/printcap file supports multiple names for print queues. Samba uses the first name for each queue. Thus, if a local queue is defined using the string lp|laser|hp5000, Samba will share it using the name LP. You can't easily share a Unix printer queue under a name other than the one it uses locally, such as sharing the inkjet queue as epson860.

Samba spool directory: Because one Samba share definition handles all the printer shares, one share directory is the norm for [printers] shares. If you feel compelled to use different directories for these shares, though, you can use a variable in the directory parameter, as in directory = /var/spool/%S to use the share name as the final component of the path to the spool directory.

Custom options: If you need to use different options for different Samba printer shares, you'll have a hard time with the [printers] share. If your server handles several printers and you only need to use special options in one or two shares, though, you can use a [printers] section for most of the printers and create explicit share definitions to override specific printers. For instance, if your system has printers called laser, inkjet, and dotmatrix, you could create a [printers] section to handle the first two printers and a [dotmatrix] share to handle the third printer with its own unique settings.

Overall, a [printers] definition looks much like the definition for the [laser] queue presented earlier:

```
[printers]
    comment = All printers
    path = /var/spool/samba
    browseable = No
    writeable = No
    printable = Yes
    create mask = 0600
```

This definition will create no, one, two, three, or more printer shares, depending upon how many printers are defined locally. Note that using a [printers] share doesn't preclude using additional printer shares. For instance, you can use a [printers] share for your regular printers and also create a separate printer share definition for a fax queue, as described in the upcoming section "Creating a Local Fax Queue."

Advantages and Disadvantages of a [printers] Share

The primary advantage of using a [printers] share is that it simplifies your printer configuration job. It does this by reducing the number of printer shares you must create initially and by reducing or eliminating the need to reconfigure Samba if you add, delete, or change your local print queues. A benefit that derives from this simplification is that you're less likely to make a mistake; if you don't need to retype or cut and paste queue names and share definitions half a dozen times, you greatly reduce the chance of a typo creeping in and causing problems.

Unfortunately, the [printers] share definition isn't without its problems. The greatest of these may be its inflexibility. If your printers all require custom handling, a single [printers] share would force you to print using a single print command and other features, depriving you of capabilities or otherwise causing problems.

Another potential problem is with naming. A common convention on Unix systems is to provide multiple names, starting with short and nondescriptive names (such as lp) and working up to more descriptive names (such as hp5000). Because Samba picks the first name for each queue, this practice results in Samba clients seeing only the least informative printer names. Of course, if you pick a more informative name as each queue's first name in /etc/printcap, this problem vanishes. On the whole, though, a [printers] share can be a substantial time-saver, particularly if a print server handles more than a couple of printers.

PostScript and Non-PostScript Printers

One of the trickiest aspects of using Samba as a print server for non-Unix systems is in handling different printer languages. Unix-like computers have traditionally worked on the assumption that printers use the PostScript page description language, so Unix applications typically produce PostScript output for printing. Most Samba clients, though, such as Windows and OS/2, frequently work with non-PostScript printers. You can share such printers via Samba, but when doing so, you're faced with a choice: Do you share the printer as it is, using client printer drivers for the specific printer model, or do you configure the server to convert PostScript to the printer's native language and share the printer as if it were a PostScript model? Understanding the Unix, Samba, and client printing systems will help you understand the merits of each approach and choose which printing method to implement.

Printing to a PostScript or Ghostscript-Driven Printer

The simplest case in sharing a printer via Samba is sharing a PostScript printer. In this case, the Samba client must use a PostScript driver, so essentially you don't have any choice to make about using PostScript or a native driver; the native driver *is* a PostScript driver. A printer share such as the [laser] share shown earlier in "A Basic Printer Share Definition" will work.

NOTE PostScript was developed by Adobe, which licenses PostScript interpreters to printer manufacturers. Many midrange and high-end printers sold today support PostScript but use PostScript interpreters written by others. Such printers are sometimes called *PostScript-compatible* printers. For the purposes of this discussion, the difference between true Adobe PostScript printers and PostScript-compatible printers is unimportant. Some printers, though, are advertised as supporting PostScript but do so through a PostScript interpreter on the computer rather than on the printer. This approach is equivalent to using Ghostscript to interpret the PostScript file, and such printers are not PostScript printers for the purposes of this discussion.

If you've installed a non-PostScript printer to work from the Samba computer itself, chances are you've configured it to use Ghostscript to convert PostScript to the printer's native language. Most printer-configuration tools, including those provided with most Linux distributions, Mac OS X, and CUPS, provide point-and-click selection of a printer model, or at least of a class of printers (such as those using the Printer Control Language, or PCL). If you've configured your printer in this way and can print PostScript files to your printer using your system's native printing commands (such as lpr sample.ps), then you can treat the printer just like a PostScript native printer from Samba. Neither Samba nor Samba's clients will know or care that the underlying Unix print queue passes the file through Ghostscript in order to print.

One of the most important parts of configuring a Samba print queue is actually not a Samba configuration option at all: It's selecting, installing, and configuring a printer driver on the client. The upcoming section "Delivering Printer Drivers to Clients" describes how to use Samba to help automate this process. This section presupposes that you can get a printer driver working through more mundane methods first, though. Depending upon your OS, several sources for PostScript printer drivers exist:

The OS itself: Modern OSs invariably ship with PostScript printer drivers. Sometimes these drivers are identified as "generic PostScript" drivers, which should work with most PostScript and Ghostscript-driven printers. Other drivers are identified by the printer model.

The printer manufacturer: Printer manufacturers invariably provide drivers for their printers. Many limit their support to recent versions of Windows, though, so you may need to look elsewhere if you're using a non-Windows OS.

Adobe: The creator of PostScript makes Windows and Mac OS Classic PostScript drivers available from its Web site at http://www.adobe.com. These drivers are licensed only for use on printers that ship with PostScript interpreters licensed from Adobe, though.

CUPS: The CUPS project includes PostScript drivers for Windows NT/200*x*/XP clients, available from http://www.cups.org/software.php. These drivers are designed to be installed on a Samba server for automatic delivery to clients, as described in the upcoming section "Delivering Printer Drivers to Clients."

Third parties: Depending upon your OS, certain third parties make drivers available. Most notable of these are drivers for CUPS and other Unix printing systems, such as those available from the GIMP Print project (http://gimp-print.sourceforge.net) and TurboPrint (http://www.turboprint.de/english.html). Most of these drivers are actually geared toward creating PostScript-compatible queues for non-PostScript printers, though. Other variants of this source are drivers that ship with specific products. In some sense, most Unix applications that print qualify in this way because they include their own PostScript-generation code. The same is true of most DOS applications that support PostScript printers.

If you're using Ghostscript or can't find your model in your printer list, Apple LaserWriter drivers usually work well for monochrome printing, and QMS magicolor drivers frequently work well with color printers. You may be able to find drivers that fit your needs better than these, though; trying several drivers may be necessary if you need support for features such as multiple sheet feeders, wide-carriage printers, or printers with duplexing features.

Some drivers and printing systems, including those that ship with Mac OS Classic, Adobe's Windows drivers, and CUPS (both the CUPS drivers for Windows and CUPS used on Unix clients), support PostScript Printer Definition (PPD) files. These files are supplements to a generic PostScript printer driver. The PPD file tells the driver about a printer's characteristics, such as how wide its margins must be, what its maximum resolution is, and so on. If a client's printer driver uses a PPD file, you can install the driver once and then install different PPD files for each printer available to the client, thus saving space on printer drivers. Adobe provides PPDs for many printers at http://www.adobe.com/products/printerdrivers/winppd.html, and most PostScript printer manufacturers make PPD files available for their models, as well. The Linux Printing Web site contains more information about PPDs, including additional pointers on where to find them, at http://www.linuxprinting.org/ppd-doc.html. (Despite this Web site's name, it hosts information that's relevant to many non-Linux platforms.)

Once you've installed a printer driver, you should be able to modify its settings. Figure 6-1 shows the Properties dialog box for the Hewlett-Packard LaserJet 4000 driver that ships with Windows XP. You can pull up a similar dialog box by opening the Printers and Faxes tool in the Control Panel, right-clicking the object for the Windows printer queue, and picking Properties from the resulting pop-up menu. You can adjust various options from the tabs across the top of this dialog box. Many of these tabs also sport buttons, such as Printing Preferences in Figure 6-1, that open new dialog boxes on which you can set more options. Although the details differ from one OS to another, and even from one driver to another, dialog boxes such as these enable you to customize many features of your printer driver. You may be able to fix problems, such as stray form feeds when print jobs end, print resolutions set too low, and so on, from these dialog boxes.

Figure 6-1. Most OSs provide dialog boxes from which you can adjust many printer driver settings.

One common problem results when client drivers place Control+D characters or mode-switching commands to tell the printer to enter PostScript mode at the start of print jobs. Such features confuse some Unix print queues, resulting in the printing of PostScript code rather than the desired formatted output. In Samba 2.2.*x* and earlier, you can overcome this problem by including a postscript = Yes parameter in the Samba printer share definition. This parameter tells Samba to add a PostScript comment (%!) to the start of each print job, which usually convinces the local print queue to treat the file as a PostScript file rather than a plain-text file. This parameter has been removed from Samba 3.0, though, so if you're using a recent version of Samba, you can't use this workaround. If you suspect you're having problems because of incorrectly identified PostScript files, try these solutions:

Set client driver options: Try looking for options in the client-side driver to disable the addition of Control+D characters or other extraneous material to the PostScript output. Such options can be buried quite deep in the printer driver settings, though.

Try new client drivers: Try another source for a client printer driver; one driver may work better than another. If your driver uses PPD files, try a different one, even if it means switching from a PPD file designed for your printer to another printer's PPD file.

Use a raw queue: Many Unix print queues try to autodetect the file type, which is part of the problem. If your printer is a PostScript model, you should be able to use it via a *raw* queue, which does absolutely no processing on the input files. If you're using a Ghostscript-driven printer, try using a simpler filter on a custom queue—a filter that always passes the data through Ghostscript, rather than trying to detect the file type, should do the job.

Modify the `print` command: Some printing systems enable you to turn off the print filters, which are the scripts or other programs that try to identify and modify files to be printed, by passing a special parameter to the printing system. You can create a custom `print command` parameter that includes this option, in which case the queue acts much like a raw queue.

Printing to a Non-PostScript Printer

You have two choices for how to use a non-PostScript printer from a Samba client:

Use Ghostscript: You can configure a conventional Unix print queue, which processes input as PostScript and passes it through Ghostscript to convert it to the printer's native format. Using such a queue from Samba is just like using a true PostScript printer, as described in the preceding section, "Printing to a PostScript or Ghostscript-Driven Printer."

Use a raw queue: You can configure a raw queue to the printer in question. This queue won't touch the contents of the file to be printed. When using such a queue, you use the printer's native drivers on your clients.

Selecting which method to use isn't easy. The next section, "Choosing a Printing Method," addresses this question. For now, though, consider the requirements for sharing a printer using a raw queue. Fundamentally, you need two things to do this:

A raw queue: You must create a queue on the Samba server that won't modify the files being sent through it for printing. Many Unix printing systems use *smart filters*, which attempt to identify the file type and print it. Unfortunately, most smart filters become confused by files intended for at least some types of printers. Some smart filters can correctly identify some file types, though, such as PCL files. If your smart filter handles such files, you can use a single local queue for both PostScript and native-driver printing.

Client drivers: You must install drivers for the printer on the client computers, just as you would for PostScript drivers. In fact, you can use many of the same sources for both types of drivers. In particular, your OS and the printer manufacturer are good sources. Other sources, such as the GIMP Print project for Unix-like OSs, can also be important for some platforms.

Once you install the client drivers and configure a raw queue, you should be able to print, using most or all of the client driver's normal features, as if the printer were connected directly to the client computer. Some printers and drivers provide features that rely upon bidirectional communication, though, and these features won't work when using the printer via a Samba server. For instance, options to read the amount of ink or toner available in a printer won't work. You must rely upon Unix tools such as the Printer Utility Program (PUP; http://pup.sourceforge.net) to control these aspects of printers directly from the Samba server computer.

Some printers support both PostScript and some other printing method, such as PCL. In such cases, you have a choice about what client drivers and printing method to use, just as you would if the printer were connected directly to the client. In many respects, the choice of which method to use mirrors the decision of whether to use a raw queue and native drivers or a Ghostscript-driven queue and PostScript drivers on a non-PostScript printer.

Choosing a Printing Method

If you want to share a non-PostScript printer, you must decide whether to share the printer using a raw queue and non-PostScript client drivers or a queue that uses Ghostscript and PostScript client drivers. Each approach has its advantages and disadvantages:

Samba server configuration: Configuring the Samba server to convert Post-Script into a printer's native format can be easy or tricky, depending upon the printer and the server OS's printer configuration tools. Check the Linux Printing Web site's printer list (http://www.linuxprinting.org/printer_list.cgi) for information about configuring specific printer models.

Ghostscript printer support: In extreme cases, Ghostscript may not support your printer. Check the Linux Printing Web site for details. If your printer isn't supported, you may still be able to share it from Samba but only using a raw queue and native client drivers. In extreme cases, though, you may not be able to share the printer at all. A few models (mostly very low-end laser printers) require bidirectional communication with Windows drivers to operate. Such printers can't be shared via Samba.

CPU requirements: When printing text or raster graphics (that is, graphics described in terms of lines, circles, and so on), Ghostscript converts the text or raster graphics into bitmap graphics for the benefit of the printer. This operation takes a certain amount of CPU time, and the CPU requirements of this conversion increase with higher printer resolutions and when printing color files. By contrast, when using native client drivers and a raw queue, the server's job doesn't consume much CPU time, but the clients may need to create a bitmap. Thus, if you're using an old computer as a print server, raw queues with native client drivers can improve printing performance. If your server has a fast CPU, though, this difference may not be important or may even favor Ghostscript-driven queues and PostScript drivers.

Network bandwidth requirements: Many low-end printers ship with very primitive support for fonts and raster graphics. When printing to such devices using native drivers, clients must create a bitmap describing the page, even if the page is filled with nothing but text. Such bitmaps will chew up a lot of bandwidth on your network, which can degrade network performance. PostScript files, by contrast, are usually much smaller, which can speed network transfers. This effect is likely to be much smaller, or conceivably even reversed, when printing bitmapped graphics files such as scanned documents or digital photographs.

Support for printer features: Many printers provide features such as different printer resolutions, duplexers, multiple paper trays, and so on. Accessing these features from a Ghostscript-driven queue can be difficult. If you need to do so, you may need to create multiple queues (both local printer queues on the server and Samba shares accessing these queues). Each queue calls Ghostscript with options to set a particular resolution or sends a special file to enable or disable a printer feature. By contrast, if you use a raw queue and native client drivers, those native drivers usually provide more direct access to these features.

Print quality: When printing to a non-PostScript printer using Ghostscript, it's Ghostscript that's most responsible for the output's quality. Ghostscript provides excellent drivers for some printers but not for others. Thus, print quality can swing either way, favoring a Ghostscript queue and PostScript drivers or a raw queue and native drivers.

PostScript compatibility: Some clients need PostScript compatibility in their printers. For instance, some page layout programs work best with PostScript printers. If you use such programs, setting up Samba with Ghostscript-driven queues can be an inexpensive way to convert cheap non-PostScript printers into PostScript-compatible printers. On the other hand, some sites rely on advanced or exotic PostScript features, and for such sites, nothing short of a printer using a genuine Adobe PostScript interpreter will do.

Print consistency: Some client programs have a tendency to reformat documents if you switch your default printer. This event can be extremely disorienting and can add to your workload if you must modify a document's formatting to get it to print properly on a new printer. If you use nothing but Ghostscript-driven queues, you can standardize on a single PostScript driver for all your clients (assuming they all run the same OS), which can create more consistent formatting across printers, even if they're very different printers.

Overall, I recommend trying to print using both raw and Ghostscript-driven queues. If your Unix print queue is smart enough to correctly identify PostScript and the printer's native language, you can install both a PostScript and a native driver on the client and link both of them to one Samba printer share.

If your Unix print queue misidentifies files in the printer's native format, you can create two Unix print queues, link them to two Samba printer shares, and install two printer drivers on the client. You can also create multiple Ghostscript-driven queues, each of which activates different printer features, to test how Ghostscript manages these features.

It's entirely possible that neither approach will be a clear winner. For instance, you might prefer a Ghostscript-driven queue for text files and a native queue for graphics files. In such a case, you can leave both queues installed and running and let users select the best queue on a job-by-job basis.

Using the *print command* Parameter

The print command parameter is conventionally used for adjusting a Samba printer share to pass custom parameters to a print queue, use an exotic printing system, or the like. Such uses of this parameter can help Samba do precisely what you want it to do. This parameter is unusually flexible, though. By specifying a command that's only marginally related to printing, or even completely unrelated to printing, you can create a Samba "printer" share that does other tasks, such as faxing, creating Adobe Portable Document Format (PDF) files, or backing up data to tape or CD-R. The following sections describe printing and related uses of print command. Chapter 14 and Chapter 16 expand upon this theme by describing the use of print command for tasks that aren't related to printing.

Tweaking the Printing Command for a Fussy Queue

Normally, if you've set the printing parameter correctly, Samba sets print command to a reasonable default. Sometimes, though, you might want to adjust this default. For instance, you might want to create a share that automatically prints multiple copies of the print job, that adds or omits a header, or that sets the name of the print job to some specific value. Table 6-1 shows the default values for print command based on the printing parameter's setting. To modify these values, you should first consult your printing system's documentation; for instance, you might type man lpr to learn how lpr works on your system.

As an example, suppose you're using CUPS on the print server, and you want to create a Samba share that prints two copies of a file and submits the job using the lowest available priority so that the job won't disrupt more important print jobs. A look at the CUPS man page for the lp command shows that the -n option, followed by the number of copies, does the first task; and -q, followed by a priority value between 1 and 100, does the second. Examining Table 6-1, you see that the default value for print command with CUPS is lp -d'%p' %s; rm %s. You can modify this value, adding your custom options, and enter the following parameter in your share definition:

```
print command = lp -c -d'%p' -n 2 -q 1 %s; rm %s
```

TIP If you compiled Samba with the --enable-cups option and set printing = CUPS, the server won't accept a print command parameter; instead it uses the CUPS API for all printing. If you have problems getting print command to work, you might try setting printing to some other value and then tweaking the print command even for shares that wouldn't ordinarily need such modifications.

When setting print command, remember that Samba doesn't automatically delete the files submitted by the clients. The rm %s command that comes at the end of print command in this example does this job. If your print spooler doesn't remove the print job, be sure to include this option, lest your Samba server's available disk space be consumed by old print jobs.

In addition to submitting jobs via typical printing commands such as lp or lpr, you can use more exotic printing systems or create your own printing scripts. For instance, if your network includes a printer that understands AppleTalk but not other protocols, you can install the Netatalk package (http://netatalk.sourceforge.net or http://rsug.itd.umich.edu/software/netatalk.html) and use its pap command to submit print jobs to the AppleTalk printer:

```
print command = pap -p lwriter %s; rm %s
```

If you find yourself creating an unusually long command, you can write a script and call it. For instance, you might write a script that submits a print job, sends an e-mail about it to a specific account, and enters information about the print job in a database for accounting purposes. You can use such a script much as you would any other printing command.

If you customize your print command, particularly via tools that don't match those set via your printing parameter, you should keep in mind that other support functions may not work correctly. For instance, no matter what your printing system, if you use pap for submitting print jobs, the lprm command, lpq command, and similar ancillary commands won't be set correctly. In some cases, you may not be able to set appropriate substitutes. Netatalk's printing client programs lack equivalents for most of these Samba parameters, for instance. This eventuality won't prevent Samba from accepting print jobs or printing them, but it will reduce clients' ability to monitor and control the status of their print jobs.

Using print command *to Achieve Greater Ends*

In addition to tweaking the printing mechanism or using unusual printing systems that aren't directly supported by Samba, print command enables you to accomplish highly unusual printing or printing-like tasks. For instance, you can create a fax queue or a share that creates PDF files. Creating such shares can greatly simplify certain tasks; for instance, you can omit modems or PDF-generation software on most clients in favor of an ordinary PostScript printer driver (which might be used by other printer shares, too).

Creating a Fax Share

A fax share enables a Samba server with a fax modem to handle outgoing faxes for any number of clients. The key to a fax share is the use of a custom print command line that calls a script or program to send a fax when fed an input file. Of course, a fax share must deal with a couple of unusual requirements:

Sending a fax: You must configure the Samba server in such a way that it can send a fax. This means the server must have a fax modem, as well as fax software, such as HylaFAX (http://www.hylafax.org) or mgetty+sendfax (http://alpha.greenie.net/mgetty/).

Determining a fax number: The program called by print command must have some way of determining the telephone number to which the fax should be sent. This task can be handled in several ways. One approach uses a script to scan the input file for a fax number and send it automatically. Of course, this approach then requires that the fax number be encoded in the input file in some form that the script can parse. A second approach is to use a bidirectional tool to send a query back to the client to obtain the fax number. The following sections describe this approach in more detail.

Creating a Local Fax Queue

To prepare a Samba fax queue using the popular mgetty+sendfax and a tool to enable Windows clients to provide fax numbers, you must first install and configure mgetty+sendfax. To do so, follow these steps:

1. **Install mgetty+sendfax**: You can obtain this software package from its Web site. It also ships with many Unix-like OSs, usually under a name such as mgetty, mgetty-fax, mgetty+sendfax, or mgetty-sendfax.

2. **Locate the mgetty+sendfax configuration files**: If the software came with your OS, its configuration files may reside in /etc/mgetty, /etc/mgetty+sendfax, or a similar location. If you compile the software yourself, the configuration files will reside in /usr/local/etc/mgetty+sendfax by default.

3. **Set a header**: The faxheader file contains information that appears at the top of each fax page. You should change the string not configured to your fax number so recipients know who has sent the fax.

4. **Edit sendfax.config**: This configuration file contains configuration options for several faxing features. Most of these options are well commented, so peruse the configuration file and change anything that seems necessary. Of particular interest are the fax-devices option, which sets the device file associated with your fax modem, and the fax-id line, which sets your fax number to be reported to the receiving fax machine.

5. **Edit faxrunq.config**: This configuration file tells the fax queue software (faxrunq) how to process faxes. As with sendfax.config, these options are well commented. You should pay particular attention to the fax-devices line, which should match the option of the same name in sendfax.config.

6. **Authorize users to fax**: The fax.allow configuration file contains the names of users who should be allowed to send faxes, one username per line. You may want to create a special account for faxing—say, faxuser. Add this username to fax.allow. Also, check the permissions on the /var/spool/fax/outgoing directory. Your chosen fax user should be able to write to this directory. Some installations assign this directory to a group called fax, give group write access to the directory, and add all fax users to this group.

7. **Launch faxrunqd**: This daemon monitors the fax queue directory (usually /var/spool/fax/outgoing) for fax jobs. When they appear, the daemon sends the faxes on their way. If you installed mgetty+sendfax from a package provided with your OS, chances are it came with a SysV or other startup script to launch faxrunqd. If not, you can create a startup script yourself or launch the daemon from a local startup script. This process is akin to launching Samba, as described in Chapter 3, except that you can't use a super server to handle faxrunqd. For testing purposes, you can simply type **faxrunqd &** as root.

Just as with ordinary printer queues, you should test your fax queue locally before attempting to use it from a Samba client. If you can't send a fax, you should troubleshoot faxing on the Samba server before you proceed with installing Samba-specific fax software. To send a fax from the system on which mgetty+sendfax is installed, you can use the sendfax program, but this program requires an appropriately formatted file for sending. This file must be in the fax G3 format. To generate such a file, you can use Ghostscript to convert a PostScript file to G3 format:

```
$ gs -dNOPAUSE -dBATCH -sOutputFile=sample.g3 -sDEVICE=faxg3 sample.ps
```

This command converts the *sample.ps* file into *sample.g3*, which is suitable for input to sendfax. Of course, you must have a PostScript file for this conversion, but that's easy to come by—most Unix programs that can print can create PostScript files. You can then send the fax using a command like this:

```
$ faxspool 555-0226 sample.g3
```

This command sends the *sample.g3* file to the fax machine at 555-0226. Of course, you should adjust the telephone number and filename in a way that's suitable for you. If all goes well, the system should, after a delay of up to a minute, send the fax to the fax machine whose telephone number you specified. The delay occurs because faxrunqd checks the outgoing spool directory only every minute or so. If the fax isn't sent or doesn't appear correctly, start debugging. Common problems include missing authorization in the fax.allow file, a faxrunqd daemon that's not running, and serial port or modem drivers that aren't loaded. If you have problems, you might also want to try using the sendfax command rather than faxspool. The sendfax command sends the fax immediately, without first spooling it and involving faxrunqd. If you can send the fax using sendfax, then concentrate on authorization and faxrunqd-related issues. If you can't send the fax using sendfax, then chances are the problem is with the serial port configuration or settings specific to your fax modem, such as those set in sendfax.config.

Installing Respond

Once you've gotten faxing working, at least minimally, you can begin integrating the faxing system and Samba. One tool for this is Respond (http://www.boerde.de/~horstf/), which includes a Perl script to run on the Unix box as a Samba printing command and a program to run on a Windows box to collect fax-specific information from the user. To install Respond, follow these steps:

1. **Download the Perl script**: The Perl script is called printfax-*x.y*.pl, where *x.y* is the version number. Hereafter, I refer to this script as printfax.pl; you can rename it or change subsequent references, as you see fit.

2. **Install the Perl script**: Place the Perl script in some convenient location on your Samba server, such as /usr/local/bin. Be sure the script is executable. You must also have a Perl interpreter installed. Most Unix-like systems ship with one, or you can go to http://www.perl.com to locate a version for your OS.

3. **Download the Respond program**: This program is a Windows executable file. It contains no special installer program, but you'll have to extract the main file with unzip or an equivalent program.

4. **Install the Respond program**: Copy the RESPOND.EXE program to the Startup folder on any Windows system from which you want to be able to send a fax. You should then either reboot or manually launch Respond.

CAUTION   The Respond program is a server that runs on the Windows computer. This server is quite simple; when contacted, it merely presents a dialog box to the user and returns the information that the user enters. Nonetheless, running servers unnecessarily can be a security risk, particularly when the computers in question are exposed directly to the Internet. Therefore, I recommend using Respond only on networks that are well protected by a firewall.

Creating a Samba Fax Share

The actual Samba fax share is fairly straightforward. This share looks much like any other Samba printer share, but it uses the print command parameter to pass the received PostScript file through the printfax.pl script. This script in turn contacts the client to receive the fax number and sends the result as a fax. You can use the force user parameter to have the share send faxes using the account you created earlier for this purpose. If you don't do this, you'll need to authorize all your users to send faxes by adding their names to the fax.allow file. The share looks like this:

```
[fax]
    comment = Fax
    path = /var/spool/samba
    force user = faxuser
    printable = Yes
    print command = ( /usr/local/bin/printfax.pl %I %s %U %m; rm %s ) &
```

Once you've entered this share, or one modeled after it, into your smb.conf file and restarted Samba, you can try using the fax share from a Windows client on which you've installed the Respond software. To do this, of course, you must first install a PostScript printer driver and point it at the FAX share. (The upcoming section "Delivering Printer Drivers to Clients" describes printer driver installation in more detail.) Once you've done this, try printing a test document. The Print Test Page button in the Windows print queue's Properties dialog box should do nicely. If all goes well, you'll see a dialog box such as the one shown in Figure 6-2. (On some systems, the dialog box won't pop up immediately; instead, a new item will appear in the Windows task bar. Click it to see the Respond dialog box.) Enter the requested information, and click OK to send the fax. The receiver's fax number is the most important piece of information; the other fields are much less important. Be sure to include the area code if the number isn't local, as well as any digits required to dial an outside line or a long-distance number.

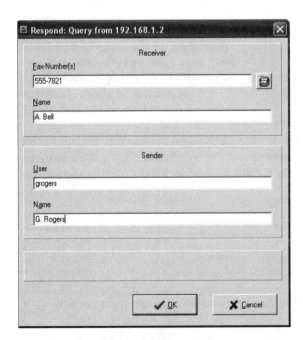

Figure 6-2. Respond's purpose is to obtain fax-specific information and return it to the Perl script running on the Samba server.

If all goes well, the Samba server should send the fax within a minute or so of you clicking OK on the client. If your network is particularly busy, though, you might encounter delays as a result of network congestion. A delay can also occur if other fax jobs are in the queue.

The Respond Web site includes some ancillary programs, such as scripts you can use as values for the lpq command and lprm command parameters. The readme.txt file provides additional information about this package, including debugging information.

One problem with the Respond solution is that it doesn't work for non-Windows clients, at least not in the same way it works for Windows clients. Other options are available, but they tend to be very delicate and awkward. For instance, you can write a script to scan the PostScript file for a fax number and then send the file to that number. A Web search turns up several examples of such scripts, but the ones I've found are old and don't work as advertised. If you want to use a Samba computer as a fax server for non-Windows clients, you may want to investigate HylaFAX, which provides such functionality directly, without using Samba.

Creating a PDF-Generation Queue

Today's demand for documents that can be moved electronically is substantial and has spawned quite a few file formats—plain text, HTML, various word processor file formats, PostScript, and so on. One format that's particularly well suited to repro-ducing the contents of a printed document is PDF. This format, created by Adobe, is loosely related to PostScript although it's different in many details. One of the most important of these details is that PDF files are compressed, which makes them a far better choice for distribution via the Internet, where download times can be an important limitation for PostScript.

Assorted vendors, including Adobe, produce PDF-generation tools. These tools often look like printer drivers to programs, enabling you to generate a PDF file from any application, much as you would print to a printer. If you've ever considered acquiring such tools, you may be interested to know that you can use Samba to do the job—or more precisely, you can use Samba with some substantial help from Ghostscript and other tools on the host OS.

The key that unlocks Samba's ability to generate PDF files is the fact that Ghost-script can do so. Thus, you can create a Samba printer share that calls Ghostscript via the print command parameter. Ghostscript can convert the PostScript generated by the client's printer driver into a PDF file. A share that accomplishes this goal looks like this:

```
[smbpdf]
    comment = PDF Generator
    path = /var/spool/samba
    printable = Yes
    print command = gs -dNOPAUSE -dBATCH -q -sDEVICE=pdfwrite \
                    -sOutputFile=%H/%s.pdf %s; rm %s
```

When this share receives a PostScript file to be printed, it passes it through Ghostscript (gs) using the specified parameters. Of particular interest are the -sDEVICE=pdfwrite option, which tells Ghostscript to create a PDF file, and the

`-sOutputFile=%H/%s.pdf` option, which tells Ghostscript to store the file in the user's home directory using the submitted filename with a `.pdf` extension added.

In practice, a user will print to the share as if it were any other printer share; it will be indistinguishable from other printer shares from the clients, except for the share name and comment. Soon after sending a file to the printer, though, a new file will appear in the user's home directory. Unfortunately, this file will most likely have a very ugly name, such as `smbprn.00000011.Rf1uvj.pdf`. You can give the PDF file a prettier name by changing `%s.pdf` to something else, but such a change is likely to increase the probability of a name collision. For instance, using `your-file.pdf` as the filename will work, but if a user tries creating several PDFs in sequence, only the last one will be available because each job will replace the preceding job. Of course, users can change the names of the PDFs they generate just as they can change the names of other files.

Depending upon the size and type of the file and the speed of the Samba server, PDF generation can take anywhere from a fraction of a second to several minutes. The output file will be as good as Ghostscript produces. Because Ghostscript and typical Windows PostScript printer drivers don't support all PDF features, you won't be able to control some PDF features if you use this method of generation. Ghostscript is also best at handling the standard set of PostScript and PDF fonts (Times, Helvetica, and Courier) or fonts embedded in the PostScript file in PostScript Type 1 form. TrueType fonts are frequently embedded in files in such a way that Ghostscript converts them to bitmap format. The result frequently prints fairly well, at least on typical home or office printers, but the fonts don't scale well to screen resolutions, so they look chunky and are slow to appear. Such fonts also aren't likely to look the best on high-resolution printing equipment, such as image setters. Keeping these facts in mind, and adjusting your use of fonts appropriately, will help you get the most out of a Samba PDF-generation share.

Unlike the Respond-based fax share presented earlier, a Samba PDF-generation share like this one works as well with Mac OS, Unix, OS/2, or other clients as it does with Windows clients. You can generate a PDF from another Unix-like system with Samba by sending the file using `smbclient`:

```
$ smbclient //RUMBA/SMBPDF
added interface ip=192.168.1.3 bcast=192.168.1.255 nmask=255.255.255.0
Password:
Domain=[RINGWORLD] OS=[Unix] Server=[Samba 3.0.1]
smb: \> print sample.ps
putting file sample.ps as sample.ps (41.6 kb/s) (average 41.6 kb/s)
```

Alternatively, you can create a regular print queue on the client and tell it to use `smbprint`, which is a script that passes a file to be printed via `smbclient`. Precisely how to do this depends on your printing system and OS. Most text-based and GUI printer configuration tools on Unix-like systems include options to use an SMB/CIFS printer.

Delivering Printer Drivers to Clients

Configuring Samba to make printer shares available is only part of the task of getting printing working on a network. Another side of the story is installing printer drivers on clients. Ordinarily, if you don't take any steps but those described in earlier sections of this chapter, you can install a driver from any of the sources described earlier in "Printing to a PostScript or Ghostscript-Driven Printer." This process can be tedious, though, and Samba provides a way to automate the process: You can tell Samba where to look for printer drivers for Windows clients. When the clients try to use the share, they can automatically download and install the drivers. This process can be a great time-saver when you're setting up a network with many clients.

NOTE Automating printer driver delivery is most important for Windows clients. Unix-like systems tend to assume that the printer is a PostScript model, so no printer driver delivery is necessary; simply configure your queues as PostScript queues (using Ghostscript, if necessary), and tell the clients that the printers are PostScript models. This procedure works well for Mac OS clients, as well. Furthermore, you may want to use another printing protocol when your printing clients are Unix-like systems. Chapter 1 describes the LPD and IPP systems, which are popular methods of printer sharing in the Unix world.

Installing Drivers Manually

On a network with few clients, or at least with few clients of each type, you might be satisfied to install drivers manually on each client. This approach has the advantage of simplifying your Samba configuration, but it doesn't scale well to networks with more than a handful of clients. To use this approach, you must obtain printer drivers and follow whatever installation method they require for each of your clients.

TIP You can create an ordinary Samba file share in which you store printer drivers. For instance, you can download the latest drivers, extract them from their archive files (if necessary), and drop them in a read-only share called, say, [drivers]. Users can then open this share, launch the driver installation tool, and install the driver. This approach simplifies driver installation by obviating the need to keep track of a driver installation CD-ROM or download drivers from the Internet every time you add a new computer to your network. You can even create separate directories in the driver share for each printer or OS in use on your network.

As an example, consider installing drivers on a Windows XP computer. The procedure is as follows:

1. Open the Printers and Faxes item in the Control Panel. If no printers are installed, you'll see a single icon called Add Printer. If printers are already configured on the system, you'll see their icons, as well.

2. Double-click the Add Printer icon. Windows opens the Add Printer Wizard (see Figure 6-3).

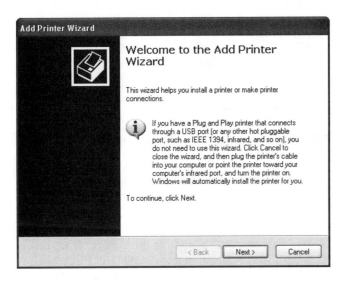

Figure 6-3. The Windows XP Add Printer Wizard enables you to install printer drivers on a single computer.

3. Click Next to continue the installation. The wizard asks if you want to install a driver for a local or a network printer. Select the network printer option.

4. Click Next. The wizard gives you the option of browsing for a printer, connecting to a printer using a NetBIOS-style computer and share name, or connecting to a printer using an Internet URL. Select the NetBIOS-style name and enter the path to the printer share, such as \\RUMBA\LASER to use the LASER share on the RUMBA printer.

5. Click Next. The Connect to Printer dialog box appears. This dialog box says you're connecting to a share that will install a printer driver.

6. Click Yes in the Connect to Printer dialog box. The dialog box disappears, and then another with the same name appears. The new incarnation informs you that a printer driver isn't available.

7. Click OK in the Connect to Printer dialog box. A new Add Printer Wizard dialog box appears in which printer manufacturers and models are listed, as shown in Figure 6-4.

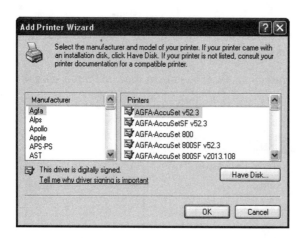

Figure 6-4. You can select drivers from a wide range of printer manufacturers using the Add Printer Wizard.

8. Click your printer manufacturer and select the printer name in the Add Printer Wizard dialog box. If your printer isn't listed, try a compatible model. For some models, you can click the Have Disk button and point to driver files on a CD-ROM, a floppy disk, or downloaded from the Internet. If you're using a non-PostScript printer that's shared from Samba using Ghostscript, try an Apple LaserWriter or QMS magicolor driver for black-and-white or color printers, respectively.

9. Click OK in the second Add Printer Wizard dialog box. Windows will copy files into position. The first Add Printer Wizard dialog box will change to ask if you want to make the new printer the default one. Pick Yes or No, as you see fit.

10. Click Next. The Add Printer Wizard presents a summary of the actions it has taken.

11. Click Finish. The Add Printer Wizard disappears.

You should now see your new printer in the Printers and Faxes window. Right-click the new printer icon, and select Properties. This action opens a Properties dialog box similar to the one shown in Figure 6-1. Click Print Test Page, and Windows will send a print job to the printer. If it doesn't print, you'll have to debug it. Check your Samba log files and evaluate any error messages you receive, either in the log file or on the Windows client. Be sure the directory pointed to by the `directory` or `path` parameter exists and can be written to by the user who's printing. If possible, try accessing the same share from another computer—perhaps another Unix or Unix-like system using `smbclient`.

Creating a [print$] Share

The key to automatic driver delivery using Samba 3.0 and later is a share called PRINT$. This name is hard-coded in Windows clients, so if you want to use automatic printer driver delivery, this is the name you *must* use. Creating this share is fairly straight-forward, but you must then install drivers into it and use the share from additional clients. The next two sections cover these tasks. For now, consider the Samba config-uration task alone.

> **NOTE** Samba 2.2.*x* and earlier included tools for automatically deliv-ering printer drivers to Windows 9*x*/Me clients. These tools were different from the ones described here for Samba 3.0. The old-style delivery mechanism relied upon the presence of a share called [printer$] and required you to manually locate and copy printer files. This procedure, along with the fact that [printer$] only worked with Windows 9*x*/Me clients, made using a [printer$] share awkward and of limited utility. By contrast, [print$] can deliver drivers to Windows 9*x*/Me or Windows NT/200*x*/XP.

The first step in defining a [print$] share is in specifying printer administrators. You accomplish this task with the share-level printer admin parameter, which accepts a comma-delimited list of users:

```
printer admin = grogers,@admin
```

This example gives grogers and members of the NT @admin group printer adminis-tration privileges. Be sure to place a parameter such as this one in the [global] section of your smb.conf file, giving a normal user printer administration access. (This parameter is share level, but chances are you want the same administrators for the PRINT$ share and all printer shares.) If you don't use this parameter, only root will have printer administration privileges. Of course, the [global] section must also contain the normal printer configuration options, and you should have at least one printer share defined.

The next step is to create a [print$] share. This share points to a directory in which printer driver files will be stored and includes a few parameters you might need to modify for your system. An example looks like this:

```
[print$]
    comment = Printer Driver Storage
    directory = /home/samba/drivers
    browseable = No
    read only = Yes
    write list = grogers,root,@admin
```

This share should be read-only to most users, but the printer administrators should be able to write files to the directory in question; hence, `write list` contains the same names that the `printer admin` parameter specifies, plus root (who's included implicitly in `printer admin`). You must, of course, create the directory specified by the `directory` parameter. Windows clients will look for printer drivers in specific subdirectories of this directory, so you must create them, too, as specified in Table 6-2.

Table 6-2. Subdirectories of the [print$] *Share*

Subdirectory Name	Client OS
win40	Windows 9*x*/Me
w32x86	Windows NT/200*x*/XP for *x*86 CPUs
w32alpha	Windows NT for Alpha CPUs
w32mips	Windows NT for MIPS CPUs
w32ppc	Windows NT for PowerPC CPUs

If your network doesn't host the more exotic versions of Windows NT that run on non-*x*86 CPUs, you can safely omit those directories. As with all Samba shares, the case of the directory names is unimportant, assuming you use the default Samba case options.

Installing Drivers into [print$]

For a server to deliver driver files automatically, you must install them on the server. Several different ways of doing this exist. The following pages emphasize driver installation via a Windows NT/200*x*/XP client, but other methods also exist.

NOTE Windows clients use Windows printer drivers installed on the Samba server. Samba doesn't run these drivers itself, and it doesn't pass them to other Unix programs (such as Ghostscript). Thus, installing Windows printer drivers in Samba won't help in a quest to print to a printer that's poorly supported in Unix.

Windows NT/200*x*/XP systems' printer driver installation routines are capable of installing drivers on an SMB/CIFS print server, including Samba servers with [print$] properly defined. The following procedure will accomplish this goal using Windows XP:

1. Using My Network Places, browse to the Samba print server and open the Printers and Faxes folder. (This folder is called the Printers folder on some earlier versions of Windows.)

2. Right-click the name of a printer for which you want to install a driver, and select the Properties item from the pop-up menu. Windows displays a dialog box stating that a printer driver isn't installed and asks if you want to install a driver.

3. Select No in response to the question about installing a driver. This action may not be intuitive, but it's necessary. In response to clicking No, Windows displays a Properties dialog box for the printer.

4. Click the Advanced tab in the Properties dialog box.

5. Click the New Driver button in the Properties dialog box. Windows launches the Add Printer Driver Wizard, which works just like the same wizard when adding a driver locally, as described earlier in "Installing Drivers Manually." Follow steps 3–11 of the procedure described in that section.

 TIP   If your server hosts multiple printer shares and you've already installed the driver you want to use for another share, you can pick the driver you want to install from the pop-down list to the left of the New Driver button rather than clicking that button and going through the Add Printer Driver Wizard procedure.

---

6. When the wizard finishes its work, click Apply or OK in the printer's Properties dialog box. If you click Cancel, the driver installation will be aborted.

At this point, drivers for the OS you used to install the drivers are installed. If you want to install drivers for additional OSs, you must take some extra steps. First, be sure you've got drivers on hand for each OS—you can obtain these drivers from a CD-ROM that shipped with the printer, from a manufacturer's Web site, or from any other source. Next, follow these steps:

1. If you've dismissed the Properties dialog box, bring it back by right-clicking the printer icon in the server's Printers and Faxes folder.

2. Click the Sharing tab in the printer's Properties dialog box.

3. Click the Additional Drivers button in the printer's Properties dialog box. The result is an Additional Drivers dialog box that shows which drivers have been installed for this share, as shown in Figure 6-5.

Figure 6-5. You must install drivers for each target OS independently.

4. Click the box next to each OS for which you want Samba to install drivers.

5. Click OK. Chances are Windows will display a Printer Drivers dialog box asking for the location of the drivers.

6. Enter the complete path to the files in the Copy Files From field, or click the Browse button to locate the directory using a file selector dialog box. When you've entered a path, click OK.

7. Chances are the system will present a list of devices that can be controlled by the driver you've selected. Select one, and click OK.

8. In the Printer Drivers dialog box, click OK. The system should copy the drivers from the location you specified to the Samba PRINT$ share.

If you select multiple OSs in step 4, you'll be asked to locate multiple sets of drivers. Be sure to point to the correct drivers in each case. If you point to an invalid driver, the system will complain and will refuse to install the driver.

Unfortunately, some drivers are shipped in a form that assumes you'll be installing the driver locally rather than to a network share. Such drivers frequently come as single .EXE files, and when you double-click these files in Windows, they launch custom installers. Such drivers can be quite difficult to install into a Samba share for automated delivery. Your best bets if you're faced with such a driver are to place the installer on a share you can access from clients for relatively simple installation from each client, to locate a more network-friendly installer from the printer manufacturer or some other source, or to use a PostScript driver (possibly even one intended for another printer) along with a Samba PostScript or Ghostscript-driven queue.

Using [print$] Drivers

Installing drivers on the Samba server doesn't obviate the need to install drivers on additional clients; however, it does greatly simplify subsequent driver installations. To install drivers on additional clients, you follow the steps outlined earlier in "Installing Drivers Manually" (making whatever minor adjustments are necessary for different versions of Windows). When you reach step 6, though, and click Yes in the Connect to Printer dialog box, the computer shouldn't squawk about a missing driver. Instead of having to locate a driver on a CD-ROM, a floppy disk, or your hard disk, the system should download the driver from the server and install it automatically.

Printing to a Samba share works the same way no matter how you installed the driver. Typically, you select a Print option from an application's File menu. Most applications then display a Print dialog box in which you can select a printer from among those you've installed. The computer processes your print job and sends it to the Samba server, which may perform additional processing before sending it to the printer.

Summary

Samba printer shares are essentially specialized file shares. Many file share configuration options apply equally well to printer shares, although some features aren't much used on printer shares. Printer shares add new features, though, some of which can be quite complex. Most important, a Samba server that shares printers must have printing working locally—or, at least, you must be able to send preformatted data to the printer, even if the Samba server is incapable of producing intelligible printouts by itself. You can then create a printer share, which uses drivers on the client to generate PostScript or printer-specific files for printing. You can install these drivers on the client without direct involvement by the Samba server, or you can use a client to install drivers on the Samba server, which can then automatically deliver the drivers to clients. A variant use of a Samba printer share is as a data-manipulation tool. You can have a Samba printer share "print" to a fax modem, create PDF files, and so on.

#### CHAPTER 7

Managing Samba Accounts

SAMBA SERVERS FREQUENTLY manage files in a way that requires user authentication and tracking. For instance, one person may store a sensitive data file on a Samba server. If another individual tries to access that file, that second user should be prevented from doing so. At the core of this functionality is the concept of an *account*—a set of data structures that help a computer identify one user or another, distinguish between each user, and separate users' data. As a multiuser OS, Unix is no stranger to the concept of an account, but Samba's use of accounts requires some adjustments to the usual Unix way of doing things. Some of these adaptations are a result of SMB/CIFS integration, but others are a consequence of Samba's extreme configurability; the Samba server offers features that interact with Unix accounts in unusual ways, independent of the SMB/CIFS protocols.

One set of account issues relates to passwords. SMB/CIFS supports both unencrypted (or cleartext) and encrypted passwords, and the proper use of Samba requires knowing when to use each type and how to configure both the server and its clients to use these passwords. Samba also offers its own unique twists on Unix permissions. Some of these options have been described in previous chapters, but their full use deserves greater elaboration. Some account features help Samba integrate with a Windows network by mapping between Unix and Windows usernames or by implementing share-level security. It's sometimes desirable to create special accounts on a Samba server to implement Samba-specific functions. Finally, this chapter looks at a few tools that ordinary users can employ to change their passwords and otherwise manage their accounts.

Using Unencrypted Passwords

Chapter 2 introduced Samba password issues. Samba 2.2.*x* and earlier used unencrypted passwords by default, as did very early versions of Windows—Windows 95 prior to OEM Service Release 2 (OSR2) and Windows NT prior to 4.0's Service Pack 3 (SP3). More recent versions of Samba and Windows use encrypted passwords by default, as described in the upcoming section "Using Encrypted Passwords."

Most networks today use encrypted passwords as a way to improve security. None-theless, there are some reasons to use unencrypted passwords, but you should be sure your reasons are good before using this less secure authentication method. If you do choose to use unencrypted passwords, you must be able to tell both Samba and your clients to use them. Linking Samba and the Unix password database together also poses certain challenges, particularly with respect to handling password case, because SMB/CIFS passwords are often case-insensitive, whereas Unix passwords are case-sensitive.

Why Use Unencrypted Passwords?

Before reconfiguring Samba or your clients to use unencrypted passwords, you should be sure your reasons for doing so are valid. Encrypted passwords are harder to compromise than unencrypted passwords, so using encryption can improve your network's security. One reason to favor unencrypted passwords is that they make for easier administration of a system that's accessed both via Samba and via other password-mediated methods (remote text-mode logins, for instance). When Samba uses unencrypted passwords, the server uses the computer's underlying authentication system, just as do other servers and login tools. Thus, using unencrypted passwords means that users can change their passwords using a single tool, and the change applies to all login methods. On the other hand, Samba provides mechanisms that enable the encrypted password tools to change the Unix password when a user changes the Samba password, so this disadvantage of encrypted passwords isn't as large as it might be.

Perhaps the strongest argument in favor of using unencrypted passwords is inertia. Suppose you have a large network that uses unencrypted passwords. As you add new clients that use encrypted passwords by default, you might find it easier to convert them to use unencrypted passwords than to add an encrypted password database to Samba and have users re-enter their passwords. Such a network might continue to use unencrypted passwords because converting it to use encrypted passwords would be a hassle. If you're in this position, and if your network is reasonably secure, the risks of using unencrypted passwords might not outweigh the hassle of converting your password system, which would involve both adding passwords for all users on Samba and modifying all your clients' defaults. On the other hand, continuing to convert new clients to use unencrypted passwords will, over the long run, entail greater effort than will a one-time conversion of your existing systems to use encrypted passwords.

If your network has some very old clients, such as Windows for Workgroups systems, they may not support encrypted passwords at all. If you configure Samba to use encrypted passwords, the server will still accept the cleartext passwords from your older clients, but those passwords (verified against the normal Unix authentication system) may not match the encrypted passwords required by newer clients (and authenticated using Samba's own encrypted password database). If the two passwords don't match, this result may be confusing to your users.

Configuring the Use of Unencrypted Passwords

In Samba, the default setting in version 2.2.*x* and earlier was to use unencrypted passwords. In Samba 3.0, though, this default has changed to use encrypted passwords. In either case, this option is controlled through the global encrypt passwords parameter, which takes a Boolean value.

To be sure you're using unencrypted passwords, enter the following line in your [global] section:

```
encrypt passwords = No
```

A more difficult task is configuring recent Windows clients to use unencrypted passwords. Windows stores its default for this option in its Registry. The simplest way to adjust this setting is by using special configuration files that come with Samba to reconfigure Windows. To do so, follow these steps:

1. **Locate the files**: The files in question have names of the form Win??_PlainPassword.reg, where ?? is a string identifying the Windows version, such as 95, 98, ME, NT4, 2000, or XP. If you downloaded the Samba source code, these files are in the docs/Registry subdirectory of the main distribution directory. If you installed Samba from a binary package, these files probably exist in a documentation directory, such as /usr/share/doc/packages/samba/Registry. Try using find to search for the files, as in find /usr -name "*.reg".

2. **Copy the files to floppy**: Copy the Registry files for all your client OSs to a FAT floppy disk. Depending upon your OS, you can do this by mounting a FAT floppy disk or by using a utility program such as mcopy, as in **mcopy WinME_PlainPassword.reg a:**.

3. **Move the floppy to the client**: Remove the floppy disk from the Samba server, and insert it in the floppy disk drive of a client.

4. **Apply the Registry patch**: Open a window on the floppy disk, and double-click the appropriate .reg file. Windows asks for confirmation that you want to add the information in the file to the Registry. Confirm the change.

5. **Reboot the client**: A reboot is necessary to apply the changed value.

Repeat steps 3–5 for each client you need to reconfigure. After you do so, your clients will be configured to use unencrypted passwords. If Samba is also configured in this way, you should be able to connect to Samba shares from the Windows clients; however, different case-sensitivity can cause problems for some combinations of clients and servers, so you may need to change some passwords or alter some Samba options related to case.

 NOTE   Using a floppy disk as a method of transferring the .reg files is a way around a chicken-and-egg problem. If your Samba server doesn't employ encrypted passwords, you won't be able to access it from recent versions of Windows, so you can't transfer the .reg files via Samba. You can, however, use some other method of data transfer, such as a File Transfer Protocol (FTP) server, a Web server, or even e-mailing the files. The key to steps 2–3 is simply to make the .reg files accessible to the clients.

Samba and Unix Passwords

Traditionally, Unix systems have stored their passwords in an encrypted form (technically, using a *hash*, which is a one-way form of encryption) in the /etc/passwd file.

Servers and login tools that require a password read this file, accept the user's password, hash the password, and compare the hashed result to the value stored in the passwd file. If the hashes match, chances are the originals also match, so the program authorizes the access. This process has several disadvantages, though, the two most important of which are as follows:

- Every program that must authenticate users must know how to hash the password. Given the prevalence of libraries to do such hashes, this problem isn't really an issue unless and until you need to change the nature of the hash—say, to improve its security or to support passwords that were previously hashed using some other system. When this happens, the task of replacing all the programs that need to authenticate users is enormous.

- Because several programs need access to nonpassword information in the file, /etc/passwd must be readable by all users. Unfortunately, password-cracking programs are commonly available and can discover poorly chosen passwords without too much trouble. Thus, the world readability of passwd is a serious security threat because any user can try cracking all the users' passwords and, on a typical multiuser system, will probably succeed for at least a few users.

For these reasons, most Unix systems today use a modified encryption system. Most important, these modified systems use *shadow passwords*, in which the password hash is moved out of the /etc/passwd file and into another file, such as /etc/shadow. This file need not be readable to all users, which provides some added protection against password cracking. Many Unix systems also employ an extra layer between programs that accept passwords and the password database. One very popular such system is the Pluggable Authentication Modules (PAM, found at http://www.kernel.org/pub/linux/libs/pam/) system, which is available for many Unix-like OSs, including Linux, Solaris, FreeBSD, Mac OS X, and others. PAM is a set of authentication libraries that can be configured independently of the programs that call it. By adding modules to PAM to handle new hashes or other authentication techniques, you can enable Unix programs to handle new authentication methods without recompiling or replacing the programs in question.

NOTE A PAM library to use a Windows NT domain controller to authenticate local users is available and is described in Chapter 10. Using this PAM library may be desirable on Windows-dominated networks on which only a few Unix systems run. It's not necessary to join Samba to a domain, although that topic is also covered in Chapter 10.

When configured to use unencrypted passwords, Samba can tie into the usual Unix authentication mechanism (direct /etc/passwd access or PAM) to determine who may access the server. In this scenario, Samba receives a password from the client and either hashes it and compares the hash to the one stored in /etc/passwd or sends the password to PAM for validation.

One potential complication to this scheme is in what constitutes a legal Unix password vs. a legal SMB/CIFS password. Unix passwords may be mixed-case and may contain letters, numbers, most punctuation symbols, and even many control characters. Depending upon the hash in use, Unix passwords may be limited to eight characters or may be up to 128 characters. DOS and Windows 9*x*/Me SMB/CIFS passwords, though, are case-insensitive. (Windows NT/200*x*/XP employs a case-sensitive password hash, though.) When configured to use unencrypted passwords, many SMB/CIFS clients nonetheless preserve password case, so this difference is unimportant. Some clients, though, convert passwords to uppercase, at least under some circumstances. Windows for Workgroups and Windows 9*x*/Me both do this with at least some SMB/CIFS protocol levels. (Windows for Workgroups converts passwords to uppercase when using the LANMAN1 protocol but doesn't touch them when using the COREPLUS protocol.) Three global parameters are particularly important in managing Samba's treatment of unencrypted passwords:

`min password length`: This parameter accepts a positive integer as a value. This integer sets the minimum password length that Samba will accept when a user changes a password. For instance, with `min password length = 5` (the default), Samba will refuse any password that's shorter than five characters. This parameter doesn't affect authentication when accessing a share, though; it only affects attempts by users to change passwords, as described in the upcoming section "User Tools for Account Maintenance." A synonym for this parameter is `min passwd length`.

`obey pam restrictions`: This Boolean parameter is new with Samba 3.0. If you compile Samba using the `--with-pam` configuration option and set this parameter to `yes`, it causes Samba to honor any restrictions on account access that PAM may report. Note that this parameter does *not* affect Samba's interactions with PAM for basic account authentication, just for post-authentication access control. The default value is `No`.

`password level`: To cope with the possibility of a password's case being changed by a client, Samba employs multiple checks of the password. First, the server checks the password as delivered by the client. Second, the server checks the password after converting it entirely to lowercase. Next, Samba tries the lowercase password but with increasing numbers of letters converted to uppercase. The `password level` parameter sets the maximum number of letters the server will try converting to uppercase. For instance, when `password level = 1`, Samba will try converting `rhythm` to `Rhythm`, `rHythm`, and so on. When `password level = 2`, Samba tries `Rhythm`, `RHythm`, `RhYthm`, and so on. The default value of `0` causes Samba to try the password as delivered and converted to lowercase but no further variants. Increasing this value increases the odds of successful legitimate logins, but it also increases the odds of a miscreant successfully guessing a password. Increasing this value also slows down login attempts—particularly when a user mistypes a password because many incorrect passwords will be tried.

None of these parameters has any meaning for encrypted passwords; they're useful only if you use cleartext passwords on your network.

Using Encrypted Passwords

Since the late 1990s, encrypted passwords have become the norm on SMB/CIFS networks. Nonetheless, you should consider whether to use them, particularly if you're configuring a new network. In most cases, using them is beneficial, but they're not without their problems. If you decide to use encrypted passwords, you must create a Samba encrypted password file to house the password hashes. Maintaining the password file becomes an issue—you must be able to add or delete users, change passwords, and so on. Furthermore, you may want to employ any of several techniques that can help you keep your Samba and Unix passwords synchronized.

Why Use Encrypted Passwords?

The traditional reason to use encrypted passwords is to increase security. Encrypting passwords makes it harder for a miscreant with access to your network wires to break into servers by using a packet sniffer to "eavesdrop" on the password while it's being exchanged. More precisely, a miscreant could monitor the challenge/response exchange used in an encrypted password login, but it wouldn't be very useful—or at least, that's the theory. In practice, the encryption system used by SMB/CIFS is variable in quality. The original LANMAN system used by Windows 9*x*/Me isn't very secure, but later hashes (favored by Windows NT/200*x*/XP) are better. You can improve the security of your network by setting lanman auth = No, which disables the poor LANMAN authentication system. You can also disable the intermediate NT LANMAN authentication by setting ntlm auth = No. This will make Samba require the newest forms of password exchanges from clients. Not all clients will work with these options set, though. Also, these options are new with Samba 3.0.

Another defense against such "sniffing" attacks is the use of a more secure encryption system layered atop SMB/CIFS, such as Secure Shell (SSH) tunneling. Chapter 11 describes such approaches. These approaches have the added benefit of encrypting all data transfers, not just the passwords. Unfortunately, they're also awkward and impractical in many cases.

 CAUTION In mid-2003, a researcher (Philippe Oechslin; http://lasecwww.epfl.ch/philippe.shtml) described a method of password cracking that stands a 99.9 percent chance of discovering an alphanumeric SMB/CIFS password within 13.6 seconds, with an average discovery time of 5 seconds. Adding punctuation increases the time to discover a password by a substantial amount, but the time is still short enough that these passwords can't be considered secure. This approach, however, works on the password as stored in hashed form on the server (or sometimes the client). When using "encrypted passwords," the password isn't actually sent over the network; instead, an encrypted challenge-response system is used. The most important practical consequence of this cracking method is that the Samba password file is *extremely* sensitive; if it falls into the wrong hands, the safest assumption is that all your server's passwords have been discovered.

Given the weakness of SMB/CIFS passwords, more important reasons to use them relate to practicality, not security. Encrypted passwords are required if you want to use a Windows domain rather than a workgroup or if you want to use a computer other than the Samba server itself for authentication—at least, within the confines of the usual SMB/CIFS network structures. Using a single computer for authentication can greatly reduce your network's administrative challenges. For instance, if you have four Samba servers, you need only change users' passwords on one server if you have the other three defer to the first one for this task.

Another practical advantage of using encrypted passwords is that Samba's encrypted password system uses the same password rules as do SMB/CIFS clients. Thus, this configuration eliminates the need for workaround parameters such as `password level`. (The `obey pam restrictions` parameter is eliminated because Samba doesn't use PAM when it uses encrypted passwords; `min password length` is also not used with encrypted passwords.) Because modern clients ship configured to only use encrypted passwords, you may find it easier to configure one or two Samba servers to use encrypted passwords than to reconfigure dozens of clients to use cleartext passwords.

Creating a Samba Encrypted Password File

The first step in using encrypted passwords in Samba is to enable their use in `smb.conf`. This is the default setting in Samba 3.0 and later, but in earlier versions, you must set the `encrypt passwords` parameter:

```
encrypt passwords = Yes
```

Once you've completed this task, you can create your encrypted password file. This file is called `smbpasswd`, and it may reside in different locations depending upon your Samba compilation options. Using stock options, the file should be in `/usr/local/samba/private`, but many precompiled binaries will look for the file in `/etc/samba`, `/etc/samba/private`, or a similar location. You can set the path and name of this file using the `smbpasswd file` parameter in `smb.conf`, as in `smbpasswd file = /etc/samba/passwords` to store the passwords in the `passwords` file in `/etc/samba`. I refer to the file as the `smbpasswd` file even if you choose to rename it in this way.

 NOTE Confusingly, `smbpasswd` is both the name of the Samba password database and the name of a utility used to manipulate this database. In this chapter, I provide enough context around my use of the word to make it clear which meaning is intended.

CAUTION The smbpasswd file's security is of utmost importance. This file should be readable only to root. As an added protection against misconfiguration, it's best to store the file in a directory that can be read only by root.

The smbpasswd file's format isn't very complicated, but because the contents are hashed passwords, you shouldn't ordinarily edit this file directly. (Chapter 2 describes this file's format.) The simplest way to create this file if it doesn't exist is to add a new user to the database using the smbpasswd utility and its -a option as root:

```
# smbpasswd -a mikhail
New SMB password:
Retype new SMB password:
unable to open passdb database.
Added user mikhail.
```

Despite the error message about being unable to open the database, the utility creates the file and adds an entry for the specified user. You can then add more users to this file, delete users when they move on, and otherwise manipulate the file. The smbpasswd utility should create a file with limited permissions to all but root, but I recommend you double-check this detail and, if necessary, use chmod to eliminate permissions to all but root, as in chmod 0600 smbpasswd.

Although using a Samba-specific smbpasswd file is the default and most typical method of storing Samba passwords, Samba does provide other options. You can set these with the passdb backend parameter, which is a new addition with Samba 3.0. The default value of this parameter is smbpasswd, but you can set it to tdbsam, ldapsam, nisplussam, or mysql to use a Trivial Database (TDB), Lightweight Directory Access Protocol (LDAP), Network Information System Plus (NIS+), or Structured Query Language (SQL) database backend, respectively. Most of these options take additional parameters, such as a pointer to a database file or server, as in passdb backend = ldapsam:ldap://localhost to point to an LDAP server running on the Samba server computer itself. Using an external database (particularly a server running on a central computer) can help coordinate user authentication for many servers. It's also a vital part of domain control when you use both primary and backup domain controllers running Samba. For this reason, Chapter 10 describes configuration details for this type of setup in more detail.

Another new authentication option with Samba 3.0 is auth methods. This parameter takes one or more values of guest (anonymous access), sam (local lookups based on NetBIOS or domain name), winbind (using the winbindd server for authentication), ntdomain (Windows NT domain lookups, deprecated in favor of winbind), or trustdomain (yet another domain lookup method). Ordinarily, you shouldn't adjust this parameter because Samba sets it to a reasonable value automatically based on the security setting. A few Samba packages set this option in their default smb.conf files, though, and you should generally leave those alone. For instance, the Mac OS X default sets auth methods = guest opendirectory, which enables Samba to tap into the Mac OS X Open Directory authentication system, thus integrating Mac OS X's local passwords and SMB/CIFS encrypted passwords.

Using smbpasswd

The smbpasswd utility is indispensable for managing Samba accounts—you can use it to add, delete, or modify accounts. This tool is similar in broad strokes to the passwd utility that many Unix-like OSs use to change passwords for their local user accounts, but certain details differ—including, of course, the database upon which the command works.

The syntax for the smbpasswd utility is as follows:

```
smbpasswd [options] [username]
```

The *username* is, naturally, the username upon which the command acts. Ordinarily, only root may specify a username; when ordinary users run the program, it acts automatically upon their own accounts. The *options* enable you to tell smbpasswd precisely what to do:

-a: This option tells the smbpasswd program to add a user to the smbpasswd database. When you use this option, the program will prompt you twice for the password. This option works only if the username is already present in the /etc/passwd file, and it extracts some information (namely, the user ID number) from that file for inclusion in the smbpasswd database. Only root may use this option.

-x: This option removes the specified user from the smbpasswd database. Only root may use this option.

-d: You can disable a user's Samba access rather than completely deleting the authentication by using this option. The smbpasswd utility writes a code in the smbpasswd file that tells the system to deny authentication to the named user. The advantage of this system is that you can subsequently reactivate the account without having to re-enter the username and password. This option doesn't work with very old smbpasswd files (those created using Samba versions earlier than 2.0). Only root may use this option.

-e: This option is the opposite of -d; it re-enables an account that's been disabled with the -d option. Only root may re-enable an account in this way.

-D *debuglevel*: This option sets the debug level, which is an integer between 0 and 10. Higher debug levels increase the level of detail logged by this tool.

-n: You can specify that an account have a *null password* by passing this option. A null password is used by accounts that shouldn't require password authentication, but you must add the null passwords = Yes parameter in the [global] section of smb.conf to enable logins from such accounts. Only root may use this option.

CAUTION   Null passwords are potentially quite risky. Use them with caution. If you want to use null passwords on some accounts, such as accounts associated with printer shares, but require authentication for other accounts, be sure to use the invalid users parameter to prevent users with null passwords from accessing shares to which they shouldn't have access. In most cases, a better approach is to use the guest ok parameter to enable access to a share without using a password. Guest accounts are described in more detail in the upcoming section "Creating Guest Accounts."

-r *remote-machine*: One of the smbpasswd utility's more flexible features is that it enables modifying the password database on remote machines, not just the local machine. For instance, if you're using the computer TAP but you want to change your password on RUMBA, you could type **smbpasswd -r RUMBA** to do so. If the *remote-machine* is a domain controller, you'll change your password on the domain. If you omit this option, the smbpasswd program operates on the database specified by passdb backend (typically the local computer's smbpasswd file).

-R *name-resolve-order*: This option overrides the name resolve order parameter in smb.conf. Pass it a comma-separated list of the strings lmhosts, hosts, wins, and bcast to tell the program to use an lmhosts file; DNS host-names; NetBIOS Name Server (NBNS), a.k.a. Windows Internet Name Service (WINS) resolution; and NetBIOS broadcasts. This option is important only if you use the -r option.

-m: Most Samba accounts are for individual users; however, some functions, particularly for domains, require that computers, rather than their users, have accounts. The -m option identifies such *machine accounts*. Only root may use this option. Chapter 10 covers its use.

-U *username*: When changing a password on a remote machine (using the -r option), you may need to specify a remote username if it's different from your local username. You do so using this option.

-h: This option displays a brief message describing how to use the smbpasswd utility.

-s: This option tells the program to not display prompts and to perform input and output using stdin and stdout. The intent is to enable the use of the smbpasswd utility from scripts.

-w *password*: If you're using Samba's experimental LDAP support, you can use this parameter to pass an LDAP administrative password.

-i: This option tells the smbpasswd utility that the account being modified is an inter-domain trust account. Such accounts contain information about other domains trusted by the domain controller.

-L: This option tells the program to run in local mode. In this mode, smbpasswd accesses the password file directly (usually it does so by contacting the smbd server and communicating with it).

Ordinarily, you won't use most of these parameters. One common use of smbpasswd is in creating accounts for new users. In such a case, you'll use the -a parameter repeatedly as root to create new smbpasswd database entries. Particularly if your system sees a lot of turnover in users, you're also likely to use the -x parameter with some frequency. Ordinary users are likely to use the command with no options from a text-mode login to change their own passwords:

```
$ smbpasswd
Old SMB password:
New SMB password:
Retype new SMB password:
Password changed for user mikhail
```

If you don't want to give ordinary users text-mode login accounts on the Samba server but you do want to enable them to change their passwords, you have several options. Described in Chapter 11, these options range from setting the login shell to the smbpasswd utility to using remote administrative tools such as the Samba Web Administration Tool (SWAT).

Linking Samba and Normal Unix Accounts

One of the problems with using encrypted passwords is that keeping those passwords synchronized with normal Unix accounts can be tricky. Several aspects of this problem are as follows:

Samba installation: When installing Samba for the first time, you may need to create dozens or hundreds of new smbpasswd database entries. This task can be a tedious one.

Account creation: When creating new accounts, you must first create a Unix account and then, if the account should be useable from Samba, add an smbpasswd database entry for the account.

Account modification: When modifying an account in any way, such as changing a password or deleting the account, you may need to make changes to both the main Unix account and the matching Samba account.

On small systems, you may find it simplest to ignore these issues. Making changes to both Unix and Samba accounts isn't too hard on an individual basis, after all, and if these changes are infrequent, the bother of linking them together in some automatic way may be greater than the effort such linkage would save. On larger systems with many users, on the other hand, it may be absolutely necessary to use various tools to help automate the process.

One of the most onerous tasks is that of Samba installation. Because the Unix and Samba password databases both use hashed passwords, it's not possible to automatically create an smbpasswd database file with correct passwords based on the normal Unix password database. A tool called mksmbpasswd or mksmbpasswd.sh used to be commonly included with Samba packages but has become less common today. This script would create an smbpasswd file from an /etc/passwd file when called like this:

```
# cat /etc/passwd | mksmbpasswd > smbpasswd
```

The resulting file would have null passwords set for all accounts and would include all accounts in the original /etc/passwd file. Unfortunately, by itself this process would do little good; you'd still need to run the smbpasswd utility to change users' passwords. One way to do this semiautomatically is to use the update encrypted = Yes global parameter in smb.conf. When this parameter is active, an unencrypted Samba login triggers an automatic entry of the password in the encrypted password database. This mechanism is useful when migrating a network from unencrypted to encrypted passwords, but it's not very useful in other situations, such as when setting up a completely new Samba network.

 CAUTION If you track down and use a mksmbpasswd script, be sure to review the smbpasswd file it creates. These scripts tend to add entries for all users in /etc/passwd, including system accounts that should not have Samba access. You can safely delete such accounts by using the -x option to the smbpasswd utility or by deleting their lines in the smbpasswd file using a text editor.

A tool that's stood the test of time for helping to integrate Unix and Samba password databases is a set of parameters and associated utilities that enable Samba to change the Unix password database whenever you change the Samba password database. You control these options through parameters in the smb.conf file:

unix password sync: This global parameter tells Samba (and the smbpasswd utility in particular) whether to change the Unix password database whenever it changes the Samba password. If this option is set to Yes, Samba uses the program specified by passwd program to change the Unix password along with the Samba password. This parameter's default value is No, which causes Samba's utilities to leave the Unix password database alone.

passwd program: This global parameter points to the program that Samba uses to change the Unix password if unix password sync = Yes. You should specify a complete path to this program. The default value is /bin/passwd. You must include the %u parameter to pass the username to this program.

passwd chat: To use a password-changing program, Samba must know what output to expect from the program and what input to provide to the program. These details vary from one program to another, and this global parameter enables you to create a "chat" script to control Samba's interactions. Spaces in this string represent breaks between what's received and what's sent. Asterisks (*) represent any character or string of characters; %o is the old password; %n is the new password; double quotes (") enclose strings that must contain spaces; and \n, \r, \t, and \s represent newlines, carriage returns, tabs, and spaces, respectively. For instance, the default passwd chat string of *new*password* %n\n *new*password* %n\n *changed* tells Samba to wait for a string containing the words new and password, in that order, and to respond with the password. The system then waits for the same string and responds with the same password. Finally, the system looks for the string changed in the output and, if it's found, assumes that the password has changed. You should study the output of your passwd program when called by root to create an appropriate passwd chat for your system.

passwd chat debug: When set to Yes, this global parameter is supposed to log exchanges with the Unix password program. This behavior is extremely dangerous because it places plain-text passwords in the Samba log files. It's an extremely useful option when debugging your passwd chat setting, though. Be sure to set this value to No or remove it (the default is No) when you've finished debugging your password chat script. Use a test account that you delete immediately after finishing your debugging so that regular users' passwords aren't logged. This parameter doesn't appear to work correctly in some versions of Samba, including at least some early 3.0.*x* releases.

pam password change: PAM provides password-changing parameters that work independently of the program specified with passwd program. If you compile Samba with PAM support (using the --with-pam compile-time option), set this global parameter to Yes, and set unix passwd sync = Yes, Samba uses the PAM password-changing mechanisms rather than the program specified with passwd program and the chat script specified with passwd chat.

If you configure your system to automatically change Unix passwords when you change Samba passwords, the result can be greatly simplified account maintenance, particularly on a system on which users change their passwords frequently. Unfortunately, this system isn't without its perils:

Dangers of root: To change users' passwords, Samba runs the Unix passwd program as root. This fact opens a potentially major security hole. If you specify a buggy script as this program, a miscreant might be able to abuse it.

Password restrictions: If the Unix passwd program imposes restrictions on the types of passwords it accepts, the password-change procedure could fail if a user provides an inappropriate password. For instance, some programs refuse passwords that are too short or that don't contain any numbers or punctuation. If your system is configured in this way, you should check your system to see how smbpasswd responds. At the very least, you should know what sort of error message the program returns if the passwd program rejects a password change.

Other errors: Unexpected errors can crop up sometimes, which can cause problems with smbpasswd failing and perhaps not reporting useful error messages.

Domain interactions: If you use a domain configuration, changing the Samba password on the domain controller can change the Unix password on the domain controller when unix password sync = Yes. This action won't, however, change the Unix passwords on other Samba servers that belong to the domain. The same limit applies to Samba servers that use security = Server but aren't technically part of a domain.

Overall, using Unix password synchronization can be a convenient time-saver in some circumstances, but it's not without its limitations. When using encrypted passwords, you should always be aware of the fact that you're dealing with two password databases. Sometimes this fact can be beneficial, but other times it can cause problems.

Managing Permissions

Experienced Unix administrators already know how to manage ownership and permissions to achieve many access control ends. You can use many of these techniques on a Samba server, provided that the server utilizes users' true usernames when logging them in. Samba provides some extra options that can be either a blessing or a curse, depending upon your experience and your needs. Knowing how to employ some of these options for private data directories, shared user directories, and read-only shares can help you manage your Samba server effectively while maintaining the appropriate level of security.

Appropriate Schemes for Read-Only Shares

Read-only file shares are some of the simplest to handle from a permissions point of view, all other things being equal. These shares typically use the read only = Yes parameter or one of its antonyms; however, as this is the default setting, these shares sometimes simply omit this parameter. Because this setting is so important, though, you may want to reiterate it for each read-only share, lest a misplaced read only = No in the [global] section make your read-only shares read/write without your knowledge.

Read-only shares might or might not reside on read-only media. For instance, you can share a CD-ROM as a read-only file share. (Attempting to share a CD-ROM as a read/write share is legal from Samba's perspective, but the practical effect will be much the same as sharing it read-only; Samba won't magically make a read-only medium writeable.) Alternatively, you can share an ordinary hard disk partition as a read-only file share. Doing so blocks users' ability to write to the share, even if they could do so if they were to log in using some other mechanism. You might create a read-only share in this way as a protection against the accidental deletion of data or malicious attacks by people who obtain passwords to your server.

TIP For added protection, you can create partitions that exactly correspond to read-only Samba shares and then mount those partitions using read-only filesystem mounting options. This approach reduces the odds of problems should you misconfigure Samba, and it provides protection against accidental or malicious data tampering via non-Samba servers. When you need to modify the contents of these partitions, you can temporarily remount them using read/write mount options.

Frequently, read-only shares contain data that should be readable to all users, such as program files, templates used by everybody on the network, and so on. In such cases, the simplest way to ensure that everybody can use the shares is to give all the files 0644 (-rw-r--r--) permissions, meaning that everybody can read the files but only the owner can write to them. (Even the owner won't be able to write to the files via Samba, though, unless you add a write list parameter and ensure that the medium is mounted for read/write access.) On the server computer, you can ensure that all files are world readable by typing the following command as root:

```
# chmod -R go+rX /path/to/shared/directory
```

This command recursively (-R) adds the read permission bit (r) for the group (g) and world (o), and it adds the execute bit to files only if the files are already directories or have at least one execute bit set (X). This command applies to */path/to/shared/ directory* and all its subdirectories.

One potential problem with this command is if you've stored files in this directory using Samba and its default permission settings, which results in files with the owner's execute bit set as a stand-in for the archive bit. The go+rX option will set the group and world execute bits. Ordinarily this isn't a problem for Samba-only use, but if you use the map hidden = Yes or map system = Yes parameters, your files will disappear from view on the clients. If this is the case, you may need to change go+rX to go+r and check each directory manually to be sure that world execute permissions are present.

If you want to restrict some files or directories so that some users can't access them, you can remove the world read permissions using chmod, as in **chmod o-r privatefile.txt** to remove the world read permissions from privatefile.txt. You must then ensure that everybody who should be able to read the file is in the file's group and that nobody who should not be able to read the file is in the group. If necessary, you can create a new group on the Unix server just for this purpose.

If some users shouldn't be able to read any files in the directory, the simplest approach is to use the invalid users parameter, as in invalid users = nosy, sneaky, which blocks the users nosy and sneaky from using the share at all. Of course, you must be sure to keep that list up to date as your user base changes. If a share contains highly sensitive data and should be readable only to a few users, a better approach might be to use the valid users parameter, which gives only the named users access to the share.

Another approach to read-only file shares is to use the `force user` parameter to give everybody equal permissions to read the files. You can then use `chown` to change the ownership of the files, if necessary, to the target owner. This approach can be a quick way to reduce the risk of running into problems down the line because of unusual permissions on some overlooked file. At the very least, if one user runs into permission problems, all users should see the same problems, which can make debugging the problem easier. On the other hand, effectively throwing away Unix's standard user and group system for managing file access makes some administrators nervous. Should a security breach occur because of a serious misconfiguration, it might be harder to track down who caused problems if you "squash" all users' access down into a single username. If you do use this approach, you should probably create a special low-privilege account just for this purpose. Give this user limited or no access to unnecessary files and directories, and be sure the user has no Unix password and so can't log in.

Appropriate Schemes for User Data Storage

Many Samba shares exist to store user data. These shares must typically provide read/write access (via `read only = No` or one of its antonyms). Such access can be trickier to configure than read-only access because the interaction of usernames, groups, and file permissions is more complex when users can create or modify files. Broadly speaking, there are two classes of user data storage: private data directories and shared data directories. Each type of storage requires its own approach to account management and security.

Users' Private Data Directories

The most common type of private data storage is via the [homes] share, which is described in Chapter 5. How best to use this share, however, depends on your specific needs.

For instance, should users have read/write, read-only, or no access to other users' shares? If users need any sort of access to other users' shares, do you need to distinguish between different groups of users? If your clients are using Windows NT/200x/XP, should they be able to modify access control lists (ACLs) to change file access on a file-by-file basis? The next sections describe appropriate options for a few specific scenarios.

NOTE   In all of the following examples, users won't be able to see other users' shares in file browsers. Users can still access other users' shares, within permission limits, by entering the share name. For instance, `grogers` can access `fastaire`'s home directory on CHARLESTON by entering **\\CHARLESTON\FASTAIRE** in a Windows file browser's address line, even though `grogers` won't see the FASTAIRE share in the CHARLESTON server's list of available shares.

Open Reading

One possible configuration is to give users full read/write access to their shares and to enable all users to read, but not write, data on other users' shares. A [homes] share that implements such a policy might look like this:

```
[homes]
    comment = Home Directories
    browseable = No
    read only = No
    nt acl support = No
    create mask = 0644
    directory mask = 0755
```

The key parameters in this share are create mask and directory mask. The values of these parameters set in this example are similar to the default values, and in fact Samba's defaults of 0744 and 0755 will work as well. (Using 0644 for create mask simply eliminates the owner execute bit, which can be confusing if files are accessed from the Unix host or via some other types of servers.) Setting nt acl support = No ensures that your permissions won't be overridden by Samba's ACL support.

Using this share, any new files and directories that a user creates will be readable, but not writeable, to all other users on the computer. If the share already contains files, their existing permissions will apply. This is true as well if a user changes permissions on the Unix server in some other way. For instance, if a user logs in using a remote login tool such as SSH, the user can change permissions on a file to 0600 (-rw-------), which will prevent other users from accessing this file. Subsequent editing of the file from a Windows client could change these permissions, though. (Some editors delete or rename the original file and create a new one in the original's place. This behavior will change the permissions on the changed file to match those specified by Samba.)

When implementing this scheme, you should be sure that the users' home directories themselves have the correct permissions. In this example, the appropriate permissions on home directories is 0755 (-rwxr-xr-x). If permissions on the home directories are more restrictive (say, 0750), some or all users may be unable to read files in other users' home directories because they won't be able to read the home directory itself. If permissions are more lenient (say, 0775), some or all users may be able to create and delete files in other users' home directories.

If world access permissions are the same as group access permissions, group ownership is unimportant. You can assign each user a unique group, create a single group (such as users) for all users, or create different groups for different classes of users (say, students, staff, and faculty). This decision is unimportant as far as Samba's home directory access is concerned. Of course, you may want to use one scheme or another to control access to other directories, as described in the upcoming section "Shared Data Directories."

Limited Read/Write Access

A second approach to home directory creation is to give certain users read/write access to other users' directories. Unlike the open-reading approach, this method requires that you define unique Unix groups. These groups can be assigned on a one-group-per-user basis (in which case you can fine-tune who may access whose shares), or you can use distinct working groups or classes of users (as in students, staff, and faculty). You can use your OS's underlying group-control tools, such as addgroup and groupmod. Consult a reference for your OS for details about how to do this.

A [homes] share to provide limited read/write access looks much like the share to provide open-read access:

```
[homes]
    comment = Home Directories
    browseable = No
    read only = No
    nt acl support = No
    create mask = 0664
    directory mask = 0775
```

This share differs from the earlier one only in the values of the create mask and directory mask parameters. These parameters enable users in the group that owns the file or directory to modify the file or directory in question.

For instance, if fastaire and grogers are both in the faculty group, they can read, create, delete, and modify files in each other's home directories, as well as subdirectories thereof. If mikhail is in the students group, though, this user won't be able to write to files in either grogers' or fastaire's home directory, although mikhail will be able to read files in these shares. As with the earlier example, of course, if non-Samba access methods are available, users can tweak these settings on a file-by-file basis.

You can adjust who may access certain directories by changing group membership. For instance, if your system has students, staff, and faculty groups, you might want to let faculty members read and write files in student and staff shares but not vice versa. You can accomplish this goal by adding all faculty members to the students and staff groups.

One drawback to giving users the ability to create files in others' directories is that the files created will be owned by whoever created them. If there's no crossover in group membership (for instance, if members of the faculty group don't also belong to the students group), this issue isn't much of a problem. The shares' owners will still have the right to create, delete, and modify files created by others of the same group. If you give some users extra privilege by giving them ownership in multiple groups, though, you could create problems. For instance, consider the system with students, staff, and faculty groups, in which faculty members belong to all three groups. If a faculty member creates a directory in a student's share and populates it with files, the new files will be owned by the faculty member and by the faculty group. Thus, the student won't be able to write to the files, create new files in the new directory, or delete the files from the new directory. Similar problems can occur if you assign one group to each user and add User A to User B's group but fail to add User B to User A's group.

You should be sure that the home directories themselves are all set with 0775 permissions when you implement this scheme and that they belong to the correct groups. If not, users might not be able to write to home directories to which they should have access, or they may be able to read or write to directories to which they shouldn't have access.

This approach is easily modified to restrict *all* access to members of other groups. Change 0664 to 0660 and 0775 to 0770, and members of other groups won't be able to read files in directories belonging to other users' groups. Changing 0664 to 0640 and 0775 to 0750 converts the nonowner write privilege to a nonowner read privilege while blocking other users from accessing files. This approach also avoids potential problems associated with files created by one user residing in another user's share.

High Security

Many file-sharing environments require high levels of security. At the extreme, users should not be able to read any files except those in their own home directories. You can implement such an approach via a share like this:

```
[homes]
    comment = Home Directories
    browseable = No
    read only = No
    nt acl support = No
    create mask = 0600
    directory mask = 0700
```

This share differs from earlier ones only in the values of the create mask and directory mask parameters. This share sets these values as low as they can go while still giving users full read/write access to their own home directories. No user will be able to read or write files in any other user's directories. (An exception is root, but Samba should not be configured to accept root logins.)

Naturally, you should ensure that users' home directories and any files they initially contain are set to appropriate modes. Typing **chmod -R og-rwx,u=rwX /home/*** as root will do this job, assuming home directories are stored in /home.

Of course, a major caveat exists to this share's security: If users can access their shares in any way that enables them to modify specific files' or directories' modes, users can overcome your security controls. If a user logs in with SSH, for instance, and uses chmod to alter permissions on a file or an entire directory tree, other users may then be able to access the first user's files. If preventing such breaches is important to you, you may want to restrict non-Samba access to the server. For instance, you could set users' login shells to point to /bin/false or some other program that will prevent access, or you could lock the account using passwd -l or a similar command (this won't affect Samba access if you use encrypted passwords). You may also want to conduct periodic checks of the permissions on files in users' home directories. The find command can do this job quite nicely:

```
# find /home -perm +0077
```

This command will find any files in /home whose group or world permissions are set higher than octal 0. This command will also find symbolic links, but for a directory that's accessed only via Samba, this fact shouldn't be a problem, and in fact any symbolic links you discover could be a sign of a security problem.

User Control

One method of access that's useful in some situations is to give users some degree of control over their files' permissions. This sort of control exists on Network File System (NFS) servers, when users log into an account via SSH or other login servers, and so on. Because most SMB/CIFS clients don't directly support most Unix security features, though, implementing it in Samba is a bit awkward. One approach is to use the inherit permissions parameter rather than create mask and directory mask:

```
[homes]
    comment = Home Directories
    browseable = No
    read only = No
    nt acl support = No
    inherit permissions = Yes
```

With this configuration, files and directories that a user creates acquire permissions based on the parent directory. Directories exactly mirror the permissions of their parents while files mirror their parent directory permissions except that their execute permissions are stripped. (Execute permissions may be added back, though, depending upon the setting of the map archive, map hidden, and map system parameters.) To take advantage of this arrangement, create home directories as follows:

Set home directory permissions: Home directory permissions should enable at least read access to everybody who should be able to read or write even a few files in the home shares. For instance, if everybody should be able to read at least some files in a home share, the home directories should have at least 0555 (-r-xr-xr-x) permissions.

Create subdirectories for specific user sets: Create subdirectories in each home directory and give them descriptive names. For instance, one subdirectory might be called private, another might be called faculty-read (for members of the faculty group to read), and so on.

Set subdirectory permissions: Set permissions on each subdirectory to match the desired security setting. For instance, type chmod 0700 private to prevent unauthorized individuals from accessing the private subdirectory. If necessary, set group ownership on specific directories, as well, as in chgrp faculty faculty-read to assign group ownership of the faculty-read directory to the faculty group.

At this point, files created via Samba in the subdirectories you've created will all have appropriate permissions, based upon the permissions on the parent directory. The result is as if you had set separate create mask and directory mask permissions for each subdirectory, which Samba doesn't actually support. Note that ownership and group ownership of the files won't be affected. For instance, setting the group of a directory to something unusual won't cause files created in that directory to have the same group ownership; they'll be the user's ordinary group or whatever group is set by the force group Samba parameter.

TIP   Setting the user's home directory permissions to prevent writing can be useful when using a scheme such as this one. This action prevents users from creating new subdirectories, which might bypass the security system, in their home directories. Users can still write to their subdirectories, but those new subdirectories will inherit their parent directories' permissions.

Using ACL Support

The ultimate in Samba permissions relies upon ACLs. Users who employ Windows NT/200x/XP clients can modify Samba ACLs to adjust who may access their files. This approach gives users substantial power over their own files' security, but with that power comes responsibility. Depending upon your user base, you might be better off using a configuration that doesn't support ACLs. With a user base that can be trusted with ACLs, though, their flexibility can be quite valuable.

CAUTION   The default value for the nt acl support parameter is Yes. Thus, if you omit the nt acl support = No parameter specified in the earlier examples, users will have greater control over their files' permissions than you might think they have.

You can change the nt acl support parameter from No to Yes in any of the preceding examples to enable ACL support. As described in Chapter 5, though, the effect depends on the filesystem you're using:

Filesystems without ACL support: Older Unix filesystems don't support ACLs. On such filesystems, enabling Samba's ACL support gives clients access to the Unix permission bits.

Filesystems with ACL support: Some relatively new filesystems (such as XFS on IRIX and Linux), some patched or very new versions of ext2fs and ext3fs on Linux, and appropriately enabled versions of FFS on FreeBSD support ACLs. When using such filesystems, clients can both adjust Unix permissions and add ACLs that can enable users to fine-tune their files' and directories' permissions in ways that aren't possible with normal Unix permissions.

In either case, ACLs give users substantial control over the access rights to their own files. This support doesn't do anything for Windows 9x/Me clients or most other clients, though, such as Unix or Mac OS clients.

TIP In theory, setting unix extensions = Yes can provide Unix clients with access to Unix-specific filesystem features, much as nt acl support = Yes provides Windows NT/200x/XP clients with native filesystem features. Unfortunately, few SMB/CIFS clients for Unix systems support the Unix extensions, at least not as of early 2004. The most notable exception is the new CIFS driver for the 2.6.x Linux kernel. Support for other OSs may improve in the future, though.

Shared Data Directories

Sometimes you need to provide read/write access to shared data directories. Such access might provide a common area in which co-workers can exchange files or work on common files. Users might work directly on files in this area or use it as an exchange area, with the intention of enabling others to copy the files into their own home directories. In any event, such directories can be tricky to configure from a permissions perspective because of the potential for users to create files that other users might not be able to read or write, even when the intent is that others should be able to do these things. This problem is most likely to occur with directories because Samba's default permissions on new directories (0755, or -rwxr-xr-x) prevent anybody but the directory's owner from creating or deleting files in the directory.

Forcing a Common User

One simple way around the permissions problem is to use the force user parameter to give every user equal access to all the files in the directory. You might use a definition like this:

```
[common]
   comment = Common file area
   directory = /home/samba/common
   browseable = Yes
   read only = No
   force user = common
   create mask = 0644
   directory mask = 0755
```

This share relies on the existence of a user called common. That account should have no direct login permissions, either in Unix or in Samba; the account is used only indirectly via the Samba force user parameter. In this example, all files that users create will be owned by the user common and have 0644 permissions (0755 for directories). The result is that all users will be able to read and write to the COMMON share, and nobody will find any file or directory to be inaccessible—at least, assuming the ownership or permissions aren't modified from the Unix server via a text-mode login, NFS, or the like.

For this approach to work, you should ensure that the user common has full read/write access to the /home/samba/common directory. In this particular example, controlling other users' access to this directory is fairly pointless because they all have full access via Samba. You could, though, use `invalid users` or `valid users` to limit who can access this share, in which case Unix group-based permission controls might be important. If you use such controls, you might want to use `force group` as well as `force user` in the share definition.

One problem with this approach is that it limits your knowledge of who created what files on the server. All files will be owned by `common`, so learning who really created a file is likely to be difficult or impossible. This limit isn't likely to be important in day-to-day use, but it could become a problem if you discover a security breach or find that a user is causing problems for others by creating files that are too large, deleting important files, and so on.

Providing Limited Common-User Access

The approach of using `force user` to make all users look like one individual to the Samba server can be refined a bit. By adding a `valid users` or `invalid users` parameter to the share, you can control who can access a share. For instance, if you want to create a common-access share for certain users, such as supervisors or faculty members, you can create a share much like the one shown in the previous section, "Forcing a Common User," but add a `valid users` or `invalid users` parameter to restrict access to the share to the desired users.

This approach has all of the advantages and disadvantages of an all-users common-access share, but it's more flexible. You can create several such shares, providing differential access to various groups of users. These groups needn't correspond to Unix groups, as listed in /etc/group, although they can. You can list a Unix group by preceding the name with an at sign (@), as in @faculty for members of the `faculty` group. (Samba first tries to match such names against members of an NIS netgroup, and if that doesn't work, checks the local Unix groups for a matching name.)

Providing Access Using Real Usernames

A final approach to providing common access is to create a fairly ordinary file share that provides access using users' real usernames. Such a share might look like this:

```
[common]
   comment = Common file area
   directory = /home/samba/common
   browseable = Yes
   read only = No
   nt acl support = Yes
   inherit permissions = Yes
```

This particular example closely resembles the home share described in the earlier section "User Control," except that it adds support for ACLs. This ACL support is likely to be particularly important in a shared read/write directory because it enables your users to overcome minor permissions problems—at least for users who run Windows NT/200x/XP and who understand at least the basics of ACLs. For other users, the `inherit permissions = Yes` parameter enables you to create subdirectories with differing permission schemes, as described earlier in "User Control."

A variant on this system is to replace the inherit permissions = Yes parameter with parameters that force a very lenient security mode:

```
create mask = 0666
directory mask = 0777
```

These lines enable any user to read or write any file in the share, much as when employing a common-user approach. The advantage of this system is that you'll have a record of who created which files; as viewed from the Unix server itself or a Windows NT/200*x*/XP system, the username will correspond to the user who created the file or possibly the last user who edited the file.

You can also use stricter create mask and directory mask parameters, such as 0664 and 0775, respectively, to provide group restrictions on file access. Alternatively, you could use read list or write list (in conjunction with read only = Yes or read only = No, respectively), to limit who may write files to the entire share.

As always, you should take care to set appropriate permissions on the shared directory itself. For a share to which everybody should have write access, this might be 0777; or it could be something more restrictive, depending upon your needs. In the case of more restrictive permissions, you may need to attend to the directory's ownership (both user and group), as well.

Unusual Account Tricks

Some Samba options enable you to perform unusual tricks with accounts. Chapter 5 described some of these tricks, such as force user. Other tricks haven't yet been covered or deserve more attention. These include username mapping and guest accounts.

Mapping Usernames

The simplest approach to using Samba, at least from Samba's perspective, is to use Unix usernames for access. For instance, the Unix user fastaire types **fastaire** into the client as the username. This approach requires no translation of SMB/CIFS to Unix usernames, except possibly for case issues that can be addressed with the username level parameter, as described in Chapter 4.

Unfortunately, using Unix usernames isn't always possible. This is most often the case when integrating a new Samba server into an existing Windows network. Such networks frequently use long usernames with embedded spaces, such as Fred Astaire rather than fastaire. Such usernames are, at best, not traditional Unix usernames, and they may not work at all as Unix usernames. Fortunately, Samba provides a parameter for mapping between SMB/CIFS and Unix usernames: username map. This global parameter specifies a file on the Unix server that contains a list of Unix and SMB/CIFS usernames:

```
username map = /etc/samba/usermap.conf
```

The mapping file (/etc/samba/usermap.conf in this example) consists of multiple lines. Each line contains a single Unix username, an equal sign (=), and a space-delimited list of equivalent usernames. Lines that begin with hash marks (#) or semicolons (;) are treated as comments. A few additional symbols have special meanings in names to the right of the equal sign:

Quotes ("): Enclosing a name in quotes, as in "Fred Astaire", enables you to provide a name that contains a space.

Asterisks (*): An asterisk is a wildcard and stands for any username. You might use an asterisk as the right-hand field of the final username mapping line to match any mistyped or otherwise unknown username.

At signs (@): A name preceded by an at sign is interpreted as an NIS netgroup name or, if that fails, as a name for a local Unix group (typically listed in /etc/group). The name is effectively expanded to every member of the group.

The system performs mapping by going through the mapping file line by line. If a name to the right of the equal sign matches a username provided by the client, the username to the left of the equal sign is substituted and processing continues. If a line begins with an exclamation mark (!), though, processing halts if it matches. Note that the mapping rule means that a name might be mapped multiple times. For instance, consider the following lines:

```
fastaire = "Fred Astaire"
freddy = fastaire
```

If your mapping file consists of these lines, a user who logs in as Fred Astaire will be assigned the fastaire username, but that assignment will immediately be changed to freddy. In practice, of course, such a series of assignments is confusing at best and should usually be avoided. You might use it, though, if you need to compress large groups of usernames together for some reason but still provide documentation about distinctions between them should you want to separate them in the future.

 CAUTION   If you use a wildcard at the end of your mapping file, you should use exclamation marks on all preceding lines. If you don't do this, your substitutions will all collapse into the wildcard mapping.

Usernames are mapped prior to authentication. For instance, if you map Fred Astaire and freddy onto the fastaire account, users typing any of those three usernames will be authenticated against the fastaire account, including its Unix or Samba password. Thus, you probably shouldn't use this approach as a convenience to enable multiple distinct people to access a server. The force user parameter, appropriate Unix permissions settings, or appropriate use of ACLs is probably a better way to handle this situation.

TIP Windows NT/200*x*/XP systems use an account called `Administrator` as the local administrative account. If your network requires you to use a Samba server from a Windows system you're administering, you may want to create a mapping of `Administrator` onto your normal Samba account. Alternatively, you could create an `Administrator` account on the Samba server system. Do *not* map the `Administrator` account onto the Unix root account, though; doing so is a potential security risk should a client's `Administrator` account be breached.

Creating Guest Accounts

The typical configuration for Samba involves user-based authentication and access; users provide usernames and passwords associated with those usernames before they can access the server. Chapter 4 describes one partial exception to this rule in the form of share-level security. If you set `security = Share` in the `[global]` section of your `smb.conf` file, Samba doesn't require a username and tries the provided password against a series of usernames, as described in Chapter 4. This approach can be convenient in some cases, such as when you want to assign passwords to particular shares instead of maintaining a user database. You might do this on a print server, for instance.

Another way to simplify access in environments that don't require user-by-user security is to use a *guest account*. This is simply a way to give users who have *no* password (or the wrong password) limited access to the server. Guest accounts can be used in any security mode, so they're potentially applicable on a wider range of servers. You can also control which shares permit guest access, so you can open some shares (such as read-only shares to which everybody should have access or printer shares) while keeping others (such as users' home shares) private. Guest accounts are controlled through four parameters:

`map to guest`: This global parameter controls what conditions trigger an attempt to access shares using a guest account. Possible values are `Never` (Samba never attempts guest access), `Bad User` (Samba attempts guest access when a user enters an invalid username), and `Bad Password` (Samba attempts guest access when a user enters an invalid username or password). The default value is `Never`. Changing this parameter isn't required when using guest accounts with share-level security.

`guest account`: This share-level parameter specifies the account that's used for guest access. The account is typically a low-priority account and may be one you created specifically as a guest account. The default value is usually `nobody` but can be changed at compile time.

`guest ok`: You tell Samba to permit guest access to a given share by specifying `Yes` to this share-level Boolean parameter. The default value is `No`.

guest only: You can specify that a share be available *only* using guest access by providing Yes as the value to this share-level Boolean parameter. The default value is No. A synonym for this parameter is only guest.

To use guest accounts, you must do the following:

- Specify map to guest = Bad User or map to guest = Bad Password in the [global] section of your smb.conf file.

- Specify a valid guest account in the [global] section or in specific shares.

- Specify guest ok = Yes in the [global] section or in specific shares (including guest ok = Yes in the [global] section is risky, though).

The default value for guest account may work acceptably, but it's usually best to make it explicit. The nobody account might or might not be able to print, depending upon your printer configuration. Because the guest account parameter is a share-level parameter, you can use a different guest account for each share. This practice may be helpful in tracking resource use, and it may have some security benefit should guest accounts have the ability to perform unusual tasks such as faxing. No Unix guest account should have more privileges than it absolutely requires. Typically, these accounts are disabled so that users can't log into them using SSH or the console.

Guest accounts are most useful on low-security servers on trusted local networks, such as print servers or servers that deliver read-only access to common files. Rather than maintain lists of usernames and risk security breaches because of password sniffing, you can run such a server using guest accounts. Such a practice runs some risk of abuse of the local resources—say, by a miscreant submitting a print job consisting of hundreds of sheets of black pages. On the other hand, if your network is properly secured, this risk is isolated to your local users, and eliminating the need to send valid passwords may do more to help overall network security than you lose by risking jokers submitting abusive print jobs.

 CAUTION   If you enable guest accounts, be sure the server that's so configured is well isolated from the Internet at large. Using a firewall for the network as a whole is a good start. You may also want to employ firewall features on the Samba server itself or use the hosts allow or hosts deny parameters to restrict access based on IP addresses. Chapter 11 describes these measures.

User Tools for Account Maintenance

The Unix server's system administrator is responsible for most Samba account maintenance. The system administrator creates and manages the Unix accounts upon which Samba relies. The system administrator also runs the smbpasswd utility to create an smbpasswd database file and to add, delete, and modify accounts in that file. Some-times, though, users need to be able to modify their own accounts. Most important, users may need to change their own passwords.

One straightforward way to enable users to change their passwords is to enable user logins via the server's console, SSH, Telnet, Virtual Network Computing (VNC), or some other tool. Users can then run the smbpasswd utility, as described earlier in "Using smbpasswd." This use is fairly straightforward:

```
$ smbpasswd
Old SMB password:
New SMB password:
Retype new SMB password:
Password changed for user grogers
```

Unfortunately, providing this type of access may be unacceptable for any number of reasons. Most important, it requires giving users shell access to the Samba server computer. If users need such access for reasons unrelated to Samba, using it for changing Samba passwords may be acceptable; however, some networks use the Samba server computer exclusively for the Samba server programs, in which case only the system administrators should have shell access to the server. In the case of a domain configuration, this approach requires giving users shell access to the domain controller, which may be an unacceptable security risk. Another problem with this approach is that some users may find command lines intimidating and may not remember the smbpasswd command. Of course, you could create a special shell script or login message to help users out in such a situation, but some users are likely to find it difficult even with some extra help.

 CAUTION   If you provide remote logins or any other method of changing Samba passwords remotely, try to do so via encrypted protocols, such as SSH. Telnet, VNC, and most remote X-based forms of access are unencrypted. If you use encrypted passwords for their security bene-fits, forcing users to change their passwords via Telnet or some other unencrypted access tool represents a reduction in your overall network security.

An alternative to using direct shell access to change the password is to use smbpasswd from another Unix-like system, using the -r parameter to specify a remote server, as in **smbpasswd -r TAP** to change the password on the computer TAP. Of course, this specific solution requires that users have access to a client computer on which at least parts of Samba are installed. It also suffers from the difficulty issue of using smbpasswd directly on the target server. On the other hand, it at least doesn't require giving users shell access to the domain controller if you use a domain configuration.

One way to simplify access to the smbpasswd utility if you don't need to give users direct shell access to the server is to use smbpasswd as the login shell. This shell is often specified as the final item on account definition lines in the /etc/passwd file, and it typically points to /bin/sh, /bin/bash, /bin/tcsh, or a similar shell. On some Unix-like systems, you can simply change this reference to point to your smbpasswd executable. On other systems, you must also add the smbpasswd utility to a list of acceptable shells, such as /etc/shells. Some systems provide text-mode or GUI interfaces to help with one or both of these tasks; consult your system's documentation for details. The advantage of this approach is that users needn't have full shell access to the server or know the name of the smbpasswd program. When users access the server using an SSH client, they'll see the smbpasswd utility's prompt for the old Samba password, followed by prompts for the new passwords. One drawback to this approach, particularly if you don't link Samba's passwords and the underlying Unix passwords, is that users may need to remember two passwords—the Unix password and the Samba password. In fact, using the smbpasswd program as a login shell means that users will have no way to change their Unix passwords unless they're tied to their Samba passwords.

Yet another option is to use a non-Samba client to change the password. Precisely how this is done depends upon the client OS and whether the network uses a workgroup or a domain configuration. Many clients don't support changing passwords on another computer at all or only when a domain configuration is in use. For instance, in Windows 9x/Me, you can only change the password on a domain controller. Double-click the Passwords icon in the Control Panel and then click the Change Other Passwords button. Windows displays a Select Password dialog box with a Microsoft Networking option. Select this option, and click Change to change the user's domain password. Windows prompts once for the old password and twice for the new one.

A final option is to use SWAT for password changes. (Chapter 13 describes this server.) It's most useful for enabling remote configuration of the Samba server, but one of the few changes ordinary users can make with it is to change a password. When users enter **http://samba.server.name:901** into a Web browser, they're greeted by a password prompt. Users should enter their Unix usernames and passwords, whereupon they see the normal SWAT main menu but with a limited set of options, one of which is Password. Clicking this option brings up a page with password-changing options similar to those shown in Figure 7-1. Users can change their passwords on the computer to which they've connected (*samba.server.name*) using the Server Password Management area. Using the Client/Server Password Management area enables changing the password on other Samba or Windows NT/200x/XP servers. In either case, the drill is a typical password-change operation, involving typing the old password once and the new password twice. SWAT is fairly easy to use; the hardest part to remember is the :901 port number extension to the URL. Of course, if you create a bookmark on users' browsers, this feature becomes a nonissue. SWAT's biggest problem is that it uses unencrypted transmission of passwords (and all other data), which may be an unacceptable risk on a high-security network.

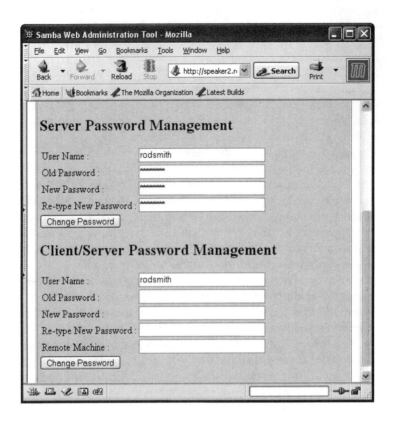

Figure 7-1. SWAT enables ordinary users to change their passwords on the Samba server or on other SMB/CIFS systems.

Summary

Samba relies upon the Unix host's accounts for many functions. As usual, the trick with Samba is in integrating the underlying Unix system with the SMB/CIFS protocols. One of the biggest issues in this respect is in encrypted passwords. Although Samba can use the Unix host's normal authentication mechanisms when using cleartext passwords, this isn't possible with encrypted passwords. Thus, when using encrypted passwords, you must maintain a Samba password database (called smbpasswd) using a special password-manipulation tool (also called smbpasswd). In addition to managing passwords, Samba operation sometimes requires the configuration of special accounts, such as guest accounts. These can be ordinary Unix accounts, but they may be accessed in unusual ways. Samba's ability to play "fast and loose" with users' identities, although very useful in setting up certain types of shares, means that you must pay careful attention to issues of user identity and security. Account maintenance also includes changing passwords on a regular basis. Several tools, ranging from the smbpasswd utility to client-side programs to SWAT, enable ordinary users to do this.

Part Three

Advanced Samba Operations

#### CHAPTER 8

Configuring a Master Browser

MANY SMB/CIFS CLIENTS, including most versions of Windows, rely upon *network browsers* to help locate resources on the network. These tools are frequently integrated tightly into the OS and make a NetBIOS network look like a filesystem directory tree, with entries for specific servers, shares on servers, and files and directories on server shares. Creating this browse tree doesn't happen effortlessly, though; it relies upon the presence of a special type of server known as a *master browser*. Samba can function as a master browser, and Samba also includes options that enable it to fine-tune the browsing functions it provides to other computers. Some of these options are fairly mundane, but others are unusual. Most notably, you can configure Samba to enable browsing across different subnets, even when your network uses a workgroup configuration— a task that Windows master browsers can't handle.

NOTE   In the context of this chapter, *browsing* refers to the tools and protocols for browsing computers and server resources using SMB/CIFS. In the broader networking world, the word *browsing* more commonly refers to Web browsers and the Hypertext Transfer Protocol (HTTP) they use. Although there are some similarities between SMB/CIFS browsing and Web browsing, the two use very different protocols and aren't interchangeable.

The Role of the Master Browser

Before delving into the minutiae of master browser configuration, you should fully understand the purpose of a master browser. This topic was introduced in Chapter 1 and has been mentioned from time to time in subsequent chapters. Now, though, it's time to look at the issue in more detail. This examination begins with a look at the reason for the existence of master browsers: the problems they're intended to solve and how they solve them. You should also understand the different forms that master browsers can take because SMB/CIFS supports two different types.

The Problem: Locating Available Resources on a Network

Consider this scenario: You know that your network hosts a network-accessible laser printer a few feet from your office door, and you want to use that printer, but it hasn't yet been installed and configured on your computer. You don't know the IP address, DNS hostname, or NetBIOS name of the server that hosts the printer. How can you learn this information so you can use the printer? This is an example of the problem that master browsers are meant to solve.

Of course, the problem of helping to locate network resources breaks down into several additional problems. Some of these problems can be solved differently on different SMB/CIFS clients, but others are solved by the design of the browsing mechanisms themselves. These subproblems include the following:

Assigning the master browser: One computer per network segment (more specifically, an IP subnet) functions as a master browser. How this computer is chosen is a matter of individual computer configurations and of the SMB/CIFS specifications.

Locating the master browser: Clients must be able to locate the master browser computer. For simplicity of configuration, this task is handled automatically; no explicit client configuration is required.

Spanning subnets: Some of the mechanisms that SMB/CIFS uses to implement browsing don't work well across subnets. Thus, additional tools are required to bridge this gap for those networks that require it.

Integrating client, network, and server resources: Some clients, including Microsoft Windows, try to present local, whole-network, and server resources in a single list, which blurs the lines between these types of resources in users' eyes. The clients perform this integration, but the protocols involved must provide enough coverage to not leave any gaps.

Addressing user interface issues: Clients that use network browsing must have some way to present this information to users. This isn't a protocol issue, but protocol design decisions do influence the client's user interface.

 NOTE   Some of these subissues actually jump the gun a bit. In principle, a browsing system might be designed that didn't involve the use of a master browser. Web browsing on the Internet works in this way, for instance, as does browsing for shared printers using the Internet Printing Protocol (IPP). The SMB/CIFS designers, though, chose a system that works using a master browser, so some of these subissues become relevant with that design.

The Solution: A Master Browser

To implement browsing, SMB/CIFS uses a centralized repository of information on network resources. This master browser collects the names of local computers that offer SMB/CIFS services. The master browser offers little more than this, though; the local computers themselves are still responsible for delivering information about their shares and of course for delivering files stored on their shares. The master browser is like a subway map, showing the different subway lines (domains or workgroups) and stops (servers). To locate a particular restaurant (share), you must consult a map at the subway stop (a browse list maintained by the target server). This may sound awkward and inefficient, and in some sense it is; however, SMB/CIFS browsing is much faster than using a subway system, and to the user, the distinctions between information from the master browser and data from the target servers are hard to find.

To a user, a master browser presents information like that shown in Figure 8-1. This figure shows the Explore view of network resources in Windows XP. You can obtain it by clicking the Start button on the desktop, right-clicking the My Network Places icon, and selecting Explore. The left pane of this window shows both network and local resources. Objects such as Desktop, My Documents, and Recycle Bin are local. My Network Places is the gateway to network resources. The Microsoft Windows Network item is the gateway to the SMB/CIFS master browser. Details differ from one network to another after that point. In the case of Figure 8-1, a single workgroup (RINGWORLD) is present and contains four computers. In Figure 8-1, one of those computers, SPEAKER, is highlighted, and the shares it contains appear in the right pane of the window. To use a resource, double-click it. (For printers, you'll then have to install a printer driver, as described in Chapter 6.) Larger networks might contain more computers, and they might be broken up into multiple domains or workgroups.

Figure 8-1. Browsing an SMB/CIFS network enables you to quickly view the computers on the network as well as the shares the network contains.

Of course, Figure 8-1 is just one view of the network. If you don't use the Explore view in Windows, you'll see the network in a somewhat different form. Other OSs may present a different view of the network. Indeed, some clients don't use browsing features at all. For instance, Samba's own smbclient requires users to enter the complete path to a share themselves, as in //RUMBA/WINPROGS to access the WINPROGS share on the RUMBA server. Even on Unix-like systems, though, GUI browsers are available, as described in Chapter 18.

At its core, a master browser is an SMB/CIFS server that collects the names of other SMB/CIFS servers. When a client scans the network for available servers, what the client really does is to ask the master browser for the names of these servers. (Actually, some networks host multiple master browsers, and on these, clients may be redirected to a backup browser. The principles are the same in any event, though.) The process works like this:

1. **Master browser assignment**: A master browser is assigned to the network. You can do this in one of two ways for local or domain master browsers, as described in the upcoming section "Assuming Master Browser Status."

2. **Server registration**: After a browser is assigned, servers register themselves with the master browser. When a new server comes online, it sends out a broadcast to register itself with the master browser, which listens for these broadcasts.

3. **Client queries**: When a user at a client tries to browse the local network, the client sends a broadcast to locate the local master browser (if required), sends a query to the local master browser or another master browser named by the local master browser, and displays the results of this query.

In principle, clients could send a broadcast asking for all servers to respond. A network designed in this way would obviate the need for a master browser, but the cost would be increased network traffic. Every time a user wanted to access a network resource (or at least browse for resources), a new broadcast would be generated, and servers would have to respond. Using a centralized server as a master browser reduces overhead.

One negative consequence of this design is that there can be delays in the appearance or disappearance of servers from the browse lists that individuals see. If a computer crashes, the master browser isn't likely to discover this fact immediately, so the crashed computer will still show up in browse lists. In theory, new computers should appear quickly, but if a client doesn't send a new request for information on available computers, new servers won't appear immediately. (Most clients provide a "refresh" option in their menus to enable users to force a check with the master browser for updated information.) Likewise, if backup master browsers are present (as in a network that spans multiple subnets), the master browsers must communicate with one another. If they don't exchange data immediately, new computers may take some time to appear on clients' browse lists when the client and server are on different subnets.

Network browsing works on computers' NetBIOS names. This fact means that browsing depends upon some form of name resolution for clients to locate servers. In SMB/CIFS, name resolution has traditionally been provided by a NetBIOS Name

Server (NBNS) or by broadcast name resolution. Increasingly, though, SMB/CIFS clients are using the traditional Domain Name System (DNS) of the Internet instead of or in addition to NBNS for name resolution. Chapter 9 describes NetBIOS name resolution in more detail.

Local vs. Domain Master Browsers

Most routers aren't configured to echo broadcasts across the subnets they serve. This fact and the fact that browsing relies upon broadcasts for important parts of its operation mean that the basic mechanism is normally restricted to individual subnets. This fact gives rise to the need for two different types of master browsers:

Local master browsers: These master browsers serve a single subnet; hence, they're designated *local master browsers*. If your network consists of a single subnet, you can get by with nothing but a single local master browser.

Domain master browsers: The traditional way to provide master browser operations across subnets is to use a domain configuration (as opposed to a workgroup configuration). The domain controller then takes on the duties of a *domain master browser*, which is a special master browser that coordinates browse lists with local master browsers on each network segment.

Figure 8-2 shows a simple three-subnet network. This network uses two local master browsers and one domain master browser (which also assumes local master browser duties for its own subnet). The domain master browser (CHARLESTON) collects data from the systems on its own subnet (BALLET and SQUARE). Each of the other subnets' master browsers does the same and reports back to CHARLESTON, which in turn propagates information on all of the subnets that report to it. Thus, for information about TAP to become available to RUMBA, CHARLESTON must collect data from WALTZ and disseminate it to CHICKENDANCE.

As a practical matter, local and domain master browsers also differ in how they obtain these roles. As described in the upcoming section "Assuming Master Browser Status," any computer can demand an *election*, which is the procedure by which a subnet's computers confer local master browser status upon one computer on the subnet. This process is handled via rules that are hard-coded in most Windows systems. Thus, you don't need to explicitly set the local master browser, although Samba provides tools that enable you to "rig" the election. Domain master browsers, by contrast, must be assigned. Normally, one computer handles both domain master browser and domain controller functions. Samba enables you to configure a domain master browser even on a network with no domain controller. These two functions are usually linked, though; a single server usually handles both functions, and in fact if a network has a primary domain controller, that system *must* also function as the domain master browser.

A variant to using a domain master browser is to use special Samba options to enable local master browsers to communicate with one another without the benefit of a domain master browser. These options are described in the upcoming section "Additional Cross-Subnet Browsing Options."

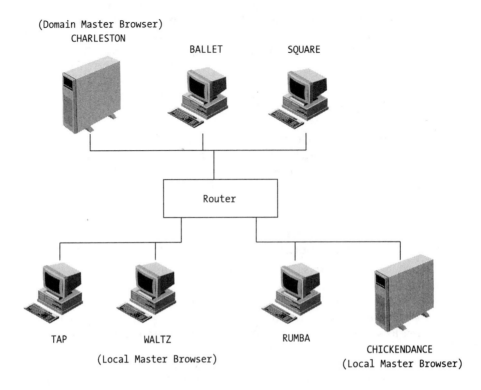

Figure 8-2. A network with subnets requires a master browser on each subnet.

Configuring Samba Browsing Status

As described in Chapter 2, Samba's master browser features are handled via the nmbd server program. You can, of course, tweak Samba's browsing options to change whether and how it tries to acquire master browser status. Another set of options influences how Samba responds to clients that attempt to learn about Samba's shares once they've found the Samba server, whether or not that server is a master browser.

NOTE   These options influence Samba's browse functioning from a server point of view. If you're using a Unix system as a client, you must rely upon the client software's browsing features to locate the network's master browser and shares on the network's servers. Most clients require no special configuration to do this; either they browse correctly or they don't offer browsing at all. Some do rely upon a correct setting of the workgroup parameter in your smb.conf file, though.

Assuming Master Browser Status

If you want to configure a Samba system to be a master browser, you must first decide whether the system should be a local master browser or a domain master browser. In the first case, you can't tell the system directly to become a local master browser; that status is decided by the outcome of a browser election. You can, however, configure Samba in such a way that it's likely to win a browser election. Telling Samba to assume domain master browser duties is a bit more straightforward in some ways, but because the domain master browser is also usually a domain controller, you should attend to the interactions of these configuration options.

Assuming Local Master Browser Status

Any computer that uses SMB/CIFS can call for a local master browser election. Most computers call for such an election only when no master browser responds to a broadcast to find one or when the last known master browser stops working. Some systems, though, including Samba, can call for a local master browser election whenever they start up or periodically thereafter, particularly if these systems are configured to prefer being the master browser.

 CAUTION Master browser elections take a few seconds to complete, and during that time, browsing won't work correctly. Thus, configuring a Samba system to insist on being a master browser when some other system will in fact win the election can cause repeated short browsing outages. If this is happening on your network, check your Samba servers' configurations, paying particular attention to the local master and preferred master parameters, both of which are described shortly.

An election begins with a computer calling for an election. The computer that calls for the election begins by broadcasting its *election criteria*—the characteristics that determine which system wins the election. Every computer that participates in the election compares its own criteria to those that have been broadcast. If a system's criteria meet or exceed those it has seen broadcast, it broadcasts its own criteria. Each system continues rebroadcasting its criteria every 200–800 milliseconds or until it sees another system broadcast criteria that match or exceed its own. Typically, then, computers that are destined to lose the election broadcast their criteria once or twice at most. When a computer broadcasts its criteria four times, it claims victory. If two or more computers claim victory, they engage in a special tie-breaking procedure.

This description omits an important detail: What are the election criteria? These criteria, ranked in order of importance from highest to lowest, are as follows:

1. **Election protocol version:** In theory, SMB/CIFS supports multiple versions of the election protocol. In practice, all systems released to date (early 2004) use version 1 of the election protocol, so this criterion is unimportant.

2. **OS levels**: Each OS is assigned a 1-byte code, and higher codes win over lower codes. Table 8-1 summarizes these codes. Samba enables you to set its OS level code via the os level parameter.

3. **PDC status**: If a computer is functioning as a primary domain controller (PDC), it wins over any computer with the same OS level and election protocol version that isn't functioning as a PDC. Note that if a PDC exists but does *not* win the local master browser election (because of a too-high OS level on another computer), browsing will fail. The PDC, if present, *must* be both the domain master browser and the local master browser for its subnet.

4. **NBNS status**: If a computer is functioning as an NBNS system, it wins the election, assuming other factors haven't determined the election.

5. **Preferred master browser**: A special flag, set via the global Boolean preferred master parameter in smb.conf, can give a computer an edge in elections.

6. **Running master browser**: The current master browser is given an edge in elections.

7. **Former master browser**: If a system used to run as a local master browser but was downgraded to backup browser status through a recent election, it's given a slight boost in the election.

8. **Running backup browser**: SMB/CIFS supports a *backup browser*, which maintains a browse list and is intended to take over browsing duties quickly if the local master browser fails. In an election, the backup browser has a tiny edge over other computers.

Table 8-1. OS Levels Used by Assorted OSs

Operating System	OS Level
Samba 2.0.5a and earlier	0
Windows for Workgroups 3.1	1
Windows 9x/Me	1
Windows NT Workstation 3.51 and 4.0	16
Windows 2000 Professional	16
Samba 2.0.6–3.0	20
Samba TNG	32
Windows NT Server 3.51 and 4.0	32
Windows 2000 Server	32
Windows XP	32

Each criterion takes precedence over all those lower in the sequence. For instance, if WALTZ has an OS level of 32 and TAP has an OS level of 16, WALTZ will beat out TAP as the local master browser, even if TAP is superior in criteria 3–8. Ordinarily, these eight criteria are enough to decide an election; however, it's possible for all eight criteria to match between two or more computers, particularly on a network with many similar systems. In such a case, the leading contenders compare two additional criteria:

1. **Up time**: The computer that's been running for the longest period of time wins the election. Samba provides no mechanism to fake a specific uptime, so you can't break a tie using this criterion.

2. **NetBIOS name**: As an absolute last resort, elections are won based on the contenders' NetBIOS names; the winner is the machine whose name comes first when they're sorted alphabetically. Because NetBIOS and NBT don't permit two computers to share a single name, this criterion guarantees a winner.

Only one system wins a local browser election. Other systems, though, may opt to function as *backup browsers*. These systems collect browse lists just as the local master browser does, but a backup browser is just that—a backup system. It may respond to browse requests if it receives them, and if the master browser becomes unavailable and a new election is held, the backup browser gets a boost in the next election. Samba can win browser elections and normally maintains browse lists and functions as a backup browser, unless you set browse list = No. Samba won't announce itself as a backup browser, though.

Given this election system, you can change a Samba server's chances of winning an election by adjusting several criteria. These criteria are all global smb.conf parameters:

local master: This parameter determines whether Samba participates in local master browser elections. When set to its default value of Yes, Samba participates, although it's not guaranteed to win. If you want to ensure that Samba doesn't participate in local master browser elections, set local master = No.

os level: Aside from local master, this parameter is the most important in determining local master browser status. Table 8-1 shows the default OS levels of several OSs and servers. Samba's default level of 20 wins local master browser elections against Windows 9x/Me and most desktop versions of Windows NT, including Windows 2000 Professional. This level loses against server versions of Windows NT and all versions of Windows XP. To ensure a Samba server wins local browser elections, set os level = 33. Using a higher value, such as 64, 65, or 99, should achieve identical results and may protect against losses to at least some other Samba systems. The highest legal value is 255.

domain logons: This Boolean parameter is the primary means of configuring a Samba server as a PDC. This topic is complex enough that Chapter 10 is devoted to it. You shouldn't change this parameter unless you fully understand its consequences. The default value is No.

wins support: This Boolean parameter enables Samba's NBNS (a.k.a. WINS) support. As with PDC support, you shouldn't activate this option lightly; read Chapter 9 first. The default value is No.

preferred master: You can tell Samba to call a local master browser election whenever it starts up with this Boolean parameter, which also sets the preferred master flag used in election criterion 5. The default value is No. A synonym for this parameter is prefered master.

browse list: This Boolean parameter tells Samba whether to maintain a browse list. If the server doesn't maintain a browse list, it won't take part in local master browser elections. This parameter's default is Yes.

Ordinarily, the default settings work well for typical servers. These servers will assume master browser status on networks containing no other Samba servers and on which clients are Windows 9*x*/Me or NT-series workstations. The default settings also cause Samba to yield master browser status to Windows NT/200*x*/XP servers. As a practical matter, I recommend leaving the default settings in place, at least initially, unless you're configuring a domain controller. If you experience browsing problems, you can adjust the Samba server's settings. If your Samba server is likely to be up more continuously than other computers, and if the network doesn't use another computer as a PDC, you can wrest local master browser status using the following parameters:

```
local master = Yes
preferred master = Yes
os level = 65
```

If a previously functioning network begins experiencing browsing problems after you add a Samba server, you should reverse these Boolean settings and set a very low OS level:

```
local master = No
preferred master = No
os level = 0
```

These settings more or less guarantee that Samba won't assume master browser duties. (In fact, either the local master = No parameter or the os level = 0 parameter alone should do the trick.) Such settings are most appropriate when a network includes a Windows NT/200*x*/XP PDC because Windows expects its PDC and master browser duties to be linked. Attempting to gain local master browser status from such a system can cause strange browsing problems.

If your subnet has multiple Samba servers, you should configure just one to take over the local master browser duties. On a multisubnet network, though, each subnet needs its own local master browser, and a Samba server can take this role on some or all of these subnets. If you use preferred master = Yes on multiple Samba servers on a single subnet, though, problems may ensue because the computer that loses the election calls for periodic new elections. Each of these new elections will briefly interrupt browsing, causing frequent (if brief) browsing problems.

If you need to know which computers serve as master browsers, you can type **nmblookup -M** *NAME* on a Samba system, where *NAME* is the workgroup or domain name in question. This command returns information on the names registered by the work-group or domain's local master browser. The result should be a report of the IP address of the local master browser for the subnet, as identified by the 0x1D resource type:

```
192.168.1.1 RINGWORLD<1d>
```

If you want to know all of the NetBIOS names registered by the local master browser, you can add -S to the query (that is, type `nmblookup -SM NAME`). The result is a node query on the master browser—a list of the types of services it offers. The result should include lines with both the NetBIOS name of the master browser and its workgroup or domain name:

```
$ nmblookup -SM RINGWORLD
querying RINGWORLD on 192.168.1.255
192.168.1.1 RINGWORLD<1d>
Looking up status of 192.168.1.1
        SPEAKER         <00> -          H <ACTIVE>
        SPEAKER         <03> -          H <ACTIVE>
        SPEAKER         <20> -          H <ACTIVE>
        .._MSBROWSE__.  <01> - <GROUP> H <ACTIVE>
        RINGWORLD       <00> - <GROUP> H <ACTIVE>
        RINGWORLD       <1b> -          H <ACTIVE>
        RINGWORLD       <1c> - <GROUP> H <ACTIVE>
        RINGWORLD       <1d> -          H <ACTIVE>
        RINGWORLD       <1e> - <GROUP> H <ACTIVE>
```

If this command reveals a computer you didn't intend to be the local master browser, you may need to study its and your intended master browser's configurations to resolve the problem. A common culprit is an `os level` parameter set too high on a Samba server that should not take on master browser duties. Another common problem is an `os level` parameter set too low on the computer that should function as the master browser.

Assuming Domain Master Browser Status

If you use a domain rather than a workgroup, you should configure one system as the domain master browser. If a Windows NT/200*x*/XP system is the domain controller, you shouldn't need to do anything special to accomplish this goal; the Windows domain controller will automatically assume domain master browser duties. In this case, you might need to ensure that your Samba systems *don't* try to take on domain master browser status, though.

If you use a Samba system as a domain controller, you should configure it as a domain master browser, as well, or browsing won't work. First, configure this system as a domain controller, as described in Chapter 10. Next, set the domain master browser option: `domain master = Yes`. This global Boolean parameter is the primary means of assigning domain master browser duties in Samba. The default value is Auto, which causes it to mimic the value of the `domain logons` parameter. To be sure it works correctly, you should change this to Yes for domain master browsers. (You may want to explicitly set domain master = No on systems that should *not* be configured as domain master browsers, too.) You should also configure the computer as you would for a local master browser, as described in the previous section, "Assuming Local Master Browser Status."

Windows computers configured to use a domain controller should be able to locate the domain master browser, assuming it's the same computer as the domain controller. Local master browsers locate the domain master browser by searching for a NetBIOS name with resource type 0x1B, which is registered by the domain master browser. If some subnets use Samba local master browsers, you can further guarantee proper communication between subnets by using the remote browse sync parameter, which is described in the upcoming section "Linking Master Browsers Across Subnets."

Once a domain master browser is properly configured, browse lists should begin to propagate across subnets. This process can take several minutes because the local master browsers collect information on local computers and periodically exchange their local lists with the domain master browser.

You can spot a domain master browser using the Samba nmblookup command, but search for resource type 0x1B by appending #1B to the workgroup name:

```
$ nmblookup -S RINGWORLD#1B
querying RINGWORLD on 192.168.1.255
192.168.1.1 RINGWORLD<1b>
Looking up status of 192.168.1.1
            SPEAKER          <00> -          H <ACTIVE>
            SPEAKER          <03> -          H <ACTIVE>
            SPEAKER          <20> -          H <ACTIVE>
            .._MSBROWSE__ .  <01> - <GROUP> H <ACTIVE>
            RINGWORLD        <00> - <GROUP> H <ACTIVE>
            RINGWORLD        <1b> -          H <ACTIVE>
            RINGWORLD        <1c> - <GROUP> H <ACTIVE>
            RINGWORLD        <1d> -          H <ACTIVE>
            RINGWORLD        <1e> - <GROUP> H <ACTIVE>
```

This command is similar to the one presented earlier that lists resources on the local master browser, but it searches for the 0x1B resource, which is associated with domain master browsers.

Enabling Browsing of Local Shares

Although configuring a Samba system as a local or domain master browser can be important, another browsing issue is equally important: configuring Samba to support browsing of local shares. Note that this part of the user's browsing experience isn't controlled by the master browser but by the servers on which the shares reside. Some parameters important for this task have been described in other chapters, particularly Chapter 4. In particular, netbios name, netbios aliases, server string, announce as, and announce version relate to how Samba identifies itself to other computers. The names you set using netbios name and netbios aliases appear in the browse lists maintained by the master browsers, and the server string may appear in users' browser windows as well. Some additional options relate to how Samba makes shares available in browse lists:

preload: This global parameter enables you to specify shares that you want to appear in browse lists, even if they otherwise wouldn't appear there. For instance, you might list specific users' home shares, as in preload = GROGERS FASTAIRE, to have those users' shares appear in browse lists presented to all users. (Ordinarily, users' home shares appear only to themselves.) A synonym for this parameter is auto services.

load printers: This global Boolean parameter is similar to a preload statement, but it tells Samba to load the names of printers defined in your /etc/printcap file or its equivalent. This parameter has an effect only if you define a [printers] share, as described in Chapter 6.

browseable: This share-level Boolean parameter enables you to specify whether a particular share is visible to clients. The default value is Yes, but you can hide a share from view by setting browseable = No. This setting does *not* make the share inaccessible, though; it simply doesn't appear in browse lists.

default service: You can specify a share that Samba opens if a user tries to access a nonexistent share with this parameter. For instance, suppose a user mistypes the share name COMMON as COMON, and no share by that name exists. If default service = HELP is set, and if a HELP share does exist, that share will open. You can use this system to provide users with more information about the server. For instance, the HELP share might include a file named README.TXT or About-This-Server.txt, which could provide information on share names. This system provides a backup for browsing. Users whose clients don't support browsing could read the information files to learn what the proper share names are. A synonym for this parameter is default.

Linking Master Browsers Across Subnets

One of the great challenges in SMB/CIFS networking is handling subnets. Because so many SMB/CIFS functions, including clients locating their master browsers, rely upon broadcasts, creating a working multisubnet SMB/CIFS network can be tricky. One of the primary functions of domains is to handle subnets. With Samba, though, it's possible to create a cross-subnet network even with a workgroup configuration, either by using a domain master browser in a configuration that's otherwise one of a workgroup or by using special Samba options that enable master browsers to communicate with one another.

Domain Cross-Subnet Browsing

In a domain configuration, local master browsers are elected via the normal procedure described earlier in "Assuming Local Master Browser Status." These local master browsers automatically contact the domain master browser and exchange browse lists with it. This exchange with the domain master browser occurs across subnet boundaries, so domain cross-subnet browsing is automatic.

NOTE A domain needn't span multiple subnets; it's possible to configure a domain that covers just one subnet. Chapter 10 describes domains, including reasons for implementing domains aside from providing cross-subnet browsing and other cross-subnet services.

In theory, no special configuration is required to implement cross-subnet browsing in a domain, aside from setting up the domain itself and the domain master browser, as described earlier in "Assuming Domain Master Browser Status." In practice, though, you might want to use the remote browse sync parameter (described shortly, in "Additional Cross-Subnet Browsing Options") on your local domain controllers when they and the domain master browser run Samba. Doing this will reduce the odds of a problem occurring because of a failure of a system to locate the domain master browser.

Similarly, the remote announce parameter (also described in "Additional Cross-Subnet Browsing Options") may be useful in a domain configuration if some servers reside by themselves on isolated subnets. As with a cross-subnet workgroup configuration, using this parameter to announce a server to a master browser will work even if the master browser in question isn't a Samba server.

Workgroups with Domain Master Browsers

Because Samba provides fine-grained control over features that are traditionally associated with domains and domain controllers, you can create a sort of hybrid between a domain and a workgroup. Specifically, you can configure the local master browser for one subnet to assume domain master browser duties by setting domain master = Yes on that computer. To do this, of course, you must ensure that a specific Samba system wins the local master browser election on its subnet so that you can include the domain master parameter in its smb.conf file. You don't need to set up the computer as a domain controller in this configuration. You do, though, need to specify a computer the handle NBNS duties because the local master browsers rely upon this form of name resolution to locate the domain master browser.

When you've configured your network in this way, most subnets have their own local master browsers. One subnet's local master browser doubles as a domain master browser, even though a full domain isn't configured. Local master browsers use the NBNS system to locate the domain master browser and exchange browse lists with it.

 NOTE Cross-subnet browsing is only half the task. When splitting a workgroup across subnets, you must also consider name resolution. Windows 9*x*/Me systems use broadcast name resolution by default, so you may need to change this configuration and set up a system to handle NBNS duties to get a workgroup functioning properly across subnets. Chapter 9 describes these tasks.

Additional Cross-Subnet Browsing Options

Samba provides a few additional options that provide browsing features. These options enable a Samba server to exchange browse lists or announce itself to a master browser with which it wouldn't ordinarily communicate. The end result is improved browsing reliability. You can even use these features to implement a workgroup that spans multiple subnets, although these options alone aren't enough to accomplish this goal. (As with a workgroup that uses a domain master browser, you must attend to name resolution issues.)

A trio of Samba parameters is the key to the server's flexibility in handling workgroups that span multiple subnets. These parameters enable local domain controllers to coordinate their browse lists without the benefit of a domain master browser and to support isolated Samba servers that want to connect to a domain that's primarily restricted to a single subnet:

remote browse sync: Pass the IP addresses of servers or networks to this global parameter, and Samba will announce itself to that address. If a Samba master browser exists there, the two systems will exchange browse lists. One important caveat with this parameter is that it enables exchanging browse lists only with other Samba servers; you can't exchange browse lists with a Windows system that becomes master browser for its subnet.

remote announce: This global parameter tells Samba to announce its presence to the IP addresses or network broadcast addresses you specify, as a member of a workgroup you specify. The format is *IP_address/WORKGROUP*, as in 192.168.8.255/FOLK to announce a system to the 192.168.8.0/24 network as a member of the FOLK workgroup. This parameter works with any master browser—Samba, Windows, or some other OS. It can also be directed at either a local master browser or a domain master browser.

enhanced browsing: This global Boolean parameter tells Samba whether to actively search for domain master browsers with which to synchronize browse lists. If set to Yes (the default), a Samba master browser will query the NBNS system for all systems that have registered names with the domain master browser code (0x1B) set. The Samba master browser then performs periodic browse synchronizations with these systems. The result is speedier and more reliable browse list maintenance. One potential downside, though, is that old workgroups and domains may never disappear from the browse list. Therefore, if you encounter this problem, you may want to set enhanced browsing = No. The enhanced browsing system works only if the remote NBNS system is a Samba server; it won't work with a Windows NBNS system.

The first two of these parameters accept one or more addresses as values. The addresses may be IP addresses corresponding to a known master browser, in which case Samba contacts that computer and that computer only. Alternatively, you can replace the appropriate bytes in the address with 255 values to send a directed broadcast (or other values if you don't use traditional Class A, B, or C addresses), which should reach the master browser for the specified subnet, even if you don't know the exact IP address or if it changes (say, because an election results in a shift).

When using a directed broadcast, though, the router between the subnets must be configured to pass such broadcasts. Not all routers are so configured, so you may need to reconfigure the router (which poses some security risks, particularly on Internet-connected networks) or find the IP address of the local master browser on the remote network. As noted in the description for remote announce, you can also add the workgroup name to the address when using that parameter.

If you want to run a workgroup across subnets, with several computers on each subnet, you can use the remote browse sync parameter to do the job. Each subnet will need a Samba computer configured as a local master browser. Each local master browser should also point to the local master browsers on other subnets. For instance, suppose your subnets use the 192.168.8.0/24, 192.168.9.0/24, and 192.168.10.0/24 IP address ranges. Suppose further that the Samba local master browsers are at 192.168.8.7 and 192.168.9.102 for the first two subnets while the address on the third is unpredictable. The local master browser on the first subnet would include a line like the following in its [global] section:

```
remote browse sync = 192.168.9.102 192.168.10.255
```

This line tells the server to exchange its browse lists with 192.168.9.102 and with whatever Samba local master browser it finds on the 192.168.10.0/24 subnet. The Samba local master browsers on the remote network should have similar parameters in their smb.conf files but pointing to the appropriate servers on what are, for them, the remote subnets.

The remote announce parameter isn't useful for linking subnets filled with multiple computers; instead, it's used to attach a lone server to a remote subnet. For instance, you might operate three distinct subnets—say, the same ones described earlier. Most computers on these subnets have no need to communicate directly with one another, but one Samba server on the 192.168.9.0/24 subnet should be accessible to clients on the other subnets. The Samba server can include the following line to ensure that it will appear in clients' browse lists on all three subnets:

```
remote announce = 192.168.8.7/FOLK 192.168.10.255/FOLK
```

This command announces the Samba server to the two master browsers specified, using the workgroup name FOLK. Because remote announce doesn't require a Samba server on the other side of the connection, you can announce a Samba server even when the remote subnet uses a Windows system as the master browser.

Summary

Although browsing isn't necessary for minimal functioning of SMB/CIFS clients and servers, it's a function that's central to most users' perceptions of SMB/CIFS networks. Browsing enables users to quickly locate servers and the shares they contain. This function relies upon the presence of one or more master browsers, which come in two varieties: local and domain. Local master browsers are chosen through an election process, and Samba provides the means to change a server's options to ensure that it wins or loses an election against specific types of servers. Domain master browsers are normally associated with domain controllers, and you tell Samba to assume this role by setting a particular parameter. In addition to ordinary master browser duties, Samba provides features that enable local master browsers to communicate with each other across subnets—a task that Windows can't handle by itself. This feature alone can make Samba an appealing addition to many networks.

#### CHAPTER 9

Configuring a NetBIOS Name Server

NAME RESOLUTION, or converting names as humans use them into numeric IP addresses as computers use them, is an important part of most networking systems. Most networking protocols today rely upon the Domain Name System (DNS) for name resolution, but this isn't true of SMB/CIFS. SMB/CIFS relies on DNS only partially and unofficially or when using "raw" SMB over TCP, as opposed to NetBIOS over TCP/IP (NBT). Instead, SMB/CIFS uses its own methods of name resolution, which include broadcasts, a file called lmhosts in which mappings are stored, and a NetBIOS Name Server (NBNS), a.k.a. the Windows Internet Name Service (WINS; this is Microsoft's name for its NBNS implementation, but the acronym is used elsewhere, including in the names of some Samba parameters). Samba can function as an NBNS system, and this chapter is devoted to describing this and other name resolution tasks.

This chapter begins with a look at NBNS functions, as well as some of the alternatives to NBNS and when NBNS is or isn't most appropriate compared to its competitors. This chapter continues with a look at Samba's NBNS options, which tell the server whether to function as an NBNS system and how to enable specific NBNS-related features. Finally, this chapter concludes with information about telling clients to use a Samba NBNS system over other name resolution methods.

Methods of Name Resolution

Depending upon the specific software in question, you can use any of several different name resolution techniques with SMB/CIFS clients and servers. Each method has its own plusses and minuses. Understanding the differences between these methods can help you pick the one that will work best for you.

NOTE　Name resolution is most important for clients, which are the computers that initiate connections and, therefore, must be able to contact the appropriate server. Depending upon how they're used, servers may never need to resolve NetBIOS names. Nonetheless, servers are usually involved in name resolution in one way or another, such as by responding to name resolution broadcasts or registering their names with NBNS systems.

Automatic Name Resolution: Broadcasts

The default method of name resolution on most older clients, including the Windows 9*x*/Me series of computers, is to use NetBIOS name resolution broadcasts. In this method of name resolution, a computer that wants to learn the IP address of another computer sends a broadcast to its entire subnet asking for the IP address of a computer with the specified name. The target computer, upon hearing such a broadcast, replies to the sender.

Broadcast name resolution has certain advantages:

Distributed computing: Broadcasts don't rely on any central name resolution computer (such as an NBNS or DNS server), so they're unaffected by failures of such computers or of the network links to them.

Automatic name assignment: Computers don't need to register their names with a central computer, so they can be configured to respond to the desired name when they start. To avoid potential conflicts, though, such as two computers both claiming the same name, a computer must broadcast its own name whenever it starts any NetBIOS-based service (such as when it boots or when Samba starts). If no computer responds with the name, the computer can keep it; otherwise, the computer can't use the name it's configured to use.

Compatibility with dynamic IP addresses: If your network uses the Dynamic Host Configuration Protocol (DHCP) to assign IP addresses, broadcast name resolution works well, even if computers' IP addresses change from time to time. Every time a computer receives a broadcast asking for its current IP address, it responds with the correct address. There's no need to change any configuration because of an altered IP address.

Compatibility with older clients: All NBT clients can use broadcast name resolution. (Some can be configured to bypass this name resolution method, though.)

Unfortunately, broadcast name resolution isn't perfect. Problems with this approach include the following:

Bandwidth use: Using broadcasts for name resolution increases the bandwidth use on the network. The increase over other methods is particularly great on Ethernet networks that use switches rather than hubs because switches direct nonbroadcast traffic more tightly than do hubs, so the scattershot of a broadcast causes traffic that wouldn't occur with a point-to-point connection. This effect tends to be fairly small, but on a large network, it may be worth considering.

Router incompatibility: Broadcasts aren't passed between subnets by most routers, so this method won't work across subnets, short of special router configurations. One exception to this rule is if you use special Samba parameters, described in the upcoming section "Samba NBNS Options," to have a Samba server function as a proxy for computers on another subnet.

Need for an extra server: Every computer that must respond by name must run a server that listens for broadcasts. In Samba, this server is nmbd (which also handles other tasks). Because broadcast name resolution is so common, though, there's no easy way to turn off the name resolution features. (In Samba, you could shut down nmbd, but this action would disrupt other Samba features provided by nmbd, including registering the computer's name with an NBNS system, if your network uses one.)

Lack of central authority: In some cases, a centralized name server computer can be an advantage. DNS, for instance, enables you to control what names appear on a subnet, so you can enforce a particular naming system from a single server. This isn't possible with NetBIOS broadcast name resolution. (In practice, NBNS implementations also don't provide this sort of control, although in theory an NBNS system could do so.)

When running normally, Samba responds to NetBIOS name broadcasts via the nmbd server. If you don't specify another name with the netbios name parameter (described in Chapter 4), Samba uses the machine name portion of the computer's hostname, as in RUMBA for rumba.example.com. Thus, when properly configured, a Samba server doesn't need any special configuration to respond correctly to NetBIOS name broadcasts.

NOTE   Technically, Samba registers several names. Many of these names are built from the NetBIOS base name (such as RUMBA) and add a single-byte code to indicate the type of service being offered, as described in the "Machine Addressing" section of Chapter 1. In Samba, you can use the netbios aliases parameter to specify additional NetBIOS base names. Other names are built from the workgroup name in a similar way. Windows systems frequently use the current local username as a base name for some service types.

When you use Samba as a client, you can specify the use of NetBIOS name broadcasts with the name resolve order parameter, as described in the upcoming section "Samba As a Client." (This parameter affects name resolution by the client, not name registration methods.) Some Windows clients use broadcasts by default, but others don't, as described in the upcoming section "Microsoft Windows."

An Alternative: A NetBIOS Name Server

Although name broadcasts work reasonably well in many cases, SMB/CIFS offers a more centralized alternative: NBNS. The idea behind NBNS is to keep many of the advantages of broadcasts while working around at least some of the deficiencies. If your network uses NBNS, one computer is set aside as an NBNS system. (The network can also host an NBNS backup server.) Instead of broadcasting their names when they start up as a protection against duplicating names, computers register their names with the NBNS system. (In practice, the two systems are often used together, so a computer configured to use NBNS will register with the NBNS system *and* respond to name resolution broadcasts.) The NBNS system approves or rejects the name registration. When attempting to resolve names, computers on an NBNS-equipped network contact the NBNS system rather than send a broadcast to the entire network. Overall, compared to broadcast name resolution, using an NBNS system offers the following advantages and disadvantages:

Fewer broadcasts: Because the NBNS system is contacted directly by all computers, the number of broadcasts used on the network as a whole is reduced, which can improve performance, particularly on Ethernet networks that use switches rather than hubs. (Hubs echo all traffic to all connected computers, so even directed traffic consumes bandwidth much like broadcasts when you use hubs.)

Router compatibility: The NBNS computer can collect IP addresses from computers on multiple subnets, which is critical if an SMB/CIFS network is to span more than one subnet.

Potential for non-SMB/CIFS integration: It's possible to use an NBNS program to tie NetBIOS names to non-SMB/CIFS protocols. For instance, you can have Samba communicate with a DNS server to add and remove NetBIOS names to a DNS server's database. The upcoming section "Linking Samba and DNS" describes this process in more detail.

Some centralized control: The centralized nature of the NBNS system means that you can exert some control over it. NBNS is designed to work fairly automatically, though, and Samba provides few options to tweak its operation, so that control is limited. This is also a potential weak point; if the NBNS system crashes, your network's name resolution may fail if you rely upon this method exclusively. (Backup servers can help in this case, and Samba tends to be quite reliable.)

Need for extra configuration: To have Samba run as an NBNS system, you must configure it as such. This task is fairly simple, though, as described in the upcoming section "Configuring Samba As an NBNS System." You must also configure your clients to use the NBNS computer, as described in the upcoming section "Configuring Clients to Use an NBNS System."

NBNS name registrations don't last forever. To clear up a name in case a computer goes down without informing the NBNS system, each name has a *time to live* (TTL). The registrant must check back with the server before its name's TTL has expired or risk losing the name to another computer. This system is similar to the way DHCP servers handle leases on IP addresses. On a well-managed network, of course, there should be no conflict for names, but if you retire a computer (and its name) and then later want to reuse the retired name, you don't want to run into problems because the name had been in use months before! (In practice, other mechanisms enable unused names to be reassigned, so expiring the name isn't the only way to manage this particular problem.)

Using lmhosts

Although it's not as common a name resolution system as broadcasts or an NBNS system, another method is supported by most SMB/CIFS implementations: lmhosts. This file is closely equivalent to the Unix /etc/hosts file. It contains a mapping of IP addresses to NetBIOS names, as shown in Listing 9-1.

Listing 9-1. Sample lmhosts *File*

```
# List SMB/CIFS machines in this file
192.168.8.27  TAP
192.168.8.29  CHARLESTON
192.168.8.30  RUMBA#20
```

Comment lines begin with hash marks (#). Other lines begin with an IP address and end with a NetBIOS name. Ordinarily, the listed name is used for any attempt to access any specific type of SMB/CIFS service; however, you can restrict a listing to apply to only one type of service by ending the name in a hash mark and a two-digit hexadecimal code for the service type. For instance, in Listing 9-1, RUMBA#20 maps the 192.168.8.30 address to the RUMBA name only for the 0x20 service. Table 1-2 in Chapter 1 lists the most common service type codes; 0x20 is for file or print services, so this entry enables users to access these services with the RUMBA name, but not others, such as Messenger (WinPopUp) services.

Samba usually stores its lmhosts file in the same directory that holds the smb.conf file. If you want to use another filename or location, you must pass the complete filename to nmbd using the -H option when you start the nmbd server. Windows 9x/Me stores its LMHOSTS file in the C:\WINDOWS directory (or the default Windows directory, if you selected a different name upon installation). Windows NT/200x/XP systems store it in the C:\WINNT\SYSTEM32\DRIVERS\ETC directory (the drive letter and WINNT directory name may differ if you installed the OS elsewhere). Windows ships with a file called LMHOSTS.SAM, which is a sample file. Rename that file or create a new LMHOSTS file to use this system. In addition to the features described earlier, Windows supports some additional features in its LMHOSTS file:

Preloading: Following a name with the string #PRE causes Windows to preload the entry—that is, to load it into the name resolution system and use the entry before attempting any other lookup method.

Domain specification: You can specify a domain by using the #DOM:*DOMAIN* addition to a name.

Nonprinting characters: You can specify nonprinting characters in names by using the backslash (\) and a hexadecimal number, as in \0x20 to specify hexadecimal 20. This notation is used instead of Samba's notation of a hash mark and a trailing hexadecimal number.

Included files: You can include an additional file by using the #INCLUDE directive at the start of a line. If you want to include multiple lines, you may, but they're normally grouped together in blocks that begin with #BEGIN_ALTERNATE and end with #END_ALTERNATE. You can use this feature to load an lmhosts file from a server, as in #INCLUDE \\TAP\PUBLIC\lmhosts to load the lmhosts file from the PUBLIC share on the TAP computer.

The lmhosts file, whether used on Windows or with Samba, tends to be a bit awkward in many respects, but it does have certain advantages. Compared to the more common broadcasts and NBNS approaches, lmhosts has these important features:

Minimal network traffic: Because the lmhosts file is local to the computer that needs to resolve names, it minimizes network traffic associated with name resolution. (If you use the #INCLUDE directive to load a file from a network server, of course, this is no longer true.)

Router compatibility: The IP addresses you specify can belong to any of your local subnets or even to computers on very distant networks. Thus, lmhosts can be useful for linking computers across subnets, particularly when you have just a few clients on scattered subnets and don't want to use an NBNS computer.

Distributed maintenance: Using local lmhosts files can create a maintenance nightmare. If your network has 100 computers, you may need to update 100 lmhosts files whenever you add a computer or change its IP address. Using #INCLUDE to point Windows systems to network-accessible lmhosts files can reduce this burden, though. For Samba systems, you could create a cron job that periodically downloads the lmhosts file from the central repository, perform this step in the Samba startup script, or permanently mount the share that holds the network lmhosts file and use a symbolic link to point to it.

Need for special configuration: Some clients need special local options set to tell them to use an lmhosts file. This issue is described in the upcoming section "Configuring Clients to Use an NBNS System."

Using DNS As a Substitute for NetBIOS Names

In principle, there's no need to use broadcasts, an NBNS system, or lmhosts for SMB/CIFS name resolution. The reason these methods exist is largely historical—before SMB/CIFS was integrated with TCP/IP and run over Ethernet, Token Ring, and other modern network hardware, NetBIOS names were used directly by the network cards of the day. NetBEUI also used its own name resolution systems. These systems were adapted and ported to TCP/IP to maintain backward compatibility. Today, though, many clients, including Samba itself and Windows NT/200x/XP, can dispense with these NetBIOS-specific tools and use the TCP/IP standard DNS for name resolution. In fact, Samba's default is to use DNS before broadcasts or an NBNS system (but after lmhosts), at least for type 0x20 (file or print service) resources. Windows 200x/XP also uses DNS in preference to other name resolution systems.

Compared to other name resolution systems, using DNS offers certain advantages and drawbacks:

Router compatibility: DNS, as part of the Internet, is extremely router-friendly; you can locate any Internet-accessible SMB/CIFS server in this way, although you may need its complete hostname (including domain name) if it's not part of your Internet domain.

Network traffic: If you run a local DNS server, DNS lookups for SMB/CIFS systems should generate a small amount of network traffic and no broadcasts (this point is comparable to NBNS lookups). Some methods of access, though, might generate a full recursive lookup, which could generate unnecessary traffic off your local network.

Name compatibility: In most cases, a computer's DNS hostname will match its NetBIOS name. In such cases, DNS can be a good stand-in for NetBIOS names. If a computer's NetBIOS name and DNS hostname are different, though, using DNS to look up the computer won't work—at least, not if you try to use the NetBIOS name. This solution is also awkward at best when you need to locate resources that use workgroup names or usernames rather than machine names because these names aren't typically registered with DNS servers.

Centralized control: Small local networks may use just one DNS server; larger networks may use two or three for redundancy. In any event, the mapping of names to IP addresses is done on very few computers. This fact makes DNS resolution at least somewhat vulnerable to outages.

IP address changes: If your systems' IP addresses change frequently, you must enter those changes on the DNS server. If you fail to do this, SMB/CIFS name lookups will fail. Methods to integrate DNS with DHCP to avoid such problems exist but are beyond the scope of this book.

Given the prevalence of DNS, this approach to name resolution is a sensible one on many networks. It's also possible to link Samba configured to perform NBNS duties to DNS so that Samba performs a DNS lookup for at least some NBNS requests. This approach is described in the upcoming section "Configuring Samba As an NBNS System." On the other hand, the assumption of matching DNS and NetBIOS names is a weak one, and some methods of accessing resources using NetBIOS names (as when using workgroup names) are unlikely to work with DNS.

NOTE Some Samba parameters accept IP addresses as values. Prior to Samba 3.0, such parameters usually also accepted DNS hostnames. As of Samba 3.0, though, Samba accepts only DNS hostnames in its parameters if the `hostname lookups` parameter is set to `Yes`. This parameter's default value is `No`, so using DNS hostnames in parameters won't work unless you change this option. This setting also affects Samba's ability to substitute a hostname for the `%M` variable when it's used in a parameter's value. The `hostname lookups` parameter doesn't affect Samba's ability to use DNS as a client; you set that feature via the `name resolve order` parameter, as described in the upcoming section "Samba As a Client."

When to Use Each Method

Most SMB/CIFS systems support at least two of these four name resolution methods, typically in series—if one method fails, the computer falls back on a second method, and perhaps then a third and fourth. Thus, the question isn't so much *which one* method to use, but *in which order* they should be tried. DNS lookups, though, aren't supported by Windows 9x/Me systems, except indirectly via a Samba NBNS system that's configured to use DNS should conventional lookups fail.

Small single-subnet networks typically work well with broadcast name resolution or lmhosts lookups. Given that broadcast name resolution is easier to configure, this is often the preferred method for networks of not much more than a dozen or so computers. Such networks aren't likely to suffer noticeable speed degradation from the broadcasts, and on a single subnet, these broadcasts should be reliable, even if computers' IP addresses change regularly. Of course, you *can* use an NBNS or DNS server on a small network, but there's little or no advantage to configuring one for SMB/CIFS use. (If you need to set up a local DNS server for other reasons, though, using it for SMB/CIFS name resolution is perfectly reasonable.)

Although lmhosts can be used on small single-subnet networks, there's seldom any reason to use it in this context over broadcasts. This method of name resolution is most useful when you have a small network with a handful of systems (particularly clients) scattered on other subnets. In such an environment, coordinating the lmhosts files usually isn't too onerous, and it's a quick way to get remote systems communicating with your central network. For instance, you could install an lmhosts file on a home computer so that a telecommuter can participate in your office network's SMB/CIFS network. (This configuration has security implications, though, because you'll need to configure your firewall to pass the telecommuter's traffic. Passwords or other sensitive data might also be intercepted and decrypted.)

Domain configurations, described in more detail in Chapter 10, almost invariably include an NBNS system. Although you can set up a Samba server as a domain controller but not handle NBNS duties, chances are you won't do so. This isn't to say that NBNS systems are restricted to domain configurations; they can be used on workgroups, as well. NBNS setups require special client configuration—the client must be informed of the IP address of the NBNS system. This requirement makes NBNS configuration more labor-intensive compared to broadcast configuration on large single-subnet networks. If your network uses DHCP to assign IP addresses, you can deliver the NBNS computer's address automatically, as described in the upcoming section "Setting Options in a DHCP Server." Not all clients use this information, though. Even Windows clients may need to be specially configured to use it. Despite these drawbacks, an NBNS system can be a major asset on midsize and large networks. The NBNS system can be accessed across routers, which is a major help in binding together large networks. The NBNS system also reduces the number of broadcasts, which reduces overall network traffic levels as well as the load on servers.

DNS is another good choice for use on midsize and large networks. Like an NBNS computer, a DNS server provides cross-subnet compatibility and reduced network loads. Samba and recent versions of Windows use DNS resolution in preference to NBNS or broadcast resolution, at least by default, so using DNS may be a good choice for these clients. This resolution works only for the server service, though, so you may need to use other name resolution methods to support other features, such as Messenger (WinPopUp). Assuming you run a local DNS server already and have configured your systems to use this server, you'll require little or no special client configuration to use DNS for SMB/CIFS—*if* the client supports DNS, which not all do.

Any name resolution method you use to break through barriers imposed by routers is likely to be just part of the solution. Many SMB/CIFS clients, including Windows, present a hierarchical view of the SMB/CIFS network via a browser. Linking remote computers into a central network's browsing system isn't always simple. You may need to resort to a domain configuration, which typically uses an NBNS system, making this approach the logical choice for name resolution. Alternatively, you can use special Samba options to announce computers for inclusion in remote networks' browsing systems. Chapter 8 covers these issues in greater detail.

Samba NBNS Options

As with most SMB/CIFS features, Samba provides a number of options related to NBNS duties and to name resolution generally. The most interesting of these options relate to configuring Samba to function as an NBNS system. Some options relate to client operations or those required in support of other Samba server functions, though.

Configuring Samba As an NBNS System

Samba's nmbd server handles NBNS duties, if called upon to do so. These smb.conf parameters affect how these features are handled:

> **wins support**: This global Boolean parameter activates or deactivates Samba's NBNS features. The default value is No, but setting this value to Yes tells Samba to collect IP address and NetBIOS name mappings and to dispense them when requested.

> **wins proxy**: Samba has the ability to respond to broadcast name resolution requests on behalf of other computers. For instance, if a Samba server receives a broadcast query asking for the IP address for CHARLESTON, and if CHARLESTON has registered its address with the server, Samba can respond to this request. This feature is activated by setting the global Boolean wins proxy parameter to Yes. This setting can improve reliability if some systems on your network are set to use broadcast queries but others are configured to use the NBNS system. The default value for this parameter is No in recent versions of Samba, but in versions prior to 2.0, the default was Yes.

> **dns proxy**: This global Boolean parameter, when set to Yes (the default), causes a Samba NBNS system to link together the NBNS and DNS lookup methods to a limited extent. If the NBNS system receives a lookup request that it can't resolve, Samba performs a DNS query, using whatever DNS server the computer is configured to use, for that name. Because NetBIOS names don't include DNS domain names, the lookup will be restricted to whatever DNS domain names the Samba server is configured to search as part of its own DNS configuration. (Typically, the /etc/resolv.conf file lists

the domains that are to be searched.) For instance, if the server is configured to search the example.com and luna.edu domains, and if it receives a lookup request for BALLET, Samba will perform DNS lookups on ballet.example.com and ballet.luna.edu.

wins partners: This parameter was a short-lived addition to early Samba 3.0.*x* versions. It was intended to aid in using Samba as a backup NBNS system, but it didn't work in practice. Even if you're using a version of Samba that officially supports this parameter, you should ignore it.

max wins ttl: This global parameter tells nmbd how long, in seconds, a name registration with the NBNS system should last. (This *lease* may be broken before that time if the original registrant doesn't respond when a new system tries to claim the name, though.) The default value is 259200, which works out to be 3 days. In other words, NBNS won't grant a lease on a name that lasts more than three days. You shouldn't need to adjust this parameter.

min wins ttl: This global parameter works much like max wins ttl, except that it sets the *minimum* time for a lease on a NetBIOS name. The default value is 21600, which works out to be six hours. You shouldn't need to adjust this parameter. (In practice, the registrant asks for a lease time; the max wins ttl and min wins ttl parameters simply set limits on the lease times that the server will grant.)

The wins proxy, dns proxy, wins partners, max wins ttl, and min wins ttl parameters are all unimportant unless you set wins support = Yes. Furthermore, in most cases, the defaults on all of these parameters are acceptable; you need only add a single line to your [global] section to enable NBNS support:

```
wins support = Yes
```

CAUTION Don't set the wins server parameter (described in the upcoming section "Telling Samba About an NBNS System") if you set wins support = Yes. The two parameters are incompatible, and Samba may behave strangely if you try to set them both.

You should set the wins support = Yes option on only one Samba server. If you configure more than one computer as an NBNS system without configuring them to exchange NetBIOS name lists, and if you point different clients at each server, name resolution is likely to become spotty. Each client may only be able to resolve names for other clients registered to the same NBNS system, or at best, the systems will use a fallback method of name resolution.

Of course, setting these parameters appropriately is only half the story; you must also tell clients to use the NBNS computer. Doing so is described in the upcoming section "Configuring Clients to Use an NBNS System."

Linking Samba and DNS

A Samba NBNS system can refer to a DNS server to locate IP addresses as a last resort if you've set the dns proxy parameter. You can turn this one-way road into a two-way road by engaging in some extra configuration, though. At the core of this possibility is the wins hook parameter, which enables you to call an external program whenever a change is made to the server's NBNS database. This global parameter accepts a single executable or script name as its value:

```
wins hook = /usr/local/bin/dns_update
```

This example calls the dns_update script, which was distributed with Samba through the 2.0.*x* series, dropped with the 2.2.*x* series, and added back with Samba 3.0. If you're using Samba 2.2.*x*, download the source code for a 2.0.*x* or 3.0.*x* package to obtain the script. Unfortunately, wins hook doesn't work with Samba 3.0.0, but this has been fixed with version 3.0.1.

The wins hook parameter sends information to the script it calls in a specific order. This information, in the order it's passed, is as follows:

Operation: The first parameter is the operation that should be performed. This is one of add, delete, or refresh to add an entry, delete an entry, or refresh an entry, respectively.

Name: This parameter is the NetBIOS name of the client.

Resource ID: Samba passes the NetBIOS resource ID, as listed in Chapter 1's Table 1-2, to the script.

TTL: This parameter is the TTL value, in seconds, negotiated by the client and server.

IP addresses: The final parameter is a space-delimited list of IP addresses. (Typically, this is just one IP address.)

If you use the dns_update script or some other prepared script, you don't need to be very concerned with the details of what information is passed to the script. This information is more important if you want to write your own script to perform some other task.

You can install the dns_update script in some convenient location (this example assumes /usr/local/bin, but you can use another location if you prefer). You must then modify the script to fit your system:

Set the domain name: You must modify the script to specify the domain to which you want the NetBIOS names added. This option is set with the DOMAIN variable, which is set to wins.example.com. by default. Note that the trailing dot in this domain name is important. To avoid problems with misconfigured NetBIOS systems overwriting other servers' names, you may want to set up a subdomain for your NetBIOS systems.

Specify the DNS server: If you use the original dns_update script, there's no need to specify a DNS server; the script (or, more precisely, the nsupdate program upon which it relies) locates the domain's official DNS server automatically and contacts it. Sometimes, though, this doesn't work, so you must modify the script, as described in the sidebar "Specifying a DNS Server for dns_update."

Specifying a DNS Server for *dns_update*

The dns_server script uses a program called nsupdate to submit changes to a domain's DNS server. Ordinarily, this tool, under direction from dns_update, updates the DNS server for the domain specified by the dns_update script's DOMAIN variable. Sometimes, though, this process goes awry. This is particularly likely to happen if you operate a private domain that's not connected to the Internet or if you want to modify your local DNS servers but not the domain's official DNS servers (the ones that are accessible to the Internet at large). In these cases, you must make an additional change to the dns_update script. To do so, first locate the following line in dns_update:

```
echo update delete $NAME.$DOMAIN
```

You'll make a change by adding a line immediately *before* this line. The new line should read as follows:

```
echo server 127.0.0.1
```

This line tells dns_update to modify the DNS server running on 127.0.0.1—that is, the local computer. If you want to modify a DNS server running on another computer, you should change 127.0.0.1 in this line to the IP address of the DNS server you want to update.

After you modify the dns_update script and point the wins hook parameter to it, you must modify your DNS server's configuration to accept updates. To do this, you should locate the zone definition for the domain or subdomain you specified in the dns_server script's DOMAIN variable. If you use the popular Berkeley Internet Name Domain (BIND) server, this definition is normally in the /etc/named.conf file and is likely to look something like this:

```
zone "example.com" {
    type master;
    file "named.example.com";
    notify no;
};
```

Various details of this definition may vary, but it should begin with a zone keyword and specify a file in which DNS records are stored. To configure the DNS server to accept updates, add a line between the curly braces like the following:

```
allow-update { 127.0.0.1; };
```

CAUTION Don't forget the semicolons (;) in this line. If you do, the entry won't work correctly!

Change the IP address (`127.0.0.1`) to match the IP address of your Samba server. (If your DNS and Samba servers are one and the same computer, `127.0.0.1` will work well.) This line tells BIND to accept updates from whatever IP address you specify.

CAUTION Telling a DNS server to accept updates from a remote computer is a potential security risk. One way to reduce the risk is to implement a challenge-response authorization system. To do so, use the key keyword and a key instead of an IP address in the allow-update line in named.conf. You must then change the call to nsupdate in the dns_update script to support passing a key via the -y or -k parameter. Consult the BIND documentation for more details about implementing this type of security. If you don't implement such restrictions, it's best to perform DNS updates only on private local networks or on a single computer using the 127.0.0.1 loopback address.

After making these changes, you'll have to restart both Samba (the nmbd server, to be precise) and your DNS server. At this point, if all goes well, new SMB/CIFS systems should appear in your domain's DNS listings when they start.

TIP Try using a Samba system other than the NBNS computer as an NBNS client to test the wins hook operation. You can have it contact the NBNS system by shutting down its nmbd server and then restarting it, which is much simpler than rebooting a Windows computer.

Unfortunately, this chain of connections is quite delicate, so chances are good you'll have problems the first time you try to implement automated DNS updates via wins hook. These are some key problem areas to check:

Samba version: Samba 3.0.0 doesn't work with `wins hook`, although versions before and after this one work properly.

Samba `wins hook` operation: Try replacing the usual `wins hook` call with a call to a simple script that echoes its parameters to a file, via a line such as `echo $1 $2 $3 $4 $5 > /tmp/winsparms.txt`. You can then check the `/tmp/winsparms.txt` file to be sure that the `wins hook` call is occurring and is receiving the correct information from the client.

Samba NBNS configuration: Your Samba server must be correctly configured to handle NBNS duties. In particular, be sure that `wins support = Yes`.

DNS `nsupdate` operation: On the DNS server, try manually entering the commands specified near the bottom of the `dns_update` script. These commands appear after `echo` keywords in the segment delimited by curly braces, as in `update delete $NAME.$DOMAIN`. When entering these commands manually, you first type **nsupdate -d** and then type the commands at its prompt, but you must change the variable names to appropriate values, as in **update delete tap.example.com.** When you're done, press the Enter key and observe the output, which should include the string `status: NOERROR`. If you see another status chances are your DNS server isn't correctly configured to accept updates, or there's been an authentication error in handling the updates.

DNS authentication: Double-check the IP addresses specified in the zone record for the domain you want to dynamically modify. If you modified the script as described in the sidebar "Specifying a DNS Server for `dns_update`," check that you entered the correct IP address and command. Also be sure that the DNS server is listening to the correct IP address. If your `named.conf` file includes a `listen-on` directive, be sure it lists the appropriate IP address, such as `127.0.0.1` if you use the loopback interface for updates on a computer with both Samba and DNS servers.

Once the system is working, it should accept updates for forward DNS lookups, but reverse DNS lookups won't be modified—at least, not with the stock `dns_update` script. In principle, you could expand this script so that it would change your domain's reverse DNS lookups, as well. On most networks on which such dynamic DNS updates are important, though, it's the forward lookups that are most important, so a lack of reverse DNS lookup mapping isn't critically important.

Telling Samba About an NBNS System

If your network uses NBNS name resolution, all your Samba servers and clients must have access to the NBNS computer. Servers must know about the NBNS system to register their names so that clients can contact them, and clients must know about the server to contact the NBNS system to resolve names. (Additional Samba name resolution options are described in the upcoming section "Samba As a Client.") If you fail to include a `wins server` line on a network that uses NBNS, clients may be unable to locate servers—either clients locating your Samba server or Samba clients locating other servers.

If Samba itself is an NBNS system (that is, if wins support = Yes), Samba uses itself for this role. For systems that aren't configured as NBNS computers, though, you must point to at least one NBNS system using the global wins server parameter. This parameter accepts one or more NBNS systems' IP addresses as its value. For instance, if your network's NBNS systems are 192.168.8.27 and 192.168.9.1, you might include the following line in your smb.conf file's [global] section:

```
wins server = 192.168.8.27 192.168.9.1
```

NOTE Instead of an IP address, you can list a DNS hostname for the NBNS system if hostname lookups = Yes. Doing so, though, makes Samba somewhat reliant on DNS. As a general rule, using IP addresses is preferable to using hostnames. You *cannot* use a NetBIOS name as the value of a wins server parameter. (Of course, if the NetBIOS name and DNS name are identical, you can use the name as a DNS name.)

The wins server line actually has two effects: First, it tells Samba (nmbd, to be precise) to register itself with the specified server or servers when Samba starts up. Second, it tells Samba clients to use the specified NBNS system for name resolution, assuming they need to do so based on the name resolve order parameter (described in the upcoming section "Samba As a Client").

The servers to which you point with wins server can be Samba servers configured with wins support = Yes or Windows systems configured as NBNS systems. In the former case, chances are you'll only list one IP address because Samba doesn't support backup NBNS operation. In principle, though, you could list the IP addresses of NBNS systems on unrelated networks. If you do this, your server will be available to clients on both networks, and your Samba clients will be able to more easily access servers on both networks.

Another option related to communicating with other NBNS systems is max ttl. This parameter tells Samba what TTL value, in seconds, to request when registering a name with a remote NBNS system. The default max ttl value is 259200, or three days. Note that the NBNS system might grant a longer or shorter TTL value than what Samba requests. (In the case of a Samba NBNS system, the max wins ttl and min wins ttl parameters, described in the earlier section "Configuring Samba As an NBNS System," are the ultimate authorities for the TTL granted to the client.)

Configuring Clients to Use an NBNS System

To use NBNS, clients must be told how to access the server. Typically, this means either giving the client the IP address of the NBNS system directly or delivering this information along with other network configuration options via DHCP. Precisely how this is done depends upon the OS in question. These options also tend to be tied up with other name resolution options, such as telling the client to use DNS instead of or in addition to NBNS.

Samba As a Client

In principle, a Samba server doesn't need to resolve NetBIOS names. When a client contacts the server, the server can and does send data back to the client via IP address, even if the server can't resolve the client's name. Nonetheless, Samba includes mechanisms to support name resolution. The smb.conf options related to name resolution (as opposed to server-side NBNS configuration) are used primarily by Samba's client programs, such as smbclient.

NOTE Programs that call libsmbclient, such as KDE's Konqueror, also use the options described here. Such programs often create an smb.conf file in the user's ~/.smb subdirectory, though, and this file's settings override the global smb.conf options.

The primary Samba name resolution option is name resolve order. This global parameter tells Samba what mechanisms to use to resolve NetBIOS names and in what order to try them. This parameter accepts four values:

lmhosts: If this value is present, Samba tries reading the lmhosts file as a name resolution mechanism.

host: This value refers to the host's native name resolution system. Typically, this system supports a combination of methods, the most important of which is DNS. Other methods may include /etc/hosts and an NIS directory. Some systems, including IRIX, Solaris, and most Linux distributions, use a file called /etc/nsswitch.conf to determine what methods are used and in what order. This method only supports lookups of names with a service type code of 0x20 (that is, the server service, which identifies file and printer shares).

wins: This value corresponds to NBNS lookups. If you use this option, you should also either point to an NBNS computer with the wins server parameter or include the wins support = Yes parameter. (In the latter case, Samba looks to itself as the NBNS system.)

bcast: To use broadcast name resolution, you should provide this value. Samba sends broadcasts to all of the interfaces listed in the interfaces parameter—normally all of the interfaces on the computer. This method of resolution is important because it's the only method that can find a local master browser. Although many Samba tools don't rely on the local master browser, some do, such as GUI network browsers. If such tools don't work, double-check that this option is present.

You can provide any set of these four name resolution codes in your name resolve order parameter. The default value is lmhosts host wins bcast, meaning that Samba checks the lmhosts file first, then tries DNS and other standard TCP/IP name resolution methods, then tries NBNS, and finally tries a broadcast. You can specify any other order you like, though, or use just a subset of these methods. For instance, you might try the following:

```
name resolve order = wins host
```

This order uses NBNS first, followed by DNS and any other locally defined lookup methods. In this example, Samba doesn't check the lmhosts file or use broadcast name resolution.

Microsoft Windows

How you configure Windows to use an NBNS system depends on the version of Windows you're running, but all versions of Windows locate the NBNS system by IP address. If your network uses DHCP for IP address assignment, you can tell Windows systems to accept the NBNS information provided by the DHCP server. (Configuring the DHCP server, in turn, is described in the upcoming section "Setting Options in a DHCP Server.")

Windows 9x/Me

Windows 9*x*/Me supports name resolution via broadcasts, NBNS, or lmhosts file. The default is to use broadcasts or, if present, an lmhosts file. To enable NBNS resolution, follow these steps:

1. Double-click the Network icon in the Control Panel. This action brings up a Network dialog box in which you can select various components (that is, drivers, network stacks, and protocols).

2. Select the TCP/IP component for your local network card. (Some systems may have more than one TCP/IP component, one for each network connection, such as one for an Ethernet card and another for a dial-up modem connection.) The Properties button should become available.

3. Click Properties. This action opens the TCP/IP Properties dialog box.

4. Click the WINS Configuration tab in the TCP/IP Properties dialog box. The result resembles Figure 9-1.

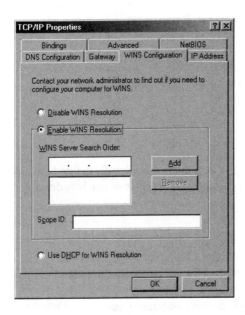

Figure 9-1. You can tell Windows 9x/Me to use NBNS by entering the server's address in your TCP/IP Properties dialog box.

5. Click the Enable WINS Resolution button. You should now be able to enter information in the WINS Server Search Order field.

6. Type the IP address of your NBNS system in the WINS Server Search Order field and then click Add. The IP address should move to the box below the WINS Server Search Order field.

7. If your network has multiple NBNS systems, repeat step 6 for any additional NBNS systems on your network.

8. Click OK in the TCP/IP Properties dialog box and then in the Network dialog box.

If you've changed your settings, Windows will tell you that you must restart to enable the changes. If you don't do so, Windows will continue using the old name resolution system until you reboot. Particularly for the first client you change, you should reboot after making these changes to be sure they work correctly. When Windows restarts, try connecting to several servers that have already been reconfigured to use NBNS.

If you configure Windows 9x/Me to use an NBNS system and if that server fails or doesn't have a listing for the requested name, Windows will automatically fall back on broadcast name resolution. In all cases, the lmhosts file, if present, may also be used.

If your network uses DHCP and you configure the DHCP server to deliver the NBNS system's address, you can have Windows use that information by selecting the Use DHCP for WINS Resolution button in the TCP/IP Properties dialog box (shown in Figure 9-1). When so configured, there's no need to enter an IP address in the WINS Server Search Order field.

Windows NT 4.0

You can configure Windows NT 4.0 to use NBNS in much the same way you can con-figure Windows 9*x*/Me. For the most part, therefore, the procedure presented in the preceding section works for Windows NT. There are some differences, though:

Administrator access: You must normally make your changes when logged in as the Administrator, the Windows administrative user.

TCP/IP Properties tabs: The TCP/IP Properties dialog box has different names on its tabs. The one you need to use is called WINS Address.

Adapter selection: You can select different NBNS options for different network adapters from the TCP/IP Properties dialog box.

NBNS IP address specification: Instead of using a WINS Server Search Order field, Windows NT provides fields to enter the primary and secondary WINS servers' IP addresses.

Using DNS and lmhosts: Windows NT provides check boxes to enable using DNS and lmhosts. Check whichever option you want to use in addition to NBNS. (You can use both if you like.)

Windows NT automatically uses NBNS information provided by a DHCP server; there's no need to explicitly enable this feature. The default settings also use lmhosts (if present) but do not use a DNS server.

Windows 200x and XP

Although Windows 200*x* and XP are derived from Windows NT, their method for setting NBNS options is different. These options are buried quite deeply in the network configuration tools. To find and change them, follow these steps:

1. Open the Control Panel.

2. Open the Network and Dial-up Connections (Windows 2000) or Network Connections (Windows XP) object.

3. Right-click the Local Area Connections object, and select Properties from the resulting context menu. The Local Area Connection Properties dialog box appears.

4. Select the Internet Protocol (TCP/IP) component, and click the Properties button. Windows displays a new dialog box called Internet Protocol (TCP/IP) Properties.

5. Click the Advanced button. The result is the Advanced TCP/IP Settings dialog box.

6. Click the WINS tab. The dialog box should resemble Figure 9-2. (This figure was captured on a Windows XP system; some details differ in Windows 200*x*.)

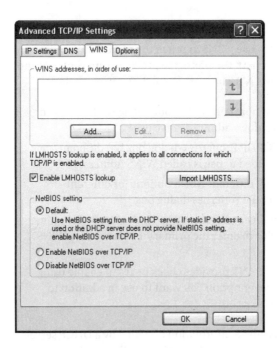

Figure 9-2. Windows 200x/XP provides finer-grained control over name resolution options than does Windows 9x/Me.

7. To add an NBNS system to the list, click the Add button. The result is the TCP/IP WINS Server dialog box.

8. Enter the IP address of your NBNS system in the TCP/IP WINS Server dialog box, and click Add. The IP address you entered should appear in the WINS Addresses, in Order of Use field of the Advanced TCP/IP Settings dialog box.

9. Repeat steps 7–8 for each additional NBNS computer on your network.

10. Click OK or Close on each of the open dialog boxes to dismiss them and implement your new settings.

By default, Windows 200*x*/XP uses DNS as a stand-in for NetBIOS name resolution and falls back on the other methods (NBNS, lmhosts, or a broadcast) as necessary. You can disable the use of lmhosts from the Advanced TCP/IP Settings dialog box if you like, but other name resolution methods aren't easy to disable.

NOTE The Advanced TCP/IP Settings dialog box provides radio buttons that support enabling or disabling use of NetBIOS over TCP/IP. These options control whether Windows uses NBT or "raw" SMB/CIFS over TCP/IP. If you select the Disable NetBIOS Over TCP/IP option, you must be sure that your Samba server supports "raw" SMB/CIFS, using port 445. Recent versions of Samba provide this support by default, but it could be disabled. If you have problems with this setting, check your Samba smb ports option; it must include the value 445 (probably in addition to 139), as in smb ports = 445 139.

Setting Options in a DHCP Server

Some NBNS clients, including Windows systems, can use information on NBNS provided by a DHCP server. To use such information, of course, the clients must be configured to use the DHCP server to obtain their IP addresses. The DHCP server must also be told about the NBNS system's IP address. Using DHCP to deliver this information can improve the reliability of your network configuration. Instead of typing NBNS systems' IP addresses into potentially hundreds of clients, you need to type it into just one server's configuration files. This fact alone reduces the odds of a typo causing problems—and if you *do* mistype the IP address, you'll learn about it more quickly and be able to correct it quite easily. Likewise, if the IP address of your NBNS system ever needs to change, you can alter it for your entire network in one fell swoop.

The most popular DHCP server for Unix systems is the Internet Software Consortium's (ISC's) server (http://www.isc.org/products/DHCP/). This software is configured via a file called dhcpd.conf, which usually appears in /etc or /usr/local/etc. This file typically begins with a series of settings that apply globally, followed by blocks beginning with the keyword subnet or host and delimited by curly braces ({}) to set options for particular IP address blocks or specific hosts.

CAUTION Don't confuse the DHCP server (dhcpd) with the DHCP client (dhcpcd). Because of the single-letter difference in these names, it's easy to mistakenly install the wrong package.

Several DHCP server options affect NetBIOS networks and NBNS features in particular. These options begin with the keyword option, and the most important of these options are as follows:

netbios-name-servers: This option lets you pass the IP addresses of one or more NBNS systems in a comma-delimited list.

netbios-node-type: This option lets you tell the DHCP clients in what order to try broadcast name resolution and NBNS-mediated name resolution. It takes a value that ranges from 1 to 8. A value of 1 means to use broadcasts alone (that is, to configure the client as a B node), and 2 means to use NBNS with no fallback on broadcasts (a P node). A value of 4 means to use broadcasts first but to fall back on NBNS (an M node), and 8 means to use NBNS with a fallback on broadcasts (an H node). In most cases, a value of 8 is the most sensible one.

Typically, you'll put these options in the first few lines of the dhcpd.conf file, before any subnet or host declarations. You can, however, put these options within these declarations to deliver customized NBNS settings to specific subnets or even specific computers. Most configuration lines in dhcpd.conf end in semicolons (;). All in all, these configuration options will resemble the following:

```
option netbios-name-servers 192.168.8.202;
option netbios-node-type 8;
```

Unfortunately, most non-Windows clients ignore DHCP-provided NBNS options. Setting these options won't do a Unix system running Samba clients any good, for instance. Even Windows 9x/Me clients must be configured to use the DHCP-provided information, as described in the preceding section "Windows 9x/Me." Thus, at first glance, it might appear that the effort saved in setting Windows to use DHCP-provided information might not be worth the hassle of configuring the DHCP server to provide this information. This may be true if your network doesn't use DHCP or if you can't readily change the DHCP information your network provides (say, if you use the simple DHCP servers included with some broadband routers). If you use a full ISC DHCP server, though, you do save keystrokes when you configure it to provide this information because you needn't enter the NBNS systems' IP addresses on all the clients. Furthermore, Windows NT/200x/XP systems automatically pick up this information by default, which simplifies their configuration if you provide this information via DHCP.

Summary

NetBIOS name resolution is complex because SMB/CIFS systems have collected four major methods of name resolution over the years, and different systems favor different methods of name resolution. Samba provides options both for its own name resolution needs, such as name resolve order, and for options related to the delivery of one of the name resolution services supported by NBT: NBNS. Samba can deliver NBNS services to Windows, Samba, and other clients. In most respects, Samba's NBNS functions work identically to those that can be provided by a Windows server, but there are some subtle differences. Samba's support for operating as a secondary NBNS system is weak at best, and you can't mix platforms for primary and backup NBNS systems. Samba can fall back on DNS as a source of information about IP addresses, which can improve reliability in some situations. With the help of some external scripts, Samba can also dynamically update a DNS server's database to include the NetBIOS names provided by clients, which can be a convenient way to provide static DNS hostnames on a network that otherwise uses dynamic IP address assignment. If you use Samba on an NBNS system, you must tell your clients how to find the NBNS computer. You can do this by entering an IP address in a configuration file or dialog box and setting appropriate name resolution orders or options. Details vary from system to system, though. In some cases, DHCP can help in this process by delivering the IP address from the main DHCP server configuration file.

Configuring a Domain Controller

MANY WINDOWS NETWORKS, particularly large networks or those that span multiple subnets, operate as *NT domains* (a.k.a. *NetBIOS domains*). Domains are like workgroups, but they offer a degree of centralized control, which is provided by the *domain controller*. The domain controller offers support functions such as centralized logons, as well as some ancillary benefits. Naturally, you can configure Samba to operate as a domain controller. A single Samba server can fill this role, but it's also possible to tie multiple computers together to provide redundancy, in case one domain controller crashes or is cut off from others because of a network problem. As with many other SMB/CIFS features, to use a domain controller, you must be able to configure your clients to use it. This task, as with many in the SMB/CIFS world, is handled differently for different client OSs.

NOTE Samba's support for more recent domain-like tools, such as Active Directory (AD), is quite limited. Samba can be a member of an AD domain, but it can't function as an AD domain controller. Samba's tools for handling the older NT-style domains are much more complete.

The Role of the Domain Controller

The core of a domain is its domain controller. In fact, in a very real sense a domain is nothing but a workgroup with a domain controller. What does a domain controller do, though? Its primary function is to centralize logon functions—that is, to authorize one system to process all logon requests for the domain. Doing this greatly simplifies administration, particularly on a network with many servers. In the process, domain controllers also take on additional duties that are peripheral to their core user authentication role.

The Problem: Providing Centralized Logons

In a workgroup, every server is responsible for authenticating users who connect to its shares. In the case of a Samba server, the system can authenticate users based on either the underlying Unix password database (when using cleartext passwords) or the

Samba encrypted password database (when using encrypted passwords). (Chapter 7 describes local Samba authentication and account management options in more detail.) In many cases, this approach works quite well, and it's certainly easy to implement on a small scale. The problem occurs when the network grows. Consider a corporate network with half a dozen servers, each of which must authenticate the same 100 users. Now consider what happens when one employee leaves the company and is replaced by another. The system administrator must remove the accounts for the old user on all six servers and add accounts for the new user on all six servers. Similar redundant changes are necessary whenever users update their passwords. A failure to make such changes is likely to result in logon failures to some servers from some clients because some SMB/CIFS clients try to use the same username/password pair on all servers.

Unless employee turnover is exceptionally low, keeping all the servers' accounts synchronized is an extremely tedious task. The problem is made worse when the network uses a peer-to-peer design, in which most workstations can share files with other workstations. Imagine trying to update the passwords, add accounts, or delete accounts on 50 computers! Doing this job just once will send you looking for an alternative. In the SMB/CIFS world, this alternative is a domain.

NOTE   NT domains are not the same as Internet domains. The upcoming section "NT Domains vs. Internet Domains" covers this distinction in more detail.

The idea behind an NT domain is to hand off all authentication duties to a single computer, the *domain controller*. In fact, two different types of NT domain controller exist. A *primary domain controller* (PDC) is the final authority on information about the domain. The *backup domain controller* (BDC) is the understudy; it takes over if the PDC fails. The BDC, when present, also typically processes most of the actual logon requests. When the distinction isn't important, I refer to the *domain controller*; otherwise, I use the appropriate abbreviation. A small domain might have only a PDC with no BDC, but larger domains frequently have both types of domain controller. Each NT domain can have just one PDC but zero, one, or more BDCs.

In a workgroup configuration, the client contacts the server and delivers authentication information to that server, including the username, the (possibly encrypted) password, and the name of the share the user wants to access. The server performs whatever security checks it deems appropriate and tells the client the outcome. If the connection was authorized, the client can then access the resource in question.

In a domain configuration, the procedure is more complex. In the simplest case (known as *pass-through authentication*), the client contacts the server (which actually doesn't need to be a full domain member) to log onto the domain. In response, the server passes the logon request onto the domain controller and passes subsequent logon data back and forth between the client and the domain controller. The domain controller grants or denies the logon request, and the server honors this outcome. In a more complex arrangement (known as *NetLogon authentication*), the server (which is known as a *domain member server* in this case) performs its own authentication of the client using data passed to it via its own secure connection to the domain controller. Essentially, the domain member server uses the domain controller as a remote authentication database. To accomplish this goal, the domain member server must be a full member of the domain, which requires additional configuration, as described in the upcoming section "Using Domain Logons."

Despite the added complexity involved in accessing a single share, a domain configuration greatly simplifies administration when a network hosts multiple servers. Using a single domain controller means that adding, deleting, or modifying user accounts need only be done on the domain controller. Domain configurations also provide additional benefits, as described in the next section, "Additional Domain Controller Duties."

NOTE   In the case of Samba servers, a domain configuration doesn't simplify matters quite as much as you might hope. Specifically, the Unix system must still have a local account for the user who's trying to access the server. Thus, you must still create and delete local accounts. If the user doesn't need non-Samba access to the server, though, you can configure these accounts to deny regular logon access, and you won't need to deal with changing user passwords on these servers. You may also be able to use Unix-style network account management tools, such as the Network Information System (NIS), to manage Unix accounts in a centralized manner. The upcoming section "Configuring Samba Clients" describes how to use a domain controller as a local account backend. You can use this configuration to eliminate the need to maintain a separate Unix account database, but this configuration entails additional setup.

Domains always use encrypted passwords. For this reason, a Samba domain controller must maintain a Samba encrypted password database, as described in Chapter 7. Samba servers that are members of a domain must also use encrypted passwords, but they don't need to maintain a local encrypted password database; instead, they pass authentication requests to the domain controller. (Configuring a Samba server as part of a domain is described in the upcoming section "Configuring Samba Servers.")

In use, domain controllers provide *domain logons*. As described in the upcoming section "Using Domain Logons," users log onto the domain. Thereafter, they have access to all a domain's resources—at least, potentially. Individual servers can restrict access to particular shares or files. The concept of a domain logon is important, though. In many respects, it's similar to logging onto a Kerberos realm or using an NIS server, but it's unlike many other server-oriented logons familiar to Unix administrators, which rely on authentication local to the server providing the service. Although individual servers can limit access by particular users or from particular clients, their deference to the domain controller makes a single logon to access any domain resource practical. On the other hand, NT domain logons are unlike Kerberos logons in that clients actually cache the passwords their users enter and reauthenticate themselves with each new server. (In Kerberos, the Kerberos logon server authenticates each system once and provides *tickets* that these systems can use for authentication.) The effects of the two systems look similar to users, but they're different under the surface.

Additional Domain Controller Duties

In addition to handling domain logons, domain controllers provide several other functions. Some of these functions involve features that are described in greater detail in other chapters of this book; these features are associated with the domain controller largely as a matter of convenience. Other functions are more closely tied to domain control in a conceptual way. In any event, these duties include the following:

NBNS functions: Domain controllers typically function as NetBIOS Name Server (NBNS) systems. You can separate these two functions in Samba, but it's usually most convenient to use a single system for both functions, particularly on smaller domains with only one domain controller. Chapter 9 describes configuring a Samba system as an NBNS system.

Domain master browser: Part of every domain is the *domain master browser*, which coordinates browse lists across different subnets and handles master browser duties on its own local subnet. You activate domain master browser and domain controller duties separately in Samba, but the two are very tightly bound together in practice. For this reason, you should always configure a domain controller as a domain master browser. Chapter 8 covers the details of master browser configuration.

Roaming profile management: A *roaming profile* is a way to store user preferences for Windows desktop configuration on a server. If you configure a domain to support roaming profiles, users who regularly log onto multiple computers can see identical desktops on all of their computers. Although you needn't store the roaming profiles on the domain controller itself, some domain controller features help implement roaming profiles. Chapter 14 describes this topic in more detail.

Domain logon scripts: You can store scripts on a server and configure Windows clients to execute these scripts when users log onto a domain. Like roaming profiles, this feature can help provide consistent features to clients. Chapter 14 covers this topic in more detail.

Time server: Computers on a domain can obtain the correct time from a domain controller, as described in Chapter 12. In both theory and practice, another computer can function as the time server, but the domain controller is usually a reliable system and, therefore, a good choice for this role.

Share server: A domain controller can hold ordinary SMB/CIFS file and printer shares, although it isn't required to do so. (A couple of near exceptions are the NETLOGON share and a share for holding roaming profiles. Neither is absolutely required for a bare-bones domain controller, but many domain functions rely upon these shares.)

Non-SMB/CIFS servers: You can run non-Samba servers on a domain controller to provide functions that aren't closely related to SMB/CIFS. For instance, you can run an NFS or Netatalk server to share files with computers that don't work well with SMB/CIFS. Chapter 1 and Chapter 12 describe some of these protocols.

Because the domain controller is so important to an SMB/CIFS network's operation, the domain controller is typically a very reliable computer. The stability of both Samba and the Unix-like OSs on which it runs makes this combination a good choice for domain controller duties. Windows NT and 200*x* are also popular choices for domain controller duty, but configuring them as such is beyond the scope of this book. (Nonetheless, if your network uses a Windows domain controller, the upcoming section "Using Domain Logons" is relevant.) Windows XP, although its heritage goes back to Windows NT and 2000, isn't able to serve as a domain controller. Windows 9*x*/Me is also incapable of functioning as a domain controller.

NOTE Windows 2000 introduced AD, which extends and replaces many traditional NT domain features. Thus, if you use a Windows 200*x* domain controller, chances are it will be built upon AD. Samba can participate as a client on an AD-controlled network but can't provide AD domain controller functions, at least not as of Samba 3.0. Windows 200*x* AD controllers also provide the older NT-style domain features but store authentication information in the AD database.

Domains vs. Workgroups

Before configuring a domain, you should be sure you need one. In many cases, a workgroup configuration will work as well, and workgroups require less in the way of configuration. Traditional benefits of domains include the following:

Domain logons: As noted earlier in "The Problem: Providing Centralized Logons," domains enable a single logon to use all of a network's servers. This feature is obviously most important when your network has several servers or uses a peer-to-peer configuration. If your network has just one or two servers, a domain will save little or no effort in managing accounts or logons compared to a workgroup.

Multiple subnets: If your network is split across two or more subnets, with routers in between, the broadcast mechanisms for name resolution and browsing upon which SMB/CIFS relies won't work. Traditionally, Windows-only networks have used a domain configuration to work around this problem, and this approach is certainly a reasonable one. Samba, though, enables you to run a domain master browser without using a full domain and provides special features that enable local master browsers to exchange browse lists, as described in Chapter 8. Using these features and an NBNS system, as described in Chapter 9, enables you to span multiple subnets with a workgroup configuration.

Improved account security: By centralizing your logons, you can eliminate redundant password files. Windows 9*x*/Me clients are notorious for storing password files locally, where they can be easily stolen. The upcoming section "Improving Windows 9*x*/Me Domain Security" describes how to reconfigure these clients so they don't unnecessarily store password files.

Account automation tools: Roaming profiles and domain logon scripts, described in Chapter 14, are available only on domains. You may be able to jury-rig something to fill a similar role in a workgroup, but doing so will require more effort.

Overall, the most compelling reasons to use a domain are to simplify account maintenance on a multiserver network and to provide account automation tools. You must evaluate your own network to determine whether the hassle of configuring and maintaining a domain controller is worth the benefits of reduced account maintenance effort and of account automation tools. One alternative way to reduce account maintenance is to consolidate several servers into one. For instance, if you've got half a dozen low-end servers, you might be able to replace them with one more powerful server. In some cases, you may also be able to convert a server to use guest accounts. For instance, you might not be terribly concerned with authentication for a system that functions only as a print server. In this case, you can set up few Samba accounts and configure the server's printer shares to use guest accounts.

 TIP   If all of your servers run Samba, a sort of partial domain configuration can work nicely. Configure one computer as a domain controller, as described in this chapter, but don't configure machine trust accounts for it. You can then configure your other Samba servers with the `security = Server` parameter. This configuration causes the Samba server to defer to the domain controller for authentication, but the server doesn't need to be part of the domain. This results in many of the benefits of domain configuration but less administrative hassle. This system does not, by itself, provide the account automation benefits, though, and adding them for Windows NT/200*x*/XP clients will require creating trust accounts for those clients, reducing the administrative effort benefits to almost nothing.

The benefits of account automation don't compare so easily to the administrative effort of handling a domain controller. These benefits apply largely to users rather than to network administrators, although providing a domain startup script can enable you to quickly modify features on all of a network's clients.

NT Domains vs. Internet Domains

If you're familiar with Internet networking, you're no doubt familiar with Internet domains. Understanding NT domains requires that you ignore everything you know about Internet domains. Despite the use of the same name for both concepts, they're completely unrelated. (They do share a few features but not enough to be very helpful in understanding NT domains.)

NT domains are far more closely related to NetBIOS workgroups than to Internet domains. Unlike Internet domains, NT domains can't be subdivided into subdomains. NT domains are purely local constructs; unless you take special steps to link domain components across subnets, they exist only on your own local network. NT domains rely upon a domain controller, which has no counterpart in Internet domains (although DNS servers are roughly analogous to NBNS systems on a domain).

As a practical matter, though, you may want to name your NT domains after the Internet domains to which they correspond. For instance, suppose you're administering the network for the luna.edu Internet domain, which has subdomains set up for each academic department—english.luna.edu, history.luna.edu, physics.luna.edu, and so on. You might create NT domains called ENGLISH, HISTORY, PHYSICS, and so on, each of which corresponds to the like-named Internet subdomain. This practice will minimize user confusion. If each Internet subdomain has just a few computers, you might use a single domain (LUNA in this case), but it might be too large if the number of subdomains is large. On a small network (say, a 12-computer network using the example.org domain), you could name the NT domain after the Internet domain (EXAMPLE in this case). Using another name, such as MYNET or STUDIO, is certainly possible, but users might mistake the NT domain name for the Internet domain name or vice versa.

Your choice of NT domain structure has security and authentication implications. If you use many local domains, users must authenticate to just one domain controller and thereafter may use resources on that domain. To use resources on another domain, the user may need to authenticate against its controller, or you may need to set up interdomain trust relationships, as described in the upcoming section "Setting Up Interdomain Trust Relationships." If you use just one large domain, though, all the users will authenticate against just one domain user database. This configuration can simplify authentication tasks but can make it harder to set up differing access rules for different groups of computers.

Configuring Samba As a Domain Controller

The core Samba domain controller options are fairly straightforward to configure. These options enable Samba to authenticate users for remote systems, provide for domain logon scripts, and so on. If your network is dominated by Windows 9x/Me systems, this set of basic features may be all you need, at least for the bulk of your network. Windows NT/200x/XP, though, uses more advanced authentication methods, and Samba requires additional options to support these clients.

Samba Domain Controller Capabilities

Samba has long supported domain controller features, but this support is incomplete. As a general rule, Samba can function quite well as a domain controller for Windows 9*x*/Me systems and can perform the most important domain-control functions for Windows NT/200*x*/XP systems. One of the most important limitations of Samba is in its support for AD, which is a newer authentication and account maintenance system than the one used with the NT-style domains that Samba implements. Although Samba 3.0 includes some AD support, its capacity to work as an AD server is still quite limited. A Samba server can authenticate itself against a Windows domain controller that uses AD, though.

Samba also provides limited or no support for a handful of Windows NT–style domain control features, such as machine policy files and group policy objects. Samba 3.0 supports most NT-style domain features, though, including the critical basic logon functions, roaming profiles, and domain logon scripts.

Samba can function as a PDC on a network with no BDC or with a Samba BDC and can function as a BDC to a Samba PDC. Samba cannot be used as a PDC with a Windows BDC or as a BDC to a Windows PDC; the protocols used for exchanging data between the PDC and the BDC are different for Samba and Windows, so the two platforms can't interact in this way. In fact, even a network with multiple Samba domain controllers is extremely difficult to configure—so much so that it's best avoided except on domains with thousands of users.

NOTE   The best way to configure a network with both a Samba PDC and a Samba BDC is to use the Lightweight Directory Access Protocol (LDAP) as an authentication backend for Samba. This configuration can be tricky and affects both the PDC and the BDC.

As a general rule, Samba makes a very good domain controller for a network that uses Windows 9*x*/Me clients. If your network uses Windows NT/200*x*/XP clients, Samba 3.0 can function as a domain controller, but it uses the NT-style domain control protocols, with limited or no support for the AD-based protocols favored by the latest versions of Windows. If you need these AD features, you may be forced to use a Windows 200*x* domain controller; however, the NT-style domain control protocols are perfectly adequate for many networks.

Samba Domain Controller Options

Conceptually, a domain controller is an ordinary Samba server that's configured to enable other computers to request authentication services. The Samba server must be configured with its own encrypted password database, and it must accept some additional parameters to support domain functions:

security = User: A Samba domain controller must be configured to provide user-level security, as opposed to share-, server-, or domain-level security. (Samba servers that do *not* function as domain controllers but that are part of the domain use domain-level security, though, as described in the upcoming section "Configuring Samba Servers.")

encrypt passwords = Yes: The password exchange between the domain controller and its clients uses encrypted passwords, so Samba must be configured to use encrypted passwords. Chapter 7 describes how to configure this feature in more detail.

passdb backend = smbpasswd: This parameter tells the server to use the Samba encrypted password file, smbpasswd, for authentication. Other valid values for a domain controller include tdbsam and ldapsam, both of which use databases maintained by outside programs. You can also specify custom "plug-in" authentication systems, and Mac OS X 10.3's default Samba uses this system, integrating Samba authentication with Mac OS X authentication. You can optionally add the guest parameter (as in passdb backend = smbpasswd, guest) to help manage guest accounts. If you omit this parameter, the system defaults to using smbpasswd for logon authentication, at least when encrypt passwords is set to Yes. The smbpasswd system is adequate for sites with a few dozen users, but it slows down when the number of users is measured in the hundreds or more.

domain logons = Yes: This global parameter is the key one for domain controller functionality; set to the default value of No, Samba won't try to function as a domain controller.

Every Samba domain controller must be configured with these global parameters as specified. The encrypted password setting also requires that the server have a Samba encrypted password file or database with appropriate user accounts set, which in turn requires that the domain controller have Unix accounts set up for all of the users. When these conditions are in place, the system will accept Windows 9*x*/Me logons to the domain specified by the workgroup parameter.

NOTE Technically, Windows 9*x*/Me servers aren't full domain members; instead, they use the domain controller as a logon server, but the Windows 9*x*/Me systems don't fully join the domain. In particular, Windows 9*x*/Me systems use pass-through authentication and don't use machine trust accounts (described in the next section, "Additional Windows NT/200*x*/XP Domain Options"), which are required for full domain membership. Windows 9*x*/Me systems may also use cleartext passwords, although this practice is both rare and discouraged for domain configurations. From the user's point of view, though, these differences are unimportant, and even most aspects of Samba configuration are identical for Windows 9*x*/Me and Windows NT/200*x*/XP.

Other global parameters set features that are linked, to one extent or another, to the domain controller functions. These features aren't strictly required for a Samba server to function as a domain controller, but they're usually set as described. Some of these options can be changed without causing serious problems, but others could cause odd behavior if they're set differently:

domain master = Yes: This parameter, described in more detail in Chapter 8, tells Samba to take on domain master browser duties. Windows systems link domain master browser and domain controller functions in one computer, so having Samba simultaneously take on both or neither is beneficial.

preferred master = Yes: This parameter, described in more detail in Chapter 8, tells Samba it should attempt to take on local master browser duties. Omitting this option or setting it to No probably won't cause major problems, but setting it to Yes on the domain controller reduces the odds of browsing problems developing.

os level = 33: As described in Chapter 8, local master browsers are *elected* via a special negotiation process that occurs on a subnet. In practice, the most important factor in determining the outcome of an election is each computer's *OS level*, which is what the parameter of the same name sets. Most Microsoft OSs set their OS levels to 32 or lower, so any os level parameter setting of 33 or greater should guarantee that Samba takes on local master browser duties. Using a value greater than 33 guarantees success even against Samba systems configured to use a value of 33, which some may mistakenly use. The top level of 255 should win against anything. In theory, separating these duties from the domain controller should work fine, but in practice it's best to keep them together. Note that the domain master browser must also win its subnet's local master browser election, as described in Chapter 8.

wins support = Yes: A Windows Internet Name Service (WINS) server, a.k.a. an NBNS system, provides name services to a network, as described in Chapter 9. Traditionally, domain controllers take on this duty, so you may want to have Samba do so if you configure Samba as a domain controller. This isn't strictly required, though.

time server = Yes: SMB/CIFS includes provisions for setting one computer's clock based on the time kept by another computer. Setting this parameter to Yes tells Samba to advertise its availability as a time server. Chapter 12 describes this parameter and other time-setting issues in more detail. A domain controller is a logical system to function as a time server, simply because it's the locus of so many other ancillary functions, but if you prefer to have another computer serve this role, or not use it at all, you can set time server = No (the default).

Once you've set the domain controller functions and restarted the Samba daemons, you should be able to use a Windows 9*x*/Me system to log onto the domain, as described in the upcoming section "Configuring Windows 9*x*/Me Clients." To get the full use out of a domain, though, you may need to configure Samba to support

Windows NT/200x/XP systems, and you may also need to configure Samba servers that are not domain controllers to use the domain controller.

In addition to these core duties, you can provide several additional parameters to set up features such as roaming profiles and domain logon scripts. Chapter 14 describes these parameters in more detail.

Additional Windows NT/200x/XP Domain Options

If your domain includes Windows NT/200x/XP systems, you'll need to do more to provide Samba support for these computers. The basic configuration described in the previous section, "Samba Domain Controller Options," still applies. You must, however, create a special Samba account, known as a *machine trust account*, for each Windows NT/200x/XP system. The computers use these accounts to authenticate themselves in addition to authenticating the individual users. Technically, the machine accounts are used only by servers, but in practice you may need to create machine trust accounts before you can join a computer to a domain, even if you intend to use the computer only as a client.

 NOTE Windows XP Home edition doesn't explicitly support domain logons. If you use this version of Windows XP, you can configure the system as for a workgroup, and it will work on a domain of the same name. To explicitly use a domain (including using the domain controller for authentication of any resources shared from the Windows XP system), you must upgrade to Windows XP Professional.

To create a machine trust account, follow these steps:

1. Set aside a Unix group to be used by the machine trust accounts. In theory, you can use an ordinary user account, but for security purposes it's best to have a special trust group. You should be able to use a group-manipulation tool to do this job; for instance, `groupadd -r trust` adds a group called `trust` on many systems. Consult your OS's documentation for details on how to add a group.

2. Create Unix system accounts as machine trust accounts for each Windows NT/200x/XP system on your network. These accounts use the NetBIOS name of the clients, but converted to lowercase and with a dollar sign ($) appended. For instance, you should create an account called `waltz$` for the WALTZ computer. These accounts should use the trust group you created in step 1 as the default group. They should not be logon accounts, so they can be configured to refuse all logons.

TIP   Some versions of Unix, such as FreeBSD, have problems creating account names that include dollar signs. If you run into this problem in step 2, create a name without the dollar sign and then use the vipw utility to manually edit the passwd file using vi to add the dollar sign.

You may need to wait a minute or so for Samba to reread its configuration file and implement the changes. Alternatively, you can pass the server a SIGHUP signal to force it to implement the changes immediately.

If you plan to add many computers to your domain, you may want to streamline this process. You can do so by using the global add machine script parameter, which tells Samba how to add Unix accounts for SMB/CIFS machine trust accounts. As an example, the following parameter works on a Red Hat Linux system:

```
add machine script = /usr/sbin/useradd -d /dev/null -g 100 -s /bin/false -M %u
```

Of course, the precise command you use will vary substantially from one OS to another. You may also need to create a custom script for the job for your system.

After you create the machine trust account, the Windows NT/200*x*/XP system can use the domain controller for authentication; however, you must first configure the system to be part of the domain, as described in the upcoming section "Configuring Windows NT/200*x*/XP Clients." If you fail to configure the Windows system to be a part of the domain, it will function as if it were on a workgroup, losing the benefits of domain membership.

 NOTE   Prior to Samba 3.0, you had to use the smbpasswd program and its -m parameter to create a machine trust account in addition to a Unix account for the machine. Samba 3.0 adds better support for the Windows machine account creation tools, though, so you can bypass this requirement.

When you add Windows NT/200*x*/XP computers to the domain, they will prompt for a username and password. You must specify a Samba administrative username and password for this role. One way to accomplish this goal is to add root to the Samba password database. This action is potentially quite risky, though. A slightly less risky approach is to create a special Unix and Samba account and then use the admin users parameter in the [global] section of smb.conf to grant this user root privileges under Samba. This approach at least has the benefit of making the username that has this power less obvious. In either case, you should use an entirely unique Samba password for this user.

TIP If possible, add all your systems at once and then comment out the admin users parameter to revoke the root privileges for the account you used to add systems to the domain. When you need to add more systems or otherwise grant administrative powers to this account, you can do so by temporarily uncommenting the admin users parameter.

Samba Domain Shares

Two shares are particularly important on domain controllers:

NETLOGON: This share contains scripts that Windows clients run when they log onto the server or domain.

PROFILES: This share holds *roaming profiles*, which enable users to store account information, such as desktop settings, on the server. The benefit of this approach is that users' desktop settings can move with them even if they don't use the same computer consistently.

Chapter 14 covers both of these topics in greater detail. Setting up these shares isn't absolutely critical for initial domain controller configuration, but you may want to get a start on it. The NETLOGON share can be read-only, but because user data is stored in roaming profiles, the PROFILES share must be read/write. (Each user's data is stored in a separate subdirectory named after the user.) The following definitions can be a good starting point for these shares, but of course you should adjust your paths appropriately:

```
[netlogon]
    directory = /home/samba/netlogon
    read only = Yes
[profiles]
    directory = /home/samba/profiles
    read only = No
    create mask = 0600
    directory mask = 0700
```

Configuring a Backup Domain Controller

On a small network (even one that spans multiple subnets), a single PDC is most likely adequate. A BDC, however, provides two features that can help improve network performance or reliability:

Reducing PDC load: If a PDC is heavily loaded, a BDC can improve overall performance by taking over many of the PDC's authentication duties. The net result can be improved network performance. Note, however, that PDC duties alone aren't likely to strain the capabilities of even a modest server on any but the largest of networks.

Reducing internetwork traffic: On a network that's distributed across subnets, placing a BDC on each subnet can reduce cross-subnet traffic associated with authentication. This feature is especially important when the subnets are widely separated from each other, as in subnets linked across the Internet via a virtual private network (VPN) configuration. Such links tend to be slow and may be unreliable, so using BDCs can improve speed and reliability.

Thus, a BDC makes the most sense on very large networks or those broken into multiple subnets by slow or unreliable links. Even in these cases, the extra configuration effort and disadvantages of maintaining a BDC may be great enough to favor finding another solution. For instance, you might be better off upgrading your PDC or off-loading non-PDC duties from the PDC onto another computer. If the PDC is doubling as a print server, set up another computer to serve that printer so that the PDC needn't be concerned with processing print jobs. If internet reliability is an issue, you might want to consider setting up two entirely separate NT domains rather than trying to integrate the two into one domain.

The core of the challenge in configuring a Samba BDC is in getting it talking to the PDC in order to exchange account information. On the surface, you might think that simply passing the smbpasswd file back and forth would be adequate, but in fact there's a problem: Suppose that a user changes a password on the PDC, and a second user changes a password using the BDC. At this point, neither system's smbpasswd file is completely up to date. Thus, the two systems would need to somehow reconcile the differences in their files. It turns out that this problem is very difficult to solve. The best solution at the moment is to use LDAP. Each Samba domain controller runs a local LDAP server and stores its authentication information in the LDAP server's database. The LDAP servers then communicate with one another. Because LDAP was designed, in part, to keep distributed databases consistent and up to date, it solves Samba's problems rather neatly—at least, in theory.

Unfortunately, LDAP configuration is extremely complex. In many respects, LDAP is more complex than Samba, so setting up LDAP to support Samba's encrypted password database and BDC configurations is quite a challenge. To make matters worse, Samba 2.2.*x* and 3.0.*x* interface to LDAP in different ways, and there are several LDAP implementations, each of which has its own requirements. One popular LDAP implementation is OpenLDAP (http://www.openldap.org), but even it varies in important ways from one version to another. For these reasons, presenting a complete guide to implementing a BDC using Samba and LDAP is impossible. If you really must do this, I recommend you study LDAP carefully. A book such as Gerald Carter's *LDAP Administration* (O'Reilly, 2003) or Brian Arkills' *LDAP Directories Explained: An Introduction and Analysis* (Addison-Wesley, 2003) can be a good starting point. You should also consult the documentation for whatever LDAP package you use. Once you're familiar with LDAP in general and your LDAP implementation in particular, look into some relevant smb.conf parameters:

ldap admin dn: This global parameter sets the distinguished name (DN) Samba uses in its interactions with the LDAP server.

ldap delete dn: This global Boolean parameter specifies whether a deletion of an entry deletes the complete entry or only the Samba-specific data.

`ldap filter`: This global parameter sets an LDAP search filter, as defined in RFC 2254, for locating usernames in the LDAP database.

`ldap group suffix`: This global parameter sets the suffix that's added to group names when they're added to the LDAP directory. The default value is to match the effect of `ldap suffix`.

`ldap idmap suffix`: This global parameter sets the suffix that's added to idmap mappings. The default is to match the effect of `ldap suffix`.

`ldap machine suffix`: This global parameter specifies where to add machine names to the LDAP tree.

`ldap passwd sync`: You can tell Samba to attempt to update the LDAP password along with the NT and LanManager passwords (Yes), to update only the NT and LanManager passwords (No), or to set only the LDAP password (Only) on password changes via Samba.

`ldap port`: This global parameter sets the TCP port number to try to use. The default is 636 if `ldap ssl = On` and 389 if `ldap ssl = Off`.

`ldap server`: Specify the fully qualified domain name of the LDAP server with this global parameter. The default value is `localhost`.

`ldap ssl`: You can tell Samba what type of Secure Sockets Layer (SSL) encryption to use with the LDAP server with this global parameter. Possible values are On to enable SSL, `Start_TLS` to enable StartTLS operation, and Off to disable encryption.

`ldap suffix`: This global parameter specifies where user and machine accounts should be added to the directory tree.

`ldap user suffix`: This global parameter sets the suffix that's added to usernames when they're added to the LDAP directory. The default value is to match the effect of `ldap suffix`.

Setting Up Interdomain Trust Relationships

Networks sometimes contain multiple domains. For instance, a university might have a separate SMB/CIFS domain for each academic department, as in PHYSICS, ENGLISH, HISTORY, and so on. Such a configuration permits localized control of user accounts, machine names, and so on. It also limits the ability of users of one domain to log onto machines on another domain; without accounts on the foreign domain, users can't use these domains' resources. This is where *interdomain trust relationships*, or *trusts* for short, come into play. Setting up trust relationships enables users to access network resources on remote domains. Samba 3.0 and later implements Windows NT 4.0–style trusts, which support one-way relationships. Thus, you can configure Samba to trust another domain's authentication decisions or be trusted by another domain. If all of your domain controllers run Samba, you need only configure trusts on the Samba domain controllers; but if one of the domain controllers runs Windows, you must configure equivalent settings in that OS.

NOTE Interdomain trusts are similar to machine trusts, which are used by the domain controller to add machines to a domain.

When to Set Up Interdomain Trusts

Interdomain trusts are very useful on midsize or large networks with modest amounts of interdomain traffic. They are, though, rather fragile; network problems can break trust relationships, shutting off remote access to servers. Microsoft's AD, which is built atop Kerberos and LDAP and is supported in Windows 2000 and later, is designed to solve some of these problems. Samba can authenticate users against an AD controller but cannot itself function as an AD controller—at least, not as of Samba 3.0. Furthermore, migrating a network to AD can be a disruptive procedure. For these reasons, many networks continue to use the older Windows NT 4.0–style domains and, when necessary, interdomain trust relationships.

NT 4.0–style domains have two important characteristics that influence your plans for how to implement interdomain trusts:

Nontransitive: Interdomain trust relationships are nontransitive—that is, they don't transfer across multiple links. For instance, suppose the PHYSICS domain is configured to trust the GEOLOGY domain, which is configured to trust the CHEMISTRY domain. In this configuration, PHYSICS doesn't automatically trust CHEMISTRY. You can explicitly configure multidomain trusts to work around this nontransitive feature. This characteristic limits the potential for damage should a user on one domain turn out to have malicious intent.

One-way: You can configure one domain to trust a second domain even if the second domain doesn't trust the first. For instance, PHYSICS might trust GEOLOGY (say, to permit GEOLOGY's users to access PHYSICS printers and shared file servers), but GEOLOGY needn't trust PHYSICS (say, because the GEOLOGY network contains no resources that the PHYSICS users need to access). You can, of course, explicitly configure a two-way relationship by configuring both domains to trust and be trusted by the other.

You should carefully consider when you need to set up a trust relationship. The usual reason for doing so is that one domain contains resources, such as large file servers or advanced printers, that are needed by a neighboring domain. For instance, if PHYSICS contains a wide-carriage printer, you might configure PHYSICS to trust the nearby GEOLOGY domain so that its users can print to the wide-carriage printer. Of course, in the case of Samba, other alternatives may exist. For instance, you could set up the print server so that it's not a full member of the PHYSICS domain but instead uses `security = server` for any shares that shouldn't be widely accessible and sets up the printer shares to accept guest access. This configuration reduces the risk of damage due to security problems on the GEOLOGY domain, loss of printing ability due to an outage of the PHYSICS or GEOLOGY domain controller, and so on.

Configuring Samba As the Trusted Domain Controller

Interdomain trusts operate using authentication mechanisms similar to those used by individual servers and workstations. The trusting domain controller contacts the trusted domain controller to establish the trust relationship. Thus, you must configure the trusted domain controller with a special interdomain trust account similar to the machine trust account described earlier in "Additional Windows NT/200x/XP Domain Options." You begin by creating a local Unix account for the trusting domain, much as you create a local Unix account for a member of a domain. Use the domain name, converted to lowercase and with a dollar sign ($) appended to the name, as the username. You must then create a Samba account using the smbpasswd command; pass the -i parameter to indicate an interdomain trust account. The smbpasswd program will ask for a password when you create the interdomain trust account. (You must remember this password and enter it on the trusting domain's PDC.) Thus, the interaction looks something like this:

```
# smbpasswd -a -i physics
New SMB password:
Retype new SMB password:
Added user physics$
```

In this example, PHYSICS is the trusting domain—it hosts resources that users of the trusted domain presumably want to use. Once you've created an interdomain trust account, the trusted domain controller will treat the specified domain something like a server that wants to authenticate users. You can create multiple interdomain trust accounts if you want multiple domains to trust your own. Each remote domain controller can in turn accept the authentication provided by your local domain controller—once it's been configured to do so, as described next.

Configuring Samba As the Trusting Domain Controller

You can configure a Samba domain controller to authorize users who have been authenticated by another domain controller. This configuration doesn't require a setting in the smb.conf file, though; instead, you accomplish this task using the net command, which is new in Samba 3.0. Specifically, you should type the following command on the Samba PDC:

```
# net rpc trustdom establish TRUSTED
```

NOTE   You should only type this command after you create an interdomain trust account, as described in the previous section. If the trusted domain has a Windows domain controller, you must perform equivalent configuration on the Windows domain controller.

In this example, *TRUSTED* is the name of the trusted domain, such as GEOLOGY if you type this command on the PHYSICS domain's PDC to have it trust the GEOLOGY domain controller. After you type this command, you'll be asked to enter the password. This is the password you created when you added the interdomain trust account, as described in the previous section (or as you did on the Windows PDC if the trusted domain has a Windows PDC). Sometimes typing this command will generate an error message that reads as follows:

```
NT_STATUS_NOLOGON_INTERDOMAIN_TRUST_ACCOUNT
```

You can safely ignore this message; it refers to the fact that the account is used for interdomain trust relationships and not for ordinary logon access. Eventually, you should see a Success message appear. Sometimes Samba takes some time to locate the domain controller and log on, particularly on large networks.

Configuring Windows for Interdomain Trusts

Interdomain trust relationships were created for Windows NT domains, and so it's only natural that Windows provides ways to implement them. In Windows NT 4.0, you can accomplish these tasks using the Domain User Manager tool. Select Policy ➤ Trust Relationships from the menu bar. You can add a domain to trust by clicking the Add button next to the Trusted Domains box. You'll then enter an NT domain name and a password. To enable other domains to trust yours, click the Add button next to the Permitted to Trust This Domain box. You can then enter the trusting domain and a password (which you must enter twice).

Windows 200x moves away from NT 4.0–style interdomain trust relationships in favor of AD. You can, however, continue to integrate Windows 200x systems in the older NT-style domains. The principles are the same as for Samba or Windows NT 4.0 systems, but the details differ. In particular, you need to open the Active Directory Domains and Trusts tool instead of the Domain User Manager tool on the Windows domain controller. To configure the domain controller to trust a Samba domain controller, right-click the name of the AD domain that will trust the Samba-controlled domain, pick Properties from the resulting pop-up dialog box, then click the Trusts tab. You should then see a box labeled Domains Trusted by This Domain. Click the Add button next to this box. You can then enter the name of the Samba-controlled domain and password. In theory, Samba should be able to trust an NT 4.0–style domain that's controlled by a Windows 200x server, but this type of operation hasn't been well tested as of Samba 3.0.1.

Using Domain Logons

Configuring a domain controller is only part of the task of creating a domain configuration. The flip side is configuring your domain clients. These domain clients include both file and print servers that should trust the domain controller and file and print clients that should join the domain. Precisely how you achieve this task varies from one OS to another. The following sections describe Windows 9*x*/Me, Windows NT/200*x*/XP, and Samba as domain clients.

Configuring Windows 9x/Me Clients

Samba's domain control features are most mature when dealing with Windows 9*x*/Me clients. These clients are also relatively straightforward to configure, although there are some tricks you should know to improve client security.

Configuring Windows 9x/Me to Log Onto a Domain

Ordinarily, once it's set up with SMB/CIFS support to function in a workgroup, Windows 9*x*/Me presents a logon prompt similar to the one shown in Figure 10-1. Note that this prompt lacks a place for a domain or workgroup name. Despite its similarity to a Unix logon prompt, this Windows 9*x*/Me prompt has no security value for the local computer; clicking Cancel bypasses this prompt and displays the local desktop. What this prompt is really doing is simply caching the username and password for subsequent network accesses. I mention these facts because they're relevant to some of the changes made in configuring the system to operate in a domain.

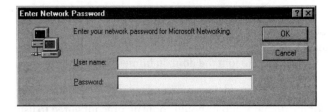

Figure 10-1. Windows 9x/Me presents a two-field logon prompt when it's configured to use a workgroup.

To configure Windows 9*x*/Me to function on a domain rather than a workgroup, follow these steps once you've logged on:

1. Open the Control Panel.

2. Open the Network item in the Control Panel.

3. Select Client for Microsoft Networks, and click Properties. You should now see the Client for Microsoft Networks Properties dialog box, as displayed in Figure 10-2.

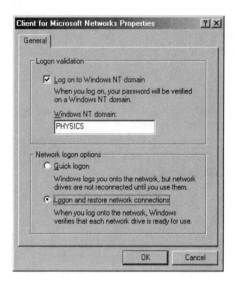

Figure 10-2. Joining a domain in Windows 9x/Me entails checking a box and entering a domain name.

4.   Check the Log On to Windows NT Domain check box, and enter the name of the domain to which the computer should belong in the Windows NT Domain field.

5.   Click OK in the Client for Microsoft Networks Properties dialog box and then in the Network dialog box. Windows will ask to reboot the computer, and you should let it do so if you want to join the domain immediately.

When the computer reboots, you'll see a new logon prompt, as shown in Figure 10-3. This prompt adds a field for the domain, and it should come up preconfigured to use the domain you specified in step 4. When you type a password, Windows contacts the domain controller and authenticates against it and then caches the username and password for future use. The Windows client is now a part of the domain.

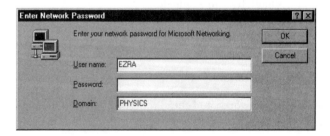

Figure 10-3. Once it's part of a domain, the Windows 9x/Me logon prompt adds a field for the domain name.

Improving Windows 9x/Me Domain Security

Unfortunately, the Windows 9*x*/Me domain logon prompt doesn't add any real local security; you can still bypass the authentication process by clicking Cancel. (If you do so, you won't be able to access resources on the domain, though, just as when you click Cancel when logging into a system configured as part of a workgroup.) What's worse, when you *do* type a password, Windows stores the password in a file called USERNAME.PWL, where USERNAME is your username. This file appears in the C:\WINDOWS directory on most systems. This file is a potential risk because a miscreant who obtains it can use its contents to break into servers on the domain. Because clicking Cancel bypasses the password prompt, obtaining this file from a Windows system is trivially easy if an intruder has just a few seconds alone with a computer. Although reconfiguring Windows 9*x*/Me to provide true logon security is well beyond the scope of this book, configuring the system to stop storing passwords in the .PWL files is simpler. To do so, begin by entering Listing 10-1 into a text editor in Windows. This file is a Windows Registry entry—it contains information that will be stored in the Windows Registry.

Listing 10-1. Windows 9x/Me Registry File Entry to Disable Password Caching

```
REGEDIT4

[HKEY_LOCAL_MACHINE\SOFTWARE\Microsoft\Windows\CurrentVersion\Policies\Network]
"DisablePwdCaching"=dword:00000001
```

 CAUTION   Be careful to enter the information in Listing 10-1 *precisely.* A typo could conceivably cause the system to change the wrong Registry data. Chances are this error won't cause any real problems, but if you're unlucky, you might overwrite some other vital data. Also, use a *Windows* text editor; Unix editors will create a file with Unix-style end-of-line characters, which will confuse Windows. Alternatively, you could enter this information using the Windows REGEDIT program and export the branch containing the entry.

Once you've created the file, save it to a file with a name ending in .REG, such as DPC.REG. You can then enter the data into the Registry in either of two ways:

- Locate the file in the Windows GUI file browser, and double-click it. If the file has a .REG extension, Windows should recognize it as a Registry file and try to load it into the REGEDIT program.

- Open a DOS prompt window, change to the directory in which the file is stored, and type **REGEDIT DPC.REG** (making any necessary changes to the filename).

In either case, Windows should pop up a dialog box asking for confirmation that you want to add the information in the file to the Registry. Click Yes to do so. You should then clean out all the `.PWL` files in `C:\WINDOWS`. You can check for these files in a DOS prompt or file manager and then delete them. For instance, typing **DELETE** **C:\WINDOWS*.PWL** will do the trick—just be sure to check for these files before using such a command. It's conceivable that some important nonpassword file has been stored with a `.PWL` extension. When you log on again, you should find that the `.PWL` files are no longer being created. This configuration can improve security by helping to keep these sensitive files out of the hands of would-be intruders.

Configuring Windows NT/200x/XP Clients

Windows NT/200x/XP is both simpler and harder to configure for operation on a domain than Windows 9x/Me. These NT-based systems are easier to configure because they provide better local security, so you don't need to reconfigure them so that they don't create `.PWL` files. They're harder to configure because their domain functions require using machine trust accounts on the domain controller. Thus, you should first review the earlier section "Additional Windows NT/200x/XP Domain Options" and create machine trust accounts on the Samba server for your NT/200x/XP computers.

NOTE Windows XP Home edition doesn't support domain configurations. If you want to use Windows XP on a domain, you must either treat the domain like a workgroup or upgrade to Windows XP Professional.

In Windows 200x/XP, you add a computer to a domain as follows:

1. Log on using the `Administrator` account. Be sure *not* to open any SMB/CIFS connections to the domain controller, such as opening any shares.

2. Open the Control Panel.

3. Double-click the System object, which opens the System Properties dialog box.

4. Click the Network Identification or Computer Name tab, depending upon the OS version you're running.

5. Click the Properties button to bring up the Identification Changes dialog box shown in Figure 10-4.

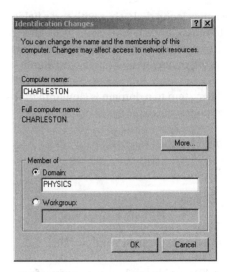

Figure 10-4. Windows 200x/XP requires entry of the NetBIOS name and domain name to join a domain.

6. If necessary, enter the NetBIOS name of the computer in the Computer Name field. (Chances are it will be set correctly.)

7. In the Member Of area, click Domain and type the domain name in the text entry field.

 CAUTION   If your computer is currently a member of a workgroup with the same name as the domain you plan to join, you should first change it to be on another workgroup. (You can make up a different workgroup name; it will only be used temporarily.) This process will require you to reboot and start again. The problem is that Windows may give you error messages concerning an inability to join the domain because of conflicting credentials or an existing connection if you try to join a domain when the machine is already a member of a workgroup of the same name.

8. Click OK to join the domain. Windows displays a dialog box in which you must enter a username and password.

9. Type the administrative username and password, and click OK. The system should respond by welcoming you to the domain. It then informs you that you must reboot the computer to join the domain.

10. Exit from the open dialog boxes, and reboot the computer.

When the system reboots, you should see a new logon dialog box with three fields rather than two. (Some systems require you to press Control+Alt+Delete to see this logon prompt.) This change parallels the change in Windows 9*x*/Me (Figure 10-1 and Figure 10-3), but a few details differ. When you log on using this system, you'll find that you're a full member of the domain.

The procedure for adding a Windows NT 4.0 system to a domain is similar to that for Windows 200*x*/XP, but there are a few differences:

- In step 3, open the Network object rather than the System object.

- In step 4, the tab is called Identification.

- In step 5, the button you click is called Change.

- In step 7, you should be sure that the Create a Computer Account in the Domain check box is checked. (This box isn't available in Windows 200*x*/XP.)

Unlike Windows 9*x*/Me, Windows NT/200*x*/XP provides real logon security; if you don't have a password, you can't simply cancel out of the logon prompt to gain access to the computer. You can, though, bypass the domain logon and instead use the local user database. To do this, select the computer name in the new Log On To field that appears in the logon prompt. To use the domain logon database, select your domain from the list that appears.

NOTE To perform administrative tasks on your Windows system, you may need to log onto the local computer rather than the domain. To work around this limitation, you could create an Administrator account on the Samba server. This account should *not* have any special privileges on the Samba server, though; it should be an ordinary account or even one with less than the usual privileges.

Configuring Samba Servers

If your network hosts multiple Samba servers, you can have these servers defer to the domain controller for authentication tasks. Creating this configuration requires setting four global parameters in smb.conf:

password server: This parameter points to the IP address or DNS hostname of the domain controller. (If you use a DNS hostname, you must also set hostname lookups = Yes.) If the domain has a PDC and one or more BDCs, you can list them all, separated by spaces. If you set password server = *, Samba will attempt to locate the domain controller for the domain whose name is specified with the workgroup parameter.

domain logons: You should ensure that this parameter is set to No on all Samba servers that aren't domain controllers. This setting is the default, so it shouldn't be a problem, but you should double-check it nonetheless.

encrypt passwords: Domain configurations require this parameter to be set to Yes for both the domain controller and its clients. (The default value for this parameter is No for Samba 2.2.*x* and earlier but Yes for Samba 3.0 and later.)

security: This parameter specifies how Samba authenticates users. Two values will work. The first, Server, causes Samba to defer all authentication decisions to the domain controller. The Samba server isn't a full member of the domain, though; it uses the pass-through authentication method described earlier in "The Problem: Providing Centralized Logons." The second option, Domain, causes Samba to fully join the domain and use the NetLogon authentication system. This setting requires some additional changes, described shortly.

If you want your system to be a full member of a domain (via security = Domain), you must join the system to the domain. This process is akin to the one described earlier for Windows NT/200*x*/XP systems but is done via the net command, which takes a wide variety of arguments and subarguments. This command illustrates the specific options needed for this task:

```
# net join member -U adminuser
```

In this example, *adminuser* is the administrative user account described earlier in "Additional Windows NT/200*x*/XP Domain Options." The net command takes other important information from the smb.conf file. Most notably, the domain name (set in the workgroup parameter) and the DNS hostname or IP address of the domain controller (set in the password server parameter) are important. After you type the command, you'll be prompted to enter the password for *adminuser*. Once you've successfully joined the domain, you should restart Samba to be sure it uses the new configuration.

If a user attempts to log onto the Samba server and that attempt fails when using a domain configuration, Samba falls back on its local authentication system (typically an smbpasswd file). Whether or not the domain controller authenticates a user, the Samba server must have a local Unix account for the user; without that account, Samba can't handle local security settings for the user and so will reject the logon attempt.

If you want to add local accounts automatically, you have two options:

- Configure Winbind on the Samba server, as described in the next section, "Configuring Samba Clients." Local Unix accounts will then be built "on the fly" from the domain controller's account database.

- Use the add user script parameter to have Samba run a local script for adding local users to the local user database whenever Samba successfully authenticates a user via the domain controller but no local Unix account exists.

The first option has the advantage of being more dynamic—there's no need to explicitly delete accounts on each Samba server as users leave; when the accounts vanish on the domain controller, they also vanish on the local Unix systems. (Files created by users won't vanish automatically, though.) You can better fine-tune the account creation via a local script, though, and in most cases this option is easier to configure.

Configuring Samba Clients

You can configure a Unix system to use an SMB/CIFS domain controller (either a Samba server or a Windows NT/200x server) as an authentication mechanism for controlling local access. That is, when a user logs onto the Unix system, the Unix system will use the domain controller for authentication. This process relies upon the integration of several components: the Name Service Switch (NSS), Pluggable Authentication Modules (PAM), a server known as Winbind, and of course an SMB/CIFS domain controller. Once configured in this way, your Unix system won't need to maintain a local user database except for purely local accounts that have no NT domain counterparts, such as root and nobody. You can still define ordinary users locally, though; you don't need to abandon any current user configuration if you decide to implement Winbind. You can use Winbind as a supplemental system or for adding future users.

NOTE   As of Samba 3.0.1, Winbind configuration is only officially available for AIX, IRIX, Linux, and Solaris, largely because the OS must support both NSS and PAM.

Preparing Your System

The first thing you should do is prepare your system for disaster. If anything goes wrong when you try to configure your system as described here, you may not be able to log on to correct the problem. You may want to have a root logon session running so that you can correct problems if they appear. You should also back up all the files you modify, especially those in the PAM configuration directory (typically /etc/pam.d). Finally, you should have an emergency boot system ready in case you need to boot up and repair any damage done to your configuration.

Verify that you have both NSS and PAM installed. PAM is typically configured through files in /etc/pam.d; if that directory is present and filled with files, chances are your system uses PAM. NSS uses /etc/nss.conf as its configuration file on most systems, so verify that it's present.

NOTE Some systems use a PAM configuration file called /etc/pam.conf rather than files in a directory called /etc/pam.d. The two approaches are similar except that the pam.conf file places the name of the service at the start of each line rather than relying on the filename for this information.

You should also verify that the necessary Samba components are installed on your system. Look for libnss_winbind.so and pam_winbind.so. If they aren't present, look for appropriate binary packages or compile these components from source code. You can find the source in the source/nsswitch subdirectory of the Samba source code distribution. You may need to create a symbolic link from libnss_winbind.so to libnss_winbind.so.2 on some systems. The pam_winbind.so file should be installed with other PAM modules, probably in /lib/security or /usr/lib/security.

One vital part of the preliminary configuration is in setting up Samba. In particular, you should read the preceding section "Configuring Samba Servers" and set up the system as described there—both the smb.conf entries and joining the SMB/CIFS domain. Once this is done, shut down your Samba servers—smbd, nmbd, and winbindd. You should also add a few Winbind-specific options to smb.conf's [global] section:

winbind separator: This parameter sets the character that separates domain names from usernames. The default value is a backslash (\), but it's frequently set to a plus sign (+). The + setting causes problems on some glibc-based systems, though.

winbind cache time: This parameter sets the time in seconds that the system will hold authentication information before querying the server again. The default value is 300 (five minutes), but you may want to reduce this value when testing the system.

template shell: To provide information normally found in /etc/passwd but not maintained by NT domain controllers, the system must fill in some information. One of these vital elements is the default shell for users, and this parameter sets it. The default value is /bin/false, which is safe from a security point of view but perhaps not very useful as a practical matter. If you want to give users shell access, you should set this value to /bin/bash, /bin/csh, or some other valid shell on your system. If you're only configuring Winbind as a way around maintaining local Unix accounts for Samba operations, leaving the default of /bin/false should work well.

template homedir: Another vital Unix-specific account element is the user's home directory. The default value of this parameter is /home/%D/%U, where %D stands for the domain name and %U stands for the username.

template primary group: This option sets the primary group of the virtual accounts created by Winbind. The default value is nobody.

winbind enum users: Normally, Winbind supports various system calls that enable programs to enumerate users. This support can be sluggish, though, so you may want to disable it by setting this parameter's value to No, particularly if you've got many users. On the other hand, disabling user enumeration causes some programs, such as finger, to misbehave. This parameter's default value is, therefore, Yes.

winbind enum groups: This parameter has an effect similar to winbind enum users, but it applies to groups rather than users.

winbind use default domain: If set to Yes, this global parameter causes Winbind to drop the domain component of usernames in most operations. The default action of No can be awkward because it requires users to log on using names that include domain names, such as PHYSICS+fastaire. Setting this option to Yes reduces this username to fastaire.

idmap uid: Specify a range of user IDs (UIDs) with this parameter, separated by a dash. The system will assign users UIDs within this range. The default value is undefined.

idmap gid: This parameter works much like idmap gid, but it sets the range of group IDs (GIDs) assigned to users. The default value is undefined.

 CAUTION   Be sure that no existing users or groups have UIDs or GIDs that overlap with those specified by the idmap uid and idmap gid parameters. If such users exist, the results can be quite strange.

You can leave many of these parameters at their default values, although you must set the idmap uid and idmap gid parameters to reasonable values for your system. As a general rule, adding parameters such as the following to the [global] section of smb.conf should work well for testing purposes:

```
winbind separator = +
winbind cache time = 5
idmap uid = 1000-20000
idmap gid = 1000-20000
template shell = /bin/bash
template homedir = /home/%U
```

Each of these options may need adjustment because of specific features of your system. Furthermore, you should probably remove or increase the winbind cache time parameter once you're done testing basic operations.

Configuring NSS

If your Samba binary package or Samba source compilation installed libnss_winbind.so, you shouldn't need to do anything special to set it up, except possibly creating a link called libnss_winbind.so.2. If you can't find this library, though, you should track it down and install it, probably to /lib, /usr/local/lib, or a similar library location. If you need to do this or create a link, you may need to run ldconfig to tell your computer about the new library.

Once you've installed the library, you must edit the /etc/nsswitch.conf file. Examine this file and look for lines beginning with the words passwd and group. These lines tell the system where to look for information relating to accounts, groups, and so on. You should add the string winbind to the passwd and group lines. This addition tells the system to use Winbind to obtain information about UID mapping, user shells, and so on. Typically, files will be the first entry on each of these lines; this tells the system to look at local files first. Some systems include other options, such as nisplus or compat, which enable additional authentication methods, such as an NIS+ server. Adding winbind after existing entries gives local files and other existing authentication tools precedence over Winbind lookups, which means you can override the domain controller for specific and important accounts, such as root. The result of this change might look something like this:

```
passwd: files winbind
shadow: files
group: files winbind
```

Testing Winbind

Once the preliminary steps are out of the way, it's time to start the winbindd server and test its basic functions. This server runs on the local computer (the domain client) and serves as an interface between the domain controller and PAM. You can launch the server manually by typing its name as root, perhaps with its complete path:

```
# /usr/local/samba/bin/winbindd
```

When running the server permanently, you may want to add the -B parameter, which causes it to run as two separate daemons, one of which answers queries from clients and the other of which handles the local cache. The result can be faster and more accurate responses.

How you run Winbind on a permanent basis depends on your OS. Chapter 3 describes several methods of running Samba. As a server, winbindd is similar, but it's best run from a SysV or local startup script. You can create a separate Winbind SysV startup script or start it in your regular Samba startup script, as you see fit. Be sure to start winbindd after you start smbd and nmbd, though, if your system runs these servers.

Once Winbind is running, you can test its functioning with the wbinfo command. A good starting point is to use the -u parameter, which tells the program to display all the accounts accessible from the server:

```
# wbinfo -u
PHYSICS+ezra
PHYSICS+grogers
PHYSICS+fastaire
PHYSICS+mikhail
```

NOTE This example assumes you didn't change the default value of winbind use default domain. If you set this parameter to Yes, you won't see the domain name or separator (+ in this example) in the wbinfo -u output.

If you receive information about users with this test, try testing with getent, which retrieves entries from the administrative database—in other words, as configured via /etc/nsswitch.conf. Type **getent passwd** to recover your username list. The result should be the contents of your /etc/passwd file followed by constructed entries based on the output of wbinfo -u, using UIDs, shells, and so on defined in smb.conf.

NOTE The getent passwd output shows the home directories associated with each account. Depending upon the purpose of the computer and the SMB/CIFS-authenticated accounts, these directories may need to exist. Creating them, setting their ownership and permissions, and perhaps populating them with standard Unix starter files may be worth doing at this point. Alternatively, you can use a PAM module called pam_mkhomedir.so to create home directories on the fly, as described shortly.

Configuring PAM

At this point, you can begin configuring PAM to work with Winbind to authenticate users. If you haven't already done so, you should back up your /etc/pam.d directory, which contains PAM configuration files (or /etc/pam.conf, if your system uses that file). You should also ensure that the pam_winbind.so file is installed, as described earlier in "Preparing Your System."

To modify PAM configurations, edit the PAM files associated with any logon services that should accept Winbind (and, hence, SMB/CIFS domain controller) authentication to include lines such as the following:

```
auth      sufficient   /lib/security/pam_winbind.so
account   sufficient   /lib/security/pam_winbind.so
```

These lines, placed within groups of similar lines, should enable logons via whatever service is specified; however, some systems may require further adjustments or may benefit from other tweaks. Results are highly dependent upon your system's PAM configurations, which vary greatly. Consult the PAM section of the User Authentication HOWTO document (http://www.tldp.org/HOWTO/User-Authentication-HOWTO/) for more information on PAM and its configuration.

If a service requires that a home directory exist, you may want to add another line to its service definition. This line calls the pam_mkhomedir.so module, which creates a home directory for the user when the user is authenticated if such a directory doesn't exist:

```
session  required  /lib/security/pam_mkhomedir.so skel=/etc/skel umask=0027
```

You can change the skeleton directory (skel=/etc/skel) and umask values (umask=0027) as you see fit. Once this line is added to a service definition, a home directory is created, if necessary, for any user who successfully authenticates, whether the authentication method is Winbind or something else.

What logon services should you modify to support Winbind? The answer is entirely up to you. For a typical workstation, you'd start with login for text-mode logons and one or both of xdm and gdm for GUI logons. You might also want to modify such popular servers as sshd for remote SSH logons, pop and imap for POP and IMAP e-mail servers, and ftp or a similar file for an FTP server. (Telnet logons are mediated by the login module.) Chances are you don't need or want to change such PAM configuration files as su or sudo, which are related to root authentication—the root account is probably best handled locally. Another tool that's conspicuous by its absence is Samba—Samba only uses PAM for authentication when it's configured to use cleartext passwords, so there's little point to configuring it to use Winbind for authentication.

Using the Configuration

To test the configuration, you can attempt to log onto the computer using whatever server you've configured to use Winbind. For instance, if you change the login tool, you can try to log on at the console or via Telnet. The result might look like this:

```
login: PHYSICS+grogers
Password:
Last login: Fri Jan 30 2004 14:23 on tty2
$
```

One point to note about this logon is that it includes the domain name and separator as part of the username. The domain doesn't make it into the user's home directory name unless you include the %D variable as part of the template homedir parameter, though. If you don't want to have to specify the domain name as part of the username, set winbind use default domain = Yes. You can then omit the domain name and separator; for instance, grogers alone would log the user into the computer in the preceding example.

I recommend you test all the logon methods you've configured to use Winbind, using both local and SMB/CIFS domain usernames. Doing these tests will ensure that everything's working as it is or, if it isn't, enable you to track down the problem and fix it before you put the system into production.

Summary

Domains have long played an important role in Windows networking. These structures are like the simpler workgroups, but they add a centralized authentication server, which can greatly simplify network administration by reducing the need for tedious account maintenance on multiple computers. Samba can function as a domain controller by adding a few parameters to the `smb.conf` file. The tricky parts of domain configuration lie elsewhere, though. Setting up a backup domain controller with Samba is technically possible, but in practice it's extremely difficult. Configuring interdomain trust relationships can expand the usefulness of domains but requires special configuration of both domain controllers. Using domains requires configuring clients and noncontroller servers to use the domain, and this task can be tricky in some cases. The most awkward of these tasks is using an SMB/CIFS domain controller for native Unix authentication—a procedure that's possible and even desirable in some situations but is a bit tedious to configure.

#### CHAPTER 11

Securing Samba

EVERY MONTH SEEMS to bring a new security horror story reported in the mainstream press. Perhaps a new worm is on the loose, infecting computers via bugs or poor configuration of popular servers. Perhaps the problem is an attack that brought down a high-profile Web site. Whatever the case, these stories serve as reminders that you shouldn't take computer security lightly. Fortunately, as of early 2004, no major attacks have involved Samba, but that doesn't mean such attacks might not occur in the future. What's more, Samba has had its share of security problems in the past, and small-scale attacks that don't reach the mainstream media are certainly possible.

Many chapters of this book mention security consequences of particular options. This chapter, though, is devoted to this topic. It begins with a look at a few general security measures. These procedures affect overall system security, but some of them interact with Samba's security measures in important ways. Next up is a look at a crude method of access control: Samba provides methods to block or allow particular IP addresses, which can serve as a defense against outside attacks. If such restrictions aren't sufficient, Samba's next line of defense is passwords, so understanding how passwords are compromised and how to implement good password policies on your system is important. Next up is a description of methods of encrypting all the traffic that Samba exchanges, which can make efforts to snoop on data exchanges fruitless. Finally, the chapter concludes with a few words about keeping up to date in a changing security world.

NOTE The mainstream media use the word *hacker* to refer to computer miscreants. This word has an older and more honorable meaning as referring to those who enjoy and are good at programming. Many of the people who developed Samba consider themselves hackers in this positive sense. For this reason, I use the word *cracker* to refer to those who break into computers or otherwise intentionally disrupt their operation.

Non-Samba Security Measures

Installing fancy locks and unbreakable glass on your home's windows can be useful security measures, but they're pointless if you leave your front door wide open. Similarly, paying careful attention to Samba security is important, but if the computer has other security flaws, the Samba security alone will be pointless. The following sections examine a few important general-purpose security considerations, including some that interact with Samba security features: addressing physical security, setting up firewalls, removing unnecessary servers, and removing unnecessary accounts.

NOTE This section can only scratch the surface of general Unix security. To learn more, you should consult a book dedicated to the topic, such as Simson Garfinkel, Gene Spafford, and Alan Schwartz's *Practical Unix & Internet Security, 3rd Edition* (O'Reilly, 2003).

Physical Security Considerations

One of the most important rules in computer security is that a cracker with physical access to a computer can do anything. In an extreme case, a miscreant could walk off with the computer or literally smash it to pieces. Less extreme violations include copying data from the hard drive (bypassing normal OS security mechanisms), installing unauthorized software, and altering system settings to give the attacker more complete remote access than you intended. Thus, you should ensure that your Samba server is as secure from physical attack as possible.

Just how secure should you make the system, though? One of the problems with security is that it's not absolute. A computer doesn't fall cleanly into a category of *secure* or *insecure*; it falls somewhere on a security scale. At one end are systems that are wide open to the most trivial attacks; at the other end are systems that are very difficult to break into. The more secure a system is, though, the harder it is to configure and, often, use the system. In the case of physical security, impediments to break-ins take the form of fairly ordinary physical objects—literal locks, bolts, doors, bars, and so on. Some physical security measures are more computer-specific, and some may be procedural. All of these measures, though, are designed to restrict who can physically touch a computer or in what way authorized personnel may do so. Common physical security measures include the following:

Building security: General security on the building in which the computer resides is important. Ideally, random people can't come and go from the building; they'll need passes of some sort. The quality of door locks, window design, and so on can affect building security, as well. Unfortunately, you can't always make wholesale changes to building security, and some buildings must be open to the public. A public library becomes useless if it's locked down against the general public, for instance.

Room security: The room in which the Samba server is located should be secured against unauthorized access. Even in the case of public buildings, such security is often possible. Attention to door materials, door locks, window locks, and so on is advisable. If possible, place the server in a room that has no windows or at least one whose windows aren't easily reached. Some Samba servers must operate in public or semipublic spaces, though. A print server might need to be in an open environment, for instance. (Sometimes you can put a print server in a locked room or closet and put its printers outside, though.)

Intrusion detection: Particularly if your site is unattended on a regular basis, you may want to install a burglar alarm system. This will help deter burglars and other miscreants and may help you catch them if they break in nonetheless.

Bolts and chains: If a computer must be exposed to the public, or as an added security measure even if the computer is in a locked room, you can purchase security kits that enable you to chain a computer to a desk or wall. These kits can protect against a miscreant stealing a computer. Such kits aren't likely to be very effective against a determined and well-equipped thief, though.

Case antitamper hardware: One of the problems of physical security is keeping unauthorized individuals from accessing your hard disk with their own tools. After security on the building and room, your main protection against this threat is antitamper hardware on the computer. These measures can be as simple as unusual screws on computer cases that require special tools to unscrew. Another common measure is a lock on the case itself, such as a hinge that prevents the case from opening until it has been unbolted. Like bolts and chains, these measures aren't likely to be effective against a determined thief—particularly one who's willing to deface the hardware. They might slow down somebody who wants surreptitious access to your data, though.

Removable media: Removable media (floppy drives, CD-ROM drives, and so on) are a potential Achilles' heel. Depending upon the computer's Basic Input Output System (BIOS) settings, intruders might be able to reboot the computer with their own OS to access your data. Likewise, these drives may give miscreants a way to cart off sensitive data, bypassing any firewalls or other network security measures you put in place. All in all, it's best to have as few removable media drives as possible on a server. Portable removable media drives are also a threat. Attackers might come equipped with Universal Serial Bus (USB) devices for retrieving data. To some extent, you can protect yourself against such attacks by removing support for these drives from your OS and/or BIOS. This protection isn't likely to be perfect, though, particularly once the attacker has full physical access to the computer.

BIOS settings: All computers follow certain startup procedures, even before the OS is involved. Many computers offer options that can be set to modify these procedures. For instance, most *x*86 systems have BIOSs that can be protected by a password. Without the password, you can't change BIOS settings or even boot the computer. Using such settings can help prevent miscreants from booting their own OSs to access your data. It's usually possible to override these settings via a jumper on the motherboard, though, so they're only as good as your computer antitamper devices.

Hard disk data encryption: In very high-security environments, all the data on the hard disk is encrypted, preventing it from being usable without a password. This practice can protect your data from being abused should an intruder steal the hard disk. This practice is uncommon on Unix systems, though, and most popular Unix-like OSs lack encrypting filesystems.

Procedural measures: You should clearly define a security policy, including factors such as who is authorized to be in particular rooms, how access to a building or room is controlled (via a card reader, a passcode on a lock, a security guard, and so on), how often to update passcodes, and so on. Remember that people are likely to try to bypass security if they think it's too onerous. You might do better with a lower level of security that's actually honored than a nominally tight security level that's routinely disrupted by inconvenienced legitimate users.

Backup security: Don't forget to protect your backups! If your computer contains sensitive data, your backups have that data, too. If security around your backups is lax, a thief could take a backup, copy it, and return it the next day, and you might be none the wiser. Note that backups contain sensitive data such as your password files, and the normal Unix security mechanisms don't apply to backups, so a miscreant can easily read these files.

When designing your physical security, you must decide which measures are appropriate for which computers. Public Samba clients might need physical chains to prevent theft, whereas you might focus on solid doors, locks, and BIOS security for servers housed in a server room. Servers that house sensitive data (such as domain controllers) may need more protection than those that don't (such as printer servers). Your budget and the needs of your users also come into play. Few individuals can afford to hire security guards to control access to their home computers, for instance.

Setting Up a Firewall

Traditionally, a *firewall* has been a computer that sits between two or more networks and controls access between those networks. Typically, one of these networks is the Internet at large, and the other is your private network, as depicted in Figure 11-1. You may notice that this placement is identical to that of a router, and in fact firewall software often does run on a network's router.

Firewalls come in several varieties, but you can categorize most in one of two ways:

Packet filters: Some firewalls function as *packet filters*, meaning that they block individual TCP/IP packets based on their source or destination addresses, source or destination ports, or other low-level features. Packet filter firewalls aren't able to analyze data streams at a very high level because each packet contains very little data. On the other hand, this class of firewall consumes little CPU power, so it won't degrade network performance very much.

Proxy filters: A *proxy filter* is a software component that intercepts network accesses on a high level, assembles complete requests and replies, analyzes the request or reply, and passes it to its destination or blocks it depending upon the results of the analysis. Proxy filters consume more CPU time than do packet filters, and they sometimes require clients to be rewritten to support the software. On the other hand, they can perform fairly sophisticated filtering, such as removing ads from Web pages.

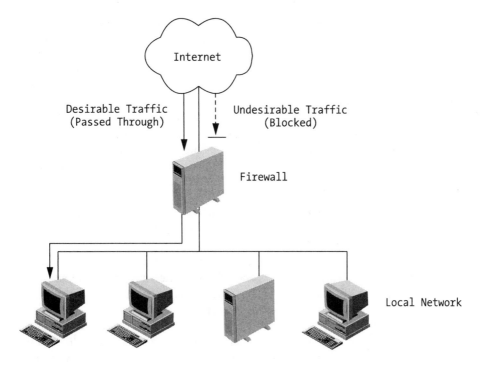

Figure 11-1. Firewalls function as gatekeepers of network traffic, controlling what types of data can pass.

For the purposes of protecting a Samba server, packet filters are the most useful type of firewall. By controlling access to a Samba server's ports, you can control access to the Samba server itself, based on the would-be client's IP address or other features of the packets. This exercise is most useful for protecting a Samba server (and other SMB/CIFS servers) from unauthorized outside access. Typically, only local users should access a Samba server, so all remote access attempts should be blocked. Sometimes, though, you may want to enable particular remote users. For instance, if certain employees frequently work at home and have broadband Internet connections with static IP addresses, you could create firewall rules that enable these users to reach the Samba server from those IP addresses, but block all other external IP addresses.

One fact about firewall configuration that's often overlooked is that firewalls, and particularly packet filter firewalls, can control access in both directions. You might want to prevent local users from accessing remote SMB/CIFS servers. One reason to do this is to prevent abuses by "bad apples" who use your local network. Another is to help prevent the spread of worms, some of which take advantage of flaws in Windows SMB/CIFS implementations.

Although Figure 11-1 shows a firewall running as a separate computer to protect an entire network, other configurations are possible. For instance, you can run a firewall on the local Samba server itself. Such a configuration protects only the Samba server computer (unless this system doubles as a router) and may prevent that system from being used to abuse other systems. One advantage of this setup is that it can differentiate between computers on your local network. For instance, you might block access from your local DHCP server if it shouldn't be running an SMB/CIFS client. This configuration can help prevent abuses should your DHCP server be compromised. Some networks use multiple layers of firewall protection. Some computers might reside behind a firewall that does only minimal filtering, and a second subnet might use a firewall that performs much stronger filtering.

Broadly speaking and in general, if you use a firewall on a router, as depicted in Figure 11-1, you should configure the firewall to block all incoming and outgoing traffic related to SMB/CIFS. As described in Chapter 1, SMB/CIFS used via NetBIOS over TCP/IP (NBT) can use UDP and TCP port 137, UDP port 138, and TCP port 139 (although in practice, TCP port 137 isn't used). Thus, you should block all of these ports. To be sure you don't err in your selection of UDP or TCP ports, block both UDP and TCP ports 137–139. Also as described in Chapter 1, SMB/CIFS can optionally work without the benefit of NetBIOS, in which case it uses TCP port 445, so you may want to block it (and UDP port 445, for good measure). Some additional Samba-related tools might require blocking, too. For instance, if you run the Samba Web Administration Tool (SWAT), it uses TCP port 901. The Respond fax helper program described in Chapter 6 runs on TCP port 5555 by default but on client systems.

So how do you configure a firewall? The answer depends on the OS running on the firewall computer. Most Unix-like OSs ship with tools that enable them to function as firewalls, but the details of how they're configured differ. Likewise, if you're running a non-Unix OS as the firewall computer, how you configure it depends on its firewall products. (Several third-party firewall packages are available for Windows, for instance.) Small networks may be protected by dedicated broadband routers, which must be configured according to the products' documentation. Larger networks may use more expensive dedicated products, which likewise should have their own documentation. Because these firewall products vary so greatly, you should consult your OS's or router's documentation to learn how to do it. On Unix-like systems, though, you'll generally create a script that repeatedly calls a tool to set up firewall rules for each port and direction you want to block.

The procedure for protecting a single Samba server is similar to the procedure for protecting your network. One important difference is that you protect a single Samba server via a script that runs on the server computer itself. Another difference is that the firewall rules are designed to block unauthorized incoming packets directed at the server computer, as opposed to packets directed at (or coming from) any computer on your network.

NOTE   Samba includes security features that can block unauthorized IP addresses from accessing the computer, as described in the upcoming section "Restricting Access by IP Address." This feature is at least partially redundant with firewall features running on the server computer itself, but if you're concerned about security, you should implement both security measures. Doing so provides redundancy in case of an error or bug; if one system fails, the other should continue protecting the computer. Also, each system has slightly different features and capabilities. For instance, a firewall can prevent unauthorized attempts to contact outside servers, which Samba's configuration alone can't do.

Removing Unnecessary Servers

Even servers written by experienced programmers usually have bugs, and sometimes these bugs can allow unauthorized individuals to gain access to the computer. Sometimes the level of access granted is small, but skilled crackers may be able to exploit limited access to gain additional access or to simply wreak havoc—say, by creating symbolic links in Samba shares that point to sensitive files or by enabling the cracker to cause Samba to crash. Thus, every server your computer runs is a potential security risk, and you should shut down all servers that aren't strictly necessary.

 NOTE   Removing unnecessary servers requires that you modify, or at least check, the basic startup configuration of your computer and its servers. Chapter 3 covers some of this material with respect to Samba, and other servers can be started in much the same way as Samba, so you may want to review Chapter 3. Unfortunately, some details are very OS-specific, so you should also review your OS's documentation regarding methods of launching servers.

Unfortunately, shutting down unnecessary servers is more easily said than done. You must be able to determine what servers are running, determine how they're being launched, determine how to prevent them from being launched, and shut them down on a one-time basis. If you're familiar with your system, you should already have a good idea of what's running; however, if you've just taken over a system you didn't configure yourself, or if you've just installed an OS on a computer, you may not know precisely what's running. You can take the following steps to learn what's running and shut down servers that shouldn't be running:

Run a local port scan: On most Unix-like systems, the netstat utility returns a great deal of information about local network operations. When fed appropriate parameters, it can tell you what ports are in use by what programs. Unfortunately, the precise syntax to use depends on the OS in question. For instance, in Linux, typing netstat -lp produces a list of sockets that are open for listening and the process IDs (PIDs) associated with them. In FreeBSD, typing netstat -aA | grep LISTEN produces a similar listing, but no PIDs are present; instead, the first column is a socket number. You can grep on the output of fstat to find the socket number, as in fstat | grep c7bc3b40 to find the process that owns socket c7bc3b40. You may need to consult your local documentation to learn how best to use netstat and any related tools to locate running servers. Note that this procedure is likely to identify a super server for any servers that are run via that super server.

Run a remote port scan: You can scan the computer from another computer to locate open ports. To do so, you must use a port scanning tool, such as Nmap (http://www.insecure.org/nmap/). Fully describing the use of this or similar tools is beyond the scope of this book, though; consult your port scanner's documentation for details. Note that a port scan may not detect servers that are protected by firewalls.

 CAUTION Although port scans can be an important and legitimate system administration tool, they're also popular cracking tools. Running port scans on computers or networks without authorization is likely to be a violation of your network's security policies. If you run a port scan on a network or computer you don't own, be sure to obtain written permission from an appropriate individual first. If you fail to do so, you could end up fired, without Internet access, or even answering for your actions in court.

Check servers run from your super server: Chapter 3 described how to run Samba from a super server. Other servers can be run in the same way, and you can check your super server configuration (the /etc/inetd.conf file for inetd or the /etc/xinetd.conf file and contents of the /etc/xinetd.d directory for xinetd) for signs of unnecessary servers. As a general rule, no server run from a super server is vital for the basic operation of a computer, so if you disable all such servers, your computer will still function. Of course, some super server–mediated servers are vital for the duties of particular computers, so disabling such servers mistakenly can cause problems—just not problems that will prevent the computer from booting.

Check for SysV startup scripts: Many Unix-like systems use SysV startup scripts, as described in Chapter 3. You can check your SysV startup script configuration for unnecessary servers; however, many SysV startup scripts start tools that aren't servers, and some may be important to normal system functioning. Thus, you shouldn't disable SysV startup scripts unless you know they don't do anything vital for normal system operations.

Check local startup scripts: If your computer uses local startup scripts, as described in Chapter 3, you should review them for evidence of servers being started. As with SysV startup scripts, though, local startup scripts can launch nonserver programs and programs vital to the basic functioning of a computer. Thus, you shouldn't disable items you find in these scripts unless you know what they do.

Kill servers: If you've identified a running server by PID, you can kill it with the kill command, as in `kill 32810` to kill process 32810. This action won't prevent the server from running again if you restart the computer, though, and in the case of servers launched from a super server, it will kill a single session at best. This procedure is, therefore, incomplete, but it's still helpful if you've disabled a server's startup script but need to kill whatever process is running. In the case of servers launched from SysV startup scripts, you may be able to pass the startup script a `stop` parameter to shut down the server.

Overall, disabling unnecessary programs is a bit of an art. Several ways of tracking them down and disabling them exist. No method is perfect and simple, but by combining these methods, and particularly paying careful attention to local and remote port scans, you should be able to identify and shut down unwanted servers that could pose a security risk to a Samba system.

Removing Unnecessary Accounts

When users leave an organization, their computer accounts should normally be disabled or deleted. Doing so prevents former users from abusing their access, as might happen if a fired employee bears a grudge, for instance. Just as important, disused accounts are potential targets for crackers. If a cracker manages to obtain a password to an old account, the cracker can break in, even if the account hasn't been used in years.

In the case of a Samba server, you must remember to remove both the Unix account and (if Samba is configured to use encrypted passwords) the encrypted password entry. You should delete the Samba encrypted password information first. You can do this using the smbpasswd command and its -x option:

```
# smbpasswd -x bill
```

This example deletes the bill user's entry from the Samba password database. Once this is done, you should delete the Unix account, which can be done with a utility called rmuser, userdel, or something similar. Sometimes the accounts can be deleted by directly editing the /etc/passwd or /etc/shadow files and deleting the lines that correspond to the accounts you want to delete. Consult your OS's documentation for details.

Restricting Access by IP Address

Security is best applied in layers. If one layer fails to work, another layer should work. Non-Samba measures, such as using firewalls and removing unnecessary servers, represent a first layer in the Samba defenses, albeit a complex layer. A second layer is Samba's built-in IP address restrictions. These restrictions work something like a firewall's or super server's restrictions, but you apply them via several Samba parameters:

interfaces: You can tell Samba to listen only to particular network interfaces with this global parameter, which takes an interface name (such as eth0 for a Linux Ethernet interface or vr0 for a VIA Rhine Ethernet board in FreeBSD), the server's IP address on a specific interface, or a network/netmask pair for an interface (as in 192.168.7.0/24) as a value. This parameter by itself does little good; you must use it in conjunction with bind interfaces only to limit the interfaces to which Samba listens.

bind interfaces only: This global Boolean parameter is used in conjunction with interfaces. Set bind interfaces only = Yes to restrict access to the interfaces specified via the interfaces parameter. The nmbd and smbd servers are affected differently by this parameter. The nmbd server rejects access attempts based on the client's claimed IP address, whereas smbd uses the actual interface hardware. Thus, nmbd could at least theoretically be tricked by an attacker who's not on the claimed interface. Ordinarily, this risk is low because nmbd doesn't grant direct access to the server computer's filesystem, but if a security bug were present in nmbd, it could become an issue.

hosts allow: This share-level parameter sets the IP addresses of computers that may access the share (or the server, if it's listed in the [global] section). A synonym for this parameter is allow hosts.

hosts deny: This share-level parameter sets the IP addresses of computers that may *not* access the share (or the server, if it's listed in the [global] section). A synonym for this parameter is deny hosts.

These last two parameters deserve more elaboration because the forms of their options can be complex. These parameters are designed to let you allow or deny access to individual computers, entire networks, and even arbitrary sets of computers, much as can be done with the TCP Wrappers package. The two parameters take the same forms; they differ in whether they treat the specified computers as white listed or black listed. Specific methods of listing computers are as follows:

Individual IP addresses: You can list IP addresses, as in hosts allow = 192.168.7.79, which grants only the computer at 192.168.7.79 access to the share.

Individual hostnames: You can list a DNS hostname, as in hosts allow = goodguy or hosts allow = goodguy.example.com.

Network IP addresses: You can specify an entire network of computers by providing a partial IP address and terminating it in a dot (.) or by providing an IP address/netmask pair, as in hosts allow = 192.168.7. or hosts allow = 192.168.7.0/255.255.255.0.

Network domain name: You can specify an entire network of computers by providing a DNS domain name preceded by a dot, as in hosts allow = .example.com, which grants all computers in the example.com domain access to the share.

Network NIS name: If your network uses a Network Information Service (NIS) server, you can provide an NIS name for a group of systems preceded by an at sign (@), as in hosts allow = @goodguys.

Combinations: You can list multiple individual computers or groups of computers by separating their identifications with spaces, commas, or tabs. For instance, hosts allow = 192.168.7.79 .example.com grants access to 192.167.7.79 and all computers in the example.com domain.

Exceptions: The keyword EXCEPT enables you to specify exceptions to a network address. For instance, hosts allow = 192.168.7. EXCEPT 192.168.7.89 grants access to all computers in the 192.168.7.0/24 network except for 192.168.7.89.

NOTE   If you use Samba 3.0 and want to use hostnames or domain names in your hosts allow or hosts deny values, you must also set hostname lookups = Yes in the global section of smb.conf. This parameter's default value is No although the man page for Samba 3.0.0 and 3.0.1 incorrectly states that the default value is Yes.

Normally, you'll use only hosts allow or only hosts deny. If you use hosts allow, all computers not explicitly listed are denied access to the share; if you use hosts deny, all unlisted computers are granted access. If you use both parameters and a computer is listed by both, hosts allow takes precedence. Thus, if you want to create exceptions to a rule in hosts allow, be sure to use the EXCEPT keyword.

For best security, I recommend using a hosts allow line in your [global] section to prevent outsiders from accessing your system. You may also want to block access by some computers on your own network that shouldn't be accessing your server, such as your router. For instance, if your local network is 192.168.7.0/24 and your router is at 192.168.7.1, you might enter the following line:

```
hosts allow = 192.168.7. EXCEPT 192.168.7.1
```

If necessary, you can add external computers before the EXCEPT keyword if they should be granted access, as with telecommuters. In general, using IP addresses is better than using hostnames or domain names because hostnames and domain names are typically resolved with the help of a DNS server, which might be compromised. A cracker who can change a domain's DNS listings can, therefore, gain entry to your Samba server if you rely on hostnames or domain names.

Password Issues

SMB/CIFS relies very heavily upon passwords for authentication. Therefore, it's important that you understand the strengths and weaknesses of passwords and how to shore up those weaknesses against attack. Unfortunately, this aspect of system security depends to a great extent upon your users' cooperation, so you must educate them about good password practices.

How Passwords Are Compromised

A password-protected server is, at best, only as secure as its passwords. Such servers frequently have many users, and this fact increases the odds that a cracker will obtain a password. Crackers can do so in many different ways:

Password sniffing: If a cracker can install a network sniffer on your network, either by gaining physical access and installing a computer for the purpose or by compromising a single computer, the cracker can monitor your network traffic in search of passwords. Wireless networks are unusually susceptible to such sniffing, particularly if their encryption is disabled. The risk of sniffing is greatest when Samba is configured to use cleartext passwords, but the SMB/CIFS password encryption algorithms are weak, so you shouldn't consider them to be proof against crackers.

Stolen password files: If a cracker can somehow steal the Samba password file (smbpasswd), the cracker can easily decrypt most of the passwords in that file. You should, therefore, protect this file very carefully. Worse, some versions of Windows, and potentially other OSs, store SMB/CIFS passwords on their hard disks, which makes them vulnerable to theft. Windows 9*x*/Me systems are particularly vulnerable because their security is so easily breached if an individual has physical access to the computer. Chapter 10 describes how to configure Windows 9*x*/Me in a domain to reduce the severity of this threat.

Stolen passwords on paper: Passwords should never be written down, but sometimes they are. A miscreant might steal or rummage through a purse or wallet, an open desk drawer, and so on to locate a person's password.

Dumpster diving: If people who write down their passwords subsequently throw away the paper on which their passwords are written, somebody can rummage through the garbage to find them—a practice known as *dumpster diving*. To protect against this practice, passwords should never be written down, but if they are, the paper should be destroyed by burning it or at least shredding it rather than simply throwing it away.

Shoulder surfing: To be useful, passwords must be typed into a computer. A person who watches another person do this may be able to follow the key presses and learn the password. This risk is obviously greatest in public and semipublic environments, such as university computing centers and corporate cubicle farms. To protect against this risk, users should be wary of individuals hovering near computers and should shield the keyboard with their bodies to block prying eyes.

Lucky guesses: In the movies, passwords are invariably broken by a cracker making a lucky guess—using the victim's pet's name, a birthday, or the like. Such techniques can certainly work but only against very poor passwords. As described in the upcoming section, "Generating Good Passwords," easily guessed strings should *never* be used for passwords.

Shared passwords: Some passwords are meant to be shared. If your Samba server functions only as a print server, for instance, you might use share-level security and give everybody in the office the password to the printer. A miscreant is likely to find it easy to obtain this password, so the defense rests on the server side. Make sure the password is unique and ensure that the printer share account can't be abused to gain further access to the system. Some servers have multiple administrators, and it's common to share the root password among them, which can become a major security headache if just one administrator slips up or engages in unauthorized activities. Try to limit who has the root password, and change it frequently.

Social engineering: Crackers sometimes ask their targets for their passwords, and surprisingly enough, the soon-to-be victims often volunteer this information. Of course, the crackers don't announce themselves as such; they lie. They claim they're system administrators investigating a problem for which the target's password is necessary, ask to use an account for a few minutes to browse the Web, or some such. This practice is known as *social engineering*, and it's sometimes used in conjunction with other techniques. For instance, a cracker might go dumpster diving for an office directory and then claim to be some specific person within the organization. The obvious protection against social engineering is to never reveal passwords to anybody. Be sure your users know you have no cause to ask for a password, and neither does anybody else.

Understanding these methods of compromising passwords is the first step toward combating them. Protecting against many of these attacks is as simple as not doing whatever thing it is that makes them vulnerabilities. Thus, you should be sure that all your users understand these pitfalls and know to avoid them. Other vulnerabilities, such as the potential for harm should a password file fall into the wrong hands, require more in the way of administrative and technical safeguards.

No matter how an attacker obtains a password, it's useless once the user changes it. Thus, you should encourage your users to change their passwords frequently—a topic that's elaborated upon in the upcoming section "Changing Passwords."

Generating Good Passwords

Some forms of attack require recovering a password from an encrypted password database. Technically, though, the password isn't decrypted because it's encoded using a *hash*—a one-way translation of the password. Hashes can't be undone, but attackers can try encoding every word in a dictionary until they find one that matches the encrypted password entry. The attacker can then use the found password to gain entry to the computer. This approach is known as a *dictionary attack*.

In years past, dictionary attacks were successful only against passwords that were real and common words. As computers improved, though, crackers were able to add variants, such as words with a number added, common misspellings, and words from many languages, to their dictionaries. These variants add time to the search, but as computers have sped up, the total time has gone down. In mid-2003, a new cracking technique was announced that could crack an SMB/CIFS password in an average of just five seconds. (See http://lasecwww.epfl.ch/abstract_AdvancedNTCracker.shtml for some basic information about this technique.) If an attacker is using this technique and has access to a Samba encrypted password database or a password file stored on a Windows computer, the system is no longer secure. Nonetheless, you can take some steps to generate a password that's less vulnerable to guessing or attacks that operate in other ways:

1. **Select a base**: The password base should not be a single word, but it can be two unrelated words added together (as in *bunpen*, from *bun* and *pen*) or a personally meaningful and unique acronym (as in *yiwttd*, for *yesterday I went to the dentist*). The longer the base you select, the better. Six characters should be considered an absolute minimum length. An acronym is arguably a better base than a word pair. *Do not* use one of my examples as your base; because they've been published, they may appear in crackers' dictionaries.

2. **Reverse a word**: If you chose a two-word base, reverse one of the words. For instance, *bunpen* might become *bunnep*.

3. **Add digits and punctuation**: Add digits and punctuation to the password. Use at least two digits or symbols, at least one of which should not be at the start or end of the password. For instance, your password might become *bu3n^nep* or *y#iwt7td*.

4. **Randomize case**: Change the case of some letters of the password. The examples might then become *bU3N^neP* or *Y#iWT7td*. This modification isn't likely to be very important for Samba because Windows 9*x*/Me passwords are case-insensitive. If the password is used elsewhere, though, such as in normal Unix logins, it can improve security.

At this point, your password should resemble complete gibberish, but you should be able to re-create it relatively easily. The key press pattern will be difficult for a shoulder surfer to discern, particularly if you use a mixed-case password. With the important exception of the latest SMB/CIFS password-cracking tools, dictionary attacks are unlikely to succeed. Random guessing by hand (as in trying your pet's name) will get the attacker nowhere. In short, the password should be as secure as a password can be, short of being completely random. (In theory, completely random passwords are a good idea, but in practice they're not because users tend to write them down.)

Whatever you do, you should be sure to never use certain classes of words as passwords or even as bases for passwords generated as just described:

Names of family, friends, or pets: Such names are frequently early attempts in any password-guessing attempt and may appear in crackers' dictionaries.

Personal identification codes and numbers: Don't use your birthday, Social Security number, home address, telephone number, or any similar information in your passwords. Likewise, don't use such numbers belonging to friends, family members, or pets.

Names of favorite books, TV shows, characters, and so on: Anybody who knows you well and who tries to break into your account might try using names or other information associated with your favorite fiction, music, and so on.

Powerful referents: Particularly for the root account, a common mistake is to use a powerful referent, such as *God*, as the password.

Your username: Another common mistake is to use your own username as the password. Crackers are sure to try this early in the process.

Another password: Ideally, you shouldn't use the same password on multiple computers. Unfortunately, the proliferation of password-protected Web sites makes this advice impossible to follow for people with average memories who use more than a trivial number of such sites. (Password-management tools, such as those included in recent Web browsers, help, but at the expense of storing passwords on users' hard disks.) Nonetheless, you shouldn't reuse sensitive passwords, such as those for home directories, on a Samba server.

Related words in the base: If you use a word pair as the base, make the words completely unrelated, as are *bun* and *pen* in the earlier example. Related words, such as *white* and *house*, are likely to appear together in crackers' dictionaries.

Any single word in any language: Don't think that using a word from a non-English language will protect you; crackers' dictionaries frequently combine words from many languages.

Changing Passwords

Avoiding common password-generation mistakes and following a few simple steps to obscure your password can go a long way in making your system more secure. Of course, even the best-selected passwords can be compromised, so another step is to change the passwords frequently. This practice will ensure that crackers have a narrow window of opportunity for abusing any passwords they might steal. Users can change their Samba passwords in several different ways:

Remote password changes using Windows 9*x*/Me via GUI: If your computer is part of a domain, you can change your password on the domain controller using Windows 9*x*/Me. To do so, open the Passwords icon in the Control Panel and click the Change Other Passwords button. Select Microsoft Networking in the resulting Select Passwords dialog box, and click Change. You can then type the new password in the resulting password-change dialog box.

Remote password changes using Windows 9*x*/Me via text mode: Whether or not a Windows 9*x*/Me computer is part of a domain, you can change a remote system's password using the NET command. Specifically, typing NET PASSWORD *SERVER username* in a DOS prompt window changes the password for *username* on the *SERVER* computer. (Windows prompts for the old password and twice for the new password.)

Remote password changes in Windows NT/200*x*/XP: Windows NT/200*x*/XP also has password-changing tools, but they don't work quite the same as the Windows 9*x*/Me tools, and they vary amongst the members of the NT/200*x*/XP family. You can access the GUI tools from the User Accounts item or the Users and Passwords item in the Control Panel. (The name varies with the precise version of the OS.) The NET command's syntax is NET USER *username* password /*DOMAIN*, where *username* is the username and *DOMAIN* is the domain name. In any event, the Windows computer must be a member of the domain to change the password.

Samba server logons and smbpasswd: If an ordinary user logs onto a Unix account (using a console logon, Telnet, SSH, or other remote logon method) and types smbpasswd, the program prompts the user to change the password. The process works much like the process to change the local password using the passwd utility.

Remote password changes using smbpasswd: If users have access to one Unix system and want to change the password on another (say, a Samba client and a Samba domain controller), smbpasswd can also be used, but the remote system's NetBIOS name must be specified with the -r parameter. For instance, typing smbpasswd -r TANGO changes the user's password on the TANGO server.

Use of SWAT: The SWAT package, described in greater detail in Chapter 13, provides ordinary users with the means to change passwords via a Web browser. To do so, enter the server's DNS hostname, a colon, and **901** in the browser's URL field, as in **http://tango:901** to access the tango server. The system responds by prompting for a username and password. Ordinary users can enter their own usernames and passwords. Clicking the Password item then enables users to enter the old and new password in the Server Password Management area. Entering this information along with another computer's name in the Client/Server Password Management area changes the password on the specified server.

Each of these methods has its advantages and disadvantages. The remote login methods (including Telnet or SSH logins and to a lesser extent SWAT) require the user to have full login access, which might be abused by miscreants. (In the case of SWAT, the user's shell could be set to /bin/false or some other bogus value, preventing remote shell access; however, the account must still have an active password.) Telnet and SWAT require the password to be sent over the local network unencrypted, but SSH provides excellent encryption for the password change.

You can enable users to change their passwords via a remote login protocol such as Telnet or SSH without providing shell access to the server. To do so, set the user's shell to smbpasswd. In most cases, you do this by setting the final field of the user's /etc/passwd entry to point to the program:

```
amanda:x:504:504::/home/amanda:/usr/bin/smbpasswd
```

In some cases, you must also add the smbpasswd program to a file that identifies valid user shells, such as /etc/shells. Some OSs don't respond well to direct changes to the /etc/passwd file, so you may need to use a tool, such as usermod, to change this configuration. Consult your OS's documentation for details.

In any event, after you've set up the account to use smbpasswd as the default shell, a user who attempts to log in will be asked for a username and a Unix password. If the login is successful, smbpasswd runs and asks the user for the current Samba password and then prompts for the new one twice. Once the process is done, the session terminates.

One of the problems with remote login methods that require a regular Unix account and password is that either users must remember two passwords (for Unix and Samba) or you must configure the system to change the Unix password when the Samba password changes. You can achieve the latter effect by setting unix passwd sync = Yes and setting the passwd program parameter appropriately for your system, as described in Chapter 7.

How often should passwords be changed? This question has no simple answer. Some sites take an extreme position and implement *one-time-use passwords*, which as their name suggests can be used just once. Such passwords are typically used in extremely high-security environments. Samba provides no explicit support for one-time-use passwords, so if you need to implement such a system, you'll need to create custom tools to automatically change passwords after each login. Most sites make do with policies that promote much less frequent password changes—perhaps once every one to three months. As with other security measures, there's no fixed value for frequency of password change that produces perfect results; you must balance the inconvenience of having to change passwords with the benefits in terms of increased difficulty for would-be crackers.

Enforcing Good Password Practices

The trickiest part of setting up good password security is in getting your users to cooperate. Left to their own devices, most users would set their passwords to poor values, reuse passwords on dozens of systems, and leave them unchanged for years. Your challenge as a Samba administrator is to curb these tendencies.

Perhaps your best tool in promoting good password practices is education. Tell your users how to generate good passwords that are nonetheless easy to remember and inform them why they shouldn't use very simple and easily guessed passwords. Tell them why passwords should be changed frequently and why they shouldn't share them with others. Such educational measures, perhaps coupled with occasional reminders to change passwords, can help curb some of the worst password-related problems. To go further, you must resort to various measures that are intrusive or coercive in one way or another.

Some Unix systems provide mechanisms to expire their local passwords. When you use this feature, passwords will simply stop working on a specified date unless they're changed, which can be an effective tool for enforcing frequent password changes. Unfortunately, Samba doesn't provide any easy way to implement such a policy for its encrypted passwords. If you use unencrypted passwords, you can use the underlying Unix expiration mechanism, but unless your users log in using Telnet, SSH, or the like, they won't be informed of the impending password expiration. If your users regularly log in using one of these mechanisms and you use encrypted Samba passwords, you could enable the local password-expiration tools but tell users to use smbpasswd or a similar tool to change both passwords at once. (Of course, you must then use Samba's tools to tie the two systems together.)

Short of having a system administrator audit all your users' passwords (a practice that's potentially dangerous, should the auditor be untrustworthy) or assigning randomly generated passwords (which is risky because they're hard to remember and, therefore, likely to be written down), it's impossible to guarantee that all users enter good passwords. Some Unix password-changing tools submit entered passwords to checks of certain kinds and won't accept passwords that don't pass their tests. For instance, such systems may reject passwords that fall under a certain length or that don't have at least a specified number of punctuation symbols or numbers. The min password length parameter and its synonym, min passwd length, enforce a minimum-length requirement for passwords changed via the smbpasswd program, but Samba provides no easy-to-use mechanism for enforcing other requirements.

Bypassing Passwords

The focus of this chapter is on improving security; however, you might want to bypass Samba's security measures from time to time. For instance, if you're running a small print server on a private network behind a strong firewall, you might not be too concerned about outsiders abusing the printer shares to break into the computer, and using passwords on the printer shares may be inconvenient.

 CAUTION Even if you're not too concerned about a compromised print server or the like, you should consider the effects of a cracker having full run of the print server computer. Could this system be used to attack other computers on your network? If the answer is *yes* (as it usually is), you may want to attend to the print server's security more carefully than you might if it were just the print server computer itself at stake.

If you decide you want to bypass passwords, several methods are available, some of which have been described in previous chapters. In particular, Chapter 7 describes guest accounts. You can set up one or more shares to accept guest access and then use them with any username or password you like. Other parameters that can bypass Samba's normal security include the following:

hosts equiv: This global parameter specifies a file that contains the names of computers, and optionally usernames, that can be trusted to authenticate their own users. When you use this parameter, Samba won't require valid passwords from users on those computers. Each line of the file consists of a computer hostname optionally followed by a list of usernames that should be trusted.

use rhosts: This global parameter has an effect similar to hosts equiv, but the file holding the names of the trusted computers is the .rhosts file in users' home directories. Thus, you're effectively giving access control to the users themselves. This parameter has been removed from Samba 3.0.

These parameters both make Samba work much like rlogin, rcp, and similar Unix commands. These tools have fallen out of favor because of their poor security features, and the same problems exist when using Samba with hosts equiv or use rhosts.

Using Encryption with Samba

The usual mode of operation for SMB/CIFS, and hence for Samba, is to pass all data, with the possible exception of passwords, over the network unencrypted. This practice is perfectly reasonable on most small wired networks, but sometimes a greater degree of security is in order. The following sections investigate the problem and possible solutions to it, starting with a look at when the lack of encryption is a problem. Three solutions to this problem are using Secure Sockets Layer (SSL) encryption, using a Secure Shell (SSH) tunnel, and using a Virtual Private Network (VPN).

TIP   Encrypting all data can be a CPU-intensive process and is tedious to configure. In many cases, a much simpler but less complete solution is to change your network hardware. In particular, Ethernet hubs are susceptible to data sniffing. Any computer connected to a hub can monitor all the traffic to or from any other computer on the same hub. Converting your network to use Ethernet switches rather than hubs greatly reduces the severity of this problem because switches direct packets to only the true target computer, thus making sniffers on other computers largely ineffective. (Switches can't completely eliminate sniffing, though; broadcast packets can still be sniffed, and switches' targeted packet delivery can sometimes be disabled. Switches also won't help if a sniffer resides on the source or destination computer itself.) In the case of wireless networks, ensure that your network hardware is configured to encrypt all data, but be aware that wireless encryption protocols are themselves far from perfect.

The Problem: Lack of Encryption on SMB/CIFS Data Transfers

SMB/CIFS is typically used on local networks, and most people don't bother with encrypting their local network traffic. The unstated assumption is that the "bad guys" don't have direct access to your network wires. This assumption isn't always valid, though. Sometimes the crackers lie in wait disturbingly close to home. They could be corporate spies, disgruntled employees, or true remote crackers who've managed to compromise one of your systems. Although rare, there are also cases where SMB/CIFS is used over the Internet at large. In this case, the packets may traverse a dozen or more computers and their networks, any one of which could hold an unauthorized sniffer. Eavesdropping on wireless networks is extremely easy if they're unencrypted, as many are; a cracker can sit in a car with a laptop computer and listen in on your local wireless data transfers.

In all of these cases, the normal unencrypted mode of operation for SMB/CIFS is a liability. An intruder might be able to steal any data transferred via Samba, such as employee evaluations, product schematics, legal documents, and so on. An intruder can potentially intercept documents as they're being loaded, saved, copied, or printed.

Encryption helps protect sensitive data by making unauthorized decryption difficult to the point of impossibility. A typical workstation, or even a small cluster of them, would have to work for months, years, or centuries to decrypt most modern encryption techniques. (To be sure, governments and very large businesses can afford the computing power to do the job more quickly, but even they can't do it in anywhere near real time.)

NOTE   Data encryption, as described here, is somewhat different from password encryption as practiced by SMB/CIFS and in the Unix password database. Encrypted passwords use *hashes*, which are one-way data transformations. Once hashed, it's mathematically impossible to recover the original data using the hashed password alone. Crackers do the job by encrypting random words until they find a match. Encryption for entire data transfer sessions must be reversible, and much more data is encrypted, which makes the decryption task harder—the sort of dictionary attack that works with password databases won't work on an encrypted SMB/CIFS connection.

Unfortunately, SMB/CIFS wasn't built with encryption in mind, so using it isn't as simple as setting a Samba parameter or two. Configuring encryption requires taking special steps, and you'll lose some functionality. The practice will also chew up some CPU time on both the clients and the server, thus increasing your network hardware requirements. Therefore, you shouldn't embark on the task of encrypting your data lightly. You must decide whether encrypting your data is worth the effort involved. In most cases, it's not. Most local networks are well enough protected from outside attackers that your main concern is local users. (A partial exception is wireless networks, but these can usually be configured to use encryption via low-level network configuration options.) Although local security shouldn't be taken lightly, chances are good that would-be local data thieves have easier ways of stealing data than sniffing the network wire. This is particularly true if you replace any hubs your network uses with switches. If your network is *not* protected from the outside world, you should invest your time and effort into doing so by installing a firewall and other security measures. This action will have far greater impact on your overall network security than encrypting your Samba traffic alone. Most methods of encrypting SMB/CIFS data handle only TCP traffic. This means that name resolution and browsing won't work, at least not using the encrypted connections.

Of course, there are exceptions to this rule. One is if your network carries extraordinarily sensitive data. If this is the case, though, you probably have a security expert on hand to help secure your network. Another condition when you might want to encrypt your SMB/CIFS traffic is if that traffic is unusually exposed, say because it's being routed between offices over the Internet. In both of these cases, encrypting some or all of your local network traffic, including your Samba traffic, may make sense.

You may want to consider encryption as falling into two distinct categories. The first is local encryption—encryption of data on your own local network segment. The second category is encryption of traffic that passes between networks. Although both categories share many commonalities in configuration, each has its own unique features.

First Solution: SSL

One solution for encrypting your network data is to use SSL. Through the 2.2.*x* Samba series, the server included native support for SSL. This support was often omitted from binary packages but could be compiled by issuing the `--with-ssl` option to the `configure` script when compiling the server.

Actually using Samba's SSL support required installing an SSL package, such as OpenSSL (`http://www.openssl.org`), obtaining or creating *certificates* (digitally signed files that can be used by SSL to prove a system's identity) for each client and the server, and enabling various global `smb.conf` parameters, most of which began with `ssl`. Each client also had to be configured with compatible software. Typically, these programs functioned like local proxy servers—they would accept connections from the client to itself but pass the data, using SSL encryption, to the server. This entire process, from Samba configuration through to client configuration, was fairly tedious, but the result was that a Samba server could communicate with a Samba client or with an appropriately configured Windows client using a secure connection. If the concern was with an Internet connection, two servers could function as, in effect, proxies for each other's networks, providing encrypted connections across the Internet and unencrypted local connections.

Unfortunately for fans of SSL, this option has been removed from Samba 3.0. If you've implemented SSL encryption in Samba 2.2.*x* or earlier and want to upgrade to Samba 3.0, you'll have to either abandon your upgrade plans or find some other way to implement encryption.

Second Solution: SSH

Even for Samba 2.2.*x* and earlier, an alternative to SSL encryption was SSH tunneling. This technique involves setting up an SSH link between the client and the server and using it to tunnel SMB/CIFS data—that is, to "piggyback" the SMB/CIFS packets on the SSH connection. Because SSH encrypts all the data it passes between systems, the SMB/CIFS data acquire all the benefits of the SSH encryption. Configuring this system requires running an SSH server on the Samba server and running an SSH client on the SMB/CIFS client or some nearby system.

Configuring the Server

Four SSH server packages are common:

SSH Tectia: The original SSH is a commercial package from SSH Communications Security (http://www.ssh.com). Originally known only as *SSH*, the official name has become *SSH Tectia* with version 4.0. This package is available as both a binary for various platforms, including AIX, HP-UX, Linux, and Solaris, and in source code form. Commercial SSH Tectia server licenses are rather pricey, though ($642 in February 2004).

OpenSSH: The second option is the open-source OpenSSH (http://www.openssh.org), which is distributed under a BSD-style license and is closely associated with the OpenBSD OS but is available for various other platforms. The OpenSSH Web site includes a page dedicated to using the server on non-OpenBSD OSs (http://www.openssh.org/portable.html). Some older Linux binaries are available from the OpenSSH site, but for the most part the assumption is that you'll obtain binaries with your OS or compile the source code yourself.

FreSSH: A second open-source SSH implementation is FreSSH (http://www.fressh.org), which uses a BSD-style license and is a completely fresh from-the-ground-up implementation of SSH.

lsh: The final common SSH server package is lsh, which is distributed under the GPL. You can learn more at http://www.lysator.liu.se/~nisse/lsh/.

NOTE   Technically, the acronym *SSH* refers only to the commercial offering or to the protocol it implements. For simplicity's sake, though, I use the term in reference to any implementation because they all have similar features. The configuration files and options described in this chapter, though, work with the commercial Tectia SSH and with OpenSSH; FreSSH and lsh may work differently.

In one form or another, most Unix-like OSs shipping in 2004 come with some form of SSH—usually OpenSSH. Check your OS's documentation to learn more, or check for a binary called sshd, which is the SSH server. Typically, the SSH server runs as a stand-alone server process, started via a SysV or local startup script, but it can be started via a super server. (Chapter 3 describes starting Samba in any of these ways, and the same methods can be applied to SSH.) Some OSs provide GUI controls that can enable various servers. The most notable of these is Mac OS X, which uses the Sharing item in the System Preferences tool to activate SSH. Figure 11-2 shows this window, with the SSH item (called Remote Login) highlighted. Be sure the box in the On column is checked.

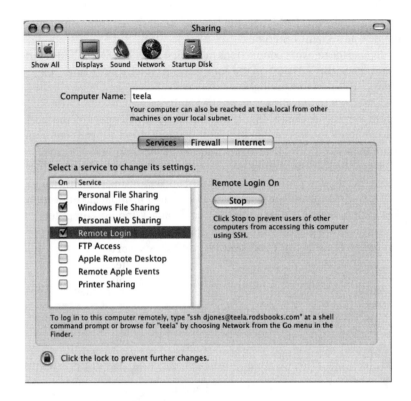

Figure 11-2. Mac OS X provides a GUI tool to activate the SSH server.

You configure the SSH server via a file called sshd_config, which is typically stored in /etc, /etc/ssh, /usr/local/etc/ssh, or a similar location. (Do not confuse this file with the ssh_config file, which configures the SSH client.) As a general rule, the default configuration will work fine for accepting forwarded SMB/CIFS traffic; however, you may want to check the file to be sure it includes this line:

```
AllowTcpForwarding yes
```

This line tells the server to accept non-SSH programs' traffic tunneled through the SSH connection. This option should be enabled by default, so if the option isn't present in your sshd_config file, it should still function fine.

Linking Individual Systems vs. Linking Networks

You can proceed with the configuration in one of two ways: linking together two individual systems or linking together a network to an individual system. You might use the first method to create encrypted connections between computers on a local network to protect against localized sniffing. The second approach ties together all the computers on a network to a server, which will typically be on a remote network.

The local network connections in this second case are unencrypted, but communication with the remote system is encrypted.

Figure 11-3 depicts the network connections in the first case. The SMB/CIFS client program contacts the SMB/CIFS port on the computer on which it's running. The SSH client listens to this port (becoming, in effect, a proxy server) and encrypts the data it receives, passing it to the SSH server on the Samba server computer. The SSH server then passes the piggybacked SMB/CIFS traffic to the Samba server on the local computer. This configuration has certain problems. For one, the client can't communicate with more than one SMB/CIFS server, at least not when using the normal ports. (You could run the SSH client and tell it to create tunnels to multiple SMB/CIFS servers using different local ports, but this is awkward and confusing.) You must also tell the SMB/CIFS client to contact the local computer in order to initiate a connection with the remote system—again, this is potentially confusing. Windows computers also have problems operating in this way; their SMB/CIFS clients tend to bind to the SMB/CIFS ports when the computer boots, so SSH can't do so.

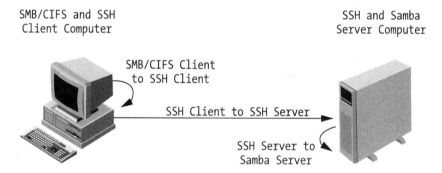

SMB/CIFS and SSH
Client Computer

SSH and Samba
Server Computer

SMB/CIFS Client
to SSH Client

SSH Client to SSH Server

SSH Server to
Samba Server

Figure 11-3. Local encryption using SSH requires having clients contact themselves using SMB/CIFS.

Figure 11-4 depicts a local network that uses an SSH-encrypted tunnel to a remote server. The local computers make what appear to be ordinary SMB/CIFS connections to the SSH client computer. (The SSH client is functioning as a proxy for the Samba server; it's listening to the SMB/CIFS port.) To the clients, it appears as though the SSH client is actually the remote Samba server. That computer, in turn, is configured just like its equivalent in Figure 11-3. It accepts the SSH connection and passes the tunneled SMB/CIFS data to its Samba server. The local connections between the SMB/CIFS clients are unencrypted, but the connection between the SSH client and the Samba server is encrypted. This configuration is a good one if you need to tie a remote office with a few computers to a central office via the Internet or some other insecure network. If you need to connect to multiple remote servers, the simplest solution is to configure multiple local SSH clients to do the job. You can also use Windows SMB/CIFS clients in this configuration, as long as the SSH client computer is running Unix or is a Windows system that does *not* run any SMB/CIFS clients or servers.

SMB/CIFS
Client Computers

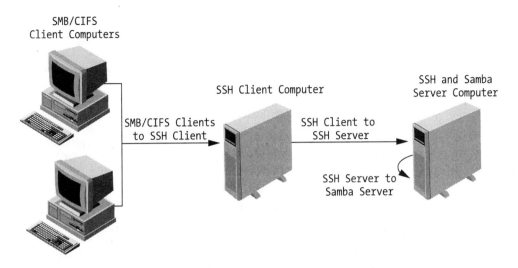

SSH Client Computer

SSH and Samba
Server Computer

SMB/CIFS Clients
to SSH Client

SSH Client to
SSH Server

SSH Server to
Samba Server

Figure 11-4. You can encrypt remote SMB/CIFS connections with the help of an SSH client.

Running a Samba server on the SSH client computer can be tricky at best. In the case of local encryption (Figure 11-3), you can do it by telling the SMB/CIFS server to not listen on the localhost (127.0.0.1) interface while configuring the SSH client to listen for SMB/CIFS connections on only that address. So configured, connections to localhost are passed to the remote system, but connections to the regular interface are handled locally. In either case, you could use nonstandard ports for tunneling the connection, but this approach won't work with all clients.

In all of these cases, you sacrifice browsing and NetBIOS name resolution because these duties are performed using UDP ports, which SSH can't forward. One workaround is to start with a configuration like the local encryption one (Figure 11-3), but configure it to run its own Samba server using the localhost/external interface dichotomy. Configure the Samba server system to mount remote shares via the encrypted connection and then share them using the local Samba server. This configuration is tricky to configure, and it will chew up more resources because the system will have to interpret every access request and re-encode it.

Configuring the SSH Client

You can obtain SSH clients from the same sources that provide SSH servers. In the case of recent Unix-like OSs, an SSH client usually ships with the OS. In addition to the reference SSH clients, many additional terminal programs have been developed that integrate SSH functionality. You can learn about many of these programs at http://www.freessh.org, which provides pointers to no-cost SSH clients.

NOTE   Don't confuse `http://www.freessh.org` with `http://www.fressh.org`; note that the number of e letters in these domain names is different. The former site provides links to free SSH implementations, especially clients. The latter site is a specific SSH client and server implementation.

In the case of Unix and Unix-like systems, you can establish an encrypted local connection to the Samba server by typing the following command on the SSH client system:

```
# ssh -N -f -L 139:target.example.com:139 user@target.example.com
```

This command creates a connection between TCP port 139 on the local computer and TCP port 139 on *target.example.com*, using the *user* account on the remote system. When used to tunnel ports below 1024, you must run this command as root. Any traffic directed at the local TCP port 139 is tunneled, with SSH encryption, to *target.example.com*'s TCP port 139. Note that this command means that the local computer can't be running a Samba server, at least not on the localhost (127.0.0.1) interface. If you want to run a Samba server on the client computer, you must change the first instance of 139 in this command to another port number and specify that port number when making connections to the remote system.

In a default configuration, after you type the preceding command, ssh will ask you for a password. Type the password belonging to *user*. SSH uses *user*'s account to establish the local connection to the local Samba server. Note that this has nothing to do with the Samba users or permissions, which can be anything the Samba server supports.

If you want to configure a Unix system as a proxy, such as the SSH client computer in Figure 11-4, you type the same command on the SSH client system; however, you must ensure that a specific line is set in the ssh_config file on that system:

```
GatewayPorts yes
```

If you omit this line, the SSH client will accept connections from only the localhost (127.0.0.1) system, so it won't be useful for tunneling connection requests from other systems, as in Figure 11-4.

In theory, a process similar to the one just described should work with Windows systems but using a Windows SSH client. Unfortunately, in practice it just doesn't work because the Windows SMB/CIFS implementations bind to TCP port 139, even when the server package is removed from the computer. Needless to say, this severely limits the utility of SMB/CIFS encryption. You can still use an encryption proxy, as in Figure 11-4, but a direct encrypted connection, as in Figure 11-3, won't work with Windows clients.

Establishing a Connection

To test the functioning of your encrypted connection, I recommend using smbclient. This program, described in more detail in Chapter 18, is a relatively straightforward client program that ships with Samba. It provides more in the way of error feedback than many SMB/CIFS client programs, so it can be a good way to test a connection.

To start, from the SSH client computer, try using smbclient to connect to a share on the server. For instance, to connect to a share called TESTSHARE using the username fastaire, you might type the following command:

```
$ smbclient //localhost/TESTSHARE -U fastaire
added interface ip=192.168.1.2 bcast=192.168.1.255 nmask=255.255.255.0
error connecting to 192.168.1.3:445 (Invalid argument)
Password:
Domain=[RINGWORLD] OS=[Unix] Server=[Samba 3.0.1]
smb: \>
```

You can omit the -U fastaire parameter if you're logged in as that user. If all goes well, you should see output similar to that shown here. You can disregard the error message about an attempt to connect to 192.168.1.3:445; this message indicates that the server wasn't listening on port 445, which is the port SMB/CIFS uses when it bypasses NetBIOS. After entering a password, the system responds with a smb: \> prompt, at which you can type FTP-style commands to view files, copy files, and so on.

If this connection attempt goes smoothly, you can try more. For instance, you might use smbmount on a Linux system to mount a remote share using the localhost address:

```
# smbmount //localhost/TESTSHARE /mnt/test -o username=fastaire
Password:
```

NOTE   The smbmount program must normally be run as root, although you can set the set user ID (SUID) bit on the program to run it as a normal user.

If you've set up the system as a proxy for your local network, as in Figure 11-4, you should then test it with other computers on that network. You can use smbclient if some of your local computers run Unix. In the case of Windows clients, you must type the complete path to the share, using the SSH client system name rather than the real target system name. Unfortunately, many Windows systems have troubles with name resolution when the SSH client system isn't using the NetBIOS name service (that is, running nmbd under Unix). If you can't seem to connect, try editing your system's lmhosts file, described in Chapter 9. Most Windows systems ship with a sample file, called LMHOSTS.SAM. On Windows 9*x*/Me systems, this file usually resides in C:\WINDOWS; in Windows NT/200*x*/XP, it's usually in C:\WINNT\SYSTEM32\DRIVERS\ETC. Copy or rename the sample file to LMHOSTS, and add an entry for your SSH client system.

Third Solution: A VPN

A third solution for data encryption is using a VPN. VPNs can provide encryption for all of the traffic passing between two network segments, each of which contains many computers. Sometimes, though, individual clients (such as computers belonging to telecommuters) are linked via VPN software to a central network.

Computers running VPN software are similar in many ways to routers, but they provide the illusion of a direct link between two networks that may actually be separated by many routers. Many VPN packages and protocols are available, including the following:

> **PPTP:** The Point-to-Point Tunneling Protocol (PPTP) ships with recent versions of Windows and is frequently used to link single clients to a central office. Various PPTP implementations for Unix-like systems exist, such as PoPToP for Linux (http://www.poptop.org; see also http://heyer.supranet.net/pptp/ for information on running PoPToP in FreeBSD), which is a PPTP server, and pptpclient (http://pptpclient.sourceforge.net), which is a client implementation for several Unix-like OSs.

> **FreeS/WAN:** This package, headquartered at http://www.freeswan.org, is a more Unix-centric VPN package. It's also more often used to link together entire networks.

> **SSH:** This program's tunneling capabilities can be combined with a slightly modified Point-to-Point Protocol (PPP) client and server to create a VPN. The VPN PPP-SSH Mini-HOWTO document (http://tldp.org/HOWTO/ppp-ssh/) describes how to create such a connection under Linux. The process is similar under other Unix-like OSs.

VPNs have the advantage of encrypting and passing all traffic between their networks, typically including both UDP and TCP. This fact means that they can support browsing features, and they don't require the use of stand-in names—you can use the network exactly as if it were a single large network, without worrying about the presence of the VPN.

VPNs typically encrypt only the connection between networks. Most VPN solutions aren't designed for use on a single network segment, although some can be configured in this way. One system serves as a VPN server, and all of the other systems use VPN client software. All traffic passes through the VPN server. This configuration can be handy if your hardware is necessarily insecure, as in a wireless network. A VPN's encryption is likely to be far better than that built into most wireless hardware. VPNs are a relatively new technology compared to most common networking tools. As such, they tend to be difficult to configure. If you need to create a VPN, you should consult documentation for whatever VPN package you choose.

Keeping Up to Date

You can spend hours securing your Samba server and do everything imaginable to make it as secure as possible. Sooner or later, though, your effort will become inadequate. This isn't because of any sort of entropy causing your settings to be undone; it's because the security world is quite dynamic. New bugs that have security implications are found every day, and sooner or later, a program you're running (perhaps even Samba itself) will be found to have a security bug. When this happens, you must update the program or configure it in such a way that the bug becomes irrelevant.

Even when new bugs don't directly affect you, other developments may, or the bugs may affect you indirectly. For instance, new worms may cause unusual amounts of traffic to be directed at your network, which can degrade performance. Knowing when to block such traffic, even if your network isn't at risk of infection, can make life easier for your users. New security products and procedures, such as biometric authentication (which uses biological scans of users to identify them) may interest you. As such technologies mature, you should be aware of them.

How, though, do you keep up to date with all of these important developments? Numerous security resources are available, many of them on the Internet. Indeed, print resources are at a distinct disadvantage over electronic resources because the time lag between events and publication can be unacceptable when a new security problem has been found. Print resources can still be useful when learning how to use new techniques and technologies, though. Some of the most valuable security resources include the following:

Security Web sites: Regularly visiting Web sites devoted to security, such as the Computer Emergency Response Team (CERT; `http://www.cert.org`), the Computer Incident Advisory Capability (CIAC; `http://www.ciac.org/ciac`), or Linux Security (`http://www.linuxsecurity.com`), can be very helpful in learning about new threats and security practices. These sites are dedicated to explaining new *exploits* (ways of breaking into computers) and their countermeasures. Some also contain useful tutorial information on security in general.

NOTE Although some resources are devoted to Linux or other OSs specifically, they may be useful even to those who use other OSs. The issues discussed are often cross-platform, at least within the Unix world.

Security mailing lists: Some security sites, such as CERT and Linux Security, maintain mailing lists. (See `http://www.cert.org/contact_cert/certmaillist.html` and `http://www.linuxsecurity.org/general/mailinglists.html` for information about joining.) If you subscribe, you'll receive advisories of new exploits soon after they're discovered.

Security newsgroups: Some Usenet newsgroups are devoted to security discussions. For instance, `comp.security.unix` hosts information on Unix security generally, and `comp.os.linux.security` covers Linux security specifically.

Samba sites and newsgroups: Samba Web sites and newsgroups can be useful security resources for Samba specifically. Any problems that directly affect Samba are likely to be described on such sites. The main Samba site, `http://www.samba.org`, is obviously prime among these sites. The SMB/CIFS and Linux Samba newsgroups, `comp.protocols.smb` and `linux.samba`, are also worth perusing.

Unix publications: Magazines devoted to Unix or specific Unix variants, such as *Sys Admin, Linux Journal,* and *Linux Magazine,* can be useful resources for learning about security generally and about up-and-coming security techniques and technologies. Security books, such as *Practical Unix & Internet Security* (mentioned earlier in this chapter) are well worth reading to learn about security generally.

Social networking: Don't overlook social, rather than computer, networks as a way to learn about security problems. If you're having a problem, discuss it with a co-worker or (if doing so wouldn't reveal confidential employer information) a friend in the field. Social networks have the advantage of being interactive; you can ask somebody about a problem and get an immediate response.

As a general rule, you should regularly visit some security Web sites and read at least one security newsgroup or mailing list. If your site is unusually security-conscious, doing more may be in order. If you're not already familiar with Unix security generally, read a book or two on the subject. Remember that security threats are constantly changing. For instance, e-mail worms were unknown before the late 1990s, but they're a major scourge on today's Internet. New security problems could emerge, and perhaps threaten Samba directly, at any point in the future. Being aware of these threats as they emerge will help you protect your server and all the other computers on your network.

In addition to keeping your own knowledge up to date, you should be sure to keep your installed software up to date. OSs are increasingly providing tools, such as Debian GNU/Linux's Advanced Package Tool (APT), that can look for, retrieve, and install updated software automatically or semiautomatically. Whether or not you use such a tool, you should look for updates to programs you run from your OS provider and other sources of the software you run. Although some updates aren't security-related and could even cause problems because of changed configurations, at least being aware of updates is important.

No matter how many tools you install to help secure your system, you should take an active hand in monitoring it. Checking Samba and other system log files, being aware of normal CPU and network loads, and generally knowing how the system operates can help you head off or at least detect problems—both security-related and more mundane. You may also want to use a tool such as Tripwire (`http://www.tripwire.org`) to help you monitor your system for unauthorized changes.

Summary

Security is a topic that extends beyond Samba. Securing a Samba server begins with physical security around the computer hardware itself. With physical access, an intruder can do just about anything, so preventing miscreants from physically touching the computer is the first step in securing it. Beyond physical security lies software security measures on your network as a whole and the Samba server computer but outside of Samba itself, such as configuring a firewall and removing unnecessary servers and accounts. Once you've handled these tasks, you can tackle Samba's own security measures. You can restrict Samba access based on IP address and deal with password and account issues. In some cases, you may want to beef up Samba's encryption techniques, which by default are quite minimal. Doing so involves adding external software, such as SSH, but this can be tedious. Finally, security issues aren't static; you should know how to keep up with security developments so you're prepared when new threats emerge.

Samba Interactions with Other Protocols

ALTHOUGH SAMBA IS an important server, it's often not the only server that runs on a computer. When Samba runs alongside another server, the two may need to interact in some way—most often because they must access the same files. Understanding how Samba interacts with other servers can, therefore, help you to avoid problems by setting up both servers so that they don't cause conflicts.

Some issues apply to many servers and other programs that might run on the computer. Other issues are very specific to particular servers. This chapter begins with a look at generic issues and then moves on to issues related to the Network File System (NFS), AppleTalk, Web servers, FTP servers, printing protocols, and time servers.

Generic File-Sharing Considerations

Many computers run several different file-sharing servers for reasons outlined shortly. Doing so can be convenient, but it also raises certain concerns. If the servers provide access to the same files, it's possible that users of the two protocols will butt heads over file access, file naming, file content, or permission issues. Understanding these issues will help you to plan a system that will minimize the potential for conflict.

Why Run Multiple File-Sharing Servers?

Samba is a very powerful file-sharing server, and clients that can communicate with Samba are available for many OSs. (Chapter 18 describes some of these clients.) Samba is not, however, perfectly adapted for use by all clients. Chapter 1 describes some of the alternatives to Samba. Knowing when to use another protocol instead of or in addition to Samba will help you keep your network running smoothly. Some reasons you might want to use other servers include the following:

> **Expensive, buggy, or nonexistent clients**: Although most OSs have good SMB/CIFS support, some don't. Mac OS Classic, for instance, ships with no support for SMB/CIFS. A commercial client/server package, DAVE (http:// www.thursby.com/products/dave.html), provides Mac OS Classic SMB/CIFS support, but this product is more expensive than one alternative: running an AppleTalk server such as Netatalk (http://netatalk.sourceforge.net) on the Samba server computer. Particularly on more exotic computers, you might find SMB/CIFS clients to be buggy or nonexistent.

Mismatched features: Some OSs work best with filesystem features that aren't supported by SMB/CIFS or Samba. The most notable example is Unix clients, which support file ownership and permission features unavailable in SMB/CIFS. Mac OS clients also use filesystem features not supported by Samba, although DAVE provides workarounds for most of these features.

 NOTE   The Samba `unix extensions` parameter enables support for some Unix-specific SMB/CIFS extensions, but client support for these features is still rare.

Not rocking the boat: If you're adding Samba to a network that already supports some other server, you may want to avoid disabling that working protocol because doing so could cause support headaches as you try to quickly transition users to SMB/CIFS. You could leave both servers and protocols running for a transition period, which could be indefinite in length.

Re-exporting files: You can run one file-sharing client on the Samba server and use the other protocol's server to re-export a share. This approach enables you to deliver files from one platform to another even when the two systems don't share a common protocol. The upcoming sections "Re-exporting SMB/CIFS and NFS," "Re-exporting SMB/CIFS and AppleTalk," and "Samba and Other Printing Protocols" describe this technique in greater detail.

On the downside, using multiple servers requires more in the way of configuration effort. It also increases your system's security vulnerability; a bug in or misconfiguration of either server could enable a cracker to access your system. For these reasons, you shouldn't run multiple servers unless doing so provides you with some real benefit.

File-Locking Issues

One issue that can cause problems is file locking. Various types of file locks exist, and Chapter 5 describes the many Samba options that relate to file locks. Generally speaking, though, file locks grant applications exclusive access to files. Typically, an application that wants to modify a file will open it with a lock, which will prevent other applications from opening the same file for write access.

The problem arises because different file-sharing protocols provide support for different types of locks. Some of these lock types may not be supported on the host OS, so if a server implements these locks itself, it may not be able to communicate this fact to other servers. The result can be file corruption or other problems when two users (or even the same user, using two protocols simultaneously) try to access the same file.

As a general rule, Samba's default locking options are reasonable both for a Samba-only system and for systems that run other file servers. In particular, `posix locking = Yes` and `kernel oplocks = Yes` are useful in synchronizing file locks across servers. (Only Linux and IRIX support kernel oplocks, though. On other platforms, Samba quietly downgrades this option to `No` if you set it to `Yes`.)

One solution to file-locking problems is to restrict the types of access users have to files. Specifically, if users don't have any real need to write files, you can create a read-only share in Samba and, if possible, in any other file-sharing protocols. If your shares have a mix of files that do and don't need to be written, consider shuffling the shares' contents to create some shares that you can share in read-only mode. If most users don't need to be able to write to a share, but some do, create the share as a read-only share and use the write list parameter to ensure that only those who need to be able to write to the share can do so. (Most other file-sharing protocols don't provide this level of control, though, so you may need to provide write access only via Samba or accept the consequences of granting a higher level of write access using other protocols.)

File-Naming Issues

Different OSs and file-sharing protocols have different file-naming conventions. As described in Chapter 2, this fact means that Samba must make changes to filenames in some cases. Chapter 5 describes some of the specific options that Samba provides to fine-tune this process. When you run multiple file-sharing servers, you may need to contend with the different needs of each file-sharing protocol and the OSs that typically function as clients for each protocol.

For instance, Mac OS Classic clients, and hence the Netatalk server, support filenames with a maximum length of 31 characters. This fact can cause problems if Samba users create longer filenames in a directory shared via both servers. In the case of Netatalk, the server (and hence the Mac OS client) will ignore the filenames that are too long. Mac OS users will, therefore, be unable to see such files. The simplest solution is usually to avoid creating files that are longer than the 31-character limit of Mac OS Classic. Of course, this solution may require educating users and perhaps renaming some files if they're in prepared file sets (say, a clip art collection you want to share with both platforms).

TIP Mac OS X clients can use AppleTalk (and hence a Netatalk server), NFS, or SMB/CIFS (and hence a Samba server). If you've migrated to Mac OS X, you can, therefore, switch to a protocol that's less restrictive in its filename features to avoid this particular problem. If you haven't upgraded any Macs on your network to Mac OS X, this may be a reason to give the new OS a try.

Filename issues extend beyond filename length. One concern has been covered in some depth in various earlier chapters: filename case. Because Unix is a case-sensitive OS, most Samba shares use case-sensitive filesystems. Unix clients that use NFS can take advantage of this fact, creating files that differ only in case, such as UPPER.TXT and Upper.Txt. Netatalk can also function in a case-sensitive fashion. Samba, however, is case-retentive but insensitive to case, at least using its default configuration. Most Samba clients will see both filenames, but an attempt to access either returns only one file's contents. As with filename length, the simplest solution to filename case issues is to avoid the problem by educating your users. Be sure that NFS, Netatalk, and Unix Samba users know not to create filenames that differ only in case.

CAUTION Samba includes a parameter called `case sensitive` that causes the server to treat filename case in a case-sensitive manner. This parameter can be useful with Unix clients, but you shouldn't use it if Windows clients (particularly Windows 9*x*/Me clients) might access the share. Windows 9*x*/Me clients are likely to experience sporadic problems accessing or browsing to files in a case-sensitive share.

Another potential filename compatibility issue is in the characters that make up individual filenames (aside from filename case). In particular, different servers and clients may have different ways of dealing with non-ASCII characters in filenames. Such problems are most likely to crop up outside of North America or when users try to use special characters, such as copyright symbols, in filenames. (Some Mac OS programs tend to embed such characters in the folder names and filenames they create when installing the program.) Unfortunately, these problems can be quite difficult to overcome. If the problem is restricted to a few nonvital characters, your best bet is to avoid using them—which of course brings you back to educating your users about the problem. If the issue is more widespread, as in Cyrillic filenames, your best bet is to experiment with the Samba filename encoding options, `dos charset`, `unix charset`, and `unicode` (all of which are described in Chapter 5). If your non-Samba server offers similar options, experiment with them as well.

Some filename issues relate to files that you'd prefer not be visible on one platform or another. Chapter 5 described several techniques Samba provides to hide individual files or sets of files by setting the SMB/CIFS hidden bit or making files disappear completely from the client's point of view. These options include `map hidden`, `hide dot files`, `hide files`, and `veto files`. Typically, when sharing a directory with both Samba and NFS, you'll want to ensure that Samba's `hide dot files` parameter is set to `Yes` in order to prevent *dot files* (those whose names begin with dots) created by Unix clients from appearing to Samba clients, most of whom won't hide such files by default. The `hide files` and `veto files` parameters are useful for hiding arbitrary files, such as the `.AppleDouble` and `.AppleDesktop` files created by Netatalk. (These specific files are hidden by the default setting of `hide dot files`, so you'd use `hide files` to hide these files only if you change the default `hide dot files` value. Using `veto files` will cause the files you specify to completely disappear from the client.)

File Permission Issues

Chapter 5 described many Samba options related to the setting of file ownership and permissions, such as `force user`, `force group`, `force create mask`, `force directory mask`, and `inherit permissions`. Samba is extraordinarily flexible in this respect; most other file-sharing servers are very limited in their options for handling these features. NFS works like an extension of the client OS, letting clients create files and modify their permissions according to the rules in place on the client OS. Those rules are usually similar to those of the server OS. Typically, files are owned by whoever created them, and those creators can't change ownership. (`root` is an exception to this rule but one that's not normally given such access from an NFS client.) Files' owners can change the access permissions on their files, though, much as can Windows NT/200x/XP clients when Samba's access control list (ACL) support is enabled.

The Netatalk server provides much more limited access to file ownership and permissions. Netatalk gives ownership of files it creates to the account used to access the server and assigns permissions much as Samba does when Samba's `inherit permissions = Yes` parameter is set. Netatalk also uses these permissions to determine read and write access to files much as Samba does.

As a general rule, Samba's default settings interact well with both NFS and Netatalk clients. If you use Samba's special features, such as `force user` or `force create mask` to achieve special security-related effects, you should be cautious about sharing the directory via any other server. Those servers won't match Samba's flexibility, and the result could be an inability of clients of one or the other server to read files, or access granted to users who shouldn't have it.

File Content Issues

When sharing files across OSs, one issue that crops up is the format of data *within* the shared files. Even if both platforms can retrieve the files using their respective file-sharing protocols, that access will be pointless if native tools can't parse the files' data format. Unfortunately, this problem is too big for Samba to solve; the server doesn't provide any options to modify the content of files for the benefit of different types of clients. You can, however, provide education and software to help your users avoid problems in a cross-platform world. Some of the file content issues that are most likely to crop up are as follows:

Macintosh resource forks: Mac OS (especially Mac OS Classic) relies upon resource forks for many file types. (Resource forks hold special data and are described in more detail in Chapter 1.) Netatalk stores resource forks in a subdirectory called `.AppleDouble`, which as noted earlier is normally hidden from Samba clients. Sometimes, though, non-Mac users may need to access resource fork data. In most such cases, the non-Mac user has software that expects the file in a StuffIt archive or as a MacBinary or BinHex format file. Mac OS archiving software, such as StuffIt, can create such files, so Mac OS users should employ these tools to do the job. The result will be a file that the non-Mac user can process. You'll need to consult the documentation to learn precisely what format is required, though.

Macintosh file creator and type codes: Mac OS (especially Mac OS Classic) relies upon file creator and type codes to link files to software that can handle them. In Netatalk, these codes are mapped to filename extensions in a file called `AppleVolumes.system`. The default file should work well in most cases, but you may need to extend or modify it if you handle unusual file types. Doing so will ensure that Mac OS users will see the correct icons and be able to load files created by compatible Windows, Unix, or other OS programs.

Text file end-of-lines: In an American Standard Code for Information Interchange (ASCII, a.k.a. plain-text) file, each line is terminated by and end-of-line (EOL) sequence. On Unix systems, this is traditionally a single line feed (LF) character. DOS, Windows, and OS/2 all use a carriage return/line feed (CR/LF) pair. Mac OS has traditionally used a single CR as its EOL character. This mish-mash means that transferring plain-text files can be a challenge. Some programs, including most full-featured editors, can handle any of these EOL forms. Others, though, may become confused and create effects such as *stair-stepping* (in which a new line appears below and to the right of the previous one) or overwriting of each line by the following line. The Netatalk server includes a configuration option (`crlf`, set in the `AppleVolumes.default` file) to convert between Mac-style and Unix-style EOLs for files with a Mac file type of `TEXT`. This option can help simplify matters, but it's not perfect, and it won't help in Unix-to-Windows interactions. Unix utilities called `unix2dos` and `dos2unix` will perform conversions from a Unix shell; check your OS or do a Web search to find these tools for your OS. If necessary, you can load text files in a suitable editor to read them.

Formatted text files: Many file formats exist to preserve file formatting in one way or another. Three common examples are PostScript, Portable Document Format (PDF), and Hypertext Markup Language (HTML). All three are cross-platform formats, although PostScript is most often used for printing.

Office files: The ubiquitous Microsoft Office suite is compatible across both Windows and Mac OS versions of the package. If you use Netatalk for Mac OS clients and Samba for Windows clients, your Mac and Windows users can freely exchange Office files. The only trick is ensuring that an appropriate mapping of the Word `.doc`, `.xls`, and other filename extensions exists in the `AppleVolumes.system` file. Unix users can usually handle these files with OpenOffice.org (http://www.openoffice.org) or its commercial twin, Sun's StarOffice (http://www.sun.com/software/star/staroffice/). These programs are also available for Windows and Mac OS X, if you prefer to use the same program on all three platforms.

Multimedia files: Graphics files, audio files, and video files are all popular, and many formats for all of these file types exist. As a general rule, the Tagged Image File Format (TIFF), the Joint Photographic Expert Group (JPEG) format, the Graphic Interchange Format (GIF), and the Portable Network Graphics (PNG) format all work well for exchanging static graphics images. The `.wav` format (which is actually several different formats, all of which share one extension), Moving Picture Experts Group Layer 3 (MP3) format, and Ogg Vorbis formats all work well for cross-platform audio files. The Moving Picture Experts Group 2 (MPEG-2), DivX, QuickTime, and RealPlayer formats work well for cross-platform video. Some other formats also work well, but some are poorly supported on one platform or another.

Archives: When storing and compressing multiple files, Unix systems generally use tarballs, Windows systems most commonly use zip files, and Mac OS systems typically use StuffIt archives. Tools to process these files on others' platforms are fairly common, although the Unix tools for handling StuffIt files are old and unreliable. As a general rule, zip files are usually best for cross-platform work.

Ultimately, you'll have to deal with file content issues on a case-by-case basis. Every site is unique, and this book can't begin to present every possible combination of software or to present advice about handling every file format on every platform. If you can't seem to read a file created by one OS on another OS, consult the documentation of the program that created the file as well as the documentation of programs you think might be able to read the file. If necessary, perform a Web search and a search on Google Groups (http://groups.google.com) to find information on cross-platform compatibility. You may also need to look into using the creating software's export feature to save the data in a format that the reading system will be able to handle. You can overcome most such problems, but sometimes imperfectly. For instance, word processors support so many features, and often in such idiosyncratic ways, that word processor import/export functions frequently drop or corrupt certain formatting features, such as tabs, fonts, and columns. Solving or working around such problems can be an adventure in itself.

Samba and NFS

The file-sharing server with which Samba is most likely to need to coexist is NFS. This protocol and server is available for most Unix-like OSs, although details of its configuration vary from one OS to another—consult your OS's documentation if you need help configuring NFS. Two types of interactions are important: sharing the same files via both servers and using one server to share directories that are remote mounts from the other server.

When to Share with Samba and NFS

The most common type of coexistence between Samba and NFS is when both servers are used to share data that exist on the server's own hard disk. For instance, you might create a Samba [homes] share and export the /homes directory via NFS.

NOTE   In NFS parlance, the word *export* can be either a noun that refers to a directory that's shared with clients or a verb describing the act of sharing the directory. In the first sense, an NFS export is conceptually equivalent to a Samba share, although of course many details differ.

NFS is most commonly used by Unix-like OSs. It supports Unix-style ownership, permissions, hard and symbolic links, and other features common on Unix filesystems. Thus, whenever a network with a need for file sharing includes Unix-like OSs, you're likely to find NFS in use. NFS clients and servers are also available for non-Unix OSs. For instance, Thursby Systems (`http://www.thursby.com`; the makers of DAVE) sell MacNFS, which enables Mac OS Classic systems to mount NFS exports. (Mac OS X supports NFS natively.) Various NFS clients for Windows also exist, such as Microsoft's Windows Services for Unix (`http://www.microsoft.com/windows/sfu/productinfo/`), Centreline 2000's Omni-NFS (`http://www.c2000.com/products/csp_omni.htm`), and Hummingbird's NFS Maestro (`http://www.hummingbird.com/products/nc/nfs/`).

Unfortunately, most non-Unix NFS clients are commercial, and they don't provide the sort of flexibility that Samba provides. Thus, incentives to use Samba, at least for platforms for which SMB/CIFS is the native file-sharing protocol, are quite strong. This, in combination with the NFS-centric nature of Unix, makes a mixed-protocol environment for a Unix/Windows network the usual configuration.

If you want to cut down on the number of servers you run, you might consider eliminating NFS and using Samba for your Unix clients. This approach will impose certain limits, though, primarily relating to file ownership and permissions. Specifically, your users won't be able to change permissions on their files, which means they won't be able to control who can access their files. The perpetual lack or presence, depending upon settings, of the execute bit could be a problem in some cases, as well. (These limitations are less of an issue if you use Samba 3.0's new `unix extensions` parameter and have clients that support it, such as a 2.6.*x* Linux kernel.)

When using both Samba and NFS, you can configure the servers independently of each other. You can share the same directories in the same way (as in sharing `/opt/clipart` from both servers), you can share the same directories in different ways (as in sharing `/home` from NFS and creating a `[homes]` share, which shares individual home directories, from Samba), or you can share entirely different directories (as in sharing `/opt` with NFS and `/home/samba/winprogs` with Samba). Any combination of sharing methods is also valid. In typical accesses, particularly when users need only to read files, the two servers won't interfere with one another. Some of the caveats described in the earlier section "Generic File-Sharing Considerations" do apply, though. Issues surrounding file locking, file naming, permissions, and so on can raise their heads.

Re-exporting SMB/CIFS and NFS

One of the more unusual types of interaction between Samba and other file-sharing protocols is using a file server for one protocol to share a directory that's actually a mounted share from another computer, as illustrated by Figure 12-1. In this configuration, the ultimate client (called *Client for B* in Figure 12-1) can access files on the more distant server (Figure 12-1's *File Server A*) indirectly. Of course, this configuration isn't without its problems, including speed and reliability issues. Nonetheless, it can be handy in some situations. In the case of Samba and NFS, either server can export data shared via the other protocol.

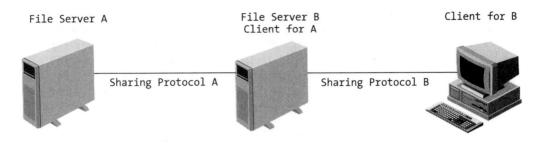

Figure 12-1. A server can share data that have in turn been mounted from another source.

NOTE   The following sections are concerned with re-exporting file shares. The upcoming section "Samba and Other Printing Protocols" describes how Samba interacts with non-SMB/CIFS printing protocols, including re-exporting printer shares.

When to Re-export Data

Re-exporting shares can be a quick and dirty way of providing access to data that clients might not otherwise be able to reach. By providing access using a different protocol than the ultimate server uses (or sometimes even the same protocol), you can overcome several problems, such as protocol incompatibilities and network obstacles. Some reasons to re-export data include the following:

Client/server protocol mismatches: If the server that houses the data you want to share doesn't support the protocol that a client must use, re-exporting the data using a supported protocol can work around this problem. For instance, suppose you've got a Windows server that houses some vital files you need to access from a Unix client that lacks proper mount support for SMB/CIFS but that can handle NFS. By enlisting the help of another Unix system with proper mount support for SMB/CIFS and an NFS server, you can give the ultimate client access to the Windows share.

Saving money: If the client or server software required for a direct connection costs money, re-exporting the data may save money by obviating the need to buy a costly new software package. For instance, if the ultimate client's NFS package is costly but SMB/CIFS support is free, and if the target server only supports NFS, using an intermediate system for re-exporting can save money.

Reliability and features: On occasion, although a single protocol may be supported by all the systems, it may be less reliable on some systems than on others or provide an incomplete feature set for some purposes. In such a case, working out a re-exporting scenario can improve reliability or provide the desired features. For instance, you might re-export an NFS mount using Samba to add Samba's username mapping features.

Overcoming network restrictions: If a network blocks one protocol but not another, you may be able to provide file-sharing support for clients that can only use the blocked protocol by setting up a system to re-export data. For instance, many broadband Internet providers block SMB/CIFS but not NFS. Using a re-export system can, therefore, enable Windows clients to access remote shares indirectly, via NFS. This sort of configuration is most helpful when sharing across the Internet at large.

 CAUTION Using re-exports to overcome network restrictions can be reasonable in some cases, but in many cases the restrictions are in place for very real and valid reasons. A network might not support a protocol as a matter of security policy, for instance, and providing covert support for that protocol might lose you your job or Internet access.

Unfortunately, re-exporting data isn't without its problems. The worst of these may be efficiency. The middle system must function as both a client and a server. Both of these functions require performing various conversions and reformatting of the file-system data. Thus, the re-exporting server will devote a certain amount of CPU time and memory to the task. If the ultimate server system were to deliver the data directly, the re-exporting server needn't be involved at all, and the load on the ultimate server wouldn't be greatly increased by supporting two protocols.

What's more, re-exporting a share means that any data transferred in service of the re-export must be sent twice—once from the ultimate server to the re-exporting server and again to the ultimate client. If two or all of these computers are on the same physical network segment, the result is increased network bandwidth consumption compared to a single direct sharing path. If the re-exporting computer straddles two networks, with the ultimate server on one network and the ultimate client on the other, though, this problem isn't so significant.

Depending upon the OSs and filesystems involved, re-exporting a share can also introduce extra problems for handling file metadata differences. In the case of NFS/Samba re-exports, this effect is likely to be small because NFS is so close to Unix in terms of the file metadata it handles. If for some reason the NFS server isn't a Unix-like system, though, you'll be dealing with Samba's workarounds for SMB/CIFS and Unix filesystem data in addition to whatever workarounds the NFS server imposes on its side of the transfer.

In the end, most of these problems translate into reduced performance for re-exported shares. Files may not transfer as quickly as they would if you were using a direct connection, and other operations (deletions, renaming, and so on) may also lag slightly. You're most likely to notice differences when transferring large files or when performing many operations in quick succession (as when copying a directory filled with small files). Because two transfers are involved, the system is more vulnerable to problems—if the re-exporting server goes down, you won't be able to make a connection, even if the ultimate server and ultimate client are both working perfectly.

In practice, re-exporting data is most useful as a temporary or low-traffic measure. For instance, suppose your network has an NFS server and another server that runs both NFS and Samba. If you find you need to access some data on the NFS server from Windows clients, it might be quicker and easier to configure a re-export share from the NFS/Samba server than to install Samba on the NFS-only server. This configuration should work fine on a short-term basis or for occasional use, but if you need regular access to the NFS-only data, you'll almost certainly be better off in the long run installing Samba on the NFS-only server and accessing the data directly.

Sharing NFS Exports with Samba

You can use Samba to share directories mounted via NFS with SMB/CIFS clients. Doing so is just like sharing any other directory on the Samba server. For instance, suppose you've mounted an NFS export at /opt on the Samba server. You could share individual directories or the entire /opt directory using an ordinary Samba share, such as the following:

```
[clipart]
    comment = Clip Art Files
    directory = /opt/clipart
    browseable = Yes
    read only = Yes
```

SMB/CIFS clients (presumably Windows systems or others that can't easily access NFS exports) would then mount the CLIPART share from the Samba server. These files, though, will be retrieved from the NFS server rather than from the Samba server's hard disk.

Of course, in order for a configuration such as this to work, you must first mount the NFS share on the Samba server. Most Unix-like systems enable you to do this automatically at boot time by creating an appropriate entry in /etc/fstab. Details vary from one OS to another, so check your OS's documentation. As an example, though, a suitable Linux /etc/fstab entry might look like this:

```
nfsserver:/opt-exp  /opt  nfs  ro  0 0
```

This line tells the system to look for the /opt-exp export on the nfsserver computer and mount it at /opt using the filesystem type code nfs and as a read-only (ro) mount. Lines to accomplish the same goal on other Unix-like OSs will be similar but will vary in some details. For instance, under FreeBSD, the ro string will be replaced by r for a read-only mount. In all cases, of course, you can change these mount options as you see fit.

After defining the NFS shares to be mounted, you must mount them the first time. In most cases, typing mount -a as root will accomplish this goal; this command causes the system to reread /etc/fstab and mount any newly defined filesystems. You should consult your mount command's man page to be sure it will do this, though. After mounting the NFS directory and defining the Samba share, you can wait a while, and Samba should automatically detect the change and begin making the new share available.

Sharing SMB/CIFS Shares with NFS

Just as you can share an NFS export via a Samba share, you can share an SMB/CIFS share via NFS—but only on OSs that support mounting SMB/CIFS shares, such as FreeBSD, Linux, and Mac OS X.

The first step in this process is to mount the SMB/CIFS share you want to export. Chapter 18, and in particular its "Mounting SMB/CIFS Shares" section, describes how to do this for several OSs. If you don't need to access the files directly on the NFS server computer, where you mount the share is somewhat arbitrary.

 CAUTION If you want to automatically mount SMB/CIFS shares to be re-exported, either the shares must have no password or you must place a password in a configuration file. Both practices are risky.

Once an SMB/CIFS share is mounted, your task becomes one of making it available via NFS. Unfortunately, NFS servers vary quite a bit in how they're configured, so details vary from one OS to another. You should consult your OS's documentation for details, but many Unix-like OSs, including FreeBSD and Linux, configure exports through a file called /etc/exports. This file consists of lines that define the directory to be exported, the systems to which each directory should be exported, and the export options. The precise format of this information varies, though. As an example, FreeBSD places options before the list of supported clients, whereas Linux places the options in parentheses after each client. For instance, in FreeBSD, you might define an export like this:

```
/opt/smbserver/cdrive -ro tango waltz
/opt/smbserver/cdrive tap
```

These lines share the /opt/smbserver/cdrive directory (which would be an SMB/CIFS mount point in this example) with the tango, waltz, and tap computers. The first two of these systems are given read-only access to the export via the -ro option, but tap is missing that option and so receives read/write access (assuming the SMB/CIFS server and Unix permissions allow that access). A similar definition in a Linux /etc/exports file looks like this:

```
/opt/smbserver/cdrive tango(ro) waltz(ro) tap(rw)
```

The ro (read-only) and rw (read/write) options follow each system's specification. Whether the default is read-only or read/write access has varied over time with Linux, so I recommend making the matter explicit.

Samba and AppleTalk

Although Mac OS X can handle NFS and SMB/CIFS, AppleTalk remains a popular file-sharing protocol on many networks. Not all Macintosh users have yet upgraded to

Mac OS X, and even for those who have, using the familiar AppleTalk remains a perfectly viable option, so why change? On such networks, coordinating the efforts of AppleTalk and SMB/CIFS servers can be quite important. In fact, the lesser support for AppleTalk on non-Apple machines and SMB/CIFS on Mac OS Classic means that the need for good coordination between AppleTalk and SMB/CIFS servers is potentially greater than the need for similar coordination between NFS and SMB/CIFS servers on mixed Unix/Windows networks.

As with mixed NFS and SMB/CIFS configurations, a common sharing approach is to deliver the same files via both protocol types. This action requires some minimal coordination between the servers but probably nothing extraordinary. More unusual and requiring more in the way of planning is the case of re-exporting data using a computer that functions as a client to one protocol and a server to the other.

When to Share with Samba and AppleTalk

AppleTalk was created by Apple for its Macintosh platform. Therefore, the vast majority of AppleTalk clients run Mac OS. (A few AppleTalk clients for other OSs, such as BeOS, do exist, though.) Chances are there's no need to run an AppleTalk server if you don't have Mac OS systems on your network. If your network has both Mac OS and Windows or other systems that normally use SMB/CIFS, and if you want to use a Unix-like server, you have several choices for how to set up file sharing:

AppleTalk only: Thursby (http://www.thursby.com) sells a product called TSStalk, which enables Windows systems to function as AppleTalk clients. You can then run an AppleTalk server to serve both platforms. This approach is likely to be costly if your network has many Windows systems, though. Also, Unix AppleTalk servers are nowhere near as flexible as Samba, so if you want to do anything even remotely complex, chances are you'll have problems.

SMB/CIFS only: This approach may be feasible if you use primarily or exclusively Mac OS X because this OS provides SMB/CIFS client support. For Mac OS Classic, though, you'll need to buy copies of Thursby's DAVE. Again, this approach can be costly.

Third protocol: You can rely upon a third protocol, such as NFS. This will require you to buy client software for both the Windows and Mac OS clients, though.

SMB/CIFS and AppleTalk: You can run the open-source Samba package to handle Windows clients and an AppleTalk server to handle Mac OS clients, or at least Mac OS Classic clients. Some Unix AppleTalk servers are open source, and Mac OS X comes with its own AppleTalk server, so this approach can be cost-effective. You won't have as much flexibility for handling the AppleTalk server configuration, though.

As a general rule, if your network has more than a few Mac OS Classic computers as well as DOS, Windows, or OS/2 computers, you're probably best off running both servers. Configuring a single AppleTalk server is easy compared with configuring dozens of DAVE clients. If you only have a handful of Mac OS Classic computers, though, you might want to rely on Samba exclusively and either upgrade those computers to Mac OS X or buy copies of DAVE. Doing so will simplify your server configuration and may have beneficial security effects—by running fewer server programs, you'll provide would-be crackers with fewer ways to attack your server computers.

If you choose to run an AppleTalk server in addition to Samba, of course, you must choose the server to run. Three options are common:

Netatalk: This package (`http://netatalk.sourceforge.net`) is an open-source AppleTalk server for Unix-like systems generally. It's not as flexible as Samba, but it handles the most common needs.

CAP: The Columbia AppleTalk Package (CAP) is an alternative to Netatalk, but it's not as popular or easy to find. Check `http://www.cs.mu.oz.au/appletalk/cap.html` for a list of FTP sites from which the software can be obtained, as well as documentation and additional links.

Mac OS X AppleTalk: Mac OS X provides an AppleTalk server that can be activated from the Sharing item in System Preferences. Select Personal File Sharing to activate the Mac OS X AppleTalk server, as shown in Figure 12-2.

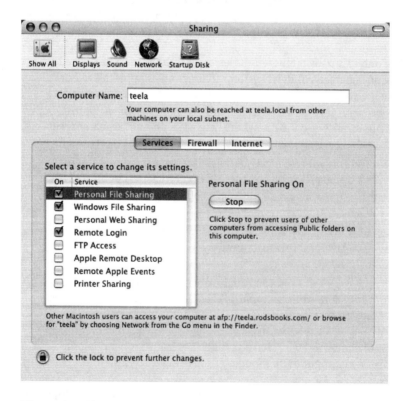

Figure 12-2. The Mac OS X Personal File Sharing server provides AppleTalk file sharing.

As a general rule, if you use Mac OS X as the server system, you'll use its AppleTalk server software, and if you use another Unix-like OS, Netatalk is the most common choice. Some administrators favor CAP, though.

The caveats concerning file sharing described earlier in "Generic File Sharing Considerations" apply to combinations of Samba and any AppleTalk server. Most important, Mac OS Classic can handle only 31-character filenames, and that OS doesn't support Unix-style ownership or permissions.

Re-exporting SMB/CIFS and AppleTalk

Just as with SMB/CIFS and NFS, it's possible to use a system as an intermediary between an SMB/CIFS server and an AppleTalk client or (with Mac OS X) between an AppleTalk server and an SMB/CIFS client. If you haven't already read it, you should read the earlier section "When to Re-export Data"; it applies to configuring a system between SMB/CIFS and AppleTalk systems as well as to a combination of SMB/CIFS and NFS. In brief, this task is best employed only temporarily or for seldom-needed shares. More direct routes produce better performance and are likely to be more reliable.

Sharing AppleTalk Shares with Samba

Re-exporting AppleTalk volumes with Samba is possible only on Mac OS X. The reason is that no other Unix-like OS supports mounting AppleTalk volumes, and without a mounted volume, you can't create a Samba share to re-export the AppleTalk files.

To mount an AppleTalk share in MacOS X, select Go ➤ Connect to Server from the Finder's main menu. This action brings up a Connect to Server dialog box in which you enter a path to the AppleTalk server. This path begins with the string afp but is otherwise similar to the path to other types of file-sharing servers. For instance, afp://granny/audio connects to the granny AppleTalk server and mounts the audio volume. This GUI tool will mount the volume at /Volumes/granny. You must then create a Samba share to re-export this directory, such as this:

```
[audio]
    comment = Audio Files
    directory = /Volumes/granny
    browseable = Yes
    read only = Yes
```

Of course, you should make whatever changes are necessary to this configuration to make it suit your needs. Samba won't be able to parse certain features that are unique to Mac OS, such as resource forks and file type and creator codes. If by some fluke a client is a Mac OS system, some of these features may become completely lost. Of course, a Mac OS client would probably connect directly to the ultimate server, so this limitation is a minor one.

Using the Mac OS GUI to mount an AppleTalk volume may make sense on a one-time basis, but to automate the process, you can use a command-line tool, mount_afp.

This program underlies the GUI mount utility. You'd type a command like this to mount an AppleTalk volume:

```
# mount_afp afp://grogers:Y#iWT7td@granny/audio /Volumes/granny
```

This command mounts the `audio` volume from the `granny` server on `/Volumes/granny` using the username `grogers` and password `Y#iWT7td`. The `/Volumes/granny` directory must exist first, so if it doesn't, be sure to create it. You could place this command in a script and place the script in `/System/Library/StartupItems` to mount the volume at system startup. Because the script contains a password, be sure it's not readable to ordinary users.

 CAUTION   Specifying the password on the command line or in a startup script file is potentially risky because the password might be found in a command shell history, in the startup script file itself, or even in a ps listing output. (The command runs and then terminates, though, so the window of vulnerability to discovery via a ps listing is short.) When using `mount_afp` in a startup script, there's no alternative to this usage; all the information needed to connect, including the password, must be on the command line. When called manually from a shell, though, you can omit the password (and, if you like, the username) and insert the `-i` parameter, as in `mount_afp -i afp://granny/audio /Volumes/granny`. The system then prompts you for the omitted information.

Sharing Samba Shares with AppleTalk

A more popular re-export scenario involving AppleTalk is to use an AppleTalk server to re-export SMB/CIFS shares. This scenario is possible with any Unix-like system that supports mounting SMB/CIFS shares and running an AppleTalk server. Chapter 18 describes the first part of this process, mounting SMB/CIFS shares on a Unix platform. Once this task is done, you must configure the AppleTalk server to share the SMB/CIFS directory or some related directory, such as its parent or a child directory.

If you're using Netatalk, the volumes you share are configured in the `AppleVolumes.default` file, which is typically stored in `/etc/atalk`. Chances are your default file includes many lines of comments that describe the general format of entries, each of which consumes one line. As a general rule, entries take the following form:

```
/dir/to/share  "Volume Name"  [options]
```

In this case, `/dir/to/share` is the path to the directory you want to share. This will typically be the SMB/CIFS share's mount point, but it could be a parent directory or a subdirectory. The `Volume Name` is the name given to the volume. This name will appear under the icon for the volume on Mac OS clients. Finally, you can specify various options, such as `ro` (for read-only volumes), `crlf` (to perform EOL translations on text files), and `noadouble` (which defers creation of `.AppleDouble` directories until a file needs to create a resource fork). Consult the Netatalk documentation or the comments in the configuration file for information on more options.

Samba and Miscellaneous Protocols

Although Samba is frequently the server that makes the computer on which it's installed worthwhile, Samba can be a useful support tool for other protocols. Most notably, Samba can be used as a means of delivering files that will be served by other servers, such as Web or FTP servers. Used in this way, many of the caveats described earlier in "Generic File-Sharing Considerations" apply; however, some of these caveats require elaboration or modification for particular servers.

Using Samba for Web Site Control

Web servers, such as Apache (http://httpd.apache.org), Roxen (http://www.roxen.com), and thttpd (http://www.acme.com/software/thttpd/), are an extremely important part of today's Internet. In fact, some users equate the World Wide Web with the Internet; the Web is so visible that all the other protocols in use on the Internet fade away in these people's minds.

Web servers use a protocol known as the Hypertext Transfer Protocol (HTTP), which accounts for the letters http at the start of Web page addresses. HTTP is primarily a one-way delivery mechanism. Users generally request files from Web servers rather than send files to Web servers. (There are exceptions to this rule, though.) Other technical differences are important, but the one-way nature of file transfers means that those who maintain Web pages need some way to place Web pages on the Web server.

Samba, as you know by now, is a convenient tool for enabling two-way file transfers. In fact, users can directly edit files on a Samba server, without first copying the file to the client computer. These characteristics make Samba a good adjunct to a Web server to aid in editing Web pages, albeit with some important caveats. The most important of these caveats is that running a Samba server on a Web server computer can degrade the Web server's security. Web server computers, by their very nature, are typically very highly exposed; anybody on the Internet can usually access a Web server. (Private Web servers on local networks are exceptions to this rule.) In addition to simply being exposed, Web servers are typically very visible, in the sense that the Web server's hostname is known to everybody, and the server itself may be noticed because of its public content. Running Samba on a Web server computer, therefore, exposes the Samba server software to attack from the outside. You can minimize this risk by using Samba's security tools (particularly hosts allow, interfaces, and bind interfaces only, all of which are described in Chapter 11) and by setting up good firewalls between the outside world and Samba. The firewalls must restrict access to Samba's ports but not to the HTTP ports.

When using Samba as a method of controlling your Web site, you should first configure your Web server software. Consult your Web server's documentation or an appropriate book on this subject. Typically, you'll set assorted Web server options and create a directory in which you'll store your Web pages. Some servers use multiple

Web page locations, such as locations for different virtual hosts or different types of content (HTML vs. scripts, for instance). Some servers also provide users with the ability to publish personal Web pages. These pages typically reside in users' home directories. In any event, when you set up Samba, you should create one or more shares corresponding to the directory tree or directories in which the Web server's files reside. For instance, if your server stores files in /var/httpd/html and /var/httpd/cgi-bin, you could create a single share for /var/httpd or two shares, one for each directory. Either configuration will work. If you configure the Web server to give users their own Web page directories, you may want to ensure that these directories are in users' home directories (they probably are) and that they don't have directory names that begin with dots (.). Such directories would be hidden by Samba's default hide dot files = Yes parameter.

Even beyond blocking unauthorized systems from accessing Samba, security on a Samba server that's used to help maintain a Web site is extremely important. Be sure that only authorized individuals have access to the server. Chances are the entire computer will have just a handful of users, although this won't be the case on a computer that hosts many independent domains or that delivers individual users' home pages. Think out your permissions scheme carefully, consider whether you want to enable users to set ACLs on files they create, and set all Samba options appropriately.

When users create or modify Web pages, they can directly access the directories the Web server uses to deliver files. This configuration can be convenient, but it also means that if the Web site maintainers make a mistake, your online Web presence may be disrupted until that mistake can be corrected.

 TIP You may want to create a "scratch" Web site—one that's identical in as many ways as possible to your primary site but that uses different directories and perhaps a different server hostname. (Most Web servers support such virtual sites; consult your Web server's documentation for details.) Your Webmasters can then make changes to the test site and, when they're satisfied, copy the files over to the real Web site.

One feature you should be sure your users are aware of when creating Web sites with the help of Samba is case-sensitivity. Unix Web servers are invariably case-sensitive, just as Unix filesystems are. Samba, though, treats files in a case-retentive but insensitive way by default. The result is that references to other files in Web pages may behave differently if a Web designer tries testing a page by loading it via a path that uses the Samba server rather than the Web server. For instance, if a Web page specifies that it should load a graphics file called image.jpg, but if the file is stored on disk as Image.jpg, the Web server won't be able to find it. This problem isn't any worse than the problem of testing a Web page on a Windows system and then uploading it to the Web server computer via FTP or some other means, though.

CAUTION Some Samba filename-handling parameters can confuse matters further. For instance, if you use `mangled map`, Samba will change filenames in ways that might not be obvious to your users. Worst of all is if you map files that end in `.html` to end in `.htm`, although mangling `.jpeg` to `.jpg` is potentially almost as bad. In these cases, common Web page filenames are likely to look different to Samba clients as opposed to Web server clients.

Using Samba for FTP Site Control

Just as you can use Samba to maintain a Web site, you can use Samba to maintain an FTP site. Today, FTP sites are most often used to deliver moderately large files independent of or in support of Web sites. For instance, you can obtain Samba itself from FTP sites. Unlike the Web, which is based on the presumption of quick accesses to a small number of files from the server, FTP is a login-oriented protocol, so users are likely to log in, look for files, and log out after some time.

NOTE Although FTP is a login-oriented protocol, many FTP sites are *anonymous*. These sites accept logins using a username of anonymous and any password (conventionally the user's e-mail address). Anonymous FTP sites are used to deliver software to the general public, but they seldom accept uploads, at least not using the anonymous username. Other FTP sites require real usernames and enable users with regular accounts to transfer files. Samba is most likely to be useful in support of anonymous FTP sites, although you could use a combination of FTP and Samba to access your personal data on a server from different clients.

FTP is a two-way protocol—it supports uploads to the server as well as downloads from it. Why, then, would you want to use Samba to help maintain an FTP site? After all, you could maintain the site via FTP itself. The main reason is convenience. Most FTP clients are a bit clunky compared to GUI SMB/CIFS clients, such as those built into Windows and Mac OS X. If the FTP server computer also runs a Samba server, your FTP site maintenance team can easily drag and drop files between their own local hard drives and the Samba/FTP server or between directories on the server.

The basic procedure for configuring an FTP server computer with a Samba support server is similar to that for doing the same with a Web server computer. Start with configuring the FTP server, at least minimally. Set aside a directory for the server, configure its permissions and the FTP server's security as you want it, then start on the Samba server. Use whatever Samba server security features you deem appropriate.

Be sure to include heavy protections against accessing the Samba server from any but a handful of authorized clients, lest the Samba server fall under attack as a way to break into the computer.

Unless the FTP server hosts files that will be references from a Web site, you needn't be quite as concerned about filename case as you must be when configuring a Samba support server for a Web server. A typical text-mode or GUI FTP client presents filenames and requires users to type in a filename or click the file entry, so the user sees the filename and can handle whatever the case actually is. Likewise, other filename modifications shouldn't be a huge problem, with the possible exception of non-ASCII characters creeping into the filenames.

Using Samba with Other Protocols

Even the actions of protocols that aren't directly related to serving files can influence Samba. Files created through various means can appear in Samba shares, and Samba can create files that might affect other protocols. These effects can be particularly important when designing Samba's security scheme and in considering how Samba's security options affect other protocols. Examples include the following:

Login protocols: Telnet, the Secure Shell (SSH), X login tools, Virtual Network Computing (VNC), and other protocols all enable users to log in, create files, delete files, and otherwise affect Samba shares. If you enable remote logins, you should be sure that users won't be able to wreak accidental or intentional havoc by doing things that might cause problems for Samba's security model. For instance, if you use force user to simplify management of ownership in a shared directory, users might not have access to files from a remote login, or if they do have access to files, they might accidentally or intentionally render files unchangeable from Samba.

Remote administration: Some tools, such as Webmin (http://www.webmin.net), enable you to remotely administer a computer without logging in. Normally tools such as this won't cause problems for Samba, but if you use them to edit Samba configuration files, you should be aware that they may have peculiar effects, such as stripping out comments. Chapter 13 describes using such tools in more detail.

Mail and news servers: Most Unix-like systems run mail servers, if only for the delivery of local mail. News servers are less common on Samba servers, but the two can coexist. Ordinarily, Samba and mail or news servers don't interact or cause problems for each other because Samba isn't normally configured to share the mail or news spool directories. In principle, you could do so, which would enable clients to directly access these directories. Doing so is inadvisable, though; file locking and permissions issues relating to these files are tricky, and using Samba to access them is likely to cause problems. You're far better off running a Post Office Protocol (POP) or Internet Mail Access Protocol (IMAP) server to access mail remotely using common mail clients than to try to do so using Samba and an SMB/CIFS client.

DHCP servers: The Dynamic Host Configuration Protocol (DHCP) provides IP addresses and other information to clients. Chapter 9 describes how to configure a DHCP server to deliver information on a Samba NBNS system to clients, which can be a convenience. Ordinarily, Samba shouldn't be configured to give clients direct access to any DHCP files.

DNS servers: Chapter 9 describes how to configure Samba to use a DNS server as a fallback for information on computers' IP addresses, as well as how to configure Samba to deliver information on clients' NetBIOS names and IP addresses to a DNS server as the clients boot up and register themselves. There's normally no need to give Samba clients more direct access to DNS configuration files.

Using (and Not Using) Samba for Miscellaneous Administration

At first glance, it might appear that Samba could be a useful general system administration tool. Create a Samba share that points to /etc, and you can then access many of a Unix system's critical configuration files. This practice, however, is extraordinarily risky. Most of the files in /etc require root privileges to write, and some require root privileges to read. This means that you would need to authorize root Samba logons, use the force user parameter, or use the admin users parameter to give an ordinary user root privileges in /etc. Any of these courses of action are extremely risky; should security be compromised, an intruder would be able to change any aspect of your system's configuration. Even aside from these dangers, using non-Unix clients to edit Unix configuration files can be risky because of ASCII EOL issues. Some Unix tools are sensitive to EOL form, so if they see Windows- or Mac-style EOLs, these tools may not work. In a worst-case scenario, the computer might fail to boot after making such changes.

Nonetheless, you can still use Samba as a system administration or configuration tool, albeit in much more limited scopes. For instance, Chapter 9 describes linking Samba with a DNS server so that the DNS server's entries for your domain are updated as SMB/CIFS clients come online. Samba account management tools can help you maintain your local Unix accounts—particularly passwords. Overall, though, you're best off leaving system administration to the console, remote logins via secure tools such as SSH, or GUI administration tools such as Webmin (described in Chapter 13).

Samba and Other Printing Protocols

Samba printer servers may have several printers connected directly to them. These printers can be shared via Samba and any other network printing protocol supported by the server computer, such as the Line Printer Daemon (LPD) or Internet Printing Protocol (IPP). Samba can also be used, though, as an intermediate step in printer sharing—to make LPD or IPP printers available to Samba clients or to make SMB/CIFS printer shares available to LPD or IPP clients. The first case is actually rather simple to configure, but the second case is more complex. This second case can also be useful for local configuration—that is, to make SMB/CIFS printer shares available to a Unix workstation using Samba's client tools.

> **NOTE**   If you haven't already read it, you should read Chapter 6 before proceeding.

Sharing LPD or IPP Printers with SMB/CIFS Clients

Unix printing systems traditionally integrate both local printing features and the ability to handle network printing connections via LPD. The more recent IPP system, as used by the Common Unix Printing System (CUPS; http://www.cups.org), is an increasingly popular alternative. In any event, local Unix print queues tend not to distinguish between local and remote printers. Applications can print to a printer in precisely the same way no matter where the printer is located. Typically, an application prints using a program called lp or lpr, which prints to a default printer or accepts a queue name, as in **lpr -Pcanon file.ps** to print file.ps to a print queue called canon. This queue could correspond to a local printer or to a remote one; the print command is identical in either case.

> **NOTE**   User applications—particularly GUI programs—frequently hide the call to lpr or a similar program and instead present a printing dialog box. These programs still call lpr or do the work that it does, though.

When you configure a Samba printer share, you give that share the name of the print queue (typically by using the name in the share name or by relying on a [printers] share to extract the name from system files). When Samba receives a print job, it passes the job to the local printing system by using lpr or some other printing command. Thus, Samba doesn't distinguish between local or remote printers when it prints on behalf of a client. Samba doesn't even need to know which printers are local and which are remote. In many respects, this mirrors the situation with re-exporting file shares; the Samba side of the configuration needn't know that a directory actually contains files that have been mounted via some other network protocol.

Re-exporting printer shares can be handy for many of the same reasons that re-exporting file shares can be convenient. Using an intermediary system may be a way to quickly add support for printers that are shared from a computer that doesn't support SMB/CIFS. Of course, most computers that support LPD or IPP can also run Samba, so in the long run you may prefer to add Samba to the computer that actually handles the printers. Sometimes, though, using a Samba system as an intermediary has its advantages. For instance, suppose the ultimate print server has a very weak CPU, but you want to use Ghostscript to convert PostScript into a printer-specific form. In this case, using a more powerful computer as a PostScript processor for SMB/CIFS print clients can help take the load off of the ultimate print server.

The main downside to using Samba to re-export existing network print shares is the increased network traffic this practice creates. Just as with re-exported file shares, a re-exported printer share means that data must be passed across the network twice. If Samba processes PostScript into printer-specific forms, the second transfer is likely to be much larger than the first, too, so running Samba, or at least Ghostscript, on the ultimate target system will help reduce network bandwidth needs. Re-exporting a share also reduces reliability because there's one more computer that can fail. Nonetheless, as with re-exporting file shares, re-exporting printer shares can be a great convenience for temporary or seldom-used printer shares or in unusual situations in which the ultimate print server can't run Samba (or some other SMB/CIFS server) for some reason.

NOTE   Even print queues that don't involve LPD or IPP can be shared via Samba. For instance, Netatalk includes an AppleTalk print client, enabling Unix-like systems to print to networked Apple printers. You can re-export such shares or use the Samba print command parameter to call the client tools directly, re-exporting to any client that the Unix OS you use supports.

Sharing SMB/CIFS Printers with LPD Clients

Configuring an LPD print server to access an SMB/CIFS printer share requires providing a way to interface Samba's printing client tools with the LPD print queue. In the case of both the BSD LPD and LPRng print servers, the local queues are controlled through a file called /etc/printcap. Making a local print queue accessible to other systems requires making additional authentication changes, which vary from one printing system to another.

TIP   You can use CUPS, which ordinarily uses IPP, to share an SMB/CIFS printer (or IPP or other types of printer) with LPD clients. Doing so requires running a special server, called cups-lpd, which listens for LPD connections and, when it detects them, passes the LPD connection internally through an appropriate CUPS queue. The cups-lpd server sometimes ships in a separate package from CUPS proper and is typically run via the computer's super server (inetd or xinetd). Configuring a CUPS server to send data to an SMB/CIFS printer share is described in the upcoming section "Sharing SMB/CIFS Printers with IPP Clients."

Configuring a Printer in /etc/printcap

The /etc/printcap file, and the underlying utilities, were designed for specifying local printers or remote LPD printers. A typical entry in this file looks something like this:

```
lp|lp0|minolta:\
    :sd=/var/spool/lpd/minolta:\
    :mx#0:\
    :sh:\
    :lp=/dev/lp0:\
    :if=/var/spool/lpd/minolta/filter:
```

The definition officially requires a single entry to be on one line, but the backslash characters (\) function as line continuation characters—any line that ends in a backslash is officially continued on the next physical line. Thus, in some sense these six lines are really one line. Components of the printcap definition are separated by colons (:). Most options begin with a two-character option name and are followed by an equal sign (=) or hash mark (#) as an assignment operator and then a value. Specific options shown in this example are as follows:

>**Queue name:** The first line is the queue name, or lp|lp0|minolta in this example, which actually defines three queue names: lp, lp0, and minolta. All three of these names function identically.

>**Spool directory:** The sd option sets the spool directory—the directory in which the software stores files that are waiting to be printed.

>**Maximum file size:** The mx option sets the maximum file size to accept for printing. A value of 0, as in this example, stands for no limit.

>**Header suppression:** Normally, BSD LPD and LPRng print a job header at the start of each job. This header contains the job name, the name of the user who submitted the job, and so on. The sh option disables this header, which is useful for saving paper on single-user systems and in small offices but should probably be omitted in larger offices.

>**Printer device:** The lp option sets the name of the printer device file—that is, the device file to which the print job will ultimately be copied for a local printer. In the case of an LPD network printer, you don't use an lp option but instead use an rm option to specify the name of the server and an rp option to point to the name of the queue on the remote server.

>**Input filter:** The if option specifies an *input filter*, which processes the input in some way. This line often points to a *smart filter*, which attempts to identify the file type and convert it to a format that the printer can accept.

Many of these options will be the same when pointing a share to a Samba server; however, the printcap file format doesn't support any way to point the spooler at an SMB/CIFS printer share. Therefore, you'll omit the printer device options or point lp to /dev/null or some other harmless location. Instead, you must use the input filter to "hijack" the normal LPD printing system and send the file to the SMB/CIFS server via a script called smbprint, which comes with Samba.

Manually configuring a queue to use an SMB/CIFS printer share can be tricky. Fortunately, most Unix-like OSs provide printer configuration tools that can help to automate the process by providing GUI or text-mode utilities that collect the necessary information and create or modify custom scripts to do the job. Even for those that don't ship with such utilities, the most reliable way to configure a local queue to print using an SMB/CIFS share is to install a smart filter package that supports SMB/CIFS printing. One such package is Apsfilter (http://www.apsfilter.org). To use this package, you should first install it and then launch the Apsfilter configuration tool, which is called /usr/share/apsfilter/SETUP on many systems. The result is a configuration tool that asks a few questions and then presents a menu similar to the one depicted in Figure 12-3.

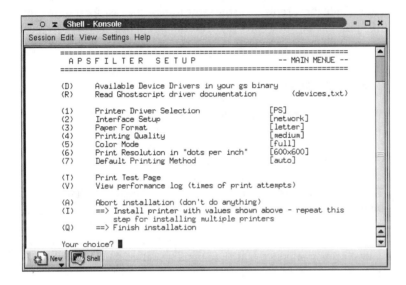

Figure 12-3. Apsfilter and other tools help you to configure a local print queue to use an SMB/CIFS printer share.

To configure a printer, select option 1, Printer Driver Selection, which lets you select the type of printer you're using (PostScript or various Ghostscript drivers). Once you've done this, Apsfilter returns to the setup menu, and you can select option 2, Interface Setup. The system gives several choices for the type of interface to use, one of which is Windows / NT (Samba). Select this option, and Apsfilter asks for information such as the server's NetBIOS name, the share name, and so on. When you're done, Apsfilter returns to the setup menu shown in Figure 12-3. If you like, you can adjust other options, such as the print quality and color mode. I recommend printing a test page, which will test your configuration. If all works, select the I option to install the printer configuration. You may also want to double-check your configuration by printing a file from the server computer by using the lpr command, as in lpr -Pminolta test.ps to print the test.ps file to the minolta printer.

CAUTION To print to an SMB/CIFS printer share, your system must store a username and password on the hard disk. This practice is a potential security risk for the print server. If possible, use a dedicated printing account on that server with limited nonprinting access. With some configuration tools, you can tell the system to use a guest account in which the password isn't stored on the disk. This method, though, requires that the server be configured to accept guest access to the printer share.

Apsfilter is something of a lowest-common-denominator printer configuration tool. Many Unix-like OSs include flashier GUI tools, such as SUSE Linux's YaST and YaST2. Ultimately, though, these tools all do the same thing—they ask for information on your SMB/CIFS printer share and enter that information in text files that the local printing system's smart filters can handle.

Authorizing Remote Access with BSD LPD

If you want to use Samba as a re-exporting print server, enabling LPD systems without Samba to print to the SMB/CIFS printer, you must then configure your system's LPD server to accept remote connection attempts. You can most easily accomplish this task if you use BSD LPD. With this printing system, you should edit the /etc/hosts.lpd file, which consists of a series of lines with hostnames, IP addresses, or other computer specifications. The safest way to use this file is to list the IP addresses of all the clients that should be able to print. You can substitute hostnames, but doing so means that your server will rely upon the DNS server for authentication, such as it does with BSD LPD. If your network uses a Network Information System (NIS) server, you can specify an NIS netgroup by placing a plus sign and an at sign (+@) before the NIS netgroup name, as in +@print to enable members of the print group to print.

 CAUTION Instead of using /etc/hosts.lpd, you can use /etc/ hosts.equiv to authorize remote hosts to access the print server. This configuration, however, is extremely risky because /etc/hosts.equiv also authorizes remote use of several other servers. Ideally, none of these servers will be installed, but if they are, you might be giving too much access to remote hosts if you use /etc/hosts.equiv. As a general rule, you should delete /etc/hosts.equiv or make sure it's completely empty.

After configuring your printers in this way, the printers you specify in /etc/ hosts.lpd should be able to print to the SMB/CIFS printers using LPD via the re-exporting server. You can accomplish local configuration on the ultimate clients using Apsfilter or more OS-specific GUI tools, or you can configure a queue by manually editing /etc/printcap—you'll point the ultimate clients to the re-exporting server's queue by using the rm and rp options in /etc/printcap.

CAUTION BSD LPD doesn't provide any built-in method of user authentication beyond the IP address, hostname, or other machine-centric systems. You can't easily restrict access to particular users, for instance, and no password is required to print. You should, therefore, be *very* cautious about what systems you authorize to print. A too-broad definition might enable miscreants to waste paper and toner or ink by printing reams of black pages. Worse, a security flaw might enable outsiders to abuse the server to gain fuller access to the system.

Authorizing Remote Access with LPRng

LPRng's access control mechanism is much more complex than that of BSD LPD, although it's still based on IP addresses. This server uses a file called /etc/lpd.perms to determine which systems may print. You should consult its documentation for details of how this system works. As a starting point, though, you may want to locate a line in this file that reads DEFAULT ACCEPT and add lines such as the following just before this line:

```
ACCEPT SERVICE=X SERVER
ACCEPT SERVICE=X REMOTEIP=172.23.78.16
REJECT SERVICE=X NOT REMOTEIP=192.168.12.0/24
```

These lines tell LPRng to accept connections from the server itself and to reject them from any system that's not 172.23.78.16 or on the 192.168.12.0/24 network. (You would change these addresses to suit your needs, of course.) To add to the list of acceptable servers, add additional ACCEPT lines prior to the REJECT line. Be sure you enter these lines in order; after the REJECT line, the system will reject all systems that haven't been authorized in previous lines. (Omitting the NOT in the REJECT line will cause the system to reject accesses from the specified IP address or network. If DEFAULT ACCEPT is also set, omitting NOT in the REJECT line will also tell the system to accept other accesses.)

After making these changes and restarting the printer daemon, an LPRng system should accept remote printer accesses for printing to an SMB/CIFS printer share. You should test printing from one of the client systems, which can be running BSD LPD, LPRng, or any other LPD-compatible printing system. Specify the re-exporting server using the rm and rp options in /etc/printcap, or use a printer configuration tool to help define the share.

Sharing SMB/CIFS Printers with IPP Clients

IPP is associated primarily with CUPS, which is one of the most flexible printing systems for Unix-like OSs. CUPS is now the default printing system on most major Linux distributions and on Mac OS X, and it's available for other Unix-like OSs. Most CUPS configuration tasks can be performed using its GUI configuration tool, which is accessible via a Web browser on port 631. Thus, you should enter http://localhost:631 in a Web browser on the CUPS server. The result is a list of administrative tasks. Click the

Manage Printers link, and you'll see a list of printers you've installed locally or that CUPS has autodetected, as shown in Figure 12-4.

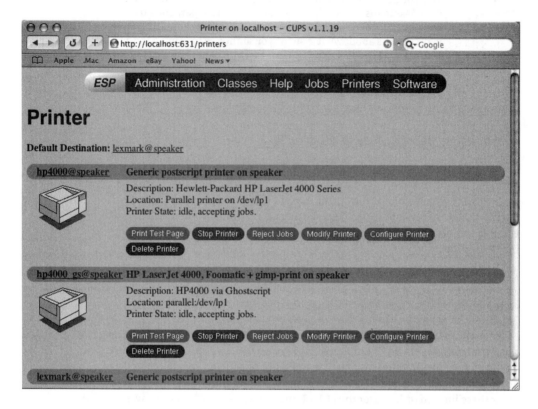

Figure 12-4. CUPS provides a Web-based printer administration tool.

TIP Before adding an SMB/CIFS printer, check that it doesn't already appear in the printer list. If the SMB/CIFS server happens to be using CUPS or some other IPP software, CUPS might autodetect the share as an IPP share and print using IPP.

To add an SMB/CIFS printer, follow these steps:

1. Scroll to the bottom of the list of printers, and click the Add Printer button. (This button isn't visible in Figure 12-4.)

NOTE On some systems, CUPS will ask for a username and password at this point. Enter **root** and the root user's password.

2. The server displays a screen asking for the name, location, and description of the printer. These fields don't hold any truly vital configuration information; they exist to help you identify the printer when you look at the printer list in the future and when you select a printer to which you want to print. Enter appropriate values, and click the Continue button.

3. CUPS asks you to select a device from a drop-down list. Depending upon the options that ship with your version of CUPS and your hardware's configuration, you're likely to see anywhere from a handful to more than a dozen options. Select the option called Windows Printer via SAMBA, and click Continue.

4. The server asks for a device URI. The field will probably have smb pre-entered. Type the complete path to the SMB/CIFS printer share, starting with smb://; for instance, you might type `smb://grogers:Y#iWT7td@TAP/MINOLTA` to print to the MINOLTA share on the TAP server using the grogers username and a password of Y#iWT7td. (You can omit the username, password, and the at sign and colon that follow them if the share accepts guest accesses.) Click Continue.

CAUTION   To print to an SMB/CIFS printer, CUPS must store the username and password on disk, although it will hide that information from its own printer configuration screens as a security measure. Try to create a special printing account on the SMB/CIFS server to minimize the risk.

---

5. CUPS asks for the make of your printer. In a default installation, this list will be quite short, but you can add software packages to expand the CUPS driver set. (These drivers, when installed, call Ghostscript to convert PostScript to a format suitable for your printer.) Make a selection, and click Continue.

6. CUPS asks for a model. Select a model number, and click Continue.

7. The system should conclude that the printer has been created.

At this point, you can click the printer name to go to a page describing the printer and click the Print Test Page item to test the printer's operation. If the system doesn't print, review the preceding steps. From the printer description page, click Show Completed Jobs to see if CUPS thinks it has successfully printed the test document.

One of the beauties of CUPS is that CUPS servers can automatically communicate with one another and exchange printer lists. This discovery process (known as *browsing*, although it bears little relationship to either SMB/CIFS browsing or Web browsing) means that you may not need to do any explicit configuration on the CUPS clients to point them to the newly defined SMB/CIFS shares. It may take a minute or two for clients to discover the new printer, though.

Despite the automatic discovery process, you may need to configure access control systems on both the CUPS server and its clients. Both tasks are handled through the cupsd.conf file, which usually resides in /etc/cups. (You may need to edit this file on the server and the clients.) On the server, you should check the <Location /printers> section, which begins with a line of that name and ends with a </Location> line. The lines in between specify what computers may access the printers defined on the server. A typical configuration that enables browsing from a local subnet looks like this:

```
<Location /printers>
Order Deny,Allow
Deny From All
BrowseAllow from 127.0.0.1
BrowseAllow from 172.23.78.16
BrowseAllow from 192.168.12.0/24
Allow from 127.0.0.1
Allow from 172.23.78.16
Allow from 192.168.12.0/24
Allow From @LOCAL
</Location>
```

This definition tells the server to set a default closed policy (Deny From All) but to accept browsing and other accesses (the BrowseAllow and Allow lines) from 127.0.0.1 (that is, the computer itself), 172.23.78.16, and the 192.168.12.0/24 network.

Earlier in the file, you should look for a line that begins Browsing. On any CUPS system that should search for other IPP servers, you should set this value to On. On both the server and the client, you may need to set the BrowseAddress directive, which tells the system what network to query for CUPS servers. The two of these options together look like this:

```
Browsing On
BrowseAddress 192.168.12.255
```

Samba and NTP

Samba is primarily a file and print server, but the package includes support for various additional functions. Some of these, such as NetBIOS Name Server (NBNS) and domain control functionality, are complex enough that they merit their own chapters in this book. Others, though, merit much less coverage. One of these lesser functions is Samba's built-in *time server* functionality. A time server is a network server that can tell other computers what time it is. Time servers can be very useful on networks with many computers; by setting the time in an automated or semiauto-mated fashion, you can save yourself or your users some effort in setting many computers' clocks when they drift, as computer clocks inevitably do. More important, some tools rely upon accurate time settings, so keeping clients' and servers' clocks synchronized can help make these tools run more smoothly. For instance, many software development tools use the time stamps on files to determine which files to compile whenever a project is rebuilt. If two systems' clocks differ, attempts to recompile a program can result in wasted time as a computer unnecessarily recom-piles a file that hasn't changed or frustration as the system fails to recompile a file that has changed.

You may want to configure one computer as a time server for your network. You can use another protocol, the Network Time Protocol (NTP), to set that computer's clock to a veridical time source outside of your network, such as one set from an atomic clock. You can then synchronize your other computers' clocks to your network's primary time server clock.

Using Samba's Built-in Time Server

Samba's built-in time server enables users of remote systems to set their clocks based on the time on the Samba server system. Configuring Samba to function as a time server is fairly straightforward. Using the server from a Windows client to set the time also requires typing only one command, although configuring Windows to do this task on a regular basis creates the potential for some pitfalls. You can even use Samba's net command to set the time on a Samba system to the time maintained by another Samba or Windows computer, although in most cases using NTP is a better choice on a Unix system.

The main Samba parameter that influences its SMB/CIFS time server behavior is the global time server parameter. Setting this option to Yes causes Samba to advertise its presence as a time server. If you don't set this option (it defaults to No), Samba will still respond to time server queries directed at it, but the server won't advertise its time server capabilities.

You can use a Samba time server with the NET command in Windows and specifically with its TIME subcommand. To set the time on a client to the time maintained by a Samba server, type the following command in a DOS prompt window:

```
C:\> NET TIME \\SERVER /SET /YES
```

Change *SERVER* to the NetBIOS name of the server you want to use as a reference time source. The result will be that the client will change its clock setting to match that of the Samba server. The precision of the SMB/CIFS time protocol isn't as good as NTP's (described in the next section, "Configuring NTP on a Samba Server"), but it's good enough for most clients.

NOTE   If you just want to view the server's time but not set it on the client, omit the /SET parameter. You can also omit the *SERVER* name, as in **NET TIME /SET /YES**, to have the client locate a time server. Doing so requires that Samba use time server = Yes or that a non-Samba server have equivalent options set. Omitting the server name also means that the client might happen to synchronize its clock to a system with an inaccurate clock. If you specify the time server computer, you can at least point to a system that's likely to maintain an accurate time.

Samba 3.0 adds its own net command, which is modeled partly on the Windows NET command. If you've installed Samba 3.0 on a Unix-like client, therefore, you can use the net command to adjust the Unix system's clock. The syntax to do so, though, is slightly different from the syntax that Windows uses. Specifically, to set the clock on the client system, you should type the following:

```
# net time set -S SERVER
```

An ordinary user can use this command without the set parameter to display the time on the server without setting the local clock. Normally, only root can use the command with the set option to set the local clock.

 NOTE The net time set command sets the system clock using the date command, which typically adjusts a software clock that the OS maintains while it's booted. Most hardware, including *x*86 hardware, provides a hardware clock, as well. Using net set time might not adjust this hardware clock, so you may need to adjust that using another command, such as hwclock. Typing hwclock --systohc --utc will often work if your hardware clock is set to Coordinated Universal Time (UTC) and hwclock --systohc --localtime will often work if your hardware clock is set to local time. Consult your local documentation for details.

One way to make effective use of a Samba time server is to configure your clients to synchronize their clocks to the server when they boot. For Windows clients, you can accomplish this task through a startup batch file. Two possibilities should work well for this job:

Startup batch file: Create a batch file (say, TIMESET.BAT) that contains nothing but the NET SET \\SERVER /SET /YES line and place it in the Windows Startup folder. (Right-click the Start menu, select Open, and open the Programs folder to reveal this folder in the Windows GUI.) Programs in this folder execute automatically when the system boots or the user logs on, so this is a good location for this file.

Network logon script: If you use a domain configuration, you can place the NET SET \\SERVER /SET /YES command in a domain's network logon script. Chapter 14 describes these scripts.

Either way, the Windows client will synchronize its clock to the Samba server whenever the client boots or a user logs on. In most environments, this will produce a good enough time synchronization. If you wanted to do something similar with a Unix client, though, your best bet would be to place the command in a cron job that you would call on a regular basis—probably somewhere between once an hour and once a day. NTP is a better tool for use on Unix clients, though, as well as for any system for which keeping the most accurate time at all times is important. One of the most important of these systems, naturally, is the computer that functions as your Samba time server.

Configuring NTP on a Samba Server

NTP is perhaps the most popular time protocol on the Internet at large. The system as a whole is configured hierarchically. At the top are so-called *stratum 0* time sources. These are devices that measure time directly (such as atomic clocks) or at least that obtain their time more or less directly from such sources (such as clocks that set their time from signals embedded in the Global Positioning System, or GPS, signals). Stratum 0 time sources aren't directly accessible via the Internet; instead, they link to *stratum 1* time servers. These servers in turn allow *stratum 2* servers to set their time based on the stratum 1 server's clocks. *Stratum 3* servers synchronize to stratum 2 servers and so on. At most of these levels, an NTP server functions as both a server to lower-tier servers and as a client to higher-tier servers. The fact that a server at any given stratum can have many different clients means that the benefits of a few expensive atomic clocks can spread to thousands or millions of computers. Each stratum jump degrades the accuracy of the clock setting but not by enough to be important for most purposes. Even a stratum 4 or 5 system is likely to be accurate to well under a second of the source clock's time.

On Unix-like systems, the most popular NTP software is known as NTP and can be obtained from http://www.ntp.org. Many Unix-like OSs ship with this server, but it's often disabled by default. When activated, the NTP server runs as a daemon and synchronizes the computer's clock with one or more external time servers. The NTP daemon periodically checks back with its source systems and adjusts the local time to keep the local clock synchronized. In fact, an NTP server can use multiple upstream NTP servers. This redundancy enables the local NTP server to spot *false tickers* (NTP servers that are delivering the wrong time) and provides a fallback in case a server goes offline for a while. By calibrating the local clock every few minutes, an NTP server can fine-tune a local clock's settings so that it's accurate to within a fraction of a second at all times. A system so configured can even maintain a more accurate time for an extended period in the event of a complete network failure because NTP can keep data about the local system clock's tendency to drift and compensate accordingly.

To use NTP, you should first check for it on your system. The main server file is called ntpd (it's xntpd on some older versions), and it's likely to be stored in /usr/sbin or /usr/local/sbin. The server is configured through a file called ntp.conf, which is usually stored in /etc. Look for this file and edit it. Many systems ship with default files that set assorted values, but the most important lines look like this:

```
server  127.127.1.0    # local clock
fudge   127.127.1.0 stratum 10
server atomic.pangaea.gov
server tempus.luna.edu
server time.example.com
```

These example lines tell NTP about four servers. The first of these (127.127.1.0) refers to the computer's own clock. It's used as a fallback in case the other servers can't be reached, but it's likely to be a poor fallback position. Many configurations omit this reference. If you include it, be sure you also include the fudge line, which tells the system to assign a stratum number of 10 to the local clock. This configuration keeps the local clock from being treated as more accurate than the real time servers. (Of course, if you really do synchronize to a stratum 10 or worse NTP server, you should adjust the value on the `fudge` line appropriately.)

The next three lines tell NTP about three time servers to which it should synchronize itself—`atomic.pangaea.gov`, `tempus.luna.edu`, and `time.example.com` in this example. Few networks need to synchronize to as many as three external servers, but if maintaining an accurate time is important, using three, at least initially, may be helpful. If one server's time signal is spurious, NTP will be able to spot this problem and discard the bad source. After you monitor the process, you can trim the number of servers if you like. For a small network, and if you don't mind if the time is off by a second or two, you might use just one source from the start.

What sources do you use, though? Check `http://www.eecis.udel.edu/~mills/ntp/servers.html` for a list of stratum 1 and stratum 2 NTP servers. Unless your network is very large (more than 100 systems is a commonly cited rule-of-thumb criterion) and needs highly accurate time signals, you should *not* use stratum 1 time servers. These servers are best used to set public stratum 2 servers, which are accessible to the public at large. Read the list of stratum 2 servers and pick a few candidates. These servers should be near to you in network topology and should be publicly accessible. You might also look for less-public servers to which you have legitimate access. For instance, many ISPs operate NTP servers, as do businesses and universities with large internal networks. A few computer companies operate NTP servers for their customers, and you may already find their NTP servers preconfigured in your default `ntp.conf` file.

Once you have a list of candidate servers, try using `ping` and `traceroute` to try to determine which servers are closest to you and produce the lowest latencies (response times). As a general rule, the quicker the responses to `ping` and the fewer the number of intervening systems in a `traceroute`, the better the source is. This is because NTP works, in part, by measuring the time between sending a packet to the NTP server and receiving a reply. The system uses this information to estimate the time for each leg of the trip, which is important in setting the time correctly. The shorter the latencies, therefore, the smaller the likely error in setting the time.

Once you've set the servers in the `ntp.conf` file, you should start or restart the server. Look for a running process called `ntpd`, and restart it if it's running. If it's not, look for an NTP SysV startup script or a commented-out call to the server in a local startup script. NTP must run continuously to work well, so you should run it from a SysV or local startup script, not from a super server. Chapter 3 describes using these startup methods for Samba, and the process is similar for NTP.

TIP   Once started, `ntpd` will exit if it finds that the system clock is off by more than about 17 minutes from what its upstream sources say it should be. If you know your clock is wrong and want to have `ntpd` fix the problem, launch it with the `-g` option, which forces it to set the clock even if it's off by a large amount.

After starting ntpd, you can monitor its operation by using the ntpq program. The most useful monitoring command is peers, which returns a list of the computers to which the NTP server has synchronized itself, along with statistics about them:

```
ntpq> peers
     remote           refid      st t when poll reach   delay   offset  jitter
==============================================================================
 LOCAL(0)        LOCAL(0)        10 l   16   64  377    0.000    0.000   0.008
+atomic.pangaea. clock.pangaea.e  2 u  662 1024  277   44.335   -4.151  26.844
*tempus.luna.edu npt3.navy.luna.  2 u  781 1024  377   33.009   -5.177   0.701
+time.example.co tick.example.ed  2 u  685 1024  377   45.299   -5.761   1.477
```

This example shows the names of the three systems to which the NTP server has synchronized—atomic.pangaea.gov, tempus.luna.edu, and time.example.com (two of these names have been truncated to fit the display), as well as the names of *their* reference servers (in the refid column). The st column indicates the stratum of the remote servers—two for all of them, making the system being configured in this example a stratum 3 server. The polling interval (under poll) is the time in seconds between time checks, and other columns provide additional information. The asterisk next to tempus.luna.edu indicates that it has been selected as the primary source. The other two are still good (as indicated by the plus signs next to their names) and are being used as backups and sanity checks for the primary source's signal.

If your network has many Unix-like systems, you can install NTP on all of them. Use one or two local systems as time servers for your entire network and configure the rest of the systems so that their NTP servers point to your primary NTP server. Chances are you'll want to make your network's primary NTP server the one you use for Samba's time server, too, although you could configure your network differently. Certainly the degradation in accuracy created by a single-level stratum increase, particularly on a local network, is unlikely to be very important.

One additional point deserves mention. Instead of using NET TIME to synchronize a Windows NT/200x/XP system to a Samba server's time, you can use a variant to set the time to that maintained by an NTP server:

```
C:\> NET TIME /SETSNTP:time.server
```

This command sets the time to that maintained by *time.server*, using the Simple NTP (SNTP) protocol, which is a subset of the full NTP. If a server runs both NTP and Samba, there's little reason to favor one form over the other for its clients except that Windows 9x/Me systems don't support the SNTP option. You might use this option if an NTP server that doesn't run Samba is closer to the system whose time you want to set, though.

Summary

No network protocol is an island. Samba is no exception to this rule; it interacts with other protocols in various ways, ranging from delivery of the same files using multiple protocols to more subtle effects regarding login protocols and the like. By far the greatest potential for important interactions comes with other file sharing protocols, though. Two file-sharing servers are likely to be used in similar ways by clients and to access overlapping sets of files. Ensuring that the protocols don't cause problems for each other is, therefore, quite important in this situation. Fortunately, Samba's defaults work fairly well in most cases, although you might want to tweak some configurations to obtain improved results. Samba can also be used to re-export directories or printers, serving as an intermediary between two otherwise incompatible systems. Finally, Samba can deliver the correct time to an entire network of computers, helping to keep your many computers' clocks synchronized.

Part Four
Samba Tips and Tricks

#### CHAPTER 13

Using GUI Configuration Tools

MOST OF THIS BOOK focuses on administering Samba via its text-based configuration files—mainly smb.conf. Many tools enable Samba configuration via point-and-click interfaces, though. These tools can be very helpful for new Samba administrators or for those who don't need to do much with the server. Even experienced administrators might find these tools helpful for quick jobs or in unusual circumstances, such as when administering an unfamiliar Samba system. These tools have the advantage of preventing configuration errors caused by mistyped parameter names, incorrect parameter placement, and so on. They can't prevent more fundamental errors, though, such as creating a read/write share when a read-only one would be more appropriate. Also, some of these tools provide access to a very limited range of Samba options; you may have no choice but to delve into the raw configuration files to accomplish certain tasks.

This chapter covers three main tools or tool classes: OS-specific tools, Webmin, and the Samba Web Administration Tool (SWAT). The OS-specific tools described in this chapter are those that ship with Mac OS X and Red Hat Linux. As a general rule, these tools are the least flexible, but they're often the most convenient for new administrators. Webmin is a third-party add-on package that supports administering much more than Samba on a wide range of platforms. SWAT ships with Samba and provides the most complete Samba administration of any GUI tool. Both Webmin and SWAT support administration locally and from remote computers.

Using OS-Specific Tools

Several Unix-like OSs, and particularly those that aim to be friendly to desktop users, provide facilities to configure Samba using their OS-wide GUI configuration tools. These tools vary substantially in how they work, so if you don't see your OS in this chapter, you may want to consult its documentation to learn about any tools it might provide. If such utilities exist, chances are they'll be similar to the tools described here in broad strokes although not in the details.

Mac OS X Tools

Mac OS X 10.2 and later ship with Samba and include at least minimal GUI configuration tools. Mac OS X 10.3 ships with Samba 3.0, but earlier versions of Mac OS X ship with earlier versions of Samba. If you're running an earlier version of Mac OS X, you can still install and run Samba, but you'll need to activate and configure it through some means other than utilities provided with the OS.

Mac OS X's default Samba configuration tools are quite limited. To begin, you must start the Samba server. Mac OS X enables you to do so by using the Sharing panel in System Preferences. Locate the Windows File Sharing item in the Services tab and be sure it's enabled (as indicated by a check mark in the box in the On column). Figure 13-1 demonstrates this configuration. When this service is active, Mac OS X runs Samba via xinetd, as described in Chapter 3. Mac OS X provides separate smbd and nmbd files in /etc/xinetd.d to launch these servers; the GUI tools change the disable lines in these files to activate or deactivate the servers.

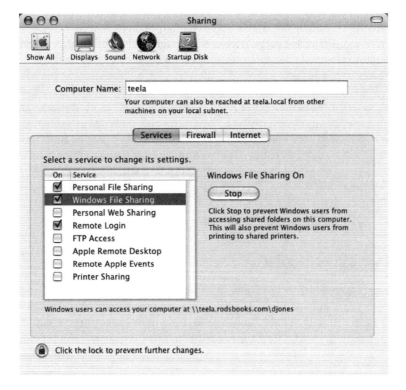

Figure 13-1. Mac OS X provides a GUI tool to activate Samba, but this tool provides no means of configuring Samba's features.

Of course, activating Samba isn't all that's required to use it. Mac OS X's Samba configuration file (/etc/smb.conf) ships with a default encrypt passwords setting of Yes, so you must store SMB/CIFS encrypted passwords. Mac OS X 10.2 requires you to set a Samba encrypted password using smbpasswd or the Accounts pane in System Preferences. Using the latter GUI tool, select a user and be sure the Allow User to Log In from Windows option is checked. If it's not (it isn't by default), check it. You'll then be asked to enter a password.

Mac OS X 10.3 uses a special auth methods option in smb.conf to provide for better integration of Samba and Mac OS X passwords. For this reason, no special password configuration is required once you've activated the Samba server. When you log in, use your normal Mac OS X username and password. The usual Mac OS X account management tools keep the passwords synchronized.

These GUI tools are the only ones provided with Mac OS X for Samba configuration. Notably absent from these tools is any way to set important global options (such as the machine's workgroup) or to define shares. The default configuration sets the system to operate in a workgroup called WORKGROUP and creates a [homes] share and a [printers] share. To do anything more complex, you must either edit smb.conf by hand or use other GUI tools, such as Webmin or SWAT.

NOTE   A third-party open-source package, the Samba Server Package (SSP; http://xamba.sourceforge.net/ssp/) provides an extension to the standard Mac OS GUI Samba configuration tools for Mac OS X 10.1 and 10.2. The package's primary author has abandoned development of SSP, though, so it doesn't work with Mac OS X 10.3, at least not as of February 2004. Somebody else might conceivably pick up SSP development in the future, though, so it might be worth checking the Web site.

Red Hat Linux Tools

Red Hat Linux has long shipped with Samba configuration tools. Some versions used a program called Linuxconf (http://www.solucorp.qc.ca/linuxconf/), which is a general-purpose Linux administration tool similar to Webmin in many ways. Red Hat has been moving away from Linuxconf for some time, though, in favor of custom administration tools. For instance, recent versions, such as Red Hat 9 and Fedora 1, use their own Samba Server Configuration tool. This program is installed from a package called redhat-config-samba, and you can launch it by typing its name (**redhat-config-samba**) in an xterm window or by selecting Server Settings ➤ Samba Server from the Red Hat menu. (If you launch this program as a non-root user, it will ask you for the root password before proceeding.) The result is the Samba Server Configuration window shown in Figure 13-2 although the list of shares may be empty or contain entries not shown in Figure 13-2.

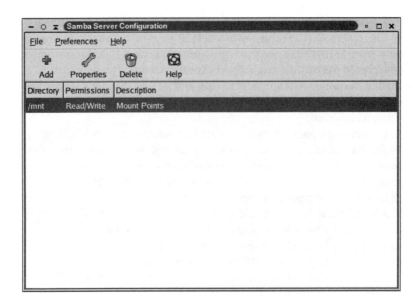

Figure 13-2. Red Hat's Samba Server Configuration tool presents a list of shares in its main window and hides global configuration options in its menus.

CAUTION Samba Server Configuration tends to choke on options it doesn't understand. Unfortunately, this includes some perfectly valid options. For instance, the tool uses `path` rather than `directory`, and if a configuration file includes a `directory` parameter, Samba Server Configuration will fail to load. If the program doesn't load, launch it from an xterm or similar window and examine the text output. Near the end should be an error message that identifies the line the program couldn't parse. You may be able to get the program working by manually editing the file to remove or change the line.

Samba Server Configuration provides two dialog boxes you can use to change global Samba options and to modify Samba accounts:

Server Settings: Pick Preferences ➤ Server Settings to bring up the Server Settings dialog box. You can set the server's workgroup, a description, and a few security options using this dialog box.

Samba Users: Pick Preferences ➤ Samba Users to bring up the Samba Users dialog box. This dialog box displays a list of users in the `smbpasswd` file and enables you to add, delete, or edit an account. (Editing an account, in this context, means changing its password.)

To add a share, click the Add icon in the icon bar or select File ➤ Add Share from the menu. To edit an existing share, select it from the list and click the Properties icon in the icon bar or select File ➤ Properties from the menu bar. Either way, the result is a dialog box like the one shown in Figure 13-3. (It's called Edit Samba Share if you edit an existing share, but it's called Create Samba Share if you choose to create a new share.) Using this dialog box, you can change the directory to be shared, change a description, set permissions to read-only or read/write, and restrict access to particular users. When creating new shares, Samba Server Configuration bases the share name on the name of the shared directory, and you can't change this value.

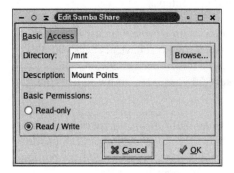

Figure 13-3. Samba Server Configuration provides very basic share-creation and share-editing options.

Overall, Samba Server Configuration is a useful tool for creating simple shares on a simple server. This package provides no support for more sophisticated Samba options, though. To use those features, you'll need to edit smb.conf manually or use other tools, such as Webmin or SWAT.

Using Webmin

The first of the cross-platform GUI configuration tools for Samba is Webmin. Its functionality isn't limited to Samba configuration; it's designed to handle a wide variety of servers, basic startup systems, and so on. It does this by using configuration modules designed for specific servers and OSs. Webmin can make a good tool for handling Samba in addition to many other OS components. As a Web-based tool, you can access Webmin from a Web browser running on the server computer itself or, depending upon how it's configured, from other computers.

CAUTION Running Webmin poses at least a small security risk. Any server such as Webmin may have a bug or misconfiguration that could leave your system vulnerable to outside attacks. Using Webmin's configuration options to restrict the client IP addresses it will serve can help reduce this risk. So can firewall rules on the server itself or your subnet's router. (Chapter 11 describes firewall configuration with respect to Samba. Similar measures are useful for Webmin.)

Obtaining and Installing Webmin

Webmin is available from http://www.webmin.com and ships with many Unix-like OSs. The list of supported OSs is available on the Webmin site and includes FreeBSD, NetBSD, OpenBSD, many Linux distributions, Mac OS X, Solaris, IRIX, and more. If your OS ships with Webmin, you may want to install it from an OS-specific package, such as an RPM Package Manager (RPM) file for many Linux distributions. If not, or if you prefer to use the original Webmin, follow these steps:

1. Ensure that Perl5 is installed on your system. The perl binary is usually stored in /usr/bin or /usr/local/bin. If you don't have it, check your OS distribution medium. If you can't find it there, check http://www.perl.com to find it—either for a prepared package for your OS or for the source code you can compile locally.

2. If desired, install a Secure Sockets Layer (SSL) encryption package, such as OpenSSL, which is available from http://www.openssl.org and ships with many Unix-like OSs. Doing so will enable you to select the SSL encryption option, which greatly enhances Webmin's security.

3. Download the Webmin tarball from its Web site. I used webmin-1.110.tar.gz as a reference for this description, but a more recent version may be available to you.

4. Change to a destination subdirectory, such as /usr/local, and uncompress the tarball. On most platforms, typing **tar -xvfz webmin-1.110.tar.gz** (or a modified version to fit the filename of your archive) will work. Chances are you'll need to be root to do this; although you can install Webmin in a user directory, for security reasons it's best to install the package into a system directory.

5. Change into the resulting Webmin directory, webmin-1.110 in this example.

6. As root, type **./setup.sh**. This command launches the setup script, which installs Webmin on your system and configures it. The script asks for various pieces of information, such as the location of perl, the port on which it should run (the default is 10,000), a username and password, and whether to use SSL encryption. During this process, Webmin should correctly identify your OS. If it doesn't, check to be sure that Webmin supports your OS. You might be able to get away with configuring Webmin for an earlier version of your OS or for a very closely related one, but such an attempt might produce strange errors.

A couple of points about Webmin security deserve attention:

Username and password: Webmin asks for a login username (the default is admin) and password. It's best to use an unusual name and unique password to make it harder for miscreants to guess how to access your Webmin server, should they be able to connect to it. For instance, if you use wadm as the username, outsiders aren't likely to be able to guess the username used to break in, even if they somehow guess the correct password.

SSL encryption: If possible, use the SSL encryption option. Doing this will encrypt your administrative username and password, as well as other Webmin traffic, improving security. If you enable SSL encryption, Webmin will *not* respond to unencrypted connection attempts.

At this point, Webmin should have started itself running and (if you so specified during step 6) set itself up to run when the system restarts. Typically, it does this by creating SysV startup scripts, but details vary from one OS to another. You can therefore move on to accessing Webmin, tightening its security a bit, and using it.

Accessing Webmin

Immediately after being installed, Webmin is configured to accept logins from any address. For instance, to access Webmin installed on tap.example.com, you'd enter https://tap.example.com:10000 into any Web browser's URL field, on any computer. (If you elected not to use SSL encryption, though, you'd use http:// rather than https:// at the start of the URL.) If you want to access Webmin from the server computer itself, you can substitute localhost for tap.example.com. In any event, if you enabled SSL encryption, your Web browser will notify you that it can't authenticate the site's *certificate*. This is because SSL works, in part, by using encryption that relies upon cryptographic *signatures* contained in a certificate. These signed certificates are issued by a handful of authorities, but unless you obtain and install such a certificate, the one issued by Webmin will appear suspicious to Web browsers. In this specific case, there really isn't a problem, so you should tell the browser to accept the certificate. The precise form this notification takes varies from one browser to another; Figure 13-4 shows one example, from Galeon 1.3.3.

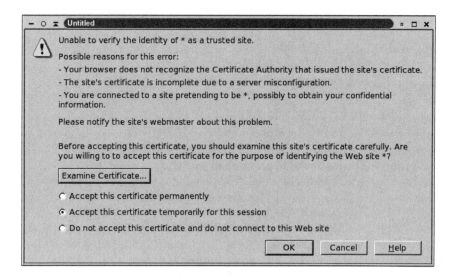

Figure 13-4. When Webmin uses SSL encryption, Web browsers will complain that they can't verify the server's identity.

CAUTION Accepting certificates that your Web browser can't authenticate is generally a risky practice. If your browser presents such a notice when you're using a commercial Web site, it could mean that the site has been compromised and any private data you send is being intercepted by a cracker. (On the other hand, it could also mean that your browser's list of certificate authorities is merely outdated.) In the case of Webmin, though, you can be reasonably certain that the server is who it should be, particularly if you're accessing it via the localhost address.

Once you accept the certificate, Webmin presents you with a login page in which you enter the username and password you specified when configuring the server. If you enter this information correctly, you'll see the main Webmin page, as shown in Figure 13-5. The options along the top (Webmin, System, Servers, and so on) control broad configuration categories. When you select one, new options appear below this strip, such as Change Language and Theme, Usermin Configuration, and Webmin Actions log in Figure 13-5.

Figure 13-5. Webmin breaks system configuration down into several categories, each of which is accessible from the main menu.

To begin, you may want to restrict Webmin to accept only local accesses. You can do so by selecting the Webmin Configuration option and then the Port and Access option on the resulting page. This brings up the Port and Access page, shown in Figure 13-6. Change the Listen on IP Address option from All to the data entry box, type 127.0.0.1 in this box, and click Save. This action will make Webmin accessible to only the local computer, and only if you enter localhost or 127.0.0.1 in the URL entry field of your browser. Such a configuration is good from a security point of view, but if you want to use Webmin for remote administration, it won't do. In that case, you should leave the original configuration alone and use firewall rules to restrict access to port 10,000 (or some other port, if you run Webmin on another port) so that only the clients you'll use for the purpose can access Webmin.

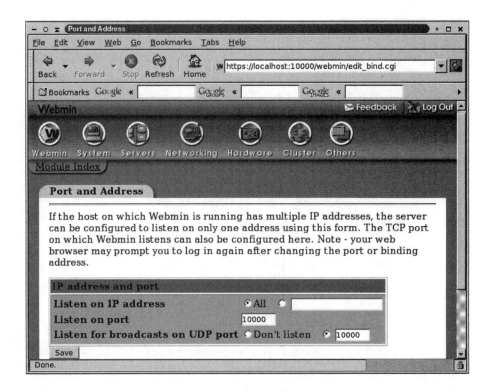

Figure 13-6. For added security, you can configure Webmin to listen on only certain ports and addresses.

After changing any option in Webmin, be sure to click the Save button. If you forget this step and back out of the window using your browser's arrow buttons, Webmin will discard your changes. (More precisely, Webmin won't even *receive* your changes; they'll be present in your Web browser but will never be sent.)

Using Webmin for Samba Administration

After configuring Webmin to accept only local connections (if you decide to do this), click the Servers item in the top list of Webmin modules. This link reveals the servers you can configure through Webmin. One of these modules should be Samba Windows File Sharing. Click this item to bring up the main Samba configuration module, shown in Figure 13-7.

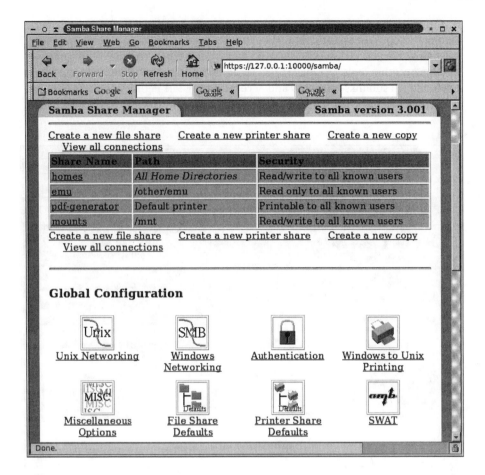

Figure 13-7. Webmin's Samba configuration module includes many options and categories.

The Webmin Samba configuration module displays quite a few options—more than Figure 13-7 can show. Options accessible from this page include the following:

Share Manager: At the top of the page is a list of all the shares defined on the server. Click the name of a share to configure it, as described shortly, or click one of the share creation options above the share list to create a new share.

Global Configuration: The next section of options leads to assorted global configuration pages. The categories are described in more detail shortly.

Samba Users: The next section (not visible in Figure 13-7) provides user administration capabilities, such as the capacity to change passwords.

Samba Management: Two buttons at the bottom of the page (not visible in Figure 13-7) enable you to stop or restart Samba.

Compared to the Samba management of Mac OS X and Red Hat's Samba Server Configuration tools, Webmin provides very thorough share management options. As shown in Figure 13-8, this tool lets you set the share name, directory, and comment, as do many other tools. This page provides additional options, though. Many of these are hidden in sublinks—Security and Access Control, File Permissions, File Naming, and Miscellaneous Options.

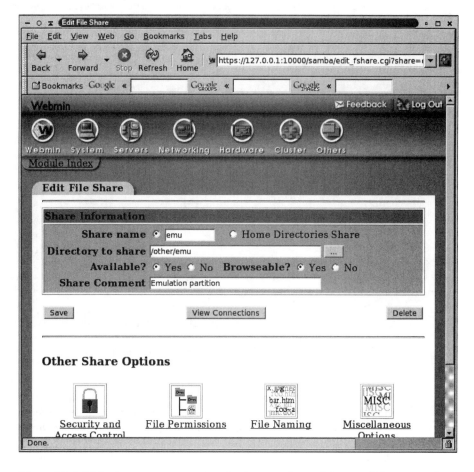

Figure 13-8. Webmin supports most Samba share options, giving you better control over your Samba server than many other GUI tools.

The links in the Global Configuration area provide the ability to tune most of Samba's [global] configuration options, as well as many share-level parameters that are frequently set in the [global] section. The two most important links are the Windows Networking and Authentication options. Figure 13-9 shows the Windows Networking Options page. It enables you to set the critical workgroup name, as well as setting NBNS/WINS server options, the OS level, and other important features. The Authentication area provides options to enable or disable Samba's use of encrypted passwords, specify a password chat, and set up a username mapping list.

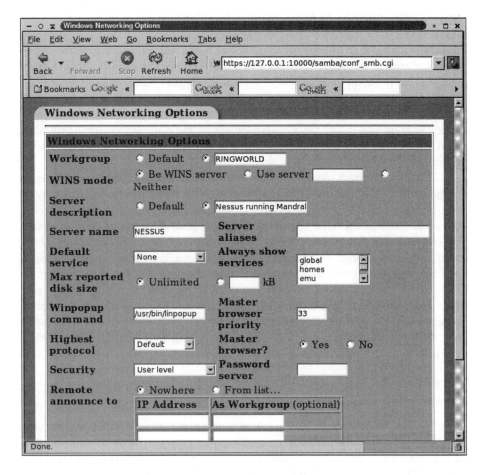

Figure 13-9. Many important global Samba options appear in the Windows Networking area of Webmin.

In the Samba Users area, Webmin provides several links to user management tools. The most important of these in everyday use is probably the Edit Samba Users and Passwords link, which brings up a list of Samba users. Click a username to change a password or set various account options, such as disabling the account or making the account a machine trust account. Note that these options don't modify the smb.conf file itself; instead, they use Samba configuration tools, such as smbpasswd, to modify other Samba files.

NOTE If you want to create an entirely new account, you should start with the Webmin Users and Groups link, which is accessible from the System area. After you create a local Unix account, you can add the Samba account for the user with the Webmin Samba module.

Webmin's Capabilities and Limitations

Overall, Webmin is an extremely powerful GUI configuration tool. It provides access to far more options than do most OS-specific GUI configuration tools. You can even use Webmin to set up unusual shares, such as fax shares (described in Chapter 6) or shares that use scripts (described in Chapter 14). Webmin's support for non-Samba configuration can also be a great boon if you want a general-purpose GUI system administration tool. In fact, you might consider running Webmin even if you're familiar with Samba in order to help you administer an unfamiliar OS or other servers with which you're less comfortable.

Webmin isn't perfect, of course. Its clusterings of options don't exactly match those of the smb.conf file, and some highly advanced options are presented next to very common ones, which can unnecessarily clutter the display if you don't need to use the advanced features. A few options don't appear at all; for instance, options related to domain controller duties are missing from Webmin. Webmin's support for non-Samba configuration, although an advantage, is also a drawback; an intruder who manages to break into your system via Webmin can easily change just about any subsystem that runs on your computer. Of course, an intruder who can modify the Samba configuration can quickly gain this sort of control by sharing /etc, so this problem isn't much greater than the similar problem of running any remote Samba administration tool. Webmin's support for encryption and binding only to the localhost interface can help minimize this risk, too.

Using SWAT

SWAT is an extremely powerful GUI and remote administration tool for Samba. Like Webmin, SWAT is accessible through a Web browser and can be used to administer a Samba server from the server itself or from another computer. SWAT comes with Samba although some Samba binary distributions break it off into a separate package. Accessing SWAT is similar to accessing Webmin, but some details differ. Once you're in, SWAT closely mirrors the smb.conf file's structure and options.

Installing and Running SWAT

SWAT ships with Samba, but it's not really fully integrated with Samba. If you installed Samba from source code, SWAT's source code is located in the swat subdirectory. Nonetheless, it should have compiled and installed along with everything else. If you're unsure, look for a file called swat in your Samba installation tree:

```
$ find /usr/local/samba -name swat
```

This command (or one like it, adjusted for your installation directory) should locate the swat executable. A similar command should work even if you installed Samba from a binary package, but you may need to search all of /usr, or conceivably some other directory tree, to be sure you find the file. Most binary packages put swat is /usr/sbin, though, so check there before doing a full search.

If you can't find SWAT, you can either compile and install it from the source code or look for a binary package. In the latter case, the package is likely to be called swat, samba-swat, or something similar. Check your distribution's packages to locate the correct one.

Unlike Webmin, SWAT doesn't normally run automatically after you install it although some binary packages may set up xinetd configuration files to speed along the process. Typically, SWAT is run from a super server (inetd or xinetd). Chapter 3 describes super server configuration with respect to Samba proper. The process is similar for running SWAT. To begin, you should ensure that your /etc/services file has an entry for SWAT:

```
swat      901/tcp      # Samba Web Administration Tool
```

If your system uses inetd, you should then look for a line like the following in your /etc/inetd.conf file:

```
swat stream tcp nowait.400 root /usr/sbin/swat swat
```

If this line is present but commented out (by a hash mark, #, at the start of the line), uncomment it. If this line isn't present, add it, but be aware that you may need to make some changes, such as pointing to your swat binary if it's not in /usr/sbin. You may also want to run SWAT via TCP Wrappers, which on some systems requires calling a binary called tcpd instead of swat. (TCP Wrappers then calls the server referenced in the first parameter it receives.) Consult your OS's inetd.conf documentation if you have problems.

NOTE   Some OSs ship with inetd.conf entries that differ slightly from the one shown here. In general, it's best to work starting with whatever your distribution provided if your sample inetd.conf file has such an entry.

In the case of xinetd, look for a file called swat in your /etc/xinetd.d directory. If you can't find one, type **grep -ir swat /etc/xinetd***. This command searches for SWAT configurations in less-obvious files in /etc/xinetd.d and in /etc/xinetd.conf. Once you find it, a xinetd configuration for SWAT should look something like this:

```
service swat
{
        port            = 901
        socket_type     = stream
        wait            = no
        only_from       = 127.0.0.1
        user            = root
        server          = /usr/sbin/swat
        log_on_failure  += USERID
        disable         = yes
}
```

As with inetd configurations, xinetd configurations can vary in certain details, such as the location of the swat executable and even the presence of certain options. For instance, the only_from parameter in this example restricts SWAT to accept connections from only the local computer itself. As a general rule, this is a wise security precaution, but if you need to administer your Samba system from another computer, you may want to change this option. For instance, to accept logins from the local computer and from 192.168.78.6, change the line to read as follows:

```
only_from    = 127.0.0.1 192.168.78.6
```

No matter what else you change, if you see a line that reads disable = yes, change yes to no to enable SWAT. If you leave the configuration disabled, it won't do you much good!

Whether you use inetd or xinetd, you must tell the super server to reload its configuration after you change it to include SWAT. Chapter 3 describes the process for doing so. In brief, though, you should find the process ID (PID) number for the super server (**ps ax | grep inetd** should do the trick on most systems) and then pass the SIGHUP signal to the process with kill, as in **kill -HUP 3511** if ps showed the PID to be 3511. Alternatively, systems with SysV startup scripts frequently provide restart or reload options that will completely restart their super servers or reload their configuration files. Typing something such as **/etc/rc.d/init.d/xinetd reload** should work on such systems.

CAUTION   The restart option to a SysV startup script usually shuts down the server and then restarts it. Doing this with a super server may disconnect the users of protocols mediated by the super server, so you shouldn't do it unless you're having problems with other methods of restarting or know that nobody's connected. Using the reload option to the SysV startup script or the SIGHUP signal should be safer.

SWAT and Mac OS X

Unfortunately, running SWAT with Mac OS X can be a challenge, and the challenge varies with the SWAT version. Some users of Mac OS X prior to 10.3 have found that the SWAT binary isn't installed by default although this seems to vary with Mac OS X installation method and other factors. If SWAT isn't installed, you must track it down and install it. In any event, you must add an /etc/services entry for SWAT and enable the server. To do any good, you must enable the root account and password; you can do this by typing **sudo passwd root**. You'll be asked for your administrative account password, then for a new password for root, which you'll use to administer the system via SWAT. The instructions presented in "Installing and Running SWAT" are otherwise accurate.

Mac OS X 10.3 has changed its user authentication system, and these changes appear to be incompatible with SWAT. Attempting to log in as root or as an ordinary user fail. The only way I know to use SWAT on Mac OS X 10.3 is to pass it the -a option via the server_args line in the xinetd configuration. This option, though, disables authentication and puts SWAT into a demo mode in which anybody may make changes. It's therefore inadvisable to use this option on a production server. If you absolutely require SWAT access, use this option in conjunction with a very strict only_from line, such as only_from = 127.0.0.1. A better option may be to use Webmin for GUI Samba administration with Mac OS X.

Accessing SWAT

You can access SWAT using a Web browser, much as you can access Webmin. There are two important differences, though:

- By itself, SWAT doesn't support SSL encryption, so you should specify the hostname preceded by http://, not https://. (In fact, you can omit the protocol specification with most Web browsers.)

- SWAT runs on port 901 by default, so you append :901 to the URL rather than :10000. If you change the SWAT port by modifying the super server configuration, though, you should change the URL you use to match the new port number.

In sum, the URL you use will be http://localhost:901 to access SWAT running on the local computer. Change localhost to an appropriate hostname if you want to access SWAT remotely. When you enter this URL, your browser should pop up a window asking you for a username and password. You must enter your root username and password. (If you enter an ordinary user's username and password, SWAT will let you in but will provide only a subset of its features. Ordinary users can use SWAT to check on the server's status and to change their own passwords but little else.) Unlike Webmin, SWAT doesn't maintain its own username and password; instead, it relies upon the underlying Unix authentication system to handle this task. If you enter the correct password, SWAT should display its main page, shown in Figure 13-10. The main configuration options appear in a row near the top of the window (Home, Globals, Shares, and so on in Figure 13-10). These options mirror the smb.conf file structure, with sections for global parameters, file shares, and printer shares. Additional options enable you to return to this main page (Home) check the status of the server, view the raw configuration file, and administer passwords. The Wizard option was added to Samba 2.2 and enables you to quickly configure a system based on any of several prototypes. The links below the list of options point to documentation on various Samba components.

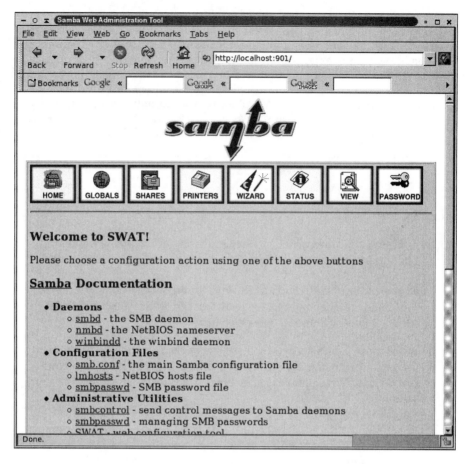

Figure 13-10. The SWAT configuration options mirror those of the Samba configuration file.

CAUTION Because SWAT doesn't support encryption, using it remotely means that your root password may be vulnerable to sniffing on your local network and on any intervening networks, depending upon your network hardware. For this reason, you should never use SWAT remotely except on secure local networks, so using the only_from parameter in a xinetd configuration to restrict remote access, as in the example presented earlier, is a good idea. Implementing similar restrictions with inetd requires configuring SWAT to work through TCP Wrappers or using local firewall rules.

Using SWAT for Samba Administration

SWAT more faithfully follows the smb.conf file's structure and option naming conventions than do most GUI Samba administration tools. As a general rule, you'll start with the Global link, which brings up the Global Variables page shown in Figure 13-11. Like several other SWAT configuration pages, this one offers a choice of views: Basic or Advanced. Figure 13-11 shows the Basic view, which provides access to the most commonly used parameters. Clicking Advanced brings up the Advanced view, which lists many more options, including quite a few very obscure ones.

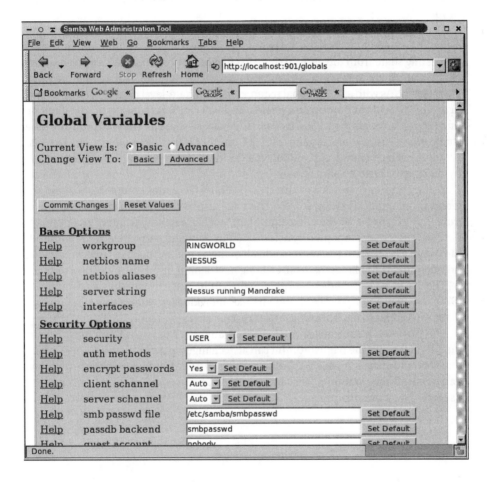

Figure 13-11. The SWAT Global Variables page displays configuration options that appear in the [global] *section of* smb.conf.

You can set most of the options in the Global area by typing a value into the text entry field or by selecting an option from a pop-up list. You can also click Set Default to set most parameters to their default values or Help to bring up another browser window with help on the item. (The help is in fact an HTML version of the smb.conf man page, scrolled to the option in question.) As with editing smb.conf directly, adjusting the workgroup name and password encryption options are the two most important settings for an initial configuration. The Global page provides access to both global-level options and those share-level options that are commonly used in the [global] section of smb.conf. When you're done making changes, click Commit Changes; if you back out using your browser's back arrow button, your changes will be lost.

When you're done changing the Global page, you can move on to share configuration. When you first click the Share link, you'll see remarkably little. You must pick an existing share from the pop-up share list to edit it or type in a new share name and click Create Share to create a new share. After you do this, the display will resemble Figure 13-12. As with editing global parameters, the share-level parameters are entered in text entry fields or pop-up entry fields, and you can set an option to its default or find help on any parameter. You can edit the [homes] share just as you'd edit any other share. When you're done, be sure to click Commit Changes to enable them. Do this *before* you select a new share, should you decide to do so. You can also delete a share by clicking the Delete Share option.

Editing printer shares is done much like editing file shares except that a slightly different set of options is available. Also, this page displays printers that are autoloaded from the /etc/printcap file or its equivalent just like ordinary printers except that their names are accompanied by asterisks (*) in the share name field. You should edit the [printers] share if you want to edit all of these; making changes to the individual printer shares will splinter them off, creating new definitions for the individual printers.

The Status page provides information on Samba, such as whether it's running (SWAT tells you about smbd, nmbd, and winbindd individually), what clients are connected to the server, and so on. You can also start or stop each server individually or as a group.

The Password page enables you to change any user's password. You must type in the username and the password. You can also change a password on another server if that server supports this access. Ordinary users can use this page to change their own passwords. Unlike Webmin, you can't use SWAT to add or delete users; you can only use it for password maintenance.

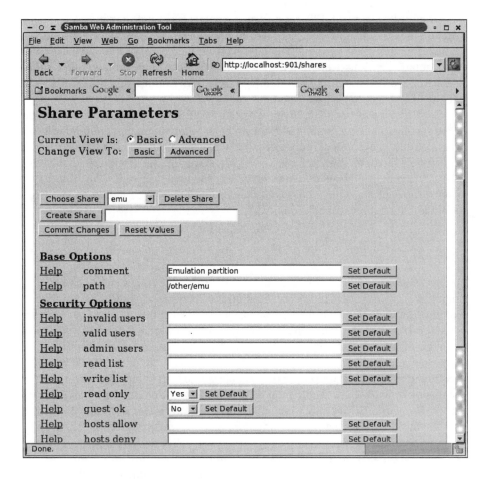

Figure 13-12. You must select a share from the drop-down list and click Choose Share or create a new share before changing share-level parameters.

SWAT's Capabilities and Limitations

SWAT provides the most complete access to Samba features of any GUI Samba administration tool. Its close mirroring of the structure of smb.conf and its features makes SWAT a good tool if you're familiar with smb.conf but can't remember an option's name; just scroll down the list of options until you find what you want. SWAT's also a better tool for learning about smb.conf than most other tools because the close parallels in structure mean that as you learn about SWAT, you also learn about smb.conf.

Despite the fact that SWAT handles more smb.conf features than most GUI configuration tools, it's not quite perfect. The most notable missing feature is the ability to handle included files. The include parameter in smb.conf enables you to place some configuration options in another file, but smb.conf doesn't support this option, so you can't edit configurations that rely upon it using SWAT. Another missing feature is the ability to add and delete user accounts.

SWAT is also a security risk. Unlike Webmin, SWAT doesn't operate with encryption. (You could access it through an SSH tunnel to add encryption, but doing so will require additional configuration on the SWAT client computer, and you'll also need to run an SSH server on the Samba server system.) Overall, SWAT is best used only from the server computer itself or at most only from your local network. SWAT doesn't provide any options to restrict its own access, so you should be sure to do so using xinetd, TCP Wrappers, or a firewall.

Summary

Most experienced Samba administrators configure their computers by directly modifying smb.conf and other configuration files using a text editor. GUI Samba administration tools are available, though, and can be helpful for new administrators, when you're unfamiliar with a system, or when you just want to be sure you don't accidentally mistype parameters or multiple-choice values. Mac OS X and Red Hat Linux are two popular examples of OSs that ship with Samba configuration tools. These tools tend to be quite bare-bones; they enable you to start or stop the server and perhaps configure a few simple shares. To do more, you'll need to move on to other tools. One of these is Webmin, which is a cross-platform tool for administering Samba and many other parts of an OS. Another tool is SWAT, which ships with Samba and supports configuring Samba alone. Both Webmin and SWAT are Web-based tools and so can be accessed from the Samba server or from other computers, depending upon how you configure them. Such Web-based tools can be convenient, but they're also potential security risks, so you should be sure to restrict access to these servers if you run them.

#### CHAPTER 14

Using Samba Scripts

SMALL'S PRIMARY PURPOSE is to function as a file and print server—to store and deliver files and make printers accessible to clients. As such, most people think of Samba as being a tool simply for file storage and printer access and perhaps as a tool to perform SMB/CIFS support functions, such as handling NetBIOS Name Server (NBNS) duties. Samba's design, though, gives it the option of performing much more dynamic tasks. In particular, Samba can run scripts or other programs under specific circumstances. This ability means that Samba can dynamically process information on behalf of clients.

One common and simple example of this capability is printer shares; when a client submits a print job, Samba calls outside programs to deliver the print job to the local printing system. This capability can be used in other ways, though—even to perform tasks that are completely unrelated to printing. Scripts can also be attached to ordinary file shares in order to perform some action before or after the user accesses the share. A few administrative functions support scripting operations, too, and these can be used in creative ways. Finally, in a domain configuration Samba can store scripts that are run by clients when they log onto the domain, which means Samba can control client operations to some extent.

Samba Script Types

Samba supports many different types of scripts. These scripts vary in their capabilities and uses. Before proceeding with descriptions of these scripts and their uses, you should know something about the capabilities of each of these script types so you know which one to use for any given purpose.

 NOTE I refer to Samba's ability to run external programs as a scripting capability because, in practice, you're likely to create a script to do whatever job you want to do. You could call a binary executable with one of these tools, though—either a standard system tool (perhaps with some arguments passed to it) or a program you write yourself in C, C++, or some other compiled language instead of writing a script. Binary programs are often less portable across different OSs and even across OS upgrades than are scripts, though, which can complicate system maintenance when you make such changes.

File Share Access Scripts

Samba can run scripts when users connect to (preexec) or disconnect from (postexec) a share. You can specify the scripts to run on a share-by-share basis and define separate connect and disconnect scripts. You can even tell Samba to execute these scripts with root privileges, although doing so is potentially quite risky. Normally, you'll write a short script to perform some specific task or simply execute a short command with this capability. Some of the things you might do with file share access scripts include the following:

Mounting a disk: If you want to share removable media, you might use the preexec script to mount the disk and postexec to unmount it.

Creating a CD-R: You can use preexec and postexec scripts to clear a directory and store its contents on a CD-R (or other removable media), respectively. This can be a good way to share a CD-R burner with an office full of users.

Backups: File share access scripts can be used as part of a backup system. This use is described in more detail in Chapter 16.

Initiating network connections: You can use Samba as a means of detecting user activity so as to perform network operations unrelated to Samba. For instance, a preexec script might launch a Virtual Network Computing (VNC) server in the user's name, enabling the user to perform GUI logons to the Samba server.

Batch data processing: You can use preexec scripts to prepare a directory tree and postexec scripts to perform processing on data files the user leaves in the directory tree. This facility can be helpful if you want to give users the ability to run data-processing tools on a fast server but don't want to give them full shell access to the server.

Logging: Samba's default logs are adequate for many purposes, but you may want some additional information, or you may want a simple summary log that shows when users have initiated Samba connections. A preexec script can be perfect for this role.

Share preparation: You can write a script that prepares a share for use in various ways. For instance, a script might check for specific permissions on critical files or back up files that might be corrupted by buggy client software or through accidental actions on the part of users.

Because Samba's share access scripts can run just about any program, their use is limited mainly by your imagination. If you want to be able to remotely trigger an action, a Samba share access script is one way to do it. Of course, it's best if the action is in some way related to the use of a Samba file share. If it's not, you might want to consider another method of launching the program, such as using Secure Shell (SSH) to launch a program remotely.

One important limitation of file access scripts is that the logout script (specified by postexec) may not be launched in a reliable or timely fashion. Depending upon the client OS and how the user accesses the share, it may be necessary to take drastic steps to control disconnection and the running of the postexec script. Methods to do this include the following:

Windows 9*x*/Me: Logging off the computer (via the Start ➤ Log Off *Username* desktop menu item) will shut down a connection. If the share is permanently mapped to a drive letter, right-clicking its icon and selecting Disconnect will also terminate the connection. You can't simply map a share and then disconnect it, though; the share must be automatically mapped when you log on for this method to work. As a last resort, shutting down or rebooting the computer will do the job.

Windows NT/200*x*/XP: These OSs are likely to terminate a connection a few seconds after you close the last window or application that's accessing the share. As with Windows 9*x*/Me, to terminate a connection if a share is mapped to a drive letter, you must right-click the drive icon and select Disconnect from the menu. Logging off should also terminate all open SMB/CIFS connections.

Unix and Samba: If you connect to a share using smbclient, exiting from the program should close the link. If you mount the share, unmounting it should do the trick.

max connections parameter: This parameter tells Samba how many connections it should accept to a share. The default value of 0 means there's no limit. Some scripted shares will function poorly if more than one user tries to use them simultaneously, though, so setting max connections = 1 may be in order. This parameter affects the running of a postexec script only in that it can prevent the script from running inappropriately. For instance, it can prevent two users from connecting to a share that uses scripts that assume only one user.

deadtime parameter: The global Samba deadtime parameter lets you set an inactivity timeout period (specified in minutes) after which a connection to a share is terminated. After this period of inactivity, Samba closes the connection and executes the postexec script, provided no files are open. (Some programs maintain open files, and such activities will defeat the deadtime parameter. Other programs, even when they seem to have open files, don't maintain open file connections to the server.) Setting a low deadtime value will ensure that the postexec script executes, even if it's after a delay of a few minutes. This parameter works with all clients.

NOTE Most SMB/CIFS clients have auto-reconnect features. If a connection is dropped unexpectedly, the client attempts to reconnect. Thus, setting a low `deadtime` shouldn't cause anything more than brief delays as clients attempt to reconnect, should they be accidentally disconnected. (One exception is Mac OS X, which tends to become confused if the server disconnects itself unexpectedly.) Of course, if the server breaks the connection before the user has finished using the share, the `postexec` script will execute prematurely, which could have very negative consequences, depending upon the purpose of the script. For instance, you probably don't want to accidentally burn a CD-R with half the files it should contain because the user was distracted by a phone call while placing files in the target directory.

Unfortunately, sometimes applications leave files open even when the user closes all the file windows. This practice can prevent the client system from closing the connection even when you instruct it to do so. If this happens, you may be forced to log out of a Windows session or even restart the computer to get the `postexec` script to execute. For users of Unix clients, the `lsof` command can be handy in locating open files on a mounted SMB/CIFS share; type `lsof | grep /path/to/share`, where */path/to/share* is the path to the mounted share. The result should be a list of the open files and the applications with which they're associated. Quit the applications, and you should be able to unmount the share.

Sometimes clients crash. When this happens, the TCP connection is eventually dropped and Samba is notified. The `postexec` script, if present, should then run.

The upcoming section "Using `preexec` and `postexec` Scripts" covers creating and using this type of script.

Magic Scripts

File share access scripts execute when a client opens or closes a share. Another type of file share–related script runs when a client writes a particular file. This script type is known as a *magic script*. These scripts are implemented by the `magic script` parameter (which points to a filename that, when written by a client, is executed as a script) and the `magic output` parameter (which defines a file to accept the script's output). Magic scripts have always been experimental, and in my experience they haven't worked since Samba 2.0.5. They may be removed from Samba in the future. All in all, they're best left unused; you can accomplish what they're designed to do in other ways that are far more reliable.

Printer Scripts

Printer scripts are specified with the `print command` parameter, which is described in Chapter 6. Unlike file share scripts, `print command` is a single script that executes once for each file that's submitted for printing. Thus, you don't need to be concerned about the unreliable disconnection of certain clients, which makes `print command` a superior method of implementing certain scripting tasks.

Printer scripts normally take a single file as an argument, although you can pass additional parameters to these scripts to have them do more. The file, though, is the one submitted as a print job. In normal printer shares, this file will be a PostScript or printer-specific file; however, as described in the upcoming section "Using `print command`," you can pass any file type to this script. This fact means you can use `print command` to perform many of the same tasks that can be handled by `preexec` and `postexec` scripts. You can burn a CD-R by passing an image file or archive with the CD-R's contents to the share, perform data processing on a single data file or archived collection of data files, and so on. In some of these cases, you must find ways to bypass the client's normal printer queue, though. This queue is likely to try to process the file using a printer driver, which will corrupt the data. (An exception is if you want to receive printer-formatted data. For instance, a queue to generate graphics files from textual documents might work well if it receives PostScript files that can be processed with Ghostscript.)

In addition to `print command`, Samba provides several ancillary parameters that point to printing support tools, such as `lpq command` and `lprm command`. Pointing these parameters to appropriate tools may be worthwhile when you need to adjust them for your printing system or when you're dealing with a nonprinting task that nonetheless maps well onto printing concepts, such as creating Portable Document Format (PDF) files from a print job. Chances are you won't need or want to use these parameters when you use `print command` in ways that aren't closely related to printing, though.

Overall, `print command` works well for batch processing tasks. Give it a file, which may in fact be an archive that contains multiple files, and the script can do just about anything with the data. This contrasts with file share access scripts, which often work best as supplements to normal file shares. Using these scripts for some nonprinting tasks is covered in the upcoming section "Using `print command`."

Processing WinPopUp Messages

SMB/CIFS incorporates a simple messaging feature referred to as the Windows Messenger Service. (In fact, two services exist that provide similar functionality.) In Windows 9*x*/Me, this service is often used via a program called WinPopUp. In Windows NT/200*x*/XP, the NET SEND command can send a message, and received messages appear automatically in small dialog boxes. A user can employ WinPopup to send a short message directly to another user. To support this functionality, Samba provides a parameter called `message command` that specifies an external program to run when Samba receives a Windows Messenger Service message. One popular tool for this purpose is called LinPopUp (`http://linpopup2.sourceforge.net`). Figure 14-1 shows LinPopUp in action.

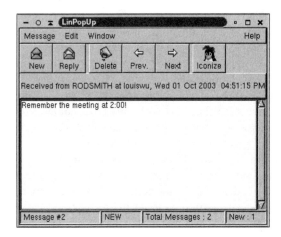

Figure 14-1. LinPopUp enables Unix users to send and receive Windows Messenger Service messages.

This command takes the usual variables (described in Chapter 2, and particularly in Table 2-1). The message that's received is actually stored in a file, so you must pass the command the %s variable (which is also used to identify a print job filename). The command should also delete the file when it's done. The following is an example that uses LinPopUp:

```
message command = /usr/bin/linpopup "%f" "%m" %s; rm %s
```

Another way to process these messages is to e-mail them. For instance, you might send the messages using the mail utility:

```
message command = mail -s "Message from %f on %m" fastaire < %s; rm %s
```

This command sends the message to the local user fastaire with a title that reads Message from USER on MACHINE, where USER is a username and MACHINE is a NetBIOS name. One problem with this approach, and indeed with WinPopUp messages generally, is that they're addressed to machines, not to users. Thus, this example hard-codes the recipient—fastaire in this case. (You could send mail to another system if you like, as in fastaire@tap.luna.edu.) LinPopUp works under the assumption that a computer has just one user. If more than one is logged on, both will see new messages appear. If multiple users access the computer sequentially, they can all see all the messages that haven't been deleted.

One problem with Windows Messenger Service messages is that receipt isn't guaranteed; you can't be sure that a message you send will be received. As a general rule, e-mail is likely to be more reliable. A few tools, such as Snort (http://www.snort.org), can send Windows Messenger Service messages regarding their operation. You might use this to help monitor security in real time, although of course very serious problems should be flagged in a more reliable way, such as scripts that will page a system administrator. You could also use the system to send messages to ordinary users concerning imminent system events, such as system reboots. Despite the fact that users aren't guaranteed to see such messages, the possibility of notifying them of the event is better than not sending any notification at all.

Administrative Control Scripts

Several administrative control parameters actually call scripts or other outside programs to do their work. For the most part, these tools are described elsewhere in this book; however, as they do enable you to call external programs, they deserve some mention in this chapter. These parameters are as follows:

`passwd program`: This parameter tells Samba what program to call to change the Unix password. It's used in conjunction with `passwd chat`, which controls the interactions with this program. It's called only when `unix password sync = Yes`.

`add user script`: The script pointed to by this parameter adds a user to the Unix account database if the SMB/CIFS authentication succeeds but no local user is found. It's intended for use on systems that rely upon a domain controller for SMB/CIFS authentication.

`delete user script`: This parameter points to a script that deletes a user from the local Unix database. It's used when an authorized Windows client deletes a user from the domain.

`add group script`: This parameter works much like `add user script` except that it points to a script that adds a local Unix group when a new user logon requires that group to be present.

`delete group script`: The script pointed to by this parameter deletes a local Unix group.

`add user to group script`: Windows user and group management tools enable adding users to groups. This script supports this feature by manipulating the Unix group database at the direction of an authorized Windows system.

`delete user from group script`: When an appropriately authorized Windows client deletes a user from a domain, the Samba server calls this script to implement the change.

`set primary group script`: This script changes the user's primary group identification at the direction of an authorized client.

`add machine script`: The script pointed to by this parameter is called when a domain controller adds a machine to its domain.

`add share command`: Samba 2.2.*x* and later supports management of shares via Windows share management tools on remote computers. To support this feature, the `add share command` parameter defines a script that does the work, including creating the necessary directory and `smb.conf` share definition.

`change share command`: In Samba 2.2.*x* and later, this parameter points to a script that can modify the features of a share on direction of an external client that's authorized to make such changes.

`enumports command`: In the context of Windows' handling of PC hardware, a *port* is an interface to a printer or other external hardware. SMB/CIFS supports a command that returns the names of available ports. Normally, Samba returns information on only one port, called the Samba Printer Port. You can specify a script that generates a list of ports, one per line, if you have a client that needs more information.

`shutdown script`: This parameter points to a script that can shut down the Samba server computer at the direction of an appropriately authorized Windows client.

`abort shutdown script`: This parameter points to a script that will abort a system shutdown when an appropriately authorized Windows client so directs.

`dfree command`: This command calculates the free disk space; it returns the total disk space in blocks, the available disk space in blocks, and optionally the block size. Normally this command goes unused, but on some OSs, such as Ultrix, Samba's internal free-space computation tools fail and cause clients to produce errors when displaying directory listings.

Most of these scripts fill very specialized roles, so you shouldn't need to set them, or at most, you'll set them to some conventional value. You might find some creative use for some of these scripts, though. For instance, you might write a script that sends you e-mail about attempts to modify user accounts as a way of alerting you to potential cracking attempts.

CAUTION   Many of these scripts—particularly those that modify accounts, shares, and other system data—run with `root` privileges. As a general rule, it's best to avoid using these scripts because a misconfiguration or error in the script could give an attacker a wedge to use in order to gain greater access to your system.

Client Scripts

If your network uses a domain configuration, you can involve Samba in the configuration of clients by providing scripts and storage space for client configuration files. Two independent features accomplish these goals:

Logon scripts: You can specify a script that Windows clients should run when they connect to the server. These scripts run on the client computer but are stored in a special share called `NETLOGON` that you must create on the server.

Roaming profiles: Windows computers store information such as desktop icons, default background images, and menu entries in a *profile*. These profiles are often stored on the local computer, but in a domain configuration, you can create a special Samba share that holds Windows computers' profiles.

Client scripts are distinctly different from other scripts described in this chapter because they don't execute on the Samba server computer. In fact, calling roaming profiles *scripts* is rather inaccurate; they're stored user configurations, not scripts. Nonetheless, both logon scripts and roaming profiles are important parts of a domain configuration, and they're often set up at the same time. Thus, describing them together is sensible.

Client scripts are most useful for helping to automatically or semi-automatically configure client computers. For instance, a logon script might set the clock on a client computer whenever a user logs on or update antivirus rules to protect the client from infection by a virus, worm, or Trojan horse. Logon scripts typically achieve the same effects on all clients, although you can customize them in various ways. Roaming profiles, by contrast, are helpful in customizing environments for individual users and enabling them to use their preferred environment no matter what workstation they use.

Client scripts are useful only on Windows systems. Client computers that run OS/2, Mac OS, or Unix don't take advantage of either logon scripts or roaming profiles. Configuring and using client scripts and roaming profiles is covered in the upcoming section "Using Client-Side Scripts."

Using *preexec* and *postexec* Scripts

The preexec, postexec, and related parameters enable you to perform particular actions whenever a user logs on or logs off. To use these parameters, though, you must understand what each of them does. Differences in timing and permissions mean that a script can have the desired effect if called in one way but no effect or the wrong effect when called in another way. You must also be able to create scripts and understand how to call them, including the potential uses of Samba variables in filenames and as script parameters. To help you understand these scripts, I present a few examples of their use.

File Share Script Parameters

Four parameters provide access to four different types of file share scripts, and two more parameters enable you to control whether Samba grants access to the share based on the output of the script. These parameters are as follows:

preexec: This parameter specifies a script that's to be launched when a user attempts to access the share. This script executes with the user's normal permissions, so it can create or modify files, launch programs, and so on, in the user's name. A synonym for this parameter is exec.

postexec: This parameter specifies a script that's to be run when the user terminates a connection to the share. Like preexec, postexec specifies a script that's to be run using the user's native permissions.

root preexec: This parameter works just like preexec except that it launches the script with root privileges. This fact enables you to do more with the scripts, but it adds danger—a buggy script could be abused by an intruder; or if the script is stored in a publicly accessible location, an intruder might be able to modify or replace the script to gain full root access to the computer.

root postexec: You can specify a script that's to be run with root privileges upon termination of a link with this parameter. As with root preexec, the security implications of this parameter are substantial.

preexec close: This Boolean parameter specifies whether the connection to the share should be terminated if the script delivers a nonzero return code. Setting preexec close = Yes enables your script to serve as an extra security measure or terminate a connection if continuing that connection would cause problems (say, because directories required by a postexec script don't exist).

root preexec close: This Boolean parameter works just like preexec close except that it applies to the root preexec script.

You can use preexec alone, postexec alone, or both in combination. The preexec script is useful for setting up a share—cleaning out old files, ensuring that directory permissions are set correctly for ordinary use, and so on. For instance, a share to create CD-Rs might use a preexec script to delete all old files from the share. The postexec script is most often used to process data the user has left in the share or to clean up files the user might have left behind. For instance, in a CD-R creation share, this script would create a CD-R image file and burn it to CD-R.

For the preexec parameters, Samba executes any root preexec command before the normal preexec command. For postexec, this relationship is reversed; root postexec is executed last.

The root variants are extremely powerful and are best avoided whenever possible. Sometimes, though, root privileges may be required to accomplish some task. For instance, you might need to use root postexec to run a CD-R burning tool. Other options are often available, though, such as using Unix ownership and permissions to enable ordinary users—or at least *one* ordinary user—to accomplish the goal, and using Samba's force user parameter or the SUID bit on a program file to run the relevant commands as a specific ordinary user.

Creating and Calling Scripts

The preexec, postexec, and root variant parameters take filenames and, optionally, parameters to be passed to the programs as values. You can specify a simple command, whether it's a script or not, or pass the name of a script or custom program that performs whatever action you like. For instance, a simple test might use a line like the following in a share definition:

```
preexec = /bin/mail -s "A user has logged on" grogers@luna.edu
```

This line tells Samba to call the mail program to send a message with a null body and the Subject line A user has logged on to grogers@luna.edu. A parameter such as this one can be handy in learning how scripting works, when clients connect and disconnect under various circumstances, and so on.

TIP If your server is equipped with a sound card, and if you can be in the same room as the server when conducting tests, try calling an audio-playing program, such as play or aplay, to have Samba play a short audio file whenever a connection is initiated or terminated. This can be a good way to learn what Samba is doing without even checking a computer screen.

You can use most of the variables described in Chapter 2 as parameters to scripts, or even as part of script filenames. For instance, suppose you want to launch a different script for every client and pass that script the name of the user who's logged on. You might use a parameter such as this:

```
preexec = /usr/local/bin/logon-%m %u
```

This example relies upon scripts whose names take the form logon-*machine*, where *machine* is the client's NetBIOS name. The resulting script could perform a task such as setting up directories required by the client for which it was created.

NOTE The %m parameter isn't always reliable. For instance, some clients make up bogus NetBIOS names, and when using SMB/CIFS over raw TCP using port 445 rather than NBT on port 139, Samba won't know the client's NetBIOS name. When this happens, Samba expands %m into the machine's IP address.

TIP If a script that uses a variable in its name isn't running when you expect, try using a simple command in a preexec parameter to discover how Samba is expanding the variable. For instance, you might use preexec = /bin/touch /tmp/test-%m.txt to discover how Samba is expanding the %m variable. After initiating a connection from a client, look for a file called /tmp/test-*machine*.txt; *machine* is how Samba has expanded the %m variable in this case.

You can write your scripts in any scripting language you like—Bash, Perl, Python, or anything else. You can even create "scripts" using a compiled language such as C or Pascal. As long as the script is executable, Samba can run it. Any parameters you pass, such as %u in the preceding example, can be accessed using the scripting language's normal methods of accessing parameters. Be sure that any script you create has its execute permission bits set, or at least one execute bit that enables the user who runs the script to do so. You can even call multiple scripts or programs by separating them with semicolons (;), much as you can at a shell prompt. (This trick can obviate the need to create what would otherwise be a simple two- or three-line script.)

One of the simplest types of scripts is a shell script, which is written in a Unix shell language, such as Bash or csh. In their simplest forms, these shell scripts are just ordinary commands you might type at a command prompt. Shell scripting languages include many common programming facilities, though, such as the ability to create loops, perform logic tests, and so on. Listing 14-1 shows a simple shell script that sends e-mail to a user. It might be the script called by the logon-%m example shown earlier.

Listing 14-1. A Sample Shell Script

```
#!/bin/sh
mail -s "You have logged in" $1@luna.edu
```

When passed a parameter consisting of the username, this script sends mail to that username (specified by the $1 variable, which stands for the first parameter) on the luna.edu mail server. This shell script begins with a line reading #!/bin/sh, which identifies the file as a script (#!) that uses the /bin/sh program as an interpreter. All Unix-like systems should have a /bin/sh program, or at least a link of that name pointing to another program. The default /bin/sh shell can vary from one OS to another, but all should be able to handle a simple shell script like Listing 14-1. If your script uses more advanced calls, you may want to specify the shell less ambiguously, as in /bin/bash on a Linux system. Doing so may make the script less portable, though. For instance, FreeBSD places its bash executable in /usr/local/bin, so if you specify /bin/bash when developing a script on a Linux system, you'll need to change the filename if you move the script to a FreeBSD system.

Examples of preexec and postexec Scripts

To give a better feel for how preexec and postexec scripts work in practice, the following sections present two examples: using these scripts to automatically mount and unmount removable media and using them to help create CD-Rs.

Mounting and Unmounting Removable Media

Suppose a computer in an open office or computing center has a removable media device, such as a DVD-ROM or magneto-optical drive, that's not common on other computers in that environment. If you want to enable any user in the area to access data stored on the appropriate removable media, you can create a fairly ordinary Samba file share to do the job. The problem, though, is that Unix systems require removable disks to be mounted before they're shared and unmounted before they can be removed from the drive. In some cases, you can configure the OS to automatically mount a device when somebody attempts to access it. This approach can work well, but another method is to have Samba do the job with a preexec script and to unmount the device with a postexec script. The resulting share looks like this:

```
[modrive]
    comment = Magneto-Optical Drive
    path = /mnt/mo
    max connections = 1
    read only = No
    preexec = mount /mnt/mo
    preexec close = Yes
    postexec = umount -l /mnt/mo
```

This share enables user access to a drive mounted at /mnt/mo. Given the comment, this drive is presumably a magneto-optical drive. Some specific points to notice about this share include the following:

- The max connections = 1 parameter ensures that the share can be accessed by only one user at a time. This can be a security measure because it prevents anybody but the current user from accessing files on the medium, and it prevents the preexec and postexec parameters from interfering with each other, unmounting the share inappropriately.

NOTE   If one user inserts a medium and another mounts the share before the first can do so, the interloper user will have access to files on the share, Unix permissions permitting.

- The preexec parameter mounts the share. This example works on a Linux system in which the /mnt/mo mount point is defined in /etc/fstab. The details of this command will need to be customized for particular systems. A program other than mount might be appropriate for some OSs. This example will mount whatever filesystems the /etc/fstab file supports. For instance, if /etc/fstab defines /mnt/mo as using the Linux vfat filesystem driver, this share will mount FAT (including VFAT) disks only. If the /etc/fstab entry specifies a filesystem type of auto, the share will support any filesystem Linux can autodetect.

- The preexec close = Yes parameter causes the connection to be terminated if the filesystem can't be mounted. This action prevents the user from, say, placing a defective (unmountable) disk in the drive, opening the share, and copying files to the mount point directory on the hard disk rather than to the removable disk.

- The postexec parameter umounts the share. The -l parameter causes a "lazy" unmount, which is necessary in Linux because this parameter is executed before Samba closes all open files on the share. A lazy unmount enables Linux to unmount the filesystem when it contains some types of open files. This option may not be available on all OSs, so check your umount command's documentation.

- Both the preexec and postexec commands in this example execute as the user who connects to the share. This will work in Linux if the /etc/fstab entry includes the user or users option. If you don't want to add this option, or if its equivalent isn't available for your OS, you could use root preexec and root postexec instead. This action might require adding mount options to the /etc/fstab entry to set permissions on FAT filesystems so that ordinary users can access them, though.

- You may want to add a global deadtime = 3 parameter to force Samba to disconnect after three minutes of inactivity, assuming no files are open on the disk. This parameter should enable users to remove the disk after three minutes of disuse, even if their clients don't explicitly close the connection. (Such a configuration is potentially risky with floppy disks, which don't lock their eject mechanisms on most computers. It's safe on most removable media, though, which are locked and can't be removed once mounted in a Unix-like OS.)

Chances are you'll need to modify this example in substantial ways to get it to work on your system. Details such as the mount and umount command parameters and their effects vary from one Unix-like OS to another. The best value for a deadtime parameter is highly site-specific and depends on local usage patterns for the share. Nonetheless, this share can be a good starting point for ordinary file access.

Creating a CD-R with a File Share

CD-Recordable (CD-R) and related media, such as CD-Rewritable (CD-RW) and various recordable DVD technologies, have become quite important since the mid-1990s. In many ways, these tools have replaced floppy disks as the physical exchange medium of choice. CD-R and related drives are not yet present on all computers, though. Particularly if your office still holds older computers, you may want to use Samba on a system with a CD-R drive to enable users on other systems to create CD-Rs.

NOTE I use *CD-R* as shorthand for *CD-R, CD-RW,* and *recordable DVD drives.* The principles described here apply to all of these recordable optical devices.

A file share that creates CD-Rs must use a preexec script to prepare the share to receive users' files and a postexec script to call Unix CD-R creation tools on the files the user has left in the share. An example share looks like this:

```
[cd-create]
    comment = CD-R Creation Share
    path = /home/samba/cd-r/files
    max connections = 1
    read only = No
    preexec = rm -r /home/samba/cd-r/files/*
    postexec = /usr/local/bin/create-cdr /home/samba/cd-r %U
```

This share relies upon a custom script, /usr/local/bin/create-cdr, to do the bulk of the work. Listing 14-2 shows a shell script that can function in this role, but of course you could modify this script in various ways. In fact, at least one aspect of the script—the call to cdrecord to copy the data to a CD-R drive—should be modified for your hardware. (The example records at 8× speed to a device on SCSI ID 4, which of course won't work if you have a CD-R burner on another SCSI ID and isn't optimal for anything but an 8× burner.) You might also want to add share access control tools, such as force user or create mask, to better manage file permissions.

Listing 14-2. Sample CD-R Creation Script

```
#!/bin/sh

# $1 = path to share parent
# $2 = username

MaxCdrSize=665600

CdrSize=`du -sk $1/files | cut -f 1`
if [ $CdrSize -lt $MaxCdrSize ]
    then
        mkisofs -J -r -o $1/cdr.iso -log-file $1/cdr.log $1/files
        cdrecord speed=8 dev=4,0 $1/cdr.iso
        cat $1/cdr.log | mail -s "CD-R Creation finished" $2@luna.edu
        rm $1/cdr.iso $1/cdr.log
    else
        mail -s "Too many files to burn CD-R ($CdrSize kilobytes)" $2@luna.edu
fi
rm -r $1/files/*
```

 NOTE The line beginning CdrSize= in Listing 14-2 uses two back-quote characters (`). This character is on the key to the left of the 1 key on most keyboards. *Do not* use ordinary single-quote characters (on the key to the left of the Enter key on most keyboards); they won't work.

In combination, the CD-CREATE share and its matching script have several characteristics that require comment:

- The intent is to use a directory of /home/samba/cd-r/files for file storage and to store temporary files, such as a CD-R image file, in that directory's parent, /home/samba/cd-r. You could, of course, rewrite the share and script to store temporary files in /tmp or some other location.

- As with the share that mounts removable media, this share uses max connections = 1 to ensure that only one user may access the share at a time. This example doesn't use a deadtime parameter to reduce potential problems caused by a user being interrupted and having a CD-R burned with partial contents. If your clients have problems disconnecting, though, you may want to add a global deadtime parameter and accept a few partially burned CD-Rs.

- The preexec line is largely a precaution; it deletes the files stored in the CD-R creation directory in case files have found their way into it. Listing 14-2 does the same when it finishes, though, so there should be no stray files. Another approach would be to track successful CD-R creation and delete files only if the CD-R has been created successfully. This approach has the potential for inter-user confusion, though—if one user attempts and fails to create a CD-R and another user then tries to access the share, the second user will see the first user's files in the share.

- The postexec parameter calls create-cdr and passes it two options: the path to the CD-R creation area and the name of the user who's creating the share. Because the former is hard-coded in the smb.conf file, it could as easily be hard-coded in the script; but passing it as a parameter gives you the option of moving this directory on your server without modifying the create-cdr script.

- The create-cdr script first checks the size of the files the user has stored using the if line. If the files total more than can be stored on a CD-R, the script aborts and sends an e-mail to the user with a title of Too many files to burn CD-R (*cdrsize* kilobytes), where *cdrsize* is the computed total size of the files.

- The mkisofs command creates an image file from the files in the /home/samba/cd-r directory and stores a log of the mkisofs output in the same directory.

- The cdrecord command then burns the CD-R image file to CD-R. The cdrecord executable may need to have its SUID bit set in order to be run by an ordinary user. Alternatively, you could perform this whole task using root preexec and root postexec, although this is much riskier from a security point of view.

- The line that begins with a cat command mails the output of the mkisofs program to the user who launched the script. The assumption is that the username on the luna.edu domain is the same as the local username.

Overall, a configuration such as that shown in this section works well for a shared CD-R creation tool. Another approach, though, is to use a Samba printer share with a custom print command. This approach has certain advantages and disadvantages, as described in the upcoming section "Using print command to Handle Nonprinting Tasks."

Using *print command*

The print command parameter's official use is to enable you to tweak the way Samba hands printing jobs to the server computer's local printing tools. With a bit of ingenuity, though, you can use this parameter to handle unusual printing-style jobs and tasks that are completely unrelated to printing.

The Role of print command

The print command parameter has a default value that depends on the value of the printing parameter. This parameter's value is mostly unimportant if you intend to use the print command parameter for more exotic purposes, though.

> **NOTE** If you've set printing = CUPS and compiled Samba with the --enable-cups compilation option, Samba bypasses the print command and tries to submit the job using CUPS-specific interfaces. Thus, if your server uses CUPS and you want to use print command, you should either compile Samba with --disable-cups or set printing to some other value and, if necessary, set print command and related parameters manually for real printers.

When a client prints a file, the client normally passes the file through a printer driver, which converts the file into a form that's suitable for the printer. When printing with Samba, this form may be PostScript, or it could be something else. In any event, the file is then passed to the Samba server much as files are transferred to file shares. Instead of storing the file on disk and then ignoring it, though, Samba stores the file in a spool directory and then calls the print command. This command normally receives the filename (using the %s variable) so that it may operate upon the print job. The default print command also deletes the file when it's done, either by an explicit call to rm as part of the print command or by including parameters to the local printing tools that cause them to delete the file.

Using print command for scripting entails diverting this normal course of events by specifying a nonprinting command. Unlike file shares and their preexec and postexec scripts, using a printer script may require you to bypass the normal share-access mechanisms on the client. Some functions, such as creating a PDF file, may work well with the output of a client's printer driver, but others, such as creating a CD-R, require data in some other form. Thus, one of the challenges of using a printer script is in bypassing the client's printer drivers. The upcoming section "Using a CD-R Creation Share" describes how to do this for one example share.

Using print command *to Handle Unusual Print Jobs*

Chapter 6 provides two examples of using print command to handle unusual tasks that are akin to print jobs: faxing data and creating PDFs. In both of these cases, the print command expects a PostScript file but processes it through means that don't involve the normal Unix print queue. Of course, other possibilities exist beyond these two. Instead of creating PDFs, you could use Ghostscript to create bitmapped graphics files, such as a series of Tagged Image File Format (TIFF) files. You could create a queue that generates PDFs and then e-mails them to a recipient, using a custom script akin to the Respond program used for faxes to obtain an e-mail address from the user. You could create a queue that generates statistics on a file, such as measures of a text's readability. All of these possibilities require creating or modifying a script, or at least calling nonscript tools (such as gs, the Ghostscript executable) in unusual ways.

Using an unusual `print command` to process text normally requires setting up a print queue on the client system that passes the file to the Samba server as PostScript or as plain American Standard Code for Information Interchange (ASCII) text. Drivers for both options are available in Windows, and Unix systems can be configured to print to SMB/CIFS queues as well, passing data in either format. Which works better depends on the nature of the share's processing. As a general rule, PostScript is good for processing that requires maintaining formatting, such as generating a fax or PDF. Text may be better for tasks that involve textual analysis, such as generating measures of readability. Some options, such as the fax share presented in Chapter 6, require special formatting or running special software on the client.

Using `print command` to Handle Nonprinting Tasks

The `print command` parameter can process data that you'd never consider printing. On the Samba server side, this configuration isn't really very different from setting up an unusual printer share; you specify the script, along with any options it needs, on the `print command` line in the share definition. You may need to bypass the printer drivers on the client to use such a share, though. As an example, consider once again the task of burning CD-Rs. The earlier section "Creating a CD-R with a File Share" described one approach to this task. This method has some limitations, though. The fact that much of the work is done by a `postexec` script means that some clients may delay processing, or if the connection is interrupted, a CD-R may be created prematurely. This method also provides very limited support for handling Unix-style permissions and ownership because this information is lost when storing files from a Unix client. A printer script, by contrast, solves both of these problems but introduces its own, such as the need for a less-than-obvious interface from the client.

Configuring a CD-R Creation Share

All printer script shares accept a single file as input. Normally, this file is a PostScript file or other file containing printer-specific data. To use such a share to process multiple files, as when creating a CD-R, you must encapsulate the multiple files in a single carrier file. On a cross-platform network, the best carrier file is normally a zip archive because tools to create zip archives are available on every OS that's likely to be able to send data to the Samba server. You could use a tarball or some other archive format if you preferred, though.

Once the server has received the file, it passes the file on to a script. The script normally extracts the archive file into a convenient directory, whereupon the multiple component files become available. The script can process the data in whatever way is convenient. In the case of this example, the processing entails burning the files to CD-R.

A pseudo-printer share that creates CD-Rs might look something like this:

```
[cd-print]
    comment = CD-R Creation via a Pseudo-Printer Share
    path = /var/spool/samba
    max connections = 1
    printable = Yes
    print command = /usr/local/bin/cdprint %H %s %U /var/spool/samba
```

This share, in turn, relies upon the cdprint script, which appears in Listing 14-3. This script is similar to Listing 14-2 but is more complex. It must extract the archive file into a temporary holding directory, which it creates in the /tmp/cdr directory. (You can change this location by altering the TempPath variable.) Before proceeding, this script deletes the original archive, which can help reduce the odds of a problem should disk space be tight. The script stores the CD-R image file in the user's home directory under a filename of the form image-*printname*.iso, where *printname* is the name of the print job on the Samba server. This file should be present for only a short period, though, because it's removed after Samba calls cdrecord to burn the CD-R.

Listing 14-3. Sample Script to Create a CD-R Using a Pseudo-Printer Share

```
#!/bin/sh
HomeDir=$1
ArchiveFilename=$2
Username=$3
SharePath=$4
TempPath=/tmp/cdr/$ArchiveFilename
MaxCdrSize=665600

mkdir -p $TempPath
cd $TempPath
unzip $SharePath/$ArchiveFilename
rm $SharePath/$ArchiveFilename

# Check to see if CD-R is small enough to burn
CdrSize=`du -sk $TempPath | cut -f 1`
if [ $CdrSize -lt $MaxCdrSize ]
    then
        mkisofs -J -r -o $HomeDir/image-$ArchiveFilename.iso \
                -log-file /tmp/$ArchiveFilename ./
        cdrecord speed=8 dev=4,0 $HomeDir/image-$ArchiveFilename.iso
        cat /tmp/$ArchiveFilename | mail -s "CD-R Creation finished" $Username
        rm $HomeDir/image-$ArchiveFilename.iso /tmp/$ArchiveFilename
    else
        mail -s "Too many files to burn CD-R ($CdrSize kilobytes)!" $Username
fi
cd ..
rm -r $TempPath
```

> **NOTE**   As with Listing 14-2, the line in Listing 14-3 beginning CdrSize= uses two back-quote characters (`` ` ``). Be sure to type these characters correctly, or the script won't work as intended.

As with the CD-R creation file share, the CD-R creation printer share can be tweaked and modified in any way that's appropriate for your system. You might change the temporary file locations to better match the distribution of free disk space on your system, for instance. Listing 14-3 does an acceptable job for many environments, but you could expand it to support creating a queue of CD-Rs to be burned, which could avoid collisions. You could configure it to recognize tarballs in addition to or instead of zip files, or even add image files to the mix, which would enable you to create image files using Windows or Mac OS CD-R tools and burn them on a CD-R drive on the Samba server.

Using a CD-R Creation Share

Using a CD-R creation printer share entails creating a zip file and passing it on to the server. You can accomplish this task in Unix using the zip archiving tool and smbclient:

```
$ cd ~/cdr-files
$ zip -r ~/cdr-files.zip *
$ cd ~
$ smbclient //SQUARE/CD-PRINT
Password:
smb: \> print cdr-files.zip
smb: \> exit
$ rm cdr-files.zip
```

In this example, files in the ~/cdr-files directory are burned to CD-R by bundling them into an archive file and transferring them to the Samba server (SQUARE) and its CD-creation share (CD-PRINT) using smbclient's print command. A similar sequence works in a Windows DOS prompt:

```
C:\> CD CDR-FILES
C:\CDR-FILES> ZIP -r ..\CDR-FILES.ZIP *
C:\CDR-FILES> CD ..
C:\> COPY CDR-FILES.ZIP \\SQUARE\CD-PRINT
C:\> DEL CDR-FILES.ZIP
```

This procedure uses the Info-ZIP package (http://www.info-zip.org), which is the same program that ships with many Unix systems, to compress the data into an archive file. You can use another zip utility if you prefer, though. The procedure then uses the COPY command to bypass the normal Windows printer queue. By copying the file directly to the CD-creation pseudo-printer share, the Windows printer drivers don't get the chance to corrupt the file contents. Of course, most Windows users aren't very comfortable with DOS prompts. One solution involves a short Windows batch file (that is, a Windows script), as shown in Listing 14-4. (You may need to change some of the paths in this listing. In particular, you should adjust the path to the zip utility to reflect its placement on your system, and of course you must adjust the name of the CD-R burning server and its share.)

Listing 14-4. A Windows Batch File to Create CD-Rs

```
C:\APPS\INFOZIP\ZIP.EXE -r C:\WINDOWS\TEMP\CDR.ZIP %1
COPY C:\WINDOWS\TEMP\CDR.ZIP \\SQUARE\CD-PRINT
DEL C:\WINDOWS\TEMP\CDR.ZIP
```

Listing 14-4 can be called by typing its name in a DOS prompt followed by the name of a directory that you want turned into a CD-R. To improve ease of use for typical Windows users, you can create a shortcut on the desktop to this batch file. Users can then drag folders to the CD-R creation batch file, and they'll be burned to CD-R on the Samba server.

Using Client-Side Scripts

Samba's scripting features enable you to turn Samba into a powerful tool for processing data, rather than simply storing and retrieving it or passing it to conventional printers. Samba also enables you to help automate tasks on the client, though. This type of scripting relies on the client's capabilities and typical client actions, rather than unusual Samba capabilities. Most of these features require you to provide pointers within Samba to particular information. The client does most of the work, although Samba stores critical client data. Domain logon scripts enable you to run specific programs on clients whenever they start up, and roaming profiles support storing user-specific data on the Samba server.

NOTE Both domain logon scripts and roaming profiles are used only by Windows clients. Unix systems provide other means to achieve similar ends, such as placing users' home directories on Network File System (NFS) servers.

Using Domain Logon Scripts

Domain logon scripts run whenever a user logs onto a domain. They're Windows batch files (with .BAT extensions, or sometimes .CMD for Windows NT/200*x*/XP). As such, you must create these files with DOS-style end-of-line characters and calling DOS/Windows tools; these files are *not* Unix scripts. (The easiest and most reliable way to create these scripts is to do so on a Windows system, using a Windows text editor. Some Unix text editors offer options to save files using DOS-style end-of-line characters, though, or you can use a tool such as unix2dos to do the conversion.) Before delving into the details of logon script creation, though, you should consider the Samba parameters that relate to it.

Domain logon scripts reside in a share called NETLOGON. You can't change the name of this share; if you want to use domain logon scripts, you must create a share of this name on the domain controller. A typical NETLOGON share looks something like this:

```
[netlogon]
    comment = Network Logon Service
    path = /home/samba/netlogon
    guest ok = No
    read only = Yes
    write list = grogers
```

This share definition is fairly straightforward. The most important detail, aside from its name, is that it's a read-only share. Ordinary users don't need to be able to write to the share, and in fact enabling them to write to the share could be dangerous. If a miscreant managed to alter the domain logon script, that miscreant could bypass security measures on workstations in order to install sniffers, log keystrokes, and so on. If any clients have privileged access to the Samba server, an intruder could take advantage of that fact to attack the server from the privileged client. In this example, the read-only nature of the share is changed for grogers via the write list parameter. This configuration enables grogers to modify the share, provided this user has write access to the /home/samba/netlogon directory and its files. You can use a configuration like this one to give yourself the ability to modify the network logon scripts from a Windows computer.

In addition to the [netlogon] share definition, you must also tell Windows clients what file from this share to use as the domain logon script. You accomplish this task with the logon script parameter, which appears in the [global] section of smb.conf:

```
logon script = LOGON.BAT
```

This line tells client computers to run LOGON.BAT from the NETLOGON share as the domain logon script. This parameter always specifies a file that's stored in the NETLOGON share; you can't point to another share. You can, however, use variables to cause different users to execute different scripts. For instance, consider this parameter:

```
logon script = LOGON-%a.BAT
```

This line causes Samba to return a domain logon script whose name takes the form LOGON-*OS*.BAT, where *OS* is the OS of the client, such as Win95 for Windows 9*x*/Me systems or Win2K for Windows 2000 systems. You can use this feature to customize the commands in a script for particular clients, users, or OSs.

If this extent of customization isn't sufficient, you can use preexec or root preexec (depending upon the access level required) to customize the logon batch files. For instance, you might use a template batch file and create a script that copies and customizes the batch file for the client, enabling particular features depending upon the time of day, network conditions, and so on. Such a script can pose some security or reliability risks, though; an error could cause clients to misbehave in various ways when they boot. Also, you may be able to accomplish the same goal with a longer

Windows batch file. The main reason to use a preexec script to customize the batch file is if you need access to Unix utilities to perform the customization.

When users log onto their computers (if they're configured to authenticate against the domain controller), they'll retrieve the domain logon scripts and execute them. This process occurs after Windows 9*x*/Me systems execute their AUTOEXEC.BAT files but before they run programs in their local Startup folders.

What should go into a domain logon script? The answer varies from one network to another. As a general rule, if you want a program to run automatically on all the computers on your domain, launching it from the domain logon script makes sense. Two common specific uses are setting the time and mapping remote shares to particular drive letters. Chapter 12 describes setting the time on Windows systems using the NET command. Typically, you'll set the time to that on the Samba domain controller, which is probably set via the Network Time Protocol (NTP). You can also use the NET command to mount a remote share to a particular drive letter and even open a window on that share by launching EXPLORER. Listing 14-5 illustrates all of these tasks.

Listing 14-5. A Sample Domain Logon Script

```
NET TIME \\TAP /SET /YES
NET USE M: \\TAP\COMMON /YES
NET USE N: \\SQUARE\HOMES /YES
EXPLORER N:
```

Listing 14-5 sets the time on the client to the time maintained by TAP, mounts two shares (\\TAP\COMMON and \\SQUARE\HOMES), and opens a window on the final mounted share. (This share, if present on a Samba server, is a home share and so will display different files for different users.) Of course, you can have a logon script perform other tasks, such as update a computer's antivirus software signatures, check a disk for errors, clean files out of C:\WINDOWS\TEMP or other temporary file locations, and so on. In fact, Windows batch files can be quite complex, and of course they can call even more complex programs, which you can store on the NETLOGON share or elsewhere. To take advantage of this capability, you can reference the program you want to run as a direct NetBIOS path, thus:

```
\\TAP\PROGRAMS\SH\SH.EXE
```

This example launches the SH.EXE program from the SH directory on the PROGRAMS share on the TAP server whenever the user logs into the computer. This can be an excellent way to launch certain programs you want running at all times on all Windows clients. A common alternative is placing the programs in individual computers' Startup folders, and this method also works well but requires more maintenance on a system-by-system basis. The beauty of a domain logon script is that you can change the behavior of all the computers on the network by changing one file.

Configuring Roaming Profiles

Roaming profiles enable client computers to store and retrieve information concerning their desktop settings on the domain controller. The benefit is that users can see their own environments—desktop background, desktop theme, and so on—from any computer they use. This feature is most important when users are likely to use a wide variety of computers, as in a university computing center. It's also useful only in domain configurations; workgroups don't support roaming profiles.

Roaming profile configuration for Windows 9*x*/Me clients is different from roaming profile configuration for Windows NT/200*x*/XP clients. (This fact also means that profiles can't be easily transported across these two platform classes.) Windows 9*x*/Me stores roaming profiles in the user's home directory, but Windows NT/200*x*/XP works better if you set aside a special share for the purpose.

Configuring Roaming Profiles for Windows 9x/Me

To tell Windows 9*x*/Me clients where their roaming profiles are, you should use the global `logon home` parameter. You specify a Windows-style network locator with this path, but you typically include Samba variables. For instance, one common configuration looks like this:

```
logon home = \\%L\%U\.winprofiles
```

Notice the Windows-style backslashes (\) that are part of the specification. Using forward slashes will cause this configuration to fail. The %L variable expands to the server's NetBIOS name, and the %U variable expands to the user's name. This configuration will work if the user's home directory is stored on the domain controller in which this definition appears. In this configuration, the profile is stored in a directory called `.winprofiles`; thus, it will be hidden from view should the user log onto Unix using a shell account, and (if you use the default `hide dot files = Yes`) the directory will be hidden from view on Windows clients, as well.

NOTE Many Unix systems include a file called `.profile` in users' home directories. This file is completely unrelated to the Windows profile, and you should be sure *not* to call the Windows profile directory `.profile`; the example presented here calls the directory `.winprofiles` to avoid this conflict.

In addition to creating a location for profiles, the `logon home` parameter tells a Windows client about the location of its home directory. Once defined, you can use the following command in Windows to mount this directory:

```
C:\> NET USE H: /HOME
```

This command mounts the home directory at `H:` (you can use another drive letter, if you prefer). To implement this feature, Samba strips the final component from the logon home value, reducing (for instance) \\%L\%U\.winprofiles to \\%L\%U. Thus, /HOME stands in for \\%L\%U.

After you set the logon home parameter, you must configure your Windows systems to use the roaming profile directory—at least, if you intend to use it. By default, Windows 9*x*/Me displays the same desktop settings for all users and won't try to use roaming profiles. To configure Windows 9*x*/Me to use a roaming profiles directory, follow these steps:

1. Open the Control Panel, and double-click the Passwords item. This action brings up the Passwords Properties dialog box.

2. Click the User Profiles tab in the Passwords Properties dialog box, as shown in Figure 14-2.

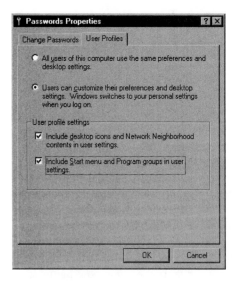

Figure 14-2. Windows 9x/Me supports customized user-by-user desktop settings or a one-desktop-for-all-users configuration.

3. Select the second radio button option (Users Can Customize Their Preferences...).

4. Select whichever of the options in the User Profile Settings you want to set. The default is to store only desktop icons and Network Neighborhood icons in the roaming profile, but you can include the Start menu items if you like.

5. Click OK. Windows tells you it must reboot to change the settings. Tell it to do so.

6. When Windows starts up again, it tells you that you haven't logged in before. Click Yes to have Windows use the roaming profile directory. You'll see a status box as Windows creates its profile.

Thereafter, when you log on using this computer, it should restore your profile from the .winprofiles directory in your home share. If you need to reinstall Windows on the computer, you won't lose your roaming profiles, although you will need to reconfigure Windows to use them. This fact alone can be a great time-saver if you spend much time tweaking your desktop options to your liking.

Configuring Roaming Profiles for Windows NT/200x/XP

In theory, Windows NT/200x/XP can store its profiles in the user's home directory. In practice, though, this is seldom done. The main reason is that Windows NT/200x/XP clients sometimes fail to disconnect from a server between logons. This failure to disconnect can cause problems if roaming profiles are stored on users' home directories. Thus, the preferred method is to create a special share for roaming profiles. A typical configuration looks something like this:

```
[profiles]
    comment = NT Profiles Directory
    directory = /home/samba/profiles
    read only = No
    create mode = 0600
    directory mode = 0700
    browseable = No
```

Because of the browseable = No parameter, this share will not appear on browse lists. The tight create mode and directory mode settings ensure that users won't be able to read others' profiles. The directory itself (/home/samba/profiles in this example) must be set with very loose permissions, though—clients will have to be able to create directories for their users in this share. In practice, 0777 permissions work well, although you might be able to get away with 0770 if all the users who will create profiles are members of a single group, which will then need group ownership of the directory.

To use this new share, you must tell Windows NT/200x/XP clients where to store their profiles. You do so with a parameter that's similar to the logon home parameter. This parameter is logon path. If you created a share called PROFILES for this purpose on the domain controller, the following line should do the job:

```
logon path = \\%L\PROFILES\%U
```

When you restart Samba and log onto a Windows NT/200x/XP domain client, the system should store your profile in a directory of the PROFILES share named after your username, as specified by the logon path parameter. This is the default configuration for a Windows NT/200x/XP system. To change this setting with recent versions of Windows, follow these steps:

1. Right-click My Computer on the desktop (or in the Start menu), and select Properties from the resulting pop-up menu. Windows displays a System Properties dialog box.

2. In Windows 2000, select the User Profiles tab. In Windows XP, select the Advanced tab and click the Settings button in the User Profiles area. The result is a User Profiles dialog box or tab, as shown in Figure 14-3.

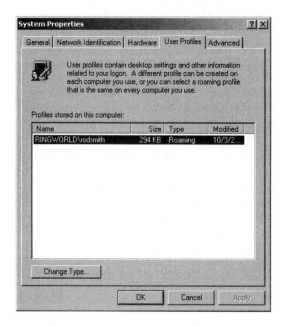

Figure 14-3. Windows NT/200x/XP defaults to using roaming profiles in a domain configuration.

3. Double-click the line corresponding to the profile you want to change. A dialog box gives you the option of using a roaming profile or a local profile.

4. Click Local Profile, and then exit from the dialog boxes.

After you make this change, your profile location won't change immediately; you must log out and then back in again to change your profile. When you do log out, though, your current profile will be stored in its new location, so your desktop will appear the same when you log back in again.

Advantages and Disadvantages of Roaming Profiles

Roaming profiles are very useful in environments in which users frequently move from one computer to another, such as public computing centers in which users aren't assigned a single computer. In such an environment, when a user logs on, the client contacts the system that holds the roaming profile and initiates a connection. The files that make up the roaming profile can then be read by the client as if they were local files. The effect is very much as if the roaming profile directory was mounted on the client in place of the local profile directory tree.

The big advantage of roaming profiles is that they untie users from specific computers, enabling them to use any of a number of computers, saving the user's desktop preferences on a central server. Without a roaming profile, users would need to reconfigure every computer with their personal preferences. This would be tedious for users and would consume a great deal of disk space if each computer had multiple users. Even on networks with few users and computers, roaming profiles have the advantage of storing the profile off of the computer, which can obviate the need to re-create desktop settings if a computer is replaced or if its OS must be reinstalled.

Roaming profiles are not without their problems, though. These include the following:

Non-networked users: If a system regularly operates without networking (such as a notebook computer), roaming profiles will cause error messages and temporary desktop settings to appear at startup. The same thing can happen if network errors cause the roaming profile directory to become temporarily inaccessible.

Multinetwork users: If a system regularly moves between networks (as in a notebook computer moving between two or more network locations), using roaming profiles means that a single user will see different desktops in each network environment.

Hardware differences: Some types of hardware differences can cause problems for roaming profiles. Display hardware is a particular problem; a profile stored using a computer with a large display will be changed when the profile is read on a computer with a smaller display.

Object referent locations: Desktop objects and Start menu items point to files, frequently on the local computer. If these files are stored in different places on different computers, the objects will become useless. For instance, suppose a desktop object for a program called BigMail points to `C:\APPS\BIGMAIL\BIGMAIL.EXE` on the computer on which a profile was created. If this profile is loaded on another computer on which BigMail is stored in `C:\Program Files\Big Mail\BIGMAIL.EXE`, then the BigMail desktop object will become useless. The bottom line is that, if you use roaming profiles, you should use care to ensure that common program files are stored in identical locations on all computers. Using a Samba share for the purpose can help minimize this problem.

Simultaneous use: If a user logs into two computers simultaneously, the computers will both try to use the profile. This is normally fine, but if the profile is changed by one computer, that change may be overwritten if the other computer saves its profile later.

Time issues: If two clients' clocks differ by enough, you might find changes made to a profile using the system with the slow clock may never be saved. You can avoid this problem by using the NET TIME *SERVER* /SET /YES command in your network logon script.

You should evaluate these potential pitfalls to decide when to use roaming profiles. As a general rule, they're best applied when users frequently use different systems that are similar in configuration, and particularly in screen size and program locations. Roaming profiles cause the most problems with portable computers and when clients vary in local software location or screen size.

Summary

Samba can be a gateway to dynamic network computing. The server supports many script types, but the two most likely to be used to support dynamic computing are file share scripts (preexec, postexec, and related tools) and printer share scripts (print command). These tools enable you to configure a server to run just about any program you choose when your users perform specific actions. The result is a great capacity for taking unusual actions, such as burning CD-Rs or performing automated computations on data sets. In addition to running programs on the Samba server computer, Samba supports tools to help run scripts on clients. In particular, you can define a domain logon script for Windows clients. You can also configure Samba to store roaming profiles, which hold a user's default desktop settings for use on any compatible computer on the network.

Migrating a Windows Domain to Samba Control

SAMBA 3.0 ADDS new features that enable you to migrate a domain from a Windows NT 4.0 domain controller to a Samba domain controller. Before embarking on such a journey, you should plan it carefully, starting with asking yourself why you want to do it. Assuming you decide a migration is worthwhile, you must use special Samba tools to copy the existing Windows domain database, as well as domain support shares and files. You must then deactivate the old domain controller, activate the new one, and perhaps make changes to client configurations.

NOTE You can migrate a domain from a Windows NT 4.0 domain controller but not from a more recent Windows 200x domain controller using Active Directory (AD)—at least, not in a way that maintains all of the AD features. You can, of course, set up a Samba domain controller with new user and machine accounts and then discontinue the Windows 200x AD domain controller, but doing so is likely to be quite disruptive.

Planning a Migration

Domain controllers hold large quantities of sensitive data, including user account information, group information, machine trust accounts, domain trust accounts, and so on. Ideally, migrating a domain from Windows NT control to Samba control involves extracting this sensitive information from the domain controller and installing it in the Samba domain controller in a seamless way. This task is nontrivial, so you shouldn't undertake it lightly. Before proceeding, you should evaluate your reasons for wanting to perform a domain migration. If you conclude that they're worth the effort, you should then consider options for how to proceed with the migration. The exact methods you choose will depend upon your priorities, such as the importance of maintaining account information.

Why Migrate a Domain?

Migrating a domain from Windows to Samba control requires a fair amount of effort, so you shouldn't undertake it lightly. Even if you want to use Samba servers to deliver the bulk of a domain's file and printer shares, you might not need to go to the effort of migrating a working Windows NT 4.0 domain controller to Samba. Samba file and print servers can function quite well on a network with a Windows domain controller. As described in Chapter 10, such a configuration is fairly straightforward and is identical whether the domain controller runs Windows or Samba.

Why, then, might you want to make the transition to Unix and Samba for domain control? Several different factors can contribute to such a decision, including the following:

Operating costs: In many cases, operating costs for Unix systems (particularly open-source Unix-like systems, such as Linux and FreeBSD) are lower than for Windows systems. This benefit is due partly to the lower up-front costs of the open-source Unix-like OSs but also relates to the ability of these OSs to run on slimmer hardware with less overhead, to costs of support contracts, and to overall OS reliability. Of course, if your site has no support contract and if the existing domain controller is operating well, you might not expect much in the way of future costs for it.

Support: Windows NT 4.0 is an aging platform that's no longer being supported by Microsoft. Thus, upgrading Windows NT 4.0 servers to something else, be it Windows 200x or Unix/Samba, is wise because it will reduce the potential for security-related problems as future bugs are discovered in Windows NT 4.0.

Reliability: Most Unix-like OSs have reputations for being more reliable than Windows NT 4.0. Of course, this issue is at least partly subjective and individual servers' reliability varies, so this factor may not be a major concern for you. In the short term, a migration could reduce reliability as you work out kinks, but in the long term it's likely to help. Note that migrating to Windows 200x may be less painful than migrating to Samba while still producing a reliability increase.

Availability of unique Samba features: In many respects, Samba is playing catch-up with Windows, particularly in terms of domain controller features; however, in some respects Samba leads Windows. For instance, you can create dynamic domain logon scripts using `preexec` scripts in the `NETLOGON` share.

Unique logon options: Samba offers several options for how to store authentication database information (`smbpasswd` file, a TDB file, LDAP, and so on). To one extent or another, these options permit integration of Unix and NetBIOS domain logons, which may improve your overall network integration.

System administration options: A Samba server can be administered via text-mode tools from the local console or a remote Secure Shell (SSH) login, via GUI tools from the console, via remote Web-based tools, and so on. This flexibility may give you options for administration (and particularly remote administration) that are important and difficult to achieve with Windows NT 4.0.

License issues: Microsoft has been making changes to its software licenses, and some people and companies are disturbed by some of these changes. For instance, some license terms may force users to upgrade software. Samba's choice of licensing under the Free Software Foundation's General Public License (`http://www.fsf.org/licenses/licenses.html#GPL`), on the other hand, imposes minimal restrictions on users (that is, individuals and companies who deploy the software), so you won't be forced into anything by using Samba. Of course, commercial Unix OSs have their own commercial license terms that may affect it (but not Samba); but you can also run Samba on an open-source OS, such as Linux or an open-source BSD.

Hardware upgrades: Although not a reason to migrate to Samba *per se*, hardware upgrades may serve as a catalyst. If you need to replace an out-moded domain controller, considering Samba in this role enables you to consider a wider range of hardware, such as a Sun server. You might even consider making the change as part of a broader hardware upgrade, even if you stick with *x*86 computers.

This list of reasons for migrating may seem compelling, and for some sites migration is certainly the best course of action. Migration isn't without its problems, though, including the following:

Potential for downtime: Any major change creates a risk of problems that will cause downtime. Taking such a risk on a domain with a handful of users might be worthwhile; if nothing else, you could switch to a workgroup configuration on a temporary basis without too much trouble. On a site with hundreds or thousands of users, though, downtime could be disastrous. In such situations, a conservative approach may be warranted, and if you decide to migrate, you should plan the migration carefully and practice the operation on a small test network. Note that problems could crop up some time after the migration, particularly if they're related to seldom-used domain features.

Lost features: Samba doesn't implement all Windows domain controller functions. In particular, Samba lacks AD server support, AD software application and access controls, AD logon scripts, AD group policy objects, machine policy objects, and the ability to coexist with Windows-based domain controllers (in primary/backup mixtures). Most of these features relate to AD, and if they're important to you, migrating to a Windows 200*x* domain controller may make more sense than trying to use Samba.

Hassle and time investment: A change in your domain controller is certain to consume a fair amount of time. That time might be better spent on other tasks, particularly if your current domain controller is working well.

Need to retrain staff: If your system administrators are familiar with Windows NT domain controller functions but not Samba, they'll need to learn Samba. Of course, if you're already running other Samba servers, this change shouldn't be too difficult; but if you don't currently run any Samba systems, you might want to start with Samba servers that do *not* function as domain controllers.

User confusion: It's possible that your users will become confused by the transition, particularly if you're forced to make changes to domain features that are readily visible to users, such as their domain usernames.

Ultimately, of course, you must make the decision of whether to migrate a domain yourself, probably in consultation with individuals in management or higher-ups in your network services department. As a general rule, if you're running a Windows NT 4.0 domain controller, migrating to something else is wise, given the lack of official support for this old OS. The question is whether this migration should be to a more recent version of Windows or to Unix/Samba. Both involve certain risks, but the Unix/Samba decision is certainly the more radical one. Migrating from Windows 200*x* to Unix/Samba entails different challenges. As of Samba 3.0, tools to perform this migration don't exist. You can extract some data using the NT 4.0 migration tools, but some AD data aren't easily extracted, and reproducing those AD functions will require using tools other than Samba, such as Kerberos, OpenLDAP, and BIND.

An Overview of Migration Options

Broadly speaking, two approaches to converting from Windows to Samba domain control exist:

True migration: This chapter focuses upon the first approach, which involves converting the database file and other important domain features from an existing Windows NT 4.0 domain controller to a Samba domain controller. In this approach, you can preserve accounts, passwords, domain logon scripts, and so on, minimizing the impact of the conversion upon users.

Disruptive replacement: A more radical approach is to remove the existing domain controller and replace it with a new one without converting the user database. You might take this approach if you want to clean out the existing user database, make wholesale changes in username policies, or otherwise make radical changes to the domain.

A domain controller replacement might fall somewhere between these two extremes. For instance, you might preserve the account database but not attempt to carry over user profiles from the old domain controller; or you might try to copy profiles but abandon the user database.

As a general rule, it's probably best to start with the least disruptive change possible. If you want to implement new features, such as setting up new shares or creating dynamic domain logon scripts, you might want to do so *after* performing a basic migration. This approach will enable you to check out the initial migration to be sure it has worked correctly. If you try to do everything at once, you might not know if a problem is due to the basic migration or a flaw in the implementation of the advanced feature. On the other hand, a series of small changes may be more confusing to your users than a single massive change.

Whatever plan you choose to implement, you should try to do as much as possible on a test system, without actually disrupting the operation of your normal network. You might even want to set up a small isolated network that's not connected to any other network to test the migration operations. Doing this will help you to uncover any problems you're likely to encounter on the regular migration, thus making the real migration go more smoothly.

Copying the Windows User Database

The trickiest part of a true migration is in copying the Windows user database from a Windows domain controller to a Samba system. Ordinarily, information such as the encrypted passwords remains on the domain controller, and Windows stores this information in different files than does Samba, so you can't simply copy the files from one computer to another. Instead, you must prepare your Unix system for the accounts it's to acquire, extract the data using a special Samba `net` command, perform tests, and clean up the configuration.

NOTE Copying the Windows user database does not, by itself, turn the Samba server into a domain controller. As a practical matter, you may need to duplicate support data, such as logon scripts and profiles, as described in the upcoming section "Copying Support Data." You must then reconfigure the Windows and Samba systems so that the Samba system takes over domain controller duties.

Preparing Samba

Before proceeding any further, you should configure Samba as a domain controller, as described in Chapter 10, but with some changes:

> `domain master` = `No`: You don't want Samba to claim domain master browser duties just yet because having two domain master browsers on one domain is likely to cause serious problems.

> `os level` = `30`: To avoid complications due to Samba claiming local master browser duties, set `os level` below the value that the Windows NT domain controller claims.

> `domain logons` = `No`: During the transition, Samba shouldn't be processing domain logon requests. After a certain point, it will be capable of doing so, but until the transition is complete, this configuration could cause strange effects on clients, such as lost user profiles.

Ultimately, you'll change all of these settings to more typical domain controller values, as described in the upcoming section "Making the Handoff." For now, though, you shouldn't set any values that might disrupt the normal operation of your existing Windows-controlled domain.

You should also prepare any file shares that the domain controller hosts. You can put off this task for a while, though. It's covered in more detail in the upcoming section "Copying Support Data."

Preparing Unix Accounts

The first step in the migration process is to prepare the Unix system with necessary account and group information. You can start with groups because they're typically few in number. If your domain relies on the presence of particular groups, be sure that they're duplicated on the Samba server computer. Use whatever tools your Unix server provides for creating new groups, such as groupadd, to create Unix accounts. You must then use the net utility and its groupmap subcommand to map domain groups to local Unix groups. This task is necessary because some Windows security tools rely on SMB/CIFS-style groups, which may not be handled automatically or by default on the new Samba domain controller.

NOTE   This section describes the use of net and its groupmap command to perform the task at hand. Appendix B covers the net command generally in more detail but the groupmap subcommand in less detail.

The net groupmap command provides a way to modify mappings between Unix and NT domain groups. This command takes several parameters. The most important are add (to add a new mapping), modify (to modify an existing mapping), unixgroup (to specify a Unix group), and ntgroup (to specify a domain group). You can obtain a listing of the current mappings by typing **net groupmap list**. The result will be a list of default mappings, such as the following:

```
Users (S-1-5-32-545) -> -1
```

This mapping shows that the domain group Users, with security identifier (SID) S-1-5-32-545, maps to no local group (indicated by the -1 at the end of this line). To modify an existing mapping, you use the modify subcommand. To add a new domain group and mapping, use the add subcommand. For instance, suppose you want to map the domain Users group to the Unix users group and then add a new group, Part Time Staff, that's linked to the ptstaff Unix group. You can accomplish these goals by typing the following commands:

```
# net groupmap modify unixgroup=users ntgroup=Users
Updated mapping entry for Users
# net groupmap add ntgroup="Part Time Staff" unixgroup=ptstaff
No rid or sid specified, choosing algorithmic mapping
Successfully added group Part Time Staff to the mapping db
```

The order of the unixgroup and ntgroup parameters is unimportant, and these examples use both orders. If the domain group name contains spaces, you should enclose the name in quotes, as in the example of the Part Time Staff group. Once you're done, type **net groupmap list** to be sure your groups have all been properly mapped.

Once you're done with this task, you can create Unix accounts for the users on the domain. If your domain has many users, you may want to obtain a list of the users and create a simple script to create all the user accounts. If users won't be logging in locally, you can set up the accounts as nonlogin accounts, so you may not need to specify usernames. Chances are you'll need to create home directories, though.

If your Windows usernames are long, mixed-case, or have spaces in them, you may need to use Samba's username mapping facility. This feature is provided by the global `username map` parameter, which is described in Chapter 7. In brief, this parameter points to a file that contains mapping pairs of Unix and Windows usernames, separated by an equals sign (=), thus:

```
fastaire = "Fred Astaire"
```

In creating user accounts, remember to create machine and (if applicable) inter-domain trust accounts, as described in Chapter 10. If you fail to create these accounts, Samba won't accept logons from Windows NT/200*x*/XP clients or authenticate users for the benefit of servers.

NOTE The total number of users and groups that a Unix-like OS can support varies from one OS to another. It's usually at least 65,536 users and 65,536 groups, though. If your site hosts an unusually large number of users, you should look into this issue in more detail.

You can avoid explicitly creating Unix accounts if you install and run Winbind on the Samba domain controller, as described in Chapter 10. In this configuration, Winbind will point back at the computer on which it runs and dynamically create Unix accounts and groups to match those stored in the Samba domain controller database. For domains with many users, the effort involved in setting up Winbind in this way is probably less than the effort required to create local Unix accounts, but on domains with few users, creating the accounts in the traditional Unix way is probably simpler.

Extracting Data from the PDC

To extract account information from the PDC and replicate it on the Samba domain controller, you must issue a single net command; however, in order for this command to be successful, you must engage in a couple of preliminary steps. This is necessary because the domain extraction command (`net rpc vampire`) "sucks" the entire user database, including passwords, from the domain controller. The domain controller won't give this information to just any computer, though. Thus, you must configure Windows to think Samba is a backup domain controller. To do so and to transfer the database, follow these steps:

1. Use the Windows NT Server Manager tool to create a BDC account for the Samba server computer.

2. On the Samba system, type net rpc join -S *NT4PDC* -w *DOMAIN* -U Administrator%*passwd*, where *NT4PDC* is the name of the PDC, *DOMAIN* is the domain name, and *passwd* is the Administrator password on the domain in question. This action joins the Samba server to the domain.

3. Migrate the user database by typing net rpc vampire -S *NT4PDC* -U Administrator%*passwd* on the Samba server, where *NT4PDC* and *passwd* have the same meanings as in step 2.

You should check the process by typing pdbedit -L. This command should print information from the local user database. It should contain entries for all your domain's users. Their names should now be stored in the Samba server's local password database (smbpasswd, a TDB database, an LDAP database, or some other local database).

It's possible that the migration didn't work perfectly. Be sure to check for errors related to username and group mapping; check that all users are accounted for in the Unix user database and that their names are mapped correctly, if necessary. You may also want to try configuring the Samba server with security = User and logging on using some migrated usernames to be sure the passwords have carried over correctly. If you can't log on, something went wrong in extracting the domain's password information.

Copying Support Data

Copying the user database and passwords from the NT domain controller to Samba is only part of the job; domain controllers typically host a lot of data outside of the user database. To completely replace a Windows domain controller, you must transfer this support data, as well as the account database. Critical components include the domain logon scripts, user profiles, user data, and public shares.

NOTE   Some support data—particularly users' home shares and, to a lesser extent, roaming profiles—are likely to change with some frequency. If you copy these data one day and don't completely change over to the new domain controller until a few days later, users are likely to lose some files. To avoid this problem, I recommend transferring these files at the last possible moment and at a time when the domain isn't being used much. The upcoming section "When to Switch Domain Control" covers the timing of domain control changes in more detail.

Copying Domain Logon Scripts

Chapter 14 describes domain logon scripts, which execute automatically when a client logs onto the domain. Naturally, if you use these scripts, you must configure Samba to deliver them to clients, as described in Chapter 14. This task entails creating a [netlogon] share, placing the logon scripts themselves in this share, and using the logon script parameter in the [global] section of smb.conf to point clients to the script they should run.

You can use the domain logon script you'd been using in Windows from Samba; just copy the file over to the Samba server's [netlogon] share once that share is created. One simple way to do this is to use the smbclient program on the new Samba system to copy the file. For instance, suppose the new [netlogon] share's directory is /home/samba/netlogon. You might type the following commands to copy the domain logon script from the existing Windows domain controller:

```
$ cd /home/samba/netlogon
$ smbclient //NT4PDC/NETLOGON
Password:
smb: \> ls
  .                          D        0  Thu Oct  2 20:24:04 2003
  ..                         D        0  Thu Oct  2 23:26:48 2003
  logon.bat                          117  Thu Oct  2 20:26:41 2003

              49197 blocks of size 131072. 23926 blocks available
smb: \> get logon.bat
smb: \> exit
```

NOTE The dollar sign ($) shell prompt character implies that this task is being performed as an ordinary user. This will work if the user in question has write privileges to the Samba [netlogon] share's directory. If not, you can temporarily give the user this privilege or perform this task as root. You may also need to specify a remote (Windows) username by passing the -U *username* parameter to smbclient.

Of course, the name of the logon script may not be the same as shown here; that's why this example uses the ls command in smbclient to determine the name of the domain logon script prior to retrieving it. Once this task is done, you may need to modify permissions on the script in order to ensure that it's readable by all the users who should be able to read it. You should also ensure that the script can't be modified except by those users who should be able to do so.

If one of your reasons for migrating to a Samba-controlled domain is to take advantage of increased Samba flexibility, you can use wildcards in the logon script parameter to point it at different logon scripts for different machines or users. Of course, doing so will require copying the main script and editing the copies to create appropriate variants. You can even use a preexec or root preexec script to create complex and customized domain logon scripts. Unless you want to make a single clean break from the old domain structure, though, I recommend putting off such tweaks until you're sure the basic Samba domain controller configuration is working.

Copying Profiles

Chapter 14 describes roaming profiles, as implemented on a Samba server. If your existing Windows NT 4.0 domain uses roaming profiles, you must decide how to handle the existing roaming profiles. Possibilities include the following:

Switching to local profiles: You can convert Windows clients to store their profiles locally. Depending upon the Windows version, doing so may automatically copy the profiles to the local hard disk, thus preserving them. This approach requires changes on all the clients, though, and if your site takes advantage of roaming profiles' advantages, this approach may be unacceptable, particularly in the long term.

Starting fresh: You can create a Samba profiles share, as described in Chapter 14, and do no more. The result will be that users will lose all their customized desktop settings, and they'll start their desktop settings from scratch. This result is probably undesirable and may be unacceptable; however, if you're implementing widespread changes in program locations or the like along with your domain controller change, this approach may be acceptable.

Copying profiles: You can copy users' profiles from the Windows domain controller to the Samba domain controller. This method requires extra work on your part, but it results in the least disruption to your users.

Roaming profiles are stored as ordinary files on the server, but they're typically manipulated using a profile manager tool. To copy them to another directory (perhaps even directly to the Samba server computer), follow these steps:

1. On the Windows NT 4.0 domain controller, right-click the My Computer icon and select User Profiles from the pop-up menu. The result is a dialog box listing the available user profiles.

2. Select the name of a user whose profile you want to export.

3. Click the Copy To button.

4. Type the path of the profile's new home (perhaps a directory on the Samba server's profile share) in the Copy Profile To field.

5. In the Permitted to Use dialog box, click Change.

6. Select the Everyone group, and click the OK button to dismiss the Permitted to Use dialog box.

7. Click OK. This action copies the profile to its new location.

You should repeat these steps for every user in the domain. The result is that the profiles will be copied to a new location. If this location isn't the final destination, you may need to copy them in some other way, such as by using `smbclient`, a Windows file browser, or a removable disk.

Steps 5 and 6 in this procedure are necessary because the Samba system isn't part of an interdomain trust relationship with the Windows domain controller. You can, of course, use Samba's own ownership and permissions tools to control who may access each user's profile. In fact, once the files are in place, you should probably go through them and use chown and chmod as necessary to set their ownership and permissions. Be sure that all users have full write privileges to whatever profiles they own, including their profile directories. For instance, the user grogers should be able to write to /home/samba/profiles/grogers (if the profile directory is /home/samba/profiles) and all its files and subdirectories. Without this permission, changes users make to their profiles after the migration will be lost.

After you copy your users' profiles, be sure to tell clients where to look for the profiles. This task is described in Chapter 14, but briefly, you use the logon home parameter for Windows 9*x*/Me clients and logon path for Windows NT/200*x*/XP roaming profiles.

Copying User Data Files

If users' home directories reside on the domain controller, you probably want to copy them to the new server. You can accomplish this task in several ways:

From the Windows server: You can create a special share on the Samba server giving access to the base of the home directory tree (typically /home) and copy users' home directories from the Windows server to the Samba server using the Windows domain controller's file browser. This solution results in a fairly straightforward drag-and-drop operation to copy home directories and should also preserve file ownership information if the Samba and Windows user databases are properly synchronized.

From a client: You can use a client to connect to both the Windows server and the Samba server and use it to copy files via a drag-and-drop operation. This process, however, consumes more network bandwidth than a direct transfer. Permissions may also be an issue; you'll either need to repeat this process for each user (which entails knowing each user's password or working around this limitation with the help of dummy accounts) or give yourself access to the directory above the home directories on both servers, including administrative privilege on both systems to enable you to copy other users' data files.

From the Samba server: You can use the smbclient program or a mount of remote shares to copy users' home directories from the Samba server. If you can create a temporary share at the base of the users' home shares on the Windows server, this operation can be fairly straightforward, particularly if your Samba server OS supports mounting; you can then use **cp -r** or a similar recursive command to copy the entire directory tree at once. This approach is likely to lose ownership and permissions information, though. Depending upon the copy options, Unix execute bits may be set or removed, which could affect the mapping of hidden, system, and archive bits.

Using direct disk access: If you can afford to bring the Windows server down, you can temporarily install its disk in the Samba server computer. If the Samba server OS can read the New Technology File System (NTFS) used by most Windows NT servers, you can then copy the files directly from one disk to another. NTFS support in Unix-like OSs isn't universal, though, and it's sometimes unreliable. Chances are you'll lose ownership and permissions information if you use this method.

Using removable media: If your Windows domain controller hosts a removable drive of sufficient capacity (a DVD burner, tape drive, or the like), you may be able to place the files on the removable media and then read them on the new Samba domain controller. Of course, this method requires compatible filesystems or tape storage formats. Some media, such as CD-R and recordable DVDs, are likely to result in lost write permissions on files, and you're also likely to lose archive, hidden, and system bits.

A variant for all of these options is to bundle the files into a carrier, such as a zip file. You can then transfer the zip file and uncompress it on the target system. This approach may simplify transfers because you need transfer only one file rather than an entire directory tree. It may also help to preserve some information, such as the write permission bit; however, you might also lose other information, such as archive, hidden, and system bits. The zip file will also consume a great deal of disk space, although you can perform the operation in small chunks (say, one user at a time) if this is an issue.

In all of these cases, you may need to rename some or all of the users' home directories once they're stored on the Samba server computer. You may also need to deal with ownership and permissions issues, particularly for the final three methods of data transfer. (In theory, copying files from the Windows system or from a Windows NT/200*x*/XP client should preserve ownership information.) ACLs may be lost in this transfer, although again, a Windows-initiated transfer should preserve ACLs if your Samba configuration supports them and if you've set up user and group information correctly on the Samba server.

 CAUTION If you created any special and temporary shares, such as a share giving access to the /home directory, remember to remove them once you've finished using them. Such shares are likely to be dangerous should they be compromised.

After you've finished copying home share data, you should try logging onto the Samba server as an ordinary user or two. (Using smbclient from the Samba server itself may be an adequate test, particularly if you're not concerned about the preservation of ACLs.) Be sure that you can read the files you should be able to read and that you can create new files, both in the root of the user's home share and in an existing subdirectory. If you can't read or create files, study the permissions carefully to learn why you can't and take whatever corrective measures are necessary.

You should also test the Samba permissions mechanism to be sure that one user can't gain an undesirable level of access to another user's files. For instance, if grogers shouldn't be able to read fastaire's files, try using the grogers account (if you have the password) to access fastaire's home share. As with testing for access that should be permitted, if you discover a problem, you should check your Unix-side permissions and smb.conf settings to discover and correct the cause.

An alternative to copying users' home directories is to leave them on the Windows domain controller. Let the Samba system take over domain control duties, but leave users' home directories on the Windows server, which will be downgraded to a conventional server rather than a domain controller. Of course, this plan is workable only if you intend to keep the Windows NT system on the network. You'll also need to reinstall Windows on the system because a Windows domain controller can't be easily downgraded to not handle domain controller duties. If you like, you can subsequently migrate this system to another Samba server.

Copying Public Shares

If the domain controller hosts general-purpose shares, such as common program file shares or printer shares, you must duplicate those shares on the Samba domain controller. (Alternatively, you could move these shares to another server, which may improve the performance of the Samba server computer. The process is similar in either case.) Copying file shares works much like copying home shares, as described in the previous section. You'll run into fewer permissions problems with file shares, though. In most cases, file shares should be readable by all users and shouldn't contain files with varying ownership. Thus, copying the files directly from one share to another, using either the Windows server or the Samba server, works well enough. You may need to tweak the permissions of the files once they're on the Samba server, but compared to tweaking permissions on users' home directories, this task is fairly straightforward. Of course, if the file share holds users' data files that they exchange with other users, the task can be much more complex.

 TIP Before transferring data files, ask your users to clean out unnecessary files. This action will reduce the amount of data that must be transferred and can simplify your task of tracking down any ownership or permissions peculiarities, particularly in common user data shares.

If your domain controller functions as a print server, you must duplicate the functionality on the Samba server. This task doesn't involve copying files, though; instead, you must create a printer share named after the original share. If you like, you can install printer drivers for the share, as described in Chapter 6. Once the switch is complete, clients can continue using the drivers they've always used; the driver installation is most important when you add new clients to your network in the future.

As with home directories, you can leave public shares on the Windows system if you intend to keep that system working on the domain in a non-domain-controller capacity. This approach has the advantage of lightening the load on the Samba server. As noted earlier, though, you'll need to reinstall the Windows OS itself to downgrade the system from domain controller status.

Making the Switch

At this point, your Samba server should be configured as a virtual clone of the Windows NT domain controller, at least from an outside point of view. The Samba server should have a copy of the NT server's user database, home directories, roaming profiles, domain logon scripts, and so on. All that's necessary is to shut down or reconfigure the Windows domain controller and reconfigure the Samba system to take over full domain control duties. Before you do this, though, you should consider the timing of a switch. An ill-timed change in domain control can cause serious disruptions for your users, even if the switch itself goes fairly smoothly.

When to Switch Domain Control

Many of the basic tasks involved in transferring domain control to Samba, such as duplicating the Windows NT account database, aren't very timing-critical. You can copy the account database on Monday and transfer the domain to Samba control on Friday, and it's possible that nobody will notice. (Of course, if any users change their passwords in this period, they'll notice, but you can probably notify your users that their recent password changes might be lost.) Other aspects of domain control transfer, such as copying users' data files, are much more timing-sensitive; you should make these changes as close to the point of switchover as possible.

The actual handoff from Windows to Samba is likely to be disruptive, no matter how carefully you plan for it. Because you'll be changing critical network resources such as users' home directories, existing users are likely to be bumped off the domain, or at least off any shares that reside on the domain controller itself. Authentication, even for accesses to servers other than either the old or the new domain controller, is likely to be disrupted. For this reason, it's important that you switch domain control at a time when the network isn't being used very much. On most networks, making the switch late at night, early in the morning, on a weekend, or on a holiday is the best choice. Of course, when is best for you depends on your local patterns of network use. For a typical nine-to-five business, any time except for the normal business hours will probably work well. For a university computing center, which is likely to be open until late at night and on weekends, an early morning conversion on a weekend may be the only choice. In extreme cases, you may need to set aside a scheduled downtime to handle the conversion.

In any event, you may want to notify your users of the change. Such notification may head off problems should a user decide to work late or early and, therefore, be in danger of losing important work as the conversion is underway. A user forewarned of the conversion could decide to work early or late on another day or to save data locally instead of or in addition to using the file server.

When planning the domain control switch time, remember to include plenty of time for copying users' home directories. Prior to making the handoff, you may want to try a dry run of the file copy simply to learn how long it will take, including any necessary cleanup of ownership and permissions. If this copying takes two hours and users start appearing at 9 a.m., don't plan to start the conversion at 7:30 a.m.; it won't be done in time. For safety, plan to start it at 5 a.m.; that will give you time for the conversion and for solving any last-minute problems.

Speaking of problems, try to perform the conversion in a way that's easy to undo. If you get started and run into problems, or if you activate the Samba domain controller and discover it's not working the way you intended, shut it down and restore the original Windows domain controller. You can then study the problem and try again at a later date.

Making the Handoff

You can convert a domain from Windows control to Samba control in either of two ways:

New machine: You can reinstall Windows on the old domain controller, keeping it on the network using its original IP address and NetBIOS name. You can then configure Samba as a domain controller using its own IP address and NetBIOS name. This approach involves minimal changes to the Samba domain controller and enables you to keep the Windows NT system in some capacity. It could require more in the way of client configuration changes, though, particularly if any important shares reside on the domain controller and are moved to the Samba system; those share names will change, and clients may need to be reconfigured to find them.

Changed identities: You can completely shut down the Windows NT system and change the identity (the NetBIOS name and probably the DNS hostname and IP address) of the Samba system to take its place. This approach requires making more extensive changes to the Samba computer, but if all goes well, the change should go virtually unnoticed to the clients, provided they aren't logged onto the domain when the switch occurs.

You should first shut down the Windows domain controller, leaving your domain without a controller. (If your domain has a BDC, shut it down, as well as the PDC.) Once you've removed the old domain controller, you can bring up the new one. In the new-machine approach, you should leave your Samba server's basic TCP/IP configuration unchanged from when it was set up. Likewise, you should leave it configured to use the same NetBIOS name. You must, though, change the parameters in the [global] section of smb.conf to identify the system as a domain controller:

```
security = User
encrypt passwords = Yes
domain logons = Yes
domain master = Yes
os level = 33
```

When you make these changes, restart Samba. Once it starts up, it should take over domain controller duties. You should be able to boot up a Windows system and log onto the domain. I recommend you perform this test as soon as possible; if there's a problem, you'll want to know about it so you can correct it quickly.

At this point, if you're satisfied with the performance of the Samba domain controller and want to use the old Windows domain controller as a normal SMB/CIFS server, you should reinstall Windows. Be careful in doing this so that you don't wipe out any vital data. (Ideally, data you want to preserve won't be on the boot partition, but you might not be so lucky.) If at all possible, though, you should delay this step until your new Samba domain controller can prove itself in actual use. If the Samba server doesn't perform as expected, you may want to restore the Windows server, which will be easier if you haven't reinstalled the OS on the computer.

If you intend your Samba server to take over the identity of the Windows NT domain controller, you should probably begin by changing your Samba server computer's IP address. Use whatever TCP/IP configuration tools your Unix OS provides for this task or edit whatever files are appropriate. You may also want to change its configured hostname so that the computer can identify itself correctly using non-SMB/CIFS protocols. Changing the hostname locally will also change the default NetBIOS name in Samba, if you didn't use the `netbios name` parameter in the `smb.conf` file. If you did use that parameter, you should change it to the new name. You should also make the other changes described earlier (particularly `domain logons`, `domain master`, and `os level`). When you bring up the system using its new IP address and restart Samba, the server should respond as a domain controller. You should be able to log onto the domain from a Windows or other client, and you should test this functionality so that you can fix any problems as soon as possible.

Changing Client Configurations

If you perform an identity-change replacement, you shouldn't need to change anything on your clients. They'll continue to contact what they believe to be the same Windows domain controller they always have, although in fact that system will now be a Unix computer running Samba. You should, however, test as many clients and user accounts as possible before regular users begin pounding on the Samba server. You might discover some peculiarities that you'll be able to correct before they cause any real problems.

If you replace the Windows domain controller by adding a Samba domain controller as a new machine, you may need to alter some client configurations. For instance, if any clients have references to the domain controller by name in their configurations (such as links to home shares on users' desktops or installed printer queues), and if the referred-to shares have moved to the new Samba domain controller, those references will have to be changed. You might be able to use a domain logon script to help make those changes automatically or at least to provide workarounds. For instance, you could add a `NET USE X: \\SERVER\SHARE /YES` command, where *X* is a local Windows drive letter, *SERVER* is the server's NetBIOS name, and *SHARE* is the share name, to link the new Samba server's share to a drive letter. This action might help users locate the new share. If your current domain logon script includes a similar command, you can simply update it for your new domain controller's name.

If your Samba domain controller takes over NBNS duties, you may need to reconfigure clients and servers to use the Samba system for NBNS functions. This process can be tedious unless you use DHCP to deliver NBNS information to clients, in which case a change to the DHCP server configuration will do the trick. Chapter 9 covers this topic.

TIP   If your changes will require altering any DHCP-delivered information, you may want to reduce the DHCP lease time prior to making your changes. This action will minimize the time that DHCP clients will have incorrect information because of the changes.

If your network hosts other Samba servers, you may need to tweak their configurations for the new domain controller. In particular, if the IP address of the new Samba domain controller doesn't match the IP address of the old Windows domain controller, you should examine the password server parameter in the [global] section of Samba servers' smb.conf files. This parameter should point to the domain controller and so may need to be changed. If this parameter's value is an asterisk (*), though, Samba should locate the domain controller automatically.

Summary

Windows NT 4.0 is an increasingly elderly platform. Some sites still use it, but those that do are well advised to consider migrating to a newer OS. Windows 200x is Microsoft's approved migration route, but Samba on Unix is another option and one with certain advantages, such as lower costs and better license terms. If you choose to migrate a domain to Samba, you should plan this migration carefully. In a technical sense, copying the user database is arguably the trickiest part of this task; however, to be complete, you must copy a lot more information from most domain controllers. This information is likely to include network logon scripts, users' roaming profiles, and ordinary file and printer shares. Some of these files (particularly users' data files) should be copied immediately before making the switch. This conversion should take place when the network is being used by as few people as possible so as to minimize problems associated with the switch. In some cases, you may need to adjust clients' configurations, but with any luck these changes will be minimal, particularly if you configure your Samba server to completely take over domain controller duties.

Samba Backups

COMPUTERS ARE IMPERFECT devices. Hard disk failures are particularly troublesome because your data are at risk. The usual protection against data loss is backups—storing copies of the data on a medium other than the main hard disk, ideally one that can be removed from the computer and stored in a safe, or even off-site. Unfortunately, although backing up a single computer usually isn't too difficult, backing up all the computers on a network can be quite a challenge. One tool that can help you overcome this challenge is Samba, and this chapter is devoted to Samba and its role in performing backups.

This chapter begins with a look at backing up the Samba server itself, including the hardware and software you're likely to want on a Samba backup server and tips on backing up Samba-specific data. This chapter then presents two ways to use Samba to back up other computers on your network: initiating the backup from the machines that are to be backed up and initiating the backup from the computer that hosts the backup hardware. Of course, backing up is useless if you don't have a way to restore data, so this chapter also looks at restoration scenarios. Finally, this chapter covers some potential pitfalls in backing up Windows systems with the help of Samba.

Backing Up a Samba Server

In a typical network backup configuration, one computer, known as the *backup server*, holds the backup hardware. Data to be backed up finds its way to the backup server in any of several different ways. The configuration of this computer is, therefore, critical to implementing a backup strategy. You must consider what backup hardware and software you want to use; inappropriate choices can make your backup task virtually impossible to implement. You should also develop a plan to back up the backup server itself; if it fails and you haven't backed it up, creating and recovering other backups may become impossible, at least temporarily. If the backup server doubles as another type of Samba server, you may also need to plan how to back up Samba-specific data stored on that server, such as SMB/CIFS hidden, system, and archive bits and access control lists (ACLs).

Backup Hardware Options

The goal of a backup is to create a redundant copy of the vital data on a computer so it can be used in case of a failure. Sometimes a second hard disk in a computer can function as a backup medium, but the problem with this approach is that a problem that affects the first disk (such as a power surge, fire, or theft) can sometimes eliminate the backup as well. For this reason, backup media should be removable and portable. For backups of limited importance, storing them near the computer but not in it may be sufficient. For extremely important backups, though, you should consider storing at least some backups off-site. Note that this implies multiple backups, and that is another important characteristic of any backup you might perform: You should keep multiple copies. If you perform a complete backup once a week, and if you keep four sets of backup media, you'll be able to refer to the backup from the week before last if last week's backup fails.

You can use just about any type of data storage device for backups. Some devices, though, are extremely slow or low in capacity and are, therefore, unsuitable for network backups. Other devices may be too expensive to be worth considering, particularly if your budget is tight. Some of the most popular backup devices include the following:

Tape: Computer tape drives have long been the traditional backup medium. Modern drives store anywhere from about 10GB–320GB per tape, which makes them adequate for backing up a single server or a few workstations, although you may need to use multiple tapes for large servers or multicomputer networks. Tape is a sequential access medium, meaning that you must read the data straight through from the beginning. (Some drives support partial exceptions to this rule, though.) Tape is reasonably fast but isn't the most reliable backup medium.

Optical media: CD-Recordable (CD-R), CD-Rewriteable (CD-RW), and various recordable DVD technologies have been gaining in popularity as backup media. These technologies can store 650MB–9.4GB per disc. This low capacity makes optical media a poor choice for backing up entire networks or large servers, but they may be adequate for backing up individual workstations, or at least their boot partitions. The near universal presence of optical media readers on workstations can also simplify data restoration.

Removable disks: Removable disks, such as floppy disks, Zip disks, LS-120 disks, and magneto-optical disks, are popular backup media for use by individuals to back up their personal data files. These disks' capacities vary from less than 1MB to about 20GB, so they're inadequate for backing up entire networks. Like optical media, though, the larger removable disks can be good choices for backing up small workstations. Removable media tend to be expensive, though.

Removable hard disks: You can purchase special mounting hardware that enables you to swap hard disks in and out of a computer much as you can insert and remove more conventional removable disks. Conventional hard disks have capacities of up to 320GB in early 2004, with higher capacities on the way. Such disks can back up the better part of a small network, and they tend to be quite fast.

Table 16-1 summarizes the features of several popular removable media technologies, arranged by order of increasing maximum capacity. (Table 16-1 doesn't consider tape changers, though; their capacities can be much higher than indicated.) Of course, the details are constantly changing. Table 16-1 shows the capacities and other information for devices that were available in early 2004; by the time you read this, more capable units may be available. Less capable devices were also available in the past, so you may encounter devices below the stated low points for a device type.

Table 16-1. Common Removable Media Devices

Device Type	Capacity	Speed	Interfaces
Floppy disk	1.2MB–2.88MB	Variable; typically 30KB/s	Floppy, USB
LS-120	120MB–240MB	4.0MB/s	ATA, USB, parallel, PC Card
CD-R and CD-RW	650MB–700MB	150KB/s–7.5MB/s	ATA, SCSI, IEEE-1394, USB
Iomega Zip disk	100MB–750MB	0.6MB/s–2.4MB/s	ATA, SCSI, USB, parallel, PC Card
Castlewood Orb	2.3GB–5.7GB	12.2MB/s–17.35MB/s	ATA, SCSI, USB, IEEE-1394
Magneto-optical	128MB–9.1GB	2MB/s–6MB/s	SCSI
Recordable DVD	4.7GB–9.4GB	4MB/s–8MB/s	ATA, SCSI, IEEE-1394, USB
Iomega Peerless	5GB–20GB	15MB/s	IEEE-1394, SCSI
Removable hard disk	20GB–320GB	10MB/s–100MB/s	ATA, SCSI, IEEE-1394, USB
Tape	10GB–320GB	2MB/s–16MB/s	Floppy, USB, parallel, ATA, SCSI

NOTE Tape drive manufacturers frequently quote capacities and speeds based on assumptions of 2:1 data compression during backup. Of course, you can apply compression to any backup medium, so you should be sure to consider this feature of specification sheets when comparing tapes with other media.

In terms of cost, you should consider both the cost of the drive (or removable mounting hardware, in the case of removable hard disks) and the cost of the media (or the disks themselves, in the case of removable hard disks). Some media, such as tapes, look very good when you consider media alone; but the cost of most tape drives is quite high (several hundred to well over a thousand dollars), which negates the cost benefits of the media themselves.

As a general rule, removable disk devices (Zip disks, LS-120 disks, and so on) are expensive; the media aren't very pricey, but they store so little data that their total costs are quite high. Optical media (CD-R, CD-RW, and recordable DVD) are inexpensive, at pennies per gigabyte, and their drives are inexpensive. This makes these media good choices for backing up limited amounts of data. You might use these drives to back up workstations' OS installations, for instance. Despite their high drive costs, tapes can be cost-effective on very large networks when you make very frequent backups. For smaller installations, though, the plummeting price of hard disks makes removable hard disks an appealing choice. A mounting kit costs about $150–$200, with a sub-$100 price for each subsequent drive. This combination, including half a dozen or a dozen 100GB–200GB hard drives, is likely to cost less than most tape drives and equivalent storage capacity in tapes. This can be a cost-effective way to back up a server or a small network, particularly if you also use optical media to store base workstation installations; the combination of optical media for "virgin" workstation installations and either tapes or removable hard disks for more frequently changing data can be an effective one.

In examining backup hardware, you should consider whether your backup needs are short-term or long-term. Short-term backups are intended to provide a quick way to recover recent data in the event of a hardware failure. Long-term backups are designed for archiving data for potential recovery months or years in the future. Optical media are widely regarded as excellent for long-term archival storage; most estimates place their lifetimes at 10–100 years, although some recent studies suggest these estimates may be optimistic. Another factor to consider in archival storage is the availability of drives to read the media. Hardware to read exotic tape or removable disk formats may be uncommon in a decade or two, but CD-ROM and DVD-ROM drives and media are so common today that readers for these devices will almost certainly be readily available for the foreseeable future.

Backup Software Options

Once you've selected your backup hardware, you must select your backup software. Samba can be a part of the overall software equation, but Samba alone can't write to the backup hardware. At a minimum, you'll need the help of your OS's kernel, including its device drivers and perhaps filesystem support. Some backup media (particularly optical devices) require additional special software to do the job.

Software for Removable Disks

Removable disks, including both low-capacity disks such as floppies and removable hard disks, are handled much as you handle disk partitions. Depending upon the OS and the medium type, you might or might not create partitions on the removable medium. For instance, Zip disks are conventionally partitioned, using the fourth primary partition for the disk's filesystem in the case of *x*86-based hardware. Floppies and magneto-optical disks, on the other hand, are typically not partitioned; they're treated as one big device.

Whether you partition the disk or not, you create a filesystem on the disk (on the partition or the raw device). What filesystem you use depends on your OS, the media type, and your specific needs. In most cases, the backup system's primary filesystem is a good choice. If you store backup files directly on the medium, the Samba server computer's OS will be able to store the files just as it would store files on its internal hard disk. Sometimes the File Allocation Table (FAT) can be a good choice, particularly if you want to read the disk back on a Windows system without the help of the Samba server. On the other hand, using FAT can lose some filesystem characteristics, such as ACLs. Sometimes storing a backup in an archive file, such as a tarball or zip file, can preserve these characteristics.

Software for Tapes

Most Unix-like OSs provide access to tape devices using device files in the /dev directory tree. For instance, under Linux the first SCSI tape device is accessed as /dev/st0 or /dev/nst0. (The first file automatically rewinds the tape after every access; the second one is a nonrewinding access file.) To store data on the tape, files are typically bundled in an archive file, then that file is copied to the tape device. In fact, popular Unix backup software such as tar, cpio, and dump provides the means to send archives directly to the tape device. A Samba backup server might send data to the tape file in any of three ways:

- Accept an archive created on the client, and copy it directly to the tape device file.

- Accept individual files, bundle them into an archive file, and send the archive to the tape device file.

- Use Samba client tools to retrieve files from backup clients, archive them, and send the resulting archive to the tape device file.

In all of these cases, the most important pieces of software you must ensure you have are drivers for the tape backup device. In most cases, you'll need a software component for the interface hardware (such as a USB port or SCSI host adapter) and a driver for tape drives generically; few tape drives require drivers customized to their specific models. In the case of Samba accepting ready-made archives, you'll also need a tool to copy the archive to the tape drive, such as cat or dd. Such tools are normally part of a Unix installation. Likewise, archive tools such as tar, cpio, and dump are part of normal Unix installations, so they can handle the second method of creating tape archives. Alternatively, you can use a third-party Unix backup tool, such as the Backup/Recovery Utility (BRU; http://www.bru.com) to perform your Unix-side backups. Samba ships with a special tar variant, called smbtar, which can retrieve files from other systems and send the archive directly to the tape drive. (The smbtar tool is actually a script that links smbclient to tar.)

In some cases, you may want to fit multiple backups on a single tape. This is most important if you want to perform incremental backups or if your tapes are big enough to hold several systems' data and you want to separate these systems. To support this feature, you can use the mt utility in conjunction with the nonrewinding tape device to move backward and forward on the tape in order to find any of the *files* (that is, backup sets) stored on the tape. Consult the mt man page to learn how to use it.

Software for Optical Media

Optical media require the help of a special program to send data to the disc. One such program is cdrecord, but other programs, such as cdrdao, can also be used. These programs send individual files to the optical medium, much as copying a file to a tape device file does. As with archiving to tape, archiving to optical media can be done in any of several ways, including:

Raw archive dump: You can dump an archive file directly to the optical medium. To read it back, you would use dd or some other utility to copy the file directly from an optical reader's device file or point the archive utility at the optical reader's device file as input. Restoration in this way works much like restoring from tape. One drawback is that restoring files directly on Windows systems may be difficult; you'll need to use the backup server computer or at least a Unix-like OS's emergency boot system on the backup client to recover files.

Archive dump in a filesystem: You can store the archive file in a filesystem (probably the common ISO-9660 filesystem) and write the filesystem to the optical medium. You can then read the archive file in any OS that supports the filesystem you used and recover files from the archive file.

Raw filesystem dump: You can store the files you want to back up directly in a filesystem and store that filesystem directly on the optical medium. The most common way to do this is to burn an ISO-9660 filesystem to the disc. ISO-9660 loses many important file characteristics, though, including the write permission bits, so this isn't a good way to back up an OS. You might back up individual projects in this way, though. You can also dump a raw ext2fs, ReiserFS, XFS, FFS, FAT, or other filesystem to optical media. This can be a good way to back up a workstation's boot OS, but it's got some problems. Most notably, the restore must be done to a partition of precisely the same size as the original. On modern systems, many partitions are also likely to be too large to fit on a single optical disc (particularly CD-R or CD-RW discs).

If you choose to store the archive in an ISO-9660 filesystem or store files directly in such a filesystem, you need the help of a program called mkisofs, which creates the filesystem as a file that can then be recorded using cdrecord or a similar program. (You can pipe the two programs together, if you like.)

 NOTE Chapter 14 presents two examples of shares that can create optical discs from files passed to Samba from a client. Either of these sample shares can be used as a type of backup share, but some critical filesystem data may be lost. Chances are you won't use such a share as a system or network backup share, but you might use these shares as starting points for designing something that's better suited to this purpose. They can also be used by individuals to back up particular working projects.

A Summary of tar

You can use any of several backup tools, such as tar, cpio, dump, BRU, or even cp, to create your backups. The details vary substantially from one tool to another, so I can't cover all of them here. Instead, this section provides an overview of just one tool: tar. This program (whose name stands for *tape archiver*) is a very popular tool for creating archive files and for performing backups. You can use tar to back up to tape, to store an archive file on a removable disk, or to create an archive file that you'll burn to an optical disk (with or without the benefit of a carrier ISO-9660 filesystem).

The tar utility takes a wide variety of parameters, which fall into two broad classes: commands and qualifiers. You use tar by typing its name followed by precisely one command and any number of qualifiers. Tables 16-2 and 16-3 summarize the most important tar commands and qualifiers, respectively.

Table 16-2. tar *Commands*

Command	Abbreviation	Description
--append	-r	Appends non-tar files to a tar file
--concatenate	-A	Appends one tar file to another
--create	-c	Creates an archive
--diff or --compare	-d	Compares files on disk to an archive's contents
--extract or --get	-x	Extracts files from an archive
--list	-t	Displays information on files in an archive
--update	-u	Appends files to an archive if the files on disk are newer than the ones in the archive

Table 16-3. Common tar *Qualifiers*

Qualifier	Abbreviation	Description
--absolute-paths	-P	Includes the leading / or ./ in archived filenames
--bzip2	-j	Uses bzip2 compression on files
--directory *dir*	-C	Changes to the specified directory before acting
--exclude *file*		Doesn't back up or restore the specified *file*
--exclude-from *file*	-X	Doesn't back up or restores files specified in *file*
--file [*host:*]*file*	-f	Uses the *file* (optionally on the specified *host*) as the tar file
--gzip or --gunzip	-z	Uses gzip compression on files
--listed-incremental *file*	-g	Performs an incremental backup using the specified *file* to store information on previously archived files

Table 16-3. Common tar *Qualifiers (Continued)*

Qualifier	Abbreviation	Description
`--multi-volume`	`-M`	Uses multiple media for the archive
`--one-file-system`	`-l`	Doesn't recurse into subdirectories on mounted filesystems
`--same-permissions`	`-p`	Preserves all ownership and permissions information
`--tape-length N`	`-L`	Specifies tape length for multivolume backups
`--verbose`	`-v`	Displays extra information on file creation, listing, or extraction

NOTE   Tables 16-2 and 16-3 present the commands and qualifiers as used by recent versions of GNU tar, which is the standard version of tar with FreeBSD, most Linux distributions, and Mac OS X. Some Unix-like OSs, though, ship with other tar variants. Some of these may not accept the verbose forms of commands and qualifiers (such as --create), only the short versions (such as -c). They may also vary in precisely what commands and qualifiers they support. If in doubt, consult your OS's tar man page or other documentation.

Normally, you'll use one command and at least one qualifier, although in theory you can omit all qualifiers for some operations. (The tar command normally defaults to accessing your tape device, so you may be able to omit the --file qualifier.) As an example, consider a backup of a system that has a root (/) partition, a /home partition, and a /usr partition:

```
# tar --create --verbose --one-file-system --file /dev/st0 / /home /usr
```

A more succinct form of this command (and one that's more likely to work on non-GNU versions of tar) uses the abbreviations for each of the tar commands and qualifiers:

```
# tar -cvlf /dev/st0 / /home /usr
```

NOTE   Some versions of tar require a single dash (-) before abbreviated commands and qualifiers, as in tar -cvlf. You can omit the dash in the popular GNU version of tar, though.

In either form, this command backs up the entire computer to the SCSI tape device at /dev/st0. Of course, you may need to adjust that device file on your system. This example uses the --one-file-system (-l) parameter to keep tar from backing up partitions other than those that are specified. For instance, if the system also had a /var partition, this command would *not* back it up. Using --one-file-system is helpful in preventing problems due to backing up mounts from remote NFS, Samba, or other file servers; mounted removable media that you don't want to back up; and virtual filesystems, such as Linux's /proc filesystem, that contain system information files that could cause a system to crash if restored inappropriately. Alternatively, you could use --exclude or --exclude-from (-X) to explicitly exclude such filesystems from being backed up.

You can use tar to back up directly to tape or create an archive file by specifying an appropriate filename, as in --file backup.tar.gz. You can place this backup file on a mounted removable disk or store the backup file on CD-R using mkisofs and cdrecord. Another option is to use tar to create a clone of a filesystem on a removable disk. To do this, you can pipe the command, like so:

```
# tar cvlf - / /home /usr | (cd /mnt/backup; tar xlf -)
```

This command backs up, then uses cd to change to the mounted backup medium, and extracts the backup. In both the backup and restore commands, using a dash (-) as the filename tells tar to back up and restore using a variant of standard output and input, so no intermediate files are created. You can achieve similar results using cp, but tar is likely to preserve more information correctly.

The --listed-incremental option can be useful in performing *incremental* backups, in which most backup operations are not complete. In an incremental backup scheme, you back up all of the files on the system fairly rarely. In between full backups, you perform incremental backups, which back up only those files that have changed recently. For instance, you might perform a full backup once a week and perform an incremental backup on other days. This approach can save space on your backup media, save network bandwidth, and save time. Incremental backups can be more difficult to restore, though; you may need to feed several backup media to the restore program to recover a system to its most recent working state.

TIP   When backing up, use the --verbose (-v) option and redirect the output to a log file. This log file will then contain information on the files stored in a given backup. This information can be very useful if you later need to restore individual files because you can locate their precise names and locations.

Backing Up the Backup Server

Once you've selected and installed your backup hardware, one of the first tasks you should undertake is to back up the system on which that hardware is installed. How you do this depends on the backup hardware and software you've chosen; the precise commands used to back up to tape will differ from those used to back up to a removable hard disk, for instance. The preceding section, "A Summary of tar," describes how to back up a computer using tar.

When you back up the backup server, be sure you *don't* back up any mounted remote filesystems unless you want them in the same backup set as the server's. The idea is to have a backup that you can use to quickly recover the backup system itself to a working state. In case of a massive network failure (say, a fire or theft of many systems), you would restore the backup server using its own backup hardware (or replacement hardware, if necessary) and then restore the clients using the restored backup server.

You should verify that you can restore data to the backup server itself. If you can't restore data locally, you won't be able to restore data to clients when the time comes. The upcoming section "Restoring Data" describes data restoration in more detail.

Backing Up Samba-Specific Data

If your backup server also has ordinary Samba shares, you may need to consider how to back up Samba-specific data. The same comments apply to some network backup scenarios. Some of the data that may be of concern are as follows:

SMB/CIFS permissions: SMB/CIFS-specific permissions, such as the hidden, system, and archive bits, may need to be backed up and restored in an appropriate way. Most Unix backup programs will handle this task appropriately, as these bits are stored in Unix execute bits, and Unix backup tools handle these bits. One notable possible exception is the archive bit, which under Windows should be cleared when a file is backed up. Ordinarily a failure to clear this bit won't cause real problems, but if you're concerned about it, you could write a backup script that performs an appropriate chmod on all the files you back up with your backup tools. Note that this action might have unintended consequences if applied inappropriately to Unix files that should have their execute bits set.

ACLs: If you've configured Samba to not support ACLs or if your filesystem doesn't support them, you don't need to worry about ACL backups. If you want to back up your ACLs, though, you must locate a backup tool that can do so. Unfortunately, most Unix backup tools ignore ACLs. One tar variant that can do this job is star (ftp://ftp.berlios.de/pub/star/).

OS-specific data: Some OSs create special directories that hold data they need. Thursby Systems' (http://www.thursby.com) DAVE for Mac OS, for instance, stores Mac OS resource forks on SMB/CIFS shares using subdirectories with the hidden bit set. Such files and directories are likely to be backed up with whatever backup tools you use and so should not pose a problem.

Of course, you should also be sure your backup includes the smb.conf file. In fact, for a server, you should probably create a separate backup of the /etc directory and any other directories that hold critical system configuration files. On some systems, /etc will fit entirely on a single floppy disk, particularly if you use compression. Using a floppy disk, or even a CD-R, Zip disk, or other low-capacity removable disk, can be a good way to handle these backups. You can quickly recover an old working configuration if you accidentally damage your configuration files.

Performing Client-Initiated Network Backups

Backup server computers frequently run server software, such as Samba, and rely upon their clients to initiate the backup process. Two common methods of implementing such a share in Samba are to use the print command parameter in a pseudo-printer share to handle data transfers and to use a pair of preexec and postexec scripts to process individual files passed to the server from a client. Both methods are similar to the CD-R creation shares described in Chapter 14.

NOTE An alternative method of initiating a backup is described in the upcoming section "Performing Server-Initiated Network Backups."

Using a print command *Backup Share*

The print command parameter, described in Chapter 6 and in Chapter 14, is a way to trigger a command that can run on the Samba server computer whenever a client sends a file to the server via a printer share. This procedure is flexible enough that you can use such shares even for nonprinter data-processing tasks, including backing up client computers. If you choose to pursue this approach, you must configure the Samba backup server and create procedures or batch files to run on the backup clients.

Creating the Pseudo-Printer Backup Share

A backup share that uses print command doesn't look very different from any other printer share. Like ordinary printer shares, this share uses the printable = Yes parameter (or one of its synonyms) to flag the share as a printer share. It also uses the print command parameter to point Samba to a script or command that does the bulk of the work:

```
[backup-pr]
    comment = Remote Backup Share
    directory = /var/spool/samba
    max connections = 1
    printable = Yes
    print command = dd if=%s of=/dev/st0; rm %s
```

This share is really quite simple, and it relies upon the client to do the bulk of the processing. The print command merely uses the dd utility to copy the file received from the client (indicated by the %s variable) to the tape device file (/dev/st0) and then to delete the received file. If the client passes a tarball to the server, the result will be a tape backup that's identical to what would have been created had the client created a backup to a tape drive connected directly to the client. Of course, the backup need not be a tarball; it could be a zip file, a StuffIt archive, an ISO-9660 filesystem image file, or anything else. This simple configuration does have some important limitations, though:

Permissions: The assumption in this [backup-pr] share is that the user has write privileges to the /dev/st0 tape device. This assumption may well be incorrect. Depending upon your network configuration, you might want to give group write privileges to the /dev/st0 file and use the force group parameter to give the user appropriate group privileges to write to this file.

Backup size: If the partition on which /var/spool/samba resides is too small to hold the backup, the process will fail. Likewise, if the backup is too large to fit on a single tape, the backup will fail. Writing a script that checks the backup size and, if necessary, dumps it to tape in parts could solve the second problem. The first isn't easily solved except perhaps by ensuring that the partition on which /var/spool/samba resides is extremely large.

Concurrent use: This share is very simple and can process only one user at a time. The max connections = 1 parameter ensures that only one user at a time will be able to access this share. This control should prevent access conflicts, but it can be awkward if many people want to back up their systems in quick succession. A more sophisticated system might create a backup queue of some sort—but swapping tapes in and out could be a problem.

Many variants on this process are possible. Chapter 14 presents a CD-R creation share that could be used for handling certain types of limited backups. A variant on this approach could take a zip file, extract its contents, and use tar or some other tool to back up the data to tape, a removable hard disk, or some other medium.

Using the Pseudo-Printer Share

Use of the pseudo-printer [backup-pr] share presented in the preceding section requires creating some type of archive file on the backup client computer and then passing that file on to the backup server. The client can be any OS that can submit a file to a Samba printer share without passing it through a print filter. One way to demonstrate the use of this share is via Samba's own smbclient program, preceded by a call to tar to create an archive:

```
# tar -cvfl backup.tar / /home /usr
# smbclient //BACKSTEP/BACKUP-PR -U backup
added interface ip=192.168.1.3 bcast=192.168.1.255 nmask=255.255.255.0
Password:
Domain=[RINGWORLD] OS=[Unix] Server=[Samba 3.0.0]
smb: \> print backup.tar
putting file backup.tar as backup.tar (402.1 kb/s) (average 402.1 kb/s)
smb: \> quit
```

After you type the print backup.tar command, the client should pause as the file is transferred and the backup server's tape drive springs into action. (If the two computers are in the same room, you'll probably be able to hear the tape drive whirring away.) Once the backup server finishes sending the file to the tape drive, you'll be able to type **quit** to exit from smbclient.

 NOTE This example doesn't use compression on the backup because most tape drives support their own compression. You could use compression to save network bandwidth at the cost of CPU time on the client (and possibly the server, if you decide to uncompress the tarball before saving it to tape). Compression might also be worthwhile if your backup share backs up to an uncompressed medium such as an optical disc.

On a Windows system, you can pass the backup job to the pseudo-printer share using the COPY command. If you want to create a tape backup in tar format, you'll have to obtain a copy of tar for Windows. You can find such ports from various sources, such as http://unxutils.sourceforge.net or http://www.cygwin.com. If you don't care about creating a tar backup, you can use a zip utility or some other tool. In any event, the process for creating the backup and copying it to the backup share looks something like this:

```
C:\> TAR -cvf D:\BACKUP.TAR C:\
C:\> COPY D:\BACKUP.TAR \\BACKSTEP\BACKUP-PR
C:\> DEL D:\BACKUP.TAR
```

These commands create a tarball on the D: drive called BACKUP.TAR, which holds the contents of the entire Windows C: drive. This backup is then copied to the BACKUP-PR share on the BACKSTEP computer, where it's dumped to tape or otherwise backed up. Of course, you should modify the specifics to suit your computer and its configuration. You can also create a batch job that does the entire task automatically by entering these commands in a script. You can then type the script name or create a shortcut to the script on the desktop and double-click it whenever you want to back up the client.

As with using the backup share on the Samba server, using this backup process on the client is not without caveats. The most important of these is that the client must possess enough free disk space for both its regular files and the temporary tarball (or other archive file) you create to hold those files. If your clients don't possess enough disk space, you may need to use another type of backup plan, such as the preexec/postexec share described next or a server-initiated backup. (You could use a file share on the backup server or another system as temporary storage, but doing so will greatly increase the network bandwidth of each backup operation.) Another potential problem is in the type of information stored in the archive file. Some archives may lack information such as the short (8.3) filenames associated with long filenames, and this information may be difficult to recover in a disaster recovery situation. Many native Windows backup tools provide workarounds for such problems, so you may want to consider using such a tool to create the archive files you pass to the backup client, even if the contents of those files aren't readily accessed from a Unix system.

Using a `preexec/postexec` *Backup Share*

A second type of backup share that you can use for client-initiated backups is an ordinary file share. The simplest case is one in which a removable disk is the backup medium. You can then create a backup share that points to the backup medium's mount point, mount the disk, and perform a drag-and-drop operation on the client's files to copy the files to the backup disk. If your backup medium is a tape or optical disc, though, you'll need to enlist the help of a `postexec` script to copy the backup files to the backup medium, and a `preexec` script may be helpful in preparing the share directory.

> **NOTE** Even if you use a removable disk, `preexec` and `postexec` scripts can be helpful in mounting and unmounting the disk. Chapter 14 presents an example of a removable disk share that handles this task automatically.

Creating the Share Script Backup Share

Chapter 14 presents a file share that includes `preexec` and `postexec` scripts to burn the share's data to a CD-R. You could use the script presented in that chapter as a starting point for a backup script, but it's probably not ideal for most backup purposes. Most important, the files are stored on an ISO-9660 CD-ROM with Rock Ridge and Joliet extensions. This format loses some critical information, such as the read-only bit. You could modify the script to bundle the files into a tarball instead of or in addition to creating an ISO-9660 image file to burn to the CD-R, though.

A similar approach works for backing up to tape. In fact, a tape backup can be simpler than an optical disc backup because a single program, such as `tar`, can send data straight from the backup directory to the backup medium. A backup share might look something like this:

```
[backup-files]
    comment = File Backup Share
    directory = /home/samba/backup
    max connections = 1
    read only = No
    preexec = rm -r /home/samba/backup/*
    postexec = cd /home/samba/backup; tar -cvlpf /dev/st0 ./; rm -r ./*
```

This share is a complete and stand-alone backup share; after the user disconnects from the share, the `postexec` parameter runs `cd` to change into the backup directory and then runs `tar` to back up the data, followed by `rm` to delete it from the server's hard disk. Of course, if you wanted to do more processing of the data, you could create a script to do the job, as the CD-R creation file share in Chapter 14 does. Your script might check that the file has actually been used, e-mail a summary of the backup activity to the user, or perform other tasks.

This example uses cd to change into the directory in which the files are stored in order to avoid storing the path to the backup directory in the archive. Storing the complete path could complicate data restoration because you would then need to restore to the same directory, which might not be convenient.

One important difference between this backup share and a pseudo-printer backup share involves where the archive is created. In a pseudo-printer share, the archive is created on the client. (Of course, the client could create an archive that's expanded and re-encoded on the backup server, as in the CD-R pseudo-printer share presented in Chapter 14.) When the client creates the final backup archive, the client is responsible for correctly encoding file metadata. When the server does the job, the server is responsible for this task. In the case of the [backup-files] share presented here, file metadata are stored on tape in the format that Samba supports, if at all. Just as when backing up a Samba server and its data, a backup share of this type may need special tools to back up ACLs. Furthermore, when you restore data, metadata may be lost unless you restore to a Samba share and then transfer the files back to the client using Windows. If you try to restore via a more direct route, you may lose some metadata.

As with the pseudo-printer backup share, the [backup-files] share requires that the user who accesses the share have write privileges to the tape device file (/dev/st0 in this example). If this isn't the case, you can use force group in conjunction with appropriate group ownership and group write privileges to /dev/st0. This solution will change the group ownership of the files in the archive, though. This change is unimportant for Windows 9x/Me clients but may cause problems when backing up Windows NT/200x/XP systems that store their own group information with files. Alternatively, you could use root postexec instead of postexec to execute the backup command as root. You should be cautious about this approach, though, particularly if you use a sophisticated script to do the job. An error in your configuration or a bug could give miscreants too much access to your system if you use root postexec.

Using the Share Script Backup Share

Using the [backup-files] share is quite straightforward: Insert a tape in the tape drive and then, on a Windows client, open a window on the BACKUP-FILES share, drag and drop the files and directories you want to back up (perhaps everything in C:), and close the window on the share. If all goes well, Windows will close the share and Samba will execute the postexec instructions, sending the data to the tape drive (or some other medium, if you're using something else).

Unfortunately, Windows clients don't always terminate their connections to the file server in a timely manner. This is particularly true of Windows 9x/Me clients. You may need to log out of the Windows client or even reboot it to terminate the connection. Alternatively, you can use the deadtime parameter to force Samba to disconnect from the client after a specified period of inactivity. Using deadtime poses a risk of early disconnection, though, particularly if a user is backing up a hodge-podge collection of files and directories and becomes distracted by a telephone call or some other activity midtask.

Plusses and Minuses of Client-Initiated Backups

The pseudo-printer and file share client-initiated backup shares vary in important ways. Nonetheless, they share many important features, including the following:

Client scheduling: Backup scheduling is handled by clients. This may be done by the users of individual machines or by network administrators. It's typically done manually, although in principle it could be done on a timed automatic basis.

Conflict avoidance: One consequence of client scheduling is that it may be difficult to avoid conflicts over access to the backup hardware, particularly on a large network. Two or more users might want to perform backups at the same time, and with only one backup device, accomplishing this goal may be impossible.

File selection: It's the client's responsibility to select which files to back up. If you use native backup software to create an archive for transfer, this isn't a problem. You might use drag-and-drop operations or nonbackup archive tools, though. In such cases, you might easily miss important system or hidden files.

Client configuration: You need not run any servers on the client. Depending upon the details of the backup share, you might not even need to install any special software at all; drag-and-drop or ordinary archive utilities might be all you need.

OS compatibility: If the clients bundle files into archives, as in the pseudo-printer backup share presented earlier, a client-initiated backup tool can work with just about any client OS. In particular, you can use one Samba server to back up another Unix system. The file share backup share presented earlier, though, would lose critical Unix permissions unless you modified it to accept files passed in an archive created on the backup client.

Security: The backup server itself is exposed to all the computers that should be able to access it. Depending upon your local network's security settings, such as the presence (or lack thereof) of a firewall, the backup server may be exposed to the Internet at large. Because clients need not run servers, they aren't greatly exposed by backup operations. Of course, unrelated factors can cause security problems for backup clients.

Server storage space: For tape and optical disc backups, the server needs enough hard disk space to store at least one complete backup. Some methods may require twice this space, or perhaps even more. If you share a removable disk as an ordinary share, though, this requirement doesn't exist.

Overall, client-initiated backups work best on small networks. One good configuration is to rely on two backup types: You as a network administrator should create backups, perhaps to optical discs, from which you can restore clients to working condition. You might use emergency Linux boot systems (described in the upcoming section "Using a Linux Emergency System to Restore Data") or client-side archiving tools such as PowerQuest's Drive Image (http://www.powerquest.com/driveimage/) to create image backups of the computers' boot partitions. You or your users could then use client-initiated backups to tape, optical discs, or removable disks to back up changes to workstations, such as locally stored user data files. In most restore situations, you could use only these workstation-change backups. In case of a complete hard disk failure, you would start with the boot partition backup to restore a working system and then use the workstation-change backup to restore user-specific data.

Performing Server-Initiated Network Backups

Client-initiated backups are a logical extension of Samba as a file and print server platform. Another approach to Samba-mediated backups is possible, though. In this configuration, the Samba backup server actually runs Samba's client tools, and the backup clients run SMB/CIFS server software. The backup server can then contact the backup clients to initiate a backup operation. Doing this requires configuring backup shares on clients and using either a special tool called smbtar or a mount of the remote share and a more conventional backup tool, such as tar. Naturally, this approach has both advantages and disadvantages over the client-initiated approach to network backups.

NOTE   The computer that holds the backup medium is frequently referred to as a *backup server* even if the backup operations require it to run client software, with the server software running on the backup clients. This terminology can be confusing.

Creating a Share on the Backup Client

A server-initiated backup requires that the backup clients be running SMB/CIFS server software. How you accomplish this goal depends on the client OS. If you're using a very obscure OS, you may need to consult its documentation for details. For Windows NT/200x/XP, Windows 9x/Me, and Unix backup clients, though, read the following sections.

NOTE   Backing up Mac OS clients using a server-initiated scheme is tricky at best. With any version of Mac OS, SMB/CIFS doesn't provide the tools needed to back up vital information, such as resource forks (for Mac OS Classic) or Unix-style permissions (for Mac OS X). You could back up data files that don't store vital information in resource forks or rely too heavily on Unix-style permissions, though. Overall, I recommend that you not even try backing up a Mac OS client using Samba server-initiated methods.

Windows NT/200x/XP Backup Clients

The first step in sharing a disk you want to back up is to install the Windows SMB/CIFS server software. In Windows 200x/XP, you can accomplish this task as follows:

1. Open the Windows Control Panel.

2. Double-click the Network Connections (Windows XP) or Network and Dial-Up Connections (Windows 200x) icon. This action opens a like-named window.

3. Right-click the Local Area Connection icon in the new window, and select Properties from the pop-up menu. The result is the Local Area Connection Properties dialog box shown in Figure 16-1.

Figure 16-1. The Local Area Connection Properties dialog box summarizes protocols supported by Windows.

4. If an item called File and Printer Sharing for Microsoft Networks is present, skip ahead to step 8.

5. If an item called File and Printer Sharing for Microsoft Networks is not present, click the Install button. This action brings up the Select Network Component Type dialog box.

6. Select Service, and click Add in the Select Network Component Type dialog box. Windows displays the Select Network Service dialog box.

7. Select File and Printer Sharing for Microsoft Networks in the Select Network Service dialog box, and click OK. You should see the File and Printer Sharing for Microsoft Networks item appear in the Local Area Connection Properties dialog box.

8. Be sure that the File and Printer Sharing for Microsoft Networks item is checked, and click Close in the Local Area Connection Properties dialog box.

These steps add the native Windows SMB/CIFS server support to the computer. Only once this support has been added can you create file shares, which the backup server will access. To create such a share, follow these steps:

1. Open the My Computer folder on the computer.

2. Right-click the icon for the drive you want to back up, and select the Sharing and Security (Windows XP) or Sharing (Windows 200x) item from the pop-up menu. The result is a Properties dialog box with the Sharing tab selected.

3. In Windows XP, the tab provides a warning that sharing an entire drive has potentially negative security consequences. Click this notice to see the real configuration dialog box, shown in Figure 16-2.

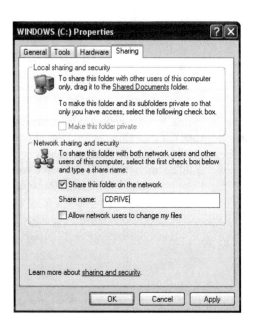

Figure 16-2. Windows provides a simple dialog box to enable sharing of a directory or disk.

4. In the Properties dialog box, check the Share This Folder on the Network button and enter a share name in the Share Name field. In Windows 200*x*, the interface is somewhat different. The window appears with a default share name of the drive letter followed by a dollar sign ($), as shown in Figure 16-3. You must click the New Share button to create a new file share. You can enter a share name and comment in the resulting dialog box.

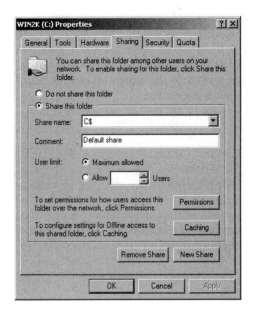

Figure 16-3. The Windows 200x share-creation dialog box is more complex than its Windows XP equivalent.

5. In Windows XP, you can opt to enable or disable write access to the share by checking or unchecking the Allow Network Users to Change My Files check box in the Properties dialog box (Figure 16-2). A backup share normally requires only read access, so this box should be unchecked. (If and when you need to restore data, though, you might need to temporarily check this box.)

6. Click OK to start sharing the drive.

CAUTION By default, Windows XP Home file shares have *no password*. This configuration is *very* dangerous and in fact is a *major* problem with using server-initiated backups with Windows XP Home. Windows XP Professional enables use of passwords but only if the Simple Sharing feature is disabled. You can do this by opening the My Computer window, selecting Tools ➤ Folder Options, clicking the View tab, and deselecting the Use Simple File Sharing option. If you must back up a Windows XP Home system, your best bet is to upgrade to Windows XP Professional. Failing that, you may want to install a third-party firewall product and use it to block access to the SMB/CIFS ports (particularly TCP ports 139 and 445) to any but the backup server computer. Unfortunately, the firewall that ships with Windows XP Home doesn't provide the fine-grained access controls required for this task.

Once file sharing is enabled, you can use the Samba backup server to back up the client, as described in the upcoming sections "Basic Principles of smbtar" and "Using tar and a Mounted Share."

Windows 9x/Me Backup Clients

Configuring Windows 9*x*/Me as a backup client is similar to configuring Windows NT/200*x*/XP, but some details differ:

- Double-clicking the Network icon in the Control Panel brings up a Network dialog box that's similar to the Local Area Connection Properties dialog box shown in Figure 16-1. This simplifies the process of getting to this point when installing SMB/CIFS server support.

- Right-clicking a drive and selecting Sharing brings up another variant on the Sharing tab of the Properties dialog box, shown in Figure 16-4. In most respects, this dialog box resembles the one used by Windows XP, but you can enter a password for read-only access, a password for read/write access, or both. By default, Windows 9*x*/XP uses what Samba calls *share-level security*, as opposed to the user-level security implemented by Windows NT/200*x*/XP. Thus, you can set different passwords for each file share you create.

- If you want to implement user-level access control, you must open the Network Control Panel, click the Access Control tab, select User-Level Access Control, and enter the NetBIOS name of a computer that will provide authentication services, such as a domain controller.

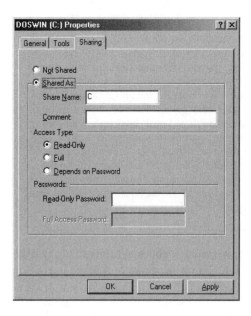

Figure 16-4. Windows 9x/Me assigns one or two passwords to each share, so you must type a password when creating a share.

Unix Backup Clients

As a general rule, using Samba for server-initiated backups of a Unix system is unwise. Because SMB/CIFS doesn't provide full support for Unix-style ownership, permissions, and other file metadata, any attempt to back up Unix-specific files via Samba will result in loss of some of this information. For this reason, it's best not to try to use Samba in this capacity, at least as a general rule. There are a few partial exceptions to this rule, though.

First, you might consider using Samba and a server-initiated backup procedure to back up files for which exact ownership and permissions are unimportant. For instance, you might use one Samba server with appropriate backup hardware to back up files that a second Samba server makes available to all users, such as a network's shared program files. In such a configuration, a hypothetical restore of the backed-up data may lose some permissions information, but because the data reside on Samba shares, this loss isn't likely to be important. One notable and important limitation of this configuration is that the Unix server itself won't be backed up via Samba, just the Samba file shares. To back up the Unix server OS itself, you'll need to use some other mechanism. Chances are you could use this mechanism to back up the Samba server's shares, as well. Thus, chances are there'd be little or no benefit to backing up the Samba shares in this way.

A second scenario involves using archiving tools on the Unix system to create a tarball or similar archive file that can then be backed up from the backup server. For instance, you might create a tarball of the computer's entire directory tree, place that tarball in a shared Samba directory, then use the Samba backup server computer to copy that tarball to tape, optical disc, or some other medium. This practice will preserve Unix ownership, permissions, and other metadata, but it's a bit awkward. To perform this backup automatically, you'd need to have some way for one system to control the other—the Samba backup server would need to trigger the archive operation, wait for the archive to appear, then back it up; or the Samba backup client would need to archive the data and then signal the Samba backup server that it's available. These problems aren't insurmountable, but chances are using a client-initiated backup would be a simpler solution, as would using non-Samba backup tools.

A final possible scenario involves using the unix extensions = Yes parameter on the Samba server running on the backup client and a backup tool running on the backup server that understands these extensions, such as the CIFS driver in the 2.6.*x* Linux kernel. In my experience, these features aren't yet mature enough (as of Samba 3.0.1 and the 2.6.1 Linux kernel) to be relied upon for backup purposes; some features are likely to be lost on restore. This problem may be eliminated in the future or if you use some SMB/CIFS client (backup server) software other than a 2.6.*x* Linux kernel, though.

If you do decide to create a Unix server-initiated backup share, you can do so just as you would create any ordinary Samba file share, as described in Chapter 5. In the case of using server-initiated backups merely to back up Samba file shares, no extra configuration is required unless file permissions issues become important. In that case, you may need to create a duplicate share with alternate security settings, use an include parameter with a variable in the filename to enable special options for the backup server computer, or otherwise customize security settings for the backup server computer. If you decide to create a share in which you'll store a tarball or other archive created on the backup client computer, you can use a fairly ordinary share definition along with some other intermachine communication method to coordinate creation of the archive and its recovery by the backup server computer.

Basic Principles of smbtar

One of the two principal methods of retrieving files from the backup client computers is a tool called smbtar. This program is a shell script that ships with Samba. The script calls the smbclient program and the tar program in order to back up the files from a backup client without actually mounting the remote system's shares on the Samba server. The smbtar utility is, therefore, useful on any computer that can run Samba, whether or not the OS is capable of mounting SMB/CIFS shares. The program has the following syntax:

```
smbtar [options] [filenames]
```

The *options* that the program accepts are as follows:

-s *server*: This is the name of the server on which the files reside—that is, the backup client computer.

-x *share*: This option identifies the name of the share that's to be backed up. The default *share* value is backup.

-X: Normally, the *filenames* you specify are ones you want to back up or restore. This option reverses the meaning; the *filenames* are ones that should be excluded from the backup or restore operation.

-d *directory*: This option tells smbtar to change to the specified directory for performing the backup or restore. You can use it to back up only part of a share or to restore files to a specified directory.

-v: This option enables verbose mode, which increases the information displayed during the program's run.

-u *username*: You specify the username to use for the connection with this option. The default is the username of whoever runs the program.

-p *password*: You can give a password to the program with this parameter. The default is no password (if the share requires one, smbtar will silently fail; you must provide the password on the command line).

-a: If you pass this parameter, smbtar will reset the SMB/CIFS archive bit on the backup client when it archives the file. This option requires write access to the backup client.

-t *tape*: This option specifies the tape device, which may be a tape device file (such as /dev/st0) or a regular file.

-b *blocksize*: You can set the tar block size, in multiples of 512 bytes, with this option. The default value is 20 (that is, 10KB). Adjusting this parameter can improve tape performance on some systems, but you'll need to experiment to learn what works best for your hardware.

-N *filename*: This option tells smbtar to back up only files that are newer than the specified file. You can use this feature to implement an incremental backup scheme by pointing the system at a log file created at the time of the last backup.

-i: Passing this option sets an incremental backup mode, in which only files with their SMB/CIFS archive bits set are backed up.

-r: The default smbtar operation is to back up a share. Passing this option initiates a restore operation.

-l *log-level*: This option sets the log level, equivalent to the -d option to smbclient.

As an example, consider the following command:

```
$ smbtar -s TAP -x CDRIVE -u grogers -p Y#iWT7td -t /dev/st0
```

This command backs up the CDRIVE share on the TAP computer. It uses the username grogers and the password Y#iWT7td. Data are stored on the /dev/st0 tape device. Of course, in practice you'll change most or all of these parameters and perhaps add more or conceivably delete one or more parameters. (For instance, you can omit the username when backing up a client that uses share-level security, such as a typical Windows 9*x*/Me system.)

This example shows a dollar sign ($) command prompt, suggesting that an ordinary user can execute it. This will work only if the user has write privileges to the backup device or file (/dev/st0 in this example). If the backup device requires root privileges, only root may execute the command.

The resulting backup is an ordinary tar backup. You can view what's on the backup by using the tar command's --list (-t) option, as in **tar -tvf /dev/st0** to view the backup stored on /dev/st0. You can also restore the backup using tar's --extract (-x) option. Of course, you may well need to restore the files to the original source, in which case using smbtar to do the job is appropriate. For instance, the following command restores files, assuming the backup client's SMB/CIFS server is running and accepts write access:

```
$ smbtar -r -s TAP -x CDRIVE -u grogers -p Y#iWT7td -t /dev/st0
```

NOTE Restoring data can pose special challenges. The upcoming section "Restoring Data" covers this topic in more detail.

One way to use smbtar is to run an automated backup schedule that backs up a few computers per night every week. For instance, suppose your network has ten computers. You could create five cron jobs, each of which backs up two computers using a script similar to Listing 16-1. This script backs up two computers and would be run once per week. One script might run at 1 a.m. on Monday, another at 1 a.m. on Tuesday, and so on. Somebody would have to swap tapes in and out each day.

Listing 16-1. Sample Script to Back Up Two Computers with smbtar

```
#!/bin/sh
smbtar -s TAP -x CDRIVE -u grogers -p Y#iWT7td -t /dev/nst0
smbtar -s WALTZ -x CDRIVE -u fastaire -p bU3N^neP -t /dev/nst0
mt -f /dev/nst0 rewind
```

CAUTION Like any automated server-initiated backup method, Listing 16-1 stores the passwords to the backup client systems in files on disk—in the case of Listing 16-1, they're stored in the backup script itself. This practice is potentially risky. To minimize the danger, ensure that the script is readable only by the user who should run it, and limit shell access to the backup server computer.

Listing 16-1 uses the nonrewinding tape device file (/dev/nst0) to store two backups on one tape. It then uses the mt utility to rewind the tape when the backup operation is complete. If you needed to restore the second backup on a tape, you'd use mt to skip past the first backup, as in **mt -f /dev/nst0 fsf 1** to skip past the first archive on the tape.

Of course, you can also use smbtar to archive files from backup clients to media other than tape. You'd specify a normal filename using the -t parameter. You can create a backup on a removable disk using this method, the result being a normal tarball on the removable medium. Alternatively, you could create the tarball in a normal hard disk directory and then use mkisofs and cdrecord to copy the tarball to an optical disc. Naturally, you can script all of these operations and run them from the cron utility if you want to perform them in an automated fashion.

Using tar and a Mounted Share

The smbtar utility was designed to back up Windows clients, and it includes a few options that take advantage of SMB/CIFS features that are designed with DOS and Windows clients in mind. The -a and -i options are two examples. These options take advantage of the SMB/CIFS archive bit to make it easier to implement an incremental backup plan. For this reason, using smbtar is a good approach to backing up Windows clients.

Sometimes, though, you might want to forego the use of smbtar. For instance, you might want to back up multiple clients in a single archive file rather than storing them as separate archives. The smbtar utility isn't designed for this task. You might also prefer using another archiving tool, such as cpio, rsync, or BRU, instead of tar. In such cases, the usual solution is to mount the remote share using the host OS's SMB/CIFS mounting tools and back up as you normally would.

NOTE Some administrators favor the dump backup utility. This tool is very filesystem-specific, though, and as of Samba 3.0, no dump tool for SMB/CIFS shares is available. Therefore, you can't use dump to back up a Windows system from another computer using SMB/CIFS.

Chapter 18 describes how to mount SMB/CIFS shares on some Unix-like OSs. You should consult that chapter for details of how to do the job. Once the share is mounted, you can back it up much as you would any other. For instance, to back up a single SMB/CIFS share in Linux, you might type the following commands:

```
# smbmount //TAP/CDRIVE /mnt/backup -o username=grogers,password=Y#iWT7td
# tar -cvlf /dev/st0 --directory /mnt/backup ./
# smbumount /mnt/backup
```

This sequence of commands is similar in effect to a single smbtar command to back up the share. It's more complex, but if you want to back up multiple shares simultaneously, you can mount them both in nearby directories (say, /mnt/tap and /mnt/waltz) and then back up both of these directories using one tar command. Of course, you'll then need to mount the shares at the same points, or at least at compatible points, should you need to restore the files, because the full or partial path to the mount points will be included in the backup archive.

Plusses and Minuses of Server-Initiated Backups

When comparing server-initiated to client-initiated backups, you need to consider the costs and benefits of each approach. Server-initiated backups have the following important characteristics:

Server scheduling: Servers handle backup scheduling, which can help you maintain a consistent backup schedule across your network, particularly if you use cron to manage the backup operation. One implication of this approach, though, is that if you perform automated backups in off hours, your backup clients must be left on at all hours, or at least overnight on nights when they're scheduled to be backed up.

Conflict avoidance: If you schedule backups automatically, you can easily avoid conflicts over access to the network hardware. As the backup server is in charge of matters, you need only develop an appropriate backup schedule and implement it at one point.

File selection: The smbtar program and Unix SMB/CIFS mount tools ignore the hidden and system bits, so hidden and system files will be backed up without problems. The actual hidden and system bits might not be properly backed up, though.

Client configuration: The backup clients need special configuration, as described earlier; they must be configured as SMB/CIFS servers.

OS compatibility: As noted earlier in "Unix Backup Clients," backing up Unix clients using a server-initiated backup and smbtar or SMB/CIFS mounting is unlikely to work well for any but very limited directory selections. Likewise, backing up Mac OS clients (either Mac OS Classic or Mac OS X) won't work well. This approach works best with Windows clients.

Backup client filesystems: Just as with OS issues, the filesystem used on the backup client can cause problems. Issues with the File Allocation Table (FAT) filesystem tend to be subtle and usually don't cause major problems. The New Technology File System (NTFS), though, can cause problems because a server-initiated backup won't capture ACLs, ownership, or some other advanced NTFS features. Options for restoring to NTFS are also more limited than are options for restoring to FAT.

Security: The backup server computer need not be greatly exposed when you use this backup method because it need not run any server software. The backup clients, though, are potentially quite exposed. This is particularly true of Windows XP Home systems, which have very poor access control mechanisms. You should use this approach to backup only when you can protect these computers in other ways, such as via firewalls.

Server storage space: The backup server computer needs little in the way of disk space, beyond what's required by the Unix OS and support software. Data are passed more or less directly from the backup clients to the backup medium. If you need to process the backup data in any way, though, such as creating intermediate files for backups to optical discs, the backup server may need more temporary storage space.

Overall, server-initiated backups can be a good choice on many networks. The scheduling flexibility alone makes this approach well worth using in order to back up clients during off hours. The security implications of running SMB/CIFS servers on all of the backup client computers is a potential problem, though. You should ensure that your local network is well protected by a firewall and set good passwords on all of the backup clients' file shares.

Another approach to using server-initiated backups is to back up workstations on an infrequent basis—say, once every six months. You can then enable the shares only when the backup is scheduled and disable them at other times. This approach is likely to be useful if workstations store little or no data locally, aside from the core OS files— that is, if you use Samba or other servers for storing all users' data files. In such an environment, restoring a backup that's several months old is unlikely to cause serious problems for users.

TIP   Some backup tools, such as the Advanced Maryland Automatic Network Disk Archiver (AMANDA; http://www.amanda.org), can help back up mixed-OS networks. AMANDA provides specialized backup client and server software for Unix systems and can use mounts of SMB/CIFS shares to back up Windows systems. AMANDA provides very sophisticated scheduling tools that can be a real boon when backing up a midsize or large network.

Restoring Data

No backup is useful if you can't restore the data in an emergency situation. For this reason, you should create data-restoration plans and test ways to do the job. Broadly speaking, data restoration falls into two categories: *partial restores*, in which you need to recover just a few files, and *complete restores*, in which you must restore a system to a working state from scratch. Partial restores are common when a user accidentally deletes a file or corrupts a single directory. Complete restores are likely to be necessary after a hardware disk failure or when an OS installation becomes irrecoverably corrupted because of a virus, worm, or user error.

Performing Partial Restores

Of the two types of restores, partial restores are the easiest to handle. When restoring to the backup server computer itself, the basic OS will still be functional, as will be most of the software, including the backup software. (If the backup software itself has been lost for some reason, you can probably reinstall it from the original files fairly easily.) In the case of network restores, both the backup server and the backup client have more or less intact files and can contact each other via the network. In either case, the result is that you can basically run the backup command in reverse.

One complication is that partial restores are, by definition, restores of a subset of the files that were backed up. For instance, a user might have deleted an important directory tree and need it back. You therefore want to restore those files and *only* those files. Restoring files that should not be restored could cause problems if the restored files overwrite newer versions of themselves.

When using tar, you can use the --extract (-x) command to extract data from the archive. You can then specify a filename or directory name as part of the command to restore only that file or directory. For instance, suppose you want to restore the /home/grogers/swing-time directory, which the user has accidentally deleted. If the backup was stored to tape, you might restore it as follows:

```
# tar -xvpf /dev/st0 --directory / home/grogers/swing-time
```

This command extracts the data using options similar to those used to create it. Note that this example uses the --directory / option to tell tar to extract data into the root (/) directory. When used in this way, you should *not* include the --one-file-system (-1) option if any of the to-be-restored files are on mounted filesystems. The filename specification (home/grogers/swing-time) omits the leading slash (/) because it's not stored in the archive by default; instead, tar relies upon the root directory location to restore the files to their correct position. Alternatively, you could restore the files to a temporary directory and then move them to their final destination. This approach has the advantage of reducing the risk of accidentally overwriting perfectly good files with older versions of themselves. In any event, after you see the files you want in the output, you can abort it by pressing Control+C.

If you don't know the exact name of the file that's to be restored, you can use tar's --list (-t) option to obtain a complete file listing. If you stored the file list in a log file during the original backup operation, you can peruse it to find the exact filename in question.

 CAUTION   If you don't specify the filename precisely, including the lack or presence of any leading slashes or dots, tar won't restore the file. Because reading through an entire backup can be a long process, this mistake can take a while to discover.

When restoring files to a remote SMB/CIFS share, you must either mount the share or use smbtar to do the restoration. In the former case, you must cd into the mounted share or use --directory to specify the restore location. In both cases, you must ensure that the client has given you write access to the share. Write access isn't normally required for backups, so you might legitimately configure your backup clients to enable read-only access. If this is so, you must reconfigure the share, at least temporarily, to provide write access. Alternatively, you might restore the files to a floppy disk, Zip disk, or a share on the Samba backup server. You can then move the removable disk to the client or read the restore share on the Samba server from the backup client to copy the files back to their original location.

Performing Complete Restores

Complete restores are a much greater challenge than are partial restores. The backup client (or, in the case of a complete restore of the backup server, the backup server OS) doesn't work at all in this case, or at best it works so poorly that you can't initiate a restore process. This fact means you'll have to take special steps to get the system recovered and to a point where it can boot. The following sections describe three complete-restore strategies: restoring data using the backup server computer alone, installing a minimal OS on the backup client and using it to restore the rest of the data, and using an emergency Linux system on the backup client to restore its normal OS. The "Restoring Bootability" section also looks at a special challenge: restoring the boot sector and core boot files of the restored OS, which may not have been restored by the principal restore process.

TIP   Always test your complete restore process. If possible, use a spare computer to test the process. Install Windows (or any other OS you intend to back up) on it, back it up, wipe its hard disk, and test your restore tools. If your network hosts multiple OSs, perform this same test with each one. Debugging a restore procedure is much less stress inducing when you have time to test it than when somebody is looking over your shoulder and demanding that the computer be made operational immediately.

Using a Local Restore Tool

One option for performing a complete restore is to install the hard disk from the backup client (or a replacement hard disk if the original disk failed) in the backup server computer itself and to use that computer's support for FAT to restore the data to the computer. To do so, follow these steps:

1. **Partition the disk:** Use your backup server or another computer to create partitions on the disk to roughly match the original disk's partitions. If you have an image backup of the original OS's boot partition made with dd, the new boot partition should exactly match the old one in size.

2. **Create a filesystem:** Create a new FAT filesystem for the C: partition of the new disk. I recommend using a Windows 9x/Me emergency floppy or third-party tool such as PowerQuest's PartitionMagic to do this job. Unix tools to create FAT filesystems are available, but Windows sometimes chokes on such filesystems. You can skip this step if your backup takes the form of a dd or other image archive. Such archives incorporate the filesystem data, so there's no need to explicitly re-create the filesystem.

3. **Install the disk:** If you haven't done so in service to steps 1 or 2, install the new disk in the Unix backup server. Normally, the new disk will be in a secondary position—on the second ATA chain, for instance. Note that this step will usually require temporarily shutting down the backup server computer.

4. **Mount the FAT partition**: Mount the FAT partition you created in steps 1 and 2. Precisely how you do this depends on your OS, but you'll normally use a command called mount or some variant of it. If you used dd to create a backup, you'll omit this step, or at most use it after step 5 to check that the data were restored correctly.

5. **Restore the data**: Use your backup tools to restore the data to the new disk. Be sure to restore to the correct location. The result should be a set of files that are virtually indistinguishable from the original.

6. **Move the disk**: After restoring data, you should unmount the new filesystem and physically move the disk to the backup client computer. Be sure to change any jumpers that need changing so that the disk operates in its appropriate position on its destination computer.

7. **Restore bootability**: If you restored from a tar or similar archive file, you'll have to restore bootability, as described in the upcoming section "Restoring Bootability." If you restored from a dd archive, you won't need to perform most of these steps, but you may need to type FDISK /MBR from a DOS floppy boot and set the primary boot partition as bootable using DOS's FDISK.

This local restore process can be effective when the backup server OS has good support for FAT and when you use FAT for your boot partition. Most Unix-like OSs have good FAT support, so the first condition is seldom a problem. The second condition is increasingly an issue, though; Windows 9*x*/Me uses FAT exclusively, but Windows NT/200*x*/XP can use either FAT or NTFS for its boot partition, with NTFS being the preferred filesystem because of its support for ACLs and other advanced features. Unfortunately, no Unix-like OSs in early 2004 include good write support for NTFS. One partial exception is Captive (http://www.jankratochvil.net/project/captive/), which enables Linux to write to NTFS using original Windows NTFS drivers. Even Captive doesn't provide full support for NTFS ACLs and similar features, though. Ultimately, this restore procedure won't work for NTFS unless the backup takes the form of a dd image. In such a case, you can restore the backup using this method.

If the backup server computer's primary duty is to handle backups, taking it down to temporarily swap a new disk into it may not be a problem. If the server performs other tasks, though, such as holding users' home directories, taking it down, even just for a few minutes to swap hardware in and out, may be unacceptable.

Using a Linux Emergency System to Restore Data

Another approach is to essentially split the functions of the local restore on the backup server across two computers. If you could run a Unix-like OS on the backup client computer, even temporarily, you could initiate a network connection between it and the backup server in order to restore data.

Fortunately, this approach is a possibility, thanks to the availability of bootable Linux emergency systems. These systems boot from a floppy disk, CD-R, or other bootable medium and run a complete Linux system. Sometimes these systems are very limited in their capabilities, but the more capable of them include support for networking protocols, including Samba. (Even if the emergency Linux system lacks Samba support, it might include an alternative, such as NFS support, that could serve for restoration purposes.) Examples of emergency Linux systems include the following:

Knoppix: This project is a CD-ROM-based Linux distribution. It boots into a fairly complete Linux system, and you can edit the Samba configuration files to provide whatever support you need to function as an emergency restore system. The official Knoppix site is at `http://www.knoppix.org`.

SUSE Live Evaluation: SUSE provides a CD-ROM-based version of its Linux distribution. This CD-ROM is intended as an evaluation version, but it can also be used to handle many emergency recovery tasks. Check SUSE's main site, `http://www.suse.com`, or the popular Linux download sites, for details.

ZipSlack: Slackware (`http://www.slackware.com`) is one of the longer-lived Linux distributions. A special version, known as ZipSlack, can run entirely from a 100MB Zip disk and so is good for emergency recovery situations. You can add any software you need, within space limits of whatever medium you use. (You can use higher-capacity Zip disks, LS-120 disks, other removable disks, or even install ZipSlack on a small emergency recovery partition on the ultimate target hard disk.)

NOTE In principle, you could create an emergency system similar to one of these Linux systems but based on FreeBSD or some other Unix-like OS. The Linux-based systems are widely available and quite capable of restoring Windows, though. For this reason, they make good emergency systems for this purpose even if you don't normally run Linux.

Once you create a Linux-based emergency restore system, you can effectively run the backup process in reverse but using Samba or Linux's SMB/CIFS mounting tools in place of their Windows equivalents. For instance, if you used a server-initiated backup with `smbtar`, you can create a FAT partition on the target disk (ideally using a Windows emergency floppy disk), mount it in Linux, and export the FAT partition. You can then initiate the restore process from the Unix backup server using `smbtar`.

This approach to restoration has many of the same problems as restoring using the backup server computer alone. In particular, Linux's write support for NTFS is very poor, so you won't be able to restore a backup created with `smbtar` or other file-by-file backup tools to NTFS. If the backup is in the form of an NTFS image file created using `dd` or something similar, though, you should be able to restore it. You're also likely to need to perform extra steps to make the system bootable again, as described in the upcoming section "Restoring Bootability."

TIP   If your network includes systems that boot from NTFS, you could try using an emergency Linux system like this to create dd images and back up those images to a backup server. In the event of a disaster, boot using the emergency Linux system and reverse the process. You can then treat the rest of the restore as if it were a partial restore, as described in the earlier section "Performing Partial Restores."

If you stored your backups on an optical disc or other medium that can be read directly on the backup client, you can use an emergency Linux system to restore the computer without the help of the backup server system. You can mount the optical disc and access the backup file just as you would any other file. With some emergency systems, though, you may need a second CD-ROM drive to accomplish this goal.

Using a Partial Installation to Restore Data

A third approach to performing complete restores is to restore part of the target OS using its original installation media and then recover the rest of the data using partial restore methods, as described in "Performing Partial Restores." This approach is likely to be awkward; because installing Windows is a task that requires constant attention, you must answer various questions throughout the process.

Once you've restored Windows and configured it to take on the identity of your "lost" system on the network, you can reverse whatever backup process you used to back up the server. One important caveat to this process is that you should not attempt to restore critical Windows files (typically stored in C:\WINDOWS or C:\WINNT); doing so could easily confuse Windows and cause the system to crash and become unbootable again. You can certainly restore ordinary user data files, though, and perhaps some applications. (Many complex applications store files in the C:\WINDOWS or similar directory, though, and so will need to be reinstalled.)

One big advantage of this system restoration approach is that it works with NTFS boot partitions. Because you use the Windows installer to install the OS, it handles the NTFS access, so your backup server OS's or emergency Linux system's capacity to read and write NTFS is irrelevant.

A variant of this partial install approach is to do a temporary or emergency install of Windows on one partition and to use it to restore your entire backup, including the C:\WINDOWS or equivalent directory, onto another partition. You can then reconfigure the system to boot the newly restored Windows system, thus recovering your original OS more or less completely.

Yet another variant of this method is to use Bart's Preinstalled Environment (BartPE) builder (http://www.nu2.nu/pebuilder/). This tool, when run from a working Windows 2003 or XP installation, will create a bootable Windows CD-R or DVD that can be used for restoring data. Use the BartPE-created disc to partition your hard disk and create FAT or NTFS partitions. You can then configure the system using whatever network client or server settings are necessary and restore the original configuration.

Restoring Bootability

Most methods of network backup restore critical filesystem files but can't handle a few key data structures used in booting a disk. In particular, most backup tools don't back up two important features:

MBR: The Master Boot Record (MBR) is the first sector on the hard disk. It holds partition table information and the *primary boot loader,* which is the first code from the hard disk that the *x*86 CPU runs. A standard *x*86 primary boot loader redirects the boot process to the boot sector of the primary partition that's marked as being bootable.

Boot partition's boot sector: The first sector of each partition is known as the *boot sector,* and it holds critical information on that partition in a format that varies from one filesystem to another. Most filesystems, including FAT and NTFS, provide space in the boot sector for code that continues the boot process. In the case of Windows, the boot sector loads a few critical files stored on the filesystem proper, and from there the boot process continues using ordinary files.

Most full-restore methods recover ordinary files but not the MBR or the boot partition's boot sector. Fortunately, restoring these sectors' data isn't very difficult, but the processes are a bit obscure. In the case of Windows 9*x*/Me, the process is as follows:

1. If you haven't already done so, prepare a Windows emergency boot disk from a working copy of the same version of Windows you're restoring, using the Startup Disk tab of the Add/Remove Programs object in the Control Panel. (Especially if you only have one or two computers running a given OS, you must be sure to do this before you run into problems!)

2. Boot the Windows emergency disk you prepared in step 1.

3. Type FDISK /MBR in the emergency Windows environment (which is really just the version of DOS upon which Windows 9*x*/Me is built). This action restores the normal *x*86 MBR.

4. Type SYS C: in the emergency Windows environment. This action restores the boot partition's boot sector.

5. Type FDISK to enter the FDISK utility.

6. Type 2 (Set Active Partition). FDISK displays a list of primary partitions.

7. Type the number of the Windows boot partition.

8. Press the Esc key until you've exited from FDISK.

When you remove the boot floppy and reboot the computer, it should boot into your newly restored Windows system. If the boot process fails very early (before any Windows logos or other Windows boot messages appear), you should review the preceding steps. If the boot process fails later in the boot process, it's possible that your backup was corrupt. Recovering from such errors can be very difficult, but Windows-specific recovery tools may be able to help.

In Windows NT/200*x*/XP, the procedure is different. You must create an emergency floppy from a working system, much as you do in Windows 9*x*/Me. Instead of booting that disk directly, though, you boot your Windows installation CD-ROM. Early in the installation process, the system gives you the option of performing recovery operations. You can restore your system to bootability using this option, possibly in conjunction with data from the emergency disk.

Windows Backup Pitfalls

Windows systems present certain challenges to backup software. Some of these challenges exist for any backup tool, whether or not it involves SMB/CIFS sharing. Other challenges are unique to Samba-mediated backups. These challenges include filename issues and handling in-use files.

Filename Concerns

As with any Samba file share, backup shares present filename challenges. Similarly, using smbtar or an OS's SMB/CIFS-mounting capabilities for server-initiated backups also poses challenges related to filenames.

One of the biggest filename issues when it comes to SMB/CIFS backups relates to the handling of short (8.3) filenames. These problems are fundamentally related to the fact that the VFAT extensions, which enable FAT to store long filenames, build upon the original short FAT filenames in a way that was designed to preserve compatibility. NTFS also includes built-in short filename features to support backward compatibility for DOS and 16-bit Windows programs. These backward compatibility features are beneficial for older programs run under Windows, but they complicate Samba and SMB/CIFS backup operations. Essentially, VFAT and NTFS provide either a short filename or a short filename and a long filename. Unix systems, though, are designed to handle just one filename, and in most cases, Unix processes just the long filename. When a restore operation occurs, the OS that handles the NTFS or VFAT filesystem creates a new short filename. This new short filename might or might not match the original, and therein lies the problem.

In Windows, it's usually possible to refer to a file by either its short or its long filename. For instance, a Windows AUTOEXEC.BAT file, a program configuration file, or the Windows Registry might refer to a file as longfilename.txt or LONGFI~1.TXT; both references will work. Now, suppose you back up this file and restore it, but when you restore it, another file called longfingernails.txt is restored in the same directory—only longfingernails.txt is restored first. Chances are it will acquire the short filename of LONGFI~1.TXT, forcing the system to give longfilename.txt the matching short filename LONGFI~2.TXT. Any references in configuration files, batch files, and so on to LONGFI~1.TXT will thereafter refer to the wrong file. This change in short filename can result in some very peculiar and program-specific problems if the program's configuration file includes a reference to short filenames. Unfortunately, such references can exist in some critical system files, including the Registry.

What can you do to avoid these problems? Unfortunately, there's very little you can do to completely eliminate the risk, but some possible ways to at least mitigate the damage include the following:

Do image backups: If you back up the system by performing an image backup—in which you back up the entire partition, filesystem and all—the restore will be identical to the original, including the short filenames. This approach is effective, but creating such backups can be a hassle. It may also be harder to restore individual files from an image backup than from a conventional backup, and restoring an image backup to a partition of a different size than the original may be tricky, depending upon the tools involved.

Avoid long filenames: If you use short filenames whenever possible, you'll minimize the chance of the problem occurring. This issue is most important for program files and the directories in which they reside, so whenever possible you should use short directory names, such as APPS rather than the default Program Files for storing program files.

Avoid similar long filenames: When you feel compelled to create files or directories with long names, be sure they're unique in their first six characters. This will more or less guarantee that they won't compete for the same short filename base.

Use long filenames in configuration files: When you create configuration file entries, batch files, and so on, refer to files by their long filenames rather than their short filenames. The long filename is usually the default for GUI tools released since 1995, but you might be tempted to use short filenames to save a bit of typing. Don't; use the full long filename.

Use the same tool for backup and restore: Different tools are likely to create short filenames in slightly different ways, so matching your backup and restore methods can minimize the chance you'll encounter a problem. Because most short filenames are created by the Windows FAT driver, restoring files using that driver whenever possible makes sense. Unfortunately, many restore methods involve using another OS for restoring files to FAT. If you use a Unix-like OS to restore files to FAT, check its VFAT options. Some offer options for how to create the VFAT "tail" (the tilde and number that help differentiate between files with otherwise similar short filenames). In particular, you should avoid the Linux nonumtail option if you use Linux to restore data. This option isn't the default, so avoiding it isn't difficult.

Reinstall programs: If you restore a system or a set of programs and encounter problems with just one program, consider reinstalling that program. Delete it using the Windows program management tools and then reinstall it. If the problem was due to mismatched short filenames, this procedure should eliminate the problem.

Overall, the likelihood of problems due to mismatched short filenames before and after restoring a system is low, particularly if you don't overuse long filenames that are similar to one another. Also, keep in mind that these problems are most likely to crop up if program directories have similar names. References to user data files are fairly rare in program and system configuration files, so if the short filenames for your budgets for 2003 and 2004 are reversed, you'll probably never even notice. The long filenames will be preserved, and as most programs rely upon the long filenames, that's what's important.

In addition to the potentially serious problem of mismatched short filenames, backing up and restoring data can also cause changes to the case of short filenames, particularly if you use different backup and restore tools or OSs. This happens because different tools have different rules for handling the case of short filenames. For instance, suppose you perform a server-initiated backup of a Windows system. If a file on this system has a short filename but the user specified all-lowercase letters when creating it, the file might have a VFAT long filename associated with it in order to preserve the case. When backed up via an SMB/CIFS server-initiated backup, the filename will be stored as an ordinary short filename. If it's subsequently restored using a VFAT driver that displays non-VFAT short filenames in lowercase, chances are the long filename attribute will *not* be created. As a result, the filename may appear with an initial capital or even in all uppercase, where previously it had been all lowercase. This change doesn't pose a problem; Windows is case-insensitive, so programs that reference the file will still find it. The change might confuse your users, though, so you should be aware of it.

Backing Up In-Use Files

Backing up a running computer can sometimes cause problems because the backup software may be unable to process files that are open and in use by other programs. For this reason, backups are best performed when few other programs are running. Unfortunately, one vital file is always in use in Windows: the Registry. This file holds critical system configuration information, such as TCP/IP settings, defaults for various applications, and more.

In my experience, the Registry is usually backed up and restored successfully, even though it's in use whenever Windows is running. Sometimes, though, the Registry backup can become corrupt. In such cases, recovering the system can be difficult. One solution to this problem is to create a backup of the Registry before backing up the computer. Creating a Registry backup requires running special Registry editing tools, such as Easy Desk Software's RegMedic (http://www.easydesksoftware.com) or the SCANREGW program that ships with Windows. The Registry backup becomes, in essence, a copy of the Registry file, but one that's not in use when the full system backup occurs. Upon restore, if the system doesn't boot fully or flaky problems occur, you can try using a Windows "safe mode" boot to restore the Registry from the backup.

Another approach to solving this problem is to back up the system from an OS other than your main Windows installation. You could create a special Windows system to use just for backups, or you could install FreeBSD, Linux, or some other OS just to handle backup tasks. Reboot into this OS whenever you want to back up the computer. When you do this, you won't have any problems because the Registry file (or any other file) is in use.

Summary

Samba can be a vital component in a network backup strategy, particularly if your network is dominated by Windows computers. The Samba server itself must be backed up, of course, particularly if you use that server to hold critical user data files or program files. Beyond backing up the server, you can back up clients either by providing special Samba backup shares or by using Samba's or your OS's SMB/CIFS client tools to back up shares created on the systems you want to back up. Either way, you should be sure to plan a restoration strategy so that you can re-create a functioning system or just restore a handful of lost files should the need arise. With a little planning, Samba-mediated backups and restores can go quite smoothly, but you should be aware of potential pitfalls such as short filename changes and problems accessing in-use files. These problems aren't usually showstoppers, and overall, Samba can be a great boon to your network backup strategy.

#### CHAPTER 17

Troubleshooting Samba

SAMBA IS A WONDERFUL TOOL when it works correctly—it enables you to deliver vital services to many clients using a robust host OS and a server that provides many configuration options. Unfortunately, Samba doesn't always work as you'd like. Problems can arise because of Samba misconfiguration, problems on other SMB/CIFS systems on the network, firewall issues, network hardware problems, and more. Tracking down problems is as much art as it is science, but this chapter looks at some of the common problems in Samba configuration and provides information on how to go about locating the source of a problem.

This chapter begins with some general troubleshooting advice—techniques and tools you can use to help narrow down the source of a problem. This chapter then moves on to a look at each of several potential trouble areas in turn: NetBIOS name problems, browsing problems, authentication problems, domain control problems, file-sharing problems, and printer-sharing problems.

NOTE The general assumption in this chapter is that a problem is Samba-specific. If you can't get any networking tools to work, you need to investigate lower-level problem sources, such as defective cables, IP address assignment, and so on. Some Samba problems can be traced to non-Samba (and even non-SMB/CIFS) causes. If many networking tools are affected, the problem is broader than those described in this chapter.

General Troubleshooting Tips

Before looking at the details of particular problems, you should learn something about the troubleshooting tools and techniques that are available to you. Knowing how to diagnose a problem will do more good than knowing about a few specific types of problems, just as knowing how to fish will do you more good than being given a single fish. The following sections look at several of these basic techniques: checking log files, using nmblookup, using testparm, testing problems using multiple systems or OSs, performing selective shutdowns, performing Internet searches, using a packet sniffer, and looking for problems with routers and firewalls.

Checking Log Files

In many cases, the first troubleshooting resource you should consult is your system's log files. These files contain critical information concerning the operation of your computer. In the case of a Samba server, these files are typically stored in /var/log/samba.

The precise filenames used are determined by the log file parameter in smb.conf. A typical entry sets this value to /var/log/samba/log.%m, which creates a separate smbd log file for each client that connects—for instance, log.tap for the TAP client, log.waltz for the WALTZ client, and so on. You may also find some files with numeric IP addresses in place of names and possibly log files for specific programs, such as log.smbd for the smbd server's operations that don't relate to specific clients and log.smbmount for the operation of the smbmount program.

 TIP   If you want to check the latest entries in a log file (as you might just after a problem occurs), try using the tail program, which displays the last few lines of a file. The default number of lines is ten, but you can change this value using the -n parameter, as in **tail -n 20 /var/log/samba/log.waltz** to display the final 20 lines of the log file.

If your Samba log files don't contain enough information to help you isolate the problem, you might consider increasing the value of the log level (a.k.a. debug level) parameter. Most working Samba installations set this value quite low—at 1 or even 0. You can increase it, though, up to a value of 10, for increased debugging output in the log files. As a practical matter, setting log level above 3 is unlikely to be helpful unless you're a Samba developer. Temporarily setting this parameter at 2 or even 3 might produce useful information for you as an administrator, though.

 CAUTION   Setting the log level too high can have negative consequences. Most important, the CPU time and disk activity involved in logging will degrade Samba's performance. The logs will also consume disk space faster. Assuming you've set the max log size parameter reasonably, the practical consequence of this effect will be that the logs will be rotated more quickly, meaning that you'll lose older information more rapidly—possibly so rapidly that the information you need will be lost before you can examine it.

If you use the Samba syslog and syslog only parameters, your Samba logs will appear in your OS's normal system logs in addition to or instead of Samba-specific log files. System log files may be called /var/log/messages, /var/log/syslog, or something similar. Consult your OS's documentation or check your syslogd server's configuration files (such as /etc/syslog.conf) to locate your system log files. Even if your Samba configuration doesn't use these files, they may contain important clues for some types of problems. For instance, if a firewall is interfering with Samba operations, it may be logging information on the packets it's discarding. Examining such logs may, therefore, be worthwhile even if Samba doesn't use them directly.

Using nmblookup

The nmblookup utility can be a useful took in diagnosing problems related to name resolution. This Samba tool can perform name lookups and can report more details than are apparent when you simply try to access a remote share by name. It has the following syntax:

```
nmblookup [options] NAME
```

Normally, NAME is a NetBIOS name—typically a machine name but sometimes a workgroup or domain name. The options you may specify include the following:

-f: This option causes nmblookup to display flags that are set in the response packet headers. It's most useful to developers or those who are intimately familiar with the SMB/CIFS protocols.

-M: You can search for a local master browser for a domain or workgroup by using this option, in which you specify the domain or workgroup name. It does this by searching for the machine with the 0x1d NetBIOS resource ID code. If you pass a dash (-) as the name, the system looks for the machine with the __MSBROWSE__ name, which is a name that local master browsers register. (In Samba 3.0.*x*, you must prefix the dash with a double dash, as in **nmblookup -M -- -.**)

-R: This option causes a recursive lookup, which can retrieve machine names from an NBNS system. This option is generally used in conjunction with -U to specify the NBNS system. For instance, **nmblookup -U namer -R TAP** locates information on the TAP computer stored on the namer NBNS computer.

-S: You can learn all of the names, including resource IDs, that are associated with a system using this parameter. This feature is most helpful when you need to learn what functions a computer serves on the network; compare the resource ID codes to those shown in Tables 1-2 and 1-3 in Chapter 1.

-r: Some versions of Windows 95 contain a bug that causes it to respond only to queries from port 137 for NetBIOS UDP packets. The -r option to nmblookup tells it to bind to this port as a workaround when dealing with affected clients. Unfortunately, only root may bind to this port, and you may only be able to use this option if nmbd is *not* running.

-T: Normally, nmblookup returns machine identifiers in the form of IP addresses. Adding this option causes nmblookup to perform reverse Domain Name System (DNS) lookups, identifying machines by their DNS names.

-A: This option works like -S, but it causes nmblookup to treat the specified NAME as an IP address.

-h: You can obtain basic usage information by passing this option.

-s *filename*: This option sets the name of the configuration file (normally smb.conf in a directory set at compile time).

-B *broadcast-address*: You can send a query to a specified broadcast address by using this option.

-U *unicast-address*: You can send a query to a specified unicast address by using this option. It's often used to specify an NBNS computer along with the -R option. (Used in this way, you must pass an IP address or DNS hostname, though, not a NetBIOS name.)

-d *level*: The nmblookup program normally uses the log level parameter in smb.conf to determine how much information to log. This option overrides the smb.conf parameter.

-i *scope*: You can set the NetBIOS scope with this option, overriding the netbios scope option in smb.conf.

The nmblookup utility can be a great diagnostic tool because it can help you see what roles a server is playing, whether a server is responding to name queries, what the master browser is on a network, and so on. For instance, the -M option can return the identity of the master browser, which can help you diagnose browsing problems:

```
$ nmblookup -MT STUDIO
querying STUDIO on 192.168.1.255
charleston.luna.edu, 192.168.1.1 STUDIO<1d>
```

This command used the -T parameter to provide a DNS hostname (charleston.luna.edu) in addition to an IP address (192.168.1.1) as part of the output, which may make it easier for you to identify the machine in question. If you didn't plan for this computer to be the master browser, you may need to reconfigure it. You can also learn about services offered by a specific computer using this command:

```
$ nmblookup -S CHARLESTON
querying CHARLESTON on 192.168.1.255
192.168.1.1 CHARLESTON<00>
Looking up status of 192.168.1.1
            CHARLESTON      <00> -           H <ACTIVE>
            CHARLESTON      <03> -           H <ACTIVE>
            CHARLESTON      <20> -           H <ACTIVE>
            .._MSBROWSE__. <01> - <GROUP> H <ACTIVE>
            STUDIO          <00> - <GROUP> H <ACTIVE>
            STUDIO          <1b> -           H <ACTIVE>
            STUDIO          <1c> - <GROUP> H <ACTIVE>
            STUDIO          <1d> -           H <ACTIVE>
            STUDIO          <1e> - <GROUP> H <ACTIVE>
```

This example shows that the CHARLESTON computer is providing quite a few different NetBIOS services, identified by the second column of the output with the two-digit hexadecimal numbers between angle brackets (<>). Comparing this output to Tables 1-2 and 1-3 in Chapter 1, you can see that the server is accepting WinPopUp messages (0x03; but note that this doesn't mean the computer necessarily *displays* the messages it receives), is offering file or printer services (0x20), is a local master browser (0x1d), is a domain master browser (0x1b), participates in browser elections (0x1e), and so on.

NOTE Windows provides a tool that's similar to nmblookup. This tool is called NBTSTAT, and it performs many of the same tasks as nmblookup, but its output is different and the details of its options are different. You might find that using NBTSTAT is simpler than using nmblookup if you need to perform checks on network functions from a Windows machine. Alternatively, you could boot the Windows machine with a Linux emergency disk similar to the ones described in the "Using a Linux Emergency System to Restore Data" section of Chapter 16.

Using testparm

The testparm utility, which ships with Samba, reviews the contents of your smb.conf file and reports any problems it discovers. These problems are mostly fairly simple and mundane ones, such as misspelling a parameter name or placing a global parameter within a share definition. The testparm utility also reports on a few issues that aren't technically incorrect configurations but that can cause problems for some clients. For instance, the tool tells you if any share names are greater than 12 characters in length, which can hide these shares from some clients.

In addition to reporting on problems, testparm displays a summary of all the options in smb.conf, stripped of comments. This summary can sometimes be useful when you're modifying a sample smb.conf file because these files sometimes contain so many comments that it becomes difficult to follow the logic of the file as a whole.

The testparm utility will *not* discover errors related to intent. For instance, if you forget to include read only = No or one of its antonyms in the definition for a share that you intend to be read/write, testparm won't discover this fact. Nonetheless, the tool is worth using after you modify a configuration, particularly if you've made extensive changes or aren't sure that the syntax for a particular parameter is correct.

Testing from Multiple OSs

Problems are sometimes OS-related. Different OS architectures, filesystems, TCP/IP stacks, server software, client software, and configuration options can all make problems appear or disappear. Thus, if you run into problems, one debugging approach you may want to try is to attempt to reproduce the problem using another OS. This advice applies both to the OS running on the server system and to the OS running on the client system. Of course, replacing an entire OS just for a test is impractical in most production environments, but you can try more limited tests:

Temporary multibooting: You can boot a computer into something other than its usual OS on a temporary basis. An emergency Linux boot CD-ROM might work well for this test if the system doesn't normally run Linux. A DOS boot floppy configured with a DOS SMB/CIFS package, as described in Chapter 18, can also be a good test platform.

Testbed systems: If the problem occurs on multiple systems, and if your network uses the same OS for all clients or all servers, you could try installing another OS on a test system and use it.

In-network OS variables: If your network supports many OSs, you can try surveying them to see if a pattern of problems emerges. For instance, if all the Windows XP systems show problems but Windows Me and Mac OS X clients function correctly, that's good evidence that the problem is related to Windows XP, or at least to your server's XP-specific configuration options, if it has any.

Evaluating the results of multi-OS testing can be tricky. Suppose you find that only one OS experiences a problem. Where do you go from there? One answer is to perform a Web search, as described in the upcoming section "Performing Internet Searches." With luck, somebody else will have noted the problem, and an online discussion will reveal a solution. You should also check your configuration for any OS-specific options or options that might affect OSs in different ways. Options related to filename case and length are common suspects. (Chapter 18 provides information on common OS-specific options and on how to use the `include` parameter in `smb.conf` to configure them.)

Selectively Shutting Down Systems

Some problems are related to the presence of specific computers on your network. For instance, a system that's misconfigured as a domain controller can wreak havoc on a network. One way to help identify such problems, and the systems that cause them, is to selectively shut down parts of the network.

In the simplest case, a binary search can help you isolate the problem fairly rapidly: Shut down half the computers on the network, and test for the problem. If it's not present, shut down all the computers you've tested and boot up the other half. If the problem appears, shut down half of the computers that are now running and look for the problem. If the problem disappears, shut down those computers and boot up the other half of the computers that were running when the problem occurred. In this way, you can isolate the problem in a rapid manner. (*Rapid*, in this context, can be many hours, though, particularly on a big network. Shutting down and rebooting many computers can be a time-consuming task!) Literally pulling the plug on networks by disconnecting hubs, switches, or routers may make for a quicker approach, but the problem can still take some time to isolate on a large network. Some types of problems may also take some time to manifest or disappear unless you reboot computers from scratch.

In practice, of course, you may not be able to perform this test, at least not in this theoretically pristine way. If your network uses a domain configuration, you'll have to leave the domain controller up at all times. The size of the network might make it difficult to perform this test in quite this way, although you might still be able to take down and bring up large subsets of the network to test for the problem. You may need to perform these tests in off hours to avoid disrupting the network, at least if the problem isn't so severe that it's making use of the network impossible. Also, keep in mind that some SMB/CIFS features will be disrupted by such changes. For instance, your computers will need to re-elect local master browsers. Thus, time will be required for the network to "settle" after such changes. All in all, this approach is most helpful on small networks. Once you move past a dozen or so computers, the problems of this approach become too great.

In practice, using other tools, such as `nmblookup` or packet sniffers, can often lead you to the source of a problem more directly than selectively shutting down parts of the network. Still, SMB/CIFS uses many highly automatic and interactive procedures, such as broadcast name resolution and master browser elections, and locating problems with these tools can sometimes be tricky using network-scanning tools.

Performing Internet Searches

Chances are good that you're not the first person to encounter a problem. Several Internet resources are available that can help you track down others who've experienced problems with Samba or with SMB/CIFS networking in general:

Web searches: Web search engines, such as Google (`http://www.google.com`), can be good ways to track down information about specific problems. Typing keywords, such as `samba connection lost`, into a search engine may turn up information in online FAQs, archived newsletters, and so on. One caveat to Web searches is that if you search on an `smb.conf` parameter name, you'll probably get many useless hits in the form of archived mailing list and Usenet newsgroup postings that include the entire contents of the poster's `smb.conf` file, even if the posting has nothing to do with your problem.

Newsgroups: Usenet newsgroups, which are accessible via newsreader programs such as Pan (`http://pan.rebelbase.com`) and Trn (`http://trn.sourceforge.net`) with the help of a news server operated by your ISP, can be good ways to find help on many topics. In particular, check out the `comp.protocols.smb` and `linux.samba` newsgroups. You can search old postings at Google Groups, `http://groups.google.com`. (You can also post new messages from this site if your ISP doesn't offer newsgroups.)

Samba mailing lists: Several Samba mailing lists exist. These are similar to Usenet newsgroups, but they're delivered via e-mail, and they're more plentiful. You can peruse their archives or join a mailing list at `http://us1.samba.org/samba/archives.html`. (The same page exists on most Samba mirror sites—replace `us1` with another mirror site code to use it instead.)

Samba's site: Samba's Web site, `http://www.samba.org`, offers many Samba-related resources, including official documentation and a bug database (accessible more directly at `https://bugzilla.samba.org`). If you think you've found an actual bug in Samba, you can report it here—but do so only after looking for information about the bug in the database itself, on the Internet at large, and so on. Many "bugs" turn out to be misconfigurations, misunder-standings of how the tool is supposed to work, and so on. Also, bugs may be fixed in more recent versions of Samba than whatever you're running, so down-loading the latest version might fix the problem—or it might not. Check the change history before going to the effort of trying a newer version of Samba.

Microsoft's site: If your problem relates to DOS or Windows clients or servers, you might want to consult Microsoft's own Web site at http://www.microsoft.com. Click the Support link or do a search on keywords that seem appropriate for the problem you're experiencing.

In practice, you can resolve many Samba problems by searching the Internet. You might learn that you've been using a parameter incorrectly, find a workaround for a bug, or learn that a bug has been fixed in a more recent version of Samba or a non-Samba package.

Using a Packet Sniffer

A *packet sniffer* is a tool that enables you to monitor data transfers at a low level. For instance, you can watch the individual packets involved in an authentication exchange to be sure that encryption is or is not being used, as appropriate. Packet sniffers can also be helpful in ensuring that packets are actually reaching their destination, as opposed to not being sent or being lost by a router, dropped by a firewall, or otherwise misplaced. As a general rule, packet sniffers are very sophisticated network diagnostic tools, but it's well worth learning how to use one.

CAUTION   Although packet sniffers are useful and legitimate network debugging tools, they're also often used by crackers to intercept clear-text passwords, steal sensitive files being transferred on a network, and so on. For this reason, many organizations have explicit policies forbidding the use of packet sniffers except under limited circumstances. Before installing and using a packet sniffer, consult this policy and obtain written permission to use the packet sniffer from an individual who has the authority to give this permission. If you install and use the packet sniffer without this permission, you could find yourself in trouble—perhaps fired or even brought up on criminal charges.

Broadly speaking, you can use packet sniffers in one of two ways:

On the client or server: When installed on the client or server computer, a packet sniffer can monitor the entire communication between the client and its server, no matter what your network hardware is. Depending upon its options, though, the packet sniffer could degrade the performance of the system on which it's installed, so running a packet sniffer on a Samba server on a regular basis isn't advisable.

On another computer: You can install a packet sniffer on a computer that's not directly involved in the transaction in order to monitor that transaction. This approach works only when your network uses hubs, a linear bus topology, or some other networking system that enables one computer to monitor the traffic to and from another computer. If your network uses Ethernet switches, this approach won't work because the switches direct traffic only to the target computer. (A packet sniffer on an unrelated computer could still pick up broadcasts, though, such as those used to initiate NetBIOS name resolution requests. The more sophisticated switches offer features that enable one port to monitor all the other ports' traffic, too.) Using another computer ensures that the performance of the computers being monitored won't be impacted.

TIP   If your network uses Ethernet switches, you could replace a switch with a hub to get around this problem on a temporary basis. This might degrade performance on that network segment, though. Another approach is to place a hub between one of the monitored computers and the switch that normally services it and place the monitoring system on another port on the hub. This approach will not seriously impact performance and will enable you to monitor all the traffic coming from and addressed to the target system.

As an example of a packet sniffer in use, consider Ethereal (http://www.ethereal.com). This program is a sophisticated packet sniffer with both text-mode and GUI controls. Completely describing its use is beyond the scope of this book, but a few pointers will get you on your way to using Ethereal as a simple packet sniffer.

To begin using Ethereal, you should first download and install it. Check the Ethereal Web site for a precompiled version for your OS or source code you can compile yourself. Ethereal also ships with many Unix-like OSs, so you may want to check your installation media. To use Ethereal to gather SMB/CIFS packet data, follow these steps:

1. As root, type **ethereal** to launch the program. The result should be a window similar to the one shown in Figure 17-1 except that it won't contain packet data.

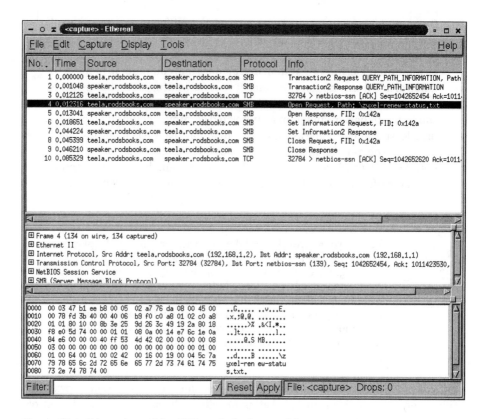

Figure 17-1. Ethereal provides GUI controls that enable you to monitor network traffic.

2. Select Capture ➤ Start or press Control+K to start a capture operation. The result is an Ethernet Capture Options dialog box in which you can set various limits on the packets Ethereal will capture. To begin with, the default options should work fine, so click OK without changing any options.

3. A new window with summaries of packet types appears. As Ethereal captures packets, it updates the numbers to reflect the captures.

4. Perform some networking task—for instance, use `ping` to test network connectivity, use a Samba client program such as `smbclient`, or initiate a connection between a Windows client and a Samba server.

5. After you've finished the tasks you want to analyze, click Stop in the packet summary window. You should now see a summary of the packets in the Ethereal window, as shown in Figure 17-1.

The Ethereal display is broken into three panes. The top pane shows a high-level summary of packets—each line corresponds to a single packet, including the source, destination, protocol, and a brief summary of the operation. Ethereal provides support for SMB/CIFS, so it can summarize packets fairly well. For instance, the highlighted line in Figure 17-1 is identified as a request to open the `zyxel-renew-status.txt` file. You can click a line to have the middle and bottom panes provide additional information about it.

The middle pane displays a *protocol tree* for the packet in question. This tree provides a hierarchical view of the data in the packet. Each line in this pane corresponds to a particular packet header. You can click the plus sign to the left of a line to provide expanded information about the header. For instance, clicking the Ethernet II item in Figure 17-1 displays the Ethernet hardware addresses and related information. The final line in Figure 17-1's middle pane, when expanded, provides detailed information about the SMB protocol data.

The bottom pane in an Ethereal display shows the raw data in the packet. This information appears in both hexadecimal numbers (the columns in the left part of the window) and in ASCII (to the right). (The first column is a hexadecimal byte count—the first byte in the 0020 line is byte 0x20, or 32, numbered starting from 0.) In most cases, the protocol tree provides information in a form that's easier to digest than the raw dump, but sometimes information will jump out at you more readily in the raw dump. For instance, the filename appears at the end of the raw dump in Figure 17-1, but you'd have to hunt for it in the protocol tree. (Of course, the filename also appears in the top pane's summary in this specific case.)

You can learn a lot about network transfers by examining the raw packets, or even just the packet headers. You can discover which systems are communicating with which others, using which protocols. This information alone may be useful in debugging Samba problems—if packets are being sent back and forth, you can rule out blockages caused by misconfigured routers, for instance. (Be careful, though; depending upon where your packet sniffer is located, it might be able to see packets that are blocked from view by the target system.) If you study the protocols, you can learn a lot by studying the packet content. Even without studying the protocols, you can spot information such as file listings or the content of files being transferred, which could be helpful if you want to verify that such information is being sent.

Depending upon your network environment and Ethereal configuration, its output might include packets to or from the host computer or between other computers on the local network segment. To gain this sort of access, the program needs root privileges; you can't run Ethereal, or any other packet sniffer, as an ordinary user on a Unix system. (DOS and Windows packet sniffers don't require special privileges, though.) The display or logging activities consume substantial CPU time and perhaps disk bandwidth as well. Thus, running the packet sniffer will degrade the system's performance.

Overall, packet sniffers are extremely powerful debugging tools, but they can be intimidating and may be best reserved for cases in which you need to study the low-level data transfer output. They can be very useful to verify that encrypted passwords are being used or to confirm that packets are making it past a router.

Looking for Router and Firewall Problems

Routers and firewalls can both cause problems for SMB/CIFS by blocking the transfer of data packets. Normally, routers are configured to facilitate the transfer of data between network segments, but some SMB/CIFS operations rely on broadcasts, in which data packets are directed at the local network as a whole rather than at specific computers. Most routers don't route broadcasts, which means that broadcast-reliant SMB/CIFS features, such as broadcast name resolution, don't work across subnets linked by routers.

Firewalls, on the other hand, are designed to selectively block data transfers. Firewall software may run on routers or may be incorporated into client or server computers. In any event, a firewall might be configured to block some or all SMB/CIFS traffic. Many ISPs and businesses, for instance, deliberately block all SMB/CIFS traffic between their networks and the Internet at large. This is done as a security measure because intruders might try to use flaws in SMB/CIFS implementations to break into computers. Worse, several computer worms and viruses, such as W32.Randex.B and W32.Deloder, exploit weak or nonexistent SMB/CIFS passwords to spread themselves. (These programs could conceivably load their software onto poorly configured Samba servers, but as of early 2004, I know of no worms that specifically target Samba systems; they're all written to install Windows program files and take over Windows servers.) By blocking TCP and UDP ports 137, 138, 139, and 445, a firewall can protect a server or an entire network from infection via this route.

CAUTION   Firewall software run on a router can block SMB/CIFS worms originating outside your network, but if one local computer becomes infected, the router's firewall can't prevent computers on the same network segment from being infected. Thus, you should not consider firewalls to be perfect protection against worms and viruses that spread via SMB/CIFS.

Unfortunately, firewalls and occasionally routers can present problems if you really do need to transfer data. One common problem is in personal firewalls, which run on individual computers to protect those computers rather than running on routers to protect all the computers on the router's network. If you don't realize a personal firewall is running on a client or server, you might encounter problems related to the firewall software. Typically, a client won't be able to contact the SMB/CIFS servers on the local network at all, or a server will be completely unresponsive to outside queries. The affected machine may work just fine with other protocols, such as the Hypertext Transfer Protocol (HTTP), which is used by Web servers and browsers, because these protocols may not be blocked. Recent versions of Windows, such as Windows XP, ship with personal firewall software, but it doesn't block SMB/CIFS traffic by default. To be sure, follow these steps:

1. Open the Network Connections item in the Control Panel.

2. Right-click the Local Area Connection item, and select Properties from the pop-up menu. The result is the Local Area Connection Properties dialog box.

3. Click the Advanced tab, and examine the Protect My Computer... check box. If it's unchecked, the firewall is completely disabled and should not be causing problems. If it's checked, though, you should continue examining its configuration.

4. Click the Settings button in the Local Area Connection Properties dialog box. The result is the Advanced Settings dialog box shown in Figure 17-2.

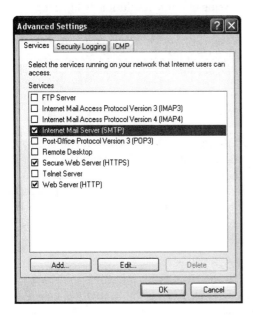

Figure 17-2. Windows XP's default firewall software enables you to pass traffic related to specific protocols.

5. Examine the list of services for anything that might refer to SMB/CIFS. If the firewall is active, by default it blocks access to an SMB/CIFS server running on the Windows system but won't block Windows' client access to other servers.

6. If you find an active firewall rule that blocks outgoing SMB/CIFS traffic, deactivate it.

7. If you want to enable access to the system's own SMB/CIFS server, create a new rule (using the Add button) to enable access to the computer's own TCP ports 139 and 445 and UDP ports 137 and 138.

NOTE Even if a Windows XP system's standard firewall isn't active, the computer could be protected by a third-party firewall product. If the Windows system and the computer to which it should be communicating are separated by a router, a firewall on the router could be causing problems. Some firewalls even run on systems other than routers, clients, or servers, so you may need to look into this possibility as well.

Firewall software on Unix systems is quite varied. Some tools used to create firewalls include IP Filter, ipfw, ipchains, and iptables. You should consult OS-specific documentation to learn how to start, stop, and reconfigure firewalls.

If a router is causing problems with browsing or name resolution by blocking broadcasts, you'll have to reconfigure the firewall to pass broadcasts, reconfigure your SMB/CIFS network into an NT domain, or use Samba-specific options to work around the firewall limitations. Chapter 8 and Chapter 9 describe these options in more detail. Chapter 10 covers domain configuration.

Fixing NetBIOS Name Problems

SMB/CIFS name resolution sometimes doesn't work at all or works only sporadically. These problems are most common on networks that span multiple subnets because routers can block the broadcast name resolution system that's the default for many computers. As with all SMB/CIFS problem types, the first step to solving the problem is in identifying it. Once you've identified the problem as such, you can begin investigating its cause and fixing the problem.

Symptoms of NetBIOS Name Problems

Name resolution problems sometimes look like total loss of connectivity. If a client can't find the IP address associated with a name, the client won't be able to link up with the server, and the result can look a lot like a crashed server, downed router, or other very serious problem.

If you can't seem to contact a remote system, you should first try accessing it using its IP address. You can do this easily using Samba's own smbclient; just substitute the IP address for the hostname:

```
$ smbclient //192.168.1.1/FASTAIRE
added interface ip=192.168.1.3 bcast=192.168.1.255 nmask=255.255.255.0
Password:
Domain=[STUDIO] OS=[Unix] Server=[Samba 3.0.0]
smb: \>
```

The same trick works with Windows clients; enter the IP address rather than the NetBIOS hostname in the Address field of a file browser window, and you should be able to access the share. You'll need to use backslashes in the share specification, though, as in \\192.168.1.1\FASTAIRE.

Another trick you can use on most OSs is to create an entry in the lmhosts file for the server you want to contact. This approach is described in Chapter 9, and it sometimes works more reliably than using a raw IP address for Windows 9x/Me clients. For this reason, you should try it if the raw IP address fails with Windows clients.

However you do this, if you can connect by using the IP address but not the NetBIOS name, it's strong evidence of a name resolution problem. Such problems sometimes affect some clients but not others. If so, take note of which clients are affected, and look for common factors. For instance, are some OSs prone to problems whereas others aren't? Are problems isolated to a particular subnet? Does the client's name resolution configuration (for instance, whether it's configured to use an NBNS system) affect the outcome? Sometimes such relationships will point directly to a solution or at least help you discover what will work.

Resolving NetBIOS Name Issues

As described in Chapter 9, SMB/CIFS clients commonly use one or more of four name resolution methods:

NetBIOS name broadcasts: Broadcast name resolution works well on small networks that don't use routers. If you're using such a network and still can't resolve names, chances are personal firewalls are blocking the name resolution broadcasts, or perhaps the clients are configured not to use them. If a system's TCP/IP netmask setting is wrong, this will also impact broadcast name resolution—some computers may ignore broadcasts from some other computers, which will disrupt normal name resolution.

NetBIOS name servers: NBNS systems resolve names for all computers on a network. NBNS systems can work across routers but only if the clients are configured to use them. If you've configured an NBNS system, as described in Chapter 9, be sure you configure your clients to use it, also as described in Chapter 9. If you've done this and have problems with all clients, chances are the server configuration is in error or a firewall is blocking traffic to the server. If only some clients are having problems, it could still be an issue on the server (clients resolving names might be using another method), or it could be that the clients need to be reconfigured. Be sure that the NBNS IP address is entered correctly on the client systems.

DNS: Some clients, such as Windows NT/200*x*/XP and Samba systems, can use DNS for name resolution instead of or in addition to broadcasts or NBNS. From the client's point of view, the process is similar to using an NBNS system, but a problem with DNS resolution will affect protocols other than SMB/CIFS. If your DNS and NetBIOS names don't match, be sure to use the DNS hostname if you use this method of name resolution.

`lmhosts`: The `lmhosts` file contains a client-side mapping of IP addresses and hostnames. This method can't be impacted by firewalls, routers, or other network problems—at least, not unless the `lmhosts` file is stored on a network share. This approach can cause problems, though, if it contains out-of-date mappings. For instance, if you move a critical server to a different subnet and if some clients have the server's old IP address in their `lmhosts` file, the server will seem to them to have dropped off the face of the earth. This problem can be very frustrating to track down if you've forgotten about the `lmhosts` file, but the recent move of the server should at least be fresh in your mind and be a big clue.

Unfortunately, Windows clients provide limited options for changing name resolution methods. These options are covered in Chapter 9, and they vary from one OS to another. You can try changing these options to see if you can get name resolution working. Samba clients (such as smbclient) can be configured to use any of these four name resolution methods in any order via the name resolve order option in smb.conf. This feature can help immensely in uncovering and fixing name resolution problems—change smb.conf to use one name resolution option alone, then another, and so on. You can map out which methods work and which ones don't in this way and configure the system to use the options that work or do further debugging to track down the problems with those that don't work.

If you're using NBNS or DNS name resolution and if your network uses a Dynamic Host Configuration Protocol (DHCP) server to deliver IP addresses to clients, be sure you've set appropriate NBNS and DNS server IP addresses in the server's configuration. You should also set the NetBIOS node type if you deliver an NBNS address via DHCP, as described in Chapter 9. If you enter the wrong IP address in the DHCP server's configuration, all of the clients will be thrown off. In the case of NBNS configuration, this error might not be immediately apparent because some or all of the clients might fall back on other name resolution methods. If some clients rely on this method, though, or if this is the only method of resolving names for some servers (as it might be in some cross-subnet domain configurations), the error will cause problems for some or all clients.

One additional smb.conf entry deserves mention, but it's mostly a last-resort workaround: wins proxy. This parameter causes Samba to forward NetBIOS name broadcast requests to an NBNS system on behalf of computers that handle only broadcasts. The result can be improved name resolution reliability, particularly if a cross-subnet network uses an NBNS server but some clients aren't configured to (or can't) use it.

Fixing Browsing Problems

Some SMB/CIFS clients, such as Samba's smbclient, require you to know the name of the server and share you want to contact. (Additional Samba tools, such as nmblookup, can provide you with this information, though.) Other clients, including Windows, support browsing, which enables users to locate shares by "browsing" through a network much as you can browse through files on the local hard disk. Browsing doesn't always work correctly, though. Several types of problems can manifest themselves as browsing issues. For instance, without functioning name resolution, you won't be able to browse to a server; and without functioning authentication, you won't be able to browse into shares on the server. The following sections describe problems that are most closely associated with browsing itself. Because browsing relies upon the presence of a functioning master browser, many browsing problems relate to Samba's master browser configuration options, and avoiding these problems is a matter of ensuring that all the Samba servers are configured properly for their roles on the network.

Symptoms of Browsing Problems

Browsing problems most frequently manifest in Windows clients because they're the most common systems that support browsing. Some GUI add-on packages for Samba support browsing, though, as do clients for some other OSs.

Chapter 8 describes how browsing works. In brief, each subnet on an SMB/CIFS network supports a local master browser. This computer is assigned local master browser status via an election process, in which the computers compare their credentials and decide which system is best suited to function as a master browser. In a small network, just one local master browser might be present. Larger networks that use domain configurations may use multiple local master browsers, one for each subnet. Such networks also typically employ a domain master browser. This system is strongly associated with the domain controller; normally the primary domain controller (PDC) also automatically assumes domain master browser duties. The local master browsers know to contact the domain master browser in order to exchange browse lists. This exchange ensures that every master browser has a complete list of the computers on the network. This list may not be current, though, because the browse lists don't propagate instantly; if a computer comes up or goes down, it may take a few minutes for that information to propagate to all the master browsers. Individual systems can locate their local master browsers automatically when they start by sending a broadcast query to which the master browser responds.

One common problem is a browse list that appears and disappears frequently; browsing will work one minute, not work the next, and work again the minute after that. The usual cause of this problem is a local master browser election in progress. If this happens infrequently, it's not a cause for concern; however, if it happens often enough that it's a real disruption, you should look into fixing the problem, as described in the upcoming section "How to Avoid Browsing Problems." A similar problem can occur if the master browser computer crashes frequently; browsing may stop working until a computer calls for a new election. Yet another cause of this type of problem is a network in which NetBIOS is bound to different protocol stacks (TCP/IP, NetBEUI, and IPX, for instance). Each protocol stack hosts a separate virtual network, and the winner of an election on one virtual network may not match the winner on another one, so a new election may then be called.

Another common master browser problem is the failure of one or more machines to appear on browse lists at all. This problem is particularly common on networks that span multiple subnets. If the local master browsers that are elected don't know how to contact the domain controller, the machines on the affected subnet won't appear on other subnets' clients, and the clients on the affected subnet won't be able to see clients on other subnets.

In all of these cases, users can still contact systems directly, even if they don't appear in the Network Neighborhood or My Network Places browsers—at least, if name resolution is working. (If it isn't, using raw IP addresses should work.) For instance, entering \\WALTZ\COMMON in the Address field of a file browser should display the contents of the COMMON share on the WALTZ server, even if WALTZ doesn't appear in the client's browse list.

> **NOTE** A problem that's closely related to browsing is an inability to browse to a server, with an error message stating that access to the IPC$ share was denied. This problem is more properly one of authentication; the IPC$ share returns information on regular shares. Under certain circumstances, clients try to access this share using the GUEST account. If a server disallows GUEST access, this attempt will fail, causing this problem.

Identifying the Master Browser

Many browsing problems trace their way back to the master browser for the network—the local master browser, the domain master browser, or both. Thus, identifying this machine is important for resolving problems. You can do this using the -M option to nmblookup, as described earlier in "Using nmblookup." This command returns the name of the local master browser:

```
$ nmblookup -MT STUDIO
querying STUDIO on 192.168.1.255
charleston.luna.edu, 192.168.1.1 STUDIO<1d>
```

This example adds the -T parameter to the mix, which causes nmblookup to return the hostname (charleston.luna.edu) as well as the IP address (192.168.1.1) of the workgroup or domain (STUDIO in this example). To be absolutely positive you've located the correct system, use a dash (-) as the name (after a double dash if you're using Samba 3.0.*x*):

```
$ nmblookup -MT -- -
querying __MSBROWSE__ on 192.168.1.255
charleston.luna.edu, 192.168.1.1 __MSBROWSE__<01>
```

This command looks for the system that has the __MSBROWSE__ name, which is an alternative way of identifying the master browser. In most cases, both commands should return the same result. Both of these methods identify the local master browser. (If the subnet hosts multiple workgroups, though, the latter method will return the local master browsers for all of the workgroups.) To find the domain master browser, use nmblookup to find the computer that returns the domain name with the 0x1b resource ID:

```
$ nmblookup -T STUDIO#1b
querying STUDIO on 192.168.1.255
charleston.luna.edu, 192.168.1.1 STUDIO<1b>
```

This command will work only if you're on the same subnet as the domain master browser, though, because it uses a broadcast to find the system. In this case, the domain master browser is the same as the local master browser. This configuration is normal and expected in a domain configuration on the same subnet as the domain controller; the domain controller will take on both local and domain master browser duties.

TIP If your network is experiencing frequent and sporadic browsing problems, you might consider calling the nmblookup commands to locate your master browser from a cron job and redirecting the output to a convenient file. (Be sure to append to the file by using the >> redirection operator rather than overwrite it, though.) You'll then have a record of changes to the master browser, which will give you clues about what's happening. For instance, if master browser duties are rotating between multiple computers, it could be that one highly electable computer is crashing or being shut down frequently. If one computer is consistently the master browser, it could be that another one is calling repeatedly for elections and then failing to win them.

How to Avoid Browsing Problems

Domain master browser status is strongly associated with the domain controller. If you use a Samba system as domain controller, be sure it has the following entry in the [global] section of its smb.conf file:

```
domain master = Yes
```

Alternatively, using Auto as the value for this parameter should also work, provided the domain logons parameter is set to Yes, which it should be for a domain controller. Just as important as setting this option correctly on the domain controller, though, is setting it correctly on other computers. Specifically, it should be No (or Auto, provided domain logons is set to No) for computers that do *not* function as domain controllers. If another computer on the network believes that it's the domain master browser, chances are you'll see some odd browsing problems.

The local master browser is selected via an election process. You can tell Samba whether to participate in this process by using the local master parameter. Computers that should never be local master browsers should have local master set to No. If a computer participates in elections, the most important criterion for winning the election is the os level parameter, which accepts an integral value between 0 and 255. This value should be low for systems that should not normally acquire master browser status but that might do so in a pinch. Windows NT/200x/XP systems have OS level values of 32, and Windows 9x/Me systems use lower values, so setting a Samba server's os level parameter to something higher than 32 guarantees that Samba will win out over a Windows system. Using os level = 33 is common, but some administrators use 64 or higher—even 255.

The preferred master parameter, when set to Yes, gives a Samba system a slight edge in local master browser elections. Just as important, the parameter causes Samba to request a local master browser election. Thus, one way to cause problems on your network is to pair preferred master = Yes with a losing os level parameter. Note that a losing os level parameter could be quite high in absolute terms. For instance, os level = 254 will lose out against a Samba server configured with os level = 255, even if that system sets preferred master = No.

In many cases, you'll want to ensure that an always-up Samba server takes on local master browser duties. When this happens in a domain configuration and when the domain controller is on another subnet, be sure to point the Samba local master browser at the domain controller using the `password server` parameter, which tells Samba where the domain controller is. If the domain controller and domain master browser is a Samba system, you may want to use the `remote browse sync` parameter, as well. This parameter, described more fully in Chapter 8, enables you to exchange browse lists with another Samba master browser. Using it provides some redundancy in your local master browser's ability to contact the domain master browser.

The `remote announce` parameter can help work around some problems, too. This parameter lets you tell a remote master browser about a single server's presence. Use it on the remote server, passing it the IP address of the master browser and the workgroup or domain to which you want to register yourself:

```
remote announce = 172.24.21.7/STUDIO
```

This command is most handy when you want to add a server that's isolated on a remote subnet. You could use it as added insurance, though, to be sure the server gets onto a workgroup or domain's browse list.

Some browsing problems are related to incorrect client configurations. Most commonly, the client's netmask is misconfigured. For instance, if a network uses a 23-bit netmask but a client is misconfigured with a 24-bit netmask, the client's broadcasts won't reach all the computers on the network. If one of the computers that the client's broadcasts don't reach is the master browser, the client won't appear on the network's browse list.

Fixing Authentication Problems

Authentication problems can be particularly frustrating: You can see a share in a browser, and you know that your client can resolve the name, but for the wrong reason—it informs you that your password is incorrect! The details of authentication problems vary greatly, but most of them are fairly obvious as such. The trouble is tracking down the cause. From a Samba perspective, the cause is often one relating to the use (or lack of use) of encrypted passwords. Beyond this problem are issues related to specific security models, each of which has unique concerns. You may also need to look into configuration of specific accounts, such as guest accounts.

Symptoms of Authentication Problems

Most authentication errors are obvious as such. Depending upon the client, you'll see a message saying that the password wasn't recognized, that there was a logon failure, or some similar wording. In most cases you'll be prompted for a username and password before you connect, although some clients (including most versions of Windows) prompt for the password when you log onto the client, so you won't need to enter a password when you connect to the share.

One unusual authentication problem, but one that's not uncommon, relates to the IPC$ share. This problem is unusual because it occurs when a client attempts to browse to the server but before opening any actual shares. Behind the scenes, SMB/CIFS uses a share called IPC$ for the exchange of commands. Normally, clients connect to this share using the username and password with which they'll eventually make subsequent connections. If the client hasn't asked for a username and password, though (and sometimes even if it has), the client tries to use the GUEST account, which normally requires no password. If this fails, the client will prompt the user for a password with which to access the IPC$ share. This message, of course, strikes most users as quite bizarre—they've never heard of this share, and they don't know what the password is for it. If you run into this problem on your network, try setting the guest account parameter explicitly in the [global] section of smb.conf. This parameter's default value is a compile-time option, but it's usually nobody. This value is also normally reasonable, but it might not be acceptable on your particular system, or the default for your Samba binaries may be something else. In either case, setting the parameter to a valid but low-privilege user should eliminate the problem.

Verifying Use of Unencrypted or Encrypted Passwords

Chapter 7 describes the use of both unencrypted and encrypted passwords in some detail. You should read that chapter to learn when to use each type of password and how to configure Samba to use the appropriate type. Some common pitfalls include the following:

Relying on defaults: The default value for the encrypt passwords parameter has changed with Samba 3.0; with Samba 2.2.*x* and earlier, it was No, and with more recent versions it's Yes. Explicitly specifying your preferred encryption setting should avoid confusion.

Mismatched client/server settings: Old versions of Windows (Windows 95 prior to OSR2 and Windows NT 4.0 prior to SP3) used unencrypted passwords only, but newer versions use encrypted passwords by default and have no fallback position. Be sure your client and server settings agree. Chapter 7 provides information on adjusting Windows clients' password encryption settings.

Missing Samba accounts: If you use encrypted passwords, be sure you create accounts for your Samba users using smbpasswd or net in addition to the underlying Unix accounts. You need *both* types of accounts to use Samba.

If there's any doubt in your mind about your settings, you might want to verify them using a packet sniffer, as described earlier in "Using a Packet Sniffer." For instance, using Ethereal, you should look for a packet that's identified as *Session Setup AndX Request* in the Ethereal top frame. The raw data for such a packet, for a cleartext logon, looks like this:

```
0000  00 50 bf 19 7e 99 00 03   47 b1 ee b8 08 00 45 00   .P?.~... G??..E.
0010  00 ab 55 52 40 00 40 06   61 a6 c0 a8 01 01 c0 a8   .?UR@.@. a??..?
0020  01 03 82 95 01 bd 4b c1   7c bd 47 93 96 ae 80 18   .....?K? |?G..?..
0030  16 d0 af d2 00 00 01 01   08 0a 1e 46 e3 54 55 a3   .???.... ...F?TU?
0040  d5 2d 00 00 00 73 ff 53   4d 42 73 00 00 00 00 08   ?-...s?S MBs.....
0050  01 48 00 00 00 00 00 00   00 00 00 00 00 00 00 00   .H...... ........
0060  69 22 00 00 02 00 0d ff   00 00 00 ff ff 02 00 69   i".....? ...??..i
0070  22 82 3f 00 00 12 00 00   00 00 00 00 00 58 00 00   ".?..... .....X..
0080  00 36 00 74 68 69 73 69   73 74 68 65 70 61 73 73   .6.thisi sthepass
0090  77 6f 72 64 00 46 41 53   54 41 49 52 45 00 52 49   word.FAS TAIRE.RI
00a0  4e 47 57 4f 52 4c 44 00   55 6e 69 78 00 53 61 6d   NGWORLD. Unix.Sam
00b0  62 61 20 33 2e 30 2e 30   00                        ba 3.0.0 .
```

NOTE Ethereal does identify the password string in its tree view, but Ethereal presents the password in a numeric form that's difficult to parse. In the end, a cleartext password is easy to spot in a raw dump.

Near the end of the data, you'll see the string thisisthepassword, which is what was typed in the password field. The username (FASTAIRE), workgroup (RINGWORLD), and other information also appears in this packet. Depending upon client and server settings, some of this information may appear in a two-byte form (Unicode), making it look more spread out in the text display. Reconfiguring the system to use encrypted passwords, the string doesn't appear in the Ethereal output; instead, the password is transformed into a format that's not easily recognized by the human eye:

```
0000  00 50 bf 19 7e 99 00 03   47 b1 ee b8 08 00 45 00   .P?.~... G??..E.
0010  00 d0 68 1b 40 00 40 06   4e b8 c0 a8 01 01 c0 a8   .?h.@.@. N??..?
0020  01 03 82 98 01 bd 70 6d   e0 15 6c 01 02 54 80 18   .....?pm ?.l..T..
0030  19 20 c9 cc 00 00 01 01   08 0a 1e 47 ca e9 55 ac   . ??.... ...G??U?
0040  e3 28 00 00 00 98 ff 53   4d 42 73 00 00 00 00 08   ?(....?S MBs.....
0050  01 48 00 00 00 00 00 00   00 00 00 00 00 00 00 00   .H...... ........
0060  88 22 00 00 02 00 0c ff   00 00 00 ff ff 02 00 01   ."......? ...??...
0070  00 00 00 00 00 52 00 00   00 00 00 58 00 00 80 5d   .....R.. ...X...]
0080  00 60 50 06 06 2b 06 01   05 05 02 a0 46 30 44 a0   .`P..+.. ...?F0D?
0090  0e 30 0c 06 0a 2b 06 01   04 01 82 37 02 02 0a a2   .0...+.. ...7...?
00a0  32 04 30 4e 54 4c 4d 53   53 50 00 01 00 00 00 15   2.0NTLMS SP......
00b0  02 08 60 09 00 09 00 20   00 00 00 07 00 07 00 29   ..`.... .......)
00c0  00 00 00 52 49 4e 47 57   4f 52 4c 44 53 50 45 41   ...RINGW ORLDSPEA
00d0  4b 45 52 55 6e 69 78 00   53 61 6d 62 61 00         KERUnix. Samba.
```

Much of the rest of the data in the packet, such as the username, workgroup name, and so on, remain unchanged. If you want to be absolutely certain that encryption is being used, you can look for packets like these. Experiment with turning encryption on and off, and try to find them. (Depending upon your clients, you may need to reconfigure the server to change the encryption sent by the client.) You should be able to identify passwords by eye when cleartext passwords are used but not when encrypted passwords are used.

NOTE Looking for cleartext passwords will help you determine whether encryption is being used but not what *type* of encryption is being used. SMB/CIFS supports several variants, some of which are better than others. Spotting this detail from packet sniffer output is possible but requires much greater familiarity with the details of the protocol.

Verifying Authentication Style

Samba supports several different methods of authenticating users: share-, user-, server-, domain-, and ADS-level. These options are set via the security parameter, which adjusts how Samba goes about trying to authenticate users. Chapter 4 describes these options in detail. Each authentication method has its own potential pitfalls, which you must take care to avoid.

Share-Level Authentication Problems

Share-level authentication is a poor match to Unix's underlying security model. As described in detail in Chapter 4, Samba tries using a series of usernames; with each attempt, Samba tries matching the provided password with that stored in its or the Unix password database (depending upon the value of the encrypt passwords parameter).

If Samba exhausts the list of users without matching the password, the server denies entry to the user. Depending upon other options used in the share and set in the [global] section of smb.conf, Samba may run out of accounts to try before authenticating the user, even if the user really should be able to gain access to the share. You should set up some sort of explicit configuration to directly map at least one username and, hence, a password to the share. Possibilities include using the guest only parameter to map the guest account password to the share, using an account named after the share, and using the username parameter to explicitly link one or more accounts to the share. Remember to create a Samba encrypted password entry for your chosen account if you enable encrypted passwords.

User-Level Authentication Problems

When you set security = User, Samba uses the normal Unix accounts for its own users. By default, Samba expects usernames passed by the client to match those on the server, but this may not be practical. In such cases, you must use a username mapping system to match up SMB/CIFS usernames to Unix usernames. This process is briefly described in the upcoming section "Configuring Special Accounts" and in more detail in Chapter 7.

Samba versions prior to 3.0 used the Unix password database for cleartext passwords and the smbpasswd file for encrypted passwords. Samba 3.0, however, has changed the authentication system substantially and added the possibility of using many additional encrypted password backends. You set these options using the passdb backend parameter. If you change this option, Samba will no longer respond to passwords stored using the original backend system, so users will suddenly find they can no longer log on.

Server-Level Authentication Problems

In server-level authentication, Samba defers to another computer (typically a domain controller) for authentication. Effectively, that server becomes the Samba encrypted password database. This system, of course, is subject to problems related to network connectivity—if the remote server goes down, Samba won't be able to authenticate users. In theory, Samba should fall back to its own local password database if this happens, but if the local database were complete, you presumably wouldn't have configured Samba to use the remote server for authentication, so this solution isn't ideal.

Another problem with server-level authentication relates to identifying the remote server. You use the password server parameter to identify this system. Be sure that a correct IP address is listed. In most cases, this mode requires that encrypt passwords be set to Yes, but this parameter can be set to No if the authentication server is also configured in this way.

Domain-Level Authentication Problems

When security = Domain, the Samba server fully joins an NT-style domain and participates in its authentication system. This mode of operation requires that you use the net utility to join the Samba server to the domain, as described in Chapter 10. The potential problems of domain-level security are similar to those of server-level security—if a network connection goes down, user authentication can suffer. Joining a Samba server to a domain can be tricky, though, so you're more likely to run into problems with this type of configuration than with server-level authentication.

ADS-Level Authentication Problems

Active Directory Services (ADS) is the latest variant on authentication domains from Microsoft. ADS adds Kerberos encryption and Lightweight Directory Access Protocol (LDAP) databases to the mix, making for a much more secure and flexible authentication system. ADS also builds its domains from DNS rather than using NT domains. Although Samba cannot yet function as an ADS server, it can defer to an ADS controller for authentication by using security = ADS. ADS servers can also emulate NT domain controllers using NT domain protocols, so setting security = Domain or security = Server should work with them, as well.

From a problem point of view, ADS-level authentication is the trickiest of the lot. It's subject to the same potential for network problems as domain- and server-level security. Configuring Samba to use ADS-level authentication requires you to install and configure Kerberos on your Samba server computer. Once configured, though, the experience to your users should be seamless, and they won't see fundamentally new security problems as a result of this configuration.

Configuring Special Accounts

Some authentication problems relate to special accounts and account-handling tools. One of these is the GUEST account, which enables access to the server without the benefit of a password. Several parameters relate to the use of a GUEST account, and each has its potential problems:

guest account: This parameter sets the Unix account name associated with the SMB/CIFS GUEST account. It's frequently set to *nobody*, but you can change this mapping in the [global] section. Setting guest account incorrectly can cause failures to log on. It can also cause failures when browsing to the server under some circumstances.

guest ok: This parameter enables guest access to a share. The default value is No, so you must set this parameter to Yes if you want to enable guest access. Failure to do so will cause problems if you want such access. At least as important, setting guest ok = Yes inappropriately can be a security risk.

guest only: This parameter tells Samba to accept *only* guest accesses to a share. Setting it to Yes on normal shares can prevent users from performing operations, such as writing to files, that they should be able to perform.

map to guest: This global parameter tells Samba when to attempt guest access. Never disables guest access, Bad User attempts guest access when the username is invalid, and Bad Password attempts guest access when the password is wrong. This final option can result in spurious guest accesses by valid users who mistype their passwords, which can result in great user confusion.

In addition to mapping user accesses onto a guest account, Samba can map accesses between usernames. This process is described in Chapter 7, but in brief, you use the username map parameter to pass a file to Samba. This file contains lines that have a Unix username, an equals sign, and an SMB/CIFS username. Samba goes through this file and, if the username passed by the user is present as the SMB/CIFS username, Samba makes the substitution and then continues. This continuation means that a single name can be substituted several times, which in turn can lead to confusion. For instance, if one line maps the username Ginger Rogers to grogers, and a subsequent line maps grogers to george, then the system will attempt to authenticate Ginger Rogers against the password stored for george. Of course, the user won't know this; to the user, it will simply appear that the server is arbitrarily refusing to accept a valid password.

One way to reduce the possibility of multi-mapping confusion is to begin each line in the username map file with an exclamation mark (!). This symbol tells Samba to stop processing at that line if a match is found.

Fixing File-Sharing Problems

File-sharing problems relate to an inability to access files on a Samba server or sometimes to an ability to access files that should not be accessible. In most cases, these problems can be traced to one of three broad classes of causes: local permissions, Samba file-access options, and file-naming options. Checking all of these, and understanding the interactions between them (particularly the first two), is important in debugging such problems.

Symptoms of File-Sharing Problems

File-sharing problems occur after you've managed to browse to a share and log onto the server; in some sense, they're the final type of problem you can encounter in the series of events that describe use of a Samba server. (This chapter also has sections on printing problems and domain controller functions, though.) File-sharing problems can manifest themselves in several ways:

Inability to access directories: You may find that you can't open some or all directories within a share. In some cases, users or computers may be denied access to entire shares.

Inability to read files: Most file shares are useless if you can't read the files they contain.

Inability to create new files: You might not be able to create files in a share or in a subdirectory of a share.

Inability to modify files: You might be able to create new files but not modify some or all existing files.

Inappropriate ability to access files or directories: Any of the preceding problems can be reversed; you might be able to access files or directories in ways that should not be permitted.

Lack of ACLs: Some networks rely on users' ability to use access control lists (ACLs) for security, and if you can't modify ACL settings, your system may be crippled.

Sporadic problems: Files or directories may become inaccessible on a seemingly random basis.

Filename issues: Files and directories may change names mysteriously, particularly between clients using different OSs. Files may disappear, particularly when using DOS clients.

Most of these problems are caused by local Unix permissions or Samba's file permissions options. Filename issues are likely an interaction between Samba's filename options and client OS limitations.

Some problems are sporadic in nature—they may occur for some users but not for others, they may occur only from some computers, or they may occur at some times and not at others. Such problems may result from the group permissions bits, or they could relate to server- or user-specific configuration files accessed via an include parameter. Temporal problems could be a symptom of broader network problems. For instance, if a router is crashing and rebooting, access may be disrupted while the router is down.

Setting Appropriate Local Permissions

As a Unix system administrator, you should already be familiar with Unix-style permissions. If you're not, review Chapter 2, which provides a brief overview of Unix ownership and permissions. Samba's default file-access procedures use Unix ownership and permissions in sensible ways. Users who log onto Samba may access files much as they would when logged on via a text-mode login tool such as SSH. Samba uses its own default file-creation modes, set via the create mask and directory mask parameters, as described in Chapter 5.

If a user reports problems accessing a specific file or directory, you should check that file or directory for appropriate permissions. Assuming you don't use Samba options to change the effective user ID, the file or directory should have permissions that enable the user to read from or, if appropriate, write to the file or directory. In a user's home share, this normally means that the file should be owned by the user in question and have at least 0400 (0600 for write access) permissions. In shared directories, the rules may be different. If all users must be able to write to the directory, you must ensure that the directory's permissions are set appropriately. You may also need to use the create mask and directory mask parameters, or set inherit permissions = Yes and set the permissions on the parent directory appropriately, in order to have all files and directories created with permissions that enable other users to read from and write to them.

If you find that the ownership or permissions for the file are off, you can correct the problem on a file-by-file basis using standard Unix tools, such as chown or chmod. For instance, you might type **chmod 0640 somefile.doc** to change the permissions on somefile.doc to enable the owner to read from and write to the file, to enable members of the file's group to read from but not write to it, and to prevent everybody else from accessing the file. The bigger problem in this case is the question of how the file was created with inadequate permissions originally. Several possibilities exist, including the following:

Samba permissions options: Your Samba configuration options, such as create mask, may be set strangely or inappropriately. These options are described in more detail shortly in "Setting Appropriate Access Options."

Non-Samba servers: A non-Samba server, such as a File Transfer Protocol (FTP) server or Netatalk, may have created the file or directory with permissions that are inappropriate for Samba access.

Remote login access: If users have shell access to the server, they can create files using the shell. The default permissions might have done the job, or the user might have issued a chmod or similar command without realizing the consequences. Similar problems can occur via remote GUI logins.

Another Samba user: Depending upon the share's permissions, another Samba user might have created the file. If the share didn't have a `force user` parameter, the result should be a file owned by another user, which in some cases might be unreadable or unwriteable to the share's primary user. Adjusting the `create mask` or `directory mask` might enable you to work around this problem. In the case of users' home shares, a better policy is probably to set Unix permissions to prevent users other than the owner from writing to the share and to create a separate file-sharing share with looser permissions. Another approach is to encourage users to share files by enabling them to "pick up" files from specific directories in others' home shares and to copy those files to their own directories.

ACL changes: If you've enabled ACL support in Samba, a user might have changed the file's permissions from a Windows NT/200*x*/XP client using the client's ACL-manipulation tools. This ACL support can be a real boon if your users understand it, but it can cause access problems if users don't understand it.

You can ask the user how the file was created and who might have accessed it and examine the ownership and group of the file for clues. Once you've determined how the file acquired the inappropriate permissions, you can take steps to correct the matter. You can change the Samba configuration or the configuration of another server, shut down an unnecessary server, change local Unix permissions, or do whatever else it takes to prevent the problem from recurring.

Problems relating to an inability to access files in the way you intend are fairly easy to spot; chances are you'll hear complaints about such problems soon enough. Problems of the opposite sort—an inappropriate ability to read or write files—may be harder to detect because you're less likely to notice these problems or receive complaints. You should perform spot checks to help find such problems, though. If ordinary users shouldn't be able to write to a directory, use an ordinary user account and attempt to do so. If particular users shouldn't be able to read a share, use such an account to be sure the share isn't readable.

ACLs can be tricky to use correctly. As noted in Chapter 5, Samba provides ACL support via the `nt acl support = Yes` parameter, but that support is partially dependent upon underlying OS features. Without explicit ACL support in the OS and its filesystem, Samba will use SMB/CIFS ACLs only as a window onto Unix-style permissions. If your users can't add other users to their files' ACLs, chances are this is the problem. Modifying Samba permissions won't get around this problem; you'll need to change your server's underlying filesystem or add a package to enable full ACLs on the existing filesystem. This support exists for some common Unix filesystems, including Linux's ext2fs and ext3fs, Linux's and IRIX's XFS, and FreeBSD's FFS. Some of these systems require patches or add-on packages to enable full ACL support, though.

Setting Appropriate Access Options

Samba provides quite a few parameters that influence the access rights granted to users. Most of these options work in concert with the underlying Unix permissions;

they modify the effective user ID of the Samba session, set Unix permissions in specified ways, and so on. These options provide a great deal of flexibility, but if they're used inappropriately they can prevent users from accessing files or grant access to users who shouldn't have it. Some of the more common options and their pitfalls include the following:

create mask: This parameter sets the mode on newly created files. Be sure this value is set appropriately in any read/write share or it will cause problems— either too great or too little access for files' owners or others. If different directories in a share should have different permissions on files created within it, either split the share into multiple shares with different create mask values or use inherit permissions and set permissions on the subdirectories appropriately.

directory mask: This parameter works just like create mask and carries the same caveats except that it applies to directories rather than files.

inherit permissions: As an alternative to create mask and directory mask, the inherit permissions parameter enables Samba to set permissions on files and directories based on the permissions of the directories in which they're created. The effect is similar to the default behavior when creating files in the default shells of many Unix systems. It carries the problem that it gives users more control over the permissions on files they create; by using subdirectories with varying permissions, users may be able to create files with inappropriate permissions, perhaps without even realizing that this is what they're doing.

force user: This parameter tells Samba to use the specified account for all file accesses and creations, rather than the user's logon account. This ability is very useful but also potentially quite dangerous and confusing. You can use this feature to simplify access to shared file directories, but doing so can make it harder to debug problems and discover who created files.

force group: This parameter works just like force user, but it affects the group ID rather than the user ID.

read only: This parameter, when set to Yes (the default), identifies a share that's read-only, even if the underlying Unix directory structure would enable users to access it. Forgetting about this parameter's default or setting it inappropriately can lead to any number of access problems. This parameter has several antonyms: write ok, writeable, and writable.

hosts allow and hosts deny: You can restrict access to a share based on a client's IP address or hostname. (Using a hostname requires setting hostname lookups = Yes.) This is a useful security feature, but it can also lead to bizarre problems if you mistype an IP address or hostname or if you add computers and forget about this restriction.

valid users and invalid users: These parameters are similar to hosts allow and hosts deny except that they work on usernames rather than client IP addresses or hostnames. Similar caveats apply, too: It's easy to forget about these restrictions or mistype a username.

read list and **write list**: These parameters provide lists of users who are exceptions to a read only = No or read only = Yes parameter on a share, respectively. Caveats are similar to those for valid users and invalid users: Forgetting the parameter or mistyping a username can cause access failures or inappropriately high access levels.

admin users: This parameter is something like a cross between valid users and force user; it grants the specified users root privileges when accessing a share. Use it sparingly, lest you open the door to abuse or a cracker. Also, if a user on this list creates files in a share, those files will be owned by root, which can have unintended consequences in terms of other users' ability to access or modify the files.

TIP   In most cases, simplicity is your friend. Trying to achieve exotic effects by implementing a complex set of Samba security options is likely to lead to problems. Samba's default security options work well in most cases and enable you to use the underlying Unix security features as they were intended. This approach of embracing simplicity can help you avoid problems or help you overcome them by simplifying your configuration if the need arises.

Fixing Naming Problems

Samba naming options are most commonly required when dealing with DOS clients, which support only short (8.3) filenames. Mac OS Classic clients are also limited in filename length, but their limit is 31 characters. Many clients, including all versions of Windows, are also limited in the filename cases they support. Some common Samba parameters, and the problems they can cause or prevent, include the following:

preserve case: This parameter, if set to Yes (the default), causes Samba to preserve the case of filenames as they're sent to the server. The result is usually desirable, but if clients have a tendency to create all-uppercase filenames, you might prefer converting them to lowercase for aesthetic reasons. Doing so can confuse some clients, though, which may not realize that the altered filename is the same as the one that was originally created.

short preserve case: This parameter works just like preserve case, but it applies only to short filenames. If you want to convert DOS filenames to lowercase, you're probably better off using short preserve case = No than preserve case = No because you'll limit the potential for damage caused by converting longer filenames to lowercase.

default case: Set this parameter's value to Upper or Lower to adjust the case as set by preserve case or short preserve case. The potential for damage is similar for both options but is present only when the case-preservation option is set to No.

`case sensitive`: Samba defaults to mimicking the lack of case-sensitivity of its primary client OSs, DOS, Windows, and OS/2. To do this, Samba must match all potential case variants of local Unix filenames. Normally this process works well, but it can hide one file of a pair that differs only in case. The best solution in most situations is to avoid creating such pairs or to rename one member of each pair if you find a pair that exists. If a client relies on these files having their names differ only in case, you can set `case sensitive` = Yes, but this setting is likely to cause problems for some clients, particularly Windows 9*x*/Me systems. Setting `case sensitive` = Yes in a file that's loaded via an `include` parameter only for systems that can handle it is appropriate, if possible.

Some other problems are rarer, at least in North America. For instance, Unicode and code page issues can cause filenames that use non-ASCII characters to become corrupted when different client OSs are used or when clients are configured in different ways. Checking that all the like-OS clients are configured identically and experimenting with the `unicode`, `unix charset`, `dos charset`, and similar options may be required to resolve such problems.

Fixing Printing Problems

Samba is a powerful printer server, but with that power comes the potential for problems. From a user's perspective, interfacing to a Samba printer share is no more difficult than interfacing to a Windows printer share. Behind the scenes, though, Samba must interface to your server's printing system, and the number of Unix printing systems complicates this task. Another potential problem is in handling PostScript vs. non-PostScript printers and inputs. Both types of printers have their own sets of problems. You may also want to investigate network and print server performance issues.

Common Printing Problems

Printer shares are basically just specialized file shares. SMB/CIFS clients communicate with both share types in similar ways, but printer shares pose their own set of unique challenges. Some of the issues regarding printer shares include the following:

Authentication: Printer share authentication follows the same rules as authentication for file shares. The trouble is that you might want to use simpler or laxer authentication on printer shares than on file shares. Using tight security on printer shares can complicate client setup by requiring users to access the printer using their own accounts or by requiring the use of special printing accounts. Using the `guest ok` = Yes parameter in printer shares can simplify authentication but at the cost of reduced security.

Lost jobs: One particularly common printing problem is lost jobs. You print from the client and nothing comes out of the printer. Tracking down just where in the system the job was lost usually helps you locate a solution.

Corrupted jobs: If you print and gibberish comes out, the data is being mis-processed. This could happen because of an incorrect print filter on the Samba server, incorrect Samba options, or an incorrect printer driver on the client.

Sluggish performance: Print jobs may be delayed for inordinate periods of time. On busy or low-performance networks, print jobs might also interfere with other network transfers, degrading overall network performance.

Because printing involves the interaction of the client's printer drivers in addition to all the other usual SMB/CIFS network elements, printing problems are more likely than many to vary strangely from one client to another. If one client can print well but another can't, and if your network doesn't have any other strange client-to-client problems, you may want to investigate printer driver differences first. Perhaps the two clients have two entirely different printer drivers or perhaps even different printer driver versions for the same printer.

Interfacing to Your Printing System

One common source of printing problems is in how Samba submits jobs to the printing system. As described in Chapter 6, the global `printing` parameter tells Samba which of several sets of printing commands to use. If you're having problems with printing, the first thing you should check is this parameter. If you're still having problems, though, you might consider setting the `print command` parameter in your printer share. This parameter enables you to adjust the command that Samba uses to submit print jobs. An example might look like this:

```
print command = lpr -r -P%p %s
```

This command submits the print job to the local printer queue using the `lpr` command, passing it the name of the print queue using `-P` (the `%p` variable expands to the print queue name), and passing the name of the print job using `%s`. The `-r` option removes the print job file when printing is complete. Of course, you must adjust this command to suit the printing system on your computer.

 TIP If you're not sure where a print job is getting lost, try using `print command = cp %s /tmp/testfile.ps; rm %s`. You can then print to the share and look for the file `/tmp/testfile.ps`. If it's not present, then something is going wrong in authentication or data transfer. If it's present, you know that Samba is at least accepting print jobs from the client, although the problem could still be on the client side. For instance, the client might be using the wrong driver, and the Unix system's print queue might be discarding the job because it can't recognize the file type.

CAUTION Remember to delete the input print job (%s) as part of your print command. If you don't, the print jobs will build up in your printer share's directory until they prevent Samba from accepting new print jobs. Using rm %s is necessary with many printing systems, but some provide options (such as -r in the preceding example) that automatically delete the print job.

If you can't seem to get any output from your printer but you're sure Samba is receiving print jobs, try printing locally on the print server computer itself. If you can do that, it's possible that something about the format of the client's print jobs is causing problems. Try capturing a print job (using a print command such as the one in the preceding Tip) and submit it for printing manually. You can also examine the contents of the print job. If you're submitting PostScript files, the first line should begin with the string %!PS-Adobe, possibly followed by additional information, such as the PostScript version. Non-PostScript files will, of course, have different content.

Some printers require a few lines of special codes to set the printer to accept PostScript before the %!PS-Adobe line. If your printer requires these lines, their absence can cause problems; but conversely, if your printer does *not* require such lines, their presence can cause problems. Your Samba server computer's print filters may also be confused by these lines. You may need to change the client's printer driver, create a "raw" local queue, or modify your local print filters to work around such problems.

Handling PostScript Output

If you're printing to a PostScript printer and using PostScript drivers on the client, you can pass the print jobs unchanged to the printer. Most print queues will do this without any problems, but sometimes a Unix print queue will misidentify a PostScript file as a non-PostScript file. The result is either a failure to print the file or a printout consisting of the PostScript source code, which includes the %!PS-Adobe string in the first few lines of text. Sometimes this misidentification occurs because the client's driver adds printer-specific mode-switching code to the file. A few drivers add Control+D characters to the start of the print job, which can also confuse print filters.

In Samba through the 2.2.*x* series, misidentification of PostScript jobs as non-PostScript could be prevented by the use of the postscript = Yes parameter, which tells Samba to add a PostScript identifier to the start of the print job. This action is enough to get the local queue to correctly handle the file as a PostScript print job. Unfortunately, this option was removed from Samba 3.0, so you can't force the issue with this version of Samba—at least, not in this way.

Another option is to set up and use a "raw" print queue. Such a queue doesn't attempt to identify the file type but instead sends the file directly to the printer. This approach will work only if you're printing to a true PostScript printer. The procedure for creating a raw print queue varies from one printing system to another. With BSD

LPD, LPRng, and other systems that use /etc/printcap for configuration, you can typically create a raw queue by deleting the if= line in the /etc/printcap definition for a queue. CUPS and many GUI configuration tools provide point-and-click options to create a raw queue; consult your printing system's documentation for more information.

Another approach to fixing problems caused by misidentified PostScript files is to change your printer driver, or at least the printer driver's options. Some drivers provide options to enable or disable the sending of Control+D characters or printer mode-switching commands. For instance, Figure 17-3 shows one Windows Me PostScript driver's advanced options dialog box. Note the check box near the bottom, called Send CTRL+D Before Job. Be sure that option is unchecked. (Sending a Control+D after the print job is unlikely to cause problems.) These options are likely to be hard to find, though, and some drivers don't provide them at all. In a worst-case scenario, you may need to switch to another driver. Chapter 6 provides information on locating drivers for your printer. In most cases, particularly for PostScript printers, more than one driver will work with a printer.

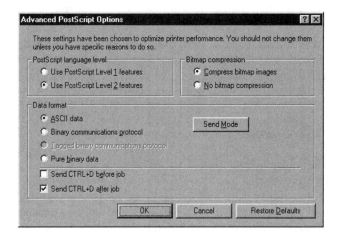

Figure 17-3. Some PostScript drivers provide options that can affect a Unix print queue's ability to correctly identify and process the file type.

If your printer is a non-PostScript model and you use Ghostscript in a Unix print queue to turn PostScript into an appropriate format, you should check that you can print ordinary PostScript directly from the Samba server computer but without using Samba. Once this is working, printing from Samba clients should work. If it doesn't, most of the same solutions for printing to genuine PostScript printers will also work. One notable exception is using a raw queue. Instead of creating a raw queue, you could try creating a queue that uses a very simple filter that blindly passes the input file through Ghostscript and out to the printer. Another approach is to switch to printer-specific drivers and use a raw queue.

Handling Non-PostScript Output

If you want to use non-PostScript printer-specific drivers on clients, your Samba server must accommodate this configuration. The usual approach is to use a raw printer queue, as described earlier. In this case, though, the raw queue is used to avoid confusing a Unix printer queue with printer-specific data it may not be able to recognize, rather than avoiding problems due to misidentified PostScript files. Most modern Unix systems' print filters, though, can identify some of the more common printers' file types. With these printers, you might be able to print to a standard queue that can recognize and process both PostScript and printer-specific output.

An overzealous print filter is likely to completely discard a print job in a format it doesn't recognize, so if you're losing print jobs and a test with a dummy print command shows that the jobs are definitely reaching the Samba system, you should look into this possibility. Try taking the print job and sending it directly to the printer's device file with cat or dd. If it prints, you can be reasonably sure that the printer queue is corrupting or discarding the print jobs.

 CAUTION Do not try using cat or dd as the Samba print command. Doing so will bypass the Unix printer queue system and is likely to cause collisions if two print jobs are submitted in quick succession. The most likely result is that the second print job will be completely lost.

Some print filters might try to process files they don't recognize as ASCII. The result could be a printout that looks like gibberish—strings of seemingly random letters, numbers, punctuation, and bizarre characters. If this happens, look into a way to bypass the print filter. Another possible explanation of a printer spewing reams of gibberish is that the wrong driver is installed on the client. A printer driver for an Epson inkjet printer is unlikely to work on a Canon printer, for instance. Even within a printer family, different models may require radically different drivers. Double-check that the correct driver is installed. You may want to try temporarily moving the printer from the print server to the client and printing directly. If that clears up the problem, then the print job is being corrupted, probably by a Unix print filter that's misidentified the file type. A few printers require bidirectional communication between themselves and their Windows drivers. Such printers won't work at all under Samba, so if you encounter this problem, you may have no choice but to replace the printer, or at least shift it to a Windows print server.

Improving Printing Performance

Getting a printer working is a major part of the job of configuring a print server. You may want to optimize printing performance, though. Several different measures of printing performance exist:

Time to print: You may want to minimize the time it takes to print a document. If you want to do so systematically, you should use a stopwatch to time how long it takes to print. A couple of specific ways to measure this time are the time between clicking the Print button in an application and the finish of the print job and the time between the printer springing to life and the final page emerging. The first measure includes client processing and network transfers, whereas the second measure is more printer-specific. Depending upon your needs, either measure might be more appropriate.

Client load: Some printer drivers consume a great deal of CPU time or RAM on the client. Typically, these drivers convert text documents into bitmaps, which are then sent to the printer. If your clients have weak CPUs or if you simply want to avoid loading them down with tasks such as printing, minimizing client CPU load may be in order. Using PostScript drivers on the client rather than printer-specific drivers will generally reduce the client load, especially when printing text documents.

Server load: If your print server computer has a weak CPU or performs non-printing tasks, you may want to minimize its CPU load. You can do this by using printer-specific drivers rather than PostScript drivers on the client, at least for non-PostScript printers. (For PostScript printers, this difference is moot.)

Network load: If your printers handle many print jobs, the network load imposed by transferring print jobs from clients to servers may be an important concern. Generally speaking, using PostScript drivers on the client will reduce network load, particularly for text documents.

Print quality: Although in some sense not a true performance measure, the quality of the output can be important. Quality is likely to differ between using native drivers on clients and using PostScript drivers on clients with Ghostscript on the server. The effects may differ between clients, particularly if they run different OSs or drivers.

Some of these measures of printing performance are likely to trade off one another. For instance, short of shifting to native PostScript printers, you can't minimize both the client and server CPU loads when printing to non-PostScript printers; one computer or the other must convert a document into a form that the printer can understand, and that process can take some time.

Broadly speaking, each of these measures can yield different results when printing text files compared to printing graphics files. The network load is particularly likely to vary greatly between these two measures when using PostScript on the client; PostScript text files are likely to be very small, but printer-specific bitmaps generated by clients for many inkjet printers can be huge, even when printing text. You may also find that different printers yield different results.

In the end, the best way to optimize your printing system is to experiment with different options on *your* network. Measure printing time, evaluate printing quality, and try to get some impression of how client, server, and CPU loads vary depending upon what type of printer drivers you use.

Fixing Domain Problems

If you use a domain configuration, your domain controller is an unusually critical component. Problems with the domain controller can wreak havoc on the entire network, even affecting the interactions of clients and servers other than the domain controller. Domain controller problems can manifest themselves in many different ways. Some problems are related to basic configuration and are easily fixed, but others are trickier to resolve.

Symptoms of Domain Controller Problems

Domain controllers play multiple roles on an SMB/CIFS network. Each of these functions can cause problems in its own way:

Domain logons: Arguably the most important function of a domain controller is processing domain logons. When the domain controller fails to process domain logons, the results closely resemble the authentication problems described earlier in "Fixing Authentication Problems." The solutions may also be similar to those for authentication problems on a server that's not a domain member.

Domain master browser: The PDC assumes domain master browser duties, and if the system has problems performing these duties, browsing problems similar to those described earlier in "Fixing Browsing Problems" will occur.

Netlogon shares: Domain controllers typically provide a share, called NETLOGON, in which network logon scripts and related files reside. If this share doesn't exist, the domain will still work, but you obviously won't be able to use the NETLOGON share's features. A misconfiguration (say, a typo in the NETLOGON share name) can result in a failure to run the network logon script.

Roaming profiles: If you don't configure roaming profiles properly, as described in Chapter 14, some clients may complain about an inability to load or store users' profiles.

Another type of problem can occur if you configure two or more computers as domain controllers for the same domain on a single network segment: Clients and domain member servers won't know which domain controller to use. This type of configuration is acceptable if one system is a PDC and the other is a backup domain controller (BDC), but when both systems are configured to be PDCs, their user databases might not match and many other issues will arise. The result can be strange authentication problems or even a failure of the correct PDC to come online. Also, as of Samba 3.0, you can't mix Samba and Windows PDCs and BDCs; if you use a BDC, it must be of the same type as the PDC.

Sometimes servers that should be members of the domain don't contact the domain controller. This problem can result in an inability to access the servers or in the servers granting access to users who've been removed from the domain. The usual cause is a failure to join the servers to the domain, as described in Chapter 10. Sometimes an authentication problem in the machine trust account can cause a problem. If a Samba server can't authenticate against the domain controller, it will fall back on its local authentication database, so you should be sure that the local Samba database is empty.

Correcting Domain Problems

You can correct most domain control problems by re-examining the domain configuration options, as described in Chapter 10. Pay particular attention to the core domain controller parameters:

> `security`: The domain controller must set `security` = `User`. Servers that are members of the domain must use `security` = `Domain`. The `security` = `Server` setting is a simpler alternative that's acceptable in many instances, but it may not be as reliable as using `security` = `Domain`, so if you experience problems, try reconfiguring the Samba server as a full domain member.
>
> `encrypt passwords`: Domain controllers must use encrypted passwords, so this option must be set to `Yes`.
>
> `domain logons`: This parameter, more than any other, defines a domain controller; it must be set to `Yes` for a domain controller. Just as important, this option must be set to `No` for all machines that are not domain controllers.
>
> `domain master`: This parameter, when set to `Yes`, defines a system as a domain master browser. This function is normally associated with domain controllers, so be sure it's set correctly.

With the exception of `encrypt passwords`, these options should all be set one way for domain controllers and the other way for all other systems on the domain. An error in either direction can cause problems, so if you're having domain controller problems, you should audit all your Samba servers' `smb.conf` files to be sure these options are set correctly.

If you're experiencing domain authentication problems, you should first try to ascertain precisely what the problem is. Are only some clients affected? Are only some servers affected? If the answer to either of these questions is *yes*, it suggests that the problem isn't in the domain controller's user accounts but in a machine trust account, a client or server configuration, or perhaps even a low-level networking problem, such as an incorrectly set netmask causing a client to be unable to locate the domain controller. If only some users can't log on but others can using the same client, the problem could be as simple as a forgotten or incorrectly typed password.

Sophisticated configurations involving LDAP or other password database backends can be tricky to diagnose and fix because so many components are involved. You might not be sure whether a problem is due to an LDAP database problem, an LDAP server problem, Samba/LDAP server communication, Samba configuration, or some other factor. In such cases, try to isolate the problem by using as simple a test as possible and working your way up. For instance, you might cut the LDAP configuration out of the picture and use a conventional `smbpasswd` database, at least for testing purposes. If users can connect using this configuration, you can rule out a large number of possibilities relating to Samba configuration and Samba/client communication. You can then try querying the LDAP database directly, logging onto the Samba server from itself, and so on. With luck, a pattern will emerge. Remember to check your log files when performing such debugging; they often provide clues about the source of a problem.

Summary

Samba problems fall into many different categories, but a few troubleshooting techniques will help you track down many different types of problems. In terms of category-specific problems, Samba issues can be broadly categorized as falling into NetBIOS name problems, browsing problems, authentication problems, file share problems, printer share problems, and domain problems. Each of these problem types has certain sets of specific symptoms, causes, and troubleshooting techniques that are likely to yield solutions. Understanding these issues will help you configure a Samba system on a network, or a network of Samba systems, efficiently and fix problems quickly when they arise.

CHAPTER 18

Using SMB/CIFS Clients

THE BULK OF THIS BOOK is devoted to the configuration and use of the Samba server software. Samba alone is only one side of the coin, though; to be useful, Samba must talk to one or more client computers. These computers can run any of many OSs, and the OS with which Samba is paired can influence how you configure Samba. What's more, particular OSs have configuration and use quirks of which you should be aware. Therefore, this chapter covers the use of several SMB/CIFS client systems. These include various Microsoft OSs, the two main lines of Mac OS, and Unix with Samba. If you're using something more exotic than these OSs, you'll need to look elsewhere for information. First, though, you may want to consider methods of setting OS-specific options in Samba.

Working with Multiple Client OSs

Some Samba settings are designed to help you work with particular OSs. Options relating to filename case and length, hiding files, and so on may work well with one client OS but poorly with another. For this reason, you may want to set options for one OS or set of OSs independently of another. The usual way of doing this is to employ the Samba `include` parameter in conjunction with an `smb.conf` variable to help you identify the client OS. The `include` parameter loads an external configuration file, effectively including it within the main file. You pass this parameter a filename, but that filename can be composed, in whole or in part, of a Samba variable. The %a variable is particularly handy in this role. This variable stands in for the architecture (that is, the OS) of the client. In practice, %a expands to one of the values shown in Table 18-1. For instance, you might set an `smb.conf` parameter like the following:

```
include = /etc/samba/%a.conf
```

Table 18-1. Interpretations of the %a Variable

Value of %a	Meaning
Samba	Samba clients (such as `smbclient`) or affiliated tools, such as a mount using most Linux, FreeBSD, or Mac OS X mounting tools
WfWg	Windows for Workgroups or DOS clients
Win95	Windows 9*x*/Me clients
WinNT	Windows NT 3.*x* and 4.0 clients

Table 18-1. Interpretations of the %a Variable (Continued)

Value of %a	Meaning
Win2K	Windows 2000 clients
Win2K3	Windows 2003 clients
WinXP	Windows XP clients
OS2	OS/2 clients
UNKNOWN	Unknown clients; includes Mac OS running DAVE, BeOS, Linux's CIFS driver, and others

An include line could go in the [global] section if you want to modify all shares, or you could place the line only in those shares that need tweaking. Either way, you would provide files called Samba.conf, WfWg.conf, Win95.conf, and so on for each client OS. (Be sure to specify the case correctly when using %a; Samba uses the underlying OS's filesystem, which is usually case-sensitive, to match the name.) These files can contain client-specific configuration options, thus tweaking the operation of Samba for particular client OSs. If a file doesn't exist that matches the template, Samba ignores the include parameter, so using it does no harm.

TIP If Samba doesn't seem to be loading the correct configuration file, try using a preexec script to create a file using the %a variable, as in preexec = touch /tmp/%a. You can then log onto the share using a particular client and see what value the %a variable produces based on the name of the file that the preexec parameter creates.

You can use the same trick to have Samba load options based on features other than the OS. For instance, you can use %R in the filename to reference the protocol version or use %m to use the client's NetBIOS name. Chapter 2, and particularly its Table 2-1, describes smb.conf variables in more detail.

Using DOS and Windows SMB/CIFS Clients

SMB/CIFS is most strongly associated with the DOS/Windows family of OSs. Therefore, it shouldn't be surprising that Samba works very well with these clients. The details vary substantially from one family to another, though. The original Microsoft Disk Operating System (DOS) is rarely used today, but it can be made to work with Samba. Windows 9*x*/Me is built upon DOS, includes native SMB/CIFS support, and works well with Samba. The Windows NT/200*x*/XP line uses a new fully 32-bit kernel and also works well with Samba.

Using DOS with Samba

First introduced in 1981, Microsoft's MS-DOS and its twin PC-DOS (sold by IBM) were built upon an earlier OS called QDOS, which was a 16-bit clone of the earlier 8-bit Control Program for Microcomputers (CP/M), which in the late 1970s was the ultimate in personal computing OSs. Because of its ancient heritage and limited base architecture, getting DOS working on modern networks can be a challenge. The software to do the job is available, but more modern OSs provide easier-to-use configuration tools.

Using DOS with Samba requires first obtaining a version of DOS; several are available. You must then obtain and install SMB/CIFS software for DOS. Only then can you actually access Samba servers from DOS. Once you've gotten basic access working, you might want to consider tweaking your Samba configuration to better suit DOS clients.

Versions of DOS

Today, DOS is really a family of products. Some of these products are related to one another, and some work better than others. The DOS family includes the following:

MS-DOS: This OS may be the most popular DOS; it was sold with most *x*86 "clone" computers through the mid-1990s and is (in disguised form) at the core of the Windows 9*x*/Me line of OSs. Microsoft has discontinued this OS, but finding a used copy, or even a new copy in a closeout bin, isn't too hard. The final version to be sold independently of Windows 9*x*/Me was MS-DOS 6.22.

PC-DOS: Originally nearly identical to MS-DOS, the IBM-branded version of the OS diverged from its Microsoft sibling in late releases. In early 2004, PC-DOS is still available from IBM, under the name *PC-DOS 2000*; check http://www.ibm.com/software/os/dos/ for details.

DR-DOS: This DOS variant bears only a loose heritage in common with MS-DOS and PC-DOS. It was originally developed by Digital Research, which created the CP/M upon which DOS was modeled. The OS changed hands several times, and version 7.03 is being sold by DeviceLogics (http://www.drdos.com) in early 2004. (The Web page promises an 8.0 release in "spring of 2004.") In changing hands, DR-DOS has changed names; at various times, it's been known as Novell DOS and Caldera OpenDOS.

FreeDOS: This project, headquartered at http://www.freedos.org, is an open-source reimplementation of DOS. In some respects, it is to DOS what Linux is to Unix. It shares no source code with the commercial DOSs but can run many of the same programs. In early 2004, the latest version is beta-9 pre-release 4, meaning that the developers don't yet consider it quite ready for release.

In principle, any of these DOS versions should work with the SMB/CIFS tools for DOS and with Samba. In practice, there may be problems with some DOS versions. (I've successfully used the tools described in this chapter with MS-DOS 6.0, DR-DOS 7.03, and FreeDOS beta-9, although the software wouldn't install on some older versions of FreeDOS.) If you can't get something to work, try a different version of DOS, a different TCP/IP protocol stack, or a different SMB/CIFS package.

Obtaining and Installing SMB/CIFS Software for DOS

One of the first challenges in accessing a Samba server from DOS is in obtaining SMB/CIFS client software. No version of DOS ships with such software, so you must obtain a copy of an SMB/CIFS package. Several packages are available (check `http://huizen.dds.nl/~jacco2/samba/dos.html` for an unofficial list), but one of the most accessible is the Microsoft Network Client for DOS. You can obtain this package from Microsoft's FTP site at `ftp://ftp.microsoft.com/bussys/Clients/MSCLIENT/` or from the `CLIENTS\MSCLIENT\DISKS` directory of the Windows NT 4.0 Server CD-ROM. Two files are present on the FTP site: `DSK3-1.EXE` and `DSK3-2.EXE`. These files are self-extracting zip archives, so you can run them in DOS or Windows or unzip them using the `unzip` command in Unix. Extract the files onto two floppy disks, one for each archive, which you'll use to install the software in DOS. The files are pre-extracted on the Windows NT 4.0 Server CD-ROM in the `DISK1` and `DISK2` subdirectories, which you should copy to two floppies. If your DOS clients have CD-ROM drives, you can also install directly from the `CLIENTS\MSCLIENT\NETSETUP` directory.

NOTE The Microsoft Network Client for DOS includes both a TCP/IP stack and SMB/CIFS client tools. The TCP/IP package doesn't include clients for protocols other than SMB/CIFS, though—not even simple and common tools such as Telnet or FTP clients. (It does come with a `PING` utility, though.) If you need to use additional TCP/IP tools, you must find them elsewhere.

Unless you're using a very old network card, chances are you'll need drivers for your card from the card manufacturer. Check any floppies or CD-ROMs that shipped with the card, or check the manufacturer's Web site. If you can't find anything, go ahead and try the installation; the Microsoft package includes drivers for some older cards, and you might luck out. If not, go back and look harder for drivers, or replace the card with one that ships with appropriate support.

To install the software, follow these steps:

1. Boot to DOS.

2. Insert the Microsoft Network Client for DOS Disk 1 in the floppy drive.

3. Run the installation program by typing **A:\SETUP.EXE** at the DOS command prompt. You should see an introductory screen telling you you're about to install the software.

4. Press the Enter key to start the installation process proper. You'll be prompted for an installation directory, which defaults to C:\NET.

5. Press the Enter key to accept the default installation directory, or enter a new one if you want to install the software elsewhere. The system does some checks and displays a list of network adapters, as shown in Figure 18-1.

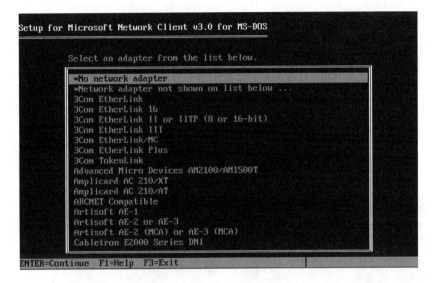

```
Setup for Microsoft Network Client v3.0 for MS-DOS


      Select an adapter from the list below.

     ┌────────────────────────────────────────────────────┐
     │ *No network adapter                                 │
     │ *Network adapter not shown on list below ...        │
     │ 3Com EtherLink                                      │
     │ 3Com EtherLink 16                                   │
     │ 3Com EtherLink II or IITP (8 or 16-bit)             │
     │ 3Com EtherLink III                                  │
     │ 3Com EtherLink/MC                                   │
     │ 3Com EtherLink Plus                                 │
     │ 3Com TokenLink                                      │
     │ Advanced Micro Devices AM2100/AM1500T               │
     │ Amplicard AC 210/XT                                 │
     │ Amplicard AC 210/AT                                 │
     │ ARCNET Compatible                                   │
     │ Artisoft AE-1                                       │
     │ Artisoft AE-2 or AE-3                               │
     │ Artisoft AE-2 (MCA) or AE-3 (MCA)                   │
     │ Cabletron E2000 Series DNI                          │
     └────────────────────────────────────────────────────┘

ENTER=Continue  F1=Help  F3=Exit
```

Figure 18-1. The Microsoft Network Client for DOS includes drivers for several older network cards.

6. If your network card is on the list, skip ahead to step 9. If not, select the second option, *Network adapter not shown on list below. This option enables you to install drivers supplied by your network card manufacturer. The next few steps assume you pick this option, which causes the program to prompt you for the location of your network drivers.

CAUTION Some network card drivers consume so much memory that it becomes impossible to run the Microsoft Network Client for DOS package on top of it; the system responds that it doesn't have enough free memory when it boots. In some cases, optimizing driver settings by hand or by using Microsoft's MEMMAKER utility can help. Other times, you may be forced to install a new network card or locate a new driver and reinstall the Network Client package. Unfortunately, you won't know until you reboot DOS whether your network card is a troublesome one.

---

7. If the drivers aren't already on the computer's hard disk, insert a floppy disk or CD-ROM containing the drivers.

8. Type the path to the directory containing the drivers, including the drive letter. Most drivers will reside in a directory called NDIS, NDIS2, or LANSVR40.DOS on the drivers floppy disk, CD-ROM, or extracted archive file. When you select a location with drivers, the system responds by displaying the driver's name or presenting you with a list of drivers in the directory you specified, much like the list in Figure 18-1 but shorter.

9. Select the appropriate driver, if necessary, and press the Enter key. The installer informs you that the drivers use memory for buffers and that you may adjust buffer parameters to improve performance.

10. If you like, press the C key to use unoptimized settings; otherwise, press the Enter key to use the default optimized settings. The program responds by prompting you to enter a username.

11. Enter the Samba username of the computer's primary user, and press the Enter key. The installer displays a summary screen similar to that shown in Figure 18-2. You'll need to make a few more changes from this point.

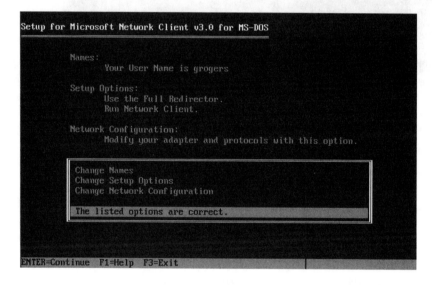

Figure 18-2. The Microsoft Network Client for DOS summary screen reveals some, but not all, critical configuration information.

12. Use the Up Arrow key to select Change Names, and press the Enter key. The result is a screen from which you can change your username, computer name, workgroup name, and domain name, as shown in Figure 18-3.

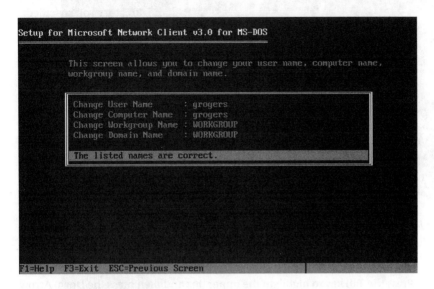

```
Setup for Microsoft Network Client v3.0 for MS-DOS

         This screen allows you to change your user name, computer name,
         workgroup name, and domain name.

      Change User Name        : grogers
      Change Computer Name    : grogers
      Change Workgroup Name   : WORKGROUP
      Change Domain Name      : WORKGROUP

      The listed names are correct.




F1=Help  F3=Exit  ESC=Previous Screen
```

Figure 18-3. You can change important NetBIOS and SMB/CIFS names from the Change Names screen.

13. Use the Up Arrow key to select the Computer Name and one or both of the Workgroup Name and Domain Name items in turn. After each selection, press the Enter key and type in the appropriate name. When you're done, highlight The listed names are correct, and press the Enter key. You'll be returned to the summary screen (Figure 18-2).

14. Pick Change Setup Options. You can configure whether to start up the software automatically and whether to log onto a domain from this menu. If you're using an old 8086 or 8088 computer, modify the Change Redir Options setting to use the basic redirector; with more sophisticated CPUs, leave the option at its default value. When you're done, exit from this screen back to the summary screen (Figure 18-2).

15. Pick the Change Network Configuration option. The result should be a network configuration screen similar to the one shown in Figure 18-4.

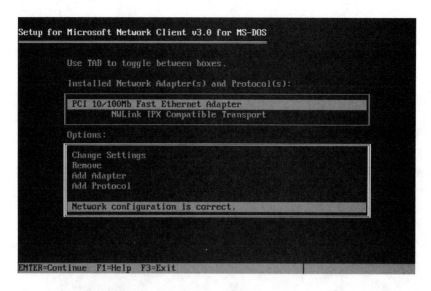

Figure 18-4. The default network settings for the Microsoft Network Client for DOS need adjustment if you want to use the software with Samba.

16. Press the Tab key to highlight the upper box and then press the Down Arrow key to select NWLink IPX Compatible Transport. Press the Tab key to highlight the lower box, then use the Up Arrow key to highlight Remove, and press the Enter key. This action removes the IPX stack that's used by default and causes the program to display a list of alternative stacks.

NOTE The PCI 10/100Mb Fast Ethernet Adapter is the name of the Ethernet adapter installed on the demonstration system. Your display is likely to show another name in this field.

17. Select Microsoft TCP/IP in the protocol list, and press the Enter key. You're returned to the network configuration screen shown in Figure 18-4 except that the line that read NWLink IPX Compatible Transport now reads Microsoft TCP/IP.

18. Select Network configuration is correct, and press the Enter key. This returns you to the summary screen (Figure 18-2).

19. Select The listed options are correct, and press the Enter key. The system should copy multiple files from the floppy disks and ask you to swap disks several times.

NOTE The program may repeatedly ask for the network card driver disk but won't seem to recognize it. If this happens, first be sure you've typed the correct path to the files on the disk. If the program continues to ask for the drivers disk, insert the Microsoft Network Client Disk 2 instead.

20. The setup program asks to reboot the computer when it finishes. Press the Enter key to do so.

When the system reboots, it should bring up a simple TCP/IP stack and SMB/CIFS client. By default, the TCP/IP stack is configured to use the Dynamic Host Configuration Protocol (DHCP) to acquire an IP address. If you want to assign the computer a static IP address, you must edit the PROTOCOL.INI file in the software's installation directory (C:\NET by default). Make the following changes to this file:

- On the line that begins IPAddress0, enter the desired IP address, substituting spaces for dots.

- Change the line that reads DisableDHCP=0 to read DisableDHCP=1.

Accessing Samba from DOS

When you boot a DOS computer with the Microsoft Network Client for DOS installed, you should see several new lines of text in the boot process describing the actions of bringing up the network interface. If you elected to join a domain, you'll also be asked for a username and password. Whether or not you joined a domain, you can use the NET command to access network shares. This command is similar to the command of the same name in Windows, but a few details differ, particularly from the Windows NT/200x/XP version. NET takes several subcommands, each of which performs some action. Some of the most important of these subcommands are as follows:

INIT: This command initializes network operations. It's run automatically from the AUTOEXEC.BAT file. (In the default configuration, this command name is expanded to INITIALIZE, which is equivalent to INIT.)

START: This command starts various network services. Like INIT, it's run from AUTOEXEC.BAT.

LOGON: You can log onto a domain or re-establish standard connections to servers on a workgroup by issuing this command.

LOGOFF: This command terminates connections to a domain's or workgroup's computers.

TIME [*SERVER***] [/SET] [/YES]:** Just as with Windows clients, you can set DOS clients' clocks using this command. The /SET parameter sets the clock (as opposed to simply displaying the time), and /YES tells NET not to display any prompts.

USE *N*: *SERVER**SHARE*: This command mounts the specified share to the specified drive letter (*N* can be any available drive letter). You can also map a DOS printer port onto a remote printer by using PRN: as the drive letter.

PRINT *SERVER**SHARE*: You can display information on queued print jobs with this command.

The most important of these subcommands is arguably USE, which enables you to access SMB/CIFS file shares. For instance, the following command makes the shares at \\WALTZ\SHARED available under the S: DOS drive letter:

```
C:\> NET USE S: \\WALTZ\SHARED
```

If you haven't already used network resources, the program may ask you if it should do so. You may also be asked to enter a username and password. Assuming you don't terminate the connection or type the wrong password, you can then see the contents of the share using the S: drive identifier:

```
C:\> DIR S:
 Volume in drive S is SHARED
 Directory of S:\

FW       TXT     56596 12-10-03  3:45p
PROJECT1       <DIR>     2-12-04 12:27p
         1 File(s)2147450880 bytes free
```

You can do almost anything with a remote SMB/CIFS share that you can do with a local hard disk—load files into applications, copy files, delete files, and so on. Of course, Samba's file permissions and other security settings play a role in what you can do.

Tweaking Samba for DOS

For the most part, Samba's default options assume that the client has mixed-case long filename support along the lines of that provided by Windows. DOS is more limiting; it works only with short (8.3) filenames. DOS clients also use only uppercase filenames, although most DOS programs are flexible enough that they can accept lowercase or mixed-case filenames. Still, you may want to pay attention to some share-level smb.conf options for DOS clients:

case sensitive: This parameter's default value of No is appropriate for DOS clients, so you should verify that it hasn't been altered.

preserve case: Samba's default setting for this parameter is Yes, which has the effect of causing files created by DOS clients to appear in all uppercase on the server itself and to most non-DOS clients. Setting preserve case = No causes the case of all files to be set to the value specified by default case. The result may be more aesthetically appealing than the usual configuration in a mixed-OS environment that includes DOS clients.

short preserve case: This parameter works just like preserve case, but it applies only to 8.3 filenames. You may want to set this parameter to No and leave preserve case = Yes if you only want to convert DOS-created filenames to lowercase. As with preserve case, this parameter relies upon the setting of default case.

default case: This parameter sets the case to which filenames are converted by preserve case and short preserve case. The default value is Lower, which most people find more aesthetically appealing than the all-uppercase filenames of DOS.

mangled names: This parameter, when set to Yes, tells Samba to generate 8.3 filenames that correspond to long filenames, thus giving DOS access to files with long filenames. Setting mangled names = No hides files with longer names from DOS, which is probably undesirable but could be a useful way to keep DOS clients from accessing certain files or directories on a share—just give them long filenames.

mangle case: If you set this parameter to Yes, Samba applies its name-mangling features when filenames differ only in case from that specified by default case. This is likely to result in strange changes in filenames, so chances are you won't want to use this parameter. (Its default value of No causes no name mangling when filename case is at odds with default case.)

mangled map: You can tell Samba to change filenames in very specified ways with this parameter, which takes filename specifications paired in parentheses as a value. For instance, mangled map = (*.html *.htm) converts filenames that end in .html so that they instead end in .htm. This parameter can be useful if a share holds many such files and you don't want to mangle the filenames in the usual ways, which are likely to change the filename in peculiar ways.

For the most part, Samba's default options work reasonably well with DOS clients. You're most likely to want to change the short preserve case parameter in a mixed-OS environment and if your users find the all-uppercase DOS filenames annoying. Bear in mind, though, that this option will prevent non-DOS clients from creating all-uppercase or mixed-case short filenames. The mangled map parameter may also be useful, particularly on shares that hold many files with long filename extensions.

CAUTION   Client programs that modify existing files, such as text editors, sometimes do so by renaming the old file and then creating a new one. When a DOS client does this on a file whose name has been mangled, the result is that the file's name will be stored on the server in mangled form—you'll lose the long filename. If you know you'll be editing files from DOS, try to use short filenames for those files.

Using Windows 3.x with Samba

The DOS and Windows OS family line is fairly convoluted. This book focuses upon the Windows 9*x*/Me and Windows NT/200*x*/XP lines as exemplars of Samba clients. The preceding section "Using DOS with Samba" describes how to use the predecessor of Windows 9*x*/Me, DOS, with Samba. Many people, though, don't think of DOS as being the predecessor to Windows 9*x*/Me; they think of Windows 3.11 and earlier in this role. Windows 3.11, though, wasn't a complete operating system; it relied upon DOS for many of its core OS features, such as filesystem handling.

You can install a DOS SMB/CIFS client on DOS and run Windows 3.11 or earlier atop this DOS installation. When you do so, Windows 3.11 gains access to the SMB/CIFS resources to which DOS has access. A special version of Windows 3.11, known as *Windows for Workgroups*, shipped with similar functionality. Windows for Workgroups used GUI configuration tools rather than the text-mode tools described earlier, though. By default, Windows for Workgroups used NetBEUI and so wouldn't work with Samba. To use it with Samba, you must download and install a free TCP/IP stack from Microsoft, available at ftp://ftp.microsoft.com/bussys/Clients/WFW/TCP32B.EXE.

Because Windows 3.11 and earlier all rely upon DOS for filesystem handling, these environments suffer from the same file-naming issues as DOS. These versions of Windows have also long been supplanted. Unless you're using particularly anemic hardware, you'll probably do better to upgrade to a more recent version of Windows.

Using Windows 9x/Me with Samba

Throughout much of the 1990s, and even a bit beyond, Samba has served primarily Windows 9*x*/Me clients. This OS family was the most common one on home and business desktops. Although Windows NT and, eventually, Windows 2000 were available during this period, these OSs were typically reserved for use on servers and high-end workstations. The Windows NT family was more expensive than the Windows 9*x*/Me family, and NT didn't handle older DOS and Windows 3.11 applications as well as Windows 9*x*/Me, which was built upon a DOS core. (Unlike Windows 3.11 and earlier, Windows 9*x*/Me ships with everything bundled in one package.) With the release of Windows XP as a new desktop OS, though, Microsoft is shifting away from the old Windows 9*x*/Me architecture. To use Windows 9*x*/Me clients with Samba, you must be sure the support is installed and know how to use the features.

Installing SMB/CIFS Support for Windows 9x/Me

Windows 95 was the first Microsoft OS to feature built-in SMB/CIFS networking features. (Windows for Workgroups included these features, but it wasn't really a complete OS.) Chances are these features will be accessible from the start, but they can be uninstalled or configured in a way that's not helpful for using the software with Samba. To check your installation and be sure it will work with Samba servers, follow these steps:

1. Open the Control Panel, and double-click the Network icon. This action produces the Network dialog box shown in Figure 18-5.

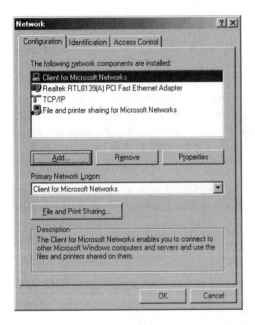

Figure 18-5. The Network Control Panel enables adding, deleting, and configuring various network drivers, stacks, and protocols.

2. If the Client for Microsoft Networks protocol is present (it's shown first in the list in Figure 18-5), skip ahead to step 6.

3. If the Client for Microsoft Networks protocol is not present, click Add. This action produces the Select Network Component Type dialog box.

4. In the Select Network Component Type dialog box, select Client and click Add. This action produces the Select Network Client dialog box shown in Figure 18-6.

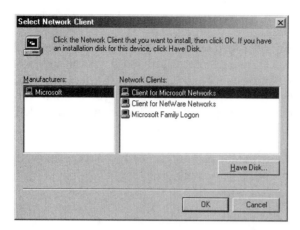

Figure 18-6. The Select Network Client dialog box provides options for several network components you might want to add.

5. In the Select Network Client dialog box, select Microsoft under Manufacturers and Client for Microsoft Networks under Network Clients and then click OK. You may be asked for disks, and once the system installs the software, you'll see the Client for Microsoft Networks component appear in the Network Control Panel.

6. In the Network Control Panel, select the Client for Microsoft Networks item and click Properties. This opens the Client for Microsoft Networks Properties dialog box shown in Figure 18-7.

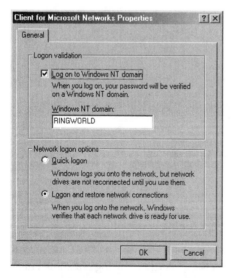

Figure 18-7. The Client for Microsoft Networks dialog box enables you to pick a workgroup or domain name, tell the system whether to log onto a domain, and specify what connections you want to restore when you log on.

7. Type your workgroup or domain name in the Windows NT Domain field and, if it's a domain, check the Log On to Windows NT Domain box. When you're done, click OK.

8. Click OK in the Network dialog box (Figure 18-5). When Windows has finished updating its files, it will inform you that it must reboot. Do so.

When the system reboots, it should be configured to provide access to SMB/CIFS servers. You'll see a logon dialog box rather than coming directly to the desktop. In a workgroup configuration, this dialog box will have two fields, one for the username and a second for the password. In a domain configuration, a third field provides a way to change the domain you log onto. The username and password you type will be used when accessing network resources.

Accessing Samba from Windows 9x/Me

In most respects, the simplest way to access Samba file shares from Windows 9x/Me is to use a GUI network browser. This browser is called My Network Places in Windows Me and Network Neighborhood in earlier versions of the OS. Figure 18-8 shows a Windows Me My Network Places window. This window provides quick access to various specific shares. There's also an icon called Entire Network, which enables you to browse all the SMB/CIFS servers on your network. Double-click it, and you'll see a list of workgroups or domains that are accessible to you. Double-click one of these, and you'll see the machines on the workgroup or domain. Double-click the name of a machine, and you'll see the resources it provides.

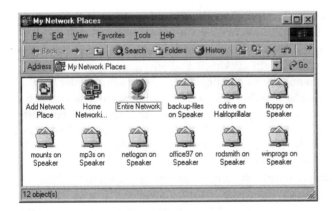

Figure 18-8. The My Network Places and Network Neighborhood browsers enable you to quickly locate network resources.

The Network Neighborhood browser of Windows 9x is similar to Windows Me's My Network Places, but it's organized slightly differently. Instead of seeing a list of shares you've accessed at the top level, Network Neighborhood shows a list of the machines in your workgroup or domain. You can still double-click the Entire Network icon to browse to other workgroups or domains, if you like.

Network browsing is accessible from most Windows applications that enable you to load and save files. The file selector dialog box provides a Look In selector that has a My Network Places or Network Neighborhood option, as shown in Figure 18-9. When you select this option, you can load or save files directly from network shares, without first opening a window on the share in question.

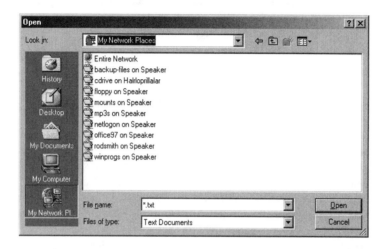

Figure 18-9. Windows' file selector dialog boxes provide easy access to SMB/CIFS resources.

You can also access shares by using many of the NET commands that DOS uses, as described earlier in "Accessing Samba from DOS." In particular, the NET USE command enables you to mount a network share to a Windows drive letter. You can achieve the same effect by browsing to a share, right-clicking it, and selecting Map Network Drive from the resulting pop-up menu. Mounting a network share on a drive letter has the advantage of making files available to older DOS and 16-bit Windows programs, which might not be able to cope with network path specifications for filenames. Particularly if the share is on another workgroup or domain than your own, it may also be quicker to browse to the share if you map it to a drive letter—the mapped drive will appear in the My Computer window, along with other drives.

Accessing Samba printers requires installing printer drivers in Windows. Most printers today ship with drivers that are installed through tools that launch when you insert a CD-ROM that ships with the printer. You can select a network printer almost as easily as you can select a local port for the printer. You can also install a printer driver on the Samba server and deliver it automatically to clients. Chapter 6 describes this task.

Using Windows NT/200x/XP with Samba

Windows NT 3.1 began the shift away from the DOS underpinnings of Windows but attempted to retain as much of the Windows look and feel as possible. With each new release in this line (Windows NT 3.5, Windows NT 4.0, Windows 2000, Windows 2003, and Windows XP), Microsoft has updated the GUI as well as the drivers and other underlying features of the OS. Most of the procedures for using Windows 9x/Me clients with Samba apply to using Windows NT/200x/XP clients, as well. Some of the details vary between the two lines, though, and even within the NT/200x/XP family, particularly with respect to enabling SMB/CIFS client support:

- You must configure the network settings using the Administrator account or another account that's authorized to perform system administration.

- You access the Network dialog box (Figure 18-5) by opening the Network Connections Control Panel or the Network and Dial-Up Connections Control Panel, right-clicking the Local Area Connection icon, and selecting Properties from the pop-up menu.

- You specify a workgroup or domain name from the System icon in the Control Panel. Click the Network Identification or Computer Name tab and then click the Properties dialog box. In some OSs, you'll also need to click a Change button. These actions will enable you to set the computer's name and the workgroup or domain to which it belongs.

Accessing SMB/CIFS servers from Windows NT/200x/XP clients works much as it does from Windows 9x/Me clients. Windows 200x/XP provide a My Network Places icon similar to the one in Windows Me, whereas earlier versions of Windows NT use a Network Neighborhood icon similar to the one in Windows 9x.

Using Mac OS SMB/CIFS Clients

Moving away from Windows, the most popular desktop OS is Mac OS (although Linux is gaining fast and by some counts may have already passed Mac OS). Mac OS is really two entirely different OSs. One is the pre-X version of Mac OS, which I refer to as *Mac OS Classic*. Mac OS Classic includes no native SMB/CIFS support, although you can add such support via a third-party package. Mac OS X, by contrast, is a Unix variant that ships with Samba and SMB/CIFS client support. Both versions of Mac OS can use Samba shares, but neither is really an optimal Samba client. Nonetheless, using SMB/CIFS from a Mac OS system can be a good way to simplify your network configuration.

Using Mac OS Classic with Samba

To use SMB/CIFS shares in Mac OS Classic, you should first understand the advantages and disadvantages of this approach. You must then obtain and install appropriate software. Only then can you begin accessing a Samba server from a Macintosh.

Even after you've gotten this far, you should understand some of the Samba settings that affect Mac OS Classic clients, as well as the clients' interactions with SMB/CIFS generally. These interactions have implications for how users can use files.

Why Use SMB/CIFS in Mac OS Classic?

Mac OS Classic isn't exactly the most obvious SMB/CIFS client; Mac OS has traditionally used its own file-sharing software, AppleShare (part of AppleTalk), which is described in Chapter 1. Nonetheless, there are reasons to use SMB/CIFS in Mac OS Classic, including the following:

Reduced number of servers: If you have just a few Mac OS Classic clients, configuring them to use SMB/CIFS may be simpler and safer than adding an AppleShare server to the systems you want the Macintoshes to access.

Availability of servers: If some of the server systems are Windows computers, the availability of AppleShare server software is an issue. Such servers are available for some versions of Windows NT/200x/XP, but they tend to be slow and awkward compared to using SMB/CIFS. Of course, you could re-export an SMB/CIFS share using a Unix SMB/CIFS client and AppleShare server, as described in Chapter 12, but this approach is awkward at best. Running an SMB/CIFS client on the Mac OS Classic system is a much cleaner approach.

Peer-to-peer environments: A special case of the preceding reason relates to a peer-to-peer environment, in which most systems function as both clients and servers. Using SMB/CIFS on Mac OS Classic makes for much simpler integration than does running AppleShare clients and servers on Windows systems.

Mac OS Classic servers: If you want to share files on the Macintosh with Windows or Unix clients, using SMB/CIFS is generally a cleaner approach than using some other server.

Using special Samba features: Suppose you want to make special Samba share features, such as a CD-R creation share, available to Mac OS Classic clients. Using an SMB/CIFS client package on the Macintosh is the simplest way to accomplish this goal.

Of course, using SMB/CIFS on Mac OS Classic isn't without its downside. Some file naming and other access quirks will manifest themselves. (The upcoming section "Tweaking Samba for Mac OS Classic" describes some of these issues.) The main SMB/CIFS package for Mac OS Classic is DAVE, which is commercial software, so if you need to implement this solution on many Macintoshes, cost is likely to be a factor. In many cases, running an AppleShare server such as Netatalk (http://netatalk.sourceforge.net) on the Unix server in addition to Samba is a better approach than running SMB/CIFS client software on the Macintosh. Upgrading to Mac OS X is also worth considering instead of purchasing DAVE; the cost is similar, although Mac OS X is more resource-intensive, and so may not be appealing on older Macintoshes. Using Mac OS X may also necessitate upgrading many additional software components.

Obtaining and Installing SMB/CIFS Software for Mac OS Classic

Thursby Software (http://www.thursby.com) makes DAVE, the SMB/CIFS client/server package for Mac OS Classic. You can download the software from Thursby's site and register to obtain an evaluation serial number. This registration will enable you to run DAVE for a few days. If you like it, you can then purchase a full version (as I write, a single copy of the full version costs $149, but bulk and educational prices are lower).

> **NOTE**   This chapter describes version 4.1 of DAVE. Some features may change with future versions of the software.

DAVE 4.1 requires Mac OS Classic 8.6 or higher with Apple's OpenTransport TCP/IP stack installed. If you need to install DAVE on an older version of Mac OS, you may be able to find an older version of DAVE that will do the job.

When you download DAVE, you'll get a BinHexed StuffIt archive, which when extracted becomes a disk image file. Double-clicking this file mounts it, assuming that the appropriate version of the standard Macintosh Disk Copy application is installed. Before proceeding further, save any open files and shut down any open applications. Launch the Installer for OS 8 and 9 in the disk image file to start the process. You'll see a few introductory windows, including a license and readme file. You'll then see an installer tool in which you can pick an easy or advanced install, switch the installation disk, and so on. Click the Install button to begin the process. You'll then be asked to restart your computer, and you should do so.

When the computer reboots, a program called the DAVE Setup Assistant launches itself, as shown in Figure 18-10. Click the right arrow button in the lower-right corner of the window to move through this tool, or click the left arrow button to move back if you decide you must change something.

Figure 18-10. The DAVE Setup Assistant guides you through the process of configuring SMB/CIFS parameters for DAVE.

Information you'll enter in this tool includes:

User identification: You must enter your name, organization, and license code. The license code is e-mailed to you from Thursby when you register. This code is long, so it's best if you cut and paste it from the e-mail.

Machine identification: You must enter your computer's NetBIOS name, workgroup or domain name, and machine description.

Network logon: You can configure DAVE to prompt for your username and password once when the system starts up rather than when you try to connect to resources.

Local file sharing: You can configure DAVE to function as an SMB/CIFS server, as well as a client, or omit the server functionality. If you choose to share files, you'll be given the opportunity to create file shares corresponding to Mac OS volumes or folders.

Accessing Samba from Mac OS Classic

Once you've installed DAVE, you can access a Samba server as follows:

1. Open the Chooser from the Apple menu. You'll see a new item in the left pane of the chooser, called DAVE Client.

2. Select the DAVE Client item in the Chooser. The result should resemble Figure 18-11. The Select a Server list on the right of the dialog box should now show other computers on your SMB/CIFS network.

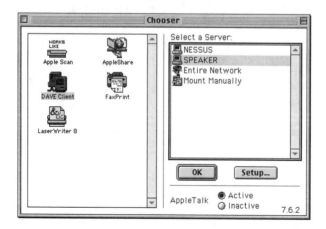

Figure 18-11. DAVE provides access controls in the Chooser similar to those provided by AppleShare.

3. Select one of the SMB/CIFS servers, and click OK. If you haven't previously logged on, DAVE will prompt for a username and password. Enter them.

4. If your username and password are accepted, DAVE presents a list of shares on the server you specified, as shown in Figure 18-12. Select all the shares you want to mount and be sure the boxes to their right have been marked and then click OK.

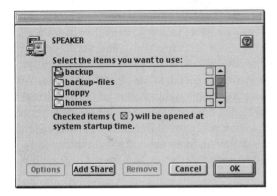

Figure 18-12. DAVE summarizes the shares you want to mount from each server.

5. Repeat steps 3–4 for any additional servers that have shares you want to access.

6. Close the Chooser. The system should mount the share or shares you specified, giving them new icons along with the icons for your local drives, removable disks, and AppleShare volumes.

At this point, you can access the Samba server's shares just as you would access any local or AppleShare volume. Files and folders appear in Macintosh windows in the usual way, you can double-click files to open them, and so on.

In addition to accessing file shares, you can print to SMB/CIFS printer shares, at least if you have the standard Apple LaserWriter driver installed. Follow the preceding instructions for adding a file share, but when you reach step 4, DAVE informs you that it's creating a new printer definition. When it finishes, an icon for the new printer will appear on the desktop.

NOTE The Apple LaserWriter driver can print to any PostScript printer, including non-PostScript printers driven by Ghostscript in Samba. If you want to print to a non-PostScript printer, be sure to set up Ghostscript to handle the job on the server. If you want to print to a non-PostScript printer on a Windows computer, you may need to create a special Samba share to re-export the printer to support PostScript. (You can do the same thing using Netatalk if you prefer.)

Tweaking Samba for Mac OS Classic

Mac OS Classic with DAVE works reasonably well with Samba. Some architectural differences deserve some elaboration, though. The first of these relates to special Macintosh filesystem features. Mac OS Classic stores two types of data with its files: data forks, which hold normal data, and resource forks, which hold special data such as icons, program code, and so on. Mac OS Classic also relies upon special file type and creator codes, each of which is four characters long, to identify the type of file (graphics, word processor, and so on) and the application that created it. To support these features, DAVE creates a special directory, called resource.frk, in each directory in which it stores files. This directory is conceptually similar to the .AppleDouble directory created by Netatalk for the same purpose, but the contents are in a different format. DAVE sets the hidden bit on the resource.frk directory, but this bit has no effect on the directory's visibility from the Samba server OS, or even from Samba's other clients, because the hidden bit maps to an executable bit that's normally set on directories. If you want to hide the resource.frk directory, you can do so with the hide files parameter:

```
hide files = resource.frk
```

For a more forceful hiding operation, you can use veto files instead; however, you should ensure that this parameter is *not* used for DAVE clients because it will make the directory inaccessible to the server that needs it. Instead, place veto files in an included configuration file that will be used only by non-DAVE clients.

 NOTE   Samba can't identify DAVE directly; instead, %a in the smb.conf file expands to UNKNOWN for DAVE clients.

Mac OS Classic is limited to filenames of 31 characters or shorter. DAVE mangles filenames that are longer than this limit, much as Samba can do for DOS clients, so you can still access them, but the filenames may be strange. Another filename issue that may crop up relates to peculiar characters in filenames. Macintosh users sometimes place characters such as trademark symbols (™) or bullets (•) in their filenames. These symbols can be changed to forms that might not be recognized on other clients or on the Samba server computer itself.

Mac OS Classic clients work fine with the default case sensitive = No option, but you can set case sensitive = Yes, and Mac OS Classic will adjust to the change and enable you to create and use files that differ only in case. Another case-related option, preserve case (and its cousin, short preserve case) should be set to the default value of Yes for DAVE clients. Mac OS Classic doesn't always respond well to filenames that change in case unexpectedly, as can happen if these parameters are set to No.

Using Mac OS X with Samba

Mac OS X is the latest incarnation of Mac OS, but it differs radically from its predecessor line; Mac OS X is built atop a Unix-like system, with a custom GUI environment that bears some resemblance to earlier versions of Mac OS but that also borrows a great deal from the defunct NeXTStep computer interface. In terms of SMB/CIFS, Mac OS X provides both client and server SMB/CIFS support. The server support comes from Samba. The client support uses SMB/CIFS kernel drivers that are independent of Samba, although some identification strings make it look like Samba (that is, %a returns Samba when a Mac OS X client connects to a Samba server).

In any event, you can access SMB/CIFS servers from Mac OS X, but it's not always the best choice for a file-sharing protocol. Sometimes it's appropriate, sometimes it's not, and knowing when to use it is your first step to doing so. If you've decided you want to use SMB/CIFS, you should know how to do so from the Mac OS X GUI. You should also understand the Samba parameters and how they interact with Mac OS X clients.

CAUTION   Mac OS X provides SMB/CIFS access to its emulated Mac OS Classic environment, which enables you to run older Mac OS programs in the new OS. Unfortunately, the SMB/CIFS access from Classic programs tends to be flaky. Classic programs may lose the ability to write to mounted shares or generally behave strangely when using SMB/CIFS shares.

Why Use SMB/CIFS in Mac OS X?

The reasons for using SMB/CIFS in Mac OS X are similar to those for using SMB/CIFS in Mac OS Classic, as outlined earlier in "Why Use SMB/CIFS in Mac OS Classic?" The twist is that, because Mac OS X is Unix-based, the best file-sharing protocol for it is generally the Unix-native Network File System (NFS), rather than AppleShare. (Mac OS X also supports AppleShare, though.) Mac OS X clients can do a good job accessing Samba servers, though, and if you don't need to control Unix-style ownership and permissions, SMB/CIFS can be a perfectly good method of providing file sharing to Mac OS X clients.

Accessing Samba from Mac OS X

Mac OS X's SMB/CIFS client tools are installed by default, so you don't need to locate and download any extra software or even run a configuration tool to be sure the software is installed. You can use the Mac OS X tools with little or no configuration; you don't need to set your workgroup or domain name, a NetBIOS name, or other options. The downside to not having to configure the tools is that the browsing features may not work as smoothly as they do in some other environments.

TIP   Setting options in the /etc/smb.conf file, and particularly the workgroup name, can improve your ability to browse the SMB/CIFS servers on your network.

To access a Samba share by name, follow these steps:

1. In the Finder, select Go ➤ Connect to Server or press Command+K. This action brings up the Connect to Server dialog box (see Figure 18-13).

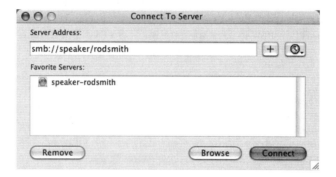

Figure 18-13. The Mac OS X Connect to Server dialog box enables you to connect to a server by name.

2. Enter the name of the server and its share in the Server Address field using the SMB URI format, smb://*SERVER*/*SHARE*.

3. Click the Connect button. A dialog box will appear asking for the workgroup or domain name, username, and password.

4. Enter the requested authentication information, and click the OK button.

If all goes well, a new window will open showing the share you've just accessed. Behind the scenes, Mac OS X has used the mount_smbfs tool to mount the share to a directory named after the share in the /Volumes directory.

To browse a workgroup or domain, you must select the Go ➤ Network (Command+Shift+K) item in the Finder's menu. The result is a view of the resources on the NetBIOS workgroup or domain specified in the smb.conf file's workgroup parameter, as shown in Figure 18-14. You can browse to these resources much as you would other local or network resources. The Mac OS X 10.3 SMB/CIFS browser isn't as reliable as browsers in some other OSs, though; it tends to be a bit slow, and servers sometimes disappear from the list. You may want to use the Go ➤ Connect to Server option and enter a URI directly rather than rely on the browser.

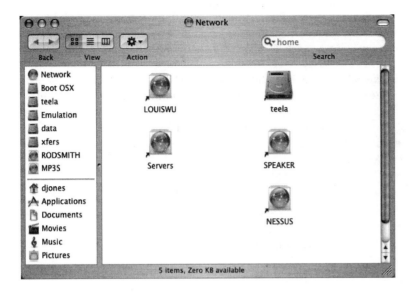

Figure 18-14. Mac OS X provides a network browser similar to the one in Windows.

You can access shared printers using the Printer Setup Utility. This tool is available from the Utilities folder in the Applications area. Once launched, it displays a list of available printers, as shown in Figure 18-15.

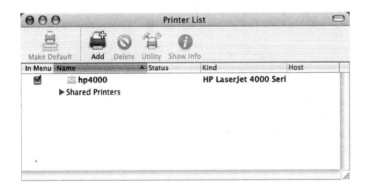

Figure 18-15. The Printer Setup Utility is Mac OS X's printer management tool.

NOTE   Mac OS X 10.2 and later use the Common Unix Printing System (CUPS) to handle printing. Instead of using the Printer Setup Utility, you can use the CUPS Web-based configuration tool, described in Chapter 12, to do the job.

The Printer Setup Utility provides fairly obvious buttons and options for adding a printer. Unfortunately, these obvious buttons and options won't quite do the job without one nonobvious extra trick. To add an SMB/CIFS printer, follow these directions:

1. Hold down the Option key while clicking the Add button in the Printer List window. Holding down the Option key is the nonobvious step that enables extra features needed to successfully add an SMB/CIFS printer. The result is a dialog box whose contents vary depending upon the setting of its first selection button. Pick Advanced for this button. The result should resemble Figure 18-16.

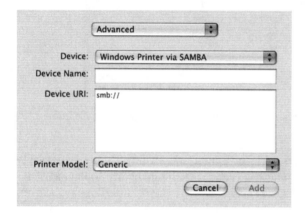

Figure 18-16. You can specify an SMB/CIFS printer by name using the Advanced printer addition tool.

2. Select Windows Printer via SAMBA in the Device button.

3. Type a name for the local printer queue in the Device Name field. This is the name by which the printer will be known locally, so use whatever you want. (Using the name of the remote queue as the local name can help to avoid confusion, though.)

4. Type the path to the printer share in the Device URI field. This path should take the form smb://*username*:*password*@*SERVER*/*SHARE*; the field begins the entry with a default value of smb://, as shown in Figure 18-16.

5. Click the Printer Model selector, and pick the make of your printer. For most selections, the dialog box will then expand to show a list of models for that manufacturer. If the share accesses a PostScript printer or passes print jobs through Ghostscript, leaving the Printer Model set to Generic should work.

6. Click the Add button. The printer should be added to the printers shown in the Printer list.

7. Exit from the Printer Setup Utility.

After making these changes, your new printer should appear in your applications' printer lists. Selecting the printer should send a print job to the print server computer. Behind the scenes, the Printer Setup Utility has modified Mac OS X's CUPS configuration to create a local queue that passes jobs on to the Samba server.

Tweaking Samba for Mac OS X

Mac OS X is basically a Unix OS and so has all of the file naming, ownership, permissions, and other issues of Unix OSs. Options you might want to set on a Samba server to help accommodate Mac OS X clients include the following:

case sensitive: You can set this option to Yes, as opposed to the usual No. Doing so isn't required, though; Mac OS X responds reasonably well to case-retentive but case-insensitive filenames.

preserve case and short preserve case: These options are best left at their default value of Yes, which causes filename case to be unchanged.

deadtime: Mac OS X doesn't respond well to shares disappearing. Sometimes you'll get a notice that the share has disappeared, but other times, the Finder may lock up. If this happens, pressing Command+Option+Esc should force the Finder to quit. Because of these problems, you should try not to set this parameter to anything but its default of 0 (which disables automatic disconnections) unless you absolutely must.

unix extensions: In theory, this parameter adds better support for Unix-specific filesystem features, such as symbolic links. As of Mac OS X 10.3, though, this parameter has no obvious effect. Using it shouldn't cause problems, but neither will it help.

NOTE   Mac OS X creates a value of Samba in a Samba server's %a variable. If you need to distinguish Mac OS X clients from other Samba clients, you'll need to do so by NetBIOS name or some other variable.

Unlike Mac OS Classic, Mac OS X doesn't make extensive use of resource forks or other Macintosh-specific filesystem features. (Mac OS Classic programs running in the Classic environment are an exception to this rule, and their needs aren't well supported by Samba.) Thus, you don't need to be concerned with the creation of resource.frk directories as you do when using DAVE with Mac OS Classic clients.

Using Unix SMB/CIFS Clients

Samba provides an SMB/CIFS client in the form of its smbclient program, which provides FTP-like access to SMB/CIFS shares. Several OSs also provide SMB/CIFS-mounting facilities, which can be used to provide more seamless integration of SMB/CIFS shares with local Unix filesystems. Numerous GUI tools have sprung up to help facilitate these interactions, so if you're more comfortable with such tools, you can use them.

Transferring Files with `smbclient`

In some respects the simplest method of using SMB/CIFS servers from Unix is to use the `smbclient` program that ships with Samba. This tool's syntax is as follows:

```
smbclient [//SERVER/SHARE] [password] [options]
```

The *SERVER* and *SHARE* are, as you might expect, the server and share names. The *SERVER* name is looked up using the order specified by the `name resolve order` parameter in `smb.conf` or by the `-R` option (described shortly). If you like, you can provide a password after the share identifier, but doing so is generally unwise because it makes the password visible in process listings. (It's provided for the benefit of scripts that might have no other means of sending the password to the utility.) The available *options* modify the operation of the utility; the most important of them are as follows:

> `-R resolve order`: This option overrides the `name resolve order` parameter from `smb.conf` and takes the same values (`lmhosts`, `host`, `wins`, and `bcast`) in order, separated by spaces.
>
> `-M MACHINE`: This option enables you to send messages using the Windows messaging (WinPopUp) system, to the specified *MACHINE*. After typing the command and pressing the Enter key, anything you type until you press Control+D is sent to the other system. Alternatively, you can pipe a message through, as in `cat message.txt | smbclient -M TAP`, which sends the message in `message.txt` to the TAP computer. You don't need to specify a server and share name in the usual way when using this option.
>
> `-h` or `--help`: This option displays summary information on how to use `smbclient`.
>
> `-I ip-address`: This option specifies an IP address to which `smbclient` should connect. If this option is present, the utility ignores the *SERVER* NetBIOS name. (You can provide a DNS hostname rather than an IP address if you like.)
>
> `-L HOST`: Pass this parameter and omit the usual server and share definitions to see a list of available shares on the *HOST* server. If *HOST* is a browser node (whether or not it's actually won a master browser election), it also returns lists of workgroups or domains and of servers within the server's own workgroup or domain.
>
> `-V`: This option causes `smbclient` to print its version number and exit.
>
> `-s filename`: Ordinarily, `smbclient` extracts some configuration options from the `smb.conf` file. You can change what file the utility uses with this parameter.
>
> `-d debuglevel`: You can set the debug level with this option, which overrides the `log level` parameter in `smb.conf`.
>
> `-N`: This option suppresses the normal prompt for a password. It's useful if you know the server won't require a password (as when using guest access) but shouldn't be used otherwise.

-k: This option enables Kerberos authentication, which is normally only useful in an Active Directory domain.

-A *filename*: Instead of passing the username and password on the command line or typing them at a prompt, you can place them in a file and pass the filename to the utility. The file should have two or three lines, containing the username, the password, and the domain name, in that order. Each line begins with an identification (username, password, or domain), then holds an equals sign, then holds the value.

CAUTION Be sure the permissions on the file you use to store the password are very restrictive—probably 0600 or tighter. If you place your password in a world-readable file (or even a group-readable file), the password could more easily fall into the wrong hands.

-U *username[%password]*: You can pass the username and, optionally, the password with this option. If you omit the *username*, Samba uses your login username. If you omit the *%password* portion, smbclient prompts for it. This option (or -A) is a practical necessity when you want to access a server using a username other than your local username.

-n *NAME*: This option sets the NetBIOS name that smbclient claims for itself when contacting the server, overriding the netbios name parameter in smb.conf.

-W *workgroup*: You can set the workgroup or domain name with this option, overriding the value set in the smb.conf file.

-T *tar-options*: You can have smbclient create tar backups of a share by passing this option along with appropriate tar options. In practice, it's easier to use the smbtar script, which is described in Chapter 16.

-c *command-string*: You can pass a series of commands to smbclient with this parameter. Ordinarily, the program prompts for commands from standard input (stdin). This option is most likely to be useful if you want to create a script that performs some complex set of actions.

A few more obscure options are also available; consult the smbclient man page for details. In practice, using smbclient is similar to using the text-mode ftp utility: You type the name of the utility, a share name, and perhaps a few extra options, whereupon you'll see an smbclient prompt and can type ftp-like commands, which include the following:

? or help: This command displays usage information.

chmod *file octal-mode*: This command changes the permissions on the specified *file*. It works only if the server supports the Unix SMB/CIFS extensions.

chown *file uid gid*: This command changes the ownership on the specified *file* to the specified numeric *uid* and *gid* values. You must know what these values are when you begin; you can't specify usernames or group names in name form.

cd [*directory*]: You can change to the specified *directory* with this command. If you omit the *directory* specification, smbclient displays your current directory within the share.

del *files*: This command deletes the requested files, which can be specified with a wildcard.

dir [*files*] or ls [*files*]: This command displays a directory listing, optionally matching whatever *files* wildcard specification you provide.

exit or quit: You can terminate a connection using this command.

get *remote-file* [*local-file*]: Transfer a file from the server to the client using this command, optionally renaming the file to the name given via the *local-file* option in the process.

lcd [*local-directory*]: This command changes the local working directory to the specified directory, or if you omit it, displays what the local working directory is.

link *source dest*: You can create a hard link from *source* to *dest* on the server using this command, provided the server supports the Unix extensions.

md *directory* or mkdir *directory*: This command creates a new directory of the specified name.

mget *files*: You can retrieve multiple files with this command, which can accept common file-naming wildcards.

mput *files*: This command uploads multiple files to the SMB/CIFS server.

print *file*: You can print a file using this command. In order to work, you must have connected to a printer share rather than a file share.

prompt [ON|OFF]: When you set this value ON, smbclient prompts for confirmation before each file transfer using mget or mput. When set to OFF, smbclient doesn't prompt for each transfer.

put *local-file* [*remote-file*]: This command sends a file from the client to the server, optionally renaming it to *remote-file* on the way.

queue: You can view information on jobs in a printer share using this command.

rd *directory* or rmdir *directory*: You can delete a directory on the server using this command.

recurse [ON|OFF]: This command toggles recursive operation on or off. When set ON, the mget and mput commands operate on entire directory trees; when OFF, the commands operate only on the current directory, not on any subdirectories it might contain. The default value is OFF.

symlink *source dest*: You can create a symbolic link on the server with this command. The server must support the Unix SMB/CIFS extensions.

tar *command*: This option runs a tar command.

This list omits a few more obscure commands, so check the `smbclient` man page if the command to do what you want isn't listed. Even with these omissions, this list of command-line options and commands can be intimidating, but in practice, use of `smbclient` for simple file transfers is fairly straightforward:

```
$ smbclient //TAP/FASTAIRE
Password:
smb: \> cd test
smb: \test\> ls
  .                              D        0  Fri May  2 23:51:49 2003
  ..                             D        0  Wed Oct 15 21:31:00 2003
  shoe                           D        0  Thu Apr 17 14:10:23 2003
  steel-toe.txt                        20483  Thu Oct 17 19:12:26 2002

              49197 blocks of size 131072. 23572 blocks available
smb: \test\> get steel-toe.txt
smb: \test\> quit
```

Of course, you can do a lot more with `smbclient` than this simple example reveals—that's what all the extra options and commands enable! Still, for basic operations, `smbclient` can be a straightforward tool, no more complex than a text-mode `ftp` client.

Mounting SMB/CIFS Shares

For added flexibility, many Unix-like OSs support tools to mount SMB/CIFS shares locally. These utilities necessarily provide options to help work around file metadata differences between SMB/CIFS and Unix. Most important, these options enable you to set ownership and permissions information for the SMB/CIFS shares. The following sections describe three commands: `smbmount`, as used in Linux; Linux's `mount`, as used with the `smb` and `cifs` filesystem options; and `mount_smbfs`, as used by FreeBSD and Mac OS X.

 NOTE The GUI Mac OS X tools for mounting SMB/CIFS shares described earlier in "Accessing Samba from Mac OS X" operate by calling `mount_smbfs`.

Using `smbmount`

The Linux `smbmount` utility enables you to mount SMB/CIFS shares on a Linux computer. The basic syntax for this command is as follows:

```
smbmount //SERVER/SHARE /mount/point [-o options]
```

As with other commands, *SERVER* and *SHARE* are the names of the server and share, as you might expect. The */mount/point* is the local mount point. The *options*, if you provide more than one, are separated by commas. They include the following:

username=*username*: You can set the username to any value you like with this option. By default, smbmount sends the name of the user who called it.

password=*password*: This option enables you to send a password on the command line for use in a script or in /etc/fstab.

credentials=*filename*: Instead of passing the username and password on the command line, you can place them in a file and pass that filename to smbmount. The file has the same format as the file associated with smbclient's -A option.

netbiosname=*NAME*: This option sets the NetBIOS name claimed by the client when it contacts the server. If you don't specify a name, the client uses the system's DNS hostname.

uid=*UID*: You can pass a User ID (UID) number or a username to the utility to have all the files on the mounted share acquire the specified ownership.

gid=*GID*: This option works just like the uid option, but it sets the group ID (GID) instead.

fmask=*mode*: You can set the permissions of files on the mounted share with this option. The default value is based on the umask when the command is called. The *mode* is an octal value, such as 0640 to set 0640 permissions.

dmask=*mode*: This option works just like fmask, but it sets the permissions of directories on the mounted share.

ip=*ip-address*: If you use this option, the client tries to contact the specified IP address, overriding the *SERVER* value. (You can also specify a DNS hostname if you like.)

workgroup=*WORKGROUP*: This option sets the workgroup name to use when contacting the server.

guest: If you include this option, smbmount won't prompt for a password, which can be helpful if you know the server doesn't require one.

ro: This option forces a read-only mount, even if the share supports read/write access.

rw: This option enables read/write access *if* the server supports it. (This option can't override a read-only option on the server.) This is the default behavior.

This list omits a few of the more obscure smbmount options; consult the smbmount man page for details. As delivered on most Linux distributions, only root may run the smbmount command. If you want to give ordinary users the ability to do so, you must set the set user ID (SUID) bit on two binaries: smbmnt and smbumount. The first of these is a helper program to smbmount and does most of the real work. The second is the tool that unmounts shares. When so configured, ordinary users can mount and unmount SMB/CIFS shares but only if they own the mount points.

In normal operation, smbmount works something like this:

```
$ smbmount //TAP/FASTAIRE ~/tap-files
Password:
```

Thereafter, the files from //TAP/FASTAIRE will be accessible from the user's ~/tap-files directory. (In this case, the presumption is that ordinary users have been granted the ability to mount SMB/CIFS shares. If not, the command would have to be run by root.) Of course, you can add more parameters if you like. If you're mounting a share as root, chances are you'll want to do so—if nothing else, you'll probably want to use the username, uid, gid, fmask, and dmask options, or at least a subset of them, to make files on the mount accessible to ordinary users.

Using Linux's mount

In addition to the smbmount utility proper, Linux's mount command provides access to the features of smbmount. Specify a filesystem type code of smbfs, and you can mount SMB/CIFS shares:

```
# mount -t smbfs //TAP/FASTAIRE /home/fastaire/tap-files \
  -o username=fastaire,uid=587
Password:
```

Ordinarily, only root may use mount. The use of mount as a frontend to smbmount can be useful as a way to automatically mount SMB/CIFS shares when the system starts. Specifically, you can create an /etc/fstab entry for an SMB/CIFS share:

```
//TAP/SHARED /mnt/tap smbfs credentials=/etc/creds/tap,uid=587 0 0
```

This line mounts the contents of //TAP/SHARED on /mnt/tap, using the username and password stored in /etc/creds/tap and giving ownership of the files to the user who has UID 587. You can add other smbmount-specific or general mount options, as well. For instance, you could use the user, users, or owner option to enable ordinary users to mount SMB/CIFS shares that are specified in /etc/fstab.

If you use the 2.6.*x* Linux kernel and have compiled the requisite driver into your kernel or as a module, you can use the cifs filesystem type code instead of smbfs. This code uses the new CIFS driver in the 2.6.*x* kernel, which interfaces with the Unix extensions support provided by Samba (via the unix extensions parameter). The utility also requires a helper application, mount.cifs, to be present in the /sbin directory. The cifs code works much like the smbfs code and accepts most of the same options. Some options are meaningless when used with cifs, though. For instance, because the Unix extensions support the transfer of UIDs and GIDs, the uid and gid options have no effect when accessing appropriately enabled servers. Another caveat is that, as of Samba 3.0.1 and the 2.6.1 kernel, the cifs option isn't as reliable as smbfs. This situation is likely to improve in the future, though. The cifs code also won't work when mounting Windows 9*x*/Me shares. When accessing Windows NT/200*x*/XP shares or others that don't support Unix extensions, some of the features won't work. On the whole, then, the cifs type code is most useful when mounting Samba shares for which unix extensions = Yes; for other servers, you're best off using smbfs. For additional information, for more up to date drivers than those that ship with current kernels, and for the mount.cifs helper application, consult the CIFS driver Web page at http://us1.samba.org/samba/Linux_CIFS_client.html (the equivalent page should appear on other Samba mirrors as well).

Between all of these options (smbmount, mount, and /etc/fstab entries), you can almost certainly find a good way to access SMB/CIFS shares from a Linux client. You can give control to users, mount only those shares you want when you want, or mount shares automatically via /etc/fstab.

 CAUTION Linux doesn't respond well to crashed SMB/CIFS servers. If you mount a share and the server on which it resides crashes, you may encounter problems with disk utilities such as df hanging. For this reason, I recommend keeping SMB/CIFS shares mounted for short periods of time and then unmounting them.

Using mount_smbfs

The mount_smbfs utility is similar in functionality to smbmount, but mount_smbfs is used in FreeBSD and Mac OS X. Its syntax is as follows:

```
mount_smbfs [options] //[workgroup;][user[:password]@]SERVER[/SHARE] /mount/point
```

The *options* provide the usual information, but in their own unique way:

-I *host*: This option overrides the *SERVER* name, connecting to the specified *host*, which may be an IP address or DNS hostname.

-N: This option tells the utility to read the user's ~/.nsmbrc file (described shortly) for configuration options, most notably the password.

-W *WORKGROUP*: This option sets the workgroup to be used when connecting to the server.

-f *mode*: You can set the permissions of files on the mounted share with this option, which takes an octal mode as a value.

-d *mode*: This option works just like -f, but it sets the permissions of directories on the mounted share.

-u *uid*: You can set the UID that will own the files on the mounted share with this option. The default is whoever owns the mount point to which the share is mounted.

-g *gid*: This option works just like -u, but it sets the group ownership of the file.

-U *username*: You can specify a username to be used for accessing the share with this parameter.

If you use the -N option, you should be sure to create a ~/.nsmbrc file, which contains lines like the following:

```
[SERVER:USERNAME:SHARE]
password=password
```

This file supports storing different information for different servers, shares, and even usernames. You can also add lines to set other options, such as workgroup=*WORKGROUP* to set the workgroup name or addr=*host* to set the server's hostname or IP address.

 CAUTION If you store your password in a ~/.nsmbrc file, be sure to set the permissions on that file to prevent any user but you from reading it. If other users can read it, somebody might be able to retrieve your passwords from the file.

Ordinarily, only root may run mount_smbfs. If you set the SUID bit on the mount_smbfs executable, though, ordinary users can run it. In use, mount_smbfs works much like Linux's smbmount, although of course the details of the parameters you use with it differ:

```
# mount_smbfs -u 1072 -f 0444 -N //fastaire@TAP/SHARED /mnt/tap
```

This command mounts the //TAP/SHARED share on /mnt/tap. When you're done using a share, you can unmount it with the umount command, just as you can unmount other filesystems.

Using GUI Tools

Many GUI tools provide easier access to SMB/CIFS shares. Most of these programs tie into smbmount, mount_smbfs, or similar tools to mount the shares on the Unix client system. As such, and because these programs are typically designed for use by ordinary users, they usually require the underlying tools to have their SUID bits set. Some utilities don't actually mount the remote shares but provide GUI drag-and-drop operations to move files between the server and the client's filesystem. Examples of these GUI tools include the following:

LinNeighborhood: This program, headquartered at http://www.bnro.de/~schmidjo/, is a Linux-only tool that provides an interface roughly akin to Network Neighborhood or My Network Places. It provides tools to help integrate it into a variety of file managers.

Kruiser: This tool is loosely associated with the K Desktop Environment (KDE) and provides basic network browsing capabilities. As of early 2004, the program hasn't been updated since 2000, though. Learn more at http://sourceforge.net/projects/kruiser/.

xSMBrowser: This program doesn't actually mount SMB/CIFS shares but does enable easy browsing of the network. You can learn more at http://www.public.iastate.edu/~chadspen/.

Gnomba: This project is yet another network browser with support for mounting shares it finds. Its home page is http://gnomba.sourceforge.net.

Jags: This is a GTK+-based SMB/CIFS network browser. It supports mounting shares using Linux's smbmount.

Konqueror: This file browser is part of the KDE project (http://www.kde.org). It doesn't yet support browsing a workgroup or domain, but it does support accessing SMB/CIFS shares by using smb:// at the start of a path specification.

These tools vary substantially in their features and modes of operation. As an example, though, consider LinNeighborhood. To use this tool, follow these steps:

1. Obtain and install the program. You can get it from its main Web site or from a site specific to your Linux distribution.

2. Launch LinNeighborhood by typing **LinNeighborhood** in an xterm window.

3. Click the Prefs button in the main window. This action brings up the Preferences dialog box, shown in Figure 18-17.

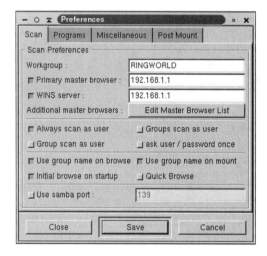

Figure 18-17. LinNeighborhood must be told certain details about your network independently of Samba.

4. Enter the information in the fields on the Scan tab of the Preferences dialog box. LinNeighborhood may be able to determine some of this information on its own, but it won't hurt to enter too much information, provided you enter it correctly.

5. If you opt to browse the network using a specific account, click the Miscellaneous tab and enter your username and, if you like, password. (The password will be saved in a cleartext configuration file, which is of course a potential security risk.) You can also specify the directory where you want LinNeighborhood to mount shares on this tab.

6. Click the Post Mount tab. If you want to have LinNeighborhood open a file browser window after mounting a share, click the Run File Manager After Mounting check box and select a file manager from the list. Alternatively, you can type a command to run, so you can launch any file manager on your system, even if it's not one that's been preconfigured in LinNeighborhood.

7. Click the Save button in the Preferences dialog box, followed by the Close button.

At this point, LinNeighborhood is configured for use. You should see an expandable list of workgroups or domains, as well as the machines in the domains and their shares, in the main LinNeighborhood window, as shown in Figure 18-18. If you click the box to the left of an item, the entry should expand, until you get to the shares themselves. When you double-click a share, LinNeighborhood pops up a small dialog box in which you can enter the username and password, followed by a bigger dialog box in which you can adjust various options, such as the mount point, the owner of mounted files, and so on. Click Mount, and LinNeighborhood will mount the share. If you opted to have a file manager open on newly mounted shares, it should do so. The pane at the bottom of the LinNeighborhood window shows the SMB/CIFS shares that are mounted on the system.

Figure 18-18. LinNeighborhood provides a GUI interface on an SMB/CIFS network, making it accessible to users who are uncomfortable with text-mode mounting tools.

Summary

Samba is primarily a server, but in order to use the server, it must be paired with one or more clients. Understanding how to operate these clients, and knowing something about their idiosyncrasies, can greatly improve your overall network reliability and utility. Potential Samba clients include DOS add-on packages, the standard clients that come with Windows, Mac OS packages, tools that ship with Samba itself, and utilities that bridge the gap between Samba and Unix filesystems.

Part Five
Appendixes

APPENDIX A

Samba Configuration Options

SMALL PARAMETERS ARE classified in one of two categories:

Global parameters: These parameters appear in the [global] section of the smb.conf file and affect the functioning of the Samba server as a whole.

Share-level parameters: These parameters can appear in individual share definitions and affect that share alone. They can also appear in the [global] section, in which case they set the default for all shares.

Tables A-1 and A-2 summarize the Samba parameters in these two categories. Most of these parameters are covered in greater depth in relevant chapters of this book. Special icons to the left of certain entries also identify particular parameters that are new with Samba 3.0 or that are no longer valid in Samba 3.0:

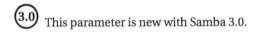 This parameter is new with Samba 3.0.

 This parameter has been removed from Samba 3.0.

Table A-1. Global Samba Parameters

	Parameter Name	Possible Values	Default Value	Description
(3.0)	abort shutdown script	Local command		Script to run to abort a scheduled server shutdown.
(3.0)	add group script	Local command		Command Samba runs to add a group to the local machine.
(3.0)	add machine script	Local command		Command Samba runs to add a local user as a machine trust account.
	add printer command	Local command		Script that adds a printer definition to the Unix host and creates a printer share for the new printer. Called from a Windows Share Manager.
	add share command	Local command		Script that adds a file share to Samba. Called from a Windows Share Manager.
	add user script	Local command		Command Samba runs to add a local user when a user successfully authenticates via a domain controller but a local account doesn't exist.
(3.0)	add user to group script	Local command		Script to add a user to a group.
	afs username map	String		String (typically containing %u) to create an AFS identifier for Samba users.
(3.0)	algorithmic rid base	Integer	1000	Base for creating RIDs for local users from local UIDs.
	allow trusted domains	Boolean	Yes	Whether or not to accept logons from clients that are members of a domain trusted by the server's domain controller.
	announce as	NT Server, NT (synonym for NT Server), NT Workstation, Win95, WfW	NT Server	OS that Samba claims to be in protocol negotiations.

Table A-1. Global Samba Parameters (Continued)

	Parameter Name	Possible Values	Default Value	Description
	announce version	Number	4.2 for Samba 2.0.*x* and earlier; 4.9 for Samba 2.2.*x* and 3.0.*x*	OS version that Samba claims to be in browse service announcements.
(3.0)	auth methods	Any combination of guest, sam, winbind, ntdomain, and trustdomain	None (methods set based on security parameter)	The set of authentication methods Samba supports; should not normally be modified.
	auto services	Share list		Synonym for preload.
	bind interfaces only	Boolean	No	If Yes, Samba listens only to the interfaces specified with the interfaces parameter.
	browse list	Boolean	Yes	Whether nmbd maintains a list of local computers for use in case it wins a local master browser election.
	change notify timeout	Integer	60	Frequency with which Samba checks for changes to directories when so requested by clients.
	change share command	Local command		Command that modifies a Samba share.
(3.0 crossed out)	character set	ISO8859-1, ISO8859-2, ISO8859-5, ISO8859-7, KOI8-R		The Unix character set. Replaced by unix charset in Samba 3.0.
(3.0 crossed out)	client code page	437, 737, 850, 852, 861, 866, 932, 936, 949, 950	850	The code page used by clients for filenames. Replaced by dos charset in Samba 3.0.
(3.0)	client lanman auth	Boolean	Yes	Whether smbclient and other Samba client tools will authenticate against servers that support only the LANMAN authentication protocol.

Table A-1. Global Samba Parameters (Continued)

	Parameter Name	Possible Values	Default Value	Description
(3.0)	client ntlmv2 auth	Boolean	No	Whether smbclient and other Samba client tools will attempt to use the more robust NTLMv2 authentication protocol.
(3.0)	client plaintext auth	Boolean	Yes	Whether smbclient and other Samba client tools will send a cleartext password if the server doesn't accept encrypted passwords.
(3.0)	client schannel	Boolean or Auto	Auto	Whether smbclient and other Samba client tools demand the use of the netlogon schannel. (Auto offers it but doesn't require its use.)
(3.0)	client signing	Auto, Mandatory, Disabled	Auto	Whether to use or require SMB signing.
(3.0)	client use spnego	Boolean	Yes	Whether to use Simple and Protected Negotiation to agree upon an authentication mechanism.
(3.0)	code page directory	Directory name	Compile-time option	The location of client code page files.
(3.0)	coding system	String		The Kanji coding system used when client code page = 932.
	config file	Filename		Name of a Samba configuration file to load in place of the current one.
	deadtime	Integer	0	Number of minutes of inactivity before Samba terminates a connection with a client. 0 represents no limit.
	debug hires timestamp	Boolean	No	If Yes, the resolution of time stamps in log files is increased to the microsecond level.

Table A-1. Global Samba Parameters (Continued)

	Parameter Name	Possible Values	Default Value	Description
	debug level	Integer between 0 and 10 or a list of *subsystem:level* pairs	0	Synonym for log level.
	debug pid	Boolean	No	If Yes, log the process ID (PID) of the Samba process along with any error or information messages. Requires debug timestamp = Yes.
	debug timestamp	Boolean	Yes	If Yes, log the time of each error or other information in the Samba log files. A synonym for this option is timestamp logs.
	debug uid	Boolean	No	If Yes, log the user ID (UID) used for operations in the Samba log files.
	default	Share name		Synonym for default service.
	default service	Share name		Share to be accessed if a requested share isn't present on the server. A synonym is default.
(3.0)	delete group script	Local command		Command that deletes a local Unix group.
	delete printer command	Local command		Command that deletes a printer from the local printer queue and from smb.conf.
	delete share command	Local command		Command that deletes a share from the smb.conf file.
(3.0)	delete user from group script	Local command		Command that deletes a user from a group.
	delete user script	Local command		Command that deletes an account from the server.
	dfree command	Local command	None (Samba internal procedures used)	Command that returns the amount of free disk space available to a share.

Table A-1. Global Samba Parameters (Continued)

	Parameter Name	Possible Values	Default Value	Description
(3.0)	disable netbios	Boolean	No	If Yes, disable NetBIOS support in Samba, using only raw SMB/CIFS over TCP/IP.
	disable spoolss	Boolean	No	If Yes, disable printing tools that better handle Windows NT/200x/XP printers.
(3.0)	display charset	ISO8859-1, ISO8859-2, ISO8859-5, ISO8859-7, KOI8-R, ASCII, UTF8	ASCII	The character set Samba uses when displaying messages on stdout and by SWAT.
	dns proxy	Boolean	Yes	Whether an NBNS system should try a DNS lookup if it can't find a requested name.
(3.0⊘)	domain admin group	Group names preceded by @ and usernames		Users and groups that are treated as members of the Domain Admins group when Samba is the PDC. Replaced in Samba 3.0.0 by mapping tools accessible from the net command.
(3.0⊘)	domain guest group	Group names preceded by @ and usernames		Users and groups that are treated as members of the Domain Guests group when Samba is the PDC. Replaced in Samba 3.0.0 by mapping tools accessible from the net command.
	domain logons	Boolean	No	Whether the computer will function as a domain controller.
	domain master	Boolean or Auto	Auto	Whether the computer will function as a domain master browser. The Auto option ties this parameter to the domain logons parameter.

Table A-1. Global Samba Parameters (Continued)

	Parameter Name	Possible Values	Default Value	Description
(3.0)	dos charset	CP437, CP737, CP850, CP852, CP861, CP866, CP932, CP936, CP949, CP950, ASCII	Varies but usually CP850 with a fallback to ASCII	The character set Samba uses when communicating with DOS clients. Supercedes client code page in Samba 3.0.0.
(3.0)	enable rid algorithm	Boolean	Yes	If Yes, algorithm to generate RIDs from Unix UIDs is enabled. This parameter is intended for developers and should not be set to No.
	encrypt passwords	Boolean	No for Samba 2.2.*x* and earlier; Yes for Samba 3.0 and later	Whether to use SMB/CIFS encrypted passwords.
	enhanced browsing	Boolean	Yes	Whether to enable master browser features that improve cross-subnet browsing.
	enumports command	Local command		Program that generates a list of printer ports (interface names) for the benefit of SMB/CIFS printing clients that need them.
(3.0)	get quota command	Local command	None (Samba uses local OS's API)	Command that returns quota information for the user accessing a share.
	getwd cache	Boolean	Yes	Whether to use a cache that improves local getwd() call performance.
	guest account	Username	Compile-time option; often nobody	The account to be used for guest accesses, as authorized by guest ok.
(3.0 crossed out)	hide local users	Boolean	No	Whether to hide the existence of local Unix users such as root from clients.
	homedir map	NIS map name		If nis homedir = Yes, the name of the NIS map from which the user's home directory can be extracted.

Table A-1. Global Samba Parameters (Continued)

	Parameter Name	Possible Values	Default Value	Description
	host msdfs	Boolean	No	Whether Samba should act as a Dfs server.
(3.0)	hostname lookups	Boolean	No	Whether to support hostnames in configuration parameters that accept IP addresses, such as hosts allow.
	hosts equiv	Filename		File that specifies hosts that should be trusted to authenticate users locally, rather than via Samba's normal mechanisms.
(3.0)	idmap backend	String		Backend database used to store SID to UID/GID mappings. If none is specified, a TDB system is used.
(3.0)	idmap gid	Dash-separated integer range		Range of GIDs Winbind uses for generated groups.
(3.0)	idmap uid	Dash-separated integer range		Range of UIDs Winbind uses for generated users.
	include	Filename		File to be included in the main configuration file. Frequently used with a filename that includes variables to customize settings for specific hosts, users, and so on.
	interfaces	Interface names	All interfaces except 127.0.0.1	List of interfaces to be used by Samba. Typically used in conjunction with bind interfaces only.
	keepalive	Integer	300	Interval in seconds between packets sent to the client to verify its continued presence.
(3.0)	kernel change notify	Boolean	Yes	Whether Samba should ask the kernel to notify it of changes in directories being used by clients.

Table A-1. Global Samba Parameters (Continued)

Parameter Name	Possible Values	Default Value	Description
kernel oplocks	Boolean	Yes	Whether local programs can break a Samba-granted oplock. As of Samba 3.0.0, supported only by Linux and IRIX.
lanman auth	Boolean	Yes	Whether Samba will accept a LANMAN authentication request.
large readwrite	Boolean	Yes	Whether Samba supports streaming 64KB operations introduced with Windows 2000.
ldap admin dn	String		The Distinguished Name (DN) used to access user account information on an LDAP server.
(3.0) ldap delete dn	Boolean	No	Whether deletion of an LDAP entry deletes the complete entry (Yes) or just the Samba-specific data (No).
ldap filter	String	(&(uid=%u) (objectclass= sambaAccount))	The search filter used to locate usernames in an LDAP directory.
(3.0) ldap group suffix	String		The suffix used when adding groups to an LDAP directory.
(3.0) ldap idmap suffix	String		The suffix used when storing idmap mappings in an LDAP directory.
(3.0) ldap machine suffix	String		Where machines are added in an LDAP tree.
(3.0) ldap passwd sync	Boolean or Only	No	Whether to synchronize LDAP passwords with NT and LANMAN passwords.
ldap port	Integer	636 if ldap ssl = On; 389 if ldap ssl = Off	Port on which Samba tries to access an LDAP server.
ldap server	DNS hostname		Hostname of the LDAP server if passdb backend = ldapsam.

Table A-1. Global Samba Parameters (Continued)

Parameter Name	Possible Values	Default Value	Description
ldap ssl	On, Off, or Start_TLS	Start_TLS	Type of encryption to use when communicating with an LDAP server.
ldap suffix	String		Where user and machine accounts are added to an LDAP directory tree.
ldap user suffix	String		Where users are added to an LDAP directory tree.
lm announce	Boolean or Auto	Auto	Whether to generate LAN Manager announce broadcasts, which are required by OS/2 systems. Auto causes Samba to generate them if it detects other systems using them.
lm interval	Integer	60	Interval, in seconds, at which LAN Manager announce broadcasts are sent, if they are sent.
load printers	Boolean	Yes	Whether Samba loads the definitions in the file specified by printcap name. To be effective, this parameter also requires the presence of a [printers] share.
local master	Boolean	Yes	Whether Samba participates in local master browser elections.
lock dir	Directory name	Compile-time option	Synonym for lock directory.
lock directory	Directory name	Compile-time option	Directory in which Samba stores files relating to max connections access controls. A synonym is lock dir.
lock spin count	Integer	2	The number of times Samba attempts to acquire a lock on a byte range within a file before reporting a failure.

(3.0)

Table A-1. Global Samba Parameters (Continued)

Parameter Name	Possible Values	Default Value	Description
lock spin time	Integer	10	The time in microseconds between attempts to acquire a lock when lock spin count is greater than 1.
log file	Filename	Compile-time option; usually files in /var/log/samba	The filename to be used for logging errors and other information. The %m variable is often used as part of the value to create separate log files for each client.
log level	Integer between 0 and 10, or list of *subsystem:level* pairs	0	The amount of information to be logged; 0 logs nothing, and 10 logs copious amounts of information. A set of subsystem names, such as winbind or auth, followed by a colon and a log level, can optionally be used to set different log levels for different Samba subsystems in Samba 3.0 and later. A synonym is debug level.
logon drive	Windows drive letter	Z:	Drive letter to which Windows NT clients map the home directory in domain logons.
logon home	String	"\\%N\%U"	Location of Windows 9*x*/Me home directories and user profiles in a domain configuration.
logon path	String	"\\%N\%U\profile"	Location of Windows NT/200*x*/XP roaming profiles.
logon script	Windows filename		Name of the domain logon script within the NETLOGON share.
lpq cache time	Local command	10	How long (in seconds) Samba stores information on jobs in the local print queue.
machine password timeout	Integer	604800	The interval in seconds between attempts to change the machine trust account password.

Table A-1. Global Samba Parameters (Continued)

	Parameter Name	Possible Values	Default Value	Description
(3.0)	mangle prefix	Integer between 1 and 6	1	Number of characters to save from the original filename in mangled filenames. Valid only when mangling method = hash2.
(3.0 crossed)	mangled stack	Integer	50	Number of filenames and their mangled equivalents to cache in memory.
	mangling method	Hash or Hash2	Hash for Samba 2.2.x and earlier; Hash2 for Samba 3.0 and later	Which of two algorithms to use for generating mangled filenames.
	map to guest	Never, Bad User, or Bad Password	Never	When to attempt a guest account access.
	max disk size	Integer	0	The maximum size, in megabytes, that Samba reports its volumes to be. A value of 0 corresponds to no limit.
	max log size	Integer	5000	The maximum size of Samba's log files, in kilobytes. A value of 0 specifies no size limit.
	max mux	Integer	50	The maximum number of outstanding SMB/CIFS operations Samba tells the client it will support.
	max open files	Integer	10000	The maximum number of open files from a single client that Samba will support.
	max protocol	CORE, COREPLUS, LANMAN1, LANMAN2, NT1	NT1	The highest SMB/CIFS protocol level supported by Samba.
	max smbd processes	Integer	0	Maximum number of smbd processes that may run simultaneously. 0 means no limit.
	max ttl	Integer	259200	The name registration time to request as an NBNS client.

Table A-1. Global Samba Parameters (Continued)

Parameter Name	Possible Values	Default Value	Description
max wins ttl	Integer	259200	The maximum time, in seconds, a name registration with an NBNS system will last.
max xmit	Integer	65535	Maximum packet size negotiated by Samba.
message command	Local command		Command to run when the server receives a WinPopUp message.
min passwd length	Integer	5	Synonym for min password length.
min password length	Integer	5	The minimum password length Samba utilities will accept when changing a password.
min protocol	CORE, COREPLUS, LANMAN1, LANMAN2, NT1	CORE	The lowest SMB/CIFS protocol level supported by Samba.
min wins ttl	Integer	21600	The minimum time, in seconds, a name registration with an NBNS system will last.
name cache timeout	Integer	660	Number of seconds DNS hostnames are stored in Samba's name resolution cache. 0 means that the cache is disabled.
name resolve order	One or more of lmhosts, host, wins, or bcast	lmhosts host wins bcast	Order in which Samba tools try various name resolution methods.
netbios aliases	String		One or more NetBIOS names the system claims, in addition to the main netbios name.
netbios name	String	The computer's DNS hostname	The name the computer claims for NetBIOS interactions with other systems.
netbios scope	String		NetBIOS scope setting; seldom used.

Table A-1. Global Samba Parameters (Continued)

	Parameter Name	Possible Values	Default Value	Description
	nis homedir	Boolean	No	Whether to retrieve users' home directory locations from an NIS map.
(3.0)	ntlm auth	Boolean	Yes	Whether the Samba server will accept NTLM encrypted password authentication attempts.
	nt pipe support	Boolean	Yes	Whether Samba permits clients to connect to the IPC$ share. This is a developer debugging option and should never be changed.
(3.0)	nt smb support	Boolean	Yes	Whether to enable NT-specific SMB/CIFS options.
	nt status support	Boolean	Yes	Whether Windows NT/200x/XP–specific status options are offered. This is a developer debugging option and should never be changed.
	null passwords	Boolean	No	If Yes, accounts with null passwords set are active and require no passwords to access. If No, attempts to log on using an account with a null password are denied.
(3.0)	obey pam restrictions	Boolean	No	Whether to obey post-authentication account and session management directives from PAM. This option is meaningful only when Samba is compiled using the --with-pam directive.
	oplock break wait time	Integer	0	Delay in milliseconds before Samba sends an oplock break request to clients.
	os2 driver map	Filename		File containing mapping of Windows NT printer driver names to OS/2 printer driver names.

Table A-1. Global Samba Parameters (Continued)

Parameter Name	Possible Values	Default Value	Description
os level	Integer	0 for Samba 2.0.5a and earlier; 20 for Samba 2.0.6 and later; 32 for Samba TNG	The OS-level code used in local master browser elections.
pam password change	Boolean	No	Whether to use PAM's password-changing tools instead of the program specified by passwd program when unix password sync = Yes.
panic action	Local command		Command to call if Samba crashes. Intended for developer use.
(3.0) paranoid server security	Boolean	Yes	Whether to refuse to use Windows NT domain controllers that accept nonguest accesses with a bad password.
(3.0) passdb backend	smbpasswd, tdbsam, nisplussam, ldapsam, or mysql	smbpasswd	System used to store encrypted Samba passwords. Most options are followed by a colon and a specification of the location of a database file or server.
passwd chat	String	*new*password* %n\n *new*password* %n\n *changed*	A "chat" string to control interactions with the local password-changing program (specified by passwd program when unix password sync = Yes).
passwd chat debug	Boolean	No	Whether to log the output of the passwd chat interaction.
(3.0) passwd chat timeout	Integer	2	Time Samba will wait for the initial response from the passwd program. Subsequent responses must appear in one-tenth this time.
passwd program	Program filename	/bin/passwd	The filename of the local Unix program that changes the local Unix password.

Table A-1. Global Samba Parameters (Continued)

Parameter Name	Possible Values	Default Value	Description
password level	Integer	0	Number of letters in a password to convert to uppercase after converting the password to lowercase when authenticating users with unencrypted passwords.
password server	NetBIOS name		NetBIOS name or IP address of a domain controller or other computer that will authenticate users when security is set to Server or Domain.
pid directory	Directory name	Compile-time option	Directory in which process ID files reside.
prefered master	Boolean or Auto	Auto	Synonym for preferred master.
preferred master	Boolean or Auto	Auto	If set to Yes, causes Samba to request a local master browser election when started and to receive a small boost in its election status.
preload	Share list		List of shares that should always be displayed to client browsers. A synonym is auto services.
preload modules	Module list		List of modules to preload into Samba before clients connect.
printcap	Filename	/etc/printcap	Synonym for printcap name.
printcap name	Filename	/etc/printcap	Filename in which printer information is stored. A synonym for this option is printcap name.
printer driver file	Filename	Compile-time option	Location of file that defines printer drivers for printer shares.

Table A-1. Global Samba Parameters (Continued)

Parameter Name	Possible Values	Default Value	Description
printing	BSD, AIX, LPRng, PLP, SysV, HPUX, QNX, SoftQ, or CUPS	Compile-time option	The printing system used on the server computer.
(3.0) private dir	Directory name	Compile-time option	Directory in which Samba stores sensitive files such as smbpasswd and secrets.tdb.
protocol	NT1, CORE, COREPLUS, LANMAN1, LANMAN2	NT1	Synonym for max protocol.
read bmpx	Boolean	No	Whether Samba supports the (rare) Read Block Multiplex SMB/CIFS command.
read raw	Boolean	Yes	Whether Samba supports the Read Raw commands, which can improve performance.
read size	Integer	16385	The size above which a data transfer must be before Samba begins writing data before the transfer is complete. This is a performance tuning parameter.
(3.0) realm	Kerberos realm name		The name of the Kerberos realm to use when accessing an ADS domain.
remote announce	IP or Network addresses and workgroup name		Addresses of remote machines or networks to which Samba should announce its presence when it starts, and periodically thereafter.
remote browse sync	IP or network addresses		Addresses of remote Samba master browsers or networks with which to exchange browse lists.

Table A-1. Global Samba Parameters (Continued)

	Parameter Name	Possible Values	Default Value	Description
	restrict anonymous	0, 1, or 2	0	Whether anonymous users can obtain user and group information—0 means that anybody can receive this information, 1 means that only authenticated users may do so, and 2 means that anonymous users are denied access completely.
	root	Directory name	/	Synonym for root directory.
	root dir	Directory name	/	Synonym for root directory.
	root directory	Directory name	/	Directory into which Samba chroots at startup. Synonyms for this option are root and root dir.
	security	Share, User, Server, or Domain	User	Sets the security model Samba uses for user authentication.
(3.0)	server schannel	Boolean or Auto	Auto	Whether the server demands that the client use the netlogon schannel. (Auto offers it but doesn't require that the client use it.)
(3.0)	server signing	Auto, Mandatory, or Disabled	Auto	Whether the server requires the client to use SMB signing.
	server string	String	Samba %v	A string that describes the Samba server. Displayed by some clients in their network browsers.
(3.0)	set primary group script	Local command		Command that sets a user's primary Unix group.
(3.0)	set quota command	Local command	None (Samba uses host OS API)	Command that sets the disk quota for a specific user.
	show add printer wizard	Boolean	Yes	Whether to display the Add Printer Wizard for the server on Windows systems.

Table A-1. Global Samba Parameters (Continued)

	Parameter Name	Possible Values	Default Value	Description
(3.0)	shutdown script	Local command		Command that shuts down the Samba server computer.
	smb passwd file	Filename	Compile-time option; usually smbpasswd in a configuration file directory	The filename (with complete path) of the file that holds the Samba encrypted password database.
(3.0)	smb ports	Port numbers	445 139	The port numbers to which smbd binds itself.
	socket address	IP address	None (connections accepted to any address)	The address to which the server listens; enables multiple servers to run on multiple virtual addresses using a single machine.
	socket options	OS-specific socket options	TCP_NODELAY	Socket options for tuning TCP/IP connections.
	source environment	Filename		File containing environment variables and their values that Samba loads when forking a process for a new user.
(3.0̸)	ssl	Boolean	No	Whether to enable SSL encryption.
(3.0̸)	ssl ca certdir	Directory name		Directory used for storing SSL CA server certificates.
(3.0̸)	ssl ca certfile	Filename		File in which SSL CA server certificates are stored.
(3.0̸)	ssl ciphers	DEFAULT, DES-CFB-M1, NULL-MD5, RC4-MD5, EXP-RC4-MD5, RC2-CBC-MD5, EXP-RC2-CBC-MD5, IDEA-CBC-MD5, DES-CBC-MD5, DES-CBC-SHA, DES-CB3-MD5, DES-CB3-SHA, RC4-64-MD5, NULL		SSL encryption systems Samba accepts.
(3.0̸)	ssl client cert	Filename		SSL client certificate (used by smbclient).

Table A-1. Global Samba Parameters (Continued)

	Parameter Name	Possible Values	Default Value	Description
(3.0)	ssl client key	Filename		SSL client key (used by smbclient).
(3.0)	ssl compatibility	Boolean	No	Workaround for bugs in older SSL implementations.
(3.0)	ssl hosts	Hostnames		Computers that must connect using SSL. If ssl = Yes and this option is unused, all computers must use SSL.
(3.0)	ssl hosts resign	Hostnames		Computers that don't need to use SSL to connect.
(3.0)	ssl require clientcert	Boolean	No	If Yes, Samba requires SSL-enabled clients to have certificates.
(3.0)	ssl require servercert	Boolean	No	If Yes, smbclient requires SSL-enabled servers to have certificates.
(3.0)	ssl server cert	Filename		File containing Samba's SSL server certificate.
(3.0)	ssl server key	Filename		File containing Samba's SSL server key.
(3.0)	ssl version	ssl2or3, ssl2, ssl3, or tls1	ssl2or3	Version of SSL Samba uses.
	stat cache	Boolean	Yes	Whether to use a cache to speed up case-insensitive name mappings.
(3.0)	status	Boolean	Yes	Whether to create a file that's used by smbstatus to display information on Samba's status. You should never need to change this parameter's default.
	syslog	Integer	1	Samba server messages lower than this value are logged to the Unix syslogd utility instead of or in addition to using Samba's own logging tools.

Table A-1. Global Samba Parameters (Continued)

	Parameter Name	Possible Values	Default Value	Description
	syslog only	Boolean	No	If Yes, Samba uses `syslogd` exclusively for logging, instead of creating its own log files.
	template homedir	Directory name	/home/%D/%U	Home directory returned by Winbind for user accounts.
(3.0)	template primary group	Unix group name	nobody	Primary group name returned by Winbind for user accounts.
	template shell	Executable filename	/bin/false	Shell returned by Winbind for user accounts.
	time offset	Integer	0	Minutes to add to the time reported to clients.
	time server	Boolean	No	Whether Samba announces itself as a LANMAN time server.
	timestamp logs	Boolean	Yes	Synonym for debug timestamp.
(3.0)	total print jobs	Integer	0	Maximum number of pending print jobs Samba will accept. 0 means no limit.
(3.0)	unicode	Boolean	Yes	Whether Samba should accept Unicode filenames from clients that try to use them.
(3.0)	unix charset	CP437, CP737, CP850, CP852, CP861, CP866, CP932, CP936, CP949, CP950, ASCII, UTF8	UTF8	The character set used by the computer on which Samba is running. Replaces `character set`.
	unix extensions	Boolean	No in Samba 2.2.*x* and earlier; Yes in Samba 3.0.0 and later	If Yes and the client so requests, Samba uses an SMB/CIFS extension that supports some Unix-style metadata, such as hard and symbolic link information.

Table A-1. *Global Samba Parameters (Continued)*

Parameter Name	Possible Values	Default Value	Description
unix password sync	Boolean	No	Whether to change the local Unix password when the Samba password is changed (via smbpasswd or similar tools).
update encrypted	Boolean	No	If Yes, an unencrypted logon triggers a password change in the Samba encrypted password database to match the unencrypted password. Requires encrypt passwords = No.
use mmap	Boolean	Yes (but No on HPUX)	Whether the Samba TDB internals can depend on a working local mmap system.
use rhosts	Boolean	No	Whether to read a user's ~/.rhosts file and provide password-free access to the specified computers and users.
use spnego	Boolean	Yes	Whether the Samba server tries to use the Simple and Protected Negotiation method of agreeing upon an authentication system.
username level	Integer	0	Number of letters in a username to convert to uppercase after converting the username to lowercase when authenticating users with unencrypted passwords.
username map	Filename		Points to a file containing a mapping of Unix user-names to SMB/CIFS usernames.
utmp	Boolean	No	Whether to create utmp or utmpx records for each connection. This action can degrade performance.
utmp directory	Directory name		Directory in which utmp or utmpx records are stored.

Table A-1. Global Samba Parameters (Continued)

	Parameter Name	Possible Values	Default Value	Description
⊘3.0	valid chars	Character list		Special characters that are valid in filenames, in addition to those determined by `client code page`.
	winbind cache time	Integer	15 in Samba 2.2.*x* and earlier; 300 in Samba 3.0.0 and later	Number of seconds Winbind will cache information before requesting an update from the domain controller.
(3.0)	winbind enable local accounts	Boolean	Yes	Whether Winbind will act as a stand-in for account management hooks such as `add user script`.
	winbind enum groups	Boolean	Yes	Whether Winbind supports group enumeration system calls.
	winbind enum users	Boolean	Yes	Whether Winbind supports user enumeration system calls.
	winbind gid	Dash-separated integer range		Synonym for `idmap gid`. Deprecated in Samba 3.0.0.
	winbind separator	Character	/	Character used by Winbind to separate the domain portion of a username from the username portion of a username.
(3.0)	winbind trusted domains only	Boolean	No	Whether to use NIS, LDAP, or rsync to locate UID information on Winbind-generated accounts.
	winbind uid	Dash-separated integer range		Synonym for `idmap uid`. Deprecated in Samba 3.0.0.
	winbind use default domain	Boolean	Yes	Whether Winbind returns the domain name as part of each username.
	wins hook	Executable filename		Script or program to be run on the server when a client registers with a Samba NBNS system.

Table A-1. Global Samba Parameters (Continued)

Parameter Name	Possible Values	Default Value	Description
(3.0) wins partners	IP address list		IP addresses of other Samba NBNS systems with which the configured servers should exchange NBNS data. This parameter should be used by developers only and has been removed from Samba 3.0.2.
wins proxy	Boolean	Yes in Samba 1.9.*x* and earlier; No in Samba 2.0 and later	If Yes, nmbd forwards broadcast name requests to an NBNS computer and proxies the response to a broadcast client.
wins server	List of IP addresses or hostnames		Computers that function as NBNS systems on the network.
wins support	Boolean	No	Whether nmbd functions as an NBNS/WINS server.
workgroup	String	WORKGROUP	The name of the workgroup to which the server belongs.
write raw	Boolean	Yes	Whether Samba supports raw write commands from clients.
wtmp directory	Directory name		Directory in which wtmp or wtmpx files are stored when utmp = Yes.

Table A-2. Share-Level Samba Parameters

Parameter Name	Possible Values	Default Value	Description
acl compatibility	WinNT, Win2K, or Auto	Auto	What type of ACL semantics to support in client/server communication.
admin users	Username list		List of users who have administrative (root) access when using a share.
afs share	Boolean	No	If Yes, assume that the share is an AFS import and enable special AFS compatibility features.
allow hosts	Computer hostnames or IP addresses		Synonym for hosts allow.
available	Boolean	Yes	Whether Samba makes the share available.
blocking locks	Boolean	Yes	If Yes, Samba can notify clients when a file lock clears.
block size	Integer	1024	Disk block size used by Samba when reporting disk space measurements to clients. This is an experimental parameter that may be removed in the future.
browsable	Boolean	Yes	Synonym for browseable.
browseable	Boolean	Yes	Whether a share appears in client browse lists. Synonym is browsable.
case sensitive	Boolean	No	Whether Samba considers filename case when opening existing files for clients. A synonym is casesignnames.
casesignnames	Boolean	No	Synonym for case sensitive.
comment	String		A comment associated with a share, visible from many browsers.

Table A-2. Share-Level Samba Parameters (Continued)

Parameter Name	Possible Values	Default Value	Description
copy	Share name		Copies defaults from another share.
create mask	Octal mode	0744	The maximum and default permissions for a file created via Samba. A synonym is create mode.
create mode	Octal mode	0744	Synonym for create mask.
csc policy	Manual, Documents, Programs, Disable	Manual	Tells clients what sorts of offline caching the server supports.
default case	Upper or Lower	Lower	Case in which filenames are stored when preserve case or short preserve case is set to No.
default devmode	Boolean	No	If Yes, Samba generates a default device mode for printer drivers, setting features such as paper size.
delete readonly	Boolean	No	Whether users may delete files to which they have no write privileges in directories to which they do have write privileges.
delete veto files	Boolean	No	Whether Samba will delete vetoed directories when they're stored in nonvetoed directories that a user tries to delete.
deny hosts	Computer hostnames or IP addresses		Synonym for hosts deny.
directory	Directory name	/tmp	The directory to be shared. A synonym is path.
directory mask	Octal mode	0755	The maximum and default permissions for a directory created via Samba. A synonym is directory mode.
directory mode	Octal mode	0755	Synonym for directory mask.

Table A-2. Share-Level Samba Parameters (Continued)

Parameter Name	Possible Values	Default Value	Description
directory security mask	Octal mode	Same as directory mask	Defines which Unix permission bits in directories may be modified via SMB/CIFS ACLs when nt acl support = Yes.
dont descend	Comma-separated directory list		List of directories Samba should show as being empty.
dos filemode	Boolean	No	Whether users may change permissions on files to which they have no write privileges in directories to which they do have write privileges.
dos filetime resolution	Boolean	No	Whether Samba should round file-creation times to the nearest two-second value.
dos filetimes	Boolean	No	Whether users who have write access to the file but who don't own it may change the file's time stamp.
exec	Local command		Synonym for preexec.
fake directory create times	Boolean	No	If Yes, Samba reports all directory creation times as January 1, 1980.
fake oplocks	Boolean	No	If Yes, Samba claims it's granted an oplock even when it hasn't. This option is unsafe except for read-only filesystems and a few other special circumstances.
follow symlinks	Boolean	Yes	Whether to follow symbolic links in shared directories.
force create mode	Octal mode	0000	The permission bits to force on when Samba clients create files.
force directory mode	Octal mode	0000	The permission bits to force on when Samba clients create directories.

Table A-2. Share-Level Samba Parameters (Continued)

Parameter Name	Possible Values	Default Value	Description
force directory security mode	Octal mode	Same as force directory mode	The permission bits to force on in directories when users change permission bits via SMB/CIFS ACLs when nt acl support = Yes.
force group	Group name		Group Samba uses for file access and creation whenever the share is accessed. A synonym for this option is group.
force security mode	Octal mode	Same as force create mode	The permission bits to force on in files when users change permission bits via SMB/CIFS ACLs when nt acl support = Yes.
force unknown acl user	Boolean	No	If Yes, Samba maps files with an unknown SID ACL to the current user's SID.
force user	Username		Username Samba uses for file access and creation whenever the share is accessed.
fstype	String	NTFS	The filesystem type string returned by Samba.
group	Group name		Synonym for force group.
guest ok	Boolean	No	If Yes, users need not give a password to access the share. Guest accesses use the privileges of the guest account. A synonym for this option is public.
guest only	Boolean	No	If Yes, only guest accesses are granted to the share (see guest ok). A synonym for this parameter is only guest.
hide dot files	Boolean	Yes	Whether to set the SMB/CIFS hidden bit on files whose names begin with a dot (.).

Table A-2. Share-Level Samba Parameters (Continued)

Parameter Name	Possible Values	Default Value	Description
hide files	Slash-separated file list		Sets the SMB/CIFS hidden bit on the specified files.
(3.0) hide special files	Boolean	No	Whether to set the SMB/CIFS hidden bit on files that have unusual file types, such as device files and sockets.
hide unreadable	Boolean	No	Whether to set the SMB/CIFS hidden bit on files to which the user lacks read access.
(3.0) hide unwriteable files	Boolean	No	Whether to set the SMB/CIFS hidden bit on files to which the user lacks write access. This parameter does *not* affect the hidden bit on directories.
hosts allow	Computer hostnames or IP addresses		If present, computers that are allowed to access the share. (If omitted, all computers are given access to the share.) A synonym is allow hosts.
hosts deny	Computer hostnames or IP addresses		Computers that are denied access to the share. A synonym is deny hosts.
inherit acls	Boolean	No	Whether to copy a parent directory's ACLs when creating a new subdirectory.
inherit permissions	Boolean	No	If Yes, overrides the create mask and directory mask parameters and sets file permissions based on the parent directory's permissions.
invalid users	Username list		Users who are denied access to the share.
level2 oplocks	Boolean	Yes	Whether Samba can down-grade an oplock to read-only oplock.
locking	Boolean	Yes	If Yes, Samba implements basic file locking features.

Table A-2. Share-Level Samba Parameters (Continued)

Parameter Name	Possible Values	Default Value	Description
`lppause command`	Local command	Depends on value of `printing` parameter	Local command to pause printing of a specific job in the local print queue.
`lpq command`	Local command	Depends on value of `printing` parameter	Local command to generate information on jobs in the local print queue.
`lpresume command`	Local command	Depends on value of `printing` parameter	Local command to reverse the effects of the `lppause` command.
`lprm command`	Local command	Depends on value of `printing` parameter	Local command to remove a print job from the local print queue.
`magic output`	Filename	`magic-script-name.out`	File in which the output of the `magic script` parameter's script is stored.
`magic script`	Filename		File that will be executed as a script when it's closed by the client. Magic scripts are experimental, tend to be unreliable, and are likely to be removed in the future.
`mangle case`	Boolean	No	Whether Samba applies filaname-mangling rules when filename case doesn't match the case specified in `default case`.
`mangled map`	Name-mapping pairs		Pairs of filename patterns to be changed, as in (`.html .htm`) to change all filenames ending in `.html` to end in `.htm`.
`mangled names`	Boolean	Yes	Whether to generate short (mangled) filenames from long filenames when a client asks for them.
`mangling char`	Character	~	The character to use in separating two components of mangled filename bases. Valid only when `mangling method = Hash`.

Table A-2. Share-Level Samba Parameters (Continued)

	Parameter Name	Possible Values	Default Value	Description
(3.0)	map acl inherit	Boolean	No	Whether to map the SMB/CIFS inherit and protected ACL entries using Unix extended attributes.
	map archive	Boolean	Yes	If Yes, Samba uses the owner execute bit to store the SMB/CIFS archive bit.
	map hidden	Boolean	No	If Yes, Samba uses the world execute bit to store the SMB/CIFS hidden bit.
	map system	Boolean	No	If Yes, Samba uses the group execute bit to store the SMB/CIFS system bit.
	max connections	Integer	0	Maximum number of connections Samba accepts to the share. A value of 0 specifies no limit.
	max print jobs	Integer	1000	The maximum number of print jobs Samba will allow in a single print queue.
(3.0)	max reported print jobs	Integer	1000	Maximum number of print jobs Samba will report to clients as being in a queue.
	min print space	Integer	0	The minimum free space, in kilobytes, required on the share's partition for Samba to accept a new print job.
(3.0)	msdfs proxy	Share specification		Share to which clients are redirected using the Dfs protocol.
	msdfs root	Boolean	No	The share is treated as a Dfs root share.
	nt acl support	Boolean	Yes	Whether to support mapping Unix ownership and permissions to SMB/CIFS ACLs. On ACL-enabled filesystems, this option also provides access to the underlying Unix ACLs.

Table A-2. Share-Level Samba Parameters (Continued)

Parameter Name	Possible Values	Default Value	Description
only guest	Boolean	No	Synonym for guest only.
only user	Boolean	No	Whether to reject logons from users who aren't on the username list.
oplock contention limit	Integer	2	Deny oplocks when the number of clients accessing a file exceeds the specified limit. Do not attempt to adjust this parameter unless you have an intimate understanding of Samba's oplock implementation.
oplocks	Boolean	Yes	Whether Samba supports opportunistic locks (*oplocks*), which enable clients to cache file accesses.
path	Directory name	/tmp	Synonym for directory.
posix locking	Boolean	Yes	Whether Samba coordinates SMB/CIFS file locks with those maintained by the OS.
postexec	Local command		Command to run when a user closes a connection to a share.
postscript	Boolean	No	If Yes, Samba adds a PostScript comment string (%!) to the start of each print job.
preexec	Local command		Command to run when a user logs onto a share. A synonym for this option is exec.
preexec close	Boolean	No	Whether to close a connection if the preexec script returns an error value.

Table A-2. Share-Level Samba Parameters (Continued)

Parameter Name	Possible Values	Default Value	Description
preserve case	Boolean	Yes	Whether to preserve the case of filenames given by clients when creating new files. If set to No, the filename is converted to the case specified by default case.
print command	Local command	Depends on value of printing parameter	The command that's used to submit a print job to the local print queue.
print ok	Boolean	No	Synonym for printable.
printable	Boolean	No	If Yes, defines a share as a printer share. A synonym for this option is print ok.
printer	Local print queue name	Share name or lp	Synonym for printer name.
printer admin	Username list	root by implication	Users who may administer printers.
printer driver	String		The name of the Windows printer driver for a share.
printer driver location	UNC path		Printer driver locations for Windows clients.
printer name	Local print queue name	Share name or lp	Name of the local print queue to which a printer share prints. A synonym for this option is printer.
profile acls	Boolean	No	Whether to dynamically change ACLs on user profiles to improve compatibility with recent Windows clients.
public	Boolean	No	Synonym for guest ok.
queuepause command	Local command	Depends on value of printing parameter	Local command to pause printing of all jobs in a local print queue.

Table A-2. Share-Level Samba Parameters (Continued)

Parameter Name	Possible Values	Default Value	Description
queueresume command	Local command	Depends on value of printing parameter	Local command to reverse the effects of the queuepause command.
read list	Username list		List of users who are restricted from writing to an otherwise read/write share.
read only	Boolean	Yes	Antonym for writeable.
root postexec	Local command		Command run as root after a connection is terminated.
root preexec	Local command		Command run as root when a connection is opened.
root preexec close	Boolean	No	Whether to close a connection if the root preexec script returns an error code.
security mask	Octal mode	Same as create mask	Defines which Unix permission bits in files may be modified via SMB/CIFS ACLs when nt acl support = Yes.
set directory	Boolean	No	If No, clients may not use the setdir command, which is only supported in Digital Pathworks clients.
share modes	Boolean	Yes	If Yes, Samba simulates several file-open options that aren't supported on Unix systems. This option should never be changed from its default.
short preserve case	Boolean	Yes	Whether to preserve the case of short (8.3) filenames given by clients when creating new files. If set to No, the filename is converted to the case specified by default case.

Table A-2. Share-Level Samba Parameters (Continued)

Parameter Name	Possible Values	Default Value	Description
strict allocate	Boolean	No	If Yes, Samba tries to allocate disk space all at once for a file's target size when creating files; if No, Samba allocates space only as it's actually needed.
strict locking	Boolean	No for Samba 2.2.*x* and earlier; Yes for Samba 3.0 and later	Whether Samba checks for file locks if a client doesn't explicitly request such a check.
strict sync	Boolean	No	If Yes, Samba honors clients' disk-sync requests, which can degrade performance but improve reliability in case of a server crash.
strip dot	Boolean	No	If Yes, dots (.) are removed from filenames that end in them.
sync always	Boolean	No	If Yes, Samba always finishes writing data before reporting it's done so. This can degrade performance but improve reliability in case of a server crash. If Yes, strict sync must also be Yes.
use client driver	Boolean	No	Whether to enable a workaround that fixes printer access problems with Windows NT/200*x*/XP clients when a client printer driver is installed. Do *not* set this option to Yes if a Windows printer driver is available on the Samba server.
use sendfile	Boolean	No	Whether to use the sendfile system call, which should improve performance. This parameter is relatively untested.

Table A-2. Share-Level Samba Parameters (Continued)

Parameter Name	Possible Values	Default Value	Description
user	Username list		Synonym for username.
username	Username list		One or more usernames that Samba is to use in authenticating the user if the client doesn't provide one. This option is often used in conjunction with security = User access configurations. Synonyms for this option are user and users.
users	Username list		Synonym for username.
valid	Boolean	Yes	Whether a share is valid; setting to No effectively disables a share.
valid users	Username list		Users who may access the share. If no list is given, all users are considered valid.
veto files	Slash-separated file list		Makes the specified files inaccessible to clients.
veto oplock files	Slash-separated file list		Files on which Samba will not grant oplocks.
(3.0) vfs object	VFS object names		Synonym for vfs objects.
(3.0) vfs objects	VFS object names		Backends used by Samba VFS I/O operations.
volume	String	The share's name	A volume name reported to clients and displayed in some clients' directory listings.
wide links	Boolean	Yes	Whether to follow symbolic links pointing outside of a share.

Table A-2. Share-Level Samba Parameters (Continued)

Parameter Name	Possible Values	Default Value	Description
writable	Boolean	No	Synonym for writeable.
write cache size	Integer	0	Size of write cache, in bytes, for oplocked files.
write list	Username list		List of users who are granted read/write access to an otherwise read-only share.
write ok	Boolean	No	Synonym for writeable.
writeable	Boolean	No	Whether to allow write access to the share. Synonyms are writable and write ok; antonym is read only.

APPENDIX B

Using *net*

MOST SAMBA FEATURES are incorporated into the Samba server itself—or more precisely, the Samba servers, because both smbd and nmbd are important to basic file server functionality, and others (such as winbindd and swat) are important for other functions. Samba ships with a few stand-alone tools that are vital adjuncts, though. Most of these, such as smbpasswd and smbclient, have been described in assorted chapters of this book. One tool, though, is new to Samba 3.0 and is complex enough that it hasn't been covered completely elsewhere. This tool is the net command, which aims to replicate many of the features of the Windows NET command.

The net command enables you to perform assorted server and domain control functions from the command line. Its syntax is complex, involving both parameters and net subcommands. The number of subcommands is quite large, and the entire suite of subcommands and parameters is intimidating, so this appendix concludes with a look at some examples of net in use, which should help you on the road to using it yourself.

The Purpose of *net*

DOS and Windows have long included a command called NET, which handles mounting and unmounting SMB/CIFS shares, setting the time from a time server, and so on. Samba 3.0's net command is modeled loosely on the DOS/Windows NET, but many of the details differ. Some features of the Samba net may seem familiar to experienced Windows users, but others won't. Broadly speaking, the functions of Samba's net include account maintenance, domain functions, server functions, and time functions. These features are described in more detail shortly.

Many of net's functions are geared toward domain operations. These functions help Samba operate on a Windows NT 4–style domain or a new Active Directory (AD) domain. Other functions are useful even in a workgroup configuration, either to control the local computer or to manage other servers on the network.

Basic *net* Syntax

The net command accepts parameters and subcommands that tell it what to do. The general syntax for the command is as follows:

```
net [ADS|RPC|RAP] commands [parameters]
```

The specification of ADS, RPC, or RAP tells the utility whether to try to communicate with other systems using AD, Remote Procedure Call (RPC), or Remote Access Protocol (RAP). In most cases, net can figure out which method to use, but if a command doesn't work, you can specify which method you want to use. A few commands work with only one or two of these communication methods. ADS is most useful on networks that use Windows 200*x* domain controllers; RPC is useful on domains controlled by Samba, Windows NT 4.0, and some Windows 2000 controllers; and RAP is useful when communicating with Windows 9*x*/Me and Windows NT 3.*x* systems. Newer systems work with the older protocols—for instance, a Windows NT 4.0 system should understand RAP as well as RPC, and a Windows 2003 system should understand all three protocols.

The *commands* are described shortly in "Using net Commands." The *parameters* modify the action of the tool. The most important of these are as follows:

-h or --help: This parameter displays help on use of net.

-s *config-file*: Normally, net takes various parameters from the smb.conf file; however, you can point the tool at another configuration file with this option.

-I *ip-address*: You can provide the IP address of a server or domain controller with this parameter.

-S *server-name*: You can specify the name of the server or domain controller with this parameter.

-w *workgroup*: This parameter sets the target workgroup or domain—the one you want to modify.

-W *workgroup*: You can specify the workgroup to which the client claims to belong with this parameter.

-n *netbios-name*: You can specify the NetBIOS name that the client claims to be with this parameter.

-U *username*: This parameter sets the username you want to use for your operations.

-P: You can tell net to query the external server using the local system's machine account using this parameter.

-l: This parameter produces long (verbose) output, providing you with more information.

-d *debuglevel*: This parameter sets the debug level; it accepts a value of from 0 to 10 and overrides the log level parameter in smb.conf.

As a general rule, you'll include one of the -I, -S, or -w parameters so that the tool knows what remote system to contact. (In the case of -w, net must scan the local network for the domain controller, which sometimes doesn't work as well as specifying a machine with -I or -S.) Sometimes net can locate the correct system to contact automatically, though. Note that these parameters are case-sensitive, and some have opposite-case equivalents, so be sure to type the case correctly!

Using *net* Commands

The bulk of the net functionality lies in its commands. Some of these commands take subcommands and additional parameters, so some of them are quite complex in and of themselves. Some are useful only in certain contexts or when the local Samba server has been prepared in some way. As of Samba 3.0.1, some commands have not yet been implemented, and these commands are not included in this list. The most important commands are the following:

CHANGESECRETPW: This command changes the machine account password for the client on the specified server. This command is potentially quite dangerous because it can break a system's ability to log onto a domain.

TIME: You can view the time on the remote server with this command. You can add several subcommands to modify its action: SYSTEM displays the time in a format that's suitable for input to /bin/date, SET runs /bin/date using the time received from the remote server, and ZONE displays the time zone on the server, expressed as hours from Universal Coordinated Time (UTC).

JOIN [*TYPE*] [*options*]: This command joins your system to a domain. *TYPE* may be MEMBER, PDC, or BDC, to specify how you'll join the domain—in most cases, MEMBER is appropriate. You must normally specify a username via the -U parameter. This username must have administrative control over the domain. In the case of a Samba domain controller, the user can be root, if you add that account to the Samba administrative database, or it can be a user who's given root privileges via the admin users option in smb.conf. The latter option is preferred because it's less of a security risk.

OLDJOIN: This command joins your system to a domain using older methods. This approach requires that a trust account for your system already exist on the domain controller.

USER: You can manipulate user accounts with this command. Passing no additional parameters lists the user accounts on the server or domain. Additional options are DELETE, which deletes the specified account; INFO, which lists the groups to which the specified user belongs; and ADD, which adds a user to the system. All of these options require a username as an additional option, and some take more options to modify their operation.

GROUP: This command is similar to USER, but it enables you to view or tweak group settings. Passing it with no additional options returns information on groups on the server. Additional options are DELETE, which deletes a group, and ADD, which adds a group.

SHARE: Typing this command alone displays all the shares available on the specified server. Available options are ADD and DELETE, which activate or deactive shares, respectively.

SESSION: You can learn about open sessions—connections to clients maintained by the server—with this command. Typing it alone produces a summary of open sessions. Additional options enable manipulations: DELETE and CLOSE are synonymous and close the specified session, and INFO displays information on the files opened by a client you specify.

SERVER: This RAP command displays information about the servers in the domain. The default is to display information in the current workgroup or domain (as specified in smb.conf), but you can add a workgroup or domain name to display information on another workgroup or domain, if the contacted system has information about that workgroup or domain.

DOMAIN: Typing this RAP command summarizes the domains and workgroups visible on the current network or available to the server you contact.

PRINTQ: This RAP command helps to manage print queues on the server. Using it with no subcommand displays information on the queues maintained by the server. Adding LIST and a queue name lists information on jobs in a specified print queue. Adding DELETE, a queue name, and a job number deletes the specified job from the queue. (These last two options appear to be broken in Samba 3.0.1.)

GROUPMEMBER: This RAP command enables you to manipulate group membership. It necessarily takes one of three commands (LIST, DELETE, or ADD) and a group name. The DELETE and ADD commands also require you to pass a username to the system.

PASSWORD: You can change the user's password on the remote system using this RAP command, which requires the username, the old password, and the new password as additional options. This command will prompt for an access password but will not prompt for the user's old or new password if you omit them from the command line.

LOOKUP: Typing this command looks up the IP address of the NetBIOS name you type. Additional options are LDAP, which looks up an LDAP server; KDC, which looks up a Kerberos domain controller; DC, which looks up a NetBIOS domain controller; and MASTER, which looks up a domain master browser.

GETLOCALSID: This command is unusual because it retrieves information from a local database—in this case, the security ID (SID) of the local machine. (The SID is a unique identifier for a user, machine, or domain.)

SETLOCALSID: You can change the local machine's SID with this command. Using this option is potentially risky, so use it only if you know what you're doing.

GROUPMAP: This command is unusually complex. It controls the mapping between Unix groups and SMB/CIFS groups. It takes subcommands called LIST, ADD, MODIFY, and DELETE, which perform the specified actions. With most, you must provide additional parameters of the form *option=value*, where *option* is unixgroup, ntgroup, rid, sid, type, or comment and where *value* is a value appropriate for the setting. This command requires administrative privileges on the server to run. An example appears in the upcoming section, "Examples of net in Use."

MAXRID: You can learn what the maximum record ID (RID) is on the server with this command.

INFO: This RPC command returns assorted information about the server queried, such as its domain, domain SID, number of users, and so on.

TESTJOIN: This command tests whether your participation in a domain is valid.

CHANGETRUSTPW: You can change the interdomain trust password with this command.

SHUTDOWN: You can shut down a remote system with this command. You can pass it several options: -t *time* is the time until the shutdown occurs, -r causes the system to reboot after it's shut down, -f forces the shutdown of all running applications, and -C *message* displays the specified message to console users. To shut down a Samba server in this way, the shutdown script parameter in smb.conf must be set to a script that will do the job.

ABORTSHUTDOWN: This command aborts the shutdown of a server. To abort the shutdown of a Samba server, the abort shutdown script in smb.conf must be set to a script that will do the job.

SAMDUMP: You can retrieve the Security Account Manager (SAM) database from a BDC or PDC using this command.

VAMPIRE: Like its namesake in folklore, this command sucks something from another entity, but the thing it sucks is the account database—users, groups, and aliases. This command is run from a BDC and is typically used as part of a procedure to extract a Windows NT domain controller's account database so that a Samba server can take over domain controller duties without having to re-create all the user accounts and passwords. This procedure is described in more detail in Chapter 15.

GETSID: You can retrieve a domain's SID and store it in the local database with this command.

LEAVE: This ADS command causes the remote system to sign off of the domain to which it belongs.

STATUS: This ADS command displays status information on the remote system's machine account. This information is intended mainly for developers; TESTJOIN is more appropriate for typical administrators.

PRINTER: You can view and modify ADS printer information with this command. Using it alone displays information on the printer whose name you specify. You can also pass the PUBLISH or REMOVE parameters, which add or remove a printer to or from an AD printer listing.

SEARCH: You can perform a standard LDAP search on an AD database with this command, which requires an LDAP search expression as a parameter.

DN: This command performs an LDAP search on an AD database. You must pass a standard LDAP distinguished name (DN).

WORKGROUP: You pass this command a Kerberos realm, and it displays the associated workgroup name.

HELP: Pass this command before (or sometimes after) another command to learn more about the specified command.

These commands aren't case-sensitive, so you needn't be too concerned with typing everything in uppercase. (This contrasts with the parameters, which are case-sensitive.) Some commands take several subcommands or options, so by the time you type everything in, the command can be quite lengthy.

Examples of *net* in Use

The preceding listings of options may be overwhelming; how you combine these commands and parameters may not be entirely obvious. A few examples should help clear up questions about how to use this command. First, consider a password change request:

```
$ net -S waltz PASSWORD grogers gr7f1tsy o70bgzw3
```

This command changes the password for the `grogers` user on the `waltz` computer from `gr7f1tsy` to `o70bgzw3`. After typing this command, you'll be asked for a password. Type the password on the server associated with the account you're using (which need not be the same as the account whose password you're changing).

CAUTION   Typing passwords on a command line is potentially risky because they're likely to be revealed by a `ps` command run by another user. Thus, changing passwords in this way is inadvisable on a multi-user system. It's even a bit risky on a single-user system; if it's been compromised, the intruder might stumble across the password-change command. This command will also be stored in any shell history file an account uses. One factor limiting the risk, though, is that this command is likely to execute quickly, so the passwords will only appear in a `ps` listing for a second or two. This factor doesn't help limit the exposure in a shell history file, though.

Another common example of `net` in use is in joining a domain. You might do this if you've set up a Samba server that isn't a domain controller but you want the system to be part of a domain. The command to do the job might look like this:

```
$ net -S waltz -U adminuser JOIN
```

This command joins the local computer to the domain controlled by the `waltz` computer, using the `adminuser` administrative account. To work with a Samba domain controller, you'll need to have created an appropriate domain trust account for the machine you're adding, or at least have configured the `add machine script` option in `smb.conf` to do the job automatically. After issuing this command, you should be able to set `security = Domain` and associated options in `smb.conf` to have the server defer to the domain controller for authentication tasks.

Yet another example of `net` in use is in modifying the group mapping database. This database is used to map Unix groups to SMB/CIFS groups. For instance, suppose you want to create a group for summer interns on your domain. You can do so by creating an appropriate Linux group (say, `interns`) and then running a command such as the following:

```
$ net -S waltz GROUPMAP ADD ntgroup="Summer Interns" unixgroup=interns
```

This command sets up a domain group called Summer Interns and associates it with the Linux group interns. Note that quotes enclose the NT group name because that name includes a space. Windows users who are added to this group will create files with interns group ownership on the Linux system and access files with interns group permissions.

You can use the net command to check or set the time. For instance, to synchronize your system's clock to the clock on another computer on the network, you might issue this command:

```
# net -S waltz TIME SET
Mon Jan 19 14:23:19 EDT 2004
```

The result of this command is a one-time setting of the system's clock. The remote computer can be running any SMB/CIFS package that supports remote time setting—a Samba server, a Windows system, DAVE, or other packages. You could call such a command in a cron job on a daily or hourly basis to keep your system's time synchronized. In most cases, though, it's preferable to run a Network Time Protocol (NTP) server on a Unix system, as described in Chapter 12. NTP will result in less drift because it runs continuously and adjusts the clock in such a way that it never shifts abruptly, even by just a second or two. Using net's time-setting capabilities might be helpful if your system is isolated from the Internet, though; you can at least use it to synchronize your Unix system's clock to one computer's clock on your local network, which will ensure that your local computers' clocks agree with one another.

Summary

Overall, the net command is a powerful tool for server and domain management. It's responsible for some of Samba 3.0's improved domain integration features, and net will undoubtedly become more powerful and important in the future. As of Samba 3.0, though, not all of its features are yet implemented, and some that are implemented are a bit awkward to use or are unreliable. Nonetheless, learning to use net will serve you well, as this command is likely to become more important for Samba administration in the future.

Index

A

H

L

forums.apress.com

FOR PROFESSIONALS BY PROFESSIONALS™

JOIN THE APRESS FORUMS AND BE PART OF OUR COMMUNITY. You'll find discussions that cover topics of interest to IT professionals, programmers, and enthusiasts just like you. If you post a query to one of our forums, you can expect that some of the best minds in the business—especially Apress authors, who all write with *The Expert's Voice*™—will chime in to help you. Why not aim to become one of our most valuable participants (MVPs) and win cool stuff? Here's a sampling of what you'll find:

DATABASES
Data drives everything.

Share information, exchange ideas, and discuss any database programming or administration issues.

INTERNET TECHNOLOGIES AND NETWORKING
Try living without plumbing (and eventually IPv6).

Talk about networking topics including protocols, design, administration, wireless, wired, storage, backup, certifications, trends, and new technologies.

JAVA
We've come a long way from the old Oak tree.

Hang out and discuss Java in whatever flavor you choose: J2SE, J2EE, J2ME, Jakarta, and so on.

MAC OS X
All about the Zen of OS X.

OS X is both the present and the future for Mac apps. Make suggestions, offer up ideas, or boast about your new hardware.

OPEN SOURCE
Source code is good; understanding (open) source is better.

Discuss open source technologies and related topics such as PHP, MySQL, Linux, Perl, Apache, Python, and more.

PROGRAMMING/BUSINESS
Unfortunately, it is.

Talk about the Apress line of books that cover software methodology, best practices, and how programmers interact with the "suits."

WEB DEVELOPMENT/DESIGN
Ugly doesn't cut it anymore, and CGI is absurd.

Help is in sight for your site. Find design solutions for your projects and get ideas for building an interactive Web site.

SECURITY
Lots of bad guys out there—the good guys need help.

Discuss computer and network security issues here. Just don't let anyone else know the answers!

TECHNOLOGY IN ACTION
Cool things. Fun things.

It's after hours. It's time to play. Whether you're into LEGO® MINDSTORMS™ or turning an old PC into a DVR, this is where technology turns into fun.

WINDOWS
No defenestration here.

Ask questions about all aspects of Windows programming, get help on Microsoft technologies covered in Apress books, or provide feedback on any Apress Windows book.

HOW TO PARTICIPATE:

Go to the Apress Forums site at **http://forums.apress.com/**.
Click the New User link.